THE CANADIAN YEARBOOK OF INTERNATIONAL LAW

2002

ANNUAIRE CANADIEN DE DROIT INTERNATIONAL

The Canadian Yearbook of International Law

VOLUME XL   2002   TOME XL

Annuaire canadien de Droit international

Published under the auspices of
THE CANADIAN BRANCH, INTERNATIONAL LAW ASSOCIATION
AND
THE CANADIAN COUNCIL ON INTERNATIONAL LAW

Publié sous les auspices de
LA SECTION CANADIENNE DE L'ASSOCIATION DE DROIT INTERNATIONAL
ET
LE CONSEIL CANADIEN DE DROIT INTERNATIONAL

UBC Press
VANCOUVER / TORONTO

Printed in Canada on acid-free paper ∞

ISBN 0-7748-0937-X
ISSN 0069-0058

National Library of Canada Cataloguing in Publication

The National Library of Canada has catalogued this publication as follows:

The Canadian yearbook of international law — Annuaire canadien de droit international

   Annual.
   Text in English and French.
   "Published under the auspices of the Canadian
Branch, International Law Association and the
Canadian Council on International Law."
   ISSN 0069-0058

   1. International Law — Periodicals.
I. International Law Association. Canadian Branch.
II. Title: Annuaire canadien de droit international.
JC 21.C3   341′.05   C75-34558-6E

Données de catalogage avant publication (Canada)

Annuaire canadien de droit international — The Canadian yearbook of international law

   Annuel.
   Textes en anglais et en français.
   "Publié sous les auspices de la Branche canadienne
de l'Association de droit international et le Conseil
canadien de droit international."
   ISSN 0069-0058

   1. Droit international — Périodiques.
I. Association de droit international. Section canadienne.
II. Conseil canadien de droit international.
III. Titre: The Canadian yearbook of international law.
JC 21.C3   341′.05   C75-34558-6F

UBC Press
University of British Columbia
2029 West Mall
Vancouver, BC V6T 1Z2
(604) 822-3259
www.ubcpress.ca

The Board of Editors, the Canadian Branch of the International Law Association, the Canadian Council on International Law, and the University of British Columbia are not in any way responsible for the views expressed by contributors, whether the contributions are signed or unsigned.

Les opinions émises dans le présent *Annuaire* par nos collaborateurs, qu'il s'agisse d'articles signés ou non, ne sauraient en aucune façon engager la responsabilité du Comité de rédaction, de la Section canadienne du Conseil canadien de droit international ou de l'Université de Colombie-Britannique.

Communications to the *Yearbook* should be addressed to:

Les communications destinées à l'*Annuaire* doivent être adressées à:

THE EDITOR, THE CANADIAN YEARBOOK OF INTERNATIONAL LAW
FACULTY OF LAW, COMMON LAW SECTION
UNIVERSITY OF OTTAWA
57 LOUIS PASTEUR
OTTAWA, ONTARIO K1N 6N5 CANADA

Contents / Matière

Book Reviews / Recensions de Livres

THE CANADIAN YEARBOOK OF INTERNATIONAL LAW

2002

ANNUAIRE CANADIEN DE DROIT INTERNATIONAL

A Hesitant Embrace:
The Application of International
Law by Canadian Courts

JUTTA BRUNNÉE AND

STEPHEN J. TOOPE

INTRODUCTION

Some ten years ago, Rosalyn Higgins mused about a "[p]sychology that disposes counsel and judge to treat international law as some exotic branch of the law, to be avoided if at all possible, and to be looked upon as if unreal, of no practical application to the real world."[1] She observed strenuous efforts on the part of the English courts not to decide cases on the basis of international law and suggested that the phenomenon was in part rooted in "legal culture."[2] She was referring not simply to whether a country's legal system was "monist" in outlook, treating international law as automatically incorporated into domestic law, or "dualist," requiring a transformation of international law into domestic law.[3] Rather, for Higgins, the approaches of domestic courts were primarily a function of the degree of familiarity of counsel and bench with international law. In most countries, international law is not viewed as an integral

---

Jutta Brunnée is Professor of Law and Metcalf Chair in Environmental Law at the University of Toronto, and Stephen J. Toope is President of the Pierre Elliott Trudeau Foundation and Professor of Law at McGill University (on leave). The views expressed should not be attributed to the foundation. We benefited from lively discussions with David Dyzenhaus, Karen Knop, and Irit Weiser about various themes explored in this article. We also thank them for their perceptive comments on earlier drafts. We also benefited from the excellent research assistance of Sean Rehaag and Ranjan Agarwal.

[1] R. Higgins, *Problems and Process: International Law and How We Use It* (New York: Oxford University Press, 1994) at 207.

[2] *Ibid.*

[3] For a brief overview on the monist and dualist models of reception, see, for example, J.H. Currie, *Public International Law* (Toronto: Irwin Law, 2001) at 199-201.

3

part of the domestic legal culture, and judges and counsel are wary to invoke it.[4]

Do Higgins's observations apply to the attitudes of Canadian courts towards international law in 2002? At first glance, one may be inclined to say that her assessment has been surpassed by the developments of the last few years, but upon closer examination, one finds that the old patterns persist, even if the manifestations are changing. Canadian courts seem to be embracing international law, employing fulsome words of endearment, but the embrace remains decidedly hesitant and the affair is far from consummated.

Our courts are certainly approaching their task of mediating the relationship between international and domestic law with new-found energy. Former Supreme Court Justice Gérard La Forest, writing in 1996, saw Canadian courts "truly becoming international courts in many areas involving the rule of law," particularly in human rights law.[5] Justice Louis LeBel, in recent comments, highlighted the role of the Supreme Court of Canada in bringing to bear — and helping to develop — an "emerging global law."[6] Indeed, Canadian courts are encountering international law in a rapidly growing number of cases, implicating a widening range of areas. These encounters involve topics as diverse as immigration and refugee law and deportation issues;[7] family law, including

[4] But see D. Dyzenhaus, M. Hunt, and M. Taggart, "The Principle of Legality in Administrative Law: Internationalisation as Constitutionalisation" (2001) 1 Oxford U. Commonwealth L. J. 5 at 7 (arguing that the reliance upon international norms in statutory interpretation and judicial review is in fact supported by the common law tradition: "It is ... precisely the common law tradition that provides the justification for what the courts are doing: and therefore our argument says to the traditionalist that he has not understood his tradition").

[5] G.V. La Forest, "The Expanding Role of the Supreme Court of Canada in International Law Issues" (1996) 34 Can. Y.B. Int'l L. 89 at 100.

[6] L. Chwialkowska, "Global Law Emerging, Judge Tells Conference — Canada Struggling to Accommodate International Treaties and Tribunals," *National Post* (13 April 2002) at A6 (citing Justice Louis LeBel of the Supreme Court of Canada). For a full version of Justice LeBel's comments, see Justice L. LeBel and G. Chao, "The Rise of International Law in Canadian Constitutional Litigation: Fugue or Fusion? Recent Developments and Challenges in Internalizing International Law" (Fifth Annual Analysis of the Constitutional Decisions of the Supreme Court of Canada, Osgoode Hall Law School, 12 April 2002) at 6 (unpublished, on file with authors).

[7] See, for example, *Suresh* v. *Canada (Minister of Citizenship and Immigration)* (2002), 208 D.L.R. (4th) 1 [hereinafter *Suresh*]; *Baker* v. *Canada (Minister of Citizenship and Immigration)*, [1999] 2 S.C.R. 817 [hereinafter *Baker*]; *Pushpanathan* v. *Canada (Minister of Citizenship and Immigration)*, [1998] 1 S.C.R. 982 [hereinafter

child abduction and support obligations;[8] environmental law;[9] and investor-state disputes under Chapter 11 of the North American Free Trade Agreement,[10] to name but a few. However, it is not only in terms of subject areas that the domestic reach of international law appears to be increasing. Recent decisions of the Supreme Court of Canada confirm that international law is potentially relevant not only to the interpretation of federal, provincial, and municipal legislation and regulation but also to the exercise of administrative discretion thereunder.[11] Finally, courts appear to recognize the relevance of international norms whether or not they have been implemented through Canadian legislation and whether or not they are binding on Canada. In *Baker* v. *Canada*, the majority of the Supreme Court held that "the values reflected in international human rights law may help inform the contextual approach to statutory interpretation and judicial review."[12]

Canadian courts, then, are grappling more and more with the "practical application" of international law. However, for all their declared openness to international law, they are not yet meeting all the challenges that domestic application poses. We venture to say that our courts are still inclined to avoid deciding cases on the basis of international law — much like Higgins observed a decade ago with respect to British courts. This does not mean that international law is given no effect or that its broad relevance is denied. The avoidance strategy is subtler. Even when they invoke or refer to international law, Canadian courts generally do not give international norms concrete legal effect in individual cases. Especially following the Supreme Court's decision in *Baker*, there appears to be a trend towards treating all of international law, whether custom or treaty, binding on Canada or not, implemented or unimplemented, in the same manner — as relevant and perhaps persuasive, but not as determinative or, dare we say, obligatory.

Pushpanathan]; *Ahani* v. *Canada (A.G.)* (2002), 58 O.R. (3d) 107 (C.A.) [hereinafter *Ahani*].

8   See, for example, *Pollastro* v. *Pollastro* (1999), 43 O.R. (3d) 497 (C.A.).

9   See, for example, *114957 Canada Ltée (Spraytech, Société d'arrosage)* v. *Hudson (Town)*, [2001] 2 S.C.R. 241 [hereinafter *Spraytech*].

10 See, for example, *Mexico* v. *Metalclad Corporation* (2001), 95 B.C.L.R. (3d) 169 (S.C.). North American Free Trade Agreement, (1993) 32 I.L.M. 289.

11 *Baker, supra* note 7; *Spraytech, supra* note 9.

12 *Baker, supra* note 7 at para. 70.

Some commentators have read *Baker* as signaling a positive paradigm shift, with the Supreme Court embracing a more nuanced search for persuasive norms, rather than focusing on binary distinctions between binding and non-binding norms.[13] We agree that subtlety is required in the evaluation of sources of legal influence. It would be misleading to see the distinction between binding and non-binding norms as a simple on-off switch. However, we caution against throwing out the entire distinction when discussing the interplay between international and domestic law. As we will illustrate, within the Canadian legal order the question of the binding quality of international law is closely intertwined with the manner in which it comes to influence the interpretation of domestic law. For domestic administrative lawyers, a more accessible way of putting the question is to ask whether or not a binding international norm is a "mandatory relevant factor" in judicial decision-making and in the exercise of administrative discretion.

We will show that, in the case of norms that are binding on Canada under international law, Canadian courts have an obligation to interpret domestic law in conformity with the relevant international norms, as far as this is possible. By contrast, norms that do not bind Canada internationally (for example, soft law or provisions of treaties not ratified by Canada) can help inform the interpretation of domestic law and, depending on the norm in question and the case at issue, may even be persuasive. Courts may, and in some cases should, draw upon such norms for interpretative purposes, but they are not strictly speaking required to do so. In short, in the domestic application of international law, the distinction between norms that bind Canada under international law and those that do not matters because of its implications for the manner in which courts should approach their interpretative tasks.

At least some of the factors that underpin the seemingly new approach of Canadian courts to international law are far more mundane than shifting paradigms, and one should be careful not to read too much into the recent cases. In part, these factors relate to the delicate balancing tasks that courts face in the application of international law.[14] Courts must balance Canada's international

---

[13] K. Knop, "Here and There: International Law in Domestic Courts" (2000) 32 N.Y.U. J. Int'l L. & Pol. 501. Knop's argument concerning the importance of persuasive authority builds on the work of H.P. Glenn, "Persuasive Authority" (1987) 32 McGill L. J. 261.

[14] See generally G. van Ert, "Using Treaties in Canadian Courts" (2000) 38 Can. Y.B. Int'l L. 3 at 4-9.

commitments, which have been made by the federal government, with the legislative supremacy over the laws that apply in Canada.[15] Similarly, courts must balance the federal government's authority to bind Canada internationally and provincial legislative jurisdiction. Finally, and not least, courts must carefully delineate their own role in giving domestic effect to international law. Treating international law as persuasive but not mandatory may be one way to manage these multiple balancing acts. International law is brought to bear on a growing range of questions, yet its potential impact is tempered — and we fear largely eviscerated — because it is merely one factor in the application and interpretation of domestic law.[16]

The inclination to temper the effect of international law may also be increased by the unease that many judges continue to feel in identifying applicable international law, particularly customary law, and in determining its precise legal effect in Canada. Noting the growing use by counsel of international law in cases before the Supreme Court, Justice LeBel observed:

Arguments are advanced before us on the basis of a bewildering number of sources, international instruments, declarations, decisions of other tribunals, and too often there is little attempt at defining the kind of law we are dealing with, or, if we are discussing international norms, customs or practice, of actually trying to establish that there is really such a practice.[17]

By treating all international norms, of whatever status and purported effect, as potentially relevant and persuasive, courts avoid the thorny details of the application of international law. In this sense, Rosalyn Higgins's assessment that a lack of familiarity with international law impedes its domestic application may well remain true for Canada.

[15] See, for example, the dissent of Justices Frank Iacobucci and Peter Cory in *Baker, supra* note 7 at para. 80 (noting that the effect of the majority's approach was "to give force and effect within the domestic legal system to international obligations undertaken by the executive alone that have yet to be subject to the democratic will of Parliament").

[16] See, for example, *Suresh, supra* note 7 at para. 46. The Supreme Court implies that soft law, unimplemented treaties, custom, and even *jus cogens* all simply help "inform" the interpretation of the Canadian Charter of Rights and Freedoms, Part I of the Constitution Act, 1982, being Schedule B to the Canada Act 1982 (U.K.), 1982, c. 11. For a detailed discussion of this aspect of the court's decision in *Suresh*, see notes 192-201 in this article and the accompanying text. In addition, see generally the second part of this article, in which we analyze the recent trends in the domestic application of international law in Canada.

[17] Quoted in Chwialkowska, *supra* note 6.

To be sure, the Supreme Court has not explicitly decided that all international law should be given persuasive, rather than mandatory, effect. Nor, we assume, did it intend for others to pull its decisions in this direction. Yet, the ambiguities in *Baker* and several other of the Supreme Court's recent decisions do provide considerable room for other courts to apply international law in ways that might end up reducing rather than increasing, and confusing rather than clarifying, its domestic impact. We are pleased, therefore, that Justice LeBel also stressed the need for more rigour "in the definition and identification of international rules and the process of internalization."[18] Indeed, he called upon lawyers and scholars to increase their efforts in this regard.

In this article, we take up the challenge. Our aim is to provide practical guidelines to assist Canadian courts in the interpretation and application of international law. We wholeheartedly agree with Justice LeBel that what is needed most in the growing domestic engagement with international law is greater analytical rigour. However, the challenge is not just one for lawyers and scholars. Courts too must approach international law in a principled and coherent manner, providing clarity as to precisely what effect is accorded to international law in a given case and why. Indeed, the judicial role is of particular importance because domestic courts influence the development not only of domestic law but of international law as well.[19] Especially in the context of customary international law, domestic courts participate in the continuous weaving of the fabric of international law. It is particularly important that Canadian courts carefully distinguish between the different threads that together make up a strong and resilient cloth. As we will argue, it is not enough to treat *all* normative threads as being potentially persuasive but not binding — over time, this approach risks weakening the fabric of the law. Our concern is that if international law is merely persuasive, it becomes purely optional and can be ignored at the discretion of the judge.

We first offer a brief overview of international law and its sources. We then review the principles that govern the internalization of international law and the approaches that Canadian courts have taken in this context. Much has been written on these topics over

---

[18] *Ibid.*

[19] According to Article 38(1)(d) of the Statute of the International Court of Justice, 26 June 1945, Can. T.S. 1945 No. 7 (entered into force 24 October 1945) [hereinafter ICJ Statute], the decisions of domestic courts are a subsidiary means for the determination of international law.

the last five years, including in the *Canadian Yearbook on International Law*.[20] Our purpose is not to retrace this literature but rather to use it to spotlight the ambiguities and potential contradictions in the judicial treatment of international law to which we have alluded. We will focus on several interrelated questions and distinctions that, we believe, are crucial to the development of a consistent approach to the application of international law in Canada: When is international law directly applicable in Canada? To what extent are the legal effects of international law in Canada dependent upon its domestic implementation? What constitutes implementation? Under what circumstances can international law that is binding *on* Canada have legal effects *in* Canada? Under what circumstances, if any, can international norms that are not binding on Canada, or not legally binding at all, have legal effects in Canada?

INTERNATIONAL LAW AND ITS SOURCES — A PRIMER FOR CANADIAN JUDGES[21]

As already suggested, some of the difficulties experienced in the domestic application of international law appear to be rooted in a

[20] See van Ert, *supra* note 14. And see E. Brandon, "Does International Law Mean Anything in Canadian Courts?" (2002) 11 J. Env. L. & Practice 397; J. Brunnée, "A Long and Winding Road: Bringing International Environmental Law into Canadian Courts" in M. Anderson and P. Galizzi, eds., *International Environmental Law in National Courts* (London: British Institute of International and Comparative Law, 2002) 45; H.M. Kindred, "The Use of Unimplemented Treaties in Canada: Practice and Prospects in the Supreme Court" in C. Carmody et al., eds., *Trilateral Perspectives on International Legal Issues: Conflict and Coherence* (Washington: American Society of International Law, 2003) 3; Knop, *supra* note 13; W.A. Schabas, "Twenty-Five Years of Public International Law at the Supreme Court of Canada" (2000) 79 Can. Bar. Rev. 174; S.J. Toope, "The Uses of Metaphor: International Law and the Supreme Court of Canada" (2001) 80 Can. Bar Rev. 534; and S.J. Toope, "Inside and Out: The Stories of International Law and Domestic Law" (2001) 50 U.N.B. L. J. 11; S.J. Toope, "Canada and International Law" (1998) 27 Can. Council Int'l L. Proc. 33; G. van Ert, *Using International Law in Canadian Courts* (New York: Kluwer Law International, 2002); I. Weiser, "Effect in Domestic Law of International Human Rights Treaties Ratified without Implementing Legislation" (1998) 27 Can. Council Int'l L. Proc. 132; and I. Weiser, "Undressing the Window: A Proposal for Making International Human Rights Law Meaningful in the Canadian Commonwealth System," September 2002 [on file with authors].

[21] This section of the article is derived from presentations made by S. Toope to the 2001 Conference of the International Association of Women Judges and by J. Brunnée and S. Toope to the annual education seminars of the Ontario Court of Appeal (June 2002) of the Federal Court of Canada (January 2003), and of

lack of familiarity with international law itself and in a resulting reluctance to engage in the identification of the applicable international law.[22] However, an inquiry into the effect of international law in Canada cannot limit itself to an examination of various principles of application. Since the relevance of these principles depends on what type of international norm is in play, a prior analytical step must provide an answer to that very question. Therefore, we begin with a brief overview on international law and a review of its main sources, both treaty and custom. We also offer some observations on the role of "soft law," a concept that has become common currency in the rhetoric of international law but that continues to confound commentators and practioners alike.[23]

---

the Supreme Court of British Columbia and Court of Appeal (March 2003). We thank the many judges whose probing questions have helped us to clarify our analysis.

[22] Others have suggested that the problem rests "in the difficulty of defining public international law." LeBel and Chao, *supra* note 6. We disagree. There is a great deal of binding international law that is well defined, with obligations that are precisely stated. Notably, many recently concluded international treaties are as specific in imposing obligations as are domestic statutes. Consider, for example, many international trade agreements, environmental treaties, and law of the sea conventions. We accept, however, that the delineation of obligations under customary international law can often — but not always — prove to be more difficult.

[23] For the purposes of this "primer," we confine ourselves to outlining the standard account of international law, which is focused upon formal sources of international law and state consent. We do so because, in domestic adjudication involving the application of international law, judges are called upon to identify binding rules according to the criteria that hold sway in international (state) practice. We do want to stress, however, that there is a lively scholarly debate on whether the sources doctrine and state consent adequately explain the operation of international law in international relations. For example, we have argued elsewhere that formal consent alone or the simple fact that a rule is binding as treaty or customary law do not necessarily ensure that the rule will influence the conduct of international actors. In our view, a norm's legitimacy and attendant persuasiveness are likely more important to its influence than its formal pedigree. See J. Brunnée and S.J. Toope, "International Law and Constructivism: Elements of an Interactional Theory of International Law" (2000) 39 Colum. J. Transnat'l L. 19; J. Brunnée and S.J. Toope, "Interactional International Law" (2001) 3 Int'l L. Forum 186; and J. Brunnée and S.J. Toope, "The Changing Nile Basin Regime: Does Law Matter?" (2002) 43 Harv. Int'l L. J. 105. See also note 210 in this article and accompanying text.

PRELIMINARY OBSERVATIONS

In practice, Article 38 of the Statute of the International Court of Justice (ICJ Statute) is the litmus test for the sources of international law.[24] Article 38 instructs the International Court of Justice (ICJ) to "decide *in accordance with international law* such disputes as are submitted to it."[25] The article thus tells the court what law it is allowed to consider and states that there are three main sources of international law: treaty, custom, and general principles.[26] The decisions of courts (including domestic courts) and doctrine (the "teachings of the most highly qualified publicists") are so-called "subsidiary" sources of law.[27]

A norm of public international law may exist in both custom and treaty.[28] In this case, the states party to the relevant treaty will be bound by the norm both as a matter of treaty law and as a matter of customary law. States not party to the treaty will be bound by the same rule as a matter of customary law only. In the words of the ICJ in *Military and Paramilitary Activities in Nicaragua (Nicaragua v. United States)*, "there are no grounds for holding that when customary international law is comprised of rules identical to those of treaty law, the latter 'supervenes' the former, so that the customary international law has no further existence of its own."[29]

The third source of international law, general principles of law, can be conceived of in a number of ways. The most intuitive, and obvious, is the borrowing of rules from national legal systems to supplement the rules found in treaty and custom. The possibility

---

[24] ICJ Statute, *supra* note 19, Article 38.

[25] *Ibid.*, Article 38(1) [emphasis added].

[26] *Ibid.*, Article 38(1)(a)-(c). There is no formal hierarchy of sources of public international law, but, in practice, the most commonly argued sources of obligation are treaty and custom. If a treaty is of relevance in a particular situation or dispute, it will usually be invoked first, largely because the existence of a treaty rule is typically easier to prove than the existence of a customary rule. See H. Kindred et al., eds., *International Law: Chiefly as Interpreted and Applied in Canada*, 6th ed. (Toronto: Emond Montgomery, 2000) at 91, 93; J. Combacau and S. Sur, *Droit international public*, 5th ed. (Paris: Montchrestien, 2001) at 44; and Q.D. Nguyen et al., *Droit international public*, 6th ed. (Paris: Librarie Générale de Droit et de Jurisprudence, 1999) at 114-15.

[27] ICJ Statute, *supra* note 19, Article 38(1)(d).

[28] See Currie, *supra* note 3 at 189-91.

[29] *Case Concerning Military and Paramilitary Activities in Nicargua (Nicaragua v. United States)*, [1986] I.C.J. Rep. 14 at 95 [hereinafter *Military Activities in Nicaragua*].

of recourse to general principles helps to ensure that there are no
"gaps" in international law and that decision-makers will not be
able to escape conclusions by invoking *non liquet*.[30] From this perspective, general principles are derived from the application of a
more or less rigorous comparative law methodology.[31] An alternative view is that general principles reflect the underlying "natural
law."[32] A third view is that general principles are simply abstractions
from a variety of national, international, and doctrinal sources,
employed when functionally necessary.[33] In the work of international tribunals, including the ICJ, no specific rationale or methodology has consistently been preferred. What is clear, however, is that
general principles are rarely invoked, at least explicitly, by the ICJ.[34]
Since general principles are also rarely argued before Canadian
courts,[35] we will leave them aside for the purposes of this article.

Over the last quarter century, international law has seen a
greater degree of flexibility than ever before in the employment of
evidence as to the existence of a binding rule of law. Courts, doctrinal writers, and state negotiators seem more willing than ever to
employ a diversity of sources to prove the existence of a binding
rule. The debates swirl around issues such as whether or not resolutions of the United Nations General Assembly can serve as evidence of either state practice or of *opinio juris* for the purposes of
proving the existence of a rule of customary law;[36] the weight to be
accorded to the writings of "publicists" or the decisions of international tribunals in arguing for the existence of a binding norm;[37]
whether or not decisions of domestic tribunals can constitute state
practice;[38] the weight that should be given to the pronouncements

---

[30] See Combacau and Sur, *supra* note 26 at 105.

[31] See M. Shaw, *International Law,* 4th ed. (Cambridge: Cambridge University Press,
1997) at 77-79.

[32] See I. Brownlie, *Principles of Public International Law,* 5th ed. (Oxford: Oxford
University Press, 1998) at 15; D.J. Harris, *Cases and Materials on International
Law,* 4th ed. (London: Sweet and Maxwell, 1991) at 47.

[33] Shaw, *supra* note 31 at 79.

[34] Harris, *supra* note 32 at 47-48.

[35] But see *R. v. Finta,* [1994] 1 S.C.R. 701 at 716-17, where Justice Gerard La Forest
considered general principles of law to be an important basis for crimes against
humanity. La Forest J. was in dissent, but not on this issue.

[36] See Currie, *supra* note 3 at 173.

[37] See *Legality of the Threat or Use of Nuclear Weapons,* Advisory Opinion, [1996] I.C.J.
Rep. 226 at paras. 68-71. And see Brownlie, *supra* note 32 at 24-25.

[38] See Shaw, *supra* note 31 at 87.

of expert bodies set up under the terms of a treaty in establishing the appropriate interpretation of the treaty;[39] whether or not
declarations of principles issued by international conferences in
non-treaty form are relevant to an assessment of the existence (or
content) of a binding rule;[40] whether or not "conferences of the
parties" sitting under the terms of a specific treaty can issue binding interpretations of treaty obligations or adopt binding decisions;[41] and whether or not non-governmental organizations actually
participate in the elaboration of international law through their
participation by voice, though not by vote, in international forums
such as the United Nations Commission on Human Rights.[42] However, all of this rhetorical activity occurs within a framework that
is still defined by Article 38 of the ICJ Statute. In the practice of
international law, and in much of the literature, the role of state
consent in the creation of international law remains predominant.
Within this framework, the ultimate question is whether or not
states have agreed to a binding treaty rule or have demonstrated the
practice and *opinio juris* necessary to show the existence of a rule
of customary law.[43] General principles play a lesser role, one that
is still marked by the need to demonstrate common acceptance of
a rule by states.

INTERNATIONAL TREATIES

Much of the substantive content of contemporary international
law is now found in formal treaties. Since the early part of the
twentieth century, enormous effort has been expended in processes
of standard setting through the elaboration of multi-party treaties,
especially in the areas of human rights, trade, the law of the sea,
and the environment. Article 38(1)(a) of the ICJ Statute contains

---

[39] See, for example, the Human Rights Committee sitting under the first Optional
Protocol to the International Covenant on Civil and Political Rights, 19 December 1966, 999 U.N.T.S. 171 (entered into force 23 March 1976) [hereinafter
ICCPR].

[40] See Brownlie, *supra* note 32 at 78.

[41] See, for example, J, Brunnée, "COPing with Consent: Lawmaking under Multilateral Environmental Agreements" (2002) 15 Leiden J. Int'l L. 1.

[42] See C. Chinkin, "Human Rights and the Politics of Representation: Is There a
Role for International Law?" in M. Byers, ed., *The Role of Law in International Politics: Essays in International Relations and International Law* (New York: Oxford
University Press, 2000) 131.

[43] See Combacau and Sur, *supra* note 26 at 23.

an implicit definition of a treaty, when it specifies that the court may apply "international conventions, whether general or particular, establishing rules expressly recognized by the contesting States." The essential idea is that states are bound by what they expressly consent to. Treaties may be bilateral or multilateral. The defining features of a treaty are that it is a binding agreement between or among states and that the agreement has been reduced to writing.[44] The precise terminology is irrelevant. "Treaty" encompasses "agreement," "covenant," "charter," "convention," "pact," "statute," and other parallel terms.

According to the fundamental principle *pacta sunt servanda*, as enshrined in Article 26 of the Vienna Convention on the Law of Treaties (Vienna Convention), treaty obligations must be performed in good faith.[45] By becoming a party to a treaty, a state pledges that it will uphold and implement all the provisions of the treaty. Certain formalities govern the process of creating a binding treaty. From the perspective of an individual state, initial consent to the treaty framework is often manifested by signature. If it is so specified in the treaty, signature may give rise to binding obligations.[46] However, it is commonly the case that signing a treaty merely commits a state not to do anything to "defeat the objects and purposes" of the treaty[47] — it is not intended to signify consent to be bound by the specific obligations contained in the treaty. In such circumstances, a state is only bound by the treaty's particular terms if it ratifies the treaty according to the particular procedural requirements of its constitution. In Canada, the executive controls both the signature and the ratification of international treaties.[48] A treaty is only binding on the parties when it has entered into force.[49]

---

[44] Vienna Convention on the Law of Treaties, 23 May 1969, Can T.S. 1980 No. 37 (entered into force 27 January 1980) [hereinafter Vienna Convention], which defines "treaty" with some greater specificity in Article 2(a):

> "treaty" means an international agreement concluded between States in written form and governed by international law, whether embodied in a single instrument or in two or more related instruments and whatever its particular designation.

[45] *Ibid.*, Article 26.

[46] *Ibid.*, Article 12.

[47] *Ibid.*, Article 18.

[48] The power to conclude treaties is vested in the governor-in-council as delegated authority under the Royal prerogative. See P.W. Hogg, *Constitutional Law of Canada*, looseleaf (Scarborough, ON: Carswell, 1997) vol. 1 at para. 11.2.

[49] Vienna Convention, *supra* note 44, Article 26.

For multilateral treaties, entry into force is usually made dependent upon the deposit of a specific number of state ratifications.[50] If a particular treaty is already in force, and a state that has not previously signed the treaty wishes to join the treaty regime, the process of so doing is usually called accession,[51] but this act is essentially the same as ratification.

The issues highlighted in this brief account are directly relevant to the domestic application of a treaty rule. Before any question of application can be answered, it will be necessary to determine whether or not Canada has ratified the treaty and whether or not the treaty is in force. If the treaty is in force *and* Canada has ratified it, the treaty is binding *on* Canada as a matter of international law. However, it is important to note that this conclusion does not yet answer the question of whether the treaty is effective within the Canadian domestic legal system. We will return to this distinction in the second part of this article.

CUSTOMARY INTERNATIONAL LAW

Until relatively recently, international legal relations have been shaped principally by the evolution of customary international law. Notwithstanding the growing importance of treaty-based law, customary law still furnishes essential threads in the fabric of international law. Suffice it to point to topics as diverse as state responsibility, legal personality, territory, and human rights, where the role of customary law was, and continues to be, formidable. Furthermore, being universal in character, custom has a potentially greater normative reach than all but the most widely ratified international treaties.[52]

The existence of a binding rule of custom is proven with reference to two distinct, but inter-related, elements: state practice and *opinio juris*. The task of establishing the existence of these two elements is complex, partly because of the increasingly diverse sources that are employed in the process.[53] Indeed, we suspect that the fluidity of custom and the challenges involved in determining whether a norm has acquired customary law status go a long way

---

[50] *Ibid.*, Article 24.

[51] *Ibid.*, Article 15.

[52] A.A. D'Amato, *The Concept of Custom in International Law* (Ithaca, NY: Cornell University Press, 1971) at 12; Combacau and Sur, *supra* note 26 at 52.

[53] See notes 36-42 in this article and accompanying text.

towards explaining the reluctance of senior Canadian courts to apply customary law. The complexities notwithstanding, a number of basic points can be made regarding the identification of the two elements of customary law.

State practice can be evidenced in a number of ways. The most authoritative pronouncement on what constitutes "practice" is found in the work of the International Law Commission (ILC), which is the United Nations organ charged with the codification and progressive development of public international law. In 1950, the ILC offered the following non-exhaustive list of the forms of state practice: treaties, decisions of international and national courts, national legislation (including subsidiary regulations), diplomatic correspondence, opinions of national legal advisors, and the practice of international organizations.[54] Ian Brownlie adds to this list policy statements, press releases, official manuals on legal questions, executive decisions, military orders, governmental comments on drafts prepared by the ILC, and resolutions of the UN General Assembly touching on legal questions.[55] It will be obvious from these lists that practice may be found in the unilateral acts and pronouncements of states and in multilateral acts and statements. In either case, the practice must be weighed, relying on criteria established in the decisions of international tribunals and the writings of leading publicists.[56]

In weighing the normative value of state practice, one must consider the consistency and generality of the practice. Complete consistency of practice is certainly not necessary, but substantial consistency is. If practice is ambiguous or contradictory, no custom can emerge. Similarly, completely universal practice is not required for a custom to exist, but a general or widespread practice is.[57] There is no magic numerical formula that can be applied to determine when a practice has crossed a threshold so that it may constitute a custom (if matched with the requisite *opinio juris*). Each case must be assessed in its particular context.[58] For example, the

---

[54] "International Law Commission" in *Yearbook of the International Law Commission 1950* (New York: United Nations, 1950) at 368, Doc. UNDOC. A/CN 4/SER. A/1950.Add. 1.

[55] Brownlie, *supra* note 32 at 5.

[56] For an overview, see Shaw, *supra* note 31 at 64-66, 70-72; Nguyen, *supra* note 26 at 321-23.

[57] *The Asylum Case (Columbia v. Peru)*, [1950] I.C.J. Rep. 266 at 276-77.

[58] Brownlie, *supra* note 32 at 5.

practice of states that have a special interest in the relevant rule may be weighed with particular attention. Thus, it has always been assumed that states with long coastlines or large merchant fleets and navies have a particular role to play in the development of the law of the sea.[59] Moreover, an effort should be made to assess whether or not a practice is supported by states in different regions.[60] Practice can be both positive and negative, in that a custom may be built upon positive assertions of right through statements and actions but also can be resisted by contrary practice and rhetoric. The failure to respond to claims of other states may constitute acquiescence in those claims, thereby allowing a customary rule to be constructed.[61]

Perhaps counter-intuitively, the existence of a binding custom is not predicated on long usage. Passage of time is relevant only to an assessment of the consistency and generality of practice. It is entirely possible for a custom to emerge within months and certainly within relatively few years if the density of the practice is sufficient — that is to say, that a large number of states support or adhere to the practice, even if this support or adherence developed over a short period of time.[62] Of course, the practice must be matched with the requisite *opinio juris.*

Opinio juris, the belief that a practice is required by law, is what turns mere usage into custom. The difficulty is in proving the "subjective belief" of a fictitious "person" — the state. In most cases, the only option will be to infer the *opinio juris* from the material practice. However, the ICJ has indicated in two important judgments that it does expect independent proof of *opinio juris.*[63] Unfortunately, it did not provide guidance on how to adduce this proof. It is for this reason that some authors have suggested that practice can only give rise to custom when states match their practice with express articulations of the supposed rule of law.[64] This view is

---

[59] *North Sea Continental Shelf Cases (Germany v. Denmark* and *Germany v. The Netherlands),* [1969] I.C.J. Rep. 3 at paras. 73, 75-76 [hereinafter *North Sea Continental Shelf*].

[60] *Ibid.* at 228 (dissenting opinion of Judge Lachs).

[61] See Shaw, *supra* note 31 at 64-66, 70-72.

[62] *North Sea Continental Shelf, supra* note 59 at para. 74, and the dissenting opinion of Judge Ad Hoc Sorenson. See also Currie, *supra* note 3 at 168-70; Nguyen, *supra* note 26 at 324-25.

[63] *North Sea Continental Shelf, supra* note 59 at para. 77; *Military Activities in Nicaragua, supra* note 29 at 108-9.

[64] D'Amato, *supra* note 52 at 74-75.

wholly impractical. Although proof of *opinio juris* may be sought in the unilateral pronouncements of states, it can also be derived from declarations of intergovernmental organizations, doctrinal writings, and even from public opinion as expressed in the media and among "opinion leaders."[65] This "proof" is admittedly weak and that is why *opinio juris* is typically inferred from practice. The role of *opinio juris* in such cases is to ensure that the standard applied to the proof of the material practice is itself rigorous.

Again, the issues that we have highlighted in our brief overview are of central importance in the application of international law in Canada. A careful assessment of the elements of state practice and *opinio juris* and a determination of whether or not a norm has attained customary law status have significant implications for the manner in which the norm exerts influence within the Canadian legal system. Specifically, and as we will argue in the next section, if a norm is part of customary international law, it should also be part of Canadian law and thus directly applicable in Canada.

"SOFT LAW" OR NON-BINDING SOURCES

We must also highlight the phenomenon of "soft law," which has given rise to much confusion.[66] The term "soft law" is employed in a number of different contexts in more or less precise ways.[67] The most common meaning ascribed to the term is a non-binding written instrument setting out international principles.[68] This definition includes UN General Assembly resolutions, statements issued

---

[65] Shaw, *supra* note 31 at 382.

[66] See P. Dupuy, "Soft Law and the International Law of the Environment" (1991) 12 Mich. J. Int'l. L. 420 (beginning his article with the observation that "'[s]oft' law is a paradoxical term for defining an ambiguous phenomenon. Paradoxical because, from a general and classical point of view, the rule of law is usually considered 'hard' ... or it simply does not exist. Ambiguous because the reality thus designated, considering its legal effects as well as it manifestations, is often difficult to identify clearly"). See also P. Weil, "Vers une normativité relative en droit international?" (1982) R.G.D.I.P. 5 (denouncing the phenomenon of soft law as blurring the normativity threshold and insisting on the fact that the accumulation of non-law does not create law).

[67] See C. Chinkin, "Normative Development in the International Legal System" in D. Shelton, ed., *Commitment and Compliance: The Role of Non-Binding Norms in the International Legal System* (New York: Oxford University Press, 2000) 21 at 23-25 (with a brief survey on the enduring debate about the nature of soft law).

[68] See C. Chinkin, "The Challenge of Soft-Law: Development and Change in International Law" (1989) 38 I.C.L.Q. 850 at 850-51.

by international conferences, declarations, sets of rules, and codes of conduct. Such instruments are commonly drafted and approved by international organs and conferences, but they are not signed and ratified by states. A formal treaty may even contain soft law principles, in this case meaning norms not designed directly to condition conduct (for example, rules that use the phrasing "should" rather than "shall").[69] Soft law is based upon the premise that certain principles are important and should ideally shape international law and policy even if they are not binding. A more expansive understanding of soft law would include even the articulation of principles by individual actors with some authority in a relevant international regime (for example, the UN High Commissioner for Human Rights, a member of a treaty-monitoring body, or the leader of an influential non-governmental organization).[70]

To suggest that such statements may be within the ambit of soft law underscores that there must be a qualitative difference between obligations of states and mere desiderata. Yet, to say that soft law is not legally binding is not to say that it is without influence. Indeed, it is increasingly common for international lawyers to speak of a progression along a continuum from soft to hard law, though this progression is by no means inevitable or invariably desirable.[71] Another way of conceptualizing the operation of soft law is that it may come to play a role in what has been called "interstitial law-making," where principles (or concepts) come to influence the interpretation of binding norms because the principles are useful or even necessary to practical decision-making.[72]

There can be no doubt that one of the reasons prompting the articulation of the concept of soft law was to assist in the progressive development of binding international law. In the words of Christine Chinkin:

[69] See, for example, Article 3.3 of the United Nations Framework Convention on Climate Change, 9 May 1992, 31 I.L.M. 849 (entered into force March 21, 1994) (providing that the parties "should take precautionary measures to anticipate, prevent or minimize the causes of climate change and mitigate its adverse effects").

[70] See generally Chinkin, *supra* note 67 at 25-29.

[71] See J. Brunnée and S.J. Toope, "Environmental Security and Freshwater Resources: Ecosystem Regime Building" (1997) 91 A.J.I.L. 26 at 31-37, 58. See also K.W. Abbott and D. Snidal, "Hard and Soft Law in International Governance" (2000) 54 Int'l Org. 401 at 422.

[72] V. Lowe, "The Politics of Law-Making: Are the Method and Character of Norm Creation Changing?" in Byers, *supra* note 42, 207 at 212-17.

While soft law may not be directly used to found a cause of action it has both a legitimising and a delegitimising direct effect: it is extremely difficult for a State that rejected some instrument of soft law to argue that behaviour in conformity with it by those who accepted it is illegitimate.[73]

This comment expresses the operation of soft law perfectly. As a legal matter, states are entirely free to reject it, as it is not binding. However, because it may possess the legitimacy of wide support, it is difficult for a state to claim that others are not free to voluntarily act according to its terms. The conceptual difficulty is that ultimately, if enough states choose to behave in accordance with the new soft law norm, this pattern may destabilize an existing customary rule and allow for the evolution of a new rule of custom. For soft law to merge into binding customary law, however, the principle of state consent must operate, and the new custom must be proved following the processes described earlier. Similarly, general treaty obligations cannot be made specific purely through the operation of soft law. Although soft law statements and instruments may come to influence a treaty regime, this effect results from a more formal expression of consent by states party.

In our discussion of customary law, we stressed that the conclusion that a norm is indeed custom has significant implications for its application in Canada. It is crucial, then, that great care is taken to determine whether a given norm is customary law or soft law. The same applies, of course, to the distinction between soft law and binding treaty norms. We hasten to add that it does not follow from the soft law status of an international norm that it is necessarily without influence on Canadian law. Our point is simply that the nature and the weight of the norm, and the channels through which it comes to operate, are different. In short, in determining the domestic impact of an international norm, the question whether it is treaty, customary, or soft law cannot be side-stepped.

THE INTERPLAY OF INTERNATIONAL LAW AND DOMESTIC LAW

International treaties are not directly applicable in Canada but require transformation.[74] Beneath the surface of this straightforward

---

[73] Chinkin, *supra* note 68 at 850-51. See also J. Ellis, *Soft Law as Topos: The Role of Principles of Soft Law in the Development of International Environmental Law* (D.C.L. thesis, McGill University, 2001) [unpublished].

[74] See generally R. St. J. Macdonald, "The Relationship between International Law and Domestic Law in Canada" in R. St. J. Macdonald, G. Morris, and D.M. Johnston, eds., *Canadian Perspectives on International Law and Organization* (Toronto: University of Toronto Press, 1974) 88.

proposition, however, lies an array of twists and turns that make the domestic application of treaties complex territory to navigate. Yet, if the law concerning the interplay of treaties and Canadian domestic law is complex, the law governing the domestic application of international customary law is at best ambiguous. Whereas, in the context of treaty law, it is clear at least that the basic outlook of the Canadian constitutional framework is dualist, our senior courts have never clarified whether or not customary law is directly applicable in Canada, although most commentators assume that it is.[75]

As we will see, Canadian courts struggle not only to determine when international norms require implementation through legislation but also to determine whether such implementation has actually occurred. They wrestle as well with the implications of the common law principle that "Parliament is not presumed to legislate in breach of a treaty or in a manner inconsistent with the comity of nations and the established rules of international law."[76] In the case law, it remains unclear when this principle comes into play and how it relates to the implementation requirement. There is concern that too wide an application of the presumption would undermine the requirement that international treaties must be transformed to apply in Canada.[77] We will argue that it is also unclear exactly what effect the presumption accords to international law in Canada's domestic legal system. Is it merely to "help inform" a contextual approach to statutory interpretation and judicial review[78] or must courts, to the extent possible, interpret domestic statutes consistently with international law?[79] In this context, does it matter whether

---

[75] See, for example, Kindred, *supra* note 20 at 5; Macdonald, *supra* note 74 at 109; Schabas, *supra* note 20 at 182; van Ert, *supra* note 14 at 4. Note that a recent decision of the Superior Court of Ontario states directly that customary international law forms part of the law of Canada. See *Bouzari* v. *Iran* (May 1, 2002), Toronto 00-CV-201372 (Ont. Sup. Ct.) at para. 39 [hereinafter *Bouzari*].

[76] *Daniels* v. *R.,* [1968] S.C.R. 517 at 541. For a recent restatement of the vitality of this doctrine, see *Schreiber* v. *Canada (Attorney General),* 2002 SCC 62, para. 50 [hereinafter *Schreiber*]. See also R. Sullivan, *Driedger on the Construction of Statutes,* 3rd ed. (Markham, ON: Butterworths, 1994) at 330.

[77] See *Baker, supra* note 7 at para. 80 (per Iacobucci and Cory JJ.). And see Dyzenhaus, Hunt, and Taggart, *supra* note 4 (challenging the validity of concerns over the legitimacy of reference to international norms in the judicial review of the exercise of executive authority).

[78] *Baker, supra* note 7 at para. 70.

[79] See, for example, *National Corn Growers Association* v. *Canada (Import Tribunal),* [1992] 2 S.C.R. 1324 at 1369 [hereinafter *National Corn Growers*]. Note that *National Corn Growers* was concerned with the interpretation of a statute designed

the international norm in question is legally binding on Canada or not? Further, does the application of the presumption depend upon whether international law is used to interpret the Canadian Charter of Rights and Freedoms (Charter)[80] or ordinary statute law?

THE APPLICATION OF INTERNATIONAL TREATIES

While the power to enter into an agreement rests with the federal executive,[81] transformation generally requires legislation that enacts treaty obligations into domestic law.[82] Pursuant to *Canada (A.G.) v. Ontario (A.G.) (Labour Conventions* case), any legislative transformation, in turn, must occur within the jurisdictional framework set out by the Constitution Act 1867,[83] which implies as well that the various legislatures reserve their power to legislate in a manner inconsistent with Canada's treaty obligations.

Transformation of International Treaties

While the principle sounds simple enough, it is remarkably unclear what constitutes transformation.[84] In a narrow sense, transformation is an explicit legislative act through which Parliament or a provincial legislature adopts the treaty obligation and implements it within Canadian law. However, in practice, there are many ways in which such implementation can be accomplished. A treaty may be incorporated directly by reproducing all or part of its text

---

to implement an international treaty. However, a similar approach should apply to all statutes, whether implementing legislation or not. See note 135 in this article and accompanying text.

[80] Canadian Charter of Rights and Freedoms, *supra* note 16.

[81] See Hogg, *supra* note 48.

[82] *Francis* v. *R.,* [1956] S.C.R. 618 [hereinafter *Francis*]. See also *Capital Cities Inc.* v. *Canada (C.R.T.C.),* [1978] S.C.R. 141 [hereinafter *Capital Cities*]. But see *R.* v. *Martin* (1994), 72 O.A.C. 316 at para. 4, where the court held that a "general implementing power" could give domestic effect to an international treaty, even in the absence of express transformation. The power was granted merely "to implement an intergovernmental arrangement or commitment."

[83] *Canada (A.G.)* v. *Ontario (A.G.),* [1937] A.C. 326 (P.C.) at 347-48 (per Lord Atkin) [hereinafter *Labour Conventions* case]. See also *Arrow River and Tributaries Slide & Boom Co. Ltd.,* [1932] S.C.R. 495 at 510 (per Lamont J.) [hereinafter *Arrow River* 1932].

[84] In this paragraph, we rely on Toope, "Inside and Out," *supra* note 20 at 16. For discussions of what constitutes transformation, see also Brandon, *supra* note 20 at 407-22; Kindred, *supra* note 20 at 7-12; van Ert, *supra* note 14 at 20-25.

within a statute, either in its body or as a schedule.[85] Alternatively, a preambular statement may indicate that a given piece of legislation is passed to fulfill specific treaty commitments.[86] Less direct still is the common Canadian practice of "inferred implementation" through the enactment of new legislation or through the amendment of existing legislation.[87] Whether inferred implementation constitutes actual "transformation" is a difficult question and one that places considerable pressure on our courts to sort out the status of the treaty commitment.

Even greater difficulties arise when transformation is said to occur as a result of prior statutory, common law, or even administrative policy conformity with the new treaty obligation.[88] Whether intentionally or through mere sloppiness, Parliament has often left the status of Canadian treaties, especially human rights obligations, unclear. Whatever the case may be, lingering uncertainties about domestic implementation have not prevented the Canadian government from ratifying international human rights treaties on the basis of prior domestic law conformity.[89] Indeed, the government frequently reports to international treaty bodies that it has already implemented the treaty in question and therefore has met its international commitments. For example, in its reports to the Human Rights Committee under the International Covenant on Civil and

[85] See Sullivan, *supra* note 76 at 396. See, for example, the Comprehensive Nuclear Test Ban Treaty Implementation Act, S.C. 1988, c. 32. Even express incorporation in a statute may be read narrowly, with a court seeking the precise intention of Parliament to "transform" specific treaty provisions. In *Pfizer* v. *Canada*, [1999] 4 F.C. 441 (T.D.), the Federal Court held that referential incorporation of the Marrakech Agreement Establishing the World Trade Organization, 15 April 1994, 33 I.L.M. 15 (1994) (cast as approval of the treaty) did not constitute "transformation." On the other hand, in *R.* v. *Crown Zellerbach Canada Ltd.*, [1988] 1 S.C.R. 401, the Supreme Court relied on mere references to an international treaty to interpret the "purposes" of an act that did not expressly transform the treaty.

[86] See *R.* v. *Hydro-Québec*, [1997] 3 S.C.R. 213.

[87] See Sullivan, *supra* note 76.

[88] See the discussion of a so-called "passive incorporation" in Brandon, *supra* note 20 at 415-18.

[89] Weiser, "Effect in Domestic Law," *supra* note 20 at 132. See also Canada, Senate Standing Committee on Human Rights, *Promises to Keep: Implementing Canada's Human Rights Obligations* (Ottawa: Standing Committee on Human Rights, 2001) (Chair: Raynell Andreychuk) (acknowledging that the practice of ratification on the basis of prior conformity has rendered the application in Canada of international human rights norms uncertain).

Political Rights (ICCPR),[90] Canada has claimed implementation primarily through the Charter and related constitutional jurisprudence, complemented by various amendments to existing statutes.[91] In such cases, from the standpoint of Canadian domestic law, has the treaty been implemented? Or should courts treat it as inapplicable simply because it has not been expressly transformed?

The Effects of Implemented Treaties

In our view, all of the above variations can, in principle, transform a treaty so that courts should apply it as part of Canadian law. When a treaty has been explicitly transformed into Canadian law, its provisions should be determinative in the interpretation of domestic legislation. As Justice Michel Bastarache observed in *Pushpanathan v. Canada (Minister of Citizenship and Immigration)*, when the purpose of a statute is to implement an international treaty, "the Court must adopt an interpretation consistent with Canada's obligations under the [treaty]."[92] More specifically, a court must rely on the treaty to interpret the statute as well as on the international rules of treaty interpretation to interpret the treaty and resolve any textual ambiguities.[93] In practice, this approach has meant that interpretation will depend primarily upon the court's understanding of Articles 31 and 32 of the Vienna Convention.[94] Of course, reliance on the treaty underlying an implementing statute is subject to the prerogative of Parliament and provincial legislatures to enact legislation that deviates from Canada's treaty commitments.[95] However, given the previously mentioned common law presumption of legislative intent to act in conformity with Canada's international obligations,[96] the legislators' intent to do

---

[90] ICCPR, *supra* note 39.

[91] Human Rights Committee, *Consideration of Reports Submitted by States under Article 40 of the Covenant: Fourth Periodic Report of States Parties Due in 1995: Canada,* UN CCPROR, 1995, UN Doc. CCPR/C/103/Add.5, accessible at <http://www. unhchr.ch/tbs/doc.nsf/(Symbol)/ CCPR.C.135.En?Opendocument> (date accessed: July 4, 2002).

[92] *Pushpanathan, supra* note 7 at para. 51.

[93] *Ibid.* For a detailed discussion of the court's interpretative approach in *Pushpanathan,* see Schabas, *supra* note 20 at 180.

[94] Vienna Convention, *supra* note 44.

[95] See, for example, *Reference re Powers of Ottawa (City) & Rockcliffe Park (Village) to Levy Rates on Foreign Legations and High Commissioners Residences,* [1943] S.C.R. 208 at 231 [hereinafter *Re Foreign Legations*]; *Capital Cities, supra* note 82 at 173.

[96] See all of the sources cited in note 76.

otherwise must be manifest. This requirement is fully appropriate since, in such cases, Canada will be in breach of its international commitments and may find itself subject to international law remedies invoked by its treaty partners. Albeit in now-dated terms, these linkages are nicely expressed in the decision of the Ontario Supreme Court (Appellate Division) in *Re Arrow River and Tributaries Slide and Boom Co:*

> [U]nless the language employed in the statute is perfectly clear and explicit, admitting of no other interpretation ... The King cannot be thought of as violating his agreement with the other contracting Power; and, if the legislation can fairly be read in such a way as to reject any imputation of breaking faith, it must be so read.[97]

In cases where it is uncertain whether, or to what extent, a statute is implementing a treaty, courts can resort to various interpretative presumptions. Notably, since the Supreme Court's decision in *National Corn Growers Association* v. *Canada,*[98] it has become well established that the treaty text may not merely be relied upon to resolve a patent ambiguity in the domestic legislation but may also be drawn upon by the courts at the very beginning of their analysis in order to determine whether the domestic legislation is ambiguous.[99] The focus on ambiguity links this approach back to the abovementioned presumption of legislative intent to act consistently with Canada's international obligations.[100] Thus, unless the legislators' intent to deviate from international treaty obligations is evident, courts should not only resort to the relevant treaty to

---

[97] *Re Arrow River & Tributaries Slide & Boom Co.,* [1931] 2 D.L.R. 216 at 217 (Ont. S.C. (App. Div.)) [hereinafter *Arrow River* 1931]. The ruling was reversed on appeal to the Supreme Court, but the dictum quoted above was not contradicted. Justice John Henderson Lamont concluded that the legislation in question could not be brought into conformity with the international treaty without doing violence to the intention of the legislator, and Justice Robert Smith held that there was no inconsistency between the treaty and the legislation. See *Arrow River* 1932, *supra* note 83.

[98] *National Corn Growers, supra* note 79.

[99] The restrictive approach of *Schavernoch* v. *Canada (Foreign Claims Commission),* [1982] 1 S.C.R. 1092 at 1098 (per Estey J.) and *Capital Cities, supra* note 82 at 173 (per Laskin C.J.) (where only manifest statutory "ambiguity" would allow reference to an underlying treaty obligation for purposes of interpretation), has not recently been followed, with the Supreme Court moving to the position established in 1984 by the Ontario Court of Appeal. See *R.* v. *Palacios* (1984), 45 O.R. (2d) 269 (C.A.); *National Corn Growers, supra* note 79; *Canada (A.G.)* v. *Ward,* [1993] 2 S.C.R. 689; and *Pushpanathan, supra* note 7.

[100] See all of the sources cited in note 76.

identify ambiguities but must also strive to resolve them through an interpretation of the statute that is consistent with international law.[101] The latter presumption has been most widely invoked in Charter cases, which makes sense given that the Charter is clearly inspired by international human rights law, but nowhere does it expressly state that it is transforming international treaty commitments. With respect to the Charter, the presumption of conformity has been rephrased as an obligation to use international human rights law as "guidance" in interpretation, at least as concerns civil and political rights.[102] However, the presumption as such is of a long-standing application to ordinary statutes[103] and applies also to the common law.[104]

In cases where there has been no specific legislative transformation but Canadian law is in conformity with a treaty due to prior statutory, common law, or even administrative policy, we suggest that the treaty is also implemented for the purposes of domestic law.[105] We are mindful that courts and academic commentators

---

[101] *Arrow River* 1931, *supra* note 97. See also M. Hunt, *Using Human Rights Law in English Courts* (Oxford: Hart Publishing, 1997) at 40 ("So instead of asking if there is ambiguity which can be resolved with the 'assistance' of international law, on this approach the court should ask, having automatically considered the international law alongside the national law, whether the domestic law is unambiguously (in the sense of irreconcilably) in conflict with the international norm").

[102] *Reference re Public Service Employee Relations Act (Alberta)*, [1987] 1 S.C.R. 313 at 349 [hereinafter *Reference re Public Service*] (per Dickson C.J.C. in dissent, though not on this point). *R. v. Keegstra*, [1990] 3 S.C.R. 697 at 837-38 [hereinafter *Keegstra*] (per McLaughlin J.). For further discussion, see notes 136-43 in this article and accompanying text.

[103] See, for example, *Arrow River* 1931, *supra* note 97; *National Corn Growers*, *supra* note 79 at 1369; *R. v. Zingre*, [1981] 2 S.C.R. 392 at 409-10 (per Dickson J.); *Baker v. Canada (Minister of Citizenship and Immigration)* (1996), 142 D.L.R. (4th) 554 at para. 18 (F.C.A.); and, arguably, *Baker*, *supra* note 7. See also van Ert, *supra* note 14 at 35, 38; Schabas, *supra* note 20 at 183; and Weiser, "Effect in Domestic Law," *supra* note 20 at 133-34.

[104] The presumption was phrased in wide terms by Justice MacKay of the Federal Court in *José Pereira E. Hijos, S.A. v. Canada (A.G.)*, [1997] 2 F.C. 84 at para. 20 (T.D.):

> In construing domestic law, whether statutory or common law, the courts will seek to avoid constriction or application that would conflict with the accepted principles of international law.

See Schabas, *supra* note 20 at 184 (citing *R. v. Ewanchuk*, [1999] 1 S.C.R. 330). But see Currie, *supra* note 3 at 222-23 (suggesting that Canadian case law and literature on this issue have been contradictory).

[105] See also Brandon, *supra* note 20 at 401-7; and Kindred, *supra* note 20 at 12.

frequently note that "[i]nternational treaties and conventions are not part of Canadian law unless they have been implemented by statute," as did the majority of the Supreme Court in *Baker*.[106] The Supreme Court's restrictive majority decision in *Francis* v. *R.* is usually invoked in support of this principle.[107] However, it is worth noting the following passage in Justice Ivan Rand's ruling in that case:

Except as to diplomatic status and certain immunities and to belligerent rights, treaty provisions affecting matters within the scope of municipal law, that is, *which purport to change existing law or restrict the future action of the legislature*... must be supplemented by statutory action.[108]

More importantly, in the foundational *Labour Conventions* case, Lord Atkin observed:

Within the British Empire there is a well-established rule that the making of a treaty is an executive act, while the performance of its obligations, *if they entail alteration of the existing domestic law*, requires legislative action ... If the national executive, the government of the day, decide to incur the obligations of treaty *which involve alteration of law* they have to run the risk of obtaining the assent of Parliament to the necessary statute or statutes.[109]

This latter passage indicates that, traditionally, Canadian law did not categorically require statutory implementation and that the flat assertion that treaties are not part of Canadian law unless they have been implemented *by statute* is overly restrictive. Several commentators reach similar conclusions.[110] A more flexible approach is also implied by some recent decisions, including decisions of the Supreme Court.[111] Two considerations suggest that the approach is both correct and compatible with legitimate concerns over the

---

[106] See, for example, *Baker, supra* note 7 at para. 70. And see the majority decision of the Ontario Court of Appeal in *Ahani, supra* note 7 at para. 31 ("Absent implementing legislation, neither [the ICCPR nor its first Optional Protocol] has any legal effect in Canada.").

[107] *Francis, supra* note 82. See also the equally restrictive ruling in *Capital Cities, supra* note 82 at 173.

[108] *Francis, supra* note 82 at 626 [emphasis added]. Justice Rand (Cartwright J. concurring) was in dissent in *Francis*, but not on this point.

[109] *Labour Conventions, supra* note 83 at 347 [emphasis added].

[110] See, for example, Currie, *supra* note 3 at 209, n. 33; Kindred, *supra* note 20 at 9-12; and van Ert, *supra* note 14 at 16.

[111] See, for example, *R.* v. *Sharpe*, [2001] 1 S.C.R. 45 at para. 175 (stating that "this Court has recognized that, generally, international norms are not binding without legislative implementation").

proper roles of the executive, legislators, and the judiciary. First, where a treaty does not actually alter domestic law, the concern that the authority of Parliament or the provincial legislatures could be usurped by federal executive action seems misplaced. In any event, it remains open to Parliament or provincial legislatures to deviate from treaty provisions through explicit statutory action. Second, where no legislative action is required to bring domestic law in line with Canada's treaty commitments, it seems absurd to insist on explicit statutory implementation. This conclusion applies with even greater force when Canada, in international forums, reports its implementation of treaty commitments, as it does regularly, for example, in the human rights context. In such circumstances, Canadian courts should not defer to a subsequent government argument that the treaty obligation has no relevance because it has not been expressly transformed. Instead, they should treat Canada's commitments as having been implemented and should rely on the treaty to interpret domestic law in the manner that we have outlined earlier.

All indications are, however, that Canadian courts continue to struggle with their role in these types of cases. The recent decision of the Ontario Court of Appeal in *Ahani* v. *Canada (A.G.)* provides a vivid and illuminating case in point.[112] *Ahani* was the companion case to *Suresh* v. *Canada,* which were both decided by the Supreme Court in January 2002.[113] Before the Supreme Court, the central issue in both cases was whether or not Canada was prevented from deporting a person accused of links to terrorist activity if that person was likely to be subjected to torture in the receiving state. The court decided unanimously that deportation to torture remains possible under section 53(1)(b) of the Immigration Act, which permits the minister to deport a refugee deemed a danger to Canadian security.[114] However, the principles of fundamental justice under section 7 of the Charter will generally militate against deportation where there is evidence of a substantial risk of torture.[115] In *Suresh,* the Supreme Court found that the appellant was entitled to

---

[112] *Ahani, supra* note 7 and accompanying text.

[113] *Suresh, supra* note 7. *Ahani* v. *Canada (Minister of Citizenship and Immigration)* (2002), 208 D.L.R. (4th) 57 (S.C.C.) [hereinafter *Ahani,* SCC].

[114] Immigration Act, R.S.C. 1985, c. I-2, s. 114(2), as revised by An Act Respecting Immigration to Canada and the Granting of Refugee Protection to Persons Who Are Displaced, Persecuted or in Danger, S.C. 2001, c. 27. *Suresh, supra* note 7 at para. 79.

[115] *Suresh, supra* note 7 at para. 129.

a new deportation hearing.[116] By contrast, in *Ahani*, it held that the facts did not warrant interference with the government's determination that Ahani faced only a minimal risk of torture if returned to his native Iran.[117] Having exhausted all Canadian remedies and facing deportation, Ahani petitioned the UN Human Rights Committee under the Optional Protocol to the ICCPR.[118] The committee requested that Canada stay the deportation order until it had considered Ahani's petition. Taking the view that the committee's interim measures request was non-binding, Canada refused the request.[119] Ahani then applied to the Ontario Superior Court for an injunction restraining his deportation pending the committee's consideration of his petition. The trial judge denied the stay,[120] and the majority of the Court of Appeal declined to overturn this decision.[121]

The majority concluded that, as a matter of treaty law, access accorded to individuals to the Human Rights Committee by Canada's ratification of the Option Protocol is conditioned by two key points. First, according to the terms of the Optional Protocol, the Human Rights Committee has no power to bind Canada — even its final determination is merely recommendatory.[122] Second, in ratifying the Optional Protocol, Canada did not consent to stay domestic proceedings.[123] Thus, the appellant could not be allowed to "convert a non-binding request in a Protocol, which has never been part of Canadian law, into a binding obligation enforceable in Canada by a Canadian court."[124] The majority decision is undoubtedly correct insofar as it is based on the non-binding nature of the committee process. However, to the extent that the decision treats the ICCPR and the Optional Protocol as unimplemented,[125]

---

[116] *Ibid.* at para. 130.

[117] *Ahani*, SCC, *supra* note 113 at para. 25-26.

[118] Optional Protocol to the International Covenant on Civil and Political Rights, 16 December 1966, Can. T.S. 1976 No. 47 (entered into force 23 March 1976) [hereinafter Optional Protocol].

[119] As it has done in previous instances of such requests. See Schabas, *supra* note 20 at 194.

[120] *Ahani* v. *Canada (Minister of Citizenship and Immigration)* (2002), 18 Imm. L.R. (3d) 193 (Ont. S.C.J.).

[121] *Ahani*, *supra* note 7.

[122] *Ibid.* at para. 31.

[123] *Ibid.* at para. 32.

[124] *Ibid.* at para. 33.

[125] Note that, given the focus on the non-binding nature of the Optional Protocol's committee process, it should not have mattered, from a strictly legal standpoint,

on the principles that we have outlined earlier, it is questionable whether the majority was correct. The majority did not consider whether the two treaties might have been implicitly implemented through the Charter. Instead, it expounded the narrow view that "Canada has never incorporated either the Covenant or the Protocol into Canadian law *by implementing legislation.* Absent *implementing legislation,* neither has any legal effect in Canada."[126]

The dissent by Justice Marc Rosenberg epitomizes the lingering dissatisfaction with this conclusion and, perhaps more importantly, with some of the arguments that the Canadian government presented in this case. As we suggested earlier, in international forums, Canada routinely argues that it is in compliance with the ICCPR because of the Charter.[127] Thus, while there was no express incorporation of the treaty, we would argue that it has been implicitly incorporated into Canadian law. The same argument can be made concerning the purely procedural obligations voluntarily accepted by Canada under the Optional Protocol. As Justice Rosenberg makes clear, the mere fact that Ahani could ask the Human Rights Committee to review his situation in light of Canada's obligations under the ICCPR does not mean that a substantive remedy would have been available. However, it seems odd for Canada to agree to the procedural right to petition the committee and then, by declining the committee's request for a stay of deportation proceedings, effectively to deny it randomly in concrete cases. Has the procedural right not been incorporated into Canadian law by virtue of the government's regular engagement with the committee, both in specific cases and in fulfilling its reporting obligations? Or is the

---

whether or not the relevant provisions were implemented in Canadian law (unless, of course, Canadian law had provided a right to have deportation orders stayed pending the outcome of the Committee process).

[126] *Ahani, supra* note 7 at para. 31 [emphasis added]. The majority went on to say that a court may nonetheless rely upon international human rights commitments to interpret section 7 of the Charter in a way that is consistent with them. See also D. Dyzenhaus and E. Fox-Decent, "Rethinking the Process/Substance Distinction: *Baker v. Canada*" (2001) 51 U.T. L. J. 193 at 232-36. Dyzenhaus and Fox-Decent argue that the insistence on statutory transformation of international obligations would logically have to be matched by an insistence that common rules can only bind if they are transformed into statute law. The justification for the requirement of statutory implementation is typically rooted in supposed considerations of democratic legitimacy, which is in the requirement of majoritarian legislative action. Pointing to this logical connection reveals a fundamental flaw in the "transformation" requirement.

[127] See note 91 and accompanying text.

solemn commitment of the government nothing more than a discretion unshaped by any legal duties? When, before the Ontario Court of Appeal, the Canadian government then argued that international conventions are not binding in Canada unless specifically incorporated,[128] one cannot but question the good faith of its position.[129] Indeed, one may also share Justice Rosenberg's frustration with the government's reliance on the non-binding nature of the Human Rights Committee's process "to shield the executive from the consequences of its voluntary decision to enter into and therefore be bound by the Covenant and the Protocol."[130] Thus, although we reiterate that the majority decision on this particular point was correct as a matter of law, we have considerable sympathy for Justice Rosenberg's decision to accord to the appellant a procedural right to have a court determine whether "the balance of convenience favours his remaining in Canada."[131]

The Effects of Unimplemented Treaties

There are, of course, cases where treaties that are in force for Canada remain genuinely unimplemented in domestic law. For

---

[128] See *Ahani, supra* note 7 at para. 91 (Rosenberg dissent).

[129] See also J. Harrington, "The Year in Review: Developments in International Law and Its Application in Canada" (presentation to the Canadian Bar Association Conference on Directions in International Law and Practice, Ottawa, March 30, 2002) at 8 [unpublished, on file with authors].

[130] *Ahani, supra* note 7 at para. 92. Justice Rosenberg specifically noted his dissatisfaction with the government's insistence on the non-binding nature of the committee process when, on a government website, it asserted that

> [i]t accepts the authority of the UN Human Rights Committee to hear complaints from Canadian citizens under the *Optional Protocol to the International Covenant on Civil and Political Rights.* These undertakings strengthen Canada's reputation as a guarantor of its citizen's rights and enhance our credentials to urge other governments to respect international standards.

Ibid. at para. 103, citing Canada, Department of Foreign Affairs and International Trade, "Human Rights in Canadian Foreign Policy," accessible at <http://www.dfait-maeci.gc.ca/foreign_policy/human-rights/forpol-en.asp> (last modified September 1998). For a similar view, see Harrington, *supra* note 129 at 8-9.

[131] Justice Rosenberg would have remitted the case to the Superior Court for determination of whether the applicant would suffer irreparable harm if returned to Iran, and which of the parties would suffer greater harm from the granting of refusal of the remedy pending the outcome of the Committee process. *Ahani, supra* note 7 at paras. 107-11.

example, it is conceivable that, due to complex stakeholder debates or federal-provincial disagreements, transformation of a treaty lags behind Canada's international obligations. One can easily imagine that this scenario will unfold in the case of the Kyoto Protocol to the United Nations Framework Convention on Climate Change.[132] What is the legal effect of a genuinely unimplemented treaty in Canada?[133]

We submit that a treaty that is binding *on* Canada, while not directly applicable *in* Canada, is nonetheless subject to the presumption of legislative intent to act consistently with Canada's international obligations. As we understand this presumption, it applies to all of Canada's international obligations, be they treaty-based or rooted in customary international law.[134] This understanding leads to the inference that courts should make every effort to interpret Canadian law (legislation or the common law) so as to conform to Canada's international obligations.[135] Furthermore, the principle that domestic law should, if possible, be interpreted consistently with Canada's treaty obligations, applies not merely to implementing legislation but to all domestic law.[136]

Unfortunately, Canadian case law has not taken a consistent approach to the presumption of conformity with international law. First, there is uncertainty regarding the effect that the presumption

[132] Kyoto Protocol, December 1997, 37 I.L.M. 32 (1998), to the United Nations Framework Convention on Climate Change, *supra* note 69.

[133] We use the phrase "genuinely unimplemented treaty" to distinguish this category from the spectrum of situations in which, as we have argued, treaties are implemented, albeit not necessarily through specific statutory transformation.

[134] See notes 76 and 100-4 and accompanying text. As we will suggest later in this article, a different approach should apply to international legal norms that do not bind Canada or to international soft law. See notes 158-60 in this article and the accompanying text. For a detailed discussion of the presumption in the context of the use of human rights law by English courts, see Hunt, *supra* note 101 at 13-25, 297-324.

[135] For a detailed discussion of why the presumption should be equally applicable to legislation enacted prior to a given international commitment, see van Ert, *supra* note 14 at 38-46.

[136] See notes 103-4 in this article and the accompanying text. See also van Ert, *supra* note 14 at 35-38; Schabas, *supra* note 20 at 183; and Weiser, "Effect in Domestic Law," *supra* note 20 at 138, who argues that the presumption of conformity should apply to all statutes. However, in "Undressing the Window," *supra* note 20 at 26, n. 116, Weiser concludes that, since the Supreme Court does not mention the presumption in the bulk of its decisions involving international law, the presumption does not currently exist with respect to statutes other than implementing legislation.

produces in the context of Charter interpretation. Second, the case law, notably since *Baker*, is unclear on whether the presumption applies equally to Canada's international obligations and non-binding international norms. As far as the Charter is concerned, Supreme Court decisions appear both to invoke the presumption of conformity to interpret the Charter in light of international human rights law as well as to eviscerate the presumption in practice.[137] At the end of the day, international (human rights) law is treated as highly "relevant and persuasive," coming close to, but stopping short of, the ordinary presumption of conformity. This approach is reflected in then Chief Justice Brian Dickson's dissenting judgment in *Reference re Public Service Employee Relations Act:*

> I believe the Charter should generally be presumed to provide protection at least as great as that afforded by similar provisions in international human rights documents which Canada has ratified.
>
> In short, though I do not believe the judiciary is bound by the norms of international law in interpreting the Charter, these norms provide a relevant and persuasive source for interpretation of the provisions of the Charter, especially when they arise out of Canada's international obligations under human rights conventions.[138]

Building on the idea that international law is "relevant and persuasive," the Supreme Court has tended to draw upon international norms merely to "inform" its interpretation of the Charter, without, however, seeing itself as being required to strive for an interpretation that is consistent with international norms.[139] The cumulative effect is that international law is not treated as a base line measure, as suggested by Chief Justice Dickson, but simply as an instructive aid. Thus, in the Charter context, a weaker version of the presumption of conformity appears to have emerged. Irit Weiser argues that

---

[137] In *Keegstra, supra* note 102 at 837-38 (per McLachlin J.), even the dissenters held that section 2(b) of the Charter should be interpreted "as a matter of construction" in a manner consistent with international approaches. However, their concern was not to allow international law to restrict the full scope of Charter rights. On the latter point, see also *R. v. Cook*, [1998] 2 S.C.R. 597 at para. 148 (per Bastarache J.) [hereinafter *Cook*].

[138] *Reference re Public Service, supra* note 102 at 349 (per Dickson C.J.C. in dissent, though not on this point). See also the discussion in G.V. La Forest, "The Use of International and Foreign Materials in the Supreme Court of Canada" (1988) 17 Can. Council Int'l L. Proc. 230 at 232-33.

[139] See, for example, *Slaight Communications Inc. v. Davidson*, [1989] 1 S.C.R. 1038 at 1056-57 [hereinafter *Slaight Communications*]; *Keegstra, supra* note 102 at 837; *United States v. Burns*, [2001] 1 S.C.R. 283 at paras. 79-81; *Baker, supra* note 7 at para. 70; and *Suresh, supra* note 7 at para. 60.

this approach is the appropriate way for courts to deal with unimplemented treaties in Charter interpretation. Weiser's concern is that the ordinary presumption of conformity would effectively eliminate domestic democratic controls over the legal system and entrench the relevant international obligation. Unlike in the case of ordinary statutes, since the treaty provision would be incorporated into *Charter* interpretation, Parliament could not legislate in deviation from international law, except on the basis of section 33.[140] One might be sympathetic to this concern, notably with respect to treaty obligations that would restrict the scope of Charter rights. Yet, David Dyzenhaus argues convincingly that "democratic deficit" arguments are often rooted in impoverished conceptions of democratic governance. They typically equate democracy with majoritarian legislative action. Dyzenhaus suggests that a rich view of democratic legitimacy can account for public engagement with international and common law norms outside the framework of statutory intervention.[141] In any event, the problem pointed to by Weiser would arise only in a relatively small number of cases. We have already suggested that many human rights treaties are in fact implemented implicitly, including through the Charter itself or due to prior conformity of Canadian law. Thus, courts have considerable scope for resorting to the presumption of conformity. In cases of genuinely unimplemented treaties, the primary concern should be that international human rights law serves as a "floor" rather than a "ceiling" for the rights enshrined in the Charter. In fact, this concern, which is nicely encapsulated in the earlier quotation from Chief Justice Dickson's judgment in the 1987 *Reference re Public Service* case, has already shaped the approach of the Canadian judiciary. Canadian courts have been intent not to allow international law to restrict the scope of Charter rights.[142]

---

[140] Weiser, "Effect in Domestic Law," *supra* note 20 at 138-39. In our view, requiring the invocation of section 33 of the Charter might well be appropriate where Parliament wishes to assert an interpretation of the Charter that restricts human rights provided by an international treaty to which Canada is a party.

[141] D. Dyzenhaus, "Constituting the Rule of Law: Fundamental Values in Administrative Law" (2002) 27 Queen's L. J. 445 at 501-2. See also Dyzenhaus and Fox-Decent, *supra* note 126.

[142] See, for example, *Slaight Communications*, *supra* note 139 at 1056; and *Cook*, *supra* note 137 at para. 148 (per Bastarache J.) (emphasizing that "the presumption of statutory interpretation that Parliament intended to legislate in conformity with international law must be applied with great care in the *Charter* context. The *Charter* is the fundamental expression of the minimum obligations owed to individuals in our society; I would not be inclined to accept that

While the Supreme Court has thus built on Chief Justice Dickson's approach to international law as being potentially relevant and persuasive — rather than obligatory — sources for Charter interpretation, it has not pursued his attempt to distinguish between international norms that are binding on Canada and other international norms.[143] The court frequently cites a mixture of binding and non-binding sources, apparently according them the same interpretative weight. For example, in *Suresh*, the Supreme Court suggests that soft law, unimplemented treaties, custom, and even *jus cogens* all simply help to "inform" the interpretation of the Charter.[144] The lack of clarity on this issue has been compounded by the fact that the Supreme Court's treatment of international law as relevant and persuasive in the interpretation of the Charter seems to have carried over to the interpretation of ordinary statutes. In other words, there are some indications that this approach is implanting itself in the very context in which the presumption of conformity originated and where it should have full application — the interpretation of domestic legislation in light of Canada's international obligations.

The ambiguous state of the case law in this regard is reflected in the Supreme Court's decision in *Baker* and is carried further in subsequent decisions of the Supreme Court and other Canadian courts. One of the principal casualties of this lack of clarity is customary international law. We turn first to a more detailed discussion of the Supreme Court's decision in *Baker* as it concerns the

---

Canada's international law obligations could truncate rights defined by the *Charter*").

[143] Although Dickson did not consider international law to bind courts in Charter interpretation, he did consider it relevant to the court's interpretative task that, by ratifying a treaty, Canada "oblige[s] itself internationally to ensure within its borders the protection of certain fundamental rights and freedoms." *Reference re Public Service, supra* note 102 at 349. Note that Justice Michel Bastarache, in a recent paper, endorsed Dickson's approach. He suggested that "[t]he Supreme Court will consider inherently non-binding instruments ... as well as instruments to which Canada is a party ... The first group, like international case law, are a guide to interpretation, while the second are a "relevant and persuasive" factor in Charter interpretation." Justice M. Bastarache, "The Honourable G.V. La Forest's Use of Foreign Materials in the Supreme Court of Canada and His Influence on Foreign Courts" in R. Johnson et al., eds., *Gérard V. La Forest at the Supreme Court of Canada 1985-1997* (Winnipeg: Canadian Legal History Project, 2000) 433 at 434.

[144] *Suresh, supra* note 7 at para. 46. See also notes 192-201 in this article and the accompanying text.

effect of unimplemented international treaties. In our subsequent discussion of customary law, we will then examine how later decisions have applied the ruling in *Baker* and what the potential implications of these decisions are for the status of international custom in Canadian law.

Baker involved both the statutory basis for, and the proper scope of, ministerial discretion concerning a deportation order.[145] Ms. Baker was an illegal immigrant who had lived in Canada since 1981. In 1992, an immigration officer ordered her deportation. Since 1981, Ms. Baker had given birth to four children in Canada. They were therefore Canadian citizens. She also had four children in Jamaica. After the birth of her last child, Ms. Baker was diagnosed with paranoid schizophrenia. To prevent her deportation, and the consequent separation from her Canadian children, two of whom were under her sole care, Ms. Baker requested an exemption from the rule that one must apply for permanent residency from outside Canada. Under the Immigration Act[146] and Regulations,[147] an exception was available on humanitarian or compassionate grounds. The application was denied, and an immigration officer's notes, including disparaging comments about Ms. Baker and about Canadian immigration policy, were submitted in evidence at trial and were held to give rise to an apprehension of bias.

The Supreme Court's decision, *per* Justice Claire L'Heureux-Dubé, was complex and wide-ranging; necessarily focusing upon process standards in administrative law and upon substantive standards for judicial review. For our purposes, the central ruling was that even though Canada had never explicitly transformed its obligations under the Convention on the Rights of the Child[148] into domestic law, the immigration official was bound to consider the "values" expressed in this convention when exercising discretion. Therefore, the convention's emphasis upon "the best interests of the child" should have weighed heavily in considering Ms. Baker's application.

Of greatest interest for our discussion is how the majority arrived at the conclusion that "the values reflected in international human

---

[145] For the summary of the *Baker* case, we rely on Toope, "Inside and Out," *supra* note 20 at 19-21.

[146] Immigration Act, *supra* note 114.

[147] Immigration Regulations, S.O.R./78-172, s. 2.1.

[148] Convention on the Rights of the Child, 20 November 1989, Can. T.S. 1992 No. 3 (entered into force September 2, 1990).

rights law may help inform the contextual approach to statutory interpretation and judicial review."[149] More specifically, the central question is how the majority conceived of this principle in relation to the traditional presumption of statutory conformity with international obligations. Justice L'Heureux-Dubé supported the passage quoted earlier through the following statement, quoted from *Driedger on the Construction of Statutes:*

> [T]he legislature is presumed to respect the values and principles contained in international law, both customary and conventional. These constitute a part of the legal context in which legislation is enacted and read. *In so far as possible, therefore, interpretations that reflect these values and principles are preferred.*[150]

It would seem that the primary question for the majority with respect to the Convention on the Rights of the Child was how to give effect to the unimplemented treaty. As noted earlier, the majority took a narrow view on the question of implementation and observed that, absent implementation by Parliament, "[i]ts provisions ... have no direct application in Canadian law."[151] Yet, the "values" reflected in the convention could shape statutory interpretation. It is conceivable that, in distinguishing the convention's provisions from its values, the majority was looking for a compromise formula that would make the consideration of unimplemented treaties more broadly acceptable.[152] However, in our view, the majority erred on the side of caution, for at least two reasons.

First, while the provisions of the convention were not directly applicable *in* Canadian law, they were binding *on* Canada and, therefore, relevant to statutory interpretation through the presumption of conformity. From the standpoint of the presumption, the court did not have to distinguish between provisions and values — it could have had recourse to both. By drawing the distinction, the majority implied that Canada's international obligations, as expressed in the provisions of the unimplemented convention, are not covered by the presumption of statutory conformity. Curiously, it took this approach to the presumption, notwithstanding the very passage in *Driedger on the Construction of Statutes* that it quoted in

---

[149] *Baker, supra* note 7 at para. 70.

[150] *Ibid.* at para. 69, quoted from Sullivan, *supra* note 76 at 330 [emphasis in Supreme Court decision].

[151] *Ibid.* at para. 69. See also note 106 and accompanying text.

[152] Nonetheless, Iacobucci and Cory JJ. objected to the majority's approach to the convention. See notes 162-65 in this article and the accompanying text.

part, to support its reliance on the values expressed in the convention. In full, the relevant passage describes the scope of the presumption of conformity as follows:

[T]here are two aspects to the presumption. First, the legislature is presumed to comply with the obligations owed by Canada as a signatory [*sic*] of international instruments and more generally as a member of the international community. In choosing among possible interpretations, therefore, the courts avoid interpretations that would put Canada in breach of any of its international obligations. Second, the legislature is presumed to respect the values and principles enshrined in international law, both customary and conventional. These constitute a part of the legal context in which legislation is enacted and read. In so far as possible, therefore, interpretations that reflect these values and principles are preferred.[153]

It was fully open to the majority to hold that Canada's immigration officers were bound to consider the best interests of the child within the framework of the Immigration Act,[154] so as to interpret it in conformity with international obligations binding on Canada.[155]

Our second concern relates to the effect of the presumption of conformity on the interpretative task of the court. The Convention on the Rights of the Child should not merely have been at the court's discretion to "help inform" its interpretative effort — something less than what is required by the traditional presumption of

---

[153] Sullivan, *supra* note 76 at 330. There is some irony in the fact that the *Baker* decision, in quoting *Driedger,* deviates from the very approach that the passage suggests courts take to the presumption.

[154] Immigration Act, *supra* note 114.

[155] One might object that the court had to tread especially carefully since it was not merely interpreting a domestic statute in light of an unimplemented treaty but was also reviewing the exercise of administrative discretion granted by the statute. In other words, the court had to avoid both trespassing Parliamentary supremacy *and* unduly constraining discretionary power. While, as a general matter, both considerations deserve deference, we do not believe that the exercise of administrative discretion warrants different treatment in the context of the presumption of conformity. After all, if Parliament is presumed to intend conformity with Canada's international obligations, it makes little sense to assume that it granted administrative decision-makers discretion to ignore these obligations. Thus, in reviewing the exercise of discretion in light of applicable international law, a court would not be constraining discretion let alone usurping the role of the decision-maker. It would merely identify the statutory bounds of the discretion. See also the detailed discussion of this issue in Dyzenhaus et al., *supra* note 4 at 24-29. Dyzenhaus et al. point out that "[t]he fear of negating discretion assumes that the intention or the effect of applying the interpretative principle to discretionary power is to substitute the court's view of the merits for that of the primary decision-maker. There is no such intention, and it will not have that effect" (at 27).

conformity.[156] Instead, the court was obliged to strive, to the extent possible, for an interpretation that is consistent with the legal commitments that Canada made by ratifying the convention.[157] The difference between the provisions of the treaty and its spirit should have manifested itself in the relatively greater interpretative scope that open-textured concepts, such as "values and principles," provide. The difference should not have affected the initial onus on the court in approaching the relevant norms.

In our view, a lesser interpretative onus ("may help inform" rather than the onus to "strive to interpret consistently") would have been warranted only if the majority had seen itself as working with non-binding international norms. In other words, had the court looked to norms that were not binding on Canada, such as non-binding values and principles reflected in international treaties or other soft law, it would have quite correctly allowed statutory interpretation or judicial review to be "informed" by them. The court would then have gone beyond the traditional reach of the presumption of conformity and accepted that a broader range of international norms than Canada's international obligations are potentially relevant to the interpretation of statutes.[158] This subtle extension of international law's influence on the domestic sphere, we submit, would have been both desirable and appropriate. However, given the focus on the fact that the Convention of the Rights of the Child was an unimplemented treaty, it is not clear that the majority intended the articulation of a principle that non-binding international law can inform statutory interpretation and judicial review.[159]

From the standpoint of international law, then, the *Baker* decision puts into the spotlight two questions about the binding quality

---

[156] See also Currie, *supra* note 3 at 225. But see Kindred, *supra* note 20 at 21, who argues that the approach of the Supreme Court in *Baker* actually went beyond the principle that, to the extent possible, statutes should be interpreted in conformity with international law. According to Kindred, the judgment "demands that courts make affirmative use of international law . . . in the interpretation of domestic statutes."

[157] For a compelling discussion of the judicial obligation to interpret domestic law consistently with international law, at least as concerns human rights law, see Hunt, *supra* note 101 at 297-324.

[158] See Kindred, *supra* note 20 at 26.

[159] But it is possible to read the court's subsequent decision in *Spraytech, supra* note 9, as drawing upon *Baker* to precisely this effect. We return to this issue in our discussion of customary law in the next section of this article. See notes 182-91 in this article and the accompanying text.

of international law. How should courts approach international treaty norms that are binding on Canada but, absent implementation, are not directly applicable in Canada? How should they approach norms that do not bind Canada internationally but that nonetheless reflect important international values? Karen Knop has suggested that international law may be best seen as "foreign" law that needs to be translated into domestic systems such as Canada's and interpreted into local culture.[160] According to Knop, comparative law methodology, which seeks out persuasive authority, is better suited to the internalization of international law than an application of international law that is dependent upon a rigid distinction between binding and non-binding norms. She argues that this distinction, if applied uncritically, risks caricaturing the influence of international law as an all or nothing proposition. On the one hand, some norms risk being ignored altogether simply because they are not legally binding. On the other hand, legally binding norms produce a false sense of certainty when it is assumed that they require nothing other than "mechanical" application by a judge. According to Knop, an approach focused on persuasiveness of norms can improve the domestic application of both types of norms. In the case of non-binding norms, a search for persuasiveness is *necessary* to justify the reliance on individual norms. In the case of binding international law, it can assist the interpretative tasks inherent in applying international law. Knop interprets the majority decision in *Baker* as embracing just such a more flexible and more nuanced methodology and thus as signalling a significant and welcome shift in the approach of the Supreme Court to international law.[161]

While we agree with the argument that Knop advances regarding the pitfalls of a mechanical focus on the binding and non-binding distinction, it should be evident from the preceding discussion that we are less confident that *Baker* signals a positive shift. Our worry is that the majority decision places the Supreme Court on a path towards treating all international law as persuasive authority, which the court *may* use to "inform" its interpretation of domestic law. In other words, by treating both binding and non-binding international norms in this manner, courts move away from their duty to strive for an interpretation that is consistent with Canada's international obligations. Thus, as appealing as the comparative law metaphor may seem at first glance, it too bears risks.

---

[160] Knop, *supra* note 13 at 525.

[161] *Ibid.* at 535.

We fear that the approach, if not carefully applied as a *supple-mentary* analytical tool, could easily lead to less, rather than more, nuance. The temptation may be great to treat all international law, whether binding on Canada or not, as "optional information" and to disregard the particular interpretative onus that is placed upon courts by the presumption of conformity with Canada's international obligations. There is a significant difference between international law that is binding on Canada and other international norms. The former is not only potentially persuasive but also obligatory. This distinction matters — when we fail to uphold our obligations, we undermine the respect for law internationally. The distinction also provides the rationale for the traditional common law presumption of conformity with Canada's international obligations as well as for treating differently international norms that do not legally bind Canada. A more limited version of the presumption, treating international law as relevant and persuasive, appears to have evolved in the context of Charter interpretation. This approach may or may not be warranted in the unique circumstances of the Charter. However, the ordinary presumption of conformity should have unfettered application in all other cases. Traditionally, this presumption has applied to the interpretation of statutory and common law and there is no rationale for importing a different approach from case law regarding Charter interpretation.

For all these reasons, we also believe that the dissent of Justices Frank Iacobucci and Peter Cory in *Baker* miscast the issues at hand. For the dissenters, the majority ruling was "not in accordance with the Court's jurisprudence concerning the status of international law within the domestic legal system."[162] However, the concern of the dissenters was not merely the idea that international "values" should shape Canadian law. Rather, the real concern seems to have been that the majority transgressed the principle that an unimplemented treaty has no direct application in Canada. Thus, Justices Iacobucci and Cory considered that the majority had effected the "adoption of a principle of law which permits reference to an unincorporated convention during the process of statutory interpretation."[163] One may or may not share the dissenters' concern that this type of principle ultimately "give[s] force and effect within the domestic legal system to international obligations undertaken by the executive alone that have yet to be subject to the democratic will

---

[162] *Baker, supra* note 7 at para. 79, per Iacobucci J. (dissenting in part).

[163] *Ibid.* at para. 80.

of Parliament."[164] However, as far as the domestic effect of a binding, but unimplemented, treaty obligation is concerned, the principle in question was most certainly not "adopted" by the majority in *Baker.* As we have explained, it has long existed in the shape of the presumption of conformity with Canada's international obligations.[165]

THE APPLICATION OF CUSTOMARY INTERNATIONAL LAW

The proper application of customary international law in Canada emerged in a series of cases after *Baker* as a major question for the Supreme Court. To what extent can international customary law inform domestic legal processes?[166] The court's treatment of this question leads to new concerns about the already troubled status of customary international law in Canada. We begin with an overview on the status of customary international norms in Canadian law and then turn to the implications of the application of the *Baker* approach to customary law.

Customary International Law and Canadian Law

The status of customary international law within Canadian law is ambiguous. In 1972, Ronald St. J. Macdonald argued that until the divided and ultimately confusing judgment of the Supreme Court in *Reference re Powers of Ottawa (City) & Rockcliffe Park (Village) to Levy Rates on Foreign Legations and High Commissioners Residences*[167] (*Re Foreign Legations* case), Canadian law was relatively consistent in favouring a "monist" theory under which customary law applied in Canada of its own force.[168] Since *Re Foreign Legations,* senior Canadian courts

---

[164] *Ibid.* Once again we see revealed a narrow and majoritarian conception of democratic governance. See note 126 in this article. See also note 141 and accompanying text.

[165] Justices Iacobucci and Cory seemed to assume that this presumption applied only to the interpretation of the Charter. See *Baker, supra* note 7 at para. 81. We already explained that we believe that this assumption is wrong. See also Dyzenhaus and Fox-Decent, *supra* note 126 at 236.

[166] Indeed, it is worth noting that customary international law has seen something of a renaissance in Canadian courts. A search on legal databases by the authors in May 2002 revealed sixty-seven cases in Canadian courts citing customary law; two-thirds of these were decided during the last three years.

[167] *Re Foreign Legations, supra* note 95.

[168] Macdonald, *supra* note 74 at 109. See also van Ert, *supra* note 20 at chapter 3 (arguing that, for customary law, the monist thesis is clearly supported in Canada).

have vacillated on the application of customary international law in Canada. In some decisions, customary law seemed to be treated as part of the law of Canada and thus as being directly applicable.[169] Other decisions would appear to point in the opposite direction or to remain ambiguous.[170]

By way of contrast, within the United Kingdom, at least since the seminal judgment of Lord Denning in *Trendtex Trading Corp.* v. *Nigeria (Central Bank)*, it has been clear that customary international law operates directly within the domestic legal system to affect the obligations of the state and of private entities, as appropriate.[171] Within the United States as well, customary law can operate of its own force. In the famous words of the US Supreme Court in *Paquete Habana*:

International law is part of our law, and must be ascertained and administered by the Courts of Justice of appropriate jurisdiction, as often as questions of right depending upon it are fully presented for their determination. For this purpose, where there is no treaty and no controlling executive or legislative act or judicial decision, resort must be had to the customs and usages of civilized nations.[172]

---

[169] See, for example, *Saint John (City)* v. *Fraser-Brace Overseas Corp.*, [1958] S.C.R. 263 (seeming to favour direct incorporation); *Schreiber, supra* note 76, at paras. 48-50 (suggesting that customary law is relevant to the interpretation of domestic law and that *jus cogens* ousts ordinary customary norms and requires its direct application within domestic law); and *Mack* v. *Canada (A.G.)*, [2002] O.J. No. 3488 at paras. 18-33 (C.A.) (QL) [hereinafter *Mack*] (treating customary law as directly applicable, unless ousted by contrary domestic legislation). One could also read Justice La Forest's reasons in *Kindler* v. *Canada (Minister of Justice)*, [1991] 2 S.C.R. 779 at 835 (per La Forest J.), as at least implicitly accepting that a customary law rule could directly shape Canadian law. He emphasizes the importance of universal practice and international consensus in shaping norms that would have an impact in Canada. Save for the terminology, the analysis is close to the traditional invocation of practice and *opinio juris* as the measure of existence for customary law. In Justice La Forest's view, the norm against the death penalty was not at that time strong enough to guide domestic law — unlike norms against genocide, slavery, and torture.

[170] See *Congo* v. *Venne*, [1971] S.C.R. 997 (where changes to customary law did not operate automatically within Canadian law); *Reference Re Mining and Other Natural Resources of the Continental Shelf* (1983), 41 Nfld. & P.E.I.R. 271 (Nfld. C.A.) (implicitly requiring transformation of customary law).

[171] *Trendtex Trading Corp.* v. *Nigeria (Central Bank)*, [1977] 1 Q.B. 529 (C.A.).

[172] *The Paquette Habana*, 175 U.S. 688 (1900) at 700. Despite this clear pronouncement, courts in the United States continue to struggle with the role of customary international law in concrete cases.

It must be emphasized, as the quotation from *Paquete Habana* so clearly indicates, that even when customary international law operates of its own force, it does not preclude the lawful domestic authorities from legislating contrary to custom. We are not suggesting that international law should simply apply in Canada despite the law and policy of the duly elected governments of Canada and the provinces. Our point is that customary law should be presumed to apply unless altered, explicitly or implicitly.[173] As with treaty law, courts should strive to interpret statutes and common law, to the extent possible, in conformity with international customary law.[174] However, if the Canadian Parliament or provincial legislatures wish to ignore customary law, they are free to do so.

Given the primacy of the common law tradition in the public law of Canada, the best view appears to be that customary law can operate directly within the Canadian legal system.[175] Yet this point needs to be clarified by senior Canadian courts. Regrettably, the decisions of the Supreme Court over the last decade or so have further muddied the waters. Indeed, there have been indications over the last decade that the court was inching its way towards a dualist position *vis-à-vis* customary international law. However, the course may have been corrected in the recent *Schreiber* v. *Canada (Attorney General)* decision.[176]

In a number of important decisions, the Supreme Court did not take up the opportunity to focus its attention on customary international law. For example, in *Reference re Secession of Quebec*, the *amicus curiae* asserted that the Supreme Court would not have jurisdiction to apply "pure international law."[177] Without discussion,

---

[173] See *Schreiber, supra* note 76; *Mack, supra* note 169. See also Currie, *supra* note 3 at 204.

[174] *Schreiber, supra* note 76; *Mack, supra* note 169; and *Currie, supra* note 3.

[175] A wonderfully clear example of such direct application of customary law is the recent decision of the Ontario Superior Court of Justice in *Bouzari, supra* note 75 at para. 39. At paras. 57-73, Swinton J. provides a nuanced discussion of the prohibition on torture as *jus cogens* and of its impact on the interpretation of Canada's State Immunity Act, R.S.C. 1985, c. S-18. See also the Ontario Court of Appeal in *Mack, supra* note 169 at para. 32 (implying that customary law is directly applicable within the domestic legal system unless ousted by unambiguous legislation).

[176] *Schreiber, supra* note 76 at para. 50 (hinting that customary law is directly applicable within the domestic legal system unless ousted by unambiguous legislation).

[177] *Reference re Secession of Quebec*, [1998] 2 S.C.R. 217 [hereinafter *Quebec Secession Reference*]. See also S. J. Toope, Case Comment on *Quebec Secession Reference* (1999) 93 A.J.I.L. 519 at 523.

the Supreme Court implicitly adopted this view, leaving others to divine the implications for the status of international law. The implication could be simply that customary law becomes part of "the laws of Canada" for the purposes of the court's jurisdiction under section 3 of the Supreme Court Act.[178] However, the implication could also be that the Supreme Court cannot directly apply international customary law because it is *not* part of Canadian law. The fact that the Supreme Court's international law analysis in *Reference re Secession of Quebec* failed completely to engage with the customary law on self-determination suggests that a dualist position may implicitly have been adopted.[179]

The Baker *Approach and Customary International Law*

Baker was another missed opportunity, where the court might have helped to clarify the status of customary international law within Canadian law.[180] Rather than engage in the debate on the domestic effect of unimplemented treaties, it would have been open to the Supreme Court in *Baker* to conclude that the "best interests of the child" test had solidified as a norm of customary international law. Once again, we are left to speculate. Was the court looking to avoid the complexities of determining whether or not a customary norm indeed existed; did it wish to avoid the question whether international customary law forms part of the law of Canada;[181] or did it simply miss the customary law angle altogether?

Far more troubling than the Supreme Court's failure to engage with customary law is the shadow that the majority's approach to international norms has since cast on the status of customary law in Canada. In a number of decisions since *Baker*, the court has referred to the *Baker* approach to statutory interpretation in the

---

[178] Supreme Court Act, R.S.C. 1985, c. S-26, s. 3. See also Currie, *supra* note 3 at 204 (noting that the decision could be read "as an endorsement of the direct legal effect or relevance of customary international law").

[179] See Toope, *supra* note 177 at 523-25.

[180] See also Schabas, *supra* note 20 at 182.

[181] On this and the previous point, see LeBel and Chao, *supra* note 6 at 11 (offering the following cryptic statement: "[U]nless the impugned custom is formally ratified and adopted into national legislation, it could be difficult to situate the custom in the domestic legal order"). At the risk of pedantry, it is important to emphasize that custom cannot ever be "formally ratified" as it emerges from practice when read with the requisite *opinio juris*. And the common law tradition, in both the United Kingdom and the United States, at least, is clear that no formal adoption into national legislation is necessary.

context of questions that involved customary international law. What are the implications of linking the principle that international values and principles can help inform the interpretation of domestic law to the application of customary international law?

In *114957 Canada Ltée (Spraytech, Société d'arrosage)* v. *Hudson (Town) (Spraytech)*, the Supreme Court had to decide whether or not it was within the jurisdiction of a municipality to regulate the use of lawn chemicals. Although Justice L'Heureux-Dubé, writing for the majority, did not need to address this issue for the purposes of the decision, she chose to note that reading the relevant by-law as permitting the municipality to regulate pesticide use "is consistent with principles of international law and policy."[182] She went on to quote from her decision in *Baker* the passage that held that "the values reflected in international human rights law may help inform the contextual approach to statutory interpretation and judicial review" and that quoted *Driedger*'s rendition of the presumption of conformity with international law.[183] L'Heureux-Dubé J. concluded that the by-law respected international law's "precautionary principle,"[184] pursuant to which measures to address significant risks of environmental harm should not be postponed due to a lack of full scientific certainty.[185] She then went on to observe:

Scholars have documented the precautionary principle's inclusion "in virtually every recently adopted treaty and policy document related to the protection of the environment" ... As a result, there may be "currently sufficient state practice to allow a good argument that the precautionary principle is a principle of customary international law" ... The Supreme Court of India considers the precautionary principle to be "part of Customary International Law."[186]

In view of the fact that international environmental law has not played a significant role in Canadian courts,[187] the Supreme Court's references to the precautionary principle should be welcomed. For the purposes of our inquiry into the application of

---

[182] *Spraytech, supra* note 9 at para. 30.

[183] *Ibid.* For the text of the *Driedger* quote, see note 150 in this article and the accompanying text.

[184] *Spaytech, supra* note 9 at para. 31.

[185] The most recent and most comprehensive analysis of the precautionary principle can be found in A. Trouwborst, *Evolution and Status of the Precautionary Principle in International Law* (Boston: Kluwer Law International, 2002).

[186] *Spraytech, supra* note 9 at para. 32 [sources omitted].

[187] See Brunnée, *supra* note 20.

international law by Canadian courts, two aspects of the decision deserve closer attention.

First, although a good case can indeed be made that the precautionary principle is custom, the issue arguably remains unresolved. It is worth asking, therefore, what contribution the *Spraytech* decision might make to the further development of international law.[188] Although the court ultimately leaves open whether or not the precautionary principle has acquired customary law status, its citation of strong evidence to that effect would tend to strengthen future customary law arguments. However, by quoting a definition of the precautionary principle that is not the most widely accepted definition, the court may also end up assisting those who insist that the precautionary principle is at best emerging in international law. The Supreme Court's choice of definition may have been in part prompted by the fact that the Canadian government had actually advocated the inclusion of the precautionary principle in the Bergen Ministerial Declaration on Sustainable Development in the ECE Region, which is the document cited by the court.[189] Nonetheless, the definitional issue is of some importance because the existence of multiple textual versions of the principle is the main basis for the assertion, including very recently by Canada, that no single version has crystallized into custom.[190]

The second and, for present purposes, most important question is what message *Spraytech* sends about the linkages between the *Baker* approach and the application of customary international law in Canada. The decision could be read as implying that a customary norm merely helps to inform statutory interpretation. We assume that the court did not intend any such implication, given that it did not actually decide the question of the precautionary principle's customary law status and given that the impact on the interplay between Canadian and international law would be

---

[188] See notes 19 and 54 and the accompanying text on the role of national courts in the development of international law.

[189] See *Spraytech, supra* note 9 at para. 31, quoting from the Bergen Ministerial Declaration on Sustainable Development in the ECE Region, which can be found in (1990) 1 Y.B Int'l. Env. L. 429. The most widely cited definition is found in Principle 15 of the Rio Declaration on Environment and Development (1992) 31 I.L.M. 876.

[190] See Canada, *A Canadian Perspective on the Precautionary Approach/Principle — Proposed Guiding Principles* (September 2001) at 5, accessible at <http://www.dfait-maeci.gc.ca/tna-nac/documents/prec-discussion-e.pdf> (date accessed: July 1, 2003).

enormous. Not only would the necessary implication be that customary law is not directly applicable in Canada but the result may also be that customary international law, which is binding on Canada, is treated as if it were soft law — as a potentially relevant and persuasive source for courts' interpretative tasks but not as obligatory. We hope, therefore, that the Supreme Court intended to suggest instead that the precautionary principle can inform statutory interpretation even if it should not yet have become customary international law. If this reading is correct, the court would have confirmed a principle that, in *Baker*, it at best alluded to: that in appropriate cases, international norms that are not legally binding on Canada may inform statutory interpretation and judicial review.

In assessing the implications of the *Spraytech* decision, it is important to note that the precautionary principle, specifically the question of its legal status, was not argued by either of the principal parties to the case. Rather, the principle and its role in statutory interpretation were brought into play by some of the interveners in the case.[191] In view of this fact, the court was unlikely to go very far in its treatment of the relevant issues. Therefore, caution is warranted in drawing conclusions regarding its stance on the domestic application of customary international law and the role of the *Baker* approach. It is safe to say, however, that the *Spraytech* decision does not clarify the matter.

Another case in which the Supreme Court commented on customary law and cited its decision in *Baker* was *Suresh*.[192] Once again, we confront a case that should not be cast as the last word on the interplay of customary international law and Canadian law. Simply put, *Suresh* involved the interpretation of the Charter, and we have already argued that when the Charter is at play, the court backs away from a clear presumption of conformity. In *Suresh*, the court offered a nicely nuanced analysis of whether or not the prohibition of torture had become a norm of international *jus cogens*.[193] As the court observes, a norm of *jus cogens* is "a peremptory norm of customary international law" and emerges by general consensus of the international community.[194] Such norms prevail over other customary or treaty norms and can be modified only by a subsequent norm

---

[191] See *Factum of the Interveners, FCM et al,* September 1, 2000, Supreme Court of Canada File no. 26937 at 8-10, paras. 20-25 [on file with authors].

[192] *Suresh, supra* note 7.

[193] *Ibid.* at paras. 61-65.

[194] *Ibid.* at para. 61.

of the same character.[195] While the Supreme Court stops short of concluding that the prohibition of torture is indeed *jus cogens*,[196] it does conclude that there are "compelling indicia" that this is the case.[197] Notwithstanding strong statements about the complete illegality of torture, the court then finds that a residual discretion exists in the minister of citizenship and immigration to deport to (feared) torture, either as a result of the balancing process required by the principles of fundamental justice under section 7 or because the section 7 right of the claimant can be overridden under section 1 of the Charter on grounds of national security. However, in deference to the powerful anti-torture norm, the deportation to torture on these grounds would be permitted only in "exceptional circumstances."[198]

Although it might seem as if the Supreme Court did a masterful job in squaring the circle, it ultimately failed. The central problem with its analysis is that if the court is right that the prohibition on torture is *jus cogens* (and deportation to torture would have to be an included prohibition), no "balancing" would be appropriate. *Jus cogens* norms are a particularly compelling form of customary law and should have been directly controlling within Canadian law to preclude deportation. Still, citing, *inter alia*, its decision in *Baker*, the Supreme Court opined that

[t]he inquiry into the principles of fundamental justice is informed not only by Canadian experience and jurisprudence, but also by international law, including *jus cogens*.[199]

This formulation is consistent with the interpretative approach that the court has developed in the Charter context. Yet, even if one accepts this approach in principle, we suggest that one should question its application to a norm of *jus cogens*.[200] In part, the court's

---

[195] Vienna Convention, *supra* note 44, Article 53.

[196] *Suresh, supra* note 7 at para. 65.

[197] *Ibid.* at paras. 62-64. It is worth noting that in *Bouzari, supra* note 75 at para. 61, Swinton J. concluded without much ado that the prohibition on torture is *jus cogens*. While she noted that the Supreme Court, in *Suresh*, did not have to finally decide the issue, she felt that her conclusion was well supported by the sources set out in that decision.

[198] *Suresh, supra* note 7 at paras. 76-79.

[199] *Ibid.* at para. 46.

[200] We suggested in note 140 in this article that requiring resort to section 33 of the Charter may be appropriate where Parliament wishes to assert an interpretation of the Charter that restricts human rights provided by an international

approach may be explained by its focus on international treaty norms, in particular, those in the ICCPR and the Convention against Torture and Other Cruel, Inhuman or Degrading Treatment or Punishment.[201] Canada has ratified both treaties but has not explicitly implemented them by statute. Thus, the Supreme Court's attention may have been focused on what it deemed to be two unimplemented treaties. Nonetheless, even if the court's approach was correct with respect to these treaties as such, it should have considered the direct application of the customary prohibition on torture.

SUMMARY

We can now offer an outline of the principles that should govern the domestic application of international law in Canada as well as a summary of the approaches that Canadian courts actually take.

Customary International Law

Customary international law should be directly applicable — it is part of Canadian law. This means that Canadian courts, to the extent possible, should strive to interpret both statutes and the common law so as to be consistent with Canada's obligations under customary law. However, the approach of senior Canadian courts to customary international law is utterly unclear. There is no unequivocal statement on whether custom is part of Canadian law or not. If anything, there are some indications that our courts may be retreating from custom. The Supreme Court's decisions in *Spraytech* and *Suresh* leave room to be interpreted as suggesting that customary law, including even *jus cogens,* is not directly binding in Canada.[202] Notably the *Suresh* decision permits the inference that custom merely helps inform a contextual approach to statutory interpretation, furnishing a potentially relevant and persuasive source for this purpose, but nothing more. Indeed, in applying

---

treaty to which Canada is a party. This argument applies with even greater force when norms of *jus cogens* are at issue.

[201] Convention against Torture and Other Cruel, Inhuman or Degrading Treatment or Punishment, December 10, 1984, Can. T.S. 1987 No. 36 (entered into force June 26, 1987). The court also relied upon the Convention Relating to the Status of Refugees, 28 July 1951, Can. T.S. 1969 No. 6 (entered into force April 22, 1954), which Canada has implemented by statute.

[202] But see *Bouzari, supra* note 75 at para. 60. Swinton J. cites the Supreme Court's decision in *Suresh* in support for the proposition that customary law is directly incorporated into Canadian domestic law.

customary law in this fashion, Canadian courts would not even be treating it as binding *on* Canada. If it were so treated, custom should not merely "help inform" statutory interpretation. It should give rise to the presumption of statutory conformity with Canada's international obligations. The recent *Schreiber* decision can be read as returning the court to the possibility of direct application of customary law within Canada and to a reliance on the traditional common law presumption of conformity. However, the discussion is not unambiguous, and the court is careful to emphasize that the presumtion will rarely be applied.[203]

International Treaty Law

A treaty that has been explicitly implemented by statute is part of our domestic law and should be determinative in the interpretation of Canadian statutes. Courts must interpret implementing legislation in conformity with the underlying treaty. The interpretative effort must be focused on clarifying the meaning of the treaty and must employ the rules of treaty interpretation set out in the Vienna Convention. These principles are in fact the only ones on which there is complete agreement in the context of the domestic application of international law in Canada. Canadian courts now consistently handle the application of transformed treaties in this fashion.

Treaties can also be transformed implicitly or on account of prior conformity of Canadian law and policy with the treaty obligations (including the Charter). Such treaties should be subject to the same interpretative principles as other international obligations that are part of Canadian law. However, Canadian courts tend to rely on an unduly narrow conception of transformation, holding that treaties are not part of Canadian law unless they have been implemented by statute. As a result, they are treating this category of treaties as unimplemented.

Treaties that Canada has ratified but not implemented are not binding *in* Canada as part of domestic law. Nonetheless, because such treaties are binding *on* Canada under international law, the presumption of conformity should apply. The onus is on Canadian courts, where possible, to interpret domestic law in a manner that comports with Canada's obligations under these treaties. By contrast, apparently drawing upon the Supreme Court's Charter

---

[203] *Schreiber, supra* note 76 at para. 50. See also *Mack, supra* note 169 at para. 32.

jurisprudence, Canadian courts seem increasingly inclined to approach unimplemented treaties merely as relevant and persuasive sources that can help inform statutory interpretation. While this approach would be appropriate in the case of a treaty that Canada has not ratified, it fails to take due account of the fact that international legal obligations arise from all treaties that Canada ratifies. We argue that a principled approach to the domestic application of international treaties must reflect the legal difference between a treaty that produces obligations for Canada and one that does not.

To summarize, all forms of international law canvassed up to this point are binding *on* Canada. While only customary law and implemented treaties are binding *in* Canada and should be applied as part of Canadian law, all of Canada's international legal obligations give rise to the presumption of conformity. This does not mean that Canadian courts are reduced to applying binding international norms in mechanical fashion. Indeed, it is difficult to imagine any circumstances in which the judicial role would be exhausted by such an approach. Courts must search for compatible interpretations of domestic law with Canada's international obligations, but they are not deprived of the margins of appreciation inherent in all their interpretative tasks. Applying the presumption of conformity to all of Canada's international obligations also does not mean that the legislative authority of Parliament or the provincial legislatures would be undermined. As we have stressed at various points, with the possible exception of the Charter, for which a different interpretative approach appears to have evolved in any event, Canadian legislatures retain full control over domestic law. The presumption of conformity is to be applied only "where possible," and, of course, it can be rebutted by an explicit legislative act. If Canadian legislators choose to ignore Canada's international obligations, they can do so. However, it bears repeating that Canada would then be in breach of its international obligations, and it could suffer from the remedies accorded to other states under public international law.

International Law That Is Not Binding on Canada —
International Soft Law

Finally, there is an array of international normative statements that may not legally bind Canada but that Canadian courts may nonetheless find relevant to the interpretation of a domestic statute. For example, Canadian courts might encounter non-binding parts (such as preambular statements or provisions phrased in non-obligatory terms) of a treaty that is otherwise binding; international treaties to which Canada is not a party; decisions of international tribunals where Canada was not a party; or a range of "soft" international norms (such as declarations, codes of conduct, or principles that have not yet crystallized into custom). There is no reason why Canadian courts should not draw upon these types of norms so long as they do so in a manner that recognizes their non-binding legal quality.

We argue that these non-binding norms — and *only* these norms — should be treated as potentially relevant and persuasive sources for the interpretation of domestic law. Courts may, and in cases of particularly compelling norms *should*, draw upon such norms for interpretative purposes, but they are not strictly speaking required to do so.[204] This approach was first suggested for Charter interpretation by then Chief Justice Dickson in *Reference re Public Service*. In *Baker*, the Supreme Court may have alluded to a similar approach to ordinary statutes and the exercise of discretion under statutes, although a number of factors militate against this interpretation of the decision. However, there is good reason to read the court's decision in *Spraytech* as endorsing the principle that, in appropriate cases, non-binding international law may inform statutory interpretation and judicial review. *Spraytech* also confirms that the approach is applicable to legislative action at all jurisdictional levels — federal, provincial, and even municipal. We applaud these developments but emphasize once again that the *Baker* approach should be limited to non-binding international norms and should not be applied to Canada's customary or treaty obligations. There is no need for the *Baker* approach in the domestic application of Canada's international obligations. The ordinary presumption of

---

[204] An example of a "particularly compelling" non-binding norm might be one that is widely supported, or even close to crystallizing into customary law. Of course, one might also argue that at least some non-binding norms should not be applied by courts at all. For example, where Canada has specifically chosen not to sign a treaty, it may be inappropriate for a Canadian court to rely upon it in the interpretation of domestic law. This consideration underscores the importance of careful evaluation of each norm, its international stature, and Canada's position. It is in this very context, that an analytical focus on why the norm is relevant and why it should be persuasive can be of assistance. We are grateful to Karen Knop for the observation, offered in comments on an earlier draft, that "persuasion is not a synonym for non-binding [international law], only for the maximum status it can have [in domestic application]" [on file with authors].

conformity is available and would be the appropriate interpretative device for these cases.

Conclusion

We welcome the recent openness of the Canadian courts, particularly the Supreme Court, to international influences. However, as Justice LeBel suggested, greater precision is required in distinguishing between binding law and persuasive influences.[205] Our worry is that the inclination appears to be to treat all international law as inspirational but not obligatory. Indeed, the recent paper by Justice LeBel and Gloria Chao on the internalization of international law in Canada betrays this very inclination. The following quotation reveals exactly the assumptions that have given rise to the confusion against which the judge warns: "As international law is generally non-binding or without effective control mechanisms, it does not suffice to simply state that international law requires a certain outcome."[206] We would highlight several concerns. First, international law *is* binding. This question is separate from how it relates to a domestic legal system. Second, international law does possess so-called "control mechanisms." They simply do not look exactly the same as the mechanisms that exist in national legal systems. Moreover, the statement obscures the role that national courts play in the internalization of international law.[207] Domestic courts are in many circumstances the very "control mechanisms" that Justice LeBel suggests do not exist.[208]

Why does the distinction between binding and non-binding norms matter? Why not simplify the domestic application of international law by treating all international norms, whether binding on Canada or not, as potentially persuasive, and nothing more?

---

[205] See note 17 and accompanying text.

[206] LeBel and Chao, *supra* note 6 at 48.

[207] See H.H. Koh, "Bringing International Law Home" (1998) 35 Houston L. Rev. 623.

[208] See *ibid.* (Koh argues that the internalization of international law through domestic political and legal processes is an important avenue for implanting a genuine sense of obligation in a state, and for promoting its compliance with international law); and see H.H. Koh, "Why Do Nations Obey International Law?" (1997) 106 Yale L.J. 2599. In Justice LeBel's own reasons in *Schreiber, supra* note 76 at para. 49, he stresses that customary law or *jus cogens* might "allow domestic courts to entertain claims."

First, we want to be clear that our conclusion that it matters in domestic litigation whether or not an international norm is binding upon Canada should not lead to the inference that we believe that international soft law is inherently less valuable than binding international law — on the contrary. The simple fact that a rule is enshrined in a treaty does not necessarily mean that it will be influential in international relations. Conversely, the fact that a rule is not binding as a treaty or customary law does not necessarily mean that it cannot shape state conduct in international society.[209] In the international legal system, formal indicators alone do not account for a norm's power. Rather than operating through hierarchical processes of adjudication or enforcement, international law most commonly works horizontally, through processes such as normative discourse and negotiation among relevant actors. In these processes, a norm's legitimacy and attendant persuasiveness are likely to be more important to its influence than its formal pedigree.[210]

However, in domestic judicial processes the yardstick for legal influence is typically said to be binding law.[211] While it is true that binding rules, be they rooted in statutes or the common law (or *droit commun*), are formally the basis of parties' arguments and courts' decisions, non-binding principles and values are in fact influential, especially in constitutional adjudication, as the *Reference re Secession of Quebec*[212] makes clear. However, this influence is intentionally limited by assertions that the court is not "bound" to invoke these principles and values. We worry that by treating all international norms merely as potentially persuasive — at the

---

[209] See also our discussion of soft law in the first section of this article.

[210] See Brunnée and Toope, sources cited in note 23 of this article.

[211] It is, of course, perfectly possible — even desirable — for domestic legal processes to evade or escape from the paradigm of formally binding law. The so-called legal pluralists have explored this issue in great detail. See, for example, B. Santos, *Toward a New Common Sense: Law, Science and Politics in the Paradigmatic Transition* (London: Routledge, 1995); J. Belley, "Law as *terra incognita*: Constructing Legal Pluralism" (1997) 12(2) Canadian J. of L. & Soc'y 17; and R.A. Macdonald, "Metaphors of Multiplicity: Civil Society, Regimes and Legal Pluralism" (1998) 15 Arizona J. of Comp. & Int'l L. 69. Lon Fuller argues that even in judging, the seeming epitome of formal decision-making rooted in binding law is actually a process of mutual deliberation in which the parties and the judge articulate shared purposes. See L.L. Fuller, "Human Purpose and Natural Law" (1958) 3 Nat. L. F. 68 at 73-74; Brunnée and Toope, "Constructivism," *supra* note 23 at 43-53.

[212] *Quebec Secession Reference, supra* note 177. See also Toope, *supra* note 177 at 523. See also *Reference Re Amendment of Constitution of Canada*, [1981] 1 S.C.R. 753.

discretionary disposal of judges — courts view all international law as "soft" law, if indeed it is seen as law at all. So while international law can, in this conception, play the same role as "principles and values," it can never amount to an obligation that actually constrains the discretion of a judge. We may have a perfectly vicious circle in this case. As a result of the inclination to cast international law as "generally non-binding" and thus not as real law — recall the Justice LeBel and Chao view — courts may lean towards the *Baker* approach. In turn, the more international norms are seen as merely helpful in informing statutory interpretation, the more the initial assumptions about the "softness" of international law are reinforced.

In our view, it is important to resist the idea that the application of international law is merely an exercise in comparative law, whereby "foreign" legal norms are translated into domestic law, and may or may not be found to be persuasive. Comparative law may provide helpful supplementary methods, particularly in identifying the appropriate domestic influence of international norms that are not legally binding on Canada. However, as we have illustrated throughout this article, many international legal rules bind Canada; some are part of Canadian law. They should be treated accordingly.[213]

In applying international law, domestic courts are not merely engaged in the internalization of international norms into the domestic legal system.[214] They are also involved in the continuous

[213] In discussing binding international human rights norms, the Senate Standing Committee on Human Rights, *supra* note 89, made the following forceful observation:

> International human rights obligations are no less binding upon us than our domestic guarantees ... International human rights are not simply promises we make to other countries or to the international community as a whole. They are rights that all people have and that we have pledged to respect and implement in our country. Human rights belong to the people, not to the states who ratify the treaties. Part of the problem in Canada is that the domestic/international dichotomy that is so firmly embedded in our legal system pervades our thinking outside the courts as well.

[214] The importance of domestic internalization, in the context of international environmental law, was recently reaffirmed by leading judges from around the globe in the Johannesburg Principles on the Role of Law and Sustainable Development. United Nations Environment Programme, "Senior Judges Adopt Ground-breaking Action Plan to Strengthen World's Environment-Related Laws," News Release 2002/58 (August 27, 2002), accessible at <http://www.unep.org/Documents/Default.asp?DocumentID=259&ArticleID=3115> (date accessed: August 29, 2002).

process of the development of international law, particularly customary law. For this reason as well, it is important that Canadian courts carefully distinguish between treaty, customary, and nonbinding norms. For example, when a Canadian court concludes that a given norm has become customary international law, it actually contributes to the process of establishing evidence for the status of the norm. This contribution may consist in the analysis conducted by the court and the evidence it assembled in the process. The court's decision itself may also constitute evidence of the state practice or *opinio juris* that help build custom. By the same token, if the court's analysis is not sufficiently careful, its decision may come to undermine the crystallization of customary law[215] or the development of its normative content.[216]

For all these reasons, we return again to Justice LeBel's plea for greater rigour "in the definition and identification of international rules and the process of internalisation." In this article, we have highlighted a number of areas of ambiguity that, we believe, negatively affect both the definition and identification of international rules and their internalization into Canadian law. In their joint paper, Justice LeBel and Chao argue that

the reception of international law into the Canadian legal system must in itself form part of the argument advanced by counsel. In other words, if parties wish to rely on a certain principle of international law as binding obligation, they should endeavour to establish how that principle became binding and how it applies to their case.[217]

---

[215] See our earlier discussion of the Supreme Court's comments on the precautionary principle in *Spraytech*, *supra* note 9, and in notes 188-90 of this article and the accompanying text.

[216] In the *Quebec Secession Reference*, *supra* note 177, the Supreme Court's failure to engage with customary law and, notably, with the evolving state practice and *opinio juris* in Europe, caused it to neglect potential shifts in the right to self-determination beyond what the court considered to be the content of that right. On this point, see Schabas, *supra* note 20 at 192-93; and Toope, *supra* note 177 at 524-25. The court's opinion has since been widely referred to by other courts and academic writers from around the world. Thus, its partial analysis of the evolving right to self-determination may reinforce those voices that seek to limit the scope of the right. Our point is not that the right should be narrowly or widely construed. It is simply to illustrate that the decisions of domestic courts can have a significant impact on the development of international law. See, for example, V.P. Nanda, "Self-Determination and Secession under International Law" (2001) 29 Denv. J. Int'l L. & Pol'y 305 at 315-19 (discussing the *Quebec Secession Reference* in detail).

[217] LeBel and Chao, *supra* note 6 at 20.

We fully agree that it is incumbent upon lawyers appearing before the courts to provide detailed and rigorous arguments regarding the international norms on which they rely. Indeed, when international law arguments are employed frivolously or without appropriate nuance, it may reinforce judicial attitudes treating international law as uncertain and irrelevant. However, Canadian courts for their part must provide clear signals as to what international law will matter (custom, treaty, or soft law), when it will matter (the transformation issues), and how it will matter (the presumption issues).

Justice La Forest was right that Canadian courts are becoming international courts. This development is an under-appreciated aspect of the increasing global integration prompted by trade, by the evolution of international human rights, by attempts to address environmental degradation, and even by security concerns. Yet the current crop of judges finds itself in a strange new world and understandably resists changes in the judicial role that are not well specified and not well argued by counsel. If it is any consolation to our judges, the rise in importance of international law within Canadian courts echoes the changes in the judicial role brought about by the promulgation of the Charter.[218] In our view, Canadian judges have proven themselves to be resilient and flexible in adapting to the new world of the Charter and its effect upon domestic law. There is every reason to expect that they will be equally successful in negotiating their way through the new world of international law. So far, they have been unduly hesitant, but recent cases suggest the possibility of a warm embrace prompted by a recognition of the normative richness of the international law and a desire to contribute to its flourishing.

Sommaire

Étreinte restreinte: Application du droit international par les cours canadiennes

Les tribunaux canadiens abordent la tâche de gérer la relation entre le droit international et le droit national avec un regain d'énergie. Cependant, malgré toute l'ouverture qu'ils expriment à l'égard du droit international, les tribunaux sont encore peu enclins à statuer en vertu de celui-ci. Ceci ne signifie pas que le droit international n'a aucune portée juridique ou qu'on

---

[218] Charter, *supra* note 16.

nie la pertinence de son principe. La stratégie d'évitement est plus subtile: même lorsqu'ils ont recours au droit international ou qu'ils lui font référence, les tribunaux canadiens n'accordent généralement pas d'effet juridique aux normes internationales dans les causes individuelles. Même si le droit international est invoqué par rapport à nombre croissant de questions variées, son incidence possible est atténuée — et grandement désamorcée, craignons-nous — parce qu'elle n'est qu'un simple facteur dans l'application et l'interprétation du droit national. Dans le cadre du système juridique canadien, la question du caractère obligatoire du droit international est inextricablement liée à la manière dont celui-ci réussit à influencer l'interprétation du droit national. Lorsqu'il est question de normes qui lient le Canada en vertu du droit international, les tribunaux du pays ont l'obligation d'interpréter le droit national en respectant les normes internationales dans la mesure du possible. Par contre, les normes qui ne lient pas le Canada internationalement (par ex., le droit en gestation ou encore les dispositions de traités qui n'ont pas été ratifiés par le Canada) peuvent aider à éclairer l'interprétation du droit national et, selon la norme en question et la cause en jeu, elles peuvent même être probantes. Les tribunaux peuvent — et ils le devraient dans certains cas — faire appel à de telles normes à des fins d'interprétation, bien qu'ils ne soient pas tenus de le faire à proprement parler. Cependant, surtout à la suite du verdict de la Cour suprême dans la cause Baker, il semblerait qu'on ait tendance à traiter tout ce qui touche au droit international, qu'il s'agisse d'un usage ou d'un traité, que celui-ci lie le Canada ou non, qu'il soit mis en application ou non — peu importe — pertinent et peut-être même convaincant, mais non comme déterminant ni, osons-nous le dire, obligatoire. Ce qui nous préoccupe, c'est qu'en présence d'un droit international qui se résume à être convaincant, celui-ci devient purement facultatif et les magistrats peuvent décider de l'ignorer. Nous avançons qu'il n'est pas suffisant de traiter toutes ficelles normatives de cette manière et que cette approche risque d'affaiblir à la longue la structure du droit.

Summary

A Hesitant Embrace: The Application of International Law by Canadian Courts

Canadian courts are approaching the task of mediating the relationship between international law and domestic law with newfound energy. Yet, for all their declared openness to international law, courts are still inclined to avoid deciding cases on the basis of international law. This does not mean that international law is given no effect or that its broad relevance is denied. The avoidance strategy is more subtle: even when they invoke or refer to international law, Canadian courts generally do not give international norms concrete legal effect in individual cases. Although international law is brought to bear on a growing range of questions, its potential impact is tempered — and we fear largely eviscerated — because it is merely one factor in the application and interpretation of domestic law. Within the Canadian legal order the question of "bindingness" of international law is closely intertwined with the manner in which it comes to influence the interpretation of domestic law. In the case of norms that are binding on Canada under international law, Canadian courts have an obligation to interpret domestic law in conformity with the relevant international norms, as far as this is possible. By contrast, norms that do not bind Canada internationally (for example, soft law or provisions of treaties not ratified by Canada) can help inform the interpretation of domestic law and, depending on the norm in question and the case at issue, may even be persuasive. Courts may, and in some cases should, draw upon such norms for interpretative purposes, but they are not strictly speaking required to do so. However, especially following the Supreme Court's decision in Baker, *there appears to be a trend towards treating all of international law, whether custom or treaty, binding on Canada or not, implemented or unimplemented, in the same manner — as relevant and perhaps persuasive, but not as determinative, dare we say obligatory. Our concern is that if international law is merely persuasive, it becomes purely optional, and can be ignored at the discretion of the judge. We argue that it is not enough to treat all normative threads in this fashion — over time this approach risks weakening the fabric of the law.*

L'obligation alimentaire des pays en développement à l'égard de leurs populations: la normativité du mécanisme de développement durable

PIERRE-FRANÇOIS MERCURE

I INTRODUCTION

La communauté internationale a été incapable, depuis la création de la l'Organisation des Nations Unies pour l'alimentation et l'agriculture[1] en 1945, d'apporter des solutions durables au problème de la sécurité alimentaire des populations vulnérables de la planète, presque exclusivement localisées dans des pays en développement.[2] La conclusion d'ententes sur le sujet et la création d'organismes voués à cette cause n'ont pas donné les résultats attendus. Les enjeux économiques, exacerbés par l'ouverture des marchés, ont occulté les devoirs de coopération et de solidarité entre États. Ces devoirs existent néanmoins et les États en développement, débiteurs du droit à la nourriture à l'égard de leurs nationaux, ont

Pierre-François Mercure est Professeur à la Faculté de droit de l'Université de Sherbrooke. L'auteur tient à remercier M Hector Arguello Mena, étudiant à l'École du Barreau du Québec, pour les recherches effectuées. Ce travail a été réalisé grâce à l'appui financier du Fonds des activités de recherche de l'Université de Sherbrooke.

[1] Pour *Food and Agriculture Organisation*. L'acronyme anglais est utilisé communément afin de désigner l'organisme [ci-après FAO].

[2] Ci après PED. Sur les caractéristiques socio-économiques des PED permettant de mieux comprendre le problème de la faim, consulter: Bernard Chantebout, *Le Tiers-Monde*, Paris, Armand Colin, 1986, 183 p. Bien que le problème de la faim existe dans les PD, son ampleur y est nettement moindre. Programme des Nations Unies pour l'environnement (PNUE), *L'avenir de l'environnement mondial — 3*, Nairobi, Programme des Nations Unies pour l'environnement, 2002, 308; Najib Akesbi, *Comment nourrir le monde?* dans Alternatives économiques, Hors-Série, n° 35, 1998, 28; Jacques Diouf, *Vaincre la faim*, Le Monde diplomatique, juin 2002, 23; FAO, *L'état de l'insécurité alimentaire dans le monde 2002*, Rome, FAO, 2002: «http://www.fao.org/sof/sofi/index_fr.htm" (page consultée le 4 décembre 2002).

l'obligation d'agir conjointement pour que se matérialise leurs engagements conventionnels, malgré l'attitude désintéressée des pays
développés.[3]

Les PED ont l'obligation d'utiliser les moyens que leur propose
le droit international, susceptibles de résoudre le problème de la
faim. Le mécanisme de développement durable[4] offre des perspectives intéressantes dans ce domaine. Il donnerait un nouveau souffle aux revendications des PED, en leur permettant d'obtenir des
concessions des PD, sur des éléments du nouvel ordre économique
international[5] essentiels à l'établissement d'une véritable sécurité
alimentaire. Les PED échangeraient, en contrepartie des concessions obtenues, leur collaboration dans la résolution de problématiques globales, notamment dans le secteur de la protection de
l'environnement mondial, mais aussi dans celles issues de préoccupations engendrées par la mondialisation et la nouvelle économie.[6]

L'action prioritaire des PED, appliquant le mécanisme de développement durable, devrait viser la sécurité alimentaire, puisque la
réalisation du droit fondamental à la nourriture conditionne celle
d'autres droits de l'homme. Les paramètres du droit à la nourriture
sont aussi mieux définis que ceux d'autres droits fondamentaux,
comme le droit à la vie et le droit au développement.[7] Les disparités
entre les niveaux de développement des PED, à la source de ce que
l'on a appelé l'éclatement du Tiers-Monde,[8] ne pourraient servir

[3] Ci-après PD.

[4] Sur la question de savoir s'il a une valeur coutumière, *cf. infra* deuxième partie,
titre 2, A, *ii.*

[5] Ci-après NOEI, *cf. infra* note 80 et deuxième partie, titre 2, A, *i.*

[6] Dans des domaines où la collaboration Nord-Sud est essentielle afin de mener
une action planétaire efficace. On pourrait penser, par exemple, à la lutte anti-
terroriste. Pierre-François Mercure, *Pauvreté, développement durable et terrorisme*, Le
Devoir, 20 décembre 2001, A7. Comme le mentionne, d'ailleurs, Jean Ziegler:
"La lutte contre le terrorisme est donc nécessairement aussi une lutte contre l'extrême pauvreté, le déni de justice, la faim," Jean Ziegler, *Les nouveaux maîtres du
monde*, Paris, Fayard, 2002, p. 54.

[7] Sur le droit à la vie, consulter: William A. Schabas, *Précis du droit international des
droits de la personne*, Cowansville, Éditions Yvon Blais, 1997, 5, 7, 28, 30-31, 41,
43, 230-31. Sur le droit au développement, consulter: Gérard Blanc, *Peut-on
encore parler d'un droit du développement?* (1991) 4 J.D.I. 903 à la p. 945.

[8] Philippe Moreau Defarges, "Du Tiers-Monde aux Tiers-Mondes," dans Yves Léo-
nard, dir., *Les Tiers-Mondes*, (1995) n° 270, Les Cahiers Français, 3-9; Immanuel
Wallerstein, *C'était quoi, le Tiers-Monde?*, (2000) n° 2.684, Problèmes économiques aux pp. 19-21; François-Regis Mahieu, *Le concept de Tiers-Monde à l'épreuve du
temps*, (1995) n° 2.411, Problèmes économiques aux pp. 25-29.

de fondement à l'abdication, par certains PED, des obligations de coopération et de solidarité qui lient tous les États en développement pour la résolution d'enjeux vitaux.

C'est à travers les relations Nord-Sud, qu'un regard critique sera porté sur l'évolution du droit à la nourriture et son corollaire, la sécurité alimentaire collective des PED. Il est cependant nécessaire, afin que le travail entrepris soit complet, d'exposer préalablement le problème de la faim dans les PED (section I) et de s'interroger sur la fonction normative du droit international public dans ce domaine (section II).

II LA FAIM: UN DRAME RÉCURRENT

Dans le document portant sur le droit à l'alimentation qu'il présenta à la Commission des droits de l'homme, le 7 février 2001, le rapporteur indiquait: "la personne qui meurt de faim est victime d'un assassinat et … la sous-alimentation chronique grave et la faim relèvent de la violation du droit fondamental à la vie."[9] Il ajoutait qu'il était temps de mettre un terme "au génocide silencieux perpétré quotidiennement par la faim."[10]

Bien que les crimes de *génocide* et d'*assassinat* soient reconnus dans presque tous les États, ainsi qu'en droit international, le fait que des populations entières soient maintenues en déficit alimentaire chronique n'est sanctionné par aucune norme supra-étatique. La raison principale de cette lacune tient au fait que les PD, qui sont en grande partie responsables de l'iniquité alimentaire mondiale, refusent de collaborer à l'élaboration d'un *corpus juris* qui pourrait éventuellement les lier. Pour les PD, la faim est une problématique similaire à la pauvreté: la communauté internationale prend des mesures afin qu'il y ait amélioration graduelle de la situation et le jour viendra où le fléau sera éradiqué.

S'il est vrai que "la faim généralisée dans un monde d'abondance dérive essentiellement de la pauvreté,"[11] le droit à la nourriture devrait recevoir la priorité sur le droit à un niveau de vie décent, car le premier est un prérequis au deuxième. La réalisation du droit à la nourriture est tributaire de la solidarité humaine et "it is clear if people come to believe that hunger is intolerable, that starving to

---

[9] Rapport établi par M. Jean Ziegler. Conseil économique et social, *Le droit à l'alimentation*, E/CN.4/2001/53, 2001 à la p. 2.

[10] Assemblée générale, 56ᵉ session, *Le droit à l'alimentation, Rapport préliminaire*, A/56/210, 2001 à la p. 29.

[11] Conseil économique et social, *supra* note 9 à la p. 2.

death is an affront to human dignity, then the human right to food becomes a necessity and a reality."[12]

Le drame de la faim n'est pas la perpétuation de la situation, mais surtout, comme les spécialistes de l'alimentation le soutiennent depuis des décennies: "que l'on peut produire assez de nourriture pour éliminer la faim."[13] Cette dernière n'est pas causée par une pénurie mondiale des denrées alimentaires mais par sa répartition inégale. Selon le dernier rapport annuel de la FAO publié le 15 octobre 2002,[14] il y avait pour la période 1998-2000, 840 millions de personnes sous-alimentées,[15] dont 799 millions, soit 95 %, dans les 122 PED.[16] Plus préoccupant encore est le constat de l'organisme: "les progrès accomplis dans la lutte contre la faim sont pratiquement au point mort."[17] En effet, le nombre de personnes sous-alimentées a baissé d'à peine 2,5 millions par an entre 1990-1992 et 1998-2000; il aurait même augmenté dans la plupart des régions. La FAO indique: "si cette tendance n'est pas rapidement inversée, il ne sera pas possible d'atteindre l'objectif du Sommet

---

[12] Economic and Social Council, *The right to food*, E/CN.4/2002/58, 2002, 9. S'il est vrai que l'on peut vivre toujours pauvre, il est aussi vrai qu'on ne peut survivre bien longtemps affamé.

[13] Conseil économique et social, *supra* note 9 à la p. 2.

[14] FAO, *supra* note 2.

[15] La faim et la sous-alimentation sont des synonymes qui désignent l'insuffisance ou l'absence de calories. Il faut distinguer ces concepts de la malnutrition qui elle désigne l'insuffisance ou l'absence de micro-nutriments, essentiellement les vitamines (molécules organiques) et les minéraux (molécules inorganiques). "Les micro-nutriments sont indispensables à la vie de la cellule et surtout à l'influx nerveux. Un enfant peut avoir suffisamment de calories, mais s'il manque de micro-nutriments il subit des retards de croissance, devient victime d'infections etc." Conseil économique et social, *supra* note 9 à la p. 8. Les carences qualitatives et quantitatives en eau de consommation constitueraient des problèmes de sous-alimentation. Le droit à la nourriture inclurait le droit à la nourriture liquide, c'est-à-dire à l'eau potable, autant que celui à la nourriture solide. Conseil économique et social, *supra* note 9 à la p. 13. Sur la problématique de l'eau dans le Tiers-Monde, consulter: Centre tricontinental, *L'eau, patrimoine commun de l'humanité*, Paris, L'Harmattan, 2002, 307 p; Maude Barlow et Tony Clarke, *L'Or bleu*, Montréal, Boréal, 2002, 85-119; Louis Join-Lambert, dir., *L'eau: un bien commun?* (2001) n° 180, Revue Quart Monde, 62 pp.

[16] On retrouve 30 millions de personnes sous-alimentées dans les pays en transition et 11 millions dans les pays industrialisés. Economic and Social Council, *supra* note 12 à la p. 9.

[17] Tiré d'un communiqué de presse émis à Rome le 15 octobre 2002, *La lutte conte la faim marque le pas*: <http://www.fao.org/french/newsroom/news/2002/9620-fr.html> à la p. 1. (page consultée le 22 octobre 2002).

mondial de l'alimentation de 1996, à savoir de réduire de moitié le nombre de personnes sous-alimentées d'ici à 2015."[18]

Les enfants sont les principales victimes de la situation. En effet, un enfant sur sept né dans un PED touché par la sous-alimentation mourra avant d'avoir atteint l'âge de cinq ans. Les autres, les "crucifiés de naissance,"[19] porteront les tares héréditaires de leur mère sous-alimentée. Plus de trente pays étaient au moment de la publication du rapport de la FAO en situation d'urgence alimentaire exceptionnelle, ce qui signifie que soixante-sept millions de personnes nécessitaient une aide alimentaire immédiate.[20]

III Le rôle du droit international public

Le droit international public est sans contredit influencé par une approche heuristique intégrant les valeurs de solidarité et d'équité qui découlent du droit naturel.[21] Il procède aussi d'une volonté de refléter l'interdépendance naturelle entre le vivant et rejoint en ce sens l'objectivisme qui le définit comme: "un impératif social traduisant une nécessité née de la solidarité naturelle."[22] Il pourrait être soutenu qu'il rejoint le positivisme, sous certains aspects, où les États ont la liberté de modifier le droit naturel "afin de faciliter le consentement mutuel."[23]

Il est toutefois, à l'évidence, un système juridique tributaire des relations d'intérêts qui s'établissent entre les groupes humains. Il résulte largement des rapports de pouvoir entre les États ou les regroupements de ceux-ci, à la faveur des enjeux économiques qui conditionnent leurs actions. L'une des fonctions principales du droit international positif est "d'aider à maintenir la suprématie de la force et les hiérarchies établies sur la base de la puissance."[24] Un

---

[18] Afin de rencontrer l'objectif fixé lors du Sommet mondial de l'alimentation, le nombre de personnes sous-alimentées doit être réduit de 24 millions par an dès aujourd'hui et jusqu'en 2015. *Ibid.*

[19] Expression utilisée par Régis Debray et Jean Ziegler, *Il s'agit de ne pas se rendre,* Paris, Éditions Arléa, 1994.

[20] Debray et Ziegler, *supra* note 17 à la p. 2.

[21] Kéba Mbaye, "Introduction," dans *Droit international, bilan et perspectives,* t. 2, Paris, Pedone, 1991 à la p. 1111.

[22] L'objectivisme est défendu notamment par Georges Scelle. Nguyen Quoc Dinh, Patrick Daillier et Alain Pellet, 6ᵉ éd. *Droit international public,* Paris, L.G.D.J., 1999 à la p. 105.

[23] *Ibid.* à la p. 57.

[24] *Ibid.* à la p. 81.

tel système fait peu de place à la solidarité humaine. Toutefois, des changements sont inévitables, car:

l'histoire de l'humanité nous enseigne que toute organisation sociale basée sur une redistribution inéquitable et inacceptable (sur le plan du respect de la dignité humaine) de ressources ne peut être maintenue à long terme que par la force, ce qui condamne invariablement une telle organisation à disparaître.[25]

Puisque la principale motivation de l'État est d'assurer le mieux-être collectif, le droit international doit alors fournir un contexte propice à l'atteinte de cet objectif. Sa fonction est alors de permettre le délicat rééquilibrage de la réalisation de droits pour des personnes appartenant à des groupes particuliers et de la régression d'un certain nombre d'acquis pour d'autres. Tous les États sont concernés par cette tâche, mais les PD ont des obligations particulières à cet égard. Le défaut des PD d'accomplir leurs devoirs ne doit cependant pas écarter les PED de la responsabilité première qu'ils ont à l'égard de leurs populations. Ces dernières sont marginalisées par un ordre mondial imposé par les États développés et dont la conséquence directe est le ralentissement de la réalisation de certains droits humains fondamentaux.

La réalisation du NOEI apparaît toujours comme la seule solution de rechange à un contexte favorisant les intérêts d'une minorité et accentuant ainsi le problème de la faim. C'est parce-qu'il constitue une voie privilégiée pour assurer le développement et la sécurité alimentaire des pays du Tiers-Monde que le droit à la nourriture doit être réalisé. S'il est vrai que le sous-développement entretient la faim, il est aussi vrai que "la sous-alimentation et la malnutrition permanentes empêchent l'homme et la femme de développer leurs potentialités et de devenir économiquement actifs; elles les condamnent à une existence sociale marginale."[26] Le lien entre développement économique, NOEI et droit à la nourriture est indéniable.

La revendication formelle du NOEI par les PED s'est soldée par un échec, à cause de leur manque d'une monnaie d'échange à offrir aux PD en contrepartie de concessions de leur part. Il a en effet été revendiqué par des demandeurs n'ayant rien à proposer à des États peu motivés par des considérations d'équité. Dans un système où les intérêts économiques l'emportent sur toutes autres

[25] Michèle Jacquart, "Droits économiques , sociaux et culturels," dans *Droit international, bilan et perspectives, op. cit., supra* note 21 à la p. 1154.

[26] Conseil économique et social, *supra* note 9 à la p. 6.

considérations et qui perpétue une répartition inégale des ressources, les PED ont le droit d'opposer aux PD des revendications
conditionnelles les forçant à des changements d'attitude. Les PED
ont l'obligation d'appliquer les mécanismes juridiques aptes à la
réalisation du droit fondamental à la nourriture.

Les PD ont reproché aux PED d'avoir revendiqué le NOEI dans
un esprit d'affrontement[27] à leur égard. La revendication d'une
plus grande équité dans les relations entre États constitue une
demande légitime. On ne pourrait d'ailleurs parler véritablement
d'affrontement lorsqu'une contrepartie aux demandes est offerte
sous forme de collaboration dans certains secteurs.[28]

C'est en faisant l'historique des relations entre États débiteurs,
d'une part, et bénéficiaires de l'obligation alimentaire, d'autre part,
que seront analysés, dans une première partie, les mécanismes de
répartition des ressources alimentaires mondiales. Il sera constaté
que la situation de demandeurs dans laquelle se trouvaient les PED
à été un frein à la réalisation du droit à la nourriture. La deuxième
partie démontrera cependant que, par l'application du mécanisme
de développement durable, les PED ont l'opportunité, en exerçant
une action solidaire, d'atteindre l'objectif de la sécurité alimentaire collective.

A   L'INADÉQUATION DES MÉCANISMES DE RÉPARTITION DES
     RESSOURCES ALIMENTAIRES MONDIALES

L'adoption, par la communauté internationale, de conventions
garantissant le droit fondamental de tout individu d'être à l'abri
de la faim traduit, à première vue, une volonté de cette dernière
d'apporter des solutions véritables au problème de la faim. Les
résultats obtenus ne peuvent cependant que démontrer le succès
limité du droit positif relatif à l'humanité afin d'assurer la sécurité
alimentaire mondiale (titre 1). Ils sont en grande partie attribuables aux déficiences inhérentes au positionnement des acteurs en
présence (titre 2).

---

[27] Assia Bensalah-Alaoui, *La sécurité alimentaire mondiale,* Paris, L.G.D.J., 1989 à la
p. 327.

[28] Les PED doivent évidemment distinguer leur démarche de celle exercée par
la Corée du Nord, par exemple, qui tente d'obtenir des concessions des États-
Unis au chapitre de l'aide alimentaire et en matière énergétique, en exerçant
un chantage basé sur la relance de son programme nucléaire militaire. Mathieu
Perreault, *Le chantage nord-coréen,* La Presse, 11 janvier 2003 à la p. B3.

*1   Le succès limité du droit positif relatif à l'humanité afin d'assurer la
       sécurité alimentaire mondiale*

Les États ont tenté, dans un premier temps, d'apporter une solution au problème de la faim par la consécration du droit individuel à la nourriture. Leur effort a été vain à cause des limites de l'acception traditionnelle du droit à la nourriture comme droit de l'homme (a). La réponse à ce revers a été, dans un deuxième temps, la tentative de collectivisation de ce droit. Les résultats furent tout aussi décevants, puisque le concept de sécurité alimentaire mondiale comportait des failles importantes (b).

(a)   Les limites de l'acception traditionnelle du droit à la
       nourriture comme droit de l'homme

Le droit à la nourriture est une composante des droits de l'homme. Malgré des objectifs conventionnels bien définis (*i*), sa réalisation reste hypothétique, en raison des multiples réserves et exceptions qui réduisent grandement la portée des concepts et conséquemment la réalisation des objectifs (*ii*).

(*i*)   *Des objectifs conventionnels bien définis*

Le droit à la nourriture prend sa source dans la *Déclaration universelle des droits de l'homme*[29] adoptée en 1948. Elle stipule à son paragraphe 25(1): "Toute personne a droit à un niveau de vie suffisant pour assurer sa santé, son bien-être et ceux de sa famille, notamment pour l'alimentation." Quoique non-contraignante pour les États, cette disposition servit de base à l'élaboration de l'article 11 du *Pacte international relatif aux droits économiques, sociaux et culturels*[30] que l'on considère constituer la formulation la plus complète de ce droit. Les dispositions pertinentes de cet article sont les suivantes:

1. Les États parties au présent Pacte reconnaissent le droit de toute personne à un niveau de vie suffisant pour elle-même et sa famille, y compris une nourriture, un vêtement et un logement suffisants, ainsi qu'à une amélioration constante de ses conditions d'existence. Les États parties

---

[29] Ci-après la *Déclaration*. Texte reproduit dans Pierre-Marie Dupuy, *Les grands textes de droit international public*, 2ᵉ éd. Paris, Dalloz, 2000 à la p. 65.

[30] Texte reproduit dans P.-M. Dupuy, *ibid.* à la p. 93. Le texte du *Pacte international relatif aux droits civils et politiques* est reproduit à la p. 71. Les deux pactes visaient à mettre en application la *Déclaration* qui ne créait aucune obligation pour les États.

prendront des mesures appropriées pour assurer la réalisation de ce droit et ils reconnaissent à cet effet l'importance essentielle d'une coopération internationale librement consentie.

2. Les États parties au présent Pacte, reconnaissant le droit fondamental qu'a toute personne d'être à l'abri de la faim, adopteront individuellement et au moyen de la coopération internationale, les mesures nécessaires, y compris les programmes concrets . . .

b) Pour assurer une répartition équitable des ressources alimentaires mondiales par rapport aux besoins, compte tenu des problèmes qui se posent tant aux pays importateurs qu'aux pays exportateurs de denrées alimentaires.

L'article 11 énonce deux types de droits: le droit à une nourriture suffisante, auquel il est fait référence au paragraphe 1 et le droit fondamental à la nourriture ou droit d'être à l'abri de la faim, indiqué au paragraphe 2. Le premier serait un droit inclut dans la catégorie des droits économiques, sociaux et culturels, tandis que le deuxième, bien que constituant aussi un droit de ce type, existerait indépendamment du Pacte comme tous les droits fondamentaux qui font partie du *Jus Cogens*.[31] Le premier fixerait un objectif souhaitable à atteindre et le second un seuil minimal à respecter. Le droit d'être à l'abri de la faim est le seul droit économique et social ayant été qualifié par le Pacte de droit fondamental.[32] L'expression *droit à la nourriture* aurait un sens générique et ferait référence aux deux types de droits.

Le droit à la nourriture constitue une composante essentielle du droit à la vie, qui est un "droit somme" selon l'expression de la Commission des droits de l'homme.[33] La reconnaissance du droit à la vie dans différentes conventions impliquerait donc la reconnaissance du droit à la nourriture, puisqu'un droit somme comprend tous les droits énoncés dans la *Déclaration universelle des droits de l'homme*.[34] Le droit à la vie est consacré aux articles 3 de la Déclaration et 6 du *Pacte international relatif aux droits civils et politiques*. Le premier mentionne que "tout individu a droit à la vie, à la liberté, et à la sûreté de sa personne." Le deuxième indique que "le

---

[31] *Cf. infra*, deuxième partie, titre 1, A.

[32] A. Bensalah-Alaoui, *supra* note 27 au pp. 46-50.

[33] Rapport de la Commission des droits de l'homme, UN Doc. A/37/40 (1982), annexe V, § 1.

[34] C.E.S. *Les dimensions internationales du droit au développement comme droit de l'homme*. Rapport du Secrétaire général, Genève (35ᵉ session), 11 déc. 1978, E/CN.4/ 1334, 174 pp. et annexes.

droit à la vie est inhérent à la personne humaine." Les États doivent ainsi adopter des mesures positives afin d'y donner effet. Comme le soutien A. Bensalah-Aloui: "les États parties au Pacte qui ne prendraient pas des mesures appropriées pour faire face à la faim et à la malnutrition, seraient désormais en violation avec l'article 6."[35]

La réalisation du droit à la nourriture est donc inter-reliée, mais aussi tributaire de celle d'autres droits que l'on pourrait qualifier les uns de droits somme, matriciels[36] ou généraux; les autres de droits spécifiques. Au nombre des premiers, on dénombrerait, en plus du droit à la vie, des droits comportant un important volet économique et social: le droit à la satisfaction des droits économiques sociaux et culturels,[37] le droit à un ordre international propre à leur épanouissement;[38] le droit au développement[39] et le droit des peuples à l'autodétermination.[40] Puisque l'adoption de mesures propres à donner un sens au droit à la nourriture comporte des coûts économiques, sa réalisation dépend donc directement de l'effectivité des différents droits à caractère économique. Les droits spécifiques qui suivent conditionneraient aussi, l'accomplissement

---

[35] A. Bensalah-Alaoui, *supra* note 27 à la p.39.

[36] Expression utilisée par le représentant permanent de l'Algérie auprès des Nations Unies à Genève en ce qui concerne le droit au développement. Il indiquait que le droit à la nourriture en dérivait. Conseil économique et social, *supra* note 9 à la p. 12.

[37] Art 22, *Pacte international relatif aux droits économiques, sociaux et culturels*, *supra* note 30 à la p. 93.

[38] Art. 28, *Déclaration*, qui se lit ainsi: "Toute personne a droit à ce que règne, sur le plan social et sur le plan international, un ordre tel que les droits et libertés énoncés dans la présente Déclaration puissent y trouver plein effet," *supra*, note 29 à la p. 93.

[39] G. Blanc, *supra*, note 7. Consulter à ce sujet: *Déclaration sur le droit au développement* AG/41/128, 4 décembre 1986. La formulation la plus complète de ce droit se retrouverait dans la *Charte Africaine des droits de l'homme et des peuples*. Entrée en vigueur le 21 octobre 1986. Texte dans *International Legal Materials*, vol. XXI, n° 1, janvier 1982 aux pp. 58-68. Aussi disponible à l'adresse suivante: <http://www.droitshumains.org/Biblio/Txt_Afr/Oua_81.htm> (page consultée le 10 octobre 2002).

[40] Art. 1 commun aux deux Pactes, libellé ainsi: "Tous les peuples ont le droit de disposer d'eux-mêmes. En vertu de ce droit, ils déterminent librement leur statut politique et assurent librement leur développement économique, social et culturel."

du droit à la nourriture: droit au travail,[41] à la liberté d'association,[42] d'expression et de l'information[43] et à la santé.[44]

Les actes constitutifs de quelques organisations internationales, notamment l'OIT, l'UNESCO, l'OMS, le FIDA,[45] la FAO, ainsi que certaines conventions régionales, telles la *Charte de l'Organisation des États américains,*[46] la *Convention américaine relative aux droits de l'homme,*[47] la *Charte sociale européenne*[48] et la *Charte africaine des droits de l'homme et des peuples,*[49] font une référence implicite au droit à la nourriture. D'autres conventions le reconnaissent formellement, mais pour des domaines particuliers cependant.[50] Ainsi, pour ce qui est du droit humanitaire, le droit à la nourriture est défini et circonscrit précisément. Les quatre conventions de Genève[51] et les

---

[41] Art. 23, *Déclaration*, et art. 6 du *Pacte international relatif aux droits économiques, sociaux et culturels.*

[42] Art. 20, *Déclaration*, et art. 8 du *Pacte international relatif aux droits économiques, sociaux et culturels.*

[43] Art. 19, *Déclaration.*

[44] Art. 12, *Pacte international relatif aux droits économiques, sociaux et culturels.*

[45] Dont les acronymes signifient respectivement: Organisation internationale du travail; Organisation des Nations Unies pour l'éducation, la science et la culture; Organisation mondiale de la santé et Fonds international de développement agricole.

[46] Par. 2(e), *Charte de l'Organisation des États américains* 1952, 119 R.T.N.U. 4, 46 A.J.I.L. Supp. 43, telle qu'amendée par le *Protocole de Buenos Aires* 1970, 721 R.T.N.U. 324, [1990] R.T. Can. n° 23.

[47] Art. 26, *Convention américaine relative aux droits de l'homme* (1979), 1144 R.T.N.U. 123.

[48] Art. 11 et 16, *Charte sociale européenne* (1965), 529 R.T.N.U. 89.

[49] Par. 20(1); 22(1 et 2) et 29(1), art. 23 et 24, *Charte africaine des droits de l'homme et des peuples, supra* note 39.

[50] L'enfant, par exemple, se voit garantir une nourriture adéquate par la *Convention relative aux droits de l'enfant*, Rés. A.G.44/25, Annexe, [1992] R.T. Can. n° 3.

[51] *Convention de Genève pour l'amélioration du sort des blessés et des malades dans les forces armées en campagne*, (I^e Convention), adoptée à Genève le 12 août 1949, Comité international de la Croix-Rouge (C.I.C.R.), Manuel du mouvement international de la Croix-Rouge et du Croissant-Rouge, 13e éd., Genève, C.I.C.R, 1994, à la p. 23. *Convention de Genève pour l'amélioration du sort des blessés, des malades et des naufragés des forces armées sur mer*, (IIe Convention), adoptée à Genève le 12 août 1949, C.I.C.R., *ibid.* à la p. 48. *Convention de Genève relative à la protection des personnes civiles en temps de guerre*, (IVe Convention), adoptée à Genève le 12 août 1949, C.I.C.R., *ibid.* à la p. 141. Texte aussi reproduit dans: (1950), 75 R.T.N.U. 287, [1965] R.T. Can. n° 20.

deux protocoles additionnels[52] prévoient des dispositions assurant la fourniture d'aliments aux prisonniers de guerre, en quantité, qualité et variété suffisantes afin qu'ils se maintiennent en bonne santé.[53] Des obligations sont aussi imposées aux États à l'égard des populations civiles, lors de l'occupation de territoires, notamment en leur imposant le devoir de procurer des vivres à ces groupes et même en les tenant d'en importer de l'extérieur de pays, lorsque les ressources du territoire occupé sont insuffisantes.[54] Les États doivent de plus s'abstenir d'utiliser l'arme alimentaire à leur égard.[55]

Les obligations précitées découlent implicitement des articles 55 et 56 de la *Charte des Nations Unies*[56] qui disposent que les États[57] et l'Organisation elle-même ont l'obligation de favoriser "le relèvement des niveaux de vie, le plein emploi et des conditions de progrès et de développement dans l'ordre économique et social,"[58] ainsi que "le respect universel et effectif des droits de l'homme."[59]

Le droit à la nourriture est donc bien encadré; il comporte néanmoins certaines limites juridiques qui résultent, tantôt de l'état d'infériorité économique des PED, tantôt de la résistance des PD à l'instauration d'un véritable droit d'accès universel aux ressources alimentaires.

---

[52] *Protocole additionnel aux Conventions de Genève du 12 août 1949 relatif à la protection des victimes des conflits armés internationaux* (Protocole I), adopté à Genève le 8 juin 1977, C.I.C.R. à la p. 206. Texte aussi reproduit dans: (1979), 1125 R.T.N.U. 3, [1991] R.T. Can. n° 2; *Protocole additionnel aux Conventions de Genève du 12 août 1949 relatif aux victimes des conflits armés non internationaux* (Protocole II), adopté le 8 juin 1977, C.I.C.R., *ibid.* à la p. 141. Texte aussi reproduit dans: (1979), 1125 R.T.N.U. 3, [1991] R.T. Can. n° 2.

[53] Art 26 de la *Convention relative au traitement des prisonniers de guerre* (IIIᵉ Convention), adoptée à Genève le 12 août 1949. Voir aussi les art. 15, 51 et 72. C.I.C.R., *ibid.* à la p. 69.

[54] IVᵉ Convention, *supra* note 51, art. 55. Consulter aussi le Protocole I, *supra* note 52, art. 52 et le Protocole II, *supra* note 52, art. 14. Pour des commentaires sur ces articles, consulter: Karine Mollard-Bannelier, *La protection de l'environnement en temps de conflit armé*, Paris, Pedone, 2001 aux pp. 187-93.

[55] IVᵉ Convention, *ibid.*, art. 26.

[56] *Charte des Nations Unies*, 1945 R.T. Can. n° 7, telle qu'amendée par (1963) 557 R.T.N.U. 143, (1965) 638 R.T.N.U. 306, (1973) R.T. Can. n° 4. Texte disponible dans P.-M. Dupuy, *supra* note 29 à la p. 1.

[57] Tant conjointement que séparément, en coopération avec l'Organisation, *ibid.*, art. 56.

[58] *Ibid.*, par. 55(a).

[59] *Ibid.*, par. 55(c).

(ii)   Les réserves et exceptions réduisant la portée des concepts

L'article 11 du *Pacte international relatif aux droits économiques, sociaux et culturels* impose des obligations premières aux États[60] vis-à-vis des populations vivant sur leur territoire; elles constituent les obligations internes de l'État. Il impose aussi des obligations aux États dans leurs relations entre eux; elles constituent les obligations externes de l'État.

En ce qui regarde les premières, le droit à la nourriture suffisante est soumis à certaines limites inhérentes aux droits économiques, sociaux et culturels reconnus par le Pacte. Elles sont de deux ordres. Le droit est tributaire du principe de progressivité énoncé au paragraphe 2(1) du Pacte et il est limité en fonction de la disponibilité des ressources de l'État.[61] Relativement au premier aspect, la réalisation du droit à la nourriture ne serait ainsi que graduelle,[62] puisqu'elle dépendrait du niveau de développement des États. Cet aspect constituerait, par analogie, la traduction sur le plan des mesures à adopter, du principe de responsabilité communes mais différenciées des États dans le secteur de l'environnement.[63]

Pour ce qui est du deuxième aspect, il constituerait la contrepartie du principe de progressivité, permettant ainsi la modulation des obligations des États en fonction de leurs capacités productrices. Les gouvernements ne seraient ainsi tenus d'accorder qu'une grande importance politique et économique au droit à la nourriture. La *Déclaration de Téhéran*[64] promulgue d'ailleurs que l'écart de développement constitue un obstacle au respect effectif des droits de l'homme dans la communauté internationale. Elle y dispose aussi que chaque État doit consentir, selon ses moyens, "le maximum

---

[60] Les individus ont certaines obligations, ainsi que les 89 organisations internationales qui s'occupent d'une manière ou d'une autre de nourriture, ce qui n'est pas sans créer une certaine confusion selon A. Bensalah-Aloui. A. Bensalah-Alaoui, *supra* note 27 aux pp. 68 et 71.

[61] Ces principes ne s'appliqueraient pas au droit fondamental à la nourriture. Le principe de la disponibilité des ressources, en plus d'être mentionné au par. 2(1) du *Pacte* est aussi mentionné à l'art. 11 de la *Déclaration*.

[62] A. Bensalah-Alaoui, *supra* note 27 à la p.58.

[63] Sur ce principe consulter: Alexandre-Charles Kiss et Jean-Pierre Beurier, 2ᵉ éd., Paris, Pedone, 2000 à la p. 134.

[64] Résolution XVII, *Le développement et les droits de l'homme*, basée sur une étude intitulée: *Les fondements économiques des droits de l'homme*, UN doc. A/CONF.32/L.2, préparée pour la Conférence tenue à Téhéran en 1968.

d'efforts pour combler l'écart entre les pays industrialisés et ceux en développement."[65]

Les obligations externes de l'État comportent trois volets: le premier, un devoir de coopération internationale comprenant un devoir d'assistance et d'aide;[66] le second, un devoir d'assurer une répartition équitable des denrées alimentaires; et le troisième, un devoir de ne pas priver une population ou un individu de celles-ci.[67]

Il importe de noter, en ce qui concerne le premier volet, que le Pacte mentionne au paragraphe 11(1) que la coopération entre États doit être "librement consentie." Il faut, à cet effet, comprendre qu'elle doit être négociée quant aux formes qu'elle peut prendre et quant aux domaines où elle peut intervenir. Cette formulation aurait été adoptée comme une clause de sauvegarde afin que les pays à excédents alimentaires n'aient pas une responsabilité automatique de transfert de denrées à l'égard des pays déficitaires.[68]

L'assistance et l'aide n'impliquent donc aucune obligation à la charge de l'État. Cela signifie que les États les plus susceptibles d'agir comme des débiteurs d'une obligation alimentaire, soit les PD, n'y sont pas contraints. Pour ce qui est de l'aide, telle était d'ailleurs la portée de la réserve interprétative apportée par les États-Unis lors de la ratification du *Pacte international relatif aux droits économiques, sociaux et culturels:* "Il est bien entendu aussi que le paragraphe 1er de l'article 2 ainsi que l'article 11 ... n'impliquent aucune obligation contraignante de fournir l'aide aux pays étrangers." En ce qui regarde l'assistance, elle est très limitative, puisqu'elle ne touche que les domaines mentionnés au paragraphe 11(2) du Pacte, soit "l'amélioration des méthodes de production, de conservation et de distribution des denrées alimentaires par la pleine utilisation des connaissances techniques et scientifiques, par la diffusion de principes d'éducation nutritionnelle."

L'alinéa 11(2)b du Pacte dispose du deuxième volet. Il oblige les États à adopter des mesures "pour assurer une répartition équitable des ressources alimentaires mondiales par rapport aux besoins, compte tenu des problèmes qui se posent tant aux pays importateurs qu'aux pays exportateurs de denrées alimentaires." Cette disposition semble viser tant le droit à une nourriture suffisante, que le droit fondamental d'être à l'abri de la faim.[69]

---

[65] *Ibid.*, par. 12.

[66] Ainsi qu'un devoir d'information. A. Bensalah-Alaoui, *supra* note 27 à la p.65.

[67] *Ibid.* aux pp. 63 et s.

[68] *Ibid.* à la p. 64.

[69] *Ibid.* à la p. 66.

Ce qui semble constituer, à première vue, une globalisation des produits alimentaires, par l'emploi de l'expression "denrées alimentaires mondiales," fixe tout au plus un objectif de responsabilisation des individus, mais surtout des États, afin qu'ils consomment modérément les ressources et tiennent compte de la situation des plus démunis lors de l'élaboration de leur politique alimentaire. L'obligation s'applique surtout aux grands producteurs et exportateurs de denrées.[70] Le texte aurait comme limite juridique le principe de souveraineté permanente sur les ressources naturelles, réaffirmé par l'article 25 du Pacte, et qui servirait de fondement aux PD afin de refuser un tel droit aux bénéficiaires mentionnés. Il ne leur reconnaîtrait que la qualité de bénéficiaires d'une aide et non celle de détenteurs d'un droit.[71] Bien que généreuse à première vue à l'égard des populations des PED, cette disposition permettrait aux États de tenir compte des contraintes économiques et commerciales dans l'application des mesures de répartition équitable des ressources alimentaires. Cette exception réduit donc considérablement la portée, à première vue humaniste, de la disposition.

Le troisième volet des obligations internationales de l'État, le devoir de ne pas priver, implique de ne pas recourir aux sanctions alimentaires; de ne pas gaspiller les ressources alimentaires et finalement de ne pas endommager les facteurs naturels de production; mais au contraire de les protéger. Force est cependant de constater que les États sont en violation fréquente avec ces obligations. En ce qui concerne l'utilisation de l'arme alimentaire, il n'existe aucune disposition conventionnelle condamnant cette pratique.[72] Elle fut, par exemple, utilisée par les États-Unis pendant la guerre froide pour des céréales à destination de l'URSS,[73] puis contre l'Irak suite à la guerre du Golfe.[74]

La simple reconnaissance conventionnelle du droit à la nourriture à l'égard des individus ne constitue pas une mesure suffisante

---

[70] *Ibid.* à la p. 67.

[71] *Ibid.* à la p. 54.

[72] Sauf en temps de guerre dans les Conventions de Genève. Le recours à l'arme alimentaire à des fins commerciales est cependant condamné par l'AGNU. Voir Rés. AG 36/185 (1981), § 10. Cette prohibition ferait partie du *Jus Cogens* selon certains auteurs: *Jus Cogens in International Law, with a Projected List,* 1977, vol. 7, GA. J. Int'l & Comp. L. 609, particulièrement aux pp.625-26.

[73] Cette mesure fut cependant désapprouvée par le Conseil mondial sur l'Alimentation en 1980. Voir UN doc. WFC/1980/7, § 8.

[74] Ali Bencheneb, *Pétrole contre nourriture: l'ONU et les contrats internationaux d'assouplissement de l'embargo consécutif à la guerre du Golfe,* 1997, 4 J.D.I. 945.

afin d'assurer l'effectivité de ce droit. Afin de remédier à cette carence, la communauté internationale a élaboré le concept de sécurité alimentaire mondiale, convaincue qu'une approche globale du problème permettrait d'atteindre ce but.

(b)   Les failles du concept de sécurité alimentaire mondiale

La sécurité alimentaire des PED demeure un mirage, puisque le concept sur lequel elle se fonde ne constitue finalement que la transposition au niveau étatique du droit individuel inappliqué. Il s'agit d'une réponse inadéquate à l'échec normatif du droit individuel à la nourriture (*i*), car il a un caractère essentiellement caritatif (*ii*).

(i)   L'échec normatif du droit individuel à la nourriture

La philosophie de la FAO, à l'origine de l'élaboration du concept de sécurité alimentaire mondiale, était que le droit à la nourriture ne pouvait acquérir d'effectivité qu'à la condition qu'il s'insère dans un cadre juridique plus large permettant sa matérialisation. La FAO souhaitait que les États assument, non seulement la mise en oeuvre du droit à la nourriture, c'est-à-dire sa transposition dans leurs ordres juridiques internes, mais qu'ils agissent conjointement de façon à créer un contexte institutionnel propice à son application. Cette stratégie confirmait en quelque sorte l'échec des États à réaliser le droit à la nourriture pour le bénéfice de leurs populations.

Le droit à la nourriture, qui constituait originellement un droit individuel, a ainsi évolué au cours des années 70, sous la pression des PED, vers une conception élargie devenant aussi un droit collectif. Le concept de sécurité alimentaire,[75] développé durant cette période, servit de fondement au droit des peuples de voir se réaliser le droit à la nourriture pour chaque individu.

La formulation originelle du concept de sécurité alimentaire mondiale remonte à 1973 et est attribuable au directeur général de la FAO[76] afin de répondre à la crise alimentaire qui sévissait à cette

---

[75] Voir la définition donnée à ce concept au § 1 du *Plan d'action du Sommet mondial de l'alimentation de 1996:* "La sécurité alimentaire existe lorsque tous les êtres humains ont, à tout moment, un accès physique et économique à une nourriture suffisante, saine et nutritive, leur permettant de satisfaire leurs besoins énergétiques et leurs préférences alimentaires pour mener une vie saine et active." Conseil économique et social, *supra* note 9 à la p. 8.

[76] Les travaux du directeur de la FAO amenèrent l'adoption, en 1974, par la Conférence mondiale de l'Alimentation, de l'*Engagement sur la sécurité alimentaire*

époque.[77] Elle visait essentiellement trois objectifs: 1) la constitution de stocks de denrées; 2) l'apport d'un soutien spécifique aux PED; et 3) l'instauration de consultations intergouvernementales afin de planifier des actions à court, moyen et long terme des États et organisations internationales.[78] C'est véritablement le *Pacte de sécurité alimentaire mondiale,* adopté en 1985 par la Conférence de la FAO,[79] qui consacre le droit collectif à la sécurité alimentaire. Il globalise le droit à la nourriture en indiquant qu'il s'agit d'une "responsabilité commune de l'humanité" et insiste sur le fait que la sécurité alimentaire incombe en premier ressort aux PED eux-mêmes. Le Pacte les invite à coopérer entre eux à cet effet. Il indique aussi que la pauvreté est directement responsable de la faim. Le document formalise ainsi l'idée qui s'est développé au cours des années 70 que le droit à la nourriture est tributaire du NOEI.[80]

Le concept de sécurité alimentaire évolua donc d'une approche minimaliste fondée sur la fourniture d'approvisionnements alimentaires de base, à une approche maximaliste s'appuyant sur la satisfaction d'un droit à la nourriture. Cette dernière découlerait ou serait, à tout le moins, nécessairement liée à la reconnaissance d'autres droits économiques et sociaux dans le contexte de la revendication du NOEI.

Le concept de sécurité alimentaire mondiale, dont l'une des finalités visait l'application du droit à la nourriture, était presque exclusivement articulé, dans ses premières formulations,[81] autour de la stabilisation des approvisionnements plutôt que de la consommation humaine.[82] Il est difficile de concevoir que le droit à

---

mondiale, première convention intégrant le concept de sécurité alimentaire mondiale (ci après l'*Engagement*). Texte annexé à la Résolution 1/64 du Conseil de la FAO, vol. CL 64/REP.

[77] Voir le préambule de l'acte constitutif de la FAO et notamment le par. 1(1), l'al. 1(2)d) et l'art. 4.

[78] A. Bensalah-Alaoui, *supra* note 27 aux pp. 75-78.

[79] Dans *Document de la Conférence de la F.A.O.,* C 85/23, oct. 1985.

[80] Sur le NOEI, consulter: Mario Bettati, *Le nouvel ordre économique international,* Paris, P.U.F. 1983, 127 pp.; Wild. D. Verway, *The New International Economic Order and the Realization of the Right to Development and Welfare — A Legal Survey,* 1981, 21 I.J.I.L. 1 à la p. 78.

[81] Notamment en ce qui concerne l'*Engagement*.

[82] Cette situation est attribuable au contexte particulier des années 70 où une pénurie alimentaire était envisagée. A. Bensalah-Alaoui, *supra* note 27 à la p. 80. Le même reproche peut cependant être fait au *Plan d'action pour la sécurité alimentaire mondiale, ibid.* à la p. 87.

la nourriture puisse s'imposer sans que les modalités de son application à la personne humaine occupent une place de premier plan dans la stratégie déployée.

Le seul mérite du concept de sécurité alimentaire est d'avoir fait de la faim un problème collectif. Le droit à la nourriture, s'il avait failli dans son application aux destinataires que sont les personnes, prenait un second souffle en devenant aussi un droit pour les destinataires que constituent les États. Si l'humain n'a qu'un droit théorique à la nourriture, l'État se chargera de le revendiquer en son nom auprès de la communauté internationale. Le droit à la nourriture, tout comme le droit au développement, ne peut d'ailleurs pas être "un droit de l'homme pris comme individu s'il n'est pas d'abord un droit du peuple ou de l'État."[83]

Du point de vue des relations Nord-Sud, c'est-à-dire, si l'on considère le problème de la faim comme étant exclusivement un problème des PED,[84] le droit à la nourriture est donc un droit individuel dont les PED sont les prestataires; tandis que le droit à la couverture des besoins alimentaires des peuples, ou le droit à la sécurité alimentaire, est un droit collectif dont la communauté internationale et plus précisément les PD sont les prestataires. Ceci est conforme au droit au développement.[85]

Malgré tous les efforts de ses dirigeants, la FAO a été incapable de donner une impulsion significative aux programmes formalisant le concept, principalement à cause de la résistance des pays développés producteurs et exportateurs de denrées alimentaires. Ces derniers, les États-Unis en tête, refusaient de s'engager fermement dans des projets sur lesquels, selon eux, ils n'exerçaient pas un contrôle suffisant et qui de surcroît menaçaient dangereusement les règles du marché.[86] Le concept de sécurité alimentaire mondiale n'a ainsi jamais, sinon sur papier, véritablement recueilli l'adhésion des PD. Il demeure un concept volontariste ne faisant appel qu'à la compassion et la charité des PD.

(ii)   Un concept à caractère essentiellement caritatif

Le concept de sécurité alimentaire mondiale souffre d'une faiblesse commune à tous les concepts juridiques ayant comme objectif

[83] Mohammed Bedjaoui, "Le droit au développement," dans *Droit international, bilan et perspectives, supra* note 21 à la p. 1250.

[84] FAO, *supra* note 2.

[85] M. Bedjaoui, *supra* note 21 à la p. 1253.

[86] A. Bensalah-Alaoui, *supra* note 27 aux pp. 75-78.

une juste répartition des ressources. Il fait appel à l'équité, concept qui n'a jamais occupé une place significative sur la scène internationale et dans le comportement des États. Pour I. Brownlie, l'équité en droit international offre peu en dehors des déceptions.[87] Cette situation n'est pas étrangère, comme il sera vu, au contexte international qui prévalait jusqu'à l'avènement du concept de développement durable.[88]

Les défaillances marquées du système alimentaire mondial sont en grande partie attribuables au fait que les PED n'ont jamais obtenu de concessions des PD sur des mécanismes propres à assurer la répartition des denrées alimentaires. La préoccupation des PED était alors laissée au bon vouloir, c'est-à-dire à la bienfaisance, des PD. Au-delà des principes généreux, le constat en est un d'iniquité quant aux mesures appliquées.

Le concept de sécurité alimentaire mondiale a connu une évolution qui s'est faite en trois périodes. La première a donné naissance au concept, dont les paramètres se retrouvent dans l'*Engagement* adopté par la FAO en 1974.[89] La seconde a défini une stratégie afin de mettre en oeuvre l'*Engagement,* par la création du *Plan d'action pour la sécurité alimentaire mondiale*[90] et la dernière a posé le problème de la sécurité alimentaire mondiale dans la perspective plus large de la revendication d'un NOEI.

Les trois phases ont pour caractéristique commune leur inaptitude à créer un contexte institutionnel propre à faire progresser de façon significative la cause de la faim. Elles ont été le ferment de tentatives des États pour trouver des solutions au problème, mais les actions envisagées ne s'appuyaient que sur des souhaits. Les textes adoptés eurent un effet négligeable, voire inexistant, sur la satisfaction du droit à la nourriture, puisque leurs dispositions ne furent qu'incitatives. Cette situation est en grande partie attribuable au fait que les ententes négociées constituaient la plupart du temps des actes concertés non conventionnels.[91] Lorsqu'elles étaient contraignantes, elles étaient bien souvent violées.

---

[87] Ian Brownlie, *Legal Status of Natural Resources,* (1980) 162 R.C.A.D.I. 288.

[88] *Cf. infra* deuxième partie, titre 2, A, *i.*

[89] *Supra* note 76.

[90] Le texte du Plan figure à l'annexe F du *Rapport de la 4ᵉ session du Comité de la Sécurité alimentaire mondiale (C.S.A.),* CSA-5-11, avril 1979. C'est le d'ailleurs le CSA qui l'a adopté (CL 75/10, mai 1979).

[91] *Cf. infra* titre 2, B, *i.*

C'est toutefois au cours de la dernière période où les avancées les plus marquantes ont été réalisées, sous l'impulsion des PED, afin de réformer l'ordre international pour qu'il puisse répondre au problème de la faim. L'action des PED avait comme objectif la création de nouvelles institutions, la réforme de celles déjà existantes et l'élaboration de mécanismes juridiques et économiques nouveaux. Le concept de nouvel ordre alimentaire mondial naissait.[92] Inspiré du NOEI, il offrait la perspective de donner un nouvel élan au concept de sécurité alimentaire mondiale. Les PED espéraient que le NOAM instaurerait un système imposant des obligations internationales à la charge des États, en remplacement de celui dont le fonctionnement ne relevait que de l'altruisme des PD à l'égard des PED.[93]

Le NOAM ne vit malheureusement pas plus le jour que le NOEI, car rien ne motivait les PD à consentir à un réaménagement des rapports inter-étatiques imposant des limitations conventionnelles à leur souveraineté. La revendication du NOAM par les PED eut cependant comme conséquence positive une meilleure définition du concept de sécurité alimentaire mondiale. Cet aspect revêt une importance non négligeable afin que ce dernier s'inscrive dans le cadre de revendications susceptibles d'infléchir des comportements aux États.[94]

2   *Les déficiences inhérentes au positionnement des acteurs en présence*

La sécurité alimentaire mondiale requiert une modification du statut juridique des denrées comestibles. Ces dernières devraient être consacrées patrimoine commun de l'humanité.[95] Le changement du statut juridique des ressources est pratiquement impossible à

[92] Ci-après NOAM. *Cf. infra* deuxième partie, titre 2, A, *iii.*

[93] Comme l'objectif de l'aide publique au développement (APD) à laquelle les PD doivent consacrer 0,7 % de leur produit national brut. N.Q. Dinh et autres, *supra* note 22 à la p. 1023.

[94] Par le développement durable. *Cf. infra* deuxième partie, titre 2, A, *ii.*

[95] Ci-après PCH. À propos du concept, consulter: Sylvie Paquerot, *Le statut des ressource vitales en droit international,* Bruxelles, Bruylant, 2002, 272 p.; Kemal Baslar, *The Concept of the Common Heritage of Mankind in International Law,* La Haye, Martinus Nijhoff, 1998, 427 p.; Bekkouche, M. Adda, *La récupération du concept de patrimoine commun de l'humanité (PCH) par les pays industriels,* (1987) vol. XXI, R.B.D.I. 124 à la p. 137; Dominique Gaurier, et Pierre-Jean Hesse, *La permanence d'un mythe: patrimoine commun des pauvres ou patrimoine commun de l'humanité,* (1991) t. XI, Ann. dr. m. a.-s. 61 à la p. 88; L.F.E., Goldie, *A Note on Some Diverse Meanings of "The Common Heritage of Mankind,"* (1983) vol. 10, n° 1,

réaliser dans le contexte actuel des relations internationales (A).
De plus, les mécanismes décisionnels dans le secteur alimentaire
ont comme conséquence un affaiblissement des institutions de
l'application du droit positif (B).

(a)   L'impossibilité de l'application du concept de patrimoine
commun de l'humanité

Les PED, qui souhaiteraient que les ressources alimentaires mondiales soient consacrées PCH, ne disposent cependant pas d'une
monnaie d'échange leur permettant d'imposer le concept (*i*). De
plus, les intérêts économiques des PD sont d'une importance telle
que tout changement dans le statut des ressources alimentaires doit
être écarté pour le moment (*ii*).

(*i*)   *Le manque d'un monnaie d'échange des pays en développement
afin d'imposer le concept*

L'évolution du droit à la nourriture, mais surtout celle du concept
de sécurité alimentaire mondiale, est marquée par la recherche
d'un mécanisme juridique permettant aux denrées alimentaires
d'acquérir le statut de ressources naturelles communes. Il est rapidement apparu, par conséquent, que la satisfaction du droit collectif à la nourriture ne pouvait s'opérer que par l'application de
procédures assurant une juste distribution de ces biens, puisque la
collectivisation d'une ressource a comme corollaire une utilisation
équitable de celle-ci.

Ce souci était déjà présent chez les représentants d'États, lors des
négociations portant sur le *Pacte international relatif aux droits économiques, sociaux et culturels.* L'alinéa 11(2)b) de ce dernier indique
qu'ils devront adopter des mesures nécessaires "pour assurer une
répartition équitable des ressources alimentaires mondiales." Il a
été avancé que ce texte ouvrait la voie à "un droit d'accès aux
ressources alimentaires des pays excédentaires au profit des pays
qui accusent un déficit dans ce domaine."[96] Mais, tel qu'indiqué

S.J.I.L.C. 69 à la p. 112; Christopher C. Joyner, *Legal implications of the concept of
the common heritage of mankind,* 1986, vol. 35, Part. 1, I.C.L.Q. 190 à la p. 199;
A.-C. Kiss, *La notion de patrimoine commun de l'humanité,* 1982 t. 175, R.C.A.D.I. 99
à la p. 256; P.-F. Mercure, *L'échec des modèles de gestion des ressources naturelles selon
les caractéristiques du concept de patrimoine commun de l'humanité,* 1996-97, vol. 28,
nº 1, R.D. Ottawa 45.

[96]   A. Bensalah-Alaoui, *supra* note 27 à la p. 53.

précédemment,[97] la disposition ne constituerait qu'un objectif pour les pays donateurs, presque exclusivement des PD, à l'égard des pays bénéficiaires qui seraient compris dans la sous-catégorie des pays à faible revenu et à déficit vivrier.

C'est dans le contexte de la recherche d'un NOEI que les PED ont tenté, mais là encore sans succès, de conférer aux ressources alimentaires mondiales un statut s'apparentant à celui de PCH. La revendication non conditionnelle des PED a vite démontré ses limites, puisqu'elle se heurtait à l'opposition des PD qui y voyaient le danger de créer une catégorie particulière de "ressources naturelles partagées, "[98] par rapport à certaines autres que les PD considéraient vitales pour la pérennité de leur modèle de développement. Le premier choc pétrolier, en 1973, avait amené les PD à avancer l'idée qu'ils possédaient un droit d'accès sur les ressources pétrolières, principalement localisées dans certains PED. Le concept de PCH était présent en filigrane. Les PED concernés opposaient le principe de la souveraineté permanente sur les ressources naturelles à cette prétention,[99] comme les PED concernés le firent ultérieurement pour les ressources génétiques.[100]

L'évolution du concept de PCH suit celle de la recherche d'un NOEI par les PED, en constituant un élément indispensable à sa réalisation et en devenant même le symbole de son accomplissement.[101] La raison de la juxtaposition de ces deux notions, opérée par les PED dans leurs rapports avec les PD et visant l'établissement de nouvelles règles dans le domaine économique, s'explique par les

---

[97] *Cf. supra* titre 1, A, *ii*.

[98] Expression utilisée par P.-M. Dupuy pour qualifier les voies d'eau internationales. P.-M. Dupuy, *Droit international public*, Paris, Dalloz, 2000 à la p. 644. L'auteur utilise plutôt l'expression "ressource commune" en ce qui concerne les ressources environnementales globales, telles l'atmosphère, la stratosphère (couche d'ozone) et la diversité biologique, *ibid.* aux pp. 676 et s.

[99] Le Groupe des 77 s'opposait vivement à une telle prétention. Voir *Déclaration des ministres des affaires étrangères du Groupe des 77*, dans UN doc. A/34/533 (1979), annexe, § 4.

[100] P.-F. Mercure, *Le rejet du concept de patrimoine commun de l'humanité afin d'assurer la gestion de la diversité biologique*, (1995) vol. XXXIII A.C.D.I. 281 à la p. 304.

[101] En parlant du début des travaux de la Conférence sur le droit de la mer, René-Jean Dupuy note: "Le départ de la Conférence, en 1974, coïncidait d'ailleurs avec celui des négociations sur le nouvel ordre économique international dont le régime des fonds marins devait, pour le Tiers-Monde, marquer un modèle et un test." René-Jean Dupuy, *La clôture du système international: La Cité Terrestre*, Paris, Presses universitaires de France, 1989 à la p. 42.

similitudes qui existent entre les idéologies à la base même de ces concepts. Le contexte de réforme de l'ordre établi, engendré par les revendications des PED dans les années 60 et 70 dans le secteur économique et formalisé par le NOEI, eut comme conséquence de lier la réalisation du droit collectif à la sécurité alimentaire mondiale avec celle des revendications des PED. L'exécution de ce droit ne pouvant désormais se concrétiser qu'à partir d'un NOAM tributaire de prémices de nature économique. La revendication du NOAM resta lettre morte et les PED obtinrent, comme maigre consolation, que le droit à la sécurité alimentaire constituait une responsabilité commune de l'humanité.[102]

Il est aisé de comprendre pourquoi le NOAM et son corollaire probable, la consécration des ressources alimentaires PCH, ne s'est jamais vraiment réalisé. Les PED n'avaient pour ainsi dire rien à offrir aux PD en échange de concessions de leur part visant la réalisation graduelle ou même partielle tant du NOAM que du NOEI. Les producteurs et exportateurs de denrées alimentaires étant largement des PD, le *"Bargaining-Power* des pays en développement est particulièrement faible dans ce domaine."[103]

La reconnaissance du statut de PCH appliqué à la gestion des grands fonds marins s'est faite dans le cadre des négociations globales portant sur une multitude d'aspects du droit de la mer. Les PED avaient un pouvoir décisionnel sur plusieurs de ceux-ci; ce qui leur permit de faire des concessions sur certains d'entre eux en échange de l'application du concept de PCH.[104] Ce pouvoir décisionnel leur faisant défaut dans les négociations portant sur la Lune, ils obtinrent que l'astre soit consacré PCH, mais sans que les puissances spatiales ne devinrent parties au traité, réduisant ainsi presque à néant sa portée.[105] La consécration du concept de PCH aux ressources naturelles communes est donc toujours tributaire du *Bargaining-Power* des PED, à défaut de quoi ce sont les PD qui dictent les modalités juridiques ou pratiques de la gestion de la ressource en fonction de leurs intérêts.

---

[102] *Pacte de la sécurité alimentaire mondiale,* Document de la Conférence de la F.A.O., C 85/23, oct. 1985.

[103] A. Bensalah-Alaoui, *supra* note 27 à la p. 113.

[104] La portée du concept fut cependant fortement réduite par les PD. P.-F. Mercure, *supra* note 95 aux pp. 74 et s.

[105] *Ibid.* aux pp. 60-74.

L'embargo commercial décrété en août 1991 contre l'Irak par le Conseil de sécurité des Nations Unies, suite à l'invasion du Koweït par cet État, n'a pu être levé que par la mise en place d'un mécanisme permettant l'échange d'une ressource naturelle irakienne essentielle pour les PD: le pétrole, contre des denrées alimentaires; ce que l'on a appelé la formule "pétrole contre nourriture."[106] La population irakienne n'aurait sans doute pas bénéficié d'un approvisionnement en denrées alimentaires et médicaments nécessaires à sa survie si les PD, qui contrôlent le Conseil de sécurité, n'avaient pas manifesté d'intérêt pour l'or noir de la dictature.

L'État cubain, qui n'a jamais possédé de ressources vitales à échanger aux États-Unis, est toujours victime d'un embargo américain; "la philanthropie étant incompatible avec le commerce mondial."[107] Même dans un contexte de tensions, comme cela est le cas entre les PD et l'Irak, le commerce, ou si l'on veut l'échange, est toujours possible; il suffit simplement d'avoir quelque chose de vital à proposer aux PD.

Ces situations permettent de comprendre le peu de gains enregistrés par les PED dans le grandes négociations commerciales internationales. Agissant comme de simples spectateurs, ils se confinent dans une position où aucune concession de la part des PD n'est envisageable. Ainsi, relativement aux discussions portant sur l'ouverture des marchés "n'ayant rien à offrir, ils n'ont guère pu faire entendre leurs voix et obtenir les concessions qu'ils souhaitaient."[108]

(ii)   Les intérêts économiques des pays développés dans le domaine alimentaire

La méfiance des PD, quant à des discussions relatives à la reconnaissance d'un droit collectif à la sécurité alimentaire, s'explique par le fait que cette dernière constitue une avancée vers la consécration des ressources alimentaires PCH. La seule mention de la possibilité de rendre effectif le droit individuel à la nourriture déclenche chez les PD la même suspicion, cette fois-ci à cause de la menace que cela fait peser sur leurs intérêts commerciaux immédiats.

Les États possédant les excédents les plus importants de leurs balances commerciales dans le secteur alimentaire sont des PD et

---

[106] A. Bencheneb, *supra* note 74.

[107] *Ibid.* à la p. 947.

[108] Dominique Carreau et Patrick Juilliard, *Droit international économique*, 4ᵉ éd., Paris, LGDJ, 1998 à la p. 272.

ceux enregistrant des déficits chroniques de celles-ci sont majoritairement des PED.[109] Ainsi, les PD et les PED se sont toujours
opposés sur le droit à la sécurité alimentaire collective et la stabilité
des échanges commerciaux. Les premiers cherchent à promouvoir,
de façon générale, un marché à l'abri de contraintes qui limi-
teraient leur liberté d'intervenir dans la circulation des denrées
alimentaires et plus spécifiquement des produits agricoles.[110] Les
seconds ambitionnent d'imposer des règles à ces mouvements
au profit des États en butte avec des problèmes d'approvisionnement.[111] Il peut ainsi être affirmé :

> De l'avis unanime, le commerce international constitue à l'heure actuelle
> l'entrave extérieure majeure à la réalisation des objectifs nutritionnels et
> de développement des pays en développement. L'importance, en effet
> qu'il revêt pour la sécurité alimentaire mondiale est à l'image des blocages
> ... Nord-Sud — qu'il cristallise.[112]

Les PED ont étendu leurs revendications commerciales dans le
cadre du NOEI, aux échanges internationaux de produits alimentaires. Les mécanismes visant la création de stocks ou banques
alimentaires, soit afin d'assurer un approvisionnement constant
aux États vulnérables ou même, afin de parer à des situations
urgentes créées par des famines, se sont toujours heurtés à la
volonté des PD.[113] L'adhésion des PD à des mécanismes de ce type
s'est toujours faite à la condition qu'ils tiennent compte de leurs
intérêts commerciaux. Ainsi, l'article 7 de l'*Engagement* prévoit des
mesures de sauvegarde afin d'éviter que les dispositions relatives
à la sécurité alimentaire aient des effets négatifs sur la structure de

---

[109] Serge Cordellier, Béatrice Didiot et Sarah Netter, dir., *L'état du monde 2003*,
Montréal, La Découverte/Boréal, 2002 aux pp.587 et s.

[110] Seules deux dispositions du *General Agreement on Tariffs and Trade* (GATT) traitent des produits agricoles; les alinéas XI(2)a et c. Elles instituent une clause de
sauvegarde qui permet de déroger à la règle générale de la prohibition des
restrictions quantitatives posée par le par. XI(1). D. Carreau et P. Julliard, *supra*
note 108 à la p. 141.
Les grands pays exportateurs développés subventionnent allègrement les
producteurs.

[111] Consulter, à cet effet, la *Déclaration universelle pour l'élimination définitive de la
faim et de la malnutrition* et les 22 résolutions adoptées pour sa mise en oeuvre.
Document officiel UN/E/CONF 65/20, 1-23, Nations Unies, New York, 1975.

[112] A. Bensalah-Alaoui, *supra* note 27 à la p. 290.

[113] Il existe actuellement sept accords portant sur des produits agricoles de base.
D. Carreau et P. Julliard, *supra* note 108 aux pp. 295-96.

la production et du commerce. Les paragraphes 8(a) et (b) mentionnent de plus:

> les gouvernements devraient tenir compte tant des intérêts des pays en développement largement tributaires des exportations de produits alimentaires, que des effets pervers que peuvent avoir sur les prix mondiaux l'accumulation, la conservation et le déblocage des stocks détenus au titre du présent Engagement.

L'*Accord sur l'agriculture*[114] et la *Déclaration sur les mesures concernant les effets négatifs possibles du programme de réforme sur les pays les moins avancés (PMA) et les pays en développement importateurs nets,*[115] adoptés lors de la Conférence de Marrakech en 1994 et entrés en vigueur en 1995, prévoient des mesures timides afin de favoriser la sécurité alimentaire du Tiers-Monde. Bien que le principe général de l'Accord soit la réduction des soutiens aux produits agricoles, les exclusions sont tellement nombreuses et leur portée si large[116] que, dans les faits, l'aide agricole interne augmente dans les PD au lieu de diminuer.[117] Ces subventions constituent des aides publiques à l'exportation.[118] Les règles actuelles favorisant le libre-échange encouragent donc l'importation de denrées alimentaires dans les PED,[119] accentuant ainsi leur dépendance face aux PD. L'augmentation, dans les PED, du volume de denrées alimentaires importées contrecarre les politiques agricoles nationales, seules capables à long terme d'assurer l'autonomie alimentaire des pays pauvres. Plusieurs

---

[114] Thiébault Flory, *L'Organisation mondiale du commerce*, Bruxelles, Bruylant, 1999 aux pp. 62 et s.

[115] *Ibid.* aux pp. 69-70.

[116] Les mesures de soutien interne qui ne sont pas soumises à réduction comprennent notamment: les versements directs aux producteurs; le financement du revenu de la production; les aides à la détention de stocks publics à des fins de sécurité alimentaire; le versement au titre de l'aide régionale; la participation financière de l'État à des programmes de garantie des revenus et à des programmes établissant un dispositif de sécurité pour les revenus, *ibid.* aux pp. 65-66. Consulter aussi D. Carreau et P. Julliard, *supra* note 108 aux pp. 140-52.

[117] Le montant total des subventions accordées au secteur agricole dans les pays de l'Organisation de coopération et de développement économiques (OCDE), donc les pays développés, s'élevait à 335 milliards de dollars américains en 1998. Rien n'indique qu'elles diminueront. OCDE, Conseil des ministres, *Communiqué final Maîtriser la mondialisation*, Paris, OCDE, 27 juin 2000.

[118] Conseil économique et social, *supra* note 9 à la p. 23.

[119] Importations qu'ils ont de moins en moins la capacité de payer en raison du contexte économique général, notamment le fardeau de leur dette extérieure.

des onze autres accords adoptés à Marrakech ont des effets dévastateurs sur l'agriculture vivrière des PED.[120]

Aucun mécanisme n'a été inclu dans les règles de l'Organisation mondiale du commerce[121] afin de garantir le respect intégral du droit à la nourriture par rapport aux impératifs commerciaux. Une réévaluation du lien entre le commerce et la sécurité alimentaire s'impose[122] et "le libre commerce doit reconnaître la primauté des droits de l'homme."[123] Les participants à la conférence tenue à Doha, en novembre 2001, qui ouvre un nouveau cycle de négociations commerciales sous l'égide de l'OMC, ont décidé de ne pas considérer le droit à l'alimentation dans les pourparlers, malgré les nombreuses propositions à cet effet.[124]

Le Consensus de Washington[125] qui est constitué d'ententes informelles, de *gentleman agreements,* conclues dans les années 80 et 90 entre les principales sociétés transnationales et banques privées américaines, la Banque mondiale, le Fonds monétaire international[126] et la Réserve fédérale américaine, vise à supprimer progressivement les entraves réglementaires imposées par les États aux marchés financiers et à obtenir, à terme, leur libéralisation complète. Il comporte quatre préceptes: privatisation, déréglementation, stabilité macroéconomique et compression budgétaire.[127] Il traduit la volonté américaine de donner une forme ultra-libérale à la mondialisation. Son application menace directement le droit à la nourriture.[128]

---

[120] Mentionnons l'*Accord sur les aspects des droits de propriété intellectuelle qui touchent au commerce* (ADPIC), l'*Accord sur les mesures concernant les investissements et liés au commerce* (MIC); l'*Accord général sur le commerce des services* (AGCS).

[121] Ci-après OMC.

[122] Conseil économique et social, *supra* note 9 à la p. 23.

[123] Commission des droits de l'homme, 59e session. Exposé oral du rapporteur, 5 avril 2002. Disponible à l'adresse suivante: "http://www.unhchr.ch/huricane/ huricane.nsf/view01" à la p. 5 (page consultée le 18 octobre 2002).

[124] *Ibid.* à la p. 5 de 6 et textes sur le programme de Doha pour le développement: <http://www.wto.org/french/thewto_f/minist_f/min01_f/min01_f.htm> (page consultée le 22 janvier 2002).

[125] Sur le Consensus de Washington, consulter: Michel Beaud, *Mondialisation, les mots et les choses,* Paris, Éditions Karthala, 1999; Robert Reich, *L'Économie mondialisée,* Paris, Dunod, 1993; Samir Amin "Quelles alternatives à la dimension destructrice de l'accumulation du capital" dans *À la recherche d'alternatives — Un autre monde est-il possible?* (2001) vol. VII, n° 2, Revue Alternatives Sud, 209 pp.

[126] Ci-après, respectivement BIRD et FMI.

[127] Commission des droits de l'homme, *supra* note 123 à la p. 3.

[128] "Au droit à la nourriture s'oppose le consensus de Washington," *ibid.* à la p. 3.

Les programmes d'ajustement structurels de la BIRD et du FMI, qui imposent aux PED les préceptes du Consensus de Washington, annulent nombre des maigres progrès réalisés par les organisations spécialisées favorisant le droit à la nourriture, notamment la FAO, l'OIT, l'OMS, le PNUD et l'UNICEF.[129] Ils sont aussi bien souvent néfastes pour les cultures vivrières des PED et ont tout simplement détruit le secteur agraire de certains PED.[130]

(b)   La faiblesse des institutions de l'application du droit positif

Les conventions internationales applicables au secteur alimentaire constituent, tout au plus, la genèse d'un droit évolutif. Leur faiblesse tient au fait que les règles juridiques énoncées sont issues d'actes concertés non conventionnels (*i*). De plus, la procédure d'adoption des textes et celle de la prise de décisions constituent des limites inhérentes à la progression du secteur (*ii*).

(i)   Des règles juridiques issues d'actes concertés non conventionnels

La réalisation du droit à la nourriture comporte deux importantes limitations juridiques. La première est à l'effet que les conventions internationales consacrant ce droit sont, dans bien des cas, non contraignantes pour les États, ne constituant dans le meilleur des scénarii que des actes concertés non conventionnels ou instruments de *Soft Law*,[131] à partir desquels une coutume émergera. La deuxième tient au fait que lorsque des obligations sont imposées aux États, elles demeurent non exécutées par eux. Il s'agit d'une déficience importante du droit international public en général, mais particulièrement dans les domaines où l'on envisage une réallocation des ressources financières entre le Nord et le Sud.

---

[129] PNUD est l'acronyme du *Programme des Nations Unies pour le développement* et UNICEF celui pour *Fonds des Nations Unies pour l'enfance. Ibid.* à la p. 3.

[130] L'exemple du Niger est probant: *Report by the special Rapporteur on the right to food submitted in accordance with Commission on Human Rights resolution 2001/25, Addendum, Mission to Niger,* Economic and Social Council, *supra* note 12, Add.1, 23. Celui du Vietnam l'est tout autant. Consulter à ce sujet: Michel Chossudovsky, *La Mondialisation de la pauvreté*, Montréal, Écosociété, 1998, aux pp. 129-52. Sur les politiques du FMI consulter: Jean Stiglitz, *La grande désillusion*, Paris, Fayard, 2002 aux pp. 27-84. Sur le rôle de l'OMC consulter: Agnès Bertrand et Laurence Kalafatides, *OMC, le pouvoir invisible*, Paris, Fayard, 2002, 332 pp.

[131] Au sujet de ces ententes et sur leur force obligatoire, consulter: N.Q. Dinh et autres, *supra* note 22 aux pp. 381-89.

Les articles 22 à 27 de *la Déclaration universelle des droits de l'homme*, qui constituent les premières définitions précises des droits socio-économiques, notamment du droit à la nourriture mentionné à l'article 25, énoncent simplement des recommandations aux États, ne les soumettant ainsi à aucune obligation.[132] tel que précisé antérieurement.[133] Des juristes considèrent toutefois que la Déclaration codifierait des règles coutumières.[134] Le *Pacte international relatif aux droits économiques, sociaux et culturels* avait comme objectif de conférer une force obligatoire aux dispositions correspondantes de la Déclaration. Tel ne fut pas le résultat, dûe à des tensions qui surgirent entre les pays participants aux négociations. Ainsi, les dispositions relatives au contenu du droit à la nourriture suffisante, sont *trop vagues pour être directement exécutoires,* pour certains.[135] Pour les autres, qui verraient dans toutes les résolutions des Nations Unies relatives au droit à la nourriture l'expression d'une *opinio juris,*[136] force est de constater qu'en l'absence de mécanismes de contrôle, ces obligations sont peu ou prou exécutées.

Même le droit fondamental d'être à l'abri de la faim connaît de sérieuses difficultés d'application. Ainsi, l'affirmation du caractère primordial de ce droit ne le rend pas exécutoire, "puisque les attributs de la nature économique de ce droit l'emportent sur les caractères qui auraient dû découler du terme fondamental."[137]

Les tentatives répétées de la communauté internationale de donner une effectivité au droit à la nourriture ont toujours abouti à des échecs, car les instruments juridiques adoptés, tels l'*Engagement*, le *Plan d'action sur la sécurité alimentaire mondiale* et la *Déclaration universelle pour l'élimination définitive de la faim et de la malnutrition*[138] constituaient, tout au plus, des actes concertés non conventionnels ne comportant que des énoncés indicatifs pour les États. La nécessité de l'adhésion des PD imposait de privilégier des instruments souples dans lesquels seuls des objectifs à atteindre étaient mentionnés.

L'*Engagement* a été qualifié non pas comme un accord international, mais comme une promesse d'agir, fondée sur la confiance

---

[132] M. Jacquart, *supra* note 25 à la p. 1155.

[133] *Cf. supra,* titre 1, A, *a.*

[134] Voir le commentaire de W.A. Schabas à ce sujet. W.A. Schabas, *supra* note 7 à la p. 32.

[135] A. Bensalah-Alaoui, *supra* note 27 à la p. 57.

[136] M. Jacquart, *supra* note 25 à la p. 1162.

[137] A. Bensalah-Alaoui, *supra* note 27 à la p. 50.

[138] *Supra,* note 111.

mutuelle et la bonne foi pour atteindre un but déterminé.[139] Le *Plan d'action*, quant à lui, avait essentiellement un caractère discrétionnaire.[140] La *Déclaration* fait elle aussi appel à la seule volonté des États. Le *Pacte de la Sécurité alimentaire mondiale*, adopté en 1985 par la Conférence de la FAO, est dépourvu de toute valeur juridique. Il appelle néanmoins la Communauté internationale à s'"engager à fond" pour la sécurité alimentaire mondiale.[141] Certains PD[142] ont préféré formuler une réserve dissociant leurs gouvernements de ses dispositions, craignant qu'elles ne créent tout de même des obligations à leur égard. L'inefficacité de ces instruments a été à la mesure de leur souplesse.

La revendication d'un NOEI a, dès 1974,[143] atteint le secteur alimentaire. Jusqu'à cette date, les ententes ne comportaient aucune échéance précise sur les actions à prendre, mais à partir de ce moment, les programmes et actions entrepris se caractérisèrent de deux façons. Premièrement, la fixation de balises temporelles visant à éliminer le problème de la faim, qui créait ainsi une illusion obligataire et deuxièmement, leur report, à mesure que l'on constatait qu'elles étaient dépassées sans que des résultats probants furent atteints.

La prorogation des échéances devient la règle. Les textes sont généreux et détaillés, les mécanismes de sécurité alimentaire très élaborés, les modifications au système économique et commercial mondial mises de l'avant; mais ils constituent des promesses sans lendemains.

La *Déclaration universelle pour l'élimination définitive de la faim et de la malnutrition*, adoptée par l'Assemblée générale des Nations Unies[144] en 1974, ainsi que les vingt-deux résolutions visant sa mise

[139] A. Bensalah-Alaoui, *supra* note 27 à la p. 81.

[140] *Ibid.* à la p. 88.

[141] *Ibid.* à la p. 134.

[142] Les États-Unis, le Canada et l'Australie.

[143] Date de la tenue de la Conférence mondiale sur l'alimentation. Rés. 3180 (XXVIII) du 17 décembre 1973 de l'Assemblée générale. Il est important de mentionner aussi la tenue, à Paris du 19 au 23 juin 1978, au siège de l'UNESCO, d'une réunion d'experts sur les droits de l'homme, les besoins humains et l'instauration d'un NOEI. Celle-ci constitue le premier événement où le droit à l'alimentation a été étudié dans la perspective du NOEI. Consulter à ce sujet l'étude présentée par Keba M'Baye sur *L'émergence du droit au développement en tant que droit de l'homme dans le contexte du NOEI*, SS 78/CONF.630/8, juin 1978.

[144] Ci-après AGNU.

en oeuvre, fixaient comme objectif de purger le monde de la faim dans un délai de dix ans.[145] L'AGNU en adoptant, en 1980, la *Stratégie internationale du développement pour la troisième décennie des Nations Unies* prévoyait l'élimination de la faim et de la malnutrition assurément avant la fin du siècle.[146]

La *Déclaration de Rome sur la sécurité alimentaire mondiale* de 1996, dans laquelle les États s'engagent à exécuter le Plan d'action du Sommet[147] mentionne que doivent être clarifiés les contenus du droit à la nourriture suffisante et du droit fondamental de chacun d'être à l'abri de la faim, retrouvés dans le *Pacte international relatif aux droits économiques, sociaux et culturels* et autres instruments internationaux et régionaux pertinents.[148] Cette remise en question de la précision des textes juridiques relatifs au droit à la nourriture masque le malaise des États à faire progresser significativement la cause de la faim. Le droit à la nourriture est suffisamment circonscrit et les obligations étatiques claires. Dans son rapport annuel de 2002, la FAO notait, comme il a été souligné,[149] qu'aucun progrès n'avait été accompli depuis la tenue en 1996 à Rome du Sommet sur l'alimentation.

(ii)   Les limites fonctionnelles des mécanismes en vigueur

Si le droit à la nourriture a pour limite des instruments juridiques non-exécutoires ou non-exécutés, il souffre aussi d'une carence due à la consécration dans ceux-ci de normes minimales et vagues à la fois, accentuant d'autant la difficulté de les appliquer. Cette faiblesse tient, en grande partie, de la tendance observée depuis le début des années 70 de rechercher le consensus entre les États, par opposition à une décision découlant d'un vote à majorité simple ou à majorité qualifiée de ceux-ci, lors de négociations internationales portant sur des sujets délicats.[150] La pratique se rencontre

---

[145] Texte de la Déclaration et des 22 résolutions: *supra* note 111.

[146] A. Bensalah-Alaoui, *supra* note 27 à la p. 125. Sur cette stratégie consulter: Maurice Flory, *La troisième décennie pour le développement*, (1980) A.F.D.I. 595 à la p. 603.

[147] *La lutte contre la faim marque le pas*, *supra* note 17 à la p. 1.

[148] Objectif 7.4 de la Déclaration, Conseil économique et social, *supra* note 9 à la p. 10.

[149] FAO, *supra* note 2.

[150] Hervé Cassan, *Le consensus dans la pratique des Nations Unies*, (1974) AFDI 456 à la p. 485.

particulièrement dans des secteurs où les intérêts des PED et des PD s'opposent directement, comme dans les domaines du développement, de la protection de l'environnement global et du commerce international. Le droit à la nourriture n'échappe pas à cette règle.

Le consensus, qui devient la règle au niveau de l'adoption d'instruments juridiques internationaux abordant des problématiques Nord-Sud, implique une procédure très lente et produit des décisions ou des normes "lâches et diluées."[151] Il réduit ainsi considérablement l'impact sur la question dont est l'objet le traité ou la décision; "sans compter les réserves formelles que les États participants ont tendance à formuler au moment de la proclamation du consensus."[152]

Le consensus présente aussi l'inconvénient de traduire un compromis sur un désaccord. "L'unanimité de façade qu'il préserve cache, le plus souvent, une coalition d'insatisfaits."[153] Il a comme conséquence la consécration de normes traduisant le plus petit dénominateur commun sur lequel les parties ont pu s'entendre: "la communauté internationale des États dans son ensemble est, à l'heure actuelle, trop divisée pour qu'un consensus puisse exister entre ses membres sur davantage que le minimum, surtout si ce minimum est érigé en normes impératives auxquelles aucune dérogation n'est permise."[154] L'*Engagement* avait d'ailleurs "retenu le plus petit dénominateur commun gommant tous les aspects potentiellement litigieux. La réalisation du compromis ne fut possible qu'à ce prix."[155] Cette conséquence soulève évidemment de sérieuses questions non seulement juridiques, mais aussi éthiques, sur la ligne de partage entre nourriture suffisante et minimum vital requis.

C'est aussi la règle du consensus qui préside la prise de décisions au sein des institutions responsables de l'adoption des normes et de l'élaboration de programmes alimentaires. Tel est le cas de la FAO où le directeur général assume la tâche de dégager le consensus des États membres en conformité avec la politique générale qu'ils ont eux-mêmes approuvée.[156] L'action des institutions chargées de coordonner les programmes alimentaires est ainsi plus difficile à

---

[151] Mohamed Bennouna, "Droit international et développement," dans *Droit international, bilan et perspectives, supra* note 21 à la p. 675.

[152] *Ibid.*

[153] N.Q. Dinh et autres, *supra* note 22 à la p. 621.

[154] *Ibid.* à la p. 643.

[155] A. Bensalah-Alaoui, *supra* note 27 à la p. 83.

[156] *Ibid.* à la p. 139.

exécuter, puisque les décisions adoptées son imprécises et fixent des objectifs diffus.

B L'ACTUALISATION DE L'OBLIGATION ALIMENTAIRE IMPOSÉE AUX PAYS EN DÉVELOPPEMENT À L'ÉGARD DE LEURS POPULATIONS

La sécurité alimentaire mondiale doit être abordée par une nouvelle approche ayant comme objectif de réaliser, dans un délai raisonnable, le droit de chacun à la nourriture. La stratégie doit s'appuyer sur une redéfinition des fondements juridiques de l'action des PED (titre 1), ainsi que sur les normes du droit international public positif (titre 2).

1   La redéfinition des fondements juridiques de l'action des pays en développement

Le droit à la nourriture est un droit fondamental prioritaire et à ce titre il importe de procéder à la hiérarchisation des droits de l'homme (a). Les États doivent adopter les mesures qui s'imposent afin de le rendre effectif, compte tenu de l'évolution de la nature de l'obligation alimentaire, d'une obligation de moyens vers une obligation de résultats (b).

(a)   La hiérarchisation des droits de l'homme

Le droit à la nourriture appartient à la deuxième génération des droits de l'homme,[157] les droits économiques, sociaux et culturels. Les droits de première génération relèvent, quant à eux, des droits civils et politiques. Il s'agit essentiellement des grandes libertés — de croyance, d'expression, d'assemblée pacifique et d'association — des garanties judiciaires, telles la présomption d'innocence et la prohibition des infractions pénales rétroactives et les droits politiques.[158] Les droits de troisième génération sont constitués des droits dits de solidarité, qui sont des droits collectifs, tels le droit au développement, le droit à un environnement sain, le droit à la paix et le droit à l'application du concept de PCH.[159]

[157] L'expression "droit de l'homme" sera utilisée au lieu de "droit de la personne" puisque les instruments internationaux étudiés utilisent la première. K. Mbaye, *supra* note 21 à la p. 1119.

[158] W.A. Schabas, *supra* note 7 à la p. 39.

[159] Hector Gros Espell, "Introduction," dans *Droit international, bilan et perspectives, supra* note 21 aux pp. 1243 et s.; W.A. Schabas, *supra* note 7 à la p. 40. M. Bedjaoui mentionne que la *Charte africaine des droits de l'homme* fait du droit à la nourriture un droit collectif. M. Bedjaoui, *supra* note 83 à la p. 1125.

Cette classification ne suppose aucune hiérarchie dans les droits reconnus, la nature indivisible et interdépendante des droits définis dans les Pactes ayant été constamment affirmée par les divers organes des Nations Unies chargés de leur application.[160] La hiérarchisation des droits de l'homme implique de donner la priorité à certains d'entre eux, au détriment d'autres jugés moins urgents, tandis que leur indivisibilité signifie que les droits civils et politiques sont indissociables des droits économiques, sociaux et culturels, quant à leur réalisation. Les États rejettent toute hiérarchie des droits de l'homme, comme cela a d'ailleurs été affirmé à la conférence de Vienne de 1993.[161] L'indivisibilité des droits de l'homme, quant à elle, a été rappelée par plusieurs résolutions de l'AGNU.[162]

Néanmoins, la *Charte des Nations Unies* mentionne, dans son préambule, l'existence des droits fondamentaux.[163] Ces derniers doivent être appliqués même en l'absence d'obligations conventionnelles, puisqu'ils sont *considérés comme essentiels pour l'intégrité et l'indivisibilité de la personne humaine, au sens physique, intellectuel et moral, jouissant d'une supériorité qui, jointe à leur caractère impératif, les apparenterait au Jus Cogens.*[164] Le droit à la vie, consacré à l'article 3 de la *Déclaration universelle des droits de l'homme,* est sans conteste le plus fondamental des droits de l'homme. La réalisation du droit à la vie étant tributaire de celle du droit à la nourriture, ce dernier constituerait aussi, à l'évidence, un droit fondamental élémentaire et de première importance.[165] On peut affirmer, pour le droit à la nourriture, ce que M. Bedjaoui défendait pour le droit au développement, c'est-à-dire qu'il:

s'impose avec la force de l'évidence et trouve son fondement tout naturellement comme corollaire du droit à la vie. Si le droit au développement

---

[160] M. Jacquart, *supra* note 25 à la p. 1156.

[161] W.A. Schabas, *supra* note 7 à la p. 46.

[162] N.Q. Dinhet autres, *supra* note 22 à la p. 642.

[163] Distinction que ne fait pas la Déclaration. W.A. Schabas, *supra* note 7 à la p. 38.

[164] A. Bensalah-Alaoui, *supra* note 27 à la p. 49. Schabas indique "qu'ils font certainement partie des règles coutumières et sont probablement aussi dans cette catégorie de normes impératives que le droit international qualifie de Jus Cogens," W.A. Schabas, *supra* note 7 à la p. 45.

[165] Sous la réserve, cependant, de la distinction apportée par l'art. 11 du *Pacte international relatif aux droits économiques, sociaux, et culturels.* Seul le droit d'être à l'abri de la faim, mentionné au par. 2 de l'article constituerait un droit fondamental. *Cf. supra* première partie, titre 1, A, *a.*

ne relève pas à ce titre du Jus Cogens, une même logique voudrait alors que le génocide, qui est la négation du droit des peuples à la vie, soit permis par le droit international.[166]

La doctrine considère, de plus, que lorsque le non-respect de certains droits fondamentaux empêche la réalisation d'autres droits, il serait légitime et même obligatoire de leur donner une priorité.[167] Le droit à la nourriture apparaît donc comme un droit prioritaire parmi les droits fondamentaux, puisqu'il constitue aussi un droit indissociable du droit à un niveau de vie suffisant. En effet:

le droit à un niveau de vie suffisant constitue une condition sine qua non à la réalisation du droit à la vie, affirmé par l'article 6 du Pacte relatif aux droits civils et politiques, ce droit constitue certainement un droit prioritaire. Non pas que ce droit soit plus important que les autres mais il reste que sans la réalisation de ce droit premier dans un ordre international qui le permette, la réalisation des autres droits socio-économiques ou civils et politiques semble illusoire.[168]

A. Bensalah-Alaoui soutient: "Le droit d'être à l'abri de la faim doit primer tous les autres droits et toute autre considération, car il est le seul droit économique qui soit également un droit fondamental."[169] Il serait même juste d'affirmer que certains droits que l'on pourrait qualifier de droits à la survie immédiate, sont des droits fondamentaux prioritaires puisqu'ils conditionnent directement le droit à la vie. Outre le droit à la nourriture, on retrouverait dans cette catégorie le droit au développement et le droit à une certaine qualité de l'environnement.

Le droit à la nourriture serait un droit fondamental prioritaire, c'est-à-dire un droit qui ferait consensus entre tous les États et auquel aucune dérogation ne serait permise.[170] Le droit à la nourriture, compris dans le sens du paragraphe 11 (2) du *Pacte international relatif aux droits économiques, sociaux et culturels,* soit le droit fondamental à la nourriture, est ainsi un droit d'une réalisation intégrale et immédiate au profit de tous[171] au même titre que le

---

[166] M. Bedjaoui, *supra* note 83 à la p. 1254.

[167] M. Jacquart, *supra* note 25 à la p. 1161.

[168] *Ibid.*

[169] A. Bensalah-Alaoui, *supra* note 27 à la p. 62.

[170] On parle de droits non dérogeables, lorsque les conventions de protection des droits de la personne rendent impossible leur suspension.

[171] A. Bensalah-Alaoui, *supra* note 27 à la p. 49.

droit à la vie.[172] Ces droits constituent sans contredit le *noyau dur*
des droits de la personne.[173]

La Commission interaméricaine des droits de l'homme, se basant
sur l'article 26 relatif aux droits économiques, sociaux et culturels
de la *Convention américaine relative aux droits de l'homme*, du 22 novembre 1969, rappelle, dans son rapport de 1980, que selon l'obligation juridique contractée, les gouvernements doivent s'efforcer de
donner la "priorité aux besoins fondamentaux de santé, de nutri-
tion et d'éducation de leurs peuples."[174] Même si la hiérarchisation
des droits de l'homme est formellement rejetée, les États doivent
situer le droit à la nourriture au sommet de la pyramide des droits
fondamentaux.

(b)   L'évolution de la nature de l'obligation alimentaire d'une
      obligation de moyens vers une obligation de résultat

La nature d'obligation de résultat du droit fondamental à la
nourriture ne fait pas de doute.[175] Le niveau de développement de
l'État ne constituerait pas une limite pour sa réalisation. La situation est différente en ce qui concerne le droit à la nourriture
suffisante.[176] Ce droit, tel qu'il a été mentionné,[177] est soumis au
principe de progressivité, comme tous les autres droits économiques,
sociaux et culturels, puisque les États ne disposent pas immédiatement des ressources financières et autres, nécessaires à sa réalisation. Le devoir des États, en ce qui concerne le droit à la nourriture
suffisante, a ainsi été qualifié d'obligation de moyens.[178]

Le droit fondamental à la nourriture, qui est immédiatement
exécutoire, implique trois types de comportements: 1) ne pas priver
de son unique moyen de subsistance une personne ou un peuple;

---

[172] N.Q. Dinh et autres, *supra* note 22 à la p. 643.

[173] Expression utilisée par Schabas. W.A. Schabas, *supra* note 7 à la p. 45. Pierre-
Marie Dupuy soutient l'idée qu'il existe une tendance à la hiérarchisation des
droits de l'homme. P.-M. Dupuy, *supra* note 98 à la p. 214.

[174] A. Bensalah-Alaoui, *supra* note 27 à la p.33.

[175] *Ibid.* à la p. 60.

[176] *Ibid.* à la p. 61.

[177] *Cf. supra* première partie, titre 1, A, *b.*

[178] Il ne faudrait cependant pas conclure que l'abandon par la Commission du
droit international, dans son projet de 2001, de la distinction entre obligation
de moyens (ou de comportement) et obligation de résultat, enlève toute pertinence à celle-ci dans la réalité. Voir à ce sujet: N.Q. Dinh et autres, 7ᵉ éd. *Droit
international public*, Paris, L.G.D.J., 2002 à la p. 771.

2) les protéger contre la privation de ce moyen de subsistance, et 3) les aider lorsqu'ils sont incapables de se procurer leur propre subsistance ou sont victimes de catastrophes naturelles.[179] Le droit à la nourriture suffisante impose, quant à lui, les obligations suivantes aux États: 1) prendre des mesures appropriées, par l'adoption de programmes concrets, afin de lui donner effet;[180] 2) utiliser le maximum de ressources pour sa réalisation[181] et 3) adopter des mesures législatives afin qu'il s'accomplisse.[182]

Les deux types de droits auraient donc une portée juridique différente, d'une part, quant à leur réalisation effective et d'autre part, quant aux obligations qui en découlent. La reconnaissance du droit fondamental à la nourriture est considérée comme la première étape de celle du droit à la nourriture suffisante. Les PED ont l'obligation juridique de rendre immédiatement applicable le droit fondamental à la nourriture et de prendre sans délai des mesures afin que le droit à la nourriture suffisante s'applique.

Une certaine prudence doit être exercée dans l'interprétation de conventions internationales à partir de concepts juridiques issus du droit interne des États. La qualification d'obligations de moyens et de résultat est imprécise pour ce qui est du droit à la nourriture, car elle suppose qu'il est plus aisé pour les États de réaliser le droit fondamental à la nourriture que le droit à la nourriture suffisante. Les gouvernements rencontrent, dans les faits, des obstacles identiques à la réalisation de l'un et de l'autre. En effet, pour les PED aux prises avec des problèmes alimentaires, les deux types de droits ne peuvent vraiment s'appliquer que dans la mesure où les PD acceptent de consentir à des concessions de même nature afin de leur donner effet.

Vu sous cet angle, les considérations économiques rendraient donc les deux droits applicables progressivement. Ces droits sont, de plus, trop liés l'un à l'autre pour constituer des droits véritablement distincts dans leur réalisation. D'ailleurs, dans les PED caractérisés par des problèmes alimentaires permanents, ni l'un ni l'autre des groupes d'obligations à la charge des États ne sont pleinement respectés.

---

[179] H. Shue, *Basic Rights: Subsistence, Affluence and U.S. Foreign Policy*, Princeton, N.J., Princeton University Press, 1980 à la p. 60.

[180] Par. 11 (1 et 2) du *Pacte international relatif aux droits économiques, sociaux et culturels, supra* note 30.

[181] *Ibid.*, al. 11 (2)a) et art 2.

[182] *Ibid.*, par. 2 (1).

Si l'effectivité du droit à la nourriture suffisante répond à un contexte économique différent au Nord et au Sud, les PED ont néanmoins l'obligation de faire ce qui est envisageable maintenant, afin de créer un environnement propre à donner effet à ce droit. Le mécanisme de développement durable devrait alors nécessairement être utilisé par les PED puisqu'il permet d'atteindre ce but. Le droit à la nourriture suffisante se confondrait alors, en quelque sorte, au droit fondamental à la nourriture, puisqu'il serait possible de lui donner une certaine immédiateté dans son application. En ce sens, l'obligation alimentaire des PED constituerait une obligation de résultat pour les PED, sous la réserve de permettre au mécanisme de développement durable d'opérer des changements dans un délai raisonnable.

2   *La réalisation de la sécurité alimentaire collective à travers les normes du droit international positif*

L'application du mécanisme de développement durable au domaine alimentaire permettrait aux PED d'obtenir des concessions des PD au chapitre du NOEI, en échange de leur collaboration à la résolution de problématiques qui intéressent les PD. Les PED ont l'obligation d'assurer l'application du concept de développement durable (a). Ils ont aussi le devoir de promouvoir la mise en oeuvre de mécanismes visant l'équité alimentaire mondiale (b).

(a)   Le devoir pour les pays en développement d'assurer l'application du concept de développement durable

Les PED, constatant l'échec de leur revendication formelle du NOEI, ont utilisé les problèmes environnementaux globaux comme prétexte afin de le réactualiser dans le concept de développement durable (*i*). Ce dernier comprend le mécanisme du même nom qui a acquis une valeur coutumière (*ii*). Il serait susceptible de permettre aux PED de réaliser le NOAM (*iii*).

(*i*)   *La réactualisation du nouvel ordre économique international dans le concept de développement durable*

La revendication d'un NOEI par les PED prend son origine lors du IVe Sommet des pays Non-alignés, tenu à Alger en septembre 1973.[183]

---

[183]   Cet événement fut précédé de deux autres, importants dans la genèse du NOEI: la première Commission des Nations Unies pour le commerce et le développement (ci-après CNUCED), tenue à Genève en 1964 et la proclamation, en

Deux résolutions adoptées par l'AGNU, en 1974, précisent les demandes des PED: la *Déclaration et le programme d'action concernant l'instauration d'un NOEI* et la *Charte des droits et devoirs économiques des États*.[184] Le nouvel ordre demandé fait appel à une plus grande solidarité de la communauté internationale et promeut l'idée de traitement préférentiel accordé aux PED afin de corriger les inégalités économiques entre les États.

Une évolution se fait, à partir des années 80, dans la façon pour les PED de revendiquer l'équité à la base du NOEI. Trois facteurs expliquent cette évolution: 1) le constat du refus des PD d'accéder à leur demande d'un NOEI; 2) les graves problèmes financiers, monétaires et énergétiques qu'ils doivent résoudre[185] et 3) l'émergence de problèmes environnementaux globaux qui préoccupent les PD et qui requièrent la collaboration des PED pour leur résolution. De plus, en ce qui concerne ce dernier point:

La survenance de certains événements menaçant la survie de l'espèce humaine donna l'opportunité aux PED de revendiquer non pas la réalisation du NOEI en tant que tel mais celle de ses éléments constitutifs. En réponse à la demande de collaboration faite par les PD aux PED en vue de l'adoption de mesures propres à assurer la préservation de l'environnement à l'échelle planétaire, les PED demandèrent en échange la prise en compte de leurs revendications exprimées dans le NOEI. Dans ces nouveaux rapports de force Nord-Sud qui caractérisèrent les années 80, les PED prirent conscience qu'ils ne pouvaient faire valoir leurs doléances en faveur de leur développement, que dans un contexte de conditionnalité et qu'en ne leur trouvant la monnaie d'échange qui leur avait fait défaut jusqu'alors.[186]

Le concept de développement durable sert de fondement à leur démarche.[187] Le contenu juridique de ce dernier a été précisé depuis

---

1970, de la *Stratégie des Nations Unies pour la deuxième décennie pour le développement.* N.Q. Dinh et autres, *supra* note 178 à la p. 1012.

[184] Résolutions 3201 (S-VI) et 3202 (S-V); M. Bennouna, *supra*, note 151 à la p. 666.

[185] N.Q. Dinh et autres, *supra* note 178 à la p. 1012.

[186] P.-F. Mercure, *supra* note 100 à la p. 292. Les PED utilisèrent, jusqu'à un certain point, durant la guerre froide, la crainte de l'expansion du communisme comme condition à l'obtention de concessions de nature économique des PD à économie de marché. D'autres PED, tel Cuba, tirèrent différemment profit du contexte géopolitique mondial. Sur ces questions, consulter: Zaki Laïdi, *L'URSS vue du Tiers-Monde,* Paris, Éditions Karthala, 1984, 185 pp.

[187] Voir à ce sujet: P.-F. Mercure, *Le choix du concept de développement durable plutôt que celui de patrimoine commun de l'humanité afin d'assurer la protection de l'atmosphère,* (1996) 41 R. D. McGill 595. Sur le concept de développement durable

sa présentation originelle par la Commission mondiale sur l'environnement et le développement.[188] Il y a été fait référence fréquemment dans les travaux préparatoires de la Conférence de Rio,[189] ainsi que dans de nombreuses résolutions de l'AGNU.[190] Il a été formalisé dans cinq documents élaborés lors de la Conférence de Rio[191] et a été mentionné dans d'importantes conventions internationales suite à cette dernière.[192] Certains considèrent qu'il jouit d'une acceptation des États qui en ferait une règle coutumière,[193]

---

en général, consulter: Astrid Epiney et Martin Scheyli, *Le concept de développement durable en droit international public*, 1997, 7 R.S.D.I.P. 247 à la p. 266; Kamal Hossain, "Sustainable Development: a normative framework for evolving a more just and human international economic order, dans Subrata Roy Chowdhury *et al.*, dir., *The Right to development as a Principle of Human Right Law*, Dordrecht, Martinus Nijhoff, 1992, 259 à la p. 265; Serge Latouche, *Développement durable: un concept alibi. Main invisible et mainmise sur la nature*, 1994, t. XXXV, n° 137, Revue Tiers-Monde 77 à la p. 94; David Luff, *An overview of International Law of Sustainable Development and a confrontation between WTO Rules and Sustainable Development*, (1996) n° 1, R.B.D.I. 90 à la p. 144; Jean Masini, *Après le Sommet de la Terre: Débats sur le développement durable*, 1994, t. XXXV, n° 137, Revue Tiers-Monde 9 à la p. 29; Philippe J. Sands, *International Law in the field of Sustainable Development*, 1994, t. LXV B.Y.B.I.L. 303 à la p. 381.

188 Ci-après CMED. Rapport de la CMED, *Notre avenir à tous*, Montréal, Les éditions du fleuve, 1989, 454 pp.

189 *Conférence des Nations Unies sur l'environnement et le développement*, Rés. AG 44/228, Doc. off. AGNU, 44ᵉ sess., Supp. n° 49 (1989).

190 Consulter les références citées par D. Luff, *supra* note 187 à la p. 97.

191 *1) L'Agenda 21*, Doc. A/CONF. 151/26 (vol. III).*2) Déclaration de Rio sur l'environnement et le développement*, adoptée le 13 juin 1992. Texte reproduit dans: 31 ILM 874. Le principe 12 de cette dernière, relatif à la promotion par tous les États d'un "système économique ouvert et propre à engendrer une croissance économique et un développement durable," situe bien le contexte économique dans lequel le développement durable évoluera. *3) Convention cadre des Nations Unies sur les changements climatiques* (CCCC), adoptée à Rio de Janeiro le 9 mai 1992. Doc. NU A/AC.237/18 (Partie II)/Add. 1. Texte reproduit dans le rapport de la CMED, *supra* note 188 aux pp. 237-58. Texte anglais dans: 31 I.L.M. 849. *4) Convention sur la diversité biologique*, Doc. A/CONF. 151/26 (vol. III). *5) Déclaration sur les forêts*, adoptée à Rio de Janeiro le 14 août 1992, Doc. A/CONF. 151/26 (vol. III), *supra* note 95.

192 Par exemple l'*Accord de Marrakech*, établissant l'OMC, signé le 15 avril 1994 et la *Convention sur la désertification*, signée en octobre 1994. Le texte de l'*Accord de Marrakech* et les textes qui y sont relatifs sont publiés dans: J.F. Dennin, dir., *Law & Practice of the World Trade Organization*, New-York, Oceana Publications, 1995. Le texte de la *Convention sur la désertification* est publié dans: (1994) 33 I.L.M., 1328.

193 A.-C. Kiss et Stéphane Doumbé-Billé, *La Conférence des Nations Unies sur l'environnement et le développement*, (1992) t. XXXVIII A.F.D.I. 823. Consulter la décision

d'autres soutiennent au contraire que son contenu n'est pas suffisamment précis pour qu'il en soit ainsi.[194]

(ii)   La nature coutumière du mécanisme de développement durable

Le concept de développement durable est une notion complexe puisqu'il comporte de multiples facettes. Certains publicistes n'hésitent pas à le qualifier de "matrice conceptuelle inspirant dorénavant le droit international de l'environnement dans son ensemble."[195] Il faut distinguer les deux composantes du concept: la première concerne l'application de principes qui devront sous-tendre l'action des États dans la gestion de l'environnement. On en compte douze.[196] Il s'agit, dans ce cas, des principes de gestion de l'environnement issus du concept lui-même. La deuxième constitue le fondement même du concept, soit l'arrangement Nord-Sud sur la résolution de leurs conflits en matière d'environnement et de développement.

La deuxième composante peut être définie comme un compromis auxquels les PD et les PED arrivèrent afin qu'ils puissent faire la promotion de leurs intérêts propres. Selon l'entente convenue, les PD s'engagent à collaborer avec les PED à la réalisation des éléments constitutifs du NOEI et les PED acceptent, en contrepartie, de coopérer avec les PD à la mise en place de mesures visant la protection de l'environnement global. Elle constitue donc un mécanisme de résolution des désaccords entre les PED et les PD

---

de la Cour internationale de justice dans l'affaire relative au *Projet Gabcikovo-Nagymaros (Hongrie/Slovaquie)* Répertoire de la CIJ, 1997, 7; §140. Disponible à l'adresse Internet suivante: <http://www.icj-cij.org/cijwww/cdocket/chs/cHS> (page consultée le 12 octobre 2002).

[194] Richard L. Revesz, Philippe Sands et Richard B. Stewart, *Environmental Law, the Economy, and Sustainable Development,* Cambridge, Cambridge University Press, 2000 à la p. 374.

[195] P.-M. Dupuy, (1997) RGDIP 886. L'auteur indique aussi qu'il s'agit d'"une matrice conceptuelle définissant la perspective générale dans laquelle les principes établis ou en voie de consolidation doivent être restitués et adaptés." P.-M. Dupuy, *supra* note 98 à la p. 105; N.Q. Dinh et autres, *supra* note 22 à la p. 1253.

[196] P.-F. Mercure, *La proposition d'un modèle de gestion intégrée des ressources naturelles communes de l'humanité,* (1998) A.C.D.I. 46. Pour une analyse de chacun de ces principes, consulter D. Luff, *supra* note 187 aux pp.99-116 et A. Epiney et M. Scheyli, *supra* note 187 aux pp. 247-66. La plupart de ces principes sont mentionnés dans la *Déclaration de Rio* aux art. 2, 3, 5, 9, 11, 12-14, 21, 26 et 27. L'obligation, pour les PD, de transférer des ressources financières additionnelles vers les PED, bien que non mentionnée expressément dans la *Déclaration de Rio,* se retrouve au par. 4(7) de la CCCC, ainsi qu'au par. 20(4) de la *Convention sur la diversité biologique.*

dans la gestion des ressources naturelles communes, ce qui inclut les questions environnementales globales; et dans celles relatives au développement. Ce mécanisme est basé sur la prémisse que les PD accordent une priorité plus grande au premier aspect, tandis que les PED accordent une priorité plus grande au deuxième. Le mécanisme de développement durable serait, par conséquent, porteur des éléments constitutifs du NOEI.[197] Il permettrait à la communauté internationale d'atteindre les nouveaux objectifs qu'elle se fixe, notamment l'intégration de la protection de l'environnement dans le processus de développement.[198] Il a d'ailleurs été clairement présenté originellement dans le rapport CMED[199] comme un mécanisme devant articuler les relations Nord-Sud dans les secteurs de l'environnement et du développement.[200]

Cet aspect du concept de développement durable est particulièrement intéressant pour les PED. Il peut, en effet, servir de levier afin que puisse se réaliser leur sécurité alimentaire dans un délai raisonnable. L'application du mécanisme de développement durable à ce domaine d'activité donnerait l'opportunité aux PED d'entamer un processus d'échange avec les PD. Ils chercheraient, par ce dernier, à obtenir des concessions des PD sur des éléments du NOEI indispensables à l'atteinte de leur autonomie alimentaire collective. Les PED échangeraient, en contrepartie des concessions des PD, leur collaboration dans des secteurs qui requièrent une action concertée de tous les États. Une institutionnalisation de ces échanges serait envisageable et même souhaitable afin que ces derniers puissent s'accomplir de façon ordonnée.[201]

Si l'on part du postulat que le mécanisme de développement durable est propre à la dynamique des négociations Nord-Sud sur des enjeux globaux; on peut alors s'interroger sur l'existence ou non d'une règle coutumière, imposant l'application du mécanisme, lors de négociations internationales où les intérêts des PED et des PD s'opposent. La question est de savoir dans quels secteurs

[197] Il suffit pour se convaincre de cette affirmation de se reporter au chapitre 3 du rapport de la CMED, intitulé: *Le rôle de l'économie mondiale,* dans lequel l'organisme traite des revendications historiques des PED en faveur d'un NOEI. CMED, *supra* note 188.

[198] N.Q. Dinh et autres, *supra* note 22 à la p. 1013.

[199] CMED, *supra* note 188.

[200] Consulter à ce sujet le chapitre 3 de la première partie du Rapport intitulé: *Le Rôle de l'économie mondiale,* CMED, *ibid.* aux pp. 79-109; Voir aussi: François Rigaux, *Réflexions sur un nouvel ordre mondial,* 1991, 3 R.A.D.I.C. 653 à la p. 667.

[201] P.-F. Mercure, *supra* note 196 aux pp. 73-89.

d'activités le mécanisme de développement durable est-il susceptible de s'appliquer lors de ce type de négociations. Posé autrement, il s'agit d'identifier si le mécanisme est confiné aux questions relatives à l'environnement et au développement ou s'il pourrait s'appliquer à d'autres domaines. La réponse donnée comporte un intérêt évident, puisque reléguer les discussions portant sur la sécurité alimentaire des PED aux seuls forums où l'on discute d'environnement et de développement, constitue un handicap certain pour la promotion de cette cause.

Les constatations qui suivent recèlent les principaux éléments de la réponse:

La première est que:

le Nord a concédé au Sud, par l'adoption du mécanisme de développement durable, l'application à la pièce d'éléments de N.O.E.I., contre l'acceptation par le Sud du modèle économique véhiculé par les États industrialisés. La collaboration essentielle des pays du Tiers-Monde dans la gestion des problèmes environnementaux globaux, n'a été que le *catalyseur du marchandage* intervenu entre les deux groupes.[202]

Si les problèmes environnementaux globaux constituent la première monnaie d'échange dont disposent les PED afin d'imposer le NOEI, rien ne s'oppose à ce que le mécanisme s'impose dans tous les secteurs où la collaboration des PED est demandée par les PD.[203]

La deuxième constatation est que le concept de développement durable origine d'une philosophie qui accorde une nette prépondérance au développement des PED sur les préoccupations environnementales. C'est l'élément premier qui anime le concept et qui constitue le fondement même du mécanisme de développement durable. En effet:

La philosophie sous-jacente de ce concept s'articule autour de deux notions. La première se retrouve à l'article un de la Déclaration de Rio, soit que "les êtres humains sont au centre des préoccupations relatives au développement durable." Cette vision considère que la protection de l'environnement ne doit pas être un frein au développement économique, et place l'homme au centre du débat, l'environnement devenant

---

[202] *Ibid.* aux pp. 43-44.

[203] Que l'on pense, par exemple, aux déclarations faites par les PED à l'AGNU du 1er au 5 octobre 2001, relativement à la lutte anti-terroriste à laquelle les PD veulent les associer. Les PED élaborèrent amplement sur le thème de la pauvreté, mentionnant qu'elle constituait la cause principale du terrorisme. Ils annonçaient ainsi leurs couleurs dans les négociations d'ententes à venir sur cette question. P.- F. Mercure, *supra* note 6.

un concept extérieur à la préoccupation la plus importante pour l'homme: son développement.[204]

La deuxième notion prend sa source dans le principe quatre de la Déclaration de Rio qui dispose que "pour parvenir à un développement durable, la protection de l'environnement doit faire partie intégrante du processus de développement et ne peut être considérée isolément." La proposition initiale défendue par les PD était à l'effet que le développement devait faire partie intégrante de la protection de l'environnement. Sous la pression des pays du Sud la proposition fut inversée.[205]

On pourrait déduire de tout ceci que, puisque le mécanisme de développement durable donne une priorité au développement des PED sur les questions environnementales, cela indique implicitement que le caractère dominant du mécanisme est plus lié aux préoccupations des PED qu'à celles des PD. Cette constatation ouvre alors indéniablement la porte à l'application du mécanisme à d'autres secteurs qu'à l'environnement. Les PED entendraient ainsi faire du mécanisme de développement durable un instrument de la promotion du développement, c'est-à-dire du NOEI, quel que soit le secteur de négociation.[206]

Le mécanisme de développement durable serait donc applicable à tous les secteurs de négociations Nord-Sud où l'enjeu déterminant est le développement des PED. Il pourrait même être soutenu qu'il constitue une règle coutumière, puisqu'il serait suffisamment circonscrit. Les balises de ce mécanisme sont, en effet, d'une précision adéquate pour imposer un comportement non équivoque aux États lorsqu'ils négocient sur des enjeux Nord-Sud qui impliquent la question du développement des États de Tiers-Monde; ce qui est presque toujours le cas. La priorité des PED porte incontestablement sur cette question, comme cela a toujours été rappelé par eux, dans de nombreuses résolutions de l'AGNU.

Le rapport de la CMED, dans lequel est né le mécanisme de développement durable, jouit d'un support sans précédent de la communauté internationale sur une question concernant le développement des pays pauvres. Cette *opinio juris* déterminante, s'accompagne d'une pratique des États appliquant le mécanisme dans

---

[204] D. Luff, *supra* note 187 à la p. 98.

[205] *Ibid.* à la p. 99.

[206] Des publicistes n'hésitent d'ailleurs pas à affirmer ce qui suit: "Malgré tout, le concept de 'nouvel ordre économique international' est à l'origine de nouveaux objectifs que se fixe la communauté internationale; il a débouché, en particulier, sur la notion de 'développement durable' ..." N.Q. Dinh et autres, *supra* note 22 à la p. 1012.

les négociations, non seulement d'ententes internationales relatives à l'environnement, mais aussi dans celles se déroulant dans
d'autres secteurs où l'un des enjeux majeurs concerne, ou est lié,
au développement des PED.[207]

C'est par l'application du mécanisme de développement durable
que les droits économiques et sociaux pourront s'imposer et ainsi
permettre au droit à la nourriture de recevoir tout son sens. Même
si le commentaire de M. Jacquart à ce sujet semble relever de prémices différentes de celles exposées, il mérite d'être mentionné: "la
réalisation des droits économiques et sociaux s'inscrit désormais
dans le cadre du développement durable."[208] Ce dernier insuffle
une nouvelle dynamique dans les relations Nord-Sud où les préoccupations des deux groupes à l'égard de leurs populations peuvent
se fondre dans un objectif commun.

*(iii)   La compatibilité du nouvel ordre alimentaire mondial et du
        mécanisme de développement durable*

Le mécanisme de développement durable, qui a été conçu afin
de permettre aux PED d'obtenir des éléments du NOEI dans les
négociations relatives à la protection de l'environnement, est cependant compatible avec leurs revendications dans le secteur alimentaire. Ces dernières s'articulent, en effet, autour du concept de
NOAM qui est issu directement de la philosophie du NOEI. La
réalisation du NOAM dépend largement de celle des éléments du
NOEI. Ces ordres constituent ainsi des éléments indissociables du
réalignement des rapports socio-économiques Nord-Sud et sont, de
ce fait, perméables à l'influence du mécanisme de développement
durable.

Le NOAM est né du constat des PED, que l'appel à la solidarité
internationale dans les textes consacrant le droit à la nourriture
n'était pas entendu par les PD, ces derniers démontrant peu d'em-
pressement à agir collectivement. Les États en développement ont
alors compris que leur sécurité alimentaire ne pouvait voir le jour
sans l'instauration de stratégies alimentaires nationales. Ces dernières sont définies ainsi par le Conseil mondial sur l'alimentation: "un moyen qui permet à un pays d'arriver à un plus grand
degré d'autosuffisance alimentaire grâce à un effort intégré visant
à accroître la production vivrière, améliorer la consommation de

---

[207]   *Cf. supra* note 6.

[208]   M. Jacquart, *supra* note 25 à la p. 1170.

denrées et éliminer la faim."[209] Elles doivent constituer une part intégrale des plans globaux de développement national[210] et inclure les considérations environnementales et économiques indispensables à leur équilibre. Développées par les PED et appuyées par une solidarité Sud-Sud, les stratégies nationales visent à assurer l'autosuffisance alimentaire du Tiers-Monde.

L'application concertée des stratégies nationales dans les PED, a débouché sur le concept d'autonomie collective qui vise à mettre en oeuvre le NOAM. Ce dernier est d'ailleurs qualifié comme "un ordre où les États seraient autosuffisants et où les populations mangeraient à leur faim."[211] C'est la Conférence mondiale sur l'alimentation, tenue en 1974, à l'initiative du Mouvement des Non-alignés, qui fait de l'autosuffisance des PED l'élément central du NOAM. Les textes adoptés mettent en lumière que le meilleur moyen de parvenir à la sécurité alimentaire mondiale consiste à adopter des politiques nationales visant l'amélioration de la production alimentaire. En 1979, le *Plan d'action pour la sécurité alimentaire mondiale* suggérait des mesures afin de renforcer la capacité collective des PED, notamment par la constitution de stocks de réserve détenus aux niveaux national et régional. Les stratégies alimentaires nationales constituent donc l'alpha du NOAM et l'autonomie collective son oméga.

Imprégnés de la doctrine du NOEI, les PED visent l'autodétermination alimentaire qui a comme corollaire le libre choix d'un système alimentaire adapté à leurs besoins. La façon d'y parvenir implique une participation égalitaire des États aux décisions d'intérêt commun et une coopération entre les PED afin qu'ils soient les premiers responsables de leur développement. Le *Pacte de la sécurité alimentaire mondiale*, adopté en 1985, rappelle avec vigueur ce dernier élément, insistant sur l'importance de la réduction de la pauvreté que l'on tient pour première responsable du problème de la faim.

L'échange, par les PED, de leur soutien à la résolution des problèmes environnementaux ou autres questions requérant leur collaboration, en contrepartie de concessions des PD dans le secteur alimentaire, apparaît comme un moyen privilégié afin que se réalise un NOAM. L'application du mécanisme de développement

---

[209] A. Bensalah-Alaoui, *supra* note 27 à la p. 193.

[210] *Ibid.* à la p. 202.

[211] *Ibid.* à la p. 205.

durable permettrait que s'accomplisse le seul ordre juridique international propice au respect du droit à la nourriture. Les individus seraient même détenteurs d'un droit à la réalisation du NOAM, si l'on considère que seul ce dernier peut véritablement rendre effectif le droit à la nourriture. L'article 28 de la *Déclaration universelle des droit de l'homme,* indique: "chaque personne a droit à ce que règne, sur le plan social et sur le plan international, un ordre tel que les droits et libertés énoncés dans la présente Déclaration puissent y trouver plein effet."

(b) La mise en oeuvre de mécanismes visant l'équité alimentaire

Érigé en principes fondamentaux du droit international du développement, la solidarité et la coopération entre PED représentent, pour ces derniers, des obligations quant à la réalisation du droit à la nourriture (*i*). Les revendications des PED doivent péremptoirement s'articuler autour de la préservation d'un État fort (*ii*). Des suggestions sur l'organisation de la coopération appliquant le mécanisme de développement durable peuvent finalement être faites (*iii*).

(i)　Les fondements juridiques des obligations de coopération et de solidarité imposées aux pays en développement

L'une des plus importantes difficultés à réaliser la sécurité alimentaire mondiale tient au fait que les obligations de solidarité et de coopération entre les États, rappelées dans toutes les ententes internationales fondant le droit à la nourriture, n'ont jamais été pleinement respectées par les PD, pour les raisons exposées.[212] Les PED ont cependant des obligations de coopération et de solidarité entre eux, afin de réaliser le NOAM, puisqu'ils sont les seules entités en mesure d'assurer une représentation non équivoque aux individus les plus affectés par les pénuries alimentaires. Le fait que les PD ne coopèrent pas véritablement à la cause et ne soient pas solidaires des PED, donc qu'il ne se conforment pas au droit international, n'écarte pas les PED de leurs propres obligations. C'est parce qu'il permet de protéger le droit primaire à la vie que le droit à la sécurité alimentaire collective impose aux PED un devoir de solidarité afin qu'il se réalise, car: "certains droits, tels ceux de la troisième génération, requièrent plus que les autres cet élément de solidarité."[213]

[212]　*Cf. supra* première partie.

[213]　M. Bedjaoui, *supra* note 83 à la p. 1240.

L'une des conséquences de la modulation dans les niveaux de développement des États du Tiers-Monde est qu'il sont touchés de façon inégale par le problème alimentaire. Les obligations de coopération et de solidarité qui les lient imposent l'adoption de comportements qui transcendent leurs différences d'intérêts. Indépendamment de toute obligation légale s'adressant à eux, comment les PED espèrent-ils faire accepter aux PD le principe d'une solidarité universelle dans le secteur alimentaire, si des lézardes sillonnent leur propre solidarité?

Rédigé afin de délimiter de façon plus adéquate le contenu des articles 1 et 2 de la *Charte des Nations Unies*,[214] la *Déclaration relative aux principes du droit international touchant les relations amicales et la coopération entre les États*[215] impose un devoir de coopération aux États pour assurer le respect et la mise en oeuvre des droits de l'homme.[216] L'article 56 de la Charte des Nations Unies impose aux États membres l'obligation d'"agir conjointement ... en coopération avec l'Organisation," afin d'atteindre les buts mentionnés à l'article 55. Ce dernier dispose: "les Nations Unies favoriseront: c) le respect universel et effectif des droits de l'homme et des libertés fondamentales pour tous ..."

Le sens de l'expression "agir conjointement" est différent de celui du verbe "coopérer." La première exprime que les États doivent agir en concertation, c'est-à-dire ensemble, d'une même voix, propre à atteindre le but visé.[217] Cette obligation sous-entend celle d'être solidaire dans un projet. Le verbe "coopérer" signifie, quant à lui, apporter son concours, sa contribution.[218] Cette nuance mérite d'être soulignée puisque, lorsqu'il est mentionné à l'article 56 que: "les membres s'engagent à agir conjointement, en coopération avec l'Organisation," cela implique que la responsabilité de

---

[214] Jacques-Yvan Morin, Francis Rigaldies et Daniel Turp, *Droit international public*, tome 1, 3ᵉ éd., Montréal, Thémis, 1997 à la p. 691.

[215] *Déclaration relative aux principes du droit international touchant les relations amicales et la coopération entre les États conformément à la Charte de Nations Unies*. Dans P.-M. Dupuy, *supra* note 29 à la p. 32.

[216] Art. 1, *ibid*. Cet article fait de la coopération un moyen, contrairement à l'art. 1 de la Charte rédigé près de vingt-cinq ans auparavant qui faisait de la coopération une fin: "Réaliser la coopération internationale en résolvant les problèmes internationaux d'ordre économique, social, intellectuel ou humanitaire, en développant et en encourageant le respect des droits de l'homme et des libertés fondamentales pour tous sans distinction. *Ibid*. à la p.3.

[217] *Le Petit Robert*, Paris, Dictionnaires Le Robert, 2002 à la p. 514.

[218] *Ibid*. à la p. 645.

définir le cadre général de la stratégie visant le respect des droits de l'homme incombe aux États et à l'Organisation collaborant ensemble; mais que les moyens pour y parvenir appartiennent aux États agissant ensemble, c'est-à-dire, solidairement.

La *Déclaration universelle des droits de l'homme* donne aussi un fondement au rôle qu'auront à jouer les États par l'entremise de leurs gouvernements, afin de permettre la réalisation des droits de l'homme. Elle fait implicitement référence aux gouvernements des États en mentionnant l'expression "tous les organes de la société" dans le préambule du texte. Ce dernier dispose en effet que: "tous les organes de la société ... s'efforcent ... d'en assurer, par des mesures progressives d'ordre ... international, la reconnaissance et l'application universelles et effectives." Le préambule de la Déclaration reprend l'énoncé de l'article 56 de la Charte quant à la coopération des États avec l'Organisation, avec la différence que la Déclaration utilise le verbe "assurer," tandis que la Charte emploie le verbe "agir." Il n'y a rien d'incompatible entre ces mots, au contraire, ils sont complémentaires. Les États doivent "agir" afin d'"assurer" le respect de droits de l'homme. Les PED doivent ainsi faire tous les efforts requis afin que se concrétise la reconnaissance des droits de l'homme. L'action des PED doit évidemment accorder préséance aux droits humains fondamentaux qui sont prioritaires.

C'est aussi par l'obligation qu'ont les États, en vertu de la *Charte des Nations Unies,* de favoriser la paix, que les PED ont le devoir d'agir conjointement afin de promouvoir le NOAM. S'il est incontestable que la faim menace la paix, la FAO a démontré, sans équivoque, que la guerre est la principale source de famines.[219] Là encore, si les PD n'exercent pas leurs obligations à ce chapitre par l'intermédiaire du Conseil de sécurité, les PED ont l'obligation d'assumer les leurs en vertu de la Charte.

Ainsi, les PED auraient l'obligation d'agir conjointement, sur la base de la coopération qui implique de participer en apportant une contribution, un appui, une aide à la cause; en définissant, par exemple, une stratégie commune afin de rendre effectif le droit à la nourriture. Ils auraient aussi l'obligation d'agir, sur la base de la solidarité qui suppose de parler d'une même voix, de s'appuyer mutuellement dans la revendication des instruments de la réalisation du NOAM auprès de la communauté internationale et dans l'action qui suivra.

---

[219] FAO, *supra* note 2 à la p. 4.

(ii)   L'autonomie de l'État au centre des revendications des pays en développement

L'institution que constitue l'État doit posséder un degré d'autonomie suffisant afin de permettre la réalisation de la sécurité alimentaire collective. L'État est en effet la pierre angulaire de l'action des PED, puisqu'il est le bénéficiaire premier du droit collectif à la sécurité alimentaire, comme il a été souligné précédemment.[220] L'action des PED doit donc se faire au nom de ce droit et seul un État exerçant pleinement les attributs de la souveraineté peut en assurer le respect.

L'État est imputable aux populations sous-alimentées, de la stratégie appliquée afin que le droit collectif à la sécurité alimentaire devienne une réalité, car: "certes, dans son exercice, ce droit est intrinsèquement individuel ... Dans son mode de réalisation, il peut paraître d'abord un droit collectif."[221] Cela ne fait d'ailleurs aucun doute, puisque: "la répartition équitable des ressources alimentaires ne peut se faire à l'échelle mondiale qu'entre États."[222] Ceci est conforme au *Pacte international relatif aux droits économiques, sociaux et culturels* qui rend l'État imputable de la réalisation du droit à la nourriture. Le choix des moyens à utiliser est aussi à la discrétion de l'État. L'article 1 du *Pacte* indique:

les États s'engagent à agir ... par ... la coopération internationale ... en vue d'assurer progressivement le plein exercice des droits reconnus dans le présent Pacte par tous les moyens appropriés, y compris en particulier l'adoption de mesures législatives.

Ce sont donc les États qui sont responsables de la définition des moyens adéquats afin de réaliser le droit à la sécurité alimentaire. L'article 11 fournit une indication de ce qui peut constituer un moyen approprié. Il dispose que: "les États doivent adopter au moyen de la coopération internationale, les mesures nécessaires, y compris des programmes concrets pour assurer une répartition équitable des ressources alimentaires mondiales ..."

Le mécanisme de développement durable constitue sans contredit un "moyen approprié," c'est-à-dire, un moyen propre à atteindre l'objectif visé, qui est d'assurer l'exercice du droit collectif à la sécurité alimentaire. Il représente sans contredit, un élément

---

[220]   *Cf. supra* première partie, titre 1, B, *a*.

[221]   *Ibid.* à la p. 51.

[222]   A. Bensalah-Alaoui, *supra* note 27 à la p. 52.

d'un "programme concret" pour assurer une répartition équitable des ressources.

Les PED doivent donc adopter une position commune afin que puisse se réaliser ce droit collectif. L'État qui serait l'entité privilégiée ayant la capacité de faire valoir la sécurité alimentaire de son peuple[223] constituerait, de plus, la seule institution susceptible de mettre en branle le mécanisme de développement durable pour atteindre cet objectif.

L'obligation qu'il a de rendre effectif le droit à la nourriture, pour chacun de ses citoyens, impose à l'État d'adopter des mesures positives car: "the obligations to protect and fulfil the right to food are certainly positive obligations that require positive actions from the State."[224] L'adoption de mesures concrètes par les PED, ne peut se faire que dans le contexte d'une structure étatique disposant d'un degré de liberté suffisant quant à l'utilisation des ressources nécessaires à l'atteinte de l'objectif.[225] Le niveau requis d'indépendance des PED est sérieusement menacé par l'environnement économique contemporain. En effet: "la globalisation des marchés financiers et la presque totale libéralisation des échanges affaiblissent gravement les États nationaux; elles constituent un danger immédiat pour la venue au monde et la réalisation du droit à l'alimentation."[226]

S'il est admis que la globalisation financière et économique menace à court terme le droit à la nourriture dans les PED; il est aussi reconnu que la croissance de l'économie mondiale constitue la seule garante du développement des PED. Les obligations de coopération et de solidarité des PED doivent donc suivre deux axes, visant à assurer à l'État un degré d'autonomie adéquat pour réaliser la sécurité alimentaire collective.

Premièrement, les PED doivent s'opposer aux aspects de la mondialisation qui constituent des obstacles évidents à la réalisation du droit à la sécurité alimentaire. L'imposition, par les PD aux PED, d'un contexte économique défavorable à l'épanouissement de ce droit créerait, pour ces derniers, un devoir de veiller à l'exécution

---

[223] M. Bedjaoui, *supra* note 83. Les PED peuvent appuyer leur action en faisant valoir que la sécurité alimentaire collective constitue un pré-requis indispensable à la réalisation de droits primaires, tels le droit à la vie et le droit au développement.

[224] Economic and Social Council, *supra* note 12 à la p. 15.

[225] Conseil économique et social, *supra* note 9 à la p. 21.

[226] *Ibid.*

des éléments du NOEI indispensables à sa réalisation. Le fondement du devoir de promotion du NOEI serait que seul le modèle
économique véhiculé par ce dernier est susceptible de contrer la
vision néo-libérale de la mondialisation, qui menace directement
la sécurité alimentaire collective.[227]

Deuxièmement, les PED auraient l'obligation de contester les
politiques des PD qui utilisent les ressources financières, afin d'atteindre des objectifs incompatibles avec la paix et la sécurité internationales et qui sont ainsi rendues indisponibles pour assurer la
croissance de l'économie mondiale. La paix et la sécurité internationale sont, en effet, indissociables de la sécurité alimentaire du
Tiers-Monde. Les PED pourraient, dans un premier temps, questionner la pertinence des dépenses miliaires excessives des États
par rapport à leurs besoins réels. Ces investissements improductifs
menacent directement la croissance de l'économie mondiale et la
paix internationale.[228]

*(iii)   L'organisation des structures appliquant le mécanisme de
        développement durable*

Le principe de l'action collective des PED en matière de développement économique et social a été posé clairement, en 1955,
par vingt-neuf pays d'Asie et d'Afrique, lors de la Conférence de
Bandoeng.[229] Ce dernier, pour qu'il ait un sens, doit nécessairement faire naître des mécanismes institutionnels permettant la
réalisation des droits premiers dont sont déficitaires les PED par
rapport aux PD, avec une primauté donnée au droit à la nourriture. Bien avant l'avènement des concepts de Tiers-Monde et de
développement, douze États d'Afrique avaient d'ailleurs, dès 1945,
lors du Vᵉ Congrès panafricain, identifié le problème de la faim
comme prioritaire. En plus de dénoncer l'exploitation économique
qui empêche l'industrialisation, on y réclamait: "la lutte contre
l'alphabétisme et la sous-nutrition."[230]

---

[227] Sur les risques de la mondialisation sauvage pour l'autonomie des pays les plus
pauvres, voir: Jacques B. Gélinas, *La globalisation du monde*, Montréal, Écosociété, 1994 aux pp. 225-41; Conseil économique et social, *supra* note 9 aux
pp. 27 et s.

[228] M. Bedjaoui, *supra* note 83 à la p. 1257.

[229] Sur cette conférence, consulter S.-J. Patel, *L'autonomie collective des pays en développement*, 1976 Revue Tiers-Monde 199 à la p. 214.

[230] Guy Feuer et Hervé Cassan, *Droit international du développement*, 2ᵉ éd., Paris,
Dalloz, 1991 à la p. 10.

Les PED doivent ainsi, par une démarche solidaire, utiliser le mécanisme du développement durable afin de réaliser leur sécurité alimentaire. Le plan d'action des PED, qui devrait être approuvé par une résolution de l'AGNU, pourrait comprendre cinq étapes. Les étapes un à trois et cinq seraient réalisées par un comité spécial mis sur pied par l'AGNU au sein duquel on retrouverait des représentants des PD et des PED. La quatrième étape serait exécutée par des forums particuliers de la famille élargie du système onusien.

La première étape permettrait l'identification et la classification de tous les aspects du NOEI qui influent sur le droit à la nourriture. Elle requerrait l'étude des liens parfois complexes existant entre les deux secteurs. Il est en effet admis qu'un nombre important des volets du NOEI ont un effet plus ou moins direct sur la réalisation du droit à la nourriture; que l'on pense aux questions suivantes: le commerce des produits agricoles; l'allègement de la dette extérieure des PED et l'aide publique au développement.

C'est à la deuxième étape que se ferait le recensement de tous les éléments des problématiques globales, sur lesquelles les PED possèdent un pouvoir de négociation par rapport aux PD. Il s'agit, pour les PED, de réaliser un exercice similaire à celui qui consiste à "faire ressortir les liaisons stratégiques entre problématiques sectorielles."[231] Cette démarche est déterminante, car "la fragmentation actuelle de la problématique mondiale passe sous silence ces interdépendances et mène à des solutions proposées qui sont essentiellement sectorielles et le plus souvent inapplicables."[232]

La troisième étape consisterait à identifier les forums ou assemblées plénières d'organes subsidiaires de la famille élargie du système onusien, au sein desquels seront étudiées et discutées les revendications des PED dans le secteur alimentaire et celles des PD relativement aux problématiques qui les préoccupent.[233]

La quatrième étape permettrait aux forums de détailler la stratégie alimentaire du Tiers-Monde dans les secteurs d'activités propres à chacun des organes subsidiaires de l'ONU et de conférer un ordre de priorité aux revendications des PD et à celles des PED.

---

[231] Kimon Valaskakis, *La planète est-elle encore gouvernable?*, Le Devoir, 20 janvier 2003, A6. L'auteur, qui a été ambassadeur du Canada à l'OCDE, donne comme exemples de liaisons stratégiques à effectuer: "lier le terrorisme à l'injustice (réelle ou imaginée); lier l'économie à l'environnement et à la technologie; la gouvernance d'entreprise à la gouvernance publique."

[232] *Ibid.*

[233] *Ibid.*

À la cinquième étape, un comité spécial d'experts nommés par l'AGNU se verrait confier la délicate fonction de préparer les listes de revendications des PD et des PED, issues de la synthèse des travaux des différents forums, à partir desquelles l'échange se ferait. L'Assemblée générale adopterait une résolution sur la création d'un nouvel organe de l'ONU qui aurait comme mandat d'institutionnaliser le mécanisme de développement durable, c'est-à-dire de créer une entité dans l'Organisation où les échanges nourriture-préoccupations des PD se feraient.[234]

La démarche des PED pourrait être initiée par une structure Sud-Sud crédible auprès du Tiers-Monde dans le secteur alimentaire, en ayant démontré, d'une part, une grande efficacité dans la définition du cadre juridique de la coopération entre PED dans ce secteur[235] et ayant fait, d'autre part, la promotion active de l'établissement du NOEI. Le Mouvement des Non-alignés ou le Groupe des 77 seraient des organismes indiqués.[236] L'AGNU, qui préciserait les cinq étapes du plan d'action présenté, se verrait confier la tâche de le formaliser et d'en assurer le suivi au sein de l'Organisme. Le travail de l'AGNU serait susceptible d'atténuer le caractère de confrontation de la démarche avec les PD. Elle aura aussi l'avantage d'être discutée amplement dans une enceinte où PD et PED exprimeraient leurs opinions sur les modalités de l'application du mécanisme de développement durable.

Le Mouvement des Non-alignés a été, depuis 1961, le promoteur des idées de solidarité et d'action collective des PED. À travers une série de conférences des chefs d'États et de gouvernements et de nombreuses conférences des ministres des Affaires étrangères, il a vigoureusement dénoncé l'impérialisme et le néo-colonialisme et a insisté sur l'urgence de renforcer la solidarité Sud-Sud principalement sur le plan économique, en faisant la promotion du NOEI. C'est au sein du mouvement qu'a été développé le concept de *self-reliance* ou "autonomie individuelle et collective"[237] qui est à

---

[234] P.-F. Mercure, *supra* note 196 aux pp. 73-89.

[235] Sur la coopération Sud-Sud, consulter: Ahmed Mahiou, *Le cadre juridique de la coopération Sud-Sud,* (1993) IV, vol. 241 R.C.A.D.I. 9 à la p. 193. Consulter aussi les documents mentionnés à la section *Coopération entre pays en développement* dans: N.Q. Dinh et autres, *supra* note 22 à la p. 1018.

[236] Les pays les moins avancés (PMA), les plus pauvres des PED, sont les principales victimes des problèmes alimentaires. Ils pourraient aussi initier la démarche. Ils étaient 49 en 2001: <http://ro.unctad.org/conference/french/pma.pdf> (page consultée le 22 janvier 2003).

[237] G. Feuer et H. Cassan, *supra* note 230 à la p. 12.

l'origine de la nouvelle approche du Tiers-Monde en matière de sécurité alimentaire.

Le sommet des Non-alignés, tenu à New-York en 1983, a fermement appuyé l'idée que l'action nationale des États est un préalable essentiel à l'atteinte de la sécurité alimentaire des États concernés et que cette dernière doit s'intégrer dans un mouvement de soutien mutuel entre les PED. La conférence de Lusaka, tenue en 1970, a été le point de départ de l'élaboration progressive d'un véritable programme global traitant de tous les aspects relatifs au développement des PED, incluant leur sécurité alimentaire. On considère que le Mouvement constitue "un groupe de pression international pour la réorganisation du système économique international."[238]

Le Groupe des 77 a, quant à lui, été formé en 1964. Il réunissait alors 77 PED et en comprend actuellement 133. Organisme de réflexion et de revendication, le Groupe tient ses rencontres avant chaque session de la CNUCED et publie préalablement à celles-ci, "un programme exposant de manière détaillée l'ensemble des propositions, requêtes ou exigences du Tiers-Monde dans le domaine des relations économiques internationales." Le Groupe a adopté plusieurs déclarations et programmes d'action sur l'autonomie collective et la coopération économique entre les PED.

Déjà, lors de la tenue d'une conférence au Caire en 1962 par trente et un pays d'Asie, d'Afrique et d'Amérique; à l'origine de la naissance du Groupe, les États adoptaient une Déclaration qui définissait une position commune aux États des trois continents, sur les grands problèmes de développement. Le document insistait "sur la nécessité d'institutionnaliser à la fois l'étude des problèmes de développement et l'action des pays du Tiers-Monde"[239] et suggérait que l'ONU constitue le cadre de la résolution des problèmes du développement économique et social des PED dans un esprit de coopération internationale.

Ces initiatives eurent des échos déterminants dans le débat sur l'alimentation. La Charte d'Alger adoptée par le groupe des 77 en 1967, indique que des consultations des membres auront lieu afin de définir une position commune sur cette question. Sous la pression du groupe, la CNUCED adopte en 1968 à New-Delhi, la première résolution prise en dehors de la FAO consacrée

---

[238] *Ibid.*

[239] *Ibid.* à la p. 13.

exclusivement au problème alimentaire mondial.[240] Le groupe a
fait une déclaration, en 1980, appuyant le Conseil mondial de l'alimentation[241] qui promouvait l'adoption de stratégies nationales
alimentaires s'intégrant dans une nouvelle structure d'aide alimentaire internationale, coordonnée par les États donateurs et bénéficiaires de celle-ci.

IV CONCLUSION

L'échec des mécanismes traditionnels d'application des droits
humains fondamentaux au droit à la nourriture requiert des
PED la recherche d'autres solutions afin de le rendre effectif, car:
"tout être doué du minimum d'humanité propre à toute personne
est prêt à reconnaître qu'il est inacceptable, car immoral, de laisser
mourir de faim ses contemporains ou d'accepter qu'ils soient
physiquement ou mentalement affectés par une malnutrition
chronique."[242] Il est alors prêt à ce que le droit à la nourriture soit
reconnu et qu'il lui soit donné effet par tous les mécanismes
juridiques ayant une valeur normative.

Le fondement de l'action des PED est incontestablement moral,
mais elle a aussi des assises juridiques. La solidarité du Tiers-Monde
dans le domaine alimentaire doit transcender les différences entre
États. S'il est un domaine qui constitue une problématique commune à la grande majorité des PED et qui, de ce fait, requiert une
action concertée de leur part, c'est assurément le problème de la
faim. C'est le devoir de l'État en développement à l'égard de sa
population, qui l'oblige à échanger le NOEI qui concrétisera le
droit à la nourriture. Le NOEI constitue, en effet, le passage obligé
pour l'instauration d'un régime social où la réalisation des droits
humains fondamentaux n'est pas tributaire de la seule puissance
des certains.

Le mécanisme de développement durable est à l'origine d'un
compromis sur une méthode dynamique permettant de concilier
l'environnement et le développement, c'est-à-dire l'atteinte d'une
position mutuellement acceptée par le Sud et le Nord, par un processus d'échange entre les parties. Appliqué au domaine alimentaire, il permet aux PED d'utiliser, par conséquent, une monnaie

[240] A. Bensalah-Alaoui, *supra* note 27 à la p. 16.

[241] Le Conseil mondial sur l'alimentation (CMA) a été créé par l'AGNU afin
d'établir un système convenable visant à assurer la sécurité alimentaire mondiale. Résolution 3348 (XXIX) de l'AGNU.

[242] Economic and Social Council, *supra* note 12 à la p. 9.

d'échange qui leur faisait jusqu'alors défaut, afin que s'affirme l'obligation solidaire qu'ils ont de nourrir leurs populations.

L'inaction des PD oblige les PED à provoquer un dialogue Nord-Sud sur cette question. Si la question alimentaire ne trouve pas de défenseurs au sein des structures existantes, les pays les plus touchés par celle-ci et liés par des obligations de coopération et de solidarité dans ce domaine doivent faire valoir leurs doléances au sein d'une nouvelle structure à mettre sur pied.

Les obligations de coopération et de solidarité Sud-Sud articulées autour d'une stratégie de revendications conditionnées, permettraient donc aux PED d'obtenir des concessions déterminantes de la part des PD dans ce secteur. Cette nouvelle dynamique Nord-Sud implique une redéfinition des rapports inter-étatiques qui ne sera possible que "dans un ordre juridique international où les conceptions classiques faisant de l'État le centre du monde seront abandonnées au profit de la seule conception désormais viable faisant du monde le centre de l'État."[243]

Summary

Developing Countries' Obligation to Feed Their Populations: The Normativity of the Mechanism for Sustainable Development

The traditional legal process has been inefficient in ensuring the right to receive food in developing countries, thereby preventing the estalishment of true food security in the Third World. This situation is largely due to developed countries giving priority to their own economic interests to the detriment of the hunger problem and of the already weak negotiating power of developing countries regarding any agreement reached on this issue. The mechanism for sustainable development does, however, offer new possibilities to developing countries. The cooperation and assistance duties imposed on states under international agreements on food entitlement compel developing countries to use that mechanism to promote their interests regarding the supply of food.

---

[243] M. Jacquart, *supra* note 25 à la p. 1171.

Sommaire

L'obligation alimentaire des pays en développement à l'égard de leurs populations: la normativité du mécanisme de développement durable

Les processus juridiques traditionnels ont été inefficaces afin que se réalise le droit à la nourriture dans les pays en développement, empêchant du même coup l'instauration d'une véritable sécurité alimentaire dans le Tiers-Monde. Cette situation est en grande partie attribuable à l'attitude des pays développés d'accorder la priorité à leurs intérêts économiques, au détriment du problème de la faim et au faible pouvoir de négociation des pays en développement dans les ententes conclues sur cette question. Le mécanisme de développement durable offre cependant de nouvelles possibilités aux pays en développement. Les devoirs de coopération et de solidarité, imposés aux États par les ententes internationales portant sur le droit à la nourriture, obligent les pays en développement à utiliser ce mécanisme afin de promouvoir leurs intérêts dans le secteur alimentaire.

An Overview of International Fisheries Disputes and the International Tribunal for the Law of the Sea

TED L. MCDORMAN

INTRODUCTION

The International Tribunal for the Law of the Sea (ITLOS)[1] is a judicial body established pursuant to the 1982 United Nations Convention on the Law of the Sea[2] (LOS Convention). The LOS Convention came into legal force for its parties (which does not include the United States or Canada) in November 1994.[3] ITLOS, which is composed of twenty-one judges elected by the state parties to the LOS Convention,[4] convened its first session at its headquarters in Hamburg, Germany, in October 1996. As of December

Ted L. McDorman, Professor, Faculty of Law, University of Victoria, British Columbia. This article is a revised and updated version of a paper presented at a workshop that was held at Roger Williams University School of Law, Bristol, Rhode Island, in June 2002.

[1] The website for ITLOS is <www.itlos.org>. Not surprisingly, ITLOS has generated a considerable amount of literature. Attention is drawn to Gudmundur Eiriksson, *The International Tribunal for the Law of the Sea* (The Hague: Martinus Nijhoff, 2000); P. Chandrasekhara Rao and Rahmatullah Khan, eds., *The International Tribunal for the Law of the Sea: Law and Practice* (The Hague: Kluwer Law International, 2001); and Myron H. Nordquist and John Norton Moore, eds., *Current Marine Environmental Issues and the International Tribunal for the Law of the Sea* (The Hague: Martinus Nijhoff, 2001).

[2] Annex VI of the United Nations Convention on the Law of the Sea, done at Montego Bay, Jamaica, December 10, 1982, entered into force on November 16, 1994, reprinted in (1982) 21 I.L.M. 1261, also available at <www.un.org/Depts/los/index.htm> [hereinafter LOS Convention].

[3] The current status and the parties to the LOS Convention are accessible at <www.un.org/Depts/los/index.htm>.

[4] See LOS Convention, *supra* note 2, at Annex VI, Articles 2-5. The current membership and the results of the April 2002 election are accessible at <www.itlos.org>.

2002, ITLOS has had eleven cases on its docket since its inception,[5] all but one of which has dealt with either the arrest of fishing or fishing-related vessels or disputes between states regarding fishing arrangements.[6] The purpose of this article is to look at how and when ITLOS becomes involved in disputes, particularly fisheries disputes, and to examine briefly the international fisheries cases that have been on the ITLOS docket and the role of ITLOS in the resolution of international fisheries disputes.

INTERNATIONAL ADJUDICATION AND FISHERIES

While the number of fishery cases that have been before ITLOS may not seem impressive, this number must be considered in relation to the fact that international judicial bodies have only dealt with three international fisheries disputes over the 100-year period prior to the establishment of ITLOS. The first case was the 1893 *Bering Sea Fur-Seals* arbitration[7] between the United Kingdom (Canada) and the United States, which, while involving marine mammals rather than fish *per se*, dealt with issues common in international fisheries disputes — the extent of national jurisdiction and the ability to take action to protect the resource. The most recent example of an adjudicative tribunal directly dealing with an international fisheries dispute was the 1986 *Filleting within the Gulf of St. Lawrence between Canada and France* (*La Bretagne* arbitration).[8]

---

[5] The docket of ITLOS cases is accessible <www.itlos.org>. For an overview of the ITLOS cases, see Shabtai Rosenne, "The Case-Law of ITLOS (1997-2001): An Overview" in Nordquist and Moore, *supra* note 1, at 127-40.

[6] All the fisheries related cases are discussed in detail later in this article. The one non-fisheries case is the *MOX Plant Case (Ireland* v. *United Kingdom)*, ITLOS, Provisional Measures Order, November 13, 2001, reprinted in (2002) 41 I.L.M. 405 [hereinafter *MOX Plant* case]. All the ITLOS decisions are accessible through the ITLOS website at <www.itlos.org>.

[7] *Bering Sea Fur-Seals (Gr. Brit.* v. *U.S.)*, 1 Int'l Envtl. L. Reports 43, 67. The award is reprinted in J.B. Moore, *History and Digest of International Arbitrations to Which the United States Has Been a Party*, volume 1 (Washington, DC: Government Printing Office, 1898) at 945-51. For a recent review of the award, see Cesare P.R. Romano, *The Peaceful Settlement of International Environmental Disputes* (The Hague: Kluwer Law International, 2000) at 133-50.

[8] *Filleting within the Gulf of St. Lawrence between Canada and France*, 1986, 19 UN Reports of International Arbitral Awards 225. See generally concerning the arbitration William T. Burke, "A Comment on the 'La Bretagne' Award of July 17, 1986: The Arbitration between Canada and France" (1988) 25 San Diego L. R. 495-533; and T.L. McDorman, "French Fishing Rights in Canadian Waters: The 1986 La Bretagne Arbitration" (1989) 4 Int'l J. of Estuarine and Coastal Law 52-64.

The dispute arose over the interpretation of French fishing rights in Canadian waters set out in the 1972 Agreement between Canada and France on Their Mutual Fishing Relations, which dealt with fisheries and ocean boundaries.[9]

The third case comprises the *Fisheries Jurisdiction* cases,[10] involving Iceland, Germany, and the United Kingdom before the International Court of Justice (ICJ). This judicial decision dealt with several fisheries matters with twists. At issue was Iceland's assertion of its national jurisdiction over fishery resources in waters adjacent to its coastline to a limit of fifty nautical miles and the counterassertion by Germany and the United Kingdom that this claim was inconsistent with the then-existing international law as well as with bilateral treaty obligations. Ultimately, the ICJ held against Iceland and its fifty-nautical-mile fishing zone. The first twist in this case was that Iceland denied that the ICJ had competency over the fisheries disputes and therefore declined to participate in the hearings. Once the court decided it did have jurisdiction based upon Iceland's pre-agreement to adjudicate, Iceland declined to participate over the merits of the action. Hence, Iceland walked away from the formal, adjudicative dispute settlement. The second twist arose with the irrelevance of the ICJ judgment a few years later when the international community accepted the 200-nautical-mile fishing zone in the late 1970s.

A recent international fisheries case, which "almost" came about, involved a conflict between Canada and Spain over the arrest by Canada of a Spanish trawler (the *Estai*) outside Canada's 200-nautical-mile fishing zone in 1995.[11] Although the two countries

---

[9] Agreement between Canada and France on Their Mutual Fishing Relations, done at Ottawa, March 27, 1972 and entered into force March 27, 1972, reprinted in *National Legislation and Treates Relating to the Law of the Sea* (New York: United Nations, 1974) at 570.

[10] *Fisheries Jurisdiction (United Kingdom v. Iceland)*, Jurisdiction, [1973] I.C.J. Rep. 3; *Fisheries Jurisdiction (Germany v. Iceland)*, Jurisdiction, [1973] I.C.J. Rep 49; *Fisheries Jurisdiction (United Kingdom v. Iceland)*, Merits, [1974] I.C.J. Rep. 3; and *Fisheries Jurisdiction (Germany v. Iceland)*, Merits [1974] I.C.J. Rep. 175 [hereinafter *Fisheries Jurisdication* cases]. See generally Hannes Jonsson, *Friends in Conflict: The Anglo-Icelandic Cod Wars and the Law of the Sea* (London: C. Hurst and Company, 1982); and Jeffrey A. Hart, *The Anglo-Icelandic Cod War of 1972-1973*, Research Series no. 20 (Berkeley: Institute of International Studies, 1976). For a more recent treatment, see Romano, *supra* note 7 at 151-76.

[11] The seizure of the *Estai* is vividly portrayed in Michael Harris, *Lament for an Ocean* (Toronto: McClelland and Stewart, 1998) at 1-38. The event has resulted in considerable academic literature. A sampling includes C. Joyner and A.A. von

were quickly able to reach a bilateral agreement to defuse the intensity of the dispute,[12] Spain decided to proceed to the ICJ in order to test the international legality of the Canadian seizure and to deter the possibility of future Canadian action on the high seas. However, the court determined that it had no jurisdiction to hear the case since Canada had carefully crafted an exception to its acceptance of the compulsory jurisdiction of the ICJ to exclude court jurisdiction over the dispute with Spain.[13]

Judicial decisions dealing with ocean boundary disputes have frequently dealt indirectly with international fishing problems.[14] It

---

Gustedt, "The Turbot War of 1995: Lessons for the Law of the Sea" (1996) 11 Int'l J. Mar. & Coastal L. 425; P. Davies, "The EC/Canada Fisheries Dispute in the Northwest Atlantic" (1995) 44 I.C.L.Q. 927; Allen L. Springer, "The Canadian Turbot War with Spain: Unilateral State Action in Defense of Environmental Interests" (1997) 6 J. Env. & Dev 26-60; Jose de Yturriaga, *The International Regime of Fisheries* (Boston: Martinus Nijhoff, 1997) at 238-57; and T.L. McDorman, "Canada's Aggressive Fisheries Actions: Will They Improve the Climate for International Agreements?" (1994-5) 2(3) Can. Foreign Pol. 525-28.

[12] Canada-European Community: Agreed Minutes on the Conservation and Management of Fish Stocks and Exchange of Letters, done April 20, 1995, reprinted in (1995) 34 I.L.M. 1260.

[13] See *Fisheries Jurisdiction (Spain v. Canada)*, [1998] I.C.J. Rep. 2. In May 1994, Canada had amended its acceptance of the compulsory jurisdiction of the International Court by adding that the Court had jurisdiction over all disputes other than:

> (d) disputes arising out of concerning conservation and management measures taken by Canada with respect to vessels fishing in the NAFO Regulatory Area, as defined in the Convention on Future Multilateral Co-operation in the Northwest Atlantic Fisheries, 1978, and enforcement of such measures (see *ibid.* at para. 14.)

Canada argued that the seizure of the *Estai* arose out of conservation measures and their enforcement respecting the NAFO waters adjacent to Canadian waters. The court agreed with the Canadian characterization of the dispute and decided that the Canadian wording of its acceptance of the compulsory jurisdiction of the International Court of Justice precluded the court from examining the merits of the *Estai* controversy (see *ibid.* at para. 87). For a review of the case and the surrounding issues, see Romano, *supra* note 7 at 177-95.

[14] For example, *Case Concerning the Delimitation of the Maritime Areas between Canada and France,* June 10, 1992, reprinted in (1992) 31 I.L.M. 1148 [hereinafter *Maritime Areas between Canada and France*]. For an excellent analysis of this decision, see G.P. Politakis, "The French-Canadian Arbitration around St. Pierre and Miquelon: Unmasked Opportunism and the Triumph of the Unexpected" (1993) 8 Int'l J. Mar. & Coastal L. 105-34. Another example is *Delimitation of the Maritime Boundary in the Gulf of Maine Area (Canada/United States)*, [1984] I.C.J. Rep. 252 [hereinafter *Maritime Boundary in the Gulf of Maine*]. For an analysis of

is not uncommon that the cause of a maritime boundary dispute or the issue that is really at hand is, in fact, harvesting rights,[15] even though the judicial decision avoids focusing on the fisheries aspect in order to direct attention towards a more "neutral" consideration such as geography.[16]

It is important to note that *all* international inter-state adjudication is based on the consent of the states to utilize adjudication. The consent may arise after a dispute arises and the disputants seek adjudication as a means of dispute settlement or the consent to adjudicate may exist as a result of a compromissory clause in a treaty that binds the states to use adjudication in the event that a dispute arises. In the *Fisheries Jurisdiction* cases, for example, the ICJ found that Iceland had consented to adjudication as a result of letters exchanged with the United Kingdom and Germany.[17] Canada's ability to avoid adjudication with Spain was a result of Canada's non-consent to the specifics of the disputes being within the authority of the ICJ.[18]

---

this decision, see Douglas M. Johnston, *The Theory and History of Ocean Boundary-Making* (Kingston-Montreal: McGill-Queen's University Press, 1988) at 178-91.

[15] This was unquestionably the case in both the *Maritime Areas between Canada and France* case, *supra* note 14, and the *Maritime Boundary in the Gulf of Maine, supra* note 14. Regarding the Canada-France situation, see T.L. McDorman, "The Canada-France Maritime Boundary Case: Drawing a Line around St. Pierre and Miquelon" (1990) 84 A.J.I.L. 157 at 158-65; and T.L. McDorman, "The Search for Resolution of the Canada-France Ocean Dispute Adjacent to St. Pierre and Miquelon" (1994) 17 Dal. L.J. 35-60. With respect to the Gulf of Maine situation, see David L. Van der Zwaag, *The Fish Feud: The U.S. and Canadian Boundary Dispute* (Toronto: Lexington Books, 1983).

[16] T.L. McDorman, P.M. Saunders, and D.L. Van der Zwaag, "The Gulf of Maine Boundary: Dropping Anchor or Setting a Course?" (1985) 9 Marine Policy 90 at 101:

> The second point on which the decision might be queried is the degree to which the decision's rationale is divorced from the reason for the dispute. On any non-legal analysis of the issue, the case was not about geography but rather was centrally concerned with the allocation of rights to the use of the oceans resources ... The decision does not reflect the importance of this aspect of the dispute. Resource-related factors ... were considered only in the final part of the three-stage process ... As a result, the elements which contributed most to the creation of the dispute were given the least weight in its resolution.

[17] *Fisheries Jurisdiction* cases, *supra* note 10 at 22 and 66. See the discussion of Romano, *supra* note 7 at 164-65.

[18] *Fisheries Jurisdiction (Spain v. Canada), supra* note 13, as well as the commentary in note 13.

ITLOS: SOURCES OF STATE CONSENT IN FISHERIES MATTERS

The authority of ITLOS to deal with an international fisheries matter can arise from the dispute settlement provisions of the LOS Convention.[19] States have pre-agreed to the authority of ITLOS to deal with *certain* disputes arising from the interpretation or application of the LOS Convention simply by being parties to the LOS Convention.[20] To date, the authority of ITLOS to deal with the cases before it have arisen from the wording of the LOS Convention. ITLOS may also attain authority to deal with an international fisheries dispute through the 1995 UN Agreement for the Implementation of the Provisions of the United Nations Convention on the Law of the Sea Relating to the Conservation and Management of Straddling Fish Stocks and Highly Migratory Fish Stocks[21] (Fish Stocks Agreement). This agreement, which is linked to the LOS Convention, deals with issues concerning the conservation and management of straddling fish stocks and highly migratory fish stocks primarily in waters beyond national jurisdiction.[22] State parties to the Fish Stocks Agreement have agreed to utilize the dispute procedures of the LOS Convention, with some variations, in order to

[19] LOS Convention, *supra* note 2 at Part XV.

[20] See *ibid.* at section 4.1.1.

[21] Agreement for the Implementation of the Provisions of the United Nations Convention on the Law of the Sea Relating to the Conservation and Management of Straddling Fish Stocks and Highly Migratory Fish Stocks, done at New York, August 4, 1995, entered into force December 11, 2001, reprinted in (1995) 34 I.L.M. 1542 and at <www.un.org/Depts/los/index.htm> [hereinafter Fish Stocks Agreement].

[22] The terms straddling fish stocks and highly migratory fish stocks are undefined in the Fish Stocks Agreement. However, a listing of highly migratory fish stocks is given in the LOS Convention, *supra* note 2 at Annex I. Straddling stocks are understood to be those stocks that migrate between the national waters of a state and the high seas. Article 3(1) of the Fish Stocks Agreement indicates the restriction on its application.

There are numerous studies of the Fish Stock Agreement. See Olav Schram Stokke, ed., *Governing High Seas Fisheries* (Oxford: Oxford University Press, 2001); Andre Tahindro, "Conservation and Management of Transboundary Fish Stocks: Comments in Light of the Adoption of the 1995 Agreement for the Conservation and Management of Straddling Fish Stocks and Highly Migratory Fish Stocks" (1997) 28 Ocean Dev. & Int'l L. 28; Moritaka Hayashi, "The Straddling and Highly Migratory Fish Stocks Agreement" in Ellen Hey, ed., *Developments in International Fisheries Law* (The Hague: Kluwer Law International, 1999) at 55-83; and Peter Orebech, Ketill Sigurjonsson, and T.L. McDorman, "The 1995 United Nations Straddling and Highly Migratory Fish Stocks Agreement: Management, Enforcement and Dispute Settlement" (1998) 13 Int'l J. Mar. & Coastal L. 119-41.

deal with disputes that may arise under the agreement. The dispute settlement process contained in the Fish Stocks Agreement is inextricably linked with the dispute settlement process in the LOS Convention.[23] The Fish Stocks Agreement entered into legal force in December 2001 following the deposit of the thirtieth instrument of ratification.[24] Unlike the LOS Convention, both the United States and Canada are parties to the Fish Stocks Agreement.

ITLOS may also obtain jurisdiction over a dispute where there exists a compromissory clause in a treaty that indicates the consent of the treaty parties to the utilization of ITLOS. Such a compromissory clause is in the 1993 Agreement to Promote Compliance with International Conservation and Management Measures by Fishing Vessels on the High Seas (Compliance Agreement).[25] Article IX(3) provides that state parties can agree to utilize ITLOS for the resolution of a dispute arising under the agreement.[26] As of February

[23] See generally T.L. McDorman, "The Dispute Settlement Regime of the Straddling and Highly Migratory Fish Stocks Convention" (1997) 35 Can. Y.B. Int'l L. 57 at 64-79. See also the discussion later in this article under the headings "1995 Fish Stocks Agreement"; "ITLOS and Provisional Measures"; and "ITLOS and the Prompt Release of Fishing Vessels."

[24] The current status and parties to the Fish Stocks Agreement is accessible at <www.un.org/Depts/los/index.htm>.

[25] Agreement to Promote Compliance with International Conservation and Management Measures by Fishing Vessels on the High Seas, done at Rome, November 24, 1993, not yet in force, reprinted in (1994) 33 ILM 968 and accessible at <www.fao.org/legal/> [hereinafter Compliance Agreement]. See generally David A. Bolton, "The Compliance Agreement" in Hey, *supra* note 22 at 31-53.

[26] Compliance Agreement, *supra* note 25 at Article IX:

Settlement of Disputes

1. Any Party may seek consultations with any other Party or Parties on any dispute with regard to the interpretation or application of the provisions of this Agreement with a view to reaching a mutually satisfactory solution as soon as possible.

2. In the event that the dispute is not resolved through these consultations within a reasonable period of time, the Parties in question shall consult among themselves as soon as possible with a view to having the dispute settled by negotiation, inquiry, mediation, conciliation, arbitration, judicial settlement or other peaceful means of their own choice.

3. Any dispute of this character not so resolved shall, with the consent of all Parties to the dispute, be referred for settlement to the International Court of Justice, to the International Tribunal for the Law of the Sea upon entry into force of the 1982 United Nations Convention on the Law of the Sea or to arbitration. In the case of failure to reach agreement on referral to the International Court of Justice, to the International Tribunal for the Law of

2003, the Compliance Agreement is not yet in force, having attained only twenty-three accepting states, out of the necessary twenty-five, to bring the convention into force.[27] Both the United States and Canada are parties to the Compliance Agreement.

ITLOS can also be accessed by states (parties or non-parties to the above conventions) that agree to have ITLOS deal with a particular dispute.[28] The disputants could make this decision as they enter into an agreement (sometimes referred to as a compromise), thereby giving ITLOS the authority to deal with a certain dispute.

ITLOS: JURISDICTION IN FISHERIES DISPUTES ARISING UNDER THE LOS CONVENTION AND THE FISH STOCKS AGREEMENT

Subject to states agreeing to confer upon ITLOS the authority to deal with a specific matter, at present, the authority of ITLOS to deal with an international fisheries matter arises from the 1982 LOS Convention or the 1995 Fish Stocks Agreement. These two treaties provide ITLOS with the ability to:

• deal with *certain* "interpretation or application" disputes;
• deal with requests for the prescription of provisional measures; and
• deal with requests for the prompt release of vessels.

ITLOS AND "INTERPRETATION OR APPLICATION"
(SUBSTANTIVE) DISPUTES

Not all "interpretation or application" disputes (substantive disputes) that arise under the LOS Convention or the Fish Stocks Agreement are within the authority of ITLOS. Certain subject areas related to fisheries have been excluded entirely from compulsory adjudication, and, even where compulsory adjudication is mandated, it is not necessarily ITLOS that has the authority to be the adjudicator.

---

the Sea or to arbitration, the Parties shall continue to consult and cooperate with a view to reaching settlement of the dispute in accordance with the rules of international law relating to the conservation of living marine resources.

Respecting this compromissory clause and ITLOS, see Eiriksson, *supra* note 1 at 125-27.

[27] The current status and parties to the Compliance Agreement is accessible at <www.fao.org/legal/>.

[28] Eiriksson, *supra* note 1 at 123-25; and Tullio Treves, "The Jurisdiction of the International Tribunal for the Law of the Sea" in Rao and Khan, *supra* note 1 at 122-23.

LOS Convention

With respect to disputes dealing with the "interpretation or application" of the fisheries provisions of the LOS Convention, the role of ITLOS is restricted by the exemption in Article 297(3)(a) and the requirement that the states involved in a dispute must have pre-selected or agreed to utilize ITLOS. Article 297 of the LOS Convention explicitly excludes certain disputes from being subject to compulsory adjudication. The principal exclusion under Article 297 is the coastal state's exercise of authority over marine living resources within its 200-nautical-mile exclusive economic zone:

3(a) Disputes concerning the interpretation or application of the provisions of this Convention with regard to fisheries shall be settled in accordance with section 2, except that the coastal State shall not be obliged to accept the submission to such settlement of any dispute relating to its sovereign rights with respect to the living resources in the exclusive economic zone or their exercise, including its discretionary powers for determining the allowable catch, its harvesting capacity, the allocation of surpluses to other States and the terms and conditions established in its conservation and management laws and regulations.[29]

For disputes listed in Article 298, a state can, prior to a dispute arising, elect to exclude the dispute from compulsory adjudication. There are two important areas that a state can elect to exclude from compulsory adjudication pursuant to Article 298: maritime boundary disputes and disputes concerning military activities.[30] Where compulsory adjudication is not available as a dispute settlement process, the LOS Convention directs that, in certain situations, formal conciliation is to be employed.[31]

Consistent with the importance of consent in accepting international dispute settlement procedures and the reluctance of many states to embrace compulsory adjudication as a means of dispute settlement,[32] the LOS Convention dispute settlement regime is one

[29] This exclusion is discussed in detail in M. Dahmani, *The Fisheries Regime of the Exclusive Economic Zone* (Boston: Martinus Nijhoff, 1987) at 121-3. See also Treves, *supra* note 28 at 118-20.

[30] With respect to Article 298 of the LOS Convention, see Shabtai Rosenne and Louis B. Sohn, eds. *United Nations Convention on the Law of the Sea, 1982: A Commentary,* volume 5 (Boston: Martinus Nijhoff, 1989) at 107-41; and Treves, *supra* note 28 at 120-22.

[31] LOS Convention, *supra* note 2 at Article 297(3)(b).

[32] The negotiators of the 1982 LOS Convention had hoped to entrench compulsory judicial settlement for all oceans disputes into the treaty, but this proved to be unacceptable. See generally A.O. Adede, *The System for Settlement of Disputes under the United Nations Convention on the Law of the Sea* (Boston: Martinus Nijhoff, 1987).

of several alternative compulsory dispute resolution processes.[33] LOS Convention Articles 280-2 provide that parties can agree to utilize other peaceful means to resolve a dispute and, by so agreeing, can avoid the dispute settlement mechanisms of the LOS Convention.[34] Where avoidance under Articles 280-2 and 297-8 is not indicated, the LOS Convention provides for compulsory third party adjudication with respect to disputes regarding the "interpretation or application" of the convention. The third party adjudicative body can be the ICJ, ITLOS, an arbitral tribunal, or a special arbitral tribunal.[35] By means of a declaration, a state party can pre-select which body it wishes to utilize, or, when a dispute arises, the disputants can agree on the appropriate body. Article 287(5) of the LOS Convention states that, where disputants cannot agree on the appropriate adjudicative body to resolve a dispute, arbitration is to be used. States have shown a reluctance to utilize their option of pre-selecting their preferred compulsory adjudicative body. As

[33] There are numerous examinations of the dispute settlement regime of the 1982 LOS Convention. Attention is drawn to Alan E. Boyle, "Dispute Settlement and the Law of the Sea Convention: Problems of Fragmentation and Jurisdiction" (1997) 46 I.C.L.Q. 59-82.

[34] Articles 280, 281, and 282 are complex provisions since they create the possibility of using means to resolve disputes other than those provided for in the LOS Convention. It was the interpretation of Article 281 that was at the heart of the Arbitral Tribunal's decision in *Southern Bluefin Tuna (N.Z. v. Japan; Austl. v. Japan)*, reprinted in (2000) 39 I.L.M. 1359 and accessible at <www.oceanlaw. net/cases/tuna2a.htm> [hereinafter *Southern Bluefin Tuna* case, 2000], between Australia/New Zealand and Japan.

The Arbitral Tribunal, pursuant to the LOS Convention dispute settlement procedures, ultimately decided that it did not have jurisdiction over the subject matter of the dispute since the parties (Australia/New Zealand/Japan) had agreed, through the 1993 Convention for the Conservation of Southern Bluefin Tuna, 1819 U.N.T.S. 360 [hereinafter SBT Convention], to a separate dispute settlement process that covered the subject matter in dispute and that this agreed-upon dispute settlement process trumped that of the LOS Convention. The tribunal's award is usually seen as a blow to compulsory adjudication advocates but, perhaps, it supports the effective settlement of disputes by adjudicators. For a briefing on the decision, see Barbara Kwiatkowska, "Southern Bluefin Tuna" (2001) 95 A.J.I.L. 162-71. For a more detailed analysis of the potential impact of the decision, see Bernard H. Oxman, "Complementary Agreements and Compulsory Adjudication" (2001) 95 A.J.I.L. 277-312; and David A. Colson and Peggy Hoyle, "Satisfying the Procedural Prerequisites to the Compulsory Dispute Settlement Mechanism of the 1982 Law of the Sea Convention: Did the *Southern Bluefin Tuna* Tribunal Get It Right?" (2003) 34 Ocean Dev. & Int'l L. (in press).

[35] LOS Convention, *supra* note 2 at Article 287(1). See generally Treves, *supra* note 28 at 128-31.

of February 2003, only thirty ratifying or acceding states to the LOS Convention had indicated their preference, with nineteen of those states having accepted ITLOS.[36] To date, ITLOS has had only two cases before it that have dealt with the merits of a dispute under the LOS Convention, of which only one has resulted in a decision: (1) *M/V "Saiga" (No. 2) Case (Saint Vincent and the Grenadines* v. *Guinea)*[37] and (2) *Case Concerning the Conservation and Sustainable Exploitation of Swordfish Stocks in the South-Eastern Pacific Ocean (Chile/European Community) (Swordfish Stocks* case).[38]

Fish Stocks Agreement[39]

As has been noted earlier in this article, the dispute settlement process contained in the Fish Stocks Agreement is inextricably linked with the dispute settlement process in the LOS Convention. Article 30(1) of the Fish Stocks Agreement provides that disputes concerning "the interpretation or application" of the Fish Stocks Agreement are to be resolved using the dispute settlement regime of the LOS Convention. Thus, subject to the parties agreeing to utilize a different set of procedures under Article 280 of the LOS Convention, disputes concerning the 1995 Fish Stocks Agreement are to be subject to compulsory dispute settlement. The effect of the wording in the Fish Stocks Agreement is that disputants can utilize the dispute settlement procedures of the LOS Convention irrespective of whether the disputants are parties to the 1982 treaty.

---

[36] The declarations of states are accessible at <www.un.org/Depts/los/index.htm>.

[37] *M/V "Saiga" (No. 2) Case (Saint Vincent and the Grenadines* v. *Guinea)*, ITLOS, Judgment, July 1, 1999, reprinted in (1999) 38 I.L.M.1323 and *M/V "Saiga" (No. 2) Case (Saint Vincent and the Grenadines* v. *Guinea)*, Provisional Measures Order, March 11, 1998, reprinted in (1998) 37 I.L.M. 1202, both are accessible at <www.itlos.org> [hereinafter *M/V "Saiga" (No. 2)*). See also the discussion under the heading *"M/V "Saiga"Case"* later in this article.

[38] *Case Concerning the Conservation and Sustainable Exploitation of Swordfish Stocks in the South-Eastern Pacific Ocean (Chile/European Community)*, ITLOS, Order, Constitution of Chamber, December 20, 2000, reprinted in (2001) 40 I.L.M. 475 and *Case Concerning the Conservation and Sustainable Exploitation of Swordfish Stocks in the South-Eastern Pacific Ocean (Chile/European Community)*, ITLOS, Suspension Order, both are accessible at <www.itlos.org> [hereinafter *Swordfish Stocks* case].

[39] Several of the paragraphs in this section are drawn, with modification, from T.L. McDorman, "Global Ocean Governance and International Adjudicative Dispute Resolution" (2000) 43 Ocean & Coastal Management 255 at 260-61 and from McDorman, *supra* note 23 at 70-71.

Article 30(2) of the Fish Stocks Agreement is designed to extend
the compulsory dispute settlement provisions of the LOS Convention to disputes that arise in regard to the "interpretation or application" of regional fisheries management agreements.[40] In certain
circumstances, this innovative provision will allow for the utilization of compulsory dispute settlement under the LOS Convention
for disputes that arise under regional fisheries management agreements even where there is no dispute resolution procedures within
the regional fisheries management agreement.[41] In order for Article 30(2) to operate in this manner, the disputing states must both
be parties to the regional fisheries agreement and the Fish Stocks
Agreement, although neither disputing state need be a party to the
LOS Convention.

The Fish Stocks Agreement has adopted the same adjudicative
selection opportunities, including ITLOS, as the LOS Convention.
Article 30(3) of the agreement provides that if a state has opted for
a specific procedure under the LOS Convention, this procedure is
to be its selection for disputes arising under the Fish Stocks Agreement, unless the state accepts another procedure for agreement disputes. A non-party to the LOS Convention (such as Canada and
the United States) can, pursuant to Article 30(4), opt for one of
the procedures listed in Article 287(1) of the LOS Convention.
Article 30(4) also directs that Article 287 is to apply where a state
party to the Fish Stocks Agreement has not selected a procedure (in
other words, an arbitral tribunal is the appropriate procedure if a
state has failed to select a procedure). Only one state, Canada, has
made a pre-selection of a forum under the Fish Stocks Agreement,

---

[40] See McDorman, *supra* note 23 at 67-68. Regional fisheries management agreements are treaties entered into by states to promote the conservation and management of straddling and highly migratory fish stocks. It is through these agreements
that many of the obligations of the Fish Stocks Agreement are to be carried out.
See Orebech et al., *supra* note 22 at 121-24; and Hayashi, *supra* note 22 at 66-68.
For a general discussion of regional fisheries management organizations and a
listing of them, see Are K. Sydnes, "Regional Fisheries Organizations: How and
Why Organizational Diversity Matters" (2001) 32 Ocean Dev. & Int'l L. 349-72.

[41] McDorman, *supra* note 23 at 67. The more interesting question is the situation
where a regional fisheries management organization has dispute settlement procedures that do not involve compulsory adjudication and whether Article 30(2)
of the Fish Stocks Agreement, which directs that the compulsory adjudication
provisions of the LOS Convention, would be applicable. In the Arbitral Tribunal
Southern Bluefin Tuna case, 2000, *supra* note 34, the non-compulsory adjudication provisions prevailed over the compulsory adjudication provisions of the
LOS Convention. It has been argued that the application of Article 30(2) would
lead to a different result. See Oxman, *supra* note 34 at 306.

and Canada has elected arbitration. The United States, which is also a party to the Fish Stocks Agreement but not to the LOS Convention, has made no pre-selection.[42]

Pursuant to the Fish Stocks Agreement, ITLOS, if pre-selected by states or where agreed upon by states, could have the authority to deal with "interpretation or application" disputes regarding the Fish Stocks Agreement and regional fisheries management treaties. Two additional things are worthy of note. First, pursuant to Article 32 of the Fish Stocks Agreement, the dispute settlement procedures of the agreement do not apply to disputes that are covered by Article 297(3)(a) of the LOS Convention. Thus, similarly to the LOS Convention, ITLOS cannot deal with national measures related to fisheries matters within national 200-nautical-mile zones. Second, independent of the Fish Stocks Agreement, which deals with high seas fisheries issues, compulsory dispute settlement exists under the LOS Convention (including the possible engagement of ITLOS) with respect to the "interpretation or application" of the provisions of the LOS Convention respecting high seas fishing.[43]

ITLOS AND PROVISIONAL MEASURES[44]

Article 290(1) of the LOS Convention provides that where a dispute has been submitted to a court or tribunal, at the request of one of the parties and following the parties right to be heard, provisional measures "appropriate under the circumstances to preserve the respective rights of the parties" or "to prevent serious harm to the environment" may be prescribed. Where the dispute is submitted to ITLOS, the tribunal would have authority to deal with a provisional measures request. Article 290(5) also gives ITLOS the authority to deal with a provisional measures request if, pending the establishment of an arbitral tribunal and within two weeks of a request for provisional measures, the disputants cannot agree upon the appropriate court or tribunal to hear the request. However,

---

[42] The declarations of states are accessible at <www.un.org/Depts/los/index.htm>.

[43] See William T. Burke, *The New International Law of Fisheries* (Oxford: Clarendon Press, 1994) at 124; Dahmani, *supra* note 29 at 121; and Boyle, *supra* note 33 at 43.

[44] McDorman, *supra* note 23 at 73-75. For a more detailed examination of the issues noted in this section, see Treves, *supra* note 28 at 148-52; Eiriksson, *supra* note 1 at 121-23 and 216-23; Rodiger Wolfrum, "Provisional Measures of the International Tribunal for the Law of the Sea" in Rao and Khan, *supra* note 1 at 173-86; and Tafsir Malick Ndiaye, "Provisional Measures before the International Tribunal for the Law of the Sea" in Nordquist and Moore, *supra* note 1 at 95-101.

provisional measures may only be prescribed, modified, or revoked if ITLOS "considers that *prima facie* the tribunal which is to be constituted would have jurisdiction and that the urgency so requires."[45]

While this provisional measures authority of ITLOS appears to be limited, ITLOS has, on three occasions to date, ruled on provisional measures requests, and two of the requests were pursuant to international fisheries matters:[46]

- *M/V "Saiga" (No. 2)*; and[47]
- *Southern Bluefin Tuna (N.Z. v. Japan; Austl. v. Japan)*.[48]

Article 31(2) of the Fish Stocks Agreement tracks the wording of LOS Convention Article 290(1), recognizing that a properly seized court or tribunal may prescribe provisional measures both to preserve the rights of disputants and also "to prevent damage to the stocks in question."[49] The "fail-safe" role of ITLOS to deal with a request for provisional measures where an arbitral tribunal is not yet constituted is accepted in the Fish Stocks Agreement, albeit with a modification. The Fish Stocks Agreement modifies the role of ITLOS in provisional measures requests. Article 31(3) of the

[45] LOS Convention, *supra* note 2 at Article 290(5). Once a tribunal has been established it may modify, revoke, or affirm any provisional measures ordered by ITLOS.

[46] The non-fisheries case was the MOX *Plant* case, *supra* note 6.

[47] *M/V "Saiga" (No. 2)*, *supra* note 37.

[48] *Southern Bluefin Tuna (N.Z. v. Japan; Austl. v. Japan)*, ITLOS, Provisional Measures Order of August 27, 1999, reprinted in (1999) I.L.M. 38 1624 [hereinafter *Southern Bluefin Tuna*, 1999, cases]. See also the discussion under the heading "*Southern Bluefin Tuna* Cases" in this article.

[49] As noted in McDorman, *supra* note 23 at 73-74:

Article 31(2) refers to two additional circumstances when provisional measures may be prescribed. First, Article 7(2) of the 1995 Agreement obliges states harvesting straddling stocks both within and without a national fishing zone to adopt "compatible" conservation and management measures. Article 7(5) directs that, pending agreement on such compatible measures, states are to attempt to establish "provisional arrangements of a practical nature." Where no such arrangements are made, an aggrieved state can submit the dispute to the appropriate court or tribunal "for the purpose of obtaining provisional measures." Second, in the circumstance of a high seas enclave surrounded by the national jurisdiction of a single state, where the coastal state and the fishing states cannot agree on appropriate conservation and management measures, an aggrieved state, using Article 7(5), can seek provisional measures from the appropriate court or tribunal. The intent of the additional circumstances for the possibility of provisional measures is to pressure reluctant states to agree to interim arrangements for high seas fishing.

agreement provides that non-parties to the LOS Convention can declare their non-acceptance of the role of the LOS Convention tribunal in prescribing provisional measures. This provision ensures that states, which are not party to the 1982 LOS Convention, are not forced to interact with ITLOS. It does not appear that Canada or the United States have made such a declaration. Presumably, if such a declaration was to be made under Article 31(3), no "fail-safe" body would have jurisdiction with respect to provisional measures.[50]

ITLOS AND THE PROMPT RELEASE OF FISHING VESSELS[51]

In the same way that ITLOS is the "fail-safe" institution with respect to requests for provisional measures under the LOS Convention, ITLOS is also the "fail-safe" option for the prompt release of fishing vessels under the LOS Convention. Article 73(1) of the LOS Convention permits a coastal state to arrest foreign fishers that have, while in the arresting states' waters, allegedly violated its fisheries laws. Article 73(2) provides that arrested vessels and crews, upon posting reasonable bond or security, are to be promptly released.[52] No specific prompt release provision exists in regard to fishing or other vessels seized on the high seas, other than those seized as a result of hot pursuit,[53] since it is inconsistent with the

---

[50] See E.D. Brown, "Dispute Settlement and the Law of the Sea: the UN Convention Regime" (1997) 21 Marine Policy 17 at 30.

[51] Several of the paragraphs in this section are drawn, with modification, from McDorman, *supra* note 23 at 75-78. For a more detailed examination of the issues noted in this section, see Treves, *supra* note 28 at 152-55; and Eiriksson, *supra* note 1 at 118-21.

[52] With respect to Article 73 of the LOS Convention, see Burke, *supra* note 43 at 312-18. Specifically regarding the issue of "reasonable bond," see Edward Arthur Laing, "ITLOS Procedures and Practices: Bonds" in Nordquist and Moore, *supra* note 1 at 113-20. As will be noted later in this article, all of the ITLOS prompt release cases have involved questions of the reasonableness of the bond. For a detailed analysis, see Erik Franckx, "'Reasonable Bond' in the Practice of the International Tribunal for the Law of the Sea" (2002) 32 California Western Int'l L.J. 303-42.

[53] LOS Convention, *supra* note 2 at Article 111, codifies the criteria that must be met for hot pursuit. See E.D. Brown, *The International Law of the Sea* (Aldershot: Dartmouth, 1994) at 295-99 and Robert C. Reuland, "The Customary Right of Hot Pursuit onto the High Seas: Annotations to Article 111 of the Law of the Sea Convention" (1993) 33 Virginia J. Int'l L. 557-89. Hot pursuit was an issue dealt with by ITLOS in the *M/V "Saiga" (No. 2)* case, *supra* note 37, Judgment, at paras. 139-52.

LOS Convention for such an arrest to take place.[54] However, as one authority has written, "[i]t would seem absurd ... that the prompt release procedure should be available in cases in which detention is permitted by the Convention ... and not available in cases in which it is not permitted by it."[55] ITLOS has made no definitive statement on this issue, although there are sentences in *M/V "Saiga" Case (Saint Vincent and the Grenadines* v. *Guinea),*[56] which indicate a division of opinion among the members of ITLOS.[57] The process for dealing with the prompt release of vessels is set out in Article 292, which is part of the dispute settlement section of the LOS Convention.

Under Article 292, where a vessel has been detained and it is alleged that the detaining state has not complied with the Article 73 prompt release requirements, "the question of release from detention" may be submitted to an agreed-upon court or tribunal. If no agreement is reached within ten days of the detention, the issue may be submitted by the flag state of the arrested vessel to the court or tribunal pre-selected by the detaining state pursuant to Article 287 or, if no pre-selection has been made, to ITLOS. Thus, ITLOS is again the "fail-safe" institution. Article 292(3) indicates that the jurisdiction of ITLOS or the other body is restricted only to questions respecting the release of the vessel and crew.

Six of the international fisheries cases on the ITLOS docket have involved the prompt release of detained fishing vessels and the proper application of Article 73 of the LOS Convention:

---

[54] High seas arrests for activities that take place on the high seas are only sanctioned by the LOS Convention for piracy (Article 105) and unauthorized broadcasting (Article 109(3)). However, the right to visit a vessel on the high seas (Article 110) may also lead to seizures respecting vessels engaged in the slave trade and vessels without nationality. See generally Brown, *supra* note 53 at 299-314; and Moritaka Hayashi, "Enforcement by Non-Flag States on the High Seas under the 1995 Agreement on Straddling and Highly Migratory Fish Stocks" (1996) 9 Georgetown Int'l Env. L. Rev. 1 at 4-10.

[55] Tullio Treves, "The Proceedings Concerning Prompt Release of Vessels and Crews before the International Tribunal for the Law of the Sea" (1996) 11 Int'l J. Mar. & Coastal L. 179 at 186.

[56] *M/V "Saiga" Case (Saint Vincent and the Grenadines* v. *Guinea),* ITLOS, Prompt Release Judgment, December 4, 1997, reprinted in (1998) 37 I.L.M. 360, accessible at <www.itlos.org> [hereinafter *M/V "Saiga"* case]. See also the discussion under the heading "*M/V "Saiga"* Cases" later in this article

[57] L. Dolliver M. Nelson, "The International Tribunal for the Law of the Sea: Some Issues" in Rao and Khan, *supra* note 1 at 55.

- *M/V "Saiga";*[58]
- *"Camouco" Case (Panama* v. *France);*[59]
- *"Monte Confurco" Case (Seychelles* v. *France);*[60]
- *"Grand Prince" Case (Belize* v. *France);*[61]
- *"Chaisiri Reefer 2" Case (Panama* v. *Yemen);*[62] and
- *"Volga" Case (Russian Federation* v. *Australia).*[63]

There is some debate over whether fishing vessels seized or detained in a way that is inconsistent with the Fish Stocks Agreement or a regional fisheries management agreement would trigger Article 292 of the LOS Convention.[64] An explicit reference in the Fish Stocks

[58] *M/V "Saiga," supra* note 56. See also the discussion under the heading "*M/V "Saiga"* Cases" later in this article.

[59] *"Camouco" Case (Panama* v. *France),* ITLOS, Prompt Release Judgment, February 7, 2000, reprinted in (2000) 39 I.L.M. 666. See also the discussion under the heading ""*Camouco"* Case" later in this article

[60] *"Monte Confurco" Case (Seychelles* v. *France),* ITLOS, Prompt Release Judgment, December 18, 2000 [hereinafter *"Monte Confurco"* case]. See also the discussion under the heading ""*Monte Confurco"* Case" later in this article

[61] *"Grand Prince" Case (Belize* v. *France),* ITLOS, Prompt Release Judgment, April 20, 2001 [hereinafter *"Grand Prince"* case]. See also the discussion under the heading ""*Grand Prince"* Case" later in this article

[62] *"Chaisiri Reefer 2" Case (Panama* v. *Yemen),* ITLOS, Press Release 51, 5 July 2001, and Press Release 52, 16 July 2001 [hereinafter *"Chaisiri Reefer"* case]. See also the discussion under the heading ""*Chaisiri Reefer 2"* Case" later in this article.

[63] *"Volga" Case (Russian Federation* v. *Australia),* ITLOS, Prompt Release Judgment, December 23, 2002 [hereinafter *"Volga"* case]. See also the discussion under the heading ""*Volga"* Case" later in this article.

[64] The issue of non-flag state enforcement on the high seas was highly contentious during the negotiation of the Fish Stocks Agreement. See Hayashi, *supra* note 54 at 10-27, who describes the negotiations about this issue in detail. The final result is that, without the consent of the flag state, a fishing vessel allegedly in breach of the Fish Stocks Agreement or an appropriate regional fisheries arrangement cannot be arrested or seized on the high seas. However, Article 21 of the Fish Stocks Agreement creates the possibility of a foreign fishing vessel on the high seas being boarded, inspected, and, where "clear grounds" exist of "a serious violation," the offending vessel may be brought into port for further investigation. While "clear grounds" is not defined in the agreement, "a serious violation" is defined in detail in Article 21(11). The keys to the exercise of these powers are: that the boarding/inspection state must be a member of a regional fisheries management arrangement; that there exist clear grounds for believing that the offending vessel is violating the regional fisheries management regulations; and that the flag state does not intervene. For a detailed description of the enforcement provisions of the Fish Stocks Agreement, see Hayashi, *supra* note 54 at 10-27; and Tahindro, *supra* note 22 at 37-40. It is important to reiterate that even under Article 21, without flag state consent, an inspected vessel cannot be prosecuted. Note also Treves, *supra* note 55 at 186-87; and David H. Anderson,

Agreement to LOS Convention Article 292 was deleted at the last
moment since the negotiators decided that such a reference might
be interpreted as sanctioning vessel arrests on the high seas.[65]

Article 30(1) integrates the entire LOS Convention dispute settlement regime into disputes regarding the interpretation and application of the Fish Stocks Agreement and this integration would
apparently include Article 292.[66] Article 292 is not a perfect fit, however, in part because it presumes that the prompt release can occur
where a reasonable bond is posted, yet Article 21(12) of the Fish
Stocks Agreement requires a vessel to be released upon flag state
request without reference to the posting of a bond. Another problem with incorporating Article 292 of the LOS Convention into the
Fish Stocks Agreement is the "fail-safe" role of ITLOS. The situation could arise where ITLOS could have jurisdiction, however
temporary, with respect to the prompt release of an arrested fishing
vessel and the relevant states are not parties to the LOS Convention
and thus not technically bound by the activities of the LOS tribunal.
For prompt release, there is no equivalent to Article 31(3) in regard
to provisional measures. While there may exist problems directly
applying Article 292 to vessel detentions under the Fish Stocks
Agreement, the better view is that the procedures under Article 292
are available to disputing states where vessels are being detained in
a way that is inconsistent with the Fish Stocks Agreement.

ITLOS FISHERIES CASES: A BRIEFING[67]

M/V "*saiga*" CASES[68]

The October 1997 seizure by Guinea in Sierra Leone waters of
the tanker *M/V Saiga,* which had been refuelling fishing vessels in

---

"Investigation, Detention and Release of Foreign Vessels under the UN Convention on the Law of the Sea of 1982 and Other International Agreements" (1996)
11 Int'l J. Mar. & Coastal L. 165 at 171-74.

[65] Treves, *supra* note 55 at 187.

[66] Article 30(2) also integrates the LOS Convention dispute settlement regime into
disputes regarding regional fisheries management arrangements.

[67] The author provides short notes on the ITLOS cases to the Yearbook of International Environmental Law. What follows in this section is drawn, with modification, from these contributions.

[68] See McDorman, *supra* note 39 at 266-67. See also Eiriksson, *supra* note 1 at 287-
309; Bernard H. Oxman, "The *M/V Saiga*" (1998) 92 A.J.I.L. 278-82; and
Bernard H. Oxman and Vincent Bantz, "The *M/V Saiga* (No. 2)" (2000) 94
A.J.I.L. 140-50.

Guinean waters, led to the first employment of the dispute settlement procedures of the 1982 LOS Convention and became the first case before ITLOS. While not technically a dispute involving a fishing vessel or fish harvesting, the *M/V Saiga* was involved in assisting fishing activities (at-sea fuelling) within the 200-nautical-mile fishing zone of Guinea.

What was first brought before ITLOS was the assertion by Saint Vincent and the Grenadines, which claimed to be the state of registry of the *M/V Saiga*, that Guinea had failed to promptly release the arrested vessel as required by Article 73 of the LOS Convention. Since Guinea had made no election respecting the appropriate body for resolving disputes, Saint Vincent and the Grenadines brought their request for prompt release to ITLOS. In December 1997, ITLOS decided that it had jurisdiction to resolve the prompt release dispute and ordered that Guinea promptly release the *M/V Saiga* and its crew provided that reasonable bond or security was posted.[69] The vessel was released on February 28, 1998. With respect to the merits of the legality of the vessel seizure, Saint Vincent and the Grenadines first sought to invoke the arbitral tribunal procedure of the dispute settlement provisions of the LOS Convention. However, in February 1998, Saint Vincent and the Grenadines and Guinea agreed to submit the merits of the dispute to ITLOS.[70] In March 1998, following a request by Saint Vincent and the Grenadines, ITLOS unanimously granted provisional measures that were designed to prevent an escalation of the dispute.[71]

There were three principal issues before ITLOS in the merits phase of the *M/V "Saiga"* dispute. The first issue was whether Saint Vincent and the Grenadines could bring claims against Guinea on behalf of the seized tanker and crew. On this issue, ITLOS determined that at the relevant time Saint Vincent and the Grenadines was the state of registry of the *M/V Saiga*[72] and that the legal validity of a ship's flag was unaffected by the existence or non-existence of a "genuine link" between the vessel and the state of registry.[73] Moreover, Saint Vincent and the Grenadines could bring

---

[69] *M/V "Saiga," supra* note 56.

[70] The agreement was through an exchange of letters set out in *M/V "Saiga" (No. 2), supra* note 37, Provisional Measures, at para. 14.

[71] *Ibid.*, Provisional Measures.

[72] *Ibid.*, Judgment, at paras. 55-74. The issue of vessel flag arose because of the appearance that the *M/V "Saiga"* was only provisionally registered in Saint Vincent and the Grenadines and that the time period for the registration had expired.

a claim on behalf of the tanker's crew irrespective of the nationality of the crew.[74] The second issue was whether the Guinean customs law, which was allegedly breached by the *M/V Saiga*, which had not paid the necessary duties for fuel supplied to fishing vessels in the Guinean 200-nautical-mile zone, was consistent with the LOS Convention. Using careful wording, ITLOS held that the LOS Convention did not permit states to apply their customs laws beyond the twenty-four-nautical-mile contiguous zone.[75] Finally, the tribunal rejected the argument that the seizure was pursuant to a rightful exercise of hot pursuit[76] and accepted that "excessive force" had been used in boarding the *M/V Saiga*. Unusual in international cases, ITLOS assessed damages to be in excess of US $2 million, which was duly paid.

SOUTHERN BLUEFIN TUNA CASES[77]

On July 15, 1999, New Zealand and Australia initiated the dispute settlement provisions of the LOS Convention, notifying Japan of their intention to institute arbitral proceedings with respect to the experimental fishing for southern bluefin tuna being conducted by Japan. On July 30, 1999, New Zealand and Australia requested ITLOS to prescribe provisional measures in the dispute. On August 16, 1999, the tribunal joined the New Zealand and Australian requests into a single proceeding.[78]

The provisional measures sought by New Zealand and Australia were that Japan cease the experimental fishery; that the Japanese

---

[73] *Ibid.*, Judgment, at paras. 75-88. In regard to the genuine link concept generally, see Brown, *supra* note 53 at 286-91.

[74] *Ibid.*, Judgment, at paras. 103-9.

[75] *Ibid.*, Judgment, at paras. 110-38. This was the core issue of the judgment.

[76] *Ibid.*, Judgment, at paras. 139-52. In regard to hot pursuit, see note 53 in this article.

[77] See T.L. McDorman, "International Tribunal for the Law of the Sea (ITLOS)" (1999) 10 Y.B. Int'l Env. L. 632 at 634-35. See also Eiriksson, *supra* note 1 at 309-19; Kwiatkowska, *supra* note 34; Donald L. Morgan, "A Practitioner's Critique of the Order Granting Provisional Measures in the Southern Bluefin Tuna Cases" in Nordquist and Moore, *supra* note 1 at 173-213; Barbara Kwiatkowska, "Southern Bluefin Tuna" (2000) 94 A.J.I.L. 150-55; and Cesare Romano, "The Southern Bluefin Tuna Dispute: Hints of a World to Come . . . Like It or Not" (2001) 32 Ocean Dev. & Int'l L. 313-48.

[78] *Southern Bluefin Tuna Cases (New Zealand v. Japan; Australia v. Japan)*, Joint Proceedings Order, August 16, 1999, accessible at <www.itlos.org>.

quota be the amount last agreed upon in the Commission for the Conservation of Southern Bluefin Tuna[79] and that the experimental fishing undertaken be counted towards the Japanese quota; that the parties "act consistently with the precautionary principle" pending the resolution of the dispute; that the parties not take action to aggravate the dispute; and that the parties take no action that would prejudice the rights of the parties in carrying out a resolution of the dispute. Japan argued, among other things, that ITLOS did not have the jurisdiction to grant provisional measures in this case and, in the alternative, that the request from New Zealand and Australia should be denied and that Australia and New Zealand should be required to "urgently and in good faith recommence negotiations" with Japan. Moreover, Japan requested that ITLOS prescribe that in the event that recommenced negotiations are unsuccessful the dispute over the experimental fishery should be referred to a panel of independent scientists.[80]

Consistent with LOS Convention Article 290(5), ITLOS determined, after concluding that the arbitral tribunal would have *prima facie* jurisdiction to hear the dispute, that it had the jurisdiction with respect to the request for provisional measures. ITLOS accepted that the stock of southern bluefin tuna was "severely depleted"[81] and that there was sufficient "scientific uncertainty" that it could not assess the measures to be taken to conserve the stock.[82] Article 290(1) of the LOS Convention allows for provisional measures "to prevent serious harm to the environment," and the tribunal found "that measures should be taken as a matter of urgency to preserve the rights of the parties and to avert further deterioration of the southern bluefin stock."[83]

The tribunal prescribed that the parties take no action that might aggravate the dispute or prejudice the carrying out of any decision made on the merits by the arbitral tribunal. The tribunal further prescribed that the parties not exceed the harvest quotas that had existed between 1989 and 1997, but which had expired in 1997. Moreover, it was prescribed that each of the three states should refrain from conducting an experimental fishery without

---

[79] The Commission for the Conservation of Southern Bluefin Tuna was the organization established by the SBT Convention, *supra* note 34.

[80] See *Southern Bluefin Tuna* cases, 1999, *supra* note 48 at paras. 31-35.

[81] *Ibid.* at para. 71.

[82] *Ibid.* at paras. 79-80.

[83] *Ibid.* at para. 80.

the agreement of the other parties, but if an experimental fishery was to be conducted, the harvest amount should count against the national quota. The parties to the dispute were instructed to resume negotiations to reach new arrangements for the conservation and management of the southern bluefin tuna. The final substantive prescription from the tribunal was that Australia, New Zealand, and Japan were to undertake efforts to reach agreement with other states engaged in harvesting southern bluefin tuna in order to ensure the conservation of the stocks.[84]

Following ITLOS's decision on provisional measures, an arbitral tribunal was established, which determined, in August 2000, that it did *not* have jurisdiction to hear or decide upon the merits of the Australia-New Zealand complaint against Japan without the explicit consent of Japan.[85]

"CAMOUCO" CASE[86]

On September 28, 1999, the Panamian-flagged longliner, the *Camouco,* was arrested by a French frigate in the exclusive economic zone adjacent to France's Crozet Islands in the southern Indian Ocean. The vessel was charged under French law with numerous offences, including unlawfully fishing in the exclusive economic zone; failing to declare entry into the exclusive economic zone; concealment of vessel markings; and attempted flight. Panama came before ITLOS seeking the prompt release of the fishing vessel pursuant to Article 292 of the LOS Convention. France argued that since Panama had taken three months to seek prompt release it was estopped from raising the issue. ITLOS indicated that its prompt release jurisdiction was not contingent upon a state raising the complaint in a timely fashion.[87] Second, France argued that, as there was an appeal of the detention of the vessel current before French courts, ITLOS was without jurisdiction. ITLOS responded that its prompt release jurisdiction was without prejudice to any action taken in local courts[88] and, more generally, that the prompt

---

[84] *Ibid.* at para. 90.

[85] *Southern Bluefin Tuna* cases, 2000, *supra* note 34, Arbitral Tribunal.

[86] See T.L. McDorman, "International Tribunal for the Law of the Sea (ITLOS)" (2000) 11 Y.B. Int'l Env. L. 582 at 582-83. See also Eiriksson, *supra* note 1 at 319-30 and Bernard H. Oxman and Vincent P. Bantz, "The *Camouco* (Panama v. France)" (2000) 94 A.J.I.L. 713-21.

[87] *"Camouco"* case, *supra* note 59 at para. 54.

[88] *Ibid.* at para. 56.

release remedy was "an independent remedy and not an appeal against a decision of a national court."[89]

Ultimately, the principal issue before ITLOS was whether the bond established by the French court for release of the vessel was a "reasonable bond" as required by Articles 73(2) and 292 of the LOS Convention. ITLOS took the view that the bond of Fr 20 million francs, which had been ordered by the French court, was not "reasonable" and that what was "reasonable" was a bond of Fr 8 million francs.[90] Ultimately, this bond was tendered and the *Camouco* released.

"MONTE CONFURCO" CASE[91]

On November 8, 2000, the Seychelles-registered and licensed fishing vessel *Monte Confurco* was arrested by a French frigate in the exclusive economic zone adjacent to the Kerguelen Islands. The vessel was charged with unlawfully fishing in the exclusive economic zone; failing to declare entry into the exclusive economic zone and the amount of fish carried on board; and attempted evasion of investigation. The Seychelles came before ITLOS seeking the prompt release of the fishing vessel and master. Again, the principal issue in front of ITLOS was whether the bond of Fr 56,400,000 francs set by the local French court was "reasonable" under Articles 73(2) and 292 of the LOS Convention. In setting the bond amount, the French court had taken into account ITLOS's finding in the *"Camouco"* case.[92] Nevertheless, ITLOS took the view that the Fr 56 million francs bond was not "reasonable" and that the bond should be set at Fr 18 million francs.[93] In reaching this conclusion, ITLOS took into account the knowledge that there was significant illicit fishing in the areas adjacent to where the *Monte Confurco* had been apprehended and that under French law the alleged breaches were grave.[94] The vessel was subsequently released.

---

[89] *Ibid.* at para. 58.

[90] *Ibid.* at paras. 70 and 74.

[91] See McDorman, *supra* note 86 at 584.

[92] *"Monte Confurco"* case, *supra* note 60 at para. 41.

[93] *Ibid.* at paras. 89 and 93.

[94] *Ibid.* at paras. 79-80.

SWORDFISH STOCKS CASE[95]

This case arose from a long-standing dispute between Chile and the European Union (EU) regarding the practices of Spanish fishing vessels beyond Chile's 200-nautical-mile economic zone and Chile's actions against those vessels. More specifically, Chile alleged that EU fishing activity outside Chilean waters violated various provisions of the LOS Convention, including abuse of rights; non-conservation of high seas stocks; and the duty to cooperate with the adjacent coastal state. The EU denied these accusations and alleged that Chile had breached international law by unilaterally applying its national law to high seas fishing activity. In late 2000, Chile and the EU agreed to submit the dispute to a special five-judge chamber of ITLOS, which was duly constituted by the president of ITLOS.[96] However, in January 2001, the two sides reached a provisional agreement regarding the dispute, and, in March 2001, the case before ITLOS was suspended, as opposed to discontinued, and, as a result, it remains on the ITLOS docket.[97]

"GRAND PRINCE" CASE[98]

This prompt release case arose from another French arrest of a vessel allegedly fishing Patagonian toothfish in French waters around the Kerguelen and Crozet Islands. It was uncontested before the French court that the *Grand Prince* had violated French law by entering French waters without notification and fishing without authorization.[99] The French "court of first instance" confirmed the arrest and set the security for release of the vessel at Fr 11.4 million francs. Ten days later, the criminal court found the vessel guilty of the charges and, consistent with French law, ordered the vessel and the equipment on board to be confiscated. Belize argued that the security was unreasonable and the fact that the order of confiscation occurred only a few days after the setting of

---

[95] See McDorman, *supra* note 86 at 585; and T.L. McDorman, "International Tribunal for the Law of the Sea (ITLOS)" (2001) 12 Y.B. Int'l Env. L. 589-97.

[96] *Swordfish Stock* case, Order, Constitution of Chamber, *supra* note 38.

[97] *Ibid.*, Suspension Order.

[98] See McDorman, "International Tribunal for the Law of the Sea," *supra* note 95. See also Bernard H. Oxman and Vincent P. Bantz, "The *Grand Prince*" (2002) 96 A.J.I.L. 219-25.

[99] *"Grand Prince"* case, *supra* note 61 at para. 42.

the security amounted to a "trick" that undermined the prompt release provisions of the LOS Convention.[100]

ITLOS did not deal with these prompt release issues. Instead, it took the view that on the evidence before it Belize had not acted "at all times material to this dispute" as the flag state of the *Grand Prince*.[101] The result of this viewpoint was that ITLOS was without jurisdiction because, at the time of the Belize application for prompt release of the *Grand Prince*, the vessel was not registered in Belize and, pursuant to Article 292(2), only the state of registry of the arrested vessel can request prompt release.[102]

"CHAISIRI REEFER 2 " CASE[103]

Panama alleged that its flag vessel *Chaisiri Reefer 2* had not been released by Yemeni authorities despite a Yemen court having ordered the release and a commercial guarantee (security) having been given regarding the alleged breach of Yemeni fisheries law by the Panamanian vessel.[104] The prompt release case was discontinued before ITLOS following an exchange of notes *verbale* between Yemen and Panama indicating that the vessel had been released.[105]

"VOLGA " CASE[106]

In late 2002, the Russian Federation sought an ITLOS order of prompt release with respect to the fishing vessel *Volga*, which had been arrested by Australia for allegedly fishing illegally for Patagonian toothfish in the exclusive economic zone waters that Australia claims around Heard Island and the McDonald Islands in the Indian Ocean. The principal issues before ITLOS involved whether the wording of Article 73(2), specifically whether the requirement that a vessel be promptly released "upon the posting of reasonable bond or other security," allowed a state to condition vessel release on the fulfilment of non-financial obligations and allowed a state to

---

[100] *Ibid.* at para. 54.

[101] *Ibid.* at para. 89.

[102] *Ibid.* at para. 93.

[103] See McDorman, "International Tribunal for the Law of the Sea," *supra* note 95.

[104] *"Chaisiri Reefer 2 "* case, *supra* note 62, Press Release 51.

[105] *Ibid.*, Press Release 52.

[106] See McDorman, "International Tribunal for the Law of the Sea (ITLOS)" (2002) 13 Y.B. Int'l Env. L. (in press).

impose as part of the bond or security a "good behaviour bond," which in this instance was AU $1,000,000.

ITLOS determined that the wording of Article 73(2) restricted the conditions that could be imposed for the release of a seized vessel to the posting of a financial security.[107] Relying on the provisions of the LOS Convention, where non-financial conditions could be imposed on a vessel's release (Article 226(1)(c)) and where only financial bonds were noted (Articles 220(7) and 226(1)(b), the tribunal decided "that where the Convention envisages the imposition of conditions additional to a bond or other financial security, it expressly states so."[108] As non-financial conditions are not mentioned in Article 73(2), ITLOS decided that their imposition was inconsistent with the provision. ITLOS thereby concluded that "[t]he object and purpose of article 73, paragraph 2, read in conjunction with article 292 of the Convention, is to provide the flag State with a mechanism for obtaining the prompt release of a vessel and crew arrested for alleged fisheries violations by posting a security of a financial nature whose reasonableness can be assessed in financial terms."[109]

The tribunal also took the view that the AU $1,000,000 "good behaviour bond" was not justifiable under Article 73(2).[110] ITLOS noted that the bond under Article 73(2) was to be related to an "arrested vessel" and that a bond amount related to future good behaviour performance did not relate to an "arrested vessel."[111]

CONCLUSIONS: THE USE OF ITLOS AND THE SETTLEMENT OF INTERNATIONAL FISHERIES DISPUTES

A statistical tabulation on the fisheries cases before ITLOS reveals ten international fisheries cases on the docket of ITLOS, eight of which proceeded before ITLOS. The eight disputes that have been dealt with by ITLOS resulted in eight decisions to analyze (five requests for prompt release, two requests for provisional measures, and one decision on the merits). As noted, only in the *M/V "Saiga"* case was ITLOS required to deal with the merits of a

---

[107] *"Volga"* case, *supra* note 63 at para. 77.

[108] *Ibid.* at para. 77.

[109] *Ibid.*

[110] *Ibid.* at para. 80.

[111] *Ibid.*

dispute between the parties.[112] The one decision on the merits is misleading since the five prompt release requests, four of which were granted, also involved substantive disputes between the parties since the immediate issue in dispute was whether a seized vessel was being detained in a way that was inconsistent with Article 73 of the LOS Convention. Thus, six of the eight ITLOS fisheries decisions have involved substantive issues of interpretation or application of the LOS Convention and the resolution of an immediate dispute. Only the two requests for provisional measures can be considered to be procedural in nature rather than substantive.

A less satisfying picture of ITLOS and fisheries matters emerges when one tabulates the choices of states regarding ITLOS. It is also to be noted that ITLOS has established a Chamber for Fishery Disputes,[113] which is designed to encourage states to utilize ITLOS. As has already been noted, ITLOS has been pre-selected as the dispute settlement body of choice under the LOS Convention by only seventeen states,[114] and no state has pre-selected ITLOS under the Fish Stocks Agreement.[115] Even the compromissory clause in the Compliance Agreement targets ITLOS as a choice along with the ICJ and arbitration.[116] In two disputes, the *Swordfish Stocks* case and the *M/V "Saiga"* case, the disputants did agree to utilize ITLOS in order to deal with the merits of the dispute. However, in the *Swordfish Stocks* case, the parties were to utilize a chamber of ITLOS rather than the full tribunal, and, in the end, a temporary resolution suspended the proceedings.[117] In the *Southern Bluefin Tuna* cases, the disputing states avoided ITLOS for the merits of the dispute and proceeded to an arbitral tribunal.[118] While it is not an international fisheries case, the *MOX Plant Case (Ireland v. United Kingdom)* reflects similar patterns in that Ireland and the United Kingdom preferred to use

---

[112] *M/V "Saiga" (No. 2)*, Judgment, *supra* note 37.

[113] ITLOS, "Resolution on the Chamber for Fisheries Disputes," October 2002, accessible at <www.itlos.org>. This 2002 resolution continues the Chamber for Fisheries Disputes, which was first established in 1997 and is to be in place for three years (until the end of 2005). See Eiriksson, *supra* note 1 at 83-84 and more generally at 76-87.

[114] LOS Convention, *supra* note 2.

[115] Fish Stocks Agreement, *supra* note 21.

[116] Compliance Agreement, *supra* note 25.

[117] See the section in this article entitled "*Case Concerning Swordfish Stocks in the South-Eastern Pacific Ocean.*"

[118] See the section in this article entitled "*Southern Bluefin Tuna* Cases."

an arbitral tribunal rather than ITLOS.[119] Based on this limited sample, developed states, such as the EU, Ireland, Japan, New Zealand, and the United Kingdom — none of whom have pre-selected ITLOS — do not appear willing to utilize the full ITLOS panel.[120]

While ITLOS is potentially a cumbersome body (twenty-one judges that have to be called to Hamburg whenever a case arises), thus far, it has proven to be very agile and efficient in dealing expeditiously with requests for the prompt release of detained vessels and for provisional measures.[121] In none of the five prompt release requests has ITLOS taken more than a month from the date of filing to the rendering of a decision. In the provisional measures cases, the *M/V "Saiga"* decision took nearly two months, while the *Southern Bluefin Tuna* cases fulfilled their one-month timetable. Arguably, this efficiency bodes well for the future utilization of ITLOS in dealing with such requests.

Judicial efficiency on requests for prompt release and provisional measures, however, may have come at the expense of well-structured and reasoned decisions, which leaves ITLOS open to jurisprudential criticism that may deter states from using ITLOS. Well-structured and reasoned decisions based on the law to be applied[122] can be seen increasingly to add to the saliency and legitimacy of an international body such as ITLOS. It is a matter of argument whether adventurous "law reform" increases or decreases the saliency or legitimacy of an international adjudicative body, which must always be concerned with the consent of states to both use and abide by the results of an international tribunal.

It is important to keep in mind that ITLOS is a mechanism for the resolution of disputes and, thus, that the most important "litmus test" for ITLOS must be whether (1) disputes brought

---

119 *MOX Plant* case, *supra* note 6.

120 Australia has, however, pre-selected both ITLOS and the International Court of Justice. See note 35 in this article.

121 In regard to the procedure and timing for prompt release and provisional measures, see Eiriksson, *supra* note 1 at 205-13 and 223-25; and Tullio Treves, "The Rules of the International Tribunal for the Law of the Sea" in Rao and Khan, *supra* note 1 at 148-55.

122 LOS Convention, *supra* note 2, at Article 293(1), indicates that ITLOS is to apply the LOS Convention "and other rules of international law not incompatible with" the LOS Convention. Eiriksson, *supra* note 1 at 145-47. In regard to the law to be applied in a dispute arising under the 1995 Fish Stocks Agreement, see Article 30(5) of the Fish Stocks Agreement, *supra* note 21; and McDorman, *supra* note 23 at 72-73.

before it are resolved and (2) whether states see ITLOS as a useful mechanism for the resolution of disputes and do not concentrate on the jurisprudential purity or law reform acceptability of its decisions. While the second concern is always subject to debate, ITLOS has been successful in *resolving* the disputes[123] that have been brought before it. With the exclusion of the requests for provisional measures, ITLOS has been called upon to "resolve" six international fisheries disputes. It has issued six decisions on these disputes. In five of the six decisions, ITLOS has ordered action to be taken by a state — in four cases, this action has involved the release of a detained vessel and, in one case, the payment of compensation. In all five situations, the states complied with ITLOS's orders. In these cases, the dispute brought before ITLOS can be said to have been resolved. It is less clear in the *"Grand Prince"* case, where the prompt release request was not dealt with by ITLOS, whether the "dispute" between the states has been resolved.[124] The role of ITLOS in dispute resolution is not confined to the situations where it can be seen to have actually resolved a dispute. The provisional measures award of ITLOS and the decision of the Arbitral Tribunal in the *Southern Bluefin Tuna* cases have been seen to be instrumental in the resolution of the dispute reached by the three states.[125]

---

123 The question of when or if an international dispute can be said to be resolved is a complex one. The tip of this iceberg is noted in Christine Chinkin and Romana Sadurska, "The Anatomy of International Dispute Resolution" (1991) 7 Ohio State J. Dispute Resolution 39 at 77-78.

124 See the section in this article entitled ""*Grand Prince*"Case."

125 See Bill Mansfield, "Southern Bluefin Tuna—Comments," paper presented at the SEAPOL Inter-Regional Conference on Ocean Governance and Sustainable Development in East and Southeast Asian Seas: Challenges in the New Millennium held in Bangkok, March 21-23, 2001, accessible at <www.mft.govt.nz/support/legal/seapol.html>. Mansfield comments:

> [A] year and three quarters after the legal proceedings were filed the atmosphere in [Southern Bluefin Tuna] Commission meetings is constructive, considerable progress has been made on a number of important issues, the most important non party fishing state has given formal notice of its intention to become party to the Convention and a mechanism involving independent external scientists has been agreed for the development of a scientific programme that will help to resolve the uncertainties about the future prospects for the stock.
>
> Few of those who have been involved would have any doubt that the legal proceedings have played a major role in this turn around and yet the only formal outcome of those proceedings is a decision by the Arbitral Tribunal that it did not have jurisdiction to hear the merits of the case.
>
> . . .

More generally, examining the role, the importance, or the effectiveness of an international adjudicative body such as ITLOS solely by direct usage and results does not provide a full picture of its existing and potential importance in the resolution of disputes. The opportunity to use third-party dispute resolution processes helps to establish the expectation that disputes will be resolved peacefully, equitably, and, where necessary, by third-party adjudication. Moreover, the existence and acceptance of institutionalized international third-party dispute resolution can influence the manner, style, and immediacy of negotiations to resolve a dispute. The existence of ITLOS and the willingness of states to utilize ITLOS may have played an important role in the resolution of the disputes in the *Swordfish Stocks* case and the *"Chaisiri Reefer 2"* case, which were brought before ITLOS and then withdrawn. It is difficult to document whether the availability of ITLOS has played a role in states negotiating the resolution of disputes or in taking action so as to avoid recourse to ITLOS. Nevertheless, this availability must be seen as important in evaluating the importance and effectiveness of ITLOS. The six adjudicative decisions of ITLOS on matters of substance respecting international fisheries disputes are impressive when the history of such international adjudication is recalled. The five disputes that have been directly resolved are equally impressive. Less certain is the role that ITLOS has played in encouraging states to resolve disputes or avoiding disputes, although the constructive role that has been played in the *Southern Bluefin Tuna* cases and the action of states in the *Swordfish Stocks* case and the *"Chaisiri Reefer 2"* case indicate that this role may be considerable.

[A]ll three of the parties have in fact heard and responded to the message from the Tribunal. Following the Award by the Tribunal, Japan advised Australia and New Zealand that it wished to see a return to consensus and cooperation in the Commission. It proposed high level negotiations for that purpose and indicated that it did not intend to conduct a further unilateral EFP. The subsequent negotiations were held in a positive and constructive atmosphere and considerable further progress was made. In particular it was agreed that the way to resolve the disagreement about the appropriate nature and extent of experimental fishing was to engage independent external scientists to devise a scientific programme which would best contribute to reducing the uncertainties in relation to the stock.

In regard to the continuing work of the Commission for the Conservation of Southern Bluefin Tuna, *supra* note 79, see its website at <www.ccsbt.org>

Sommaire

Survol des différends internationaux relatifs aux pêcheries et du Tribunal international du droit de la mer

Bien que peu de différends liés aux pêcheries directement ait fait l'objet d'arbitrage international dans le passé, tous les dossiers devant le Tribunal international du droit de la mer, sauf un, avaient trait aux pêcheries. Cet article examine en premier lieu les différentes façons par lesquelles un différend relatif aux pêcheries peut aboutir devant ce Tribunal, puis les dossiers inscrits au rôle de ce Tribunal jusqu'ici. Cela a donné lieu à cinq décisions relatives à des demandes de prompte mainlevée, à deux décisions relatives à des demandes de mesures conservatoires, mais à une décision seulement sur le mérite de l'affaire. En somme, le Tribunal a joué un rôle utile dans le règlement de différends relatifs aux pêcheries, surtout si l'on considère l'historique du règlement international des différends en matière de pêcheries.

Summary

An Overview of International Fisheries Disputes and the International Tribunal for the Law of the Sea (ITLOS)

Although there have been few international adjudications dealing directly with fishing disputes in the past, all but one of the cases before ITLOS have been fisheries cases. This article first reviews the different ways in which a fisheries dispute can get before ITLOS and considers the disputes that have been on the docket of ITLOS so far. These have resulted in five decisions on requests for prompt release, two decisions on request for provisional measures, but only one decision on the merits of a dispute. The conclusion is that ITLOS has played a useful role in fisheries dispute settlement particularly when contrasted with the history of international dispute settlement for fisheries disputes.

The Impact of the
Human Rights Accountability Movement
on the International Law of Immunities

DARRYL ROBINSON

INTRODUCTION: COMPETING VALUES, EVOLVING PRIORITIES, AND DEVELOPING JURISPRUDENCE

International law has long recognized various types of immunities for persons performing certain functions, such as heads of state or diplomats. These immunities have been developed to enable discourse between states that may have very different legal systems and that may not entirely trust one another. The advent of the human rights movement, and the drive towards greater individual accountability for the most serious international crimes, has necessitated a certain re-thinking and evolution of these rules.

Until recently, however, the interaction of international criminal law and general immunities law was unresolved. The two bodies of law have co-existed as "two solitudes," containing seemingly contradictory principles. Human rights law has assumed that human rights accountability considerations are an absolute trump card, and immunities law has assumed that respect for immunities is an absolute trump card. As a result of the traditional hesitance of states to engage in sensitive prosecutions, concrete situations have not arisen that would bring these contradictory principles into conflict. Recently, as states have begun taking more committed action, situations have arisen necessitating a resolution of the precise

Darryl Robinson is a Legal Officer in the United Nations, Human Rights and Humanitarian Law Section of the Department of Foreign Affairs and International Trade, Canada. This article was drafted during the course of studies in the LL.M. program in International Legal Studies at New York University School of Law. The author's gratitude goes to the Hauser Global Scholar Program and to the Social Sciences and Humanities Research Council of Canada for making this research possible.

contours of these clashing principles, thereby contributing to the clarification and evolution of international law.

As a preliminary matter, it is critical to understand that there are legitimate interests underlying both the human rights principles and the immunities principles. One cannot understand the emerging jurisprudence if one neglects either side of the equation. Thus, there are two pitfalls to be avoided. First, some human rights lawyers have tended to assume that no form of immunity may ever be raised against allegations of genocide, crimes against humanity, or war crimes.[1] Advocates of the "no immunity" approach rely heavily on precedents such as the Rome Statute of the International Criminal Court (ICC Statute),[2] the decision of the House of Lords in *R. v. Bow Street Metropolitan Stipendiary Magistrate and Others,* ex parte *Pinochet Ugarte (Amnesty International and Others Intervening)* (*Pinochet* case), and the groundbreaking arrest warrant issued by Belgium against the Congolese foreign minister, Abdoulaye Yerodia.[3] Yet, every one of those precedents also *explicitly* affirms that some absolute immunities do continue to exist, even against charges of the most serious international crimes.[4] A pure "no

[1] See, for example, Amnesty International, *Universal Jurisdiction: The Duty of States to Enact and Implement Legislation,* September 2001, AI Index IOR 53/2001, at chapter 14, accessible at <http://www.web.amnesty.org/web/web.nsf/pages/legal_memorandum>.

[2] Rome Statute of the International Criminal Court, adopted July 17, 1998, reprinted in 37 I.L.M. 999 (1999) [hereinafter ICC Statute].

[3] *R. v. Bow Street Metropolitan Stipendiary Magistrate and Others,* ex parte *Pinochet Ugarte (Amnesty International and Others Intervening),* (No. 3), [1999] 2 All E.R. 97 (H.L.) [hereinafter *Pinochet* decision]. The Belgian warrant is discussed in *Case Concerning the Arrest Warrant of 11 April 2000 (Democratic Republic of the Congo v. Belgium),* Judgment, ICJ General List no. 121, February 14, 2002, accessible at <www.icj-cij.org> [hereinafter *Yerodia* decision].

[4] Article 27 of the ICC Statute, *supra* note 2, rejects immunities for persons once they are before the International Criminal Court [hereinafter ICC], yet Article 98 explicitly contemplates that some persons will not be surrendered to the ICC, because of their immunities, unless a waiver is obtained. See the discussion under the heading "ICC: Relinquishment through Treaty" later in this article. The *Pinochet* principle addresses *former* heads of state, whereas each one of the seven Law Lords painstakingly emphasized that had Pinochet been a *current* head of state, he would have received absolute immunity *ratione personae,* even against charges of torture or crimes against humanity. See the discussion under the heading "Inroads into Immunities Ratione Materiae: The *Pinochet* Principle" later in this article. The Belgian arrest warrant against the foreign minister of the Democratic Republic of Congo [hereinafter DRC] was a high-water mark in the efforts to ensure accountability, but even that warrant explicitly recognized that the foreign minister would have complete immunity if he came to Belgium for official

immunities" approach therefore fails to accurately explain the nuances of the law. Objective scholarship requires us to acknowledge and understand this jurisprudence and state practice in order to have a sound and complete account of the law. Likewise, effective human rights advocacy requires an appreciation of the competing values and interests that underpin immunities law in order to be able to address the concerns of states and to press for advancement in those areas where progress can be made.

Second, from the perspective of immunities lawyers, it is important to understand that immunities are neither timeless principles nor inherent rights and that immunities law is not a static field. Immunities are an exception to the normal state of affairs (whereby all individuals are accountable for their crimes), and they must be strictly justified by the purposes they serve. The traditional rationales for immunities must be critically examined, and, to the extent that immunities are rooted in legal fictions or weak rationales such as political expedience, they must be narrowed and refined. As the international community moves towards a system that is more and more based on the rule of law and human rights, and as states are more willing to accept risks in order to advance accountability, there will be a continual re-assessment and re-balancing of the scope of immunities.

The thesis of this article is that the developing jurisprudence and state practice present a coherent picture, whereby principles of immunity law are not eradicated but are gradually giving way to accommodate the imperative of accountability for international crimes. Important advances have already been made in two areas: (1) the denial of immunities *ratione materiae* for serious international crimes (under the *Pinochet* principle), and (2) the establishment of international criminal tribunals and courts, with powers to pierce even immunities *ratione personae*. The recent International Court of Justice (ICJ) decision in the *Case Concerning the Arrest Warrant of 11 April 2000 (Democratic Republic of the Congo v. Belgium)* (*Yerodia* case) reveals some of the limits for the accountability movement.[5] This article will suggest some further areas where additional development is possible.

---

business. See the discussion under the heading "The ICJ *Yerodia* Decision" later in this article. There is, in addition, a consistent state practice of respecting immunities *ratione personae* against national court proceedings, even for international crimes. See the discussion under the heading "National Jurisprudence and State Practice" later in this article.

[5] *Yerodia, supra* note 3.

CONTEXT: UNDERLYING PRINCIPLES AND PURPOSES

THE ASCENSION OF HUMAN RIGHTS AND ACCOUNTABILITY AS
INTERNATIONAL VALUES

The human rights movement, including the movement to establish individual accountability for those who commit the most serious
international crimes (such as genocide, crimes against humanity,
and war crimes), has had a dramatic effect on the perceptions and
priorities of states. Historically, states tended to give lip service to
the need to respond to serious atrocities, but were frequently content to abandon the objective of prosecution wherever it was feared
that such prosecution might complicate peace negotiations, jeopardize stability or reconciliation efforts, agitate relations, or bring
other inconveniences.[6] However, history has repeatedly brought
home the lesson that inaction in the face of mass atrocities also
carries significant costs. In addition, governmental perceptions of
the rule of non-interference in internal affairs have been reshaped
by the human rights movement, such that violations of certain basic
norms are now clearly of international concern.[7] Moreover, international law is increasingly focusing on the role of individuals, both
as victims and as perpetrators of crimes.

The result has been an impressive array of initiatives intended
to help uphold the most basic laws and to bring to justice those
who commit serious international crimes, such as genocide, crimes
against humanity, and war crimes. These initiatives include the
Nuremberg Charter,[8] the Tokyo Charter,[9] the Geneva Conventions,[10]

---

[6] See, for example, Diane F. Orentlicher, *Settling Accounts: The Duty to Prosecute
Human Rights Violations of a Prior Regime*, 100 Yale L.J. 2537 (1991).

[7] See, for example, UN Security Council Resolution 827 (1993) (International
Criminal Tribunal for the Former Yugoslavia), Resolution 955 (1994) (International Criminal Tribunal for Rwanda), and Resolution 1315 (2000) (Sierra
Leone Special Court), and see ICC Statute, *supra* note 2 at preamble and Articles
1 and 5.

[8] Agreement for the Prosecution and Punishment of the Major War Criminals of
the European Axis, Charter of the International Military Tribunal, August 8,
1945, 82 U.N.T.S. 279 [hereinafter Nuremberg Charter).

[9] Charter of the International Military Tribunal for the Far East, January 19, 1946
(General Orders No. 1), as amended, General Orders no. 20, April 26, 1946,
T.I.A.S. No. 1589 [hereinafter Tokyo Charter], accessible at <http://www.yale.
edu/lawweb/avalon/imtfech.htm>.

[10] 1949 Geneva Conventions, including Convention (I) for the Amelioration of
the Condition of the Wounded and Sick in Armed Forces in the Field, August
12,1949, 75 U.N.T.S. 31; Convention (II) for the Amelioration of the Condition

the Convention on the Prevention and Punishment of the Crime of Genocide (Genocide Convention),[11] the Convention against Torture and Other Cruel, Inhuman or Degrading Treatment or Punishment (Torture Convention),[12] the creation of the International Criminal Tribunal for the Former Yugoslavia (ICTY), the International Criminal Tribunal for Rwanda (ICTR), and the ICC. Accountability is taking a higher priority in state decision-making, as states are showing a greater willingness to insist that justice be done. It has also emboldened state practice, leading to more progressive national legislation and stronger efforts to apprehend violators.[13]

These developments bring the problems with immunities into sharper relief. Although immunities are highly effective at screening out frivolous prosecutions of state representatives, they may also help shield from justice individuals responsible for very serious crimes. Immunities run counter to the strongly felt and proper expectation that persons responsible for terrible crimes will be held accountable. It should be recalled that immunities are an extraordinary exception to the general rule that states have jurisdiction over all persons on their territories. Therefore, immunities and their underlying rationales should be strictly examined to ensure that any exception to the principle of accountability is granted only insofar as is necessary to serve more compelling societal and international interests.[14]

---

of Wounded, Sick and Shipwrecked Members of Armed Forces at Sea, August 12, 1949, 75 U.N.T.S. 85; Convention (III) relative to the Treatment of Prisoners of War, August 12, 1949, 75 U.N.T.S. 135; Convention (IV) relative to the Protection of Civilian Persons in Time of War, August 12, 1949, 75 U.N.T.S. 287 [hereinafter Geneva Conventions].

[11] Convention on the Prevention and Punishment of the Crime of Genocide, UN General Assembly Resolution 260(A)(III), UN GAOR, 3rd Sess., Supp. No. 1921, Dec. 9, 1948, 78 U.N.T.S. 227 [hereinafter Genocide Convention].

[12] Convention against Torture and Other Cruel, Inhuman or Degrading Treatment or Punishment, December 10, 1984, 1465 U.N.T.S. 85 [hereinafter Torture Convention].

[13] For example, this made possible precedent-setting developments such as the arrest of General Pinochet in 1998. See the discussion under the heading "Inroads into Immunities Ratione Materiae: The *Pinochet* Principle" later in this article.

[14] Since the drafting of this article, the author has had the benefit of reading some of the subsequently published commentaries reacting to the *Yerodia* decision and notes that others share the conceptual framework of seeking a proper "balancing" between accountability concerns and maintaining international relations:

TESTING THE RATIONALES FOR IMMUNITIES

Several rationales have historically underpinned the law of immunities. Some of these are based on legal fictions. For example, immunity was once fortified by a theory of "extraterritoriality," namely that a diplomat or other high official was not really on the receiving state's territory.[15] Another oft-cited basis was "personification," namely that the head of state "personifies" the state.[16] (This reasoning was also used in the past for diplomats, who were thought to literally represent their head of state and were therefore entitled to the same honours and privileges.)[17] Such bases are fictions, and exceptions to the urgent goal of accountability cannot be justified by fictions. Such reasoning may have had great weight in the days of monarchical governments, but today it is recognized that the head of state is indeed a person distinct from the state.[18]

Antonio Cassese, "When May Senior Officials Be Tried for International Crimes? Some Comments on the *Congo* v. *Belgium* Case" (2002) 13 Eur. J. Int'l L. 853; Steffen Wirth, "Immunity for Core Crimes? The ICJ's Judgment in the *Congo* v. *Belgium* Case" (2002) 13 Eur. J. Int'l L. 877; Bruce Broomhall, *International Justice and the International Criminal Court: Between Sovereignty and the Rule of Law,* Monographs in International Law, edited by I. Brownlie (Oxford: Oxford University Press, 2002); Paola Gaeta, "Official Capacity and Immunities" in Antonio Cassese et al, eds, *The Rome Statute of the International Criminal Court: A Commentary* (Oxford: Oxford University Press, 2002); and Claus Kress, "War Crimes Committed in Non-International Armed Conflict and the Emerging System of International Criminal Justice" (2000) 30 Israel Y.B.H.R. 103.

15 See earlier texts such as Montel Ogdon, *Juridical Bases of Jurisdictional Immunity* (Washington DC: John Byrne and Company, 1936) at 63-104 and Clifton Wilson, *Diplomatic Privileges and Immunities* (Tucson: University of Arizona Press, 1967) at 1-5.

16 See, for example, *Pinochet, supra* note 3 at 171 (Lord Millett): "The immunity of a serving head of state is enjoyed by reason of his special status as the holder of his state's highest office. He is regarded as the personal embodiment of the state itself. It would be an affront to the dignity and sovereignty of the state which he personifies and a denial of the equality of sovereign states to subject him to the jurisdiction of the municipal courts of another state ... he is not liable to be arrested or detained on any ground whatever."

Likewise, see Lord Phillips, *ibid.* at 185-86: "An acting head of state enjoyed by reason of his status absolute immunity from all legal process. This had its origin in the times when the head of state truly personified the state ... it would have been contrary to the dignity of a head of state that he should be subjected to judicial process and this would have been likely to interfere with the exercise of his duties as a head of state."

17 See Ogdon, *supra* note 15 at 105-65 and Wilson, *supra* note 15 at 1-5.

18 See *Tachiona* v. *Mugabe* 169 F. Supp. 259, US Dist. at 277 (October 30, 2001).

Another basis for immunities, particularly head of state immunities, was the need to respect the "dignity" of the head of state or the sending state.[19] Considerations of respect are of course understandable and appropriate in diplomatic relations, as a corollary of sovereign equality, but it is doubtful whether such considerations are a sufficient reason to override access to justice for victims of serious international crimes.[20]

All of these varying rationales have in reality been strongly buttressed by an important underlying consideration — political expediency.[21] The desire to avoid political embarrassment and ruptures in smooth bilateral relations is undoubtedly a weighty concern for any state. However, these are *political* considerations that states are well equipped to take into account when crafting extraterritorial criminal legislation or when deciding whether to initiate prosecutions. They are not a sound *legal* basis for barring *a priori* any possibility of prosecuting international crimes where a state is willing to do so.

Thus, it is suggested in this article that, of the various rationales suggested for immunities, only one is sufficient to justify immunities in the modern world — the *"functional necessity"* of immunities for the maintenance of international relations. Centuries of experience suggest that immunities facilitate international discourse in a world of states with differing legal, political, and philosophical outlooks and, thereby, do indeed serve important societal and international interests. The challenge is therefore in finding how to balance these competing values to best serve the human community.

---

[19] See *Schooner Exchange* v. *M'Fadden* 11 U.S. 116 at 137 (1812) as well as *Pinochet, supra* note 3 at 171 and 185-86.

[20] On the need to move away from a "dignity" rationale, see H. Lauterpacht, "The Problem of Jurisdictional Immunities of Foreign States" (1951) 28 B.Y.I.L. 220. See also Wirth, *supra* note 14 at 888.

[21] The rationale of political expediency is candidly discussed in US jurisprudence. See, for example, *Tachiona* v. *Mugabe* 169 F. Supp. 259, US Dist. at 290-91 (October 30, 2001), referring to "fraying sensibilities," "embarrassment," and "harm to diplomatic relations." See also Ogdon, supra note 15 at 59-60. In the first *Pinochet* hearing of the House of Lords, Lord Lloyd of Berwick was very concerned that "issues of great sensitivity have arisen between Spain and Chile" and "the UK is caught in the crossfire": *Pinochet, infra* note 97 at 934.

THE FUNCTIONAL NECESSITY OF FACILITATING
INTERNATIONAL RELATIONS

The law of diplomatic immunities has been described without exaggeration as "ancient"[22] — the concept is not merely hundreds, but indeed thousands, of years old.[23] Anthropological studies suggest that the immunity of envoys was one of the first principles to be established in inter-tribal relations.[24] This principle was regarded as a necessity for free communication and negotiation between diverse societies, and the strictest adherence was therefore expected and enforced. For example, when the Theban ambassador to Alexander was arrested and imprisoned in 366 BC, Thebes objected that the "outrage" was "an infringement of the law of nations" and declared war.[25]

Diplomatic immunity is granted not as a "perk" for privileged individuals but rather as a necessity to enable the continued functioning of diplomatic relations between states with very different legal traditions and political outlooks.[26] It prevents unscrupulous governments from harassing or imprisoning envoys on frivolous charges or for politicized reasons. This is particularly important when one considers that diplomatic communication is all the more critical in situations where relations are particularly strained.

Similarly, head of state immunity has also long been well recognized, although its precise parameters are less clear.[27] With respect

---

[22] See, for example, Vienna Convention on Diplomatic Relations, April 18, 1961, 500 U.N.T.S. 95 at preamble, paragraph 1 [hereinafter Vienna Convention].

[23] Linda S. Frey and Marsha L. Frey, *The History of Diplomatic Immunity* (Columbus: Ohio State Press, 1999); J. Craig Barker, *The Abuse of Diplomatic Privileges and Immunities: A Necessary Evil?* (Aldershot: Dartmouth, 1996) at 14-31, tracing "one of the oldest branches of international law" from prehistory and antiquity; Ogdon, supra note 15 at 8-20; and Grant V. McLanahan, *Diplomatic Immunity* (New York: St. Martin's Press, 1989) at 18-25.

[24] Barker, supra note 23 at 32; Frey and Frey, *supra* note 23 at 3; McLanahan, *supra* note 23 at 18-21.

[25] Ogdon, *supra* note 15 at 16.

[26] Vienna Convention, *supra* note 22 at preamble, paras. 2-4.

[27] Even its conceptual foundation is unclear. Some commentators treat it as a type of state immunity, which deals with the immunity of the state itself against foreign courts. (Significant inroads have been made in the context of *civil suits*, as opposed to criminal prosecutions, against foreign states in certain situations. This vast area is beyond the scope of this article.) Others consider it a type of diplomatic immunity. Neither of these analogies is entirely apt, so it seems most accurate to regard head of state immunity as a separate category. See,

to diplomatic immunity, centuries of frictions and incidents have produced ample state practice and relatively clear understandings of the contours of the law, which is now codified in the Vienna Convention on Diplomatic Relations (Vienna Convention).[28] With respect to head of state immunity, there is no codifying convention and, given the traditional reluctance of states to interfere with heads of state, scant state practice. Nonetheless, it is clear that serving heads of state are also accorded immunity *ratione personae*,[29] facilitating their ability to travel abroad to meet with other leaders and officials and to advance the conduct of foreign affairs.

Thus, the law of immunities is not simply a historical anomaly or vestige of sovereignty. It has enabled diplomats to work in antagonistic states in order to protect nationals and to negotiate to prevent or reduce conflicts.[30] Interaction between officials from states with historical antipathies and very different viewpoints has helped them to learn about each other, to resolve differences and reach understandings, and to negotiate treaties and build international institutions.

Immunities can even contribute to the advancement of human rights objectives. For example, immunities allow human rights rapporteurs to work in resentful states that might otherwise use spurious legal processes to inhibit their work.[31] Indeed, even the ICC

---

for example, Jerrold Mallory, "Resolving the Confusion over Head of State Immunity: The Defined Right of Kings" (1986) 86 Colum. L. Rev. 169; Jürgen Bröhmer, *State Immunity and the Violation of Human Rights* (The Hague: Martinus Nijhoff, 1997) at 29-32.

[28] Vienna Convention, *supra* note 22.

[29] Lewis, *State and Diplomatic Immunity*, 3rd edition (London: Lloyd's of London Press, 1999) at 125: "The sovereign's personal immunity at common law, whereby he may not be directly impleaded, is total, though he made waive it by an actual submission." See also Mallory, *supra* note 27 and see the *Pinochet* decision, *supra* note 3 at 179 (Millet): "[A] serving head of state or diplomat can still claim immunity ratione personae if charged with [torture] ... The nature of the charge is irrelevant; his immunity is personal and absolute." Likewise, see Lord Hope (at 152), holding that even in respect of "serious international crimes," "a head of state is still protected while in office by the immunity ratione personae." All of the lords confirmed the absolute nature of this immunity, even with respect to international crimes: *Ibid* at 111, 119-20, 152, 168-69, 179, and 181.

[30] See Barker, *supra* note 23 at 219-42, on the necessity of the diplomatic function and the necessity of immunities for the fulfilment of that function.

[31] As an illustration, consider the use in Malaysia of libel suits against a special rapporteur on the independence of judges and lawyers. That was a civil matter, but criminal measures could also be used to hinder important international

prosecutor will be heavily reliant on immunities to carry out on-site investigations in states that may be less than enthusiastic about the prospect.[32] More broadly, the negotiation of the current body of human rights treaties was made possible under the system of diplomatic relations.

FUNCTIONAL NECESSITY AND THE CONSISTENT REJECTION OF
ANY EXCEPTIONS TO IMMUNITIES *RATIONE PERSONAE*

It is important to distinguish between two types of immunity: immunity *ratione personae* and immunity *ratione materiae*. With respect to *former* heads of state and diplomats, functional necessity has only been considered to require immunity *ratione materiae* relating to their official acts while in office.[33] This immunity protects official *conduct*, not persons, so it only covers acts taken as part of the person's official functions carried out while in office. This immunity is intended to prevent other states from using criminal proceedings to do indirectly what they cannot do directly — to sit in judgment on the policies and actions of another sovereign. The balance achieved is that acts of state are protected from being adjudged in foreign courts through the indirect medium of a prosecution, while the official remains liable for his or her criminal activity in a private capacity.[34]

Immunity *ratione personae* (personal immunity) is accorded only to certain officials performing representative functions, such as

---

work, thus demonstrating the value of immunities in preventing such abuse. See, for example, Peter Bekker, "Difference Relating to Immunity from Legal Process of a Special Rapporteur of the Commission on Human Rights. Advisory Opinion" (1999) 93 Am.J. Int'l L. 913.

[32] See Lindsay Zelnicker, "Toward a Functional International Criminal Court: An Argument in Favor of a Strong Privileges and Immunities Agreement" (2001) 24 Fordham Int'l L. J. 988 .

[33] *Satow's Guide to Diplomatic Practice,* 5th edition (London: Longman, 1979) at 9: "A head of state who has been deposed or replaced or has abdicated or resigned ... will be entitled to continuing immunity in regard tc acts which he performed while head of state, provided that the acts were performed in his official capacity." This approach has now been developed by *Pinochet, supra* note 3. See the discussion under the heading "Inroads into Immunities Ratione Materiae: The *Pinochet* Principle" later in this article.

[34] As will be discussed later in this article, the *Pinochet* decision, *supra* note 3, highlights that immunities *ratione personae* do not prevent prosecution for international crimes, since the commission of such crimes cannot constitute state functions.

accredited diplomats, heads of state, and high government officials, and only for as long as the person is serving that representative role. It is a complete immunity of the beneficiary's person from the criminal jurisdiction of the receiving state and therefore applies irrespective of the charges alleged. This form of immunity admits no exception based on the seriousness of the allegations, since otherwise, unscrupulous governments could easily circumvent the immunity. As was stated in 1740 by Wicquefort,

if Princes had the Liberty of Proceeding against the Embassador who negotiates with them on any Account, or under any Colour whatsoever, the Person of the Embassador would never be in Safety; because those who should have a Mind to make away with Him would never want a Pretext.[35]

This principle of immunity without exceptions has been repeatedly tested and affirmed in state practice over the centuries. Although diplomats and high officials have generally complied with their undertaking to respect the laws and regulations of the receiving state,[36] there have been spectacular cases of gross criminal abuses by those enjoying immunity, which has at times severely strained the willingness of host states to respect such immunities.[37]

Such incidents have led at different times to spirited debates among royal advisers,[38] governmental review of the law of diplomatic immunities,[39] and draft legislation to create exceptions to diplomatic immunities.[40] Publicists and politicians have over the

[35] A. van Wicquefort, *The Embassador and His Functions*, 2nd edition (London, 1740) (translated into English by John Digby) at 251, quoted in Ogdon, *supra* note 15 at 128-29. Thus, the only remedy, regardless of the gravity of the offence, was to expel the offending diplomat.

[36] Codified in the Vienna Convention, *supra* note 22, Article 41(1).

[37] Over the centuries, diplomatic agents have been implicated in plots against monarchs, espionage, drug smuggling, and even crimes of violence such as murder.

[38] In 1571 and 1584, when ambassadors in England were detected in plots against the Crown, some urged that foreign ambassadors should lose their immunity for treason and high crimes. In the end, these arguments did not prevail and the diplomats were expelled. Similar practices were followed in other countries. See Ogdon, *supra* note 15 at 56-59.

[39] The murder of policewoman Yvonne Fletcher in the United Kingdom in 1984 provoked a massive outcry and a parliamentary review of diplomatic immunities. The review concluded, however, that attempts to renegotiate the Vienna Convention, *supra* note 22, would create more problems that it would solve. The United Kingdom therefore resolved to take firmer steps within the existing framework of diplomatic immunities. See Barker, *supra* note 23 at 135-52.

[40] Bills to limit immunity have been introduced several times over the decades in the US Congress, including in the late 1920s, 1930, 1941, and 1956. See Wilson,

years proposed various exceptions to diplomatic immunities for violent offences or offences against the laws of nations.[41] Yet, it is of the most profound significance for state practice that, in each case, the conclusion has been reached that the benefits of upholding the existing system of diplomatic immunities and diplomatic communication outweigh the disadvantages.[42] The consistent concern has been that to create any exception would provide the very loophole to be invoked by other governments acting in bad faith, or out of passion, or in retaliation for unpopular policies, thus erasing the efficacy of diplomatic immunity and the prospect for diplomatic communications in tense situations. For example, the United States State Department, responding to an unsuccessful Congressional initiative to create exceptions to diplomatic immunity, concluded: "We believe complete immunity from criminal jurisdiction assured to diplomats is fundamental to diplomatic relations. Diplomats could not perform their duties ... if they could be harassed by the receiving State bringing false charges."[43] Similarly, a UK review exploring the possibility of exceptions to diplomatic immunity concluded: "There would in any case be a risk that a restriction on immunity could in certain countries be exploited for political or retaliatory purposes against British diplomats and communities overseas."[44]

Judicial decisions have also confirmed that there is no exception to immunity from criminal jurisdiction, even for violations of the law of nations.[45] The absolute approach is now entrenched in the

---

supra note 15 at 37-38. In 1987, Jesse Helms introduced a bill to remove diplomatic immunity for crimes of violence, drug trafficking, and drunk driving. This bill was rejected as it would violate the Vienna Convention and put US diplomats at risk. McClanahan, *supra* note 23 at 167-71.

[41] Sir Edward Coke proposed that an ambassador should lose immunity for any crime *contra jus gentium,* "such as Treason, Felony, Adultery or any other crime which is against the Law of Nations," a suggestion that was not picked up in state pratice. Ogdon, *supra* note 15 at 44.

[42] See the examples in notes 38-40 in this article. Barker, *supra* note 23, after extensively reviewing state practice, concludes that, despite all of the problems immunities create, the benefits in terms of preserving the diplomatic function in volatile situations outweigh the disadvantages and that immunities are therefore a "necessary evil" (at 243-46).

[43] Ambassador Roosevelt, providing the executive branch's response to proposed US legislation to limit the immunities of foreign diplomats, quoted in Barker, *supra* note 23 at 232.

[44] *Ibid.* at 148.

[45] See, for example, the Canadian case, *Rose* v. *The King* (1946), [1947] 3 D.L.R. 618. This case allowed certain incursions into normal privileges for diplomatic

Vienna Convention, in which, after careful discussion, states established certain narrow exceptions to diplomatic immunity for civil and administrative jurisdiction but left intact complete immunity from criminal jurisdiction.[46] States have therefore restricted themselves to the established options of requesting waiver of immunity from the sending state[47] or declaring the diplomat *persona non grata* and expelling him or her back to the sending state.[48] Where a diplomat commits crimes in a private capacity, prosecution has also been recognized as an option in the event that the former diplomat subsequently returns to the territory of the host state.[49]

CONFLICTING VALUES AND THE RESPONSIBILITY PARADOX

States have denied exceptions to immunities *ratione personae* because of the concern that unscrupulous governments could abuse any exceptions created, thereby destroying the utility of immunities. At the same time, most states would agree in principle that a person responsible for serious international crimes should not be able to escape justice. These conflicting imperatives present a "responsibility paradox"; namely, even if states were willing to agree in principle that immunities *ratione personae* should not protect a person responsible for committing serious international crimes, they do not grant each other the right to make that unilateral determination. The

---

documents in extreme cases where diplomats imperilled the security of the host state (the judges therefore admitted as evidence documents that had fallen into Canada's possession). However, the foreign diplomat himself can under no circumstance be summoned before the criminal jurisdiction of the receiving state: "If the diplomat violates the law of nations, it does not follow that the other State has the right to do likewise" (at 645).

[46] Vienna Convention, *supra* note 22, Article 31(1). See Eileen Denza, *Diplomatic Law: A Commentary on the Vienna Convention on Diplomatic Relations* (New York: Oceana Publications, 1976) at 149 and 174-75.

[47] Vienna Convention, *supra* note 22, Article 32.

[48] *Ibid.*, Article 9.

[49] Barker, *supra* note 23 at 159, discusses a 1984 US policy affirming that former diplomats returning to the US could be tried for crimes in the United States unless they related to official functions: This position dovetails well with the *Pinochet* decision, *supra* note 3. There are a few other options to control abuse. Receiving states are entitled to refuse *agrément*, that is, to refuse to accept a particular individual proposed as a head of mission to the state. States can also encourage or pressure the sending state to prosecute. See the additional suggestions under the heading "Future Avenues for Development" later in this article.

challenge for human rights lawyers is how best to advance the cause of accountability, given this backdrop.

SEEDS OF CHANGE: THE SIGNIFICANCE OF THE NUREMBERG PRECEDENT

The establishment of the Nuremburg Tribunal following the Second World War was a seminal moment for the enforcement of international criminal law. In addition to establishing key precepts, the Nuremberg trials made concrete the conviction that, in order to uphold the most basic norms of humanity, individual violators must be held accountable.[50] Following the unconditional surrender by Germany, sovereign decision-making rested with the Allies, and thus immunities against "foreign" jurisdictions, or waiver thereof, were not in issue.[51] Article 7 of the Nuremberg Charter provided that "[t]he official position of defendants, whether as Heads of State or responsible officials in Government Departments, shall not be considered as freeing them from responsibility or mitigating punishment." The Tokyo International Military Tribunal, which was founded on the same basis,[52] contained a similar but somewhat attenuated provision.[53] Although it is often assumed that no heads of

---

50 "Crimes against international law are committed by men, not by abstract entities, and only by punishing individuals who commit such crimes can the provisions of international law be enforced." Judgment of the International Military Tribunal for the Trial of German Major War Criminals, Nuremberg Trial Proceedings, vol. 22, at 466.

51 Instrument of Surrender, May 8, 1945, 59 Stat. 1957, Executive Agreement Series 502, accessible at <http://www.yale.edu/lawweb/avalon/wwii/gs11.htm>. The Allies accordingly exercised sovereign functions within Germany, including making provision for the trial of all war criminals. See Declaration Regarding the Defeat of Germany and the Assumption of Supreme Authority by Allied Powers, June 5, 1945, esp. Articles 11 and 13, accessible at <http://www.yale.edu/lawweb/avalon/wwii/gero1.htm>.

52 Instrument of Surrender, September 2, 1945, accessible at <http://www.yale.edu/lawweb/avalon/wwii/j4.htm>.

53 Article 6 of the Tokyo Charter, *supra* note 9, did not refer directly to the head of state, since a special agreement had been reached not to prosecute Emperor Hirohito. Article 6 therefore simply provided: "Neither the official position, at any time, of an accused, nor the fact that an accused acted pursuant to order of his government or of a superior shall, of itself, be sufficient to free such accused from responsibility for any crime with which he is charged, but such circumstances may be considered in mitigation of punishment if the Tribunal determines that justice so requires."

state were prosecuted by these tribunals,[54] in fact, Admiral Dönitz, one of the Nuremberg defendants, had become head of state following the death of Adolf Hitler and, therefore, was the first former head of state to be convicted by an international tribunal.

The Nuremberg precedent affected the development of the law of immunities in at least two ways.[55] First, it entrenched the notion that there are serious international crimes for which special international rules apply. A key aspect is the conclusion that

[h]e who violates the laws of war cannot obtain immunity while acting in pursuance of the authority of the State, if the State in authorizing action moves outside its competence under international law.[56]

This sensible proposition provides an excellent basis for reconsidering immunities *ratione materiae*. Given that it is outside the state's competence to authorize an international crime, it is hard to see how such conduct can be authorized as an "official act" and thereby free from scrutiny. As will be discussed later in this article, this seed planted at Nuremberg was subsequently cultivated in the *Pinochet* decision of the House of Lords. However, this reasoning does not pertain to immunities *rationae personae*, since they are not at all based on purported state authorization of any particular *conduct*, but rather are based on the distinct objective of denying any pretext for interfering with envoys and thereby protecting international discourse.[57] Second, Nuremberg established an important

---

[54] See, for example, Mary Margaret Penrose, "It's Good to Be the King!: Prosecuting Heads of State and Former Heads of State under International Law" (2000) 39 Colum. J. Transnat'l L. 193 at 194-95.

[55] Some have interpreted Article 7 as meaning that those responsible for genocide, crimes against humanity, and war crimes can never benefit from immunities of any kind: See *ibid.;* Andrea Bianchi, "Immunity versus Human Rights: The *Pinochet* Case" (1999) 10 Eur. J. Int'l L. 237; and Amnesty International, *supra* note 1. This interpretation is simple and clear, as it does not require any cumbersome distinctions between immunities *ratione materiae* and immunities *ratione personae*, nor between national courts and international courts. It is also morally attractive because it seems to sweep away all obstacles to the prosecution of war criminals. However, such an interpretation is profoundly and increasingly contradicted by the applicable jurisprudence and state practice, which consistently continues to uphold certain immunities *ratione personae* regardless of the nature of the allegation. Therefore, a more sophisticated theory is necessary to take into account this jurisprudence and state practice.

[56] *Judgment of the International Military Tribunal for the Trial of German Major War Criminals* (London: His Majesty's Stationery Office, 1946) at 42.

[57] This is sensitively addressed in *The Princeton Principles on Universal Jurisdiction,* Program in Law and Public Affairs, 2001, accessible at <www.princeton.edu>,

precedent for the creation of international criminal tribunals, paving the way for the creation of the ICTY, the ICTR, and the ICC. It also established a precedent for enabling such tribunals to pierce even immunities *ratione personae.*

RELINQUISHMENT OF IMMUNITIES TO INTERNATIONAL TRIBUNALS AND COURTS

All immunities, even immunities *ratione personae,* may be waived or otherwise relinquished through the consent of a state. Even in a world where states are reluctant to authorize each other to pierce immunities, states have under various circumstances accorded such powers to international tribunals.

TRIBUNALS: RELINQUISHMENT THROUGH SECURITY COUNCIL ENFORCEMENT ACTION

The creation of the ICTY and the ICTR by the Security Council was a major step forward in the accountability movement. The power to create international tribunals is not explicitly stated in the Charter of the United Nations (UN Charter),[58] but the Security Council is given a very broad discretion under Articles 41 and 42 of the UN Charter to determine what measures are appropriate to maintain or restore international peace and security. Article 41 provides that "[t]he Security Council may decide what measures not involving the use of armed force are to be employed to give

which is the product of a working group of scholars on the principles of universal jurisdiction. Principle 5 endorses the rule that official position does not relieve a person of criminal responsibility. The commentary notes that "[t]here is an extremely important distinction between 'substantive' [*rationae materiae*] and 'procedural' [*rationae personae*] immunity"(at 48). The commentary says that the rejection of *substantive immunity*, covering conduct committed in an official capacity, "keeps faith with the Nuremberg Charter." "Nevertheless, in proceedings before national tribunals, *procedural immunity* remains in effect during a head of state's or other official's tenure in office, or during the period in which a diplomat is accredited to a host state" (at 49). Diplomats and other officials enjoy an "unqualified *ex officio* immunity" while they perform a particular role, but they are subject to prosecution once they step down. The Princeton Principles wisely take an agnostic position with respect to the *future* development of immunities *rationae personae*, suggesting that such immunities "may be in the process of erosion" and leaving open the possibility of further developments in this area.

58 Charter of the United Nations, June 26, 1945, Can. T.S. 1955 No. 7 [hereinafter UN Charter].

effect to its decisions, and it may call upon the Members of the United Nations to apply such measures." All UN member states are obligated to carry out such decisions.[59] The power of the Security Council to create international criminal tribunals is not completely free from controversy, but it has been judicially upheld and is now generally accepted.[60]

In creating the ICTY and the ICTR, the Security Council incorporated the Nuremberg provision that the official position of a defendant does not relieve the person of criminal responsibility before the Tribunals,[61] and it also ordered all states to comply with requests from the Tribunals, including requests for surrender. No exception was created for requests relating to persons otherwise enjoying immunities *ratione personae*. A state's obligation to the Security Council is paramount over all other obligations.[62] Thus, a UN member state receiving a request for the surrender of a person is obliged to comply with that request, even if the person is otherwise the beneficiary of immunities *ratione personae*, since the Security Council obligation is paramount over other obligations, including the obligation to respect immunities. By the same token, the state otherwise holding the immunities *ratione personae* is estopped from raising those immunities as a shield, by virtue of its obligations under the UN Charter (or any other treaties pledging full cooperation with the Tribunals).[63]

---

[59] *Ibid.*, Article 25.

[60] See, for example, *Prosecutor v. Tadic, Decision on the Defence Motion for Interlocutory Appeal on Jurisdiction,* Case no. IT-94-1-AR72, International Criminal Tribunal on the Former Yugoslavia [hereinafter ICTY] Appeals Chamber, October 2, 1995, relying, *inter alia,* on the principles laid down by the ICJ in *Effect of Awards of Compensation Made by the United Nations Administrative Tribunal (1953-1954),* [1954] I.C.J. Rep. at 47 (power to create tribunals). This conclusion has recently been confirmed in *Prosecutor v. Milosevic, Decision on Preliminary Motions,* November 8, 2001, Trial Chamber, Doc. IT-02-54.

[61] ICTY Statute, annex to SC Resolution 827 (1993), reprinted 32 I.L.M. 1192 (1993), Article 7(2); International Criminal Tribunal for Rwanda [hereinafter ICTR] Statute, annex to SC Resolution 955 (1994), reprinted 33 I.L.M. 1604 (1994), Article 6(2).

[62] UN Charter, *supra* note 58, Articles 25, 41, 49, and 103. See especially Article 103: "In the event of a conflict between the obligations of the Members of the United Nations under the present Charter and their obligations under any other international agreement, their obligations under the present Charter shall prevail."

[63] *Ibid.*, Articles 25, 41, 49, and 103. The situation is less clear with respect to diplomats or officials of a state not party to the UN Charter, although an argument

The Tribunals have already taken groundbreaking steps in bringing to justice the highest governmental officials. On September 4, 1998, the ICTR convicted and sentenced a former head of government, Prime Minister Jean Kambanda, to life imprisonment for genocide and crimes against humanity.[64] On May 24, 1999, Chief Prosecutor Louise Arbour established an important historic precedent by issuing the first indictment against a serving head of state, Slobodan Milosevic.[65] As discussed earlier in this article, the Tribunal's power to do so was already established by virtue of the UN Charter, but the reaction of states is nevertheless instructive. Most states welcomed the indictment, and, even among those who were critical, the criticisms focused on political arguments and not on the legality of proceeding against a current head of state.[66] The indictment, apprehension, and prosecution of Milosevic serves as a decisive precedent on the jurisdiction of a Security Council tribunal over current heads of state and other officials.

ICC: RELINQUISHMENT THROUGH TREATY

Although the establishment of ad hoc tribunals by the Security Council was an important step in the advancement of accountability, most of the international community has agreed that a more permanent and predictable approach is necessary.[67] Accordingly, the ICC Statute was adopted in Rome on July 17, 1998 and entered into force on July 1, 2002, after obtaining the necessary sixty

---

can be made based on Article 2(6) of the UN Charter and Article 4 of Security Council Resolution 827, *supra* note 7, requiring that "all States shall cooperate fully with the International Tribunal ... including the obligation of States to comply with requests for assistance or orders issued by a Trial Chamber under Article 29 of the Statute." In any event, immunities may also be relinquished through a treaty in which the state pledges to cooperate with the ICTY. See, for example, the Dayton Peace Accords, November 21, 1995, reprinted 35 I.L.M. 75 (1996), Article IX, accessible at <http://www.yale.edu/lawweb/avalon/intdip/bosnia/day01.htm>, where parties pledge to cooperate fully with the ICTY.

64 *Prosecutor* v. *Kambanda, Judgement and Sentence,* Case no. ICTR 97-23-S, September 4, 1998, accessible at <www.ictr.org>.

65 *Prosecutor* v. *Milosevic, Indictment,* Case no. IT-02-54, May 24, 1999, accessible at <http://www.un.org/icty/indictment/english/mil-ii990524e.htm>.

66 "Milosevic Indictment Threatens Peace Plan," *Toronto Star,* May 28, 1999; "Indictment Was Poorly Timed," *Montreal Gazette,* May 28, 1998.

67 The ICC Statute, *supra* note 2, has been signed by 139 states.

ratifications in only four years.[68] The ICC offers a significant solution to the "responsibility paradox" (the paradox that states agree in principle that there should be no impunity for certain crimes but are not prepared to authorize each other to set aside immunities *ratione personae.*) Although states may be hesitant to allow one "prince" to sit in judgment of another "prince," a great many states have been willing to create an impartial international court with jurisdiction limited to the most serious international crimes,[69] to invest it with multiple safeguards to prevent frivolous or political misuse,[70] and then to consent to allow it to pierce even immunities *ratione personae.* As more and more states ratify the ICC Statute, this accountability gap, created by immunities *ratione personae,* can gradually be reduced. ICC states parties are obliged to cooperate with the ICC and cannot raise substantive or procedural immunities as a bar to ICC jurisdiction over their officials.[71] Thus, many states whose laws contemplated immunities for certain officials have had to modify domestic legislation and even to amend their constitutions in order to ratify the ICC Statute.[72] This process of changing national laws in so many countries has already had a profound impact in raising awareness of issues of impunity and the need for accountability.[73]

The ICC Statute deals with immunities in Article 27 and Article 98. Article 27(1) affirms that the "official capacity as a Head of

[68] By July 1, 2003, one year after the statute's entry into force, the number of ratifications had already reached eighty-nine, demonstrating the considerable momentum behind the court. See <www.icc.gc.ca> for updates on the number of ratifications. Of course, some significant countries remain unconvinced — see, for example,"US Notification of Intent not to become a Party to the Rome Statute" (2002) 96 Am. J. Int'l L. 724 — but the global trend is otherwise an encouraging one.

[69] ICC Statute, *supra* note 2, Articles 5-9.

[70] The safeguards in the ICC Statute are too numerous to list, but examples include Articles 15-19, 22-24, 36, 40-47, 53-55, 57, 63-67, 72-73, 81-82, and 112.

[71] ICC Statute, *supra* note 2, Article 86 (obligation to cooperate), Article 89 (surrender of persons to the Court), and Article 120 (no reservations).

[72] See, for example, Claus Kress and Flavia Lattanzi, eds., *The Rome Statute and Domestic Legal Orders,* volume 1 (Baden Baden: Il Sirente, 2000).

[73] See, for example, Darryl Robinson, "The Rome Statute and Its Impact on National Laws" in Antonio Cassese *et al.*, eds., *The Rome Statute of the International Criminal Court — A Commentary* (Oxford: Oxford University Press, 2002); and see the study for the French Senate, *La Responsabilité Pénale des Chefs d'État et de Gouvernement,* September 2001, accessible at <http://www.igc.org/icc/html/French_Study.pdf>.

State or Government, a member of a Government or a parliament, an elected representative or a government official shall in no case exempt a person from criminal responsibility under this Statute." Article 27(2) specifies that "[i]mmunities or special procedural rules which may attach to the official capacity of a person ... shall not bar the Court from exercising its jurisdiction."[74] To understand the ICC Statute approach, however, Article 27(2) must be read in conjunction with Article 98(1), which provides that the ICC will not proceed with requests for surrender

which would require the requested State to act inconsistently with its obligations under international law with respect to the State or diplomatic immunity of a person or property of a third State, unless the Court can first obtain the cooperation of that third State for the waiver of the immunity.[75]

At first sight, these provisions may seem contradictory; with Article 27 denying immunities and Article 98 acknowledging immunities. However, Article 27 deals with the situation of a person once he or she has been brought before the Court. Article 98 deals with a separate, preliminary situation where a state might be requested to surrender a person to the court but that person is protected by immunities owed to a third state. Article 98 prevents a state from being placed in an impossible situation of conflict between, for example, its obligation to comply with surrender requests from the ICC and its obligation under the Vienna Convention to respect the immunities *ratione personae* of a serving diplomat of a state not party to the ICC Statute.

This does not mean that persons enjoying immunities will never arrive before the Court. First, with respect to a state's own nationals, Article 98 does not apply because it deals with conflicting obligations to a third state. Thus, state parties remain obliged to surrender their citizens (where they fail to investigate or prosecute the crime themselves).[76]

---

[74] Article 27(1) of the ICC Statute, *supra* note 2, contains the familiar principle that "official capacity as a Head of State or Government, a member of a Government or parliament, an elected representative or a government official shall in no case exempt a person from criminal responsibility under this Statute."

[75] Similarly, Article 98(2) of the ICC Statute respects obligations under international agreements pursuant to which the consent of a sending state is required to surrender a person of that State to the Court. This refers to status of forces agreements.

[76] ICC Statute, *supra* note 2, Article 17 and Article 86.

Second, where a state party is requested to surrender a national of another state party, immunities will not be an obstacle to surrender. There was a useful interpretive debate among states whether it would first be necessary to obtain the waiver of the sending state in accordance with Article 98. It was agreed that, if such a waiver were required, the sending state would in any event be obliged, as a state party, to grant that waiver as part of its duty of cooperation with the Court.[77] In any event, the prevailing interpretation was that seeking a waiver from a state party would not be necessary because, by ratifying the ICC Statute, the sending state has already relinquished any immunities *vis-à-vis* the ICC requests.[78]

Third, even with respect to officials of non-party states,[79] it must be recalled that Article 98 only inhibits surrender where there is an immunity that the requested state must respect "under international law." Thus, those individuals who only enjoy immunities *ratione materiae,* such as former heads of state and diplomats, are not immune from surrender, since serious international crimes fall outside the scope of such immunity.[80] In addition, even non-party states will lose their ability to raise immunities if the Security Council refers a matter pursuant to Chapter VII of the UN Charter, since such a referral binds all UN member states and is a paramount obligation.[81] Thus, the only scope for Article 98 is with respect to a serving official of a non-party state who holds immunities *ratione personae,* in the absence of a Security Council referral. In such a case, the state in question has not relinquished its immunities *ratione*

---

[77] *Ibid.,* Articles 27 and 86.

[78] This interpretation was confirmed in an informal document circulated by interested states after extensive discussions at the ICC Preparatory Commission ("Informal Paper by Canada and the United Kingdom" [on file with author]). There were two distinct routes by which delegations reached this conclusion. Some delegations reached this conclusion by interpreting "third state" as referring only to non-party states. Others reached this conclusion on the grounds that ICC states parties have already relinquished any immunities against ICC proceedings by virtue of ratifying Article 27 and Article 88 and thus do not possess immunities "under international law" *vis-à-vis* the ICC. See Gaeta, *supra* note 14 at 992-95; Broomhall, *supra* note 14 at 128-50; and Kress, supra note 14 at 159-61.

[79] For further discussion, see Steffen Wirth, "Immunities, Related Problems and Article 98 of the Rome Statute" (2001) 12 Crim. L. Forum 429.

[80] For more information, see the *Pinochet* decision, *supra* note 3, which is discussed later in this article.

[81] UN Charter, *supra* note 58, Articles 25, 41, and 103.

personae, and the official will retain his or her immunities until he or she leaves office.[82]

In conclusion, although the ICC Statute does not go so far as to purport to abolish immunities *ratione personae* of non-state parties, it does substantially narrow the problem created by such immunities.

INROADS INTO IMMUNITIES *RATIONE MATERIAE:* THE *PINOCHET* PRINCIPLE

National courts are in a different position from international courts because other states have not given any special consent to have their immunities set aside. Nor are national courts in the hierarchical position that would result from a Security Council referral. Thus, any authority to set aside immunities must be found in general international law.

The landmark 1999 decision of the House of Lords in the *Pinochet* case[83] was a profoundly important step in injecting important modern principles of accountability for serious international crimes into the traditionally conservative law of immunities. The *Pinochet* case defies easy summarization, because each judge delivered a separate opinion, but the basic reasoning is as follows. Each judge accepted that, whereas current heads of state are entitled to absolute immunity *ratione personae*, former heads of state are entitled only to immunity *ratione materiae* with respect to acts performed as part of their official functions while in office.[84] The centrally important principle, recognized by six of the seven judges, was that the commission of certain serious international crimes is condemned by all states as illegal and therefore cannot constitute an "official function."[85] Thus, immunities *ratione materiae* are not an obstacle to prosecution for serious international crimes. The exact contours of the rule are unclear, as some judges focused only on the crime of torture under the Torture Convention,[86] but the principle recognized in the *Pinochet* case would logically apply equally to all serious international crimes — including genocide, crimes against

---

[82] In such a case, the options are to seek a waiver, seek a Security Council referral, or wait for the person's term in office to come to completion.

[83] *Pinochet, supra* note 3.

[84] *Ibid.* at 152 and 186-87.

[85] *Ibid.* at 113 and 177-78.

[86] *Ibid.* at 113 and 168; Torture Convention, *supra* note 12.

humanity, and war crimes — since none of these crimes may be authorized by a state.[87]

It is important to situate this decision in context in order to understand what a significant step it represented. In the first hearing of the immunity issue, before the Court of Queen's Bench, three judges unanimously upheld Senator Pinochet's claims of immunity.[88] These judges applied the classically conservative and deferential approach to the law of immunities. They agreed with the proposition that "after a head of state ceases to be such, he ceases to enjoy any immunity in respect of personal or private acts but continues to enjoy immunity in respect of public acts performed by him as head of state."[89] However, these judges emphasized that Pinochet "is charged not with personally torturing or murdering victims or causing their disappearance, but with using the power of the state of which he was head to that end."[90] Given that the acts alleged were carried out solely through the apparatus of the state, the judges concluded that they could hardly be described as "private" acts and therefore had to be official acts. The judges rejected the argument that serious international crimes could not be functions of a head of state.[91] They noted that immunity from criminal jurisdiction clearly included criminal acts, as otherwise such

---

[87] The *Pinochet* rationale, *supra* note 3, adopted does not depend on "waiver" by treaty; instead it stipulates that acts condemned and prohibited as international crimes cannot at the same time be "official functions." So the rationale should apply equally to customary international law prohibitions.

Several judges said that a single act of torture would not suffice and that the crime would have to constitute a crime against humanity, that is, "widespread or systematic torture as an instrument of state policy" (see Lord Hope at 144 and 150-51). On the other hand, Lord Hutton felt that a single act of torture would suffice (at 166). One possible way to reconcile this is to suggest that for states parties to the Torture Convention, a single act of torture suffices because the state has accepted the convention definition. In addition, the principle applies to serious international crimes, namely, genocide, crimes against humanity, and war crimes. This conclusion is consistent with the conclusion reached by Cassese, *supra* note 14 at 864-65 and Kress, *supra* note 14 at 158-59.

[88] *Pinochet, supra* note 3. For pinpoint cites, reference will also be made to the page numbers in Reed Brody and Michael Ratner, eds., *The Pinochet Papers: the Case of Augusto Pinochet in Spain and Britain* (The Hague: Kluwer, 2000), which also reproduces the decision.

[89] *Pinochet, supra* note 3 at para. 56; Brody and Ratner, *supra* note 89 at 83.

[90] *Pinochet, supra* note 3 at para. 58; Brody and Ratner, *supra* note 89 at 84.

[91] *Pinochet, supra* note 3 at para. 63-65; Brody and Ratner, *supra* note 89 at 85-86.

immunity would be entirely pointless.[92] They found that an argument restricted to serious international crimes "has some attraction," but rejected the argument because it was unclear "where does one draw the line."[93] The Nuremberg Charter, the ICTY Statute,[94] and the ICTR Statute[95] were distinguished on the grounds that "these were international tribunals, established by international agreement. They did not therefore violate the principle that one sovereign state will not implead another in relation to its sovereign acts."[96]

At the first House of Lords hearing, following the intervention of *amici curiae* (including Amnesty International and others) and a more detailed review of developments in international human rights law and international criminal law, three out of five judges were persuaded that former head of state immunity did not include such serious international crimes.[97] By the time of the second House of Lords hearing on the merits of the case,[98] six out of seven judges were persuaded.

This outcome clearly reflects the impact of the human rights movement and the recognition of the need for accountability for serious international crimes. As was noted by Lord Phillips, "[h]ad the events with which this appeal is concerned occurred in the 19th century, there could have been no question of Senator Pinochet being subjected to criminal proceedings in this country in respect of acts, however heinous, committed in Chile."[99] The judges emphasized the role of individual criminal accountability in international law and developments such as the Genocide Convention, the Torture Convention, the Nuremberg Charter, the ICTY and ICTR Statutes, and the ICC Statute, such that "since the end of the second

---

[92] *Pinochet, supra* note 3 at para. 63; Brody and Ratner, *supra* note 89 at 86.

[93] *Pinochet, supra* note 3 at para. 68; Brody and Ratner, *supra* note 89 at 86.

[94] ICTY Statute, *supra* note 61.

[95] ICTR Statute, *supra* note 61.

[96] *Pinochet, supra* note 3 at para. 68; Brody and Ratner, *supra* note 89 at 87.

[97] *R. v. Bow Street Metropolitan Stipendiary Magistrate and Others, ex parte Pinochet Ugarte (Amnesty International and Others Intervening)*, (No. 1) [1998] 4 All E.R. 897 (H.L.).

[98] A re-hearing was necessitated by the perceived conflict of interest of one of the judges in the first hearing: *R. v. Bow Street Metropolitan Stipendiary Magistrate and Others, ex parte Pinochet Ugarte (Amnesty International and Others Intervening)*, (No. 2), [1999] 1 All E.R. 577 (H.L.).

[99] *Pinochet, supra* note 3 at 183.

world war there has been a clear recognition by the international community that certain crimes are so grave and so inhuman that they constitute crimes against international law and that the international community is under a duty to bring to justice persons who commit such crimes."[100]

Indeed, the very events leading to the *Pinochet* decision in the first place — the fact that Spain adopted universal jurisdiction legislation, that an indictment was made against such a prominent figure, that the United Kingdom proceeded with extradition proceedings against the former head of state of an ally — all were made possible by the dramatic movement towards individual accountability and the willingness of states to give greater priority to human rights considerations and to take greater risks in insisting that justice be done.[101] The reasoning adopted in the *Pinochet* case appears sound in law and principle, as it would indeed seem entirely contradictory to assert that the commission of a serious international crime, condemned by all states as an unacceptable breach of international law for which the individuals responsible must be punished, can at the same time constitute an "official function" of any state official. The conclusion is also sound in terms of the balancing of the imperative of accountability with the functional necessity rationale of immunities. Where an individual possesses only immunities *ratione materiae*, international law already reflects the calculation of states that such an individual is no longer playing a role that necessitates absolute immunity. Thus, the concern about frivolous prosecutions, while still real, is less pressing, since exposure to national criminal jurisdiction is already contemplated with respect to private acts. In such a context, there is no basis to insist that immunity against charges of genocide, crimes against humanity, or war crimes is somehow necessary. The reasoning of the *Pinochet* case would presumably apply to former heads to state, former diplomats, and any other officials possessing only immunity *ratione materiae*.[102] It would also apply to national or international proceedings.

---

[100] *Ibid.* at 163 (Lord Hutton).

[101] Michael Byers, "The Law and Politics of the Pinochet Case" (2000) 10 Duke J. Comp & Int'l L. 415 .

[102] See, for example, Vienna Convention, *supra* note 22, Article 37(3), giving members of the service staff of a diplomatic mission immunities only "in respect of acts performed in the course of their duties."

A Bridge Too Far: National Courts and
Immunities *Ratione Personae*

NATIONAL JURISPRUDENCE AND STATE PRACTICE

As discussed earlier, many authorities have reiterated that states
are not empowered under international law to set aside each other's
immunities *ratione personae* because the very purpose of such immunities is to offer a complete protection against national criminal
jurisdiction.[103] To create an exception would be to create a possibility of abuse and thereby defeat the purpose of the immunity.[104]
Recent cases have consistently upheld this principle even with
respect to international crimes. In *Pinochet,* each of the judges
emphasized that had Pinochet been a serving head of state, the outcome would have been different — "a head of state is still protected
while in office by the immunity *ratione personae*" even in respect of
"serious international crimes."[105] Thus, "a serving head of state or
diplomat can still claim immunity *ratione personae* if charged with
[torture] ... The nature of the charge is irrelevant; his immunity is
personal and absolute."[106] Likewise, in March 2001, the French
Cour de cassation held in the *Qaddafi* case that a serving head of
state is immune from prosecution in national courts, even in relation to serious acts of terrorism.[107] The Spanish Audienco Nacional
reached the same conclusion with respect to Fidel Castro, holding
that he could not be tried even for international crimes, as he was
a serving head of state enjoying immunities under public international law.[108] A United States court reached the same conclusion in

---

[103] See the second section in this article under the heading "Functional Necessity
and the Consistent Rejection of any Exceptions to Immunities *Ratione Personae.*"

[104] See Wicquefort, *supra* note 35.

[105] *Pinochet, supra* note 3 at 152 (Lord Hope).

[106] *Ibid.* at 179 (Lord Millett).

[107] *Cour de cassation — Chambre criminelle, Arrêt no. 1414 du 13 mars 2001,* accessible
at <http://courdecassation.fr/agenda/arrets/arrets/00-87215.htm>, holding
that "la coutume internationale s'oppose à ce que les chefs d'Etat en exercice
puissent, en l'absence de dispositions internationales contraires s'imposant
aux parties concernées, faire l'objet de poursuites devant les juridictions
pénales d'un Etat étranger" (author's informal translation: "international custom forbids, in the absence of a contrary international provision binding on
the parties concerned, that a serving head of state be subjected to prosecution
before the criminal jurisdiction of a foreign state").

[108] Order of March 4, 1999 (Doc. 1999/2723). See "Spain Rules It Has No Jurisdiction to Try Castro," *Agence-France Presse,* March 8, 1999, Doc. 1999 WL 2560095.

October 2001 in *Tachiona* v. *Mugabe*, where it was affirmed that the Torture Victim Protection Act did not override either traditional diplomatic immunities or the comparable immunity given to visiting heads of states.[109] The practice of executive branches of governments consistently adheres to this approach as well. France and Denmark were each recently urged by non-governmental organizations to prosecute serving foreign diplomats on their territory who were alleged to have committed international crimes. After examining the situation, both countries refused, on the grounds that diplomatic immunity prevents national prosecutions, regardless of the charge.[110] The legislative practice of several states also affirms this approach. For example, many states implementing the ICC Statute have set aside immunities in relation to ICC surrender proceedings but have declined to set aside immunities of foreign diplomats and heads of state in relation to national prosecutions, on the grounds that their international legal obligations do not permit them to pierce such immunities.[111] The most recent and most significant pronouncement

---

[109]   *Tachiona* v. *Mugabe*, 169 F. Supp. 259, US Dist. at 297, October 30, 2001. This case was about civil liability rather than criminal responsibility, but it canvassed various aspects of head of state and diplomatic immunity, including the complete immunity from criminal jurisdiction.

[110]   Amnesty International press release, "Amnesty International Calls on Denmark to Fulfill Its Obligations under the UN Convention against Torture," August 14, 2001, accessible at <www.web.amnesty.org> and Howard Knowles, "Amnesty Demands Gillon Investigation," *Copenhagen Post*, August 8, 2001, accessible at <http://cphpost.periskop.dk/>. Amnesty International argued that the Vienna Convention did not immunize Ambassador Carmi Gillion (of Israel) from torture charges; but the Danish government concluded that diplomatic immunity prevented prosecution. See also "Lawyer Regrets French Decision on Burkina President's Immunity from Prosecution," October 13, 2001, transcript from the British Broadcasting Corporation [on file with author], reporting on the Paris prosecution office's rejection of torture charges against the serving president of the Burkina Faso president, on the grounds that such proceedings would violate international law.

[111]   See, for example, Canada's *Crimes against Humanity and War Crimes Act*, R.S.C. 2000, c. 24, s. 48, accessible at <http://www.parl.gc.ca/36/2/parlbus/chambus/house/bills/government/C-19/C-19_4/C-19_cover-E.html>; or the United Kingdom's International Criminal Court Act (U.K.) 2001, c. 17, s. 23, accessible at <http://www.legislation.hmso.gov.uk/acts/acts2001/20010017.pdf>. See also the Canadian government's testimony before the Standing Committee on Foreign Affairs, June 1, 2000, accessible at <http://www.parl.gc.ca/InfoComDoc/36/2/FAIT/Meetings/Evidence/faitev52-e.htm> at 1140 to 1205.

of international law on the subject is the recent decision of the ICJ in the *Yerodia* decision.[112]

ICJ *YERODIA* DECISION

In 1999, Belgium amended its legislation providing universal jurisdiction over international crimes committed by anyone, anywhere, even if the perpetrator was not present in Belgium[113] and denying all immunities for such crimes.[114] On April 11, 2000, a Belgian judge issued an international arrest warrant against Mr. Yerodia, who was at the time serving as the minister for foreign affairs for the Democratic Republic of Congo (DRC). The DRC initiated proceedings against Belgium in the ICJ, arguing that the universal jurisdiction *in absentia* asserted by Belgium exceeded international law and that Belgium's non-recognition of the immunity of a serving minister of foreign affairs was a violation of international law.[115]

On February 14, 2002, the ICJ released its decision,[116] finding by thirteen votes to three that Belgium had violated a legal obligation towards the DRC "in that they failed to respect the immunity from criminal jurisdiction and the inviolability which the incumbent Minister for Foreign Affairs of the Democratic Republic of the Congo enjoyed under international law."[117] In particular, the ICJ held that the immunities *ratione personae* enjoyed by a foreign minister could not be set aside by a national court by charging them with war crimes or crimes against humanity.[118] The ICJ examined the non-immunity provisions of the Nuremberg Charter and the ICTY, ICTR, and ICC Statutes and found that these did not suggest any exception in customary international law in regard to national courts.[119]

---

[112] *Yerodia, supra* note 3.

[113] Article 7 of Belgium's *Loi relative à la répression des violations graves du droit international humanitaire* [hereinafter Belgian Law], which was adopted on February 10, 1999, reprinted 38 I.L.M. 918 (1999).

[114] *Ibid.*, Article 5(3).

[115] *The Democratic Republic of the Congo Institutes Proceedings against Belgium Concerning an International Arrest Warrant Issued by a Belgian Examining Judge against the DRC's Acting Minister for Foreign Affairs,* ICJ Press Release, October 17, 2000, accessible at <http://www.icj-cij.org/icjwww/ipresscom/iprpencobe.html>.

[116] *Yerodia, supra* note 3.

[117] *Ibid.* at para. 75.

[118] *Ibid.* at para. 56-58.

[119] *Ibid.* at para. 58.

Given the line of national decisions and state practice upholding absolute immunity *ratione personae,* as mentioned earlier in this article, the outcome of the case is not particularly surprising. Nevertheless, there are elements of the ICJ decision that are disappointing and rather regrettable. Of particular concern is the fact that the decision did not examine the nuances of state practice and *opinio juris* on the law of immunities and that it did not weigh the countervailing imperative of human rights accountability in determining the appropriate parameters of immunity. As a result, the decision went much further than was necessary to resolve the dispute in question, thereby inhibiting future development in this area.

The legal discussion of the central question of immunity was startlingly brief, even laconic.[120] Remarkably, the ICJ departed from its traditional approach of carefully reviewing state practice and *opinio juris* in order to determine customary international law. Instead, the ICJ purported to deduce international law from abstract observations about international relations. The ICJ announced that in order to determine the extent of a foreign minister's immunities under customary international law, it must "first consider the nature of the functions" exercised by a foreign minister.[121] After briefly considering these functions, which require frequent international travel, the court leapt promptly to the conclusion that "the functions of a Minister for Foreign Affairs are such that, throughout the duration of his or her office, he or she when abroad enjoys full immunity from criminal jurisdiction and inviolability." The court further deduced, *in abstractio,* that this immunity includes acts in an official capacity or private capacity, before or after the assumption of office, and whether or not the minister is on an official or private visit.[122] What is startling is that the court purported to deduce all of this from abstract reasoning rather than a review of state practice and *opinio juris,* turning the normal process of identifying customary international law upside down.[123] Had the ICJ engaged in a proper review of the sources of law, it may have found that customary international law was not at all as unequivocal as it suggests.

---

[120] *Ibid.* at paras. 51-60.

[121] *Ibid.* at para. 53.

[122] *Ibid.* at para. 55.

[123] This is not to suggest that it is inappropriate to consider rationales and policy implications underlying legal principles — indeed, the thesis of this article is the need to consider such implications — but such analysis must be a *secondary* process to evaluate or to refine rules found in recognized sources of international law.

Moreover, the general approach adopted in the judgment gives rise to concern. The judgment commenced its analysis by accepting immunities as a first, sacred principle and then dealt with accountability only briefly at the end as an afterthought.[124] This article has suggested that the rationales for bestowing immunity — namely, their functional necessity in promoting international relations — must continually be balanced against the competing value of establishing accountability for the most serious atrocities. Several judges in separate opinions criticized the judgment for failing to engage in such a balancing. For example, the Joint Separate Opinion of Judges Higgins, Kooijmans, and Buergenthal eloquently argued (very much in line with the approach advocated in this article) that there must be a "balancing of interests":

> On the one scale, we find the interest of the community of mankind to present and stop impunity for perpetrators of grave crimes against its members; on the other, there is the interest of the community of States to allow them to act freely on the inter-State level without unwarranted interference. A balance therefore must be struck between two sets of functions which are both valued by the international community. Reflecting these concerns, what is regarded as permissible jurisdiction and what is regarded as the law on immunity are in constant evolution. The weights on the two scales are not set for all perpetuity. Moreover, a trend is discernible that in a world which increasingly rejects impunity for the most repugnant offenses, the attribution of responsibility and accountability is becoming firmer ... and the availability of immunity as a shield more limited. The law of privileges and immunities, however, retains its importance since immunities are granted to high state officials to guarantee the proper functioning of the network of mutual inter-state relations, which is of paramount importance for a well-ordered and harmonious international system.[125]

This "balancing of interests" approach would have been far more satisfying and would have allowed a more sensitive and nuanced judgment. In fact, the ICJ majority went much further than necessary to decide the specific issue before it and, through its unequivocal statements on several debatable points, seems to have unnecessarily closed the door on points that would have been better left open. Two aspects are of the gravest concern.

The first is that the judgment seems to omit the monumental principle established by the *Pinochet* precedent, that former officials can be tried for serious international crimes since such crimes

---

[124] *Yerodia, supra* note 3 at paras. 60 and 61.

[125] *Ibid.* at para. 75 (Joint Separate Opinion of Judges Higgins, Kooijmans, and Buergenthal), accessible at <www.icj-cij.org>.

cannot be considered official functions.[126] The judgment merely mentions, in *obiter dicta*, that a *former* foreign minister may be tried for acts committed in a private capacity, but it neglects to mention the second critical category, serious international crimes. If this was a deliberate omission, it was an inexplicable one. The rationale on which the ICJ based its entire conclusion was the need to enable high officials to travel and carry out their official functions, and this rationale does not explain or justify the extension of sweeping immunities to *former* officials.[127] Moreover, as Antonio Cassese notes, to extend such immunities would contradict the ICJ's own jurisprudence and also contradict a point that was agreed upon between the parties.[128] The rule already existing in positive law is not only supported by state practice and *opinio juris*, but it also strikes a balance between functional necessity and accountability in a manner that best protects each value.[129] The soundest interpretation is not that the ICJ deliberately contradicted the *Pinochet* principle but rather that it simply did not touch on the question at all.[130]

The second disturbing aspect is that the ICJ extended immunity *ratione personae* to include not only official visits but also *private visits* to another country (for example, for purposes of tourism). Such a conclusion was not supported by state practice and *opinio juris* — indeed, the precedents tend against such an extension. Moreover, such a conclusion is not supported by the ostensible rationale for the rule (necessity for official functions) nor does it reflect any attempt at balancing the competing international values. This problem is discussed in greater length later in this article, as an area for re-evaluation and future development.[131]

In conclusion, it is not surprising that the ICJ upheld immunities *ratione personae*, given the long line of precedents. Yet, in many respects, the ICJ seems to have overstated the law, failed to consider state practice and *opinio juris*, failed to balance other international

---

[126] *Ibid.* at para. 60. The ICJ judgment should be interpreted not as contradicting, but rather as passing in silence, on the *Pinochet* principle.

[127] Wirth, *supra* note 14 at 881.

[128] Cassese, *supra* note 14 at 872.

[129] See *ibid.* at 874; and Wirth, *supra* note 14 at 892.

[130] An alternative solution, to regard international crimes as inherently "private acts," may raise more problems than it solves, as is discussed in Marina Spinedi, "State Responsibility versus Individual Responsibility for International Crimes: Tertium Non Datur?" (2002) 13 Eur. J. Int'l L. 895.

[131] See the section in this article under the heading "Re-evaluate the Law of Non-Official Visits".

values, and made unhelpful and unnecessary pronouncements in *obiter dicta* in areas that would have been better left for development in jurisprudence and state practice.

FUTURE AVENUES FOR DEVELOPMENT

The present situation may be summarized as follows. First, former heads of state, former diplomats, and other officials possess immunity *ratione materiae* — that is, immunity protecting their official acts. The *Pinochet* principle provides that serious international crimes prohibited by *jus cogens* cannot be regarded as "official functions" and are therefore outside the scope of such immunity. This principle is equally applicable in international and national proceedings. Although the *Pinochet* judgment is ambiguous or even contradictory as to the precise contours of this rule, the reasoning is logically applicable to all serious international crimes, including genocide, crimes against humanity, and war crimes.[132]

Second, it seems clear that immunities *ratione personae* of certain visiting officials remain opposable to all national claims of jurisdiction, as was reaffirmed in the ICJ *Yerodia* decision and in numerous other judicial decisions and instances of state practice.[133] There are, nevertheless, ways of seeking justice even against those individuals possessing immunities *ratione personae*. Although states, given their very different social, political, and legal traditions, have not been prepared to grant each other the right to set aside immunities *ratione personae*, many have agreed to grant that right to the ICC. In addition, the Security Council may create international tribunals or refer matters to the ICC and, in so doing, override immunities by virtue of its authority under the UN Charter to maintain international peace and security.[134] The remainder of this article suggests a few ways in which the goal of fighting impunity can be further advanced, given the existing legal and political framework.

---

[132] See the comments in note 87. It is suggested here that ratification of treaties should not be pivotal since certain crimes are well established under customary international law. The rationale of *Pinochet* does not depend on "waiver" by treaty, but rather on the fact that a state can hardly claim that its "official functions" include actions that it renounces and condemns as serious international crimes.

[133] See the discussion earlier in this article under the heading "A Bridge Too Far: National Courts and Immunities *Ratione Personae*."

[134] See the discussion in this article under the heading "Relinquishment of Immunities to International Tribunals and Courts."

MORE EFFECTIVE USE OF THE TOOLS AVAILABLE

The greatest gap with respect to individual accountability relates to persons with immunity *ratione personae,* particularly where their sending state is unwilling or unable to bring them to justice. One means of reducing this "accountability gap" is to continue encouraging more and more states to ratify the ICC Statute. States ratifying the ICC signal that their commitment to repudiating international crimes is so strong that they are willing to stand by their record before a trusted, independent institution and that even immunities *ratione personae* will not bar accountability. This approach strikes a sound balance, as it prevents exposure to frivolous prosecution by a world full of national courts of varying credibility, yet ensures accountability in truly legitimate cases. In addition, assuming certain Security Council members can put aside their narrow concerns,[135] the Security Council can play a valuable role in reducing the problem of immunities by referring matters to the ICC, thus imbuing it with Chapter VII enforcement powers.

A second means of reducing the accountability gap is for states to use their existing rights not to accept war criminals in situations where they would be granted immunities *ratione personae* in the first place. Traditional options open to a receiving state are (1) to refuse to accept the unacceptable representative;[136] (2) to request a waiver of immunity by the sending state;[137] and (3) to expel the unacceptable representative. States can also urge the sending state to prosecute the person in question.[138] In addition, once the official has ceased to serve a particular function (for example, is declared *persona non grata* or ceases to be an accredited diplomat or a head of state or high official), the person then loses immunities *ratione personae* and may be prosecuted for private acts or serious international crimes if the receiving state can re-acquire custody.

The obvious problem with the this set of legal responses is that a sending state may refuse to waive immunity and then fail to investigate or prosecute the official once he or she has been expelled from the host state. However, this situation need not be accepted as

---

[135] As was noted earlier in this article, the United States has emphatically indicated that it does not intend to ratify and that it is opposed to the ICC. It remains to be seen whether the United States would go so far as to veto Security Council efforts to refer situations to the ICC.

[136] Vienna Convention, *supra* note 22, Articles 4 and 5.

[137] *Ibid.,* Article 32.

[138] *Ibid.,* Article 31 (4).

such. Through greater diligence, states can give greater effect to their conventional and customary duties to bring to justice persons responsible for certain international crimes.[139] These duties constrain both the sending state and the receiving state. Where there is credible evidence supporting an allegation, it is a logical corollary of the principle *aut dedere aut judicare* that the sending state must either waive immunity or initiate its own investigation and prosecution. A sending state refusing to either waive immunity or initiate genuine investigations should be regarded as violating the letter and spirit of its obligations. Enforcement of this obligation would depend on the usual mechanisms of pressure from other states and public opinion, condemnation by the international community and mobilization of shame. The international community can and should be far more diligent in encouraging or pressuring states to comply with this basic obligation.

Likewise, receiving states must recall their duties to investigate and prosecute credible allegations regarding certain international crimes committed by persons present in their territory.[140] Where such persons enjoy immunities *ratione personae*, prosecution is not a straightforward option. However, the receiving state is still obliged to take steps in order to comply with its duty *as far as possible in the circumstances*. The receiving state may not be entitled to prosecute, but it can pursue the matter with the sending state and request a waiver of immunity. Where a waiver is refused, the person should be expelled or recalled. Moreover, since expulsion is not a sufficient response to the duty to prosecute, the receiving state should also recognize a special responsibility to follow up with the sending state to encourage genuine proceedings to be carried out.[141] Greater

---

[139] On the duty to prosecute generally, see, for example, Orentlicher, *supra* note 6; Carla Edelenbos, "Human Rights Violations: A Duty to Prosecute?" (1994) 7 Leiden J. Int'l L. 5; Naomi Roht-Arianna, "Non-Treaty Sources of the Obligation to Investigate and Prosecute" in Naomi Roht-Arianna, ed., *Impunity and Human Rights in International Law and Practice* (New York: Oxford University Press, 1995); Michael Scharf, "The Letter of the Law: The Scope of the International Legal Obligation to Prosecute Human Rights Crimes" (1996) 59 Law & Contemporary Problems 41.

[140] See, for example, the Torture Convention, *supra* note 12, Article 6; and the Geneva Convention (IV), *supra* note 10, Article 146.

[141] Some states may object that this sounds like a novel obligation, but it is important to recall that the initial obligation was *to prosecute*; so the burden of following up with another state is merely a "next best" alternative flowing from that duty.

temerity in this regard would be more faithful to a state's obligations concerning serious international crimes.

RE-EVALUATE THE LAW OF NON-OFFICIAL VISITS

The ICJ *dicta* on private visits in the *Yerodia* decision should be critically evaluated and not necessarily accepted as a correct statement of the law. First, the rationale of functional necessity for diplomatic relations, on which the majority so heavily relied, simply does not support immunities during private visits. Second, private visits have very different implications for the receiving state and involve very different considerations. Third, the ICJ failed to conduct any review of state practice or *opinio juris* on this question, and a review of such sources would have supported the opposite conclusion. Fourth, while decisions of the ICJ are undoubtedly entitled to considerable weight, these particular comments of the ICJ were *obiter dicta* and do not clearly have the support of a majority of the judges.

First, the majority's fundamental rationale, from which all of its ruminations about immunities flowed, was that exposure to proceedings "could deter the Minister from traveling internationally *when required to do so for the purposes of his or her official functions.*" This rationale is utterly inapplicable to travel unrelated to official functions. In the case of official visits, the official must go in order to perform his or her normal functions, so even a risk of frivolous prosecution could be argued to jeopardize the official's ability to carry out his or her state functions. Yet with respect to private visits, what is jeopardized is the official's ability to go skiing or shopping in another country. The urgency of the rationale is simply not as compelling. It is true, of course, that being arrested for war crimes while on holidays would dramatically impede an official's ability to carry out his or her functions. However, this consideration does not justify the extension of absolute immunities to holiday travel. A more modest alternative, which would do less damage to normal principles of accountability and jurisdiction, would be to recognize the normal rule of immunities *ratione materiae* in such situations. An official fearful of arrest for serious international crimes could avoid the inconvenient consequences of such an arrest by curtailing vacation travel (particularly to countries where he or she may be under indictment), just as anyone else is free to do. Of course, a rule providing immunity even while on holiday travel would undoubtedly be more *convenient* to foreign ministers and high officials and provide them with even greater protection. However, convenience is not a sufficient justification to frustrate accountability for genocide, crimes against humanity, and war crimes. The question is one of balancing two values: the normal rule of accountability for serious crimes and the functional necessity that justifies immunities in certain circumstances. Immunities are not supposed to be a benefit for privileged individuals but rather an exception made in order to enable diplomatic functions.[142] The argument of "functional necessity for the maintenance of international relations" is utterly inapplicable to leisure travel.

Second, a private visit is also very different from an official visit when seen from the perspective of the receiving state. Where the receiving state has welcomed the visiting dignitary (that is, invited or consented to the visit), the state is understood as warranting that full immunity will be bestowed.[143] Thus, the need for immunity is reinforced by the good faith of the receiving state in fulfilling its undertakings as host. This principle is recognized in national legislation and was elegantly articulated in the famous arrest warrant issued by Belgium against Yerodia:

Pursuant to the general principle of fairness in judicial proceedings, *immunity from enforcement must, in our view, be accorded to all State representatives welcomed as such onto the territory of Belgium (on "official visits").* Welcoming such foreign dignitaries as official representatives of sovereign States involves not only relations between individuals but also relations between States. This implies that such welcome includes an undertaking by the host State and its various components to refrain from taking any coercive measures against its guest and *the invitation cannot become a pretext for ensnaring the individual concerned* in what would then have to be labeled a trap. In the contrary case, failure to respect this undertaking could give rise to the host State's international responsibility.[144]

---

142 See Vienna Convention, *supra* note 22, preamble, para. 4. It is of course undesirable for high officials to be subject to frivolous prosecutions, but the same is true for everyone, yet this is not seen as necessitating immunities for everyone in the world. Vacationing officials should be in the same position as former officials and indeed as every other citizen. Determining the appropriate rule involves a balancing of risks or interests and in this case it seems better to side with accountability.

143 See, for example, *The Schooner Exchange* v. *M'Faddon*, 11 U.S. (7 Cranch) at 137 (1812): "A nation would justly be considered as violating its faith, although that faith might not be expressly plighted, which should suddenly and without previous notice, exercise its territorial powers in a manner not consonant to the usages and received obligations of the civilized world."

144 Quoted in *Yerodia*, *supra* note 3 at para. 68 [emphasis added].

This consideration also strongly supports the restriction of immunities *ratione personae* to situations where the high official is in the host state "at the invitation of or with the consent of" the receiving state.[145] This approach gives the receiving state the opportunity to review who its guests are to be and, if necessary, to deny access where a particular individual has a criminal history that is simply unacceptable to the receiving state.

Where the official is not on official business and has not been "welcomed" by the host state, this consideration of the host's duty is completely absent. The ICJ approach would mean that a state would be helpless to act against a high official responsible for the most horrible crimes even where that official entered the state's territory without the government's knowledge or consent. Thus, if, immediately prior to the Gulf conflict, Saddam Hussein had managed to enter the United States without the government's awareness, he would (according to the ICJ) have been entitled to holiday at Disney World and ski in Vermont, and the United States would be legally prohibited from bringing war crimes or crimes against humanity charges. The proposition is profoundly dubious.

Third, state practice does not support such an extraordinary rule. For example, the UN Convention on Special Missions provides that "[t]he Head of the sending State, when he leads a special mission, shall enjoy in the receiving State or in a third State the facilities, privileges and *immunities accorded by international law to Heads of State on an official visit,*"[146] implying that immunities depend on whether the visit is an official visit. The US Restatement of Foreign Relations Law states that "[w]hen a head of state or government comes *on an official visit* to another country, he is generally given the same personal inviolability and immunities as ... an accredited diplomat."[147]

Moreover, an examination of diplomatic immunities offers a very helpful analogy, since it has been developed over centuries and is a

---

[145] This was the wording originally appearing in the UK legislation, which may have reflected customary international law. There was a suggestion by a member of Parliament to change the provision on the rather curious grounds about concerns about heads of state outside of the United Kingdom, and agreement was reached to go along with the change. See *Pinochet, supra* note 3 at 191-92.

[146] United Nations Convention on Special Missions, December 16, 1969, Ann. to UN General Assembly Resolution 2530 (XXIV), December 8, 1969, Article 21 [emphasis added].

[147] American Law Institute, *Restatement of Foreign Relations Law, Third Edition* (St. Paul: American Law Institute, 1986) at 464, n. 14.

more clearly codified area of law. In this area, it is well established that diplomats do not enjoy immunities *ratione personae* while holidaying in third countries. Instead, immunity is granted only in the state to which he or she is accredited and in third states only during transit between his or her home country and his or her post.[148] The demands of functional necessity were not regarded as requiring any broader immunity. Even though it is equally true that the wrongful arrest of a diplomat while on holiday in a third country would ultimately impede that diplomat's official functions, this risk was not considered grave enough to justify a departure from the normal rule of individual accountability and the normal rule of state jurisdiction over persons on its territory. This approach, formed after centuries of experience and state practice, should also inform the situation for high officials.[149] Given that immunities *ratione personae* are a special exception to the normal rule of accountability, justified only by their necessity for the maintenance of international relations, the scope of such immunities should be given the narrower interpretation where there is any doubt.

Finally, this particular suggestion of the ICJ need not be regarded as part of the *ratio decidendi*. The arrest warrant could still be invalidated on the grounds that, by its broad terms, it left the foreign minister in doubt as to whether he might be arrested during official visits to various countries and, therefore, would interfere with his established immunities.[150] Moreover, a "head count" of the judges produces a surprising result. Two judges dissented on this point, and a third dissented on the ground that the matter should not have

[148] Vienna Convention, *supra* note 22, Article 40.

[149] Even if one were to conclude that the special status of the head of state justified immunity *ratione personae* even during private visits — a proposition that is doubtful — this should not be extended without reflection to other officials such as heads of government or foreign ministers. Sir Arthur Watts, "The Legal Position in International Law of Heads of States, Heads of Governments and Foreign Ministers" (1994) 3 Rec.des Cours 1 at 109, states:

> Although it may well be that a Head of State, when on a private visit to another State, still enjoys certain privileges and immunities, it is much less likely that the same is true of heads of governments and foreign ministers. Although they may be accorded certain special treatment by the host State, this is more likely to be a matter of courtesy and respect for the seniority of the visitor, than a reflection of any belief that such a treatment is required by international law.

[150] The warrant specifically allowed for immunity during official visits to Belgium but did not clearly specify that such immunity would be respected during official visits to other countries, thus producing the "chilling effect" on the minister's ability to perform his representational duties.

been addressed.[151] Three judges, while concurring in the result, expressed very strong doubts on this particular point.[152] A seventh judge, concurring in the result, provided an interesting disclaimer on the immunities point, noting that the court had not undertaken a "disquisition of the law," "perhaps not wanting to tie its hands," and that therefore "the Judgment cannot be said to be juridically constraining."[153] Thus, it is arguable that only six out of thirteen judges must be presumed to stand behind this suggested rule, so even as a *dictum* it was not adopted by a majority.

In conclusion, the approach suggested by a minority of the ICJ in *obiter dicta* should not be adopted lightly. The issue should be left open for determination by the give-and-take process of actual state practice. Moreover, a consideration of state practice and *opinio juris* to date, an examination of the analogous rules for diplomatic immunity, as well as a consideration of the policy implications and values at stake, strongly suggest that immunities *ratione personae* must be accorded only where the high official is on the territory at the invitation of, or by the consent of, the receiving state. This approach satisfies the functional necessity requirement while also respecting the normal rule of accountability and the sovereignty of the receiving state.

A PROTOCOL TO RESTRICT IMMUNITIES *RATIONE PERSONAE*?

A more radical suggestion, and one that is perhaps not yet feasible, would be to create a protocol by which states agree to restrict immunities *ratione personae* in certain cases. As discussed earlier, national and international jurisprudence and state practice have consistently upheld respect for absolute immunities *ratione personae*.[154] These immunities persist because states perceive an absolute

---

[151] *Yerodia* decision, *supra* note 3 at paras. 1-3 (Dissenting Opinion of Judge Al-Khasawneh); paras. 18-21 (Dissenting Opinion of Judge Van den Wyngaert); and para. 14 (Dissenting Opinion of Judge Oda), which are all available at <www.icj-cij.org>.

[152] For example, the Joint Separate Opinion of Judges Higgins, Kooijmans, and Buergenthal agrees that "a Minister of Foreign Affairs is entitled to full immunity during official visits" (*ibid.* at para. 83), but finds that "whether he is also entitled to immunities during private travel and what is the scope of any such immunities, is far less clear" (at para. 86).

[153] *Ibid.* at para. 6 (Separate Opinion of Judge Koroma).

[154] See the discussion in this article under the headings "Functional Necessity and the Consistent Rejection of Any Exceptions to Immunities *Ratione Personae*" and "A Bridge Too Far: National Courts and Immunities *Ratione Personae*."

rule as the only way to deny any pretext for abuse, which would have a "chilling effect" on international discourse and conflict resolution.

Ultimately, however, the question comes down to a balancing of *risks*: the risk of abuse of any exceptions versus the risk of international criminals escaping justice. The priorities and perspectives of states are evolving, and a time may soon come when a re-assessment of these risks is possible. Broadly speaking, two relevant trends are in play. First, states are attaching increasing priority to human rights considerations, leading to a greater willingness to take risks to combat impunity. Second, as international criminal law becomes clearer and more developed, the uncertainty of the "risk" involved in creating an exception becomes more manageable. Thus, it may some day be possible to create a protocol or agreement whereby states waive in advance immunities *ratione personae* with respect to credible allegations of serious international crimes, such as genocide, crimes against humanity, war crimes, and torture.[155] In order to advance such a protocol, it will be necessary to anticipate and address the natural concern of states.

The first and gravest concern of states will be the fear of abuse of any such exceptions to persecute and harass diplomats or high officials and to dispute unpopular governmental policies. One possibility to address this would be to create a mechanism for a trusted independent source to review, promptly and expeditiously, any allegations to verify that they are substantiated. In this manner, it will be possible to allay fears of abuse while enabling prosecution where there is credible evidence of a serious crime, thus serving both values: accountability and the security of international discourse.

A second concern will be the discomfort of states with the criminal procedures of other states, a concern that could be reduced through provisions on minimal procedural standards and other safeguards. Another possibility would be to allow the sending state the option of consenting to prosecution in the ICC as an alternative to prosecution in the foreign state.

A third difficulty would be determining the scope of the exceptions, especially given that states may have significant good faith

---

[155] Given the intractable problems of abuse of diplomatic immunity, it would also be desirable to consider similar exceptions for serious domestic crimes, such as murder and sexual assault, committed by diplomats in the host state. If the agreement contained the safeguards suggested here, it might overcome some of the preoccupations that have hitherto necessitated absolute immunities.

differences about the content even of *jus cogens* prohibitions.[156] This concern can be reduced as international criminal law develops, thereby providing the necessary clarity with respect to the crimes and their thresholds,[157] which could then be reflected by reference in any agreement.

It is likely that at the time of writing this article, many states would have grave hesitations about creating such exceptions to otherwise complete immunities. Twenty years ago, when the United Kingdom explored the idea of agreements to waive all immunities for certain serious crimes, the proposal met a cool reception.[158] However, "in a world which increasingly rejects impunity for the most repugnant offences,"[159] the values, priorities, and risk assessments of states are in constant evolution. States may soon re-assess the risks and recognize such an arrangement as a necessary response to a glaring lacuna in international criminal law. After all, one hundred years ago, national prosecutions of former heads of states and the relinquishment of immunities to a permanent international criminal court would have been inconceivable, and today they are a natural part of the international landscape.

---

[156] For example, Andreas Zimmerman, "Sovereign Immunity and Violations of *Jus Cogens* — Some Critical Remarks" (1995) 16 Mich. J. Int'1 L. 433, who notes potential problems flowing from the vagueness of even *jus cogens* prohibitions. For example, the European Court of Human Rights jurisprudence regards the "death row phenomenon" as "inhuman treatment," an interpretation with which the United States almost certainly does not agree. Such interpretation, while acceptable in a human rights context, would be unacceptably broad in an international criminal law context.

[157] Considerable precision and clarification is already provided in the definitions contained in the ICC Statute, *supra* note 2, Articles 5-8, which are further elaborated in the ICC Elements of Crimes, UN Doc. ICC-ASP/1/3, accessible at <www.un.org/law/icc/asp/aspfra.htm>. These are explained in further detail in Roy S. Lee et al., eds, *The International Criminal Court: Elements of Crimes and Rules of Procedure and Evidence* (Ardsley: Transnational, 2001).

[158] See discussion in note 39 of this article.

[159] *Yerodia* decision, *supra* note 3 at para. 75 (Joint Separate Opinion of Judges Higgins, Kooijmans, and Buergenthal).

Sommaire

L'effet du mouvement de responsabilité en matière des droits de la personne sur les immunités en droit international

Durant la dernière décennie, le mouvement de responsabilité en matière des droits de la personne a fait des percées remarquables dans le droit classique des immunités. Cette évolution dénote un nouvel équilibre entre le besoin de promouvoir la responsabilité et le besoin de protéger le discours international. Les progrès à cet égard sont cohérents si l'on considère les fondements du droit dans ces domaines. L'immunité ratione materiae dont jouissent les dignitaires, actuels et anciens, cherche à protéger les fonctions officielles accomplies au nom de l'État. L'arrêt de principe rendu dans l'affaire Pinochet confirme que les fonctions officielles ne peuvent inclure la commission de crimes internationaux condamnés par le droit international. Inversement, l'immunité ratione personae découle d'un autre principe. Cette forme d'immunité protège uniquement certains hauts fonctionnaires représentant leur État, pendant la durée de leur mandat seulement, ce qui facilite les visites officielles en empêchant leur arrestation, quel que soit le motif. La décision Yerodia de la Cour internationale de justice ainsi que l'évolution recente de droit confirment que cette immunité demeure absolue, sans égard à la conduite reprochée. Par contre, même cette immunité absolue peut être levée par votre d'une mesure coercive de Conseil de sécurité ou par l'acceptation de la compétence de la Cour pénal internationale.

Summary

The Impact of the Human Rights Accountability Movement on the International Law of Immunities

In the last decade, the human rights accountability movement has made remarkable inroads into the classical law of immunities. The developments strike a new equilibrium between the need to promote accountability and the need to protect international discourse. These developments form a coherent picture if one looks to the underlying rationales of these areas of law. Immunities ratione materiae, enjoyed by current and former officials, protect official functions on behalf of a state. The landmark Pinochet decision affirmed that official functions could not include the commission of international crimes condemned by international law. Conversely, immunity ratione personae flows from a different rationale. This form of immunity protects only certain high officials representing their state and only during office and facilitates official visits by precluding arrest on any grounds. The International Court of Justice Yerodia *decision and other developments confirm that this immunity remains absolute, irrespective of the conduct alleged. However, even this absolute immunity may be relinquished through Security Council enforcement action or acceptance of the jurisdiction of the International Criminal Court.*

Deployment of Troops to Prevent Impending Genocide: A Contemporary Assessment of the UN Security Council's Powers

MARK TOUFAYAN

> "If a man is killed in Paris, it is a murder; the throats of fifty thousand people are cut in the East, and it is a question."[1]
>
> — Victor Hugo

INTRODUCTION

During the First World War, as the rest of the world gazed silently in horror and disbelief, the Ottoman Empire carried out the slaughter of its non-Muslim minority Armenian population. The outright denial by many states of the genocidal killings of more than one million Armenians and the relatively low impact of these killings on modern public consciousness continues today to raise serious questions about the ability of the international community to prevent future acts of that nature.[2] It was feared that to delve into the past might reopen old wounds that were now healing — an intellectually crafted obscurantism and revisionism, which seeks nothing short of hiding, diminishing, or belittling the shattering past

Mark Toufayan, B.C.L., LL.B. (McGill), is an LL.M. candidate in International Legal Studies at New York University School of Law. This article is a revised version of an essay written under the supervision of Professor Stephen Toope in the Faculty of Law at McGill University while the author was a student enrolled in the National Program offered by the faculty. The author wishes to express his indebtedness to Professor Toope for his guidance and precious comments on earlier drafts. However, any shortcomings are strictly his own. This article is dedicated to the loving memory of Levon Hovaghimian.

[1] Quoted in V.N. Dadrian, "Genocide as a Problem of National and International Law: The World War I Armenian Case and Its Contemporary Legal Ramifications" (1989) 13 Yale J. Int'l L. 221 at 223.

[2] *Ibid.* at 225; see also L.B. Sohn and T. Buergenthal, *International Protection of Human Rights* (New York: Bobb-Merrill, 1973) at 181-92.

relating to genocide. However, more frighteningly, it set an important precedent for the subsequent Jewish Holocaust of the Second
World War. Indeed, asserting that the world would not interfere
with his "final solution," Hitler once noted: "Who, after all, speaks
today of the annihilation of the Armenians?"[3]

These events, however, planted in our minds the seeds of bitter-
ness towards such barbarity against civilization, and the world community vowed that such acts would "never again" be perpetrated.
Their aftermath gave added urgency to the task of building an institution intended not only to bring about peace but also above all
to preserve human dignity through the cooperation of nation
states.[4] This fact further prompted the United Nations (UN) General Assembly to recognize unanimously that the denial of the
right to existence of entire human groups is a crime that "shocks
the conscience of mankind, results in great losses to humanity in
the form of cultural and other contributions represented by these
human groups, and is contrary to moral law and to the spirit and
aims of the United Nations."[5] Finally, the adoption in 1948 of the
Convention on the Prevention and Punishment of the Crime of Genocide (Genocide Convention),[6] under the auspices of the United
Nations, provided the legal impetus upon which the organization
and its member states could seek to prevent and suppress genocide.
To borrow the words of Secretary General Kofi Annan, "[g]eno-
cide shaped the founding of the United Nations ... Ensuring that

---

[3] Dadrian, *supra* note 1. See also V.N. Dadrian, "The Historical and Legal Inter-
connections between the Armenian Genocide and the Jewish Holocaust: From
Impunity to Retributive Justice" (1998) 23 Yale J. Int'l L. 503.

[4] A. Roberts and B. Kingsbury, "Introduction: The UN's Roles in International
Society since 1945" in A. Roberts and B. Kingsbury, eds., *United Nations, Divided
World: The U.N.'s Roles in International Relations,* 2nd ed. (Oxford: Oxford Univer-
sity Press, 1993) at 6.

[5] UN General Assembly [hereinafter GA] Resolution 96(I), UN Doc. A/64/Add.1
at 188 (1946).

[6] Convention on the Prevention and Punishment of the Crime of Genocide, GA
Resolution 260(A)(III), UN GAOR, 3rd Sess., Supp. No. 1921, Dec. 9, 1948, 78
U.N.T.S. 227 [hereinafter Genocide Convention]. The Genocide Convention
was approved and proposed for signature and ratification or accession by GA
Resolution 260A(III) of December 9, 1948. It entered into force on January 12,
1951. In addition to the 135 state parties (including all five permanent members
of the UN Security Council), there are forty-one signatories who have not yet
ratified the treaty. The text of the convention and list of ratifications can be found
online at <http://www.un.org/Depts/Treaty/bible.htm> (date accessed: October 2, 2003).

genocide could never be repeated became, in many people's eyes, the new world Organization's most important mission."[7]

However, in the intervening decades since the entry into force of the treaty, the repeated failure of the international community to take preventive action against the vilest abomination of our species[8] has demonstrated a cynical disregard for the most "elementary considerations of humanity."[9] It has made a mockery of the Charter of the United Nations (UN Charter)[10] and the most sacred values of civilization. Yet above all, it has betrayed the political cowardice of self-interested states whose "short-sighted" policies relegate the notion of universal human rights to an "expeditious means to salve the conscience of those who proclaim themselves as 'civilized nations'."[11] This failure is further exacerbated by the total lack of effective enforcement mechanisms in international law aimed at preventing genocide. It is well known that there are two prongs to the Genocide Convention, prevention and punishment. However, while the instrument addresses the latter issue, albeit unsatisfactorily, it remains idle to the means by which states are to prevent genocide, thereby allowing perpetrators to ignore it with impunity. It is thus telling to recount the observation of Sir Hersch Lauterpacht who suggested that "[a]pparently, to a considerable extent, the Convention amounts to a registration of protest against past misdeeds of individuals or collective savagery rather than to an effective instrument of their prevention or repression."[12]

---

[7] United Nations Secretary-General Kofi Annan, *Address Commemorating the Occasion of the Fiftieth Anniversary of the 1948 Convention on the Prevention and Punishment of the Crime of Genocide*, December 9, 1998, accessible at <http://www.un.org/Docs/SG/ quotable/6822.htm>.

[8] Special Rapporteur Benjamin Withaker has described genocide as "the ultimate crime and the gravest violation of human rights it is possible to commit." See *Revised and Updated Report on the Question of the Prevention and Punishment of the Crime of Genocide Prepared by Mr. Ben Whitaker, Special Rapporteur*, UN ESCOR, 38th Sess., Supp. No. 37, at 5, UN Doc. E/CN.4/Sub.2/1985/6 (1985) [hereinafter *Whitaker Report*].

[9] This expression is borrowed from the *Corfu Channel case (United Kingdom v. Albania)*, [1949] I.C.J. Rep. 4 at 24 [hereinafter *Corfu Channel* case].

[10] Charter of the United Nations, June 26, 1945, Can. T.S. 1955 No. 7 [hereinafter UN Charter].

[11] P. Akhavan, "Enforcement of the Genocide Convention: A Challenge to Civilization" (1995) 8 Harv. H.R.J. 229 at 257.

[12] L. Oppenheim, *International Law: A Treatise*, vol. I, 8th ed. (London: Longmans and Company, 1905) at 751.

The failure to enact more far-reaching provisions in the Genocide Convention undoubtedly highlights the still relatively underdeveloped condition of international human rights law in 1948. Very few are aware though that the treaty was adopted the day before the adoption of the Universal Declaration of Human Rights,[13] which set the common standard of achievement for human civilization. Since then, however, genocide prevention has virtually gained no attention from the international community, much less the UN.[14] While genocide has repeatedly stained with blood the pages of

[13] Universal Declaration of Human Rights, GA Resolution 217 (III), UN GAOR, 3rd Sess., Supp. No. 13, UN Doc. A/810 (1948) 71.

[14] Four UN reports on genocide have been prepared during the 1985-99 period. They address specifically the issue of genocide prevention. In the *Whitaker Report, supra* note 8, which was presented to the Sub-Commission on Prevention of Discrimination and Protection of Minorities of the United Nations ECOSOC, the special rapporteur made specific recommendations on how the UN could develop a capacity to prevent genocide (para. 85). While the recommendations for the establishment of a UN High Commissioner on Human Rights and an International Criminal Court have been realized, his recommendation for the establishment of an impartial international body concerned with preventing genocide has been ignored. In the *Report by Mr. B.W. Ndiaye, Special Rapporteur on Extrajudicial, Summary or Arbitrary Executions on His Mission to Rwanda from 8 to 17 April 1993,* August 11, 1993, UN Doc. E/CN.4/1994/7/Add.1 [hereinafter *Ndiaye Report*], the special rapporteur made recommendations on how to respond to the escalating ethnic violence and the risk of genocide in Rwanda (para. 78). His report was largely ignored. In the *Report of the Secretary-General pursuant to General Assembly Resolution 53/35: The Fall of Srebrenica,* November 15, 1999, UN Doc. A/54/549 [hereinafter *Srebrenica Report*], Secretary-General Kofi Annan said the UN Security Council should have approved "more decisive and forceful action to prevent the unfolding horror" in Bosnia and that "safe areas" should never be established again without credible means of defence. The report refers to an "attempted genocide" in Bosnia. Since the conviction of perpetrators for genocide at The Hague in August 2001, the Srebrenica crime has become widely recognized as genocide. Finally, in the *Report of the Independent Inquiry into United Nations Actions during the 1994 Rwanda Genocide,* December 15, 1999 [hereinafter *Carlsson Report*], the special rapporteurs found that the UN had ignored evidence that genocide was planned and had refused to act once it began. In particular, the report is critical of the Security Council's April 21, 1994 decision to reduce the strength of the United Nations Assistance Mission for Rwanda [hereinafter UNAMIR] after the genocidal acts began and highlights the role of Kofi Annan, who was head of UN peacekeeping at the time, sharply criticizing his failure to act on a January 11, 1994 warning of the risk of genocide. The Special Rapporteurs Carlsson, Sung-Joo, and Kupolati recommended that the secretary-general should initiate an "action plan to prevent genocide" in which each part of the "United Nations system, including Member States, should examine what active steps" they should take. The plan should include a "follow-up mechanism to ensure that such steps are taken." No such

history before our passive eyes,[15] one cannot but wonder whether the efficiency and legitimacy of the world organization may ever be secured. Considering that "genocide is a crime under international law, *contrary to the spirit and aims of the United Nations* and condemned by the civilized world"[16] and that "in order to liberate mankind from such an odious scourge, *international cooperation* was required,"[17] the UN still appears to provide today the most promising venue for preventive action. Thus, it would be inconceivable to expect it to remain silent or neutral while perpetrators proceed, deliberately excising their prey from mankind under the umbrella of unrestricted sovereignty.

As the mission of the UN broadens in the post-Cold War world, the international community has increasingly recognized the need to address civil conflicts and violence within sovereign nations before they escalate. In such conflicts, one would expect an international system to be able to muster both the authority and means to take effective dampening measures. This article addresses one subset of the increasingly common scheme of "structural prevention" — prevention through the support of the UN. The author will specifically consider the authority of the UN to take coercive measures to prevent impending genocide. While most of the means at the disposal of the organization are not new, military action deployed in earlier ventures has not been conceived as preventive but rather as reactive to events. This is because restrictions on state sovereignty, whether real or perceived, have often caused the states concerned to resist preventive measures.[18] This article argues, however, that the UN is mandated in its charter to act preemptively

---

action plan has been initiated yet. The text of the report can be found online at \<http://www.ess.uwe.ac.uk/documents/RwandaReport5.htm\> (date accessed: July 22, 2003).

[15] Other than the Nazi extermination of the Jews, post-war examples of genocide that have been cited are "the Tutsi massacre of Hutu in Burundi in 1965 and 1972, the Paraguayan massacre of Aché Indians prior to 1974, the Khmer Rouge massacre in Kamputchea between 1975 and 1978, and the contemporary Iranian killings of the Bahais." See *Whitaker Report, supra* note 8 at 9-10, para. 24. Since 1985, the cataclysms in Tibet, northern Iraq, the former Yugoslavia (Bosnia), Rwanda, and, more recently, in Kosovo and East Timor, among others, may also be added to the list.

[16] Genocide Convention, *supra* note 6 at preamble [emphasis added].

[17] *Ibid.* [emphasis added].

[18] R. Gordon, "United Nations Intervention in Internal Conflicts: Iraq, Somalia and Beyond" (1994) 15 Mich. J. Int'l. L. 519 at 536-37.

to prevent human rights violations occurring solely within the borders of a sovereign state from escalating into genocide. Furthermore, through a case study of contemporary Security Council practice in the post-Cold War era, it will demonstrate that the UN has seized a mandate today to intervene militarily to uphold human rights when they are massively violated within the borders of a sovereign state, irrespective of any direct or immediate transborder effects.

With respect to the question "what can the enlightened sectors of the international community do to prevent and halt the proliferation of genocides around the planet?" we usually evade the obvious, albeit costliest answer — to stop them before, or at least while they are happening, by any means necessary — to instead focus on actions after the fact. Prevention may entail rights and obligations that are only implicit in the Genocide Convention, but the preeminence of the UN Charter gives an institutional framework to the taking of preventive measures in cases of impending genocide. In order to keep the argument as circumscribed as possible, this article will focus solely on the legitimacy of collective forcible humanitarian intervention through the Security Council in cases of threatening genocide. It is not intended however to minimize the crucial role of "early warning" mechanisms targeted at stopping the dissemination of hate propaganda, direct and public incitement by racist organizations as well as other "preparatory acts" before a situation has assumed genocidal proportions.[19]

The United Nations' Competence to Take Preventive Measures in Cases of Massive Human Rights Violations Occurring within a State

HUMAN RIGHTS PROTECTION BEYOND THE UN CHARTER PARADIGM

There was general agreement in the initial stages of the UN that the protection of human rights and fundamental freedoms on the part of international society organized through it would strengthen the authority of the organization.[20] At the same time, it became clearly apparent that the degree to which that task could be fulfilled is in itself dependent to a large extent upon the moral and political authority wielded by the UN at any given time. The UN is certainly not immune to barriers of political alliances or antagonism and

---

[19] See generally, W.A. Schabas, "Hate Speech in Rwanda: The Road to Genocide" (2000) 46 McGill L.J. 141.

[20] R. Jennings and A. Watts, eds., *Oppenheim's International Law*, vol. 2 to 4, 9th ed. (Harlow: Longman, 1993) at 991.

cumbersome bureaucratic decision-making processes, which may and have greatly undermined its effectiveness in this field. Having said that, this reality by no means entails that the organization merely represents a centre "for harmonizing the actions of nations"[21] in achieving the common end of safeguarding basic human rights. Nor does it signify that the UN has been created merely to reflect the political will and interests of all its members at any given time.[22] In *Reparation for Injuries Suffered in the Service of the United Nations*, the International Court of Justice (ICJ) indeed recognized the distinct objective legal personality of the UN, stating that "it is a subject of international law and capable of possessing international rights and duties."[23]

Of course, international subjectivity or the possession of "international legal personality" does not in itself determine what rights and obligations the organization might have under international law.[24] More particularly, in the field of human rights, the UN cannot *ipso jure* claim the possession of the same rights enjoyed by its member states nor be considered to be obligated in the same way as states under customary international law.[25] Rather, "the [international] rights and duties of an entity such as the Organization must depend on the purposes and functions as specified or implied in its constituent documents and developed in practice."[26]

Perhaps surprisingly, I would suggest that the question "what can the United Nations do?" when confronting impending genocide is not particularly controversial, even in the absence of an explicit grant of authority by the UN Charter. An analysis of the numerous human rights provisions of this document demonstrates that the UN is clearly mandated to act in response to impending genocide.

21 *Reparation for Injuries Suffered in the Service of the United Nations*, Advisory Opinion, [1949] I.C.J. Rep. 174 at 178 [hereinafter *Reparation* case].

22 *Ibid.* at 179; R. Higgins, *Problems and Process : International Law and How We Use It* (Oxford: Clarendon Press, 1994) at 46; F. Seyersted, "International Personality of Intergovernmental Organizations: Do Their Capacities Really Depend upon Their Constitutions" (1964) 4 Indian J. Int'l L. 1 at 40-43; J.A. Barberis, "Nouvelles Questions Concernant la Personnalité Juridique Internationale" (1983) 179 Rec. des Cours 145 at 219; H. Waldock, "General Course on Public International Law" (1962) 106 Rec. des Cours 1 at 140.

23 *Reparation* case, *supra* note 21 at 178. See also *Case Concerning the Legality of the Use by a State of Nuclear Weapons in Armed Conflict*, Advisory Opinion, [1996] I.C.J. Rep. 66 at 78, para. 25.

24 *Reparation* case, *supra* note 21 at 179.

25 *Ibid.* at 178.

26 *Ibid.* at 180.

In the preamble to the UN Charter, the peoples of the United Nations have expressed, among other things, their determination "to save succeeding generations from the scourge of war ... and to reaffirm faith in the fundamental human rights, in the dignity and worth of the human person, [and] in the equal rights of men and women." The UN Charter lays down, as one of the purposes of the UN, the achievement of international cooperation "in solving problems of a ... humanitarian character, and in promoting and encouraging respect for human rights and for fundamental freedoms for all without distinction as to race, sex, language, or religion."[27] The promotion of "universal respect for and observance of" these same rights and freedoms is further declared to be one of the objects of the UN in the sphere of international economic and social cooperation as a prerequisite for the creation of "conditions of stability and well-being which are necessary for peaceful and friendly relations among nations."[28] Genocide attacks these concepts at their very root and, by doing so, strikes at the foundations of international stability and security. Thus, the ordinary meaning of these provisions in light of the objects and purpose of the treaty[29] shows that the international recognition and protection of human rights and, consequently, the prevention of genocide fall squarely within the purposes and legitimate concerns of the organization.

Nevertheless, these provisions do not themselves signify a full and effective guarantee of human rights on the part of international society, much less the UN. As has become obvious to many commentators, these provisions are rhetorical in their affirmation and limit the jurisdiction of international society to a "*droit de regard*" — a right to monitor, encourage respect for, and promote fundamental human rights and freedoms from the outside rather

---

[27] UN Charter, *supra* note 10, Article 1(3). "The Purposes constitute the *raison d'être* of the Organization. They are the aggregation of the common ends on which our minds met; hence, the cause and object of the Charter to which member states collectively and severally subscribe." See L.M. Goodrich, E. Hambro, and A.P. Simons, *Charter of the United Nations. Commentary and Documents*, 3rd ed. (New York: Columbia University Press, 1969) at 20.

[28] UN Charter, *supra* note 10, Article 55(c).

[29] Vienna Convention on the Law of Treaties, 1155 U.N.T.S. 331, 1969, Article 31(1) [hereinafter Vienna Convention]. The principles of treaty interpretation contained in Articles 31-33 of the convention reflect customary international law. On this point, see Sir I.M. Sinclair, *The Vienna Convention on the Law of Treaties*, 2nd ed. (Dover, NH: Manchester University Press, 1984) at 153; *Case Concerning the Kasikili/Sedudu Island (Botswana v. Namibia)*, [1999] I.C.J. Rep. 3 at para. 18.

than to more "aggressively" enforce or implement them within the territory of non-consenting states.[30] A clear illustration of this right is the fact that the General Assembly and the variety of committees established under its auspices have extensive authority on human rights issues, but this authority is limited to debating, initiating studies, producing reports, and making recommendations.[31] The process of "implementation" thus remains largely political, primarily through bilateral and multilateral diplomacy and the marshalling of shame through excited public opinion.

However, it is now also widely accepted that respect for human rights and fundamental freedoms has an immediate impact upon the maintenance of international peace and security and undeniably influences the cooperation between states.[32] The UN Charter

---

[30] B. Simma and P. Alston, "The Sources of Human Rights Law: Custom, Jus Cogens, and General Principles" (1992) 12 Aus. Y.B. Int'l L. 82 at 98-99; E. Lane, "Demanding Human Rights: A Change in the World Legal Order" (1978) 6 Hofstra L. Rev. 269 at 279-86; and J.S. Watson, "Autointerpretation, Competence, and the Continuing Validity of Article 2(7) of the UN Charter" (1977) 71 A.J.I.L. 60 at 71-77.

[31] UN Charter, Article 13(1). The protective mechanisms envisaged here may be extremely relevant in the context of the prevention of genocide. They range from the action under the Economic and Social Council [hereinafter ECOSOC] resolutions in the case of a consistent pattern of gross and persistent violations of human rights, to public debate in the UN Commission of Human Rights and studies and reports undertaken under the aegis of the commission and its Sub-Commission on Prevention of Discrimination and Protection of Minorities. Further action may result from the operation of the procedures specified in the International Covenant on Civil and Political Rights, December 19, 1966, 999 U.N.T.S. 171, Can. T.S. 1976 No. 47, art. 4, at 6 [hereinafter ICCPR] and the International Convention on the Elimination of All Forms of Racial Discrimination, January 4, 1969, 660 U.N.T.S. 195, and under the various regional systems for human rights protection. See generally on this point, T. Meron, ed., *Human Rights in International Law: Legal and Policy Issues* (Oxford: Clarendon Press, 1984), Chapter 6; A. Vandenbosch and W.N. Hogan, *The United Nations Background, Organization, Functions, Activities* (New York: McGraw-Hill, 1952) at 96, 112; N.M. Procida, "Ethnic Cleansing in Bosnia-Herzegovina, A Case Study: Employing United Nations Mechanisms to Enforce the Convention on the Prevention and Punishment of the Crime of Genocide" (1995) 18 Suffolk Transnat'l L. Rev. 655 at 671. All of this does not make up, however, for the need for a special committee on genocide, which would be the appropriate forum for the airing of questions pertaining specifically to genocide. A recent suggestion that such an organ be created was made by the United Nations Sub-Commission on the Prevention of Discrimination and the Protection of Minorities, but it has not been taken up by bodies in a position to implement such a measure.

[32] H. Lauterpacht, *International Law and Human Rights* (London: Stevens, 1950) at 186; M. McDougal and W.M. Reisman, "Rhodesia and the United Nations: The

lays down, as another commitment of the UN, the "maintenance of international peace and security" and, to that end, the taking of "effective collective measures for the *prevention and removal of threats to peace.*"[33] Further, according to Article 2(5), "[a]ll Members shall give the United Nations assistance in any action it takes in accordance with the present Charter, and shall refrain from giving assistance to any state against which the United Nations is taking *preventive or enforcement action.*" In *Certain Expenses of the United Nations (Article 17, paragraph 2, of the Charter)*, the ICJ recognized that these enforcement and preventive measures clearly envisage action by the Security Council according to Chapter VII of the UN Charter, particularly Articles 41 and 42 whereby the council may impose sanctions and even authorize the use of force.[34] Thus, the Security Council, in addition to having the competence to debate and make recommendations on human rights matters under Chapter VI, may adopt binding decisions under Chapter VII once a determination that a threat to the peace has manifested itself has been made. As I will discuss in the next section, the latter determination may comprise cases where genocidal acts are being committed within the borders of a state.[35]

It has however been suggested that there is no provision in the UN Charter that lays down *expressis verbis* that there is an obligation resting upon nations to *enforce* an observance of human rights and fundamental freedoms. Although it may be fashionable to disparage the UN Charter and bemoan its ineffectiveness, most detractors of this document have not reviewed it carefully enough and do not know clearly what it contains. Though imperfect from the point

---

Lawfulness of International Concern" (1968) 62 A.J.I.L. 1 at 12-13, and n. 50. International instruments have declared consistently that the protection of human rights constitutes the foundation of peace — a view that GA resolutions have reiterated. See, for example, Universal Declaration of Human Rights, *supra* note 13 at preamble; United Nations, *Human Rights and Mass Exoduses*, UN GAOR, 48th Sess., Agenda Item 114(b) at 1, UN Doc. A/RES/48/139. See also P. Malanczuk, *Humanitarian Intervention and the Legitimacy of the Use of Force* (Hingham, MA: M. Nijkhoff International, 1993) at 25; J. Delbrück, "A Fresh Look at Humanitarian Intervention under the Authority of the United Nations" (1992) 67:4 Indiana L. J. 887 at 900.

[33] UN Charter, *supra* note 10, Article 1(1) [emphasis added].

[34] *Certain Expenses of the United Nations (Article 17, paragraph 2, of the Charter)*, Advisory Opinion, [1962] I.C.J. Rep. 151 at 164 [hereinafter *Certain Expenses* case].

[35] See generally O. Schachter, "International Law in Theory and Practice. General Course of Public International Law" (1982) 178 Rec. des Cours 21 at 328-29.

of view of enforcement, a juxtaposition of its relevant provisions, namely Article 55(c) and 56,[36] entails that they do in fact generate legal obligations on UN member states to actively enforce respect for human dignity and protect fundamental human rights.[37] The ICJ would appear to have recognized this fact in its advisory opinion in *Legal Consequences for States of the Continued Presence of South Africa in Namibia (South-West Africa) Notwithstanding Security Council Resolution 276* with respect to the prohibition against discrimination clause found in Article 55(c) of the UN Charter, which is of particular relevance to the position of national minorities.[38] The fact that the human rights clauses of the UN Charter and the Universal Declaration of Human Rights contain binding legal obligations was further recognized in *United States Diplomatic and Consular Staff at Tehran (United States of America v. Iran)*, with regard, at least,

[36] According to the wording of Article 56, the member states are only under an obligation to give, jointly or separately, such support to the UN to achieve the purposes delineated in Article 55 as they see fit. Article 56, however, does require the member states to cooperate with the UN in a constructive way, and obstructive policies are thus excluded. The rather limited obligatory function of Article 56 is the result of the wording of Article 55, to which it refers. The latter, which is addressed to the UN, only describes purposes (and not substantive obligations) to be achieved by means of cooperation. To this extent, Article 56 can thus only create substantive obligations (as opposed to procedural obligations) upon states in so far as Article 55 contains a corresponding basis in this respect. This is partly the case with respect to Article 55(c). Although the "universal respect for, and observance of, human rights and fundamental freedoms" has been formulated as an objective, the additional words "without distinction as to race, sex, language, or religion" already circumscribe a fixed and directly executable obligation. See on this point R. Wolfrum, "Article 56" in B. Simma *et al.*, eds., *The Charter of the United Nations: A Commentary* (Oxford: Oxford University Press, 1994) at 56-57.

[37] N. Singh, *Enforcement of Human Rights in Peace and War and the Future of Humanity* (Dordrecht: Martinus Nijhoff, 1986) at 28; B. Ramcharan, *The Concept and Present Status of the International Protection of Human Rights — Forty Years after the Universal Declaration* (Dordrecht: Martinus Nijhoff, 1988) at 59; and I. Brownlie, *Principles of Public International Law*, 4th ed. (Oxford: Clarendon Press, 1990) at 570.

[38] *Legal Consequences for States of the Continued Presence of South Africa in Namibia (South-West Africa) Notwithstanding Security Council Resolution 276 (1970)*, Advisory Opinion, [1971] I.C.J. Rep. 16 at 57, para. 131 [hereinafter *Namibia* case]. See also E. Schwelb, "The International Court of Justice and the Human Rights Clauses of the Charter" (1972) 66 A.J.I.L. 337 at 350-51 and, more generally, N. Rodley, "Human Rights and Humanitarian Intervention: The Case Law of the World Court" (1989) 38 I.C.L.Q. 321 at 323-27. The earlier view is disputed by Judge van Wynk in the *South West Africa Cases (Ethiopia v. South Africa; Liberia v. South Africa)*, Preliminary Objections, Judgment of December 21, 1962, [1962] I.C.J. Rep. 319 at 602-16 [hereinafter *South West Africa* case].

to the right not to be subjected to torture or cruel, inhuman, or degrading treatment or punishment and the right to liberty and security of the person.[39]

Arguably, the above provisions would also impose a legal obligation on the organs of the organization to act in a way that achieves the purposes set out in the UN Charter, of which the prevention of genocide is perhaps one of the most fundamental to its *raison d'être*.[40] The absence of any clear definition under these provisions is in no way indicative of an absence of legal obligation, nor is the binding nature of this obligation affected by the defectiveness of the machinery that has been provided for its enforcement.[41] The UN Charter provisions are therefore not just hortatory and programmatic. Rather, the subsequent plethora of human rights treaties is seen, at least in the fertile minds of international lawyers and human rights advocates, as supplementing their absent measure of effectiveness rather than transforming their legal and binding nature.[42]

---

[39] *United States Diplomatic and Consular Staff at Tehran (United States of America* v. *Iran),* [1980] I.C.J. Rep. 3 at 42-44, particularly at para. 91 [hereinafter *Teheran Hostages* case].

[40] In the Declaration on Principles of International Law Concerning Friendly Relations and Co-operation among States, GA Resolution 2625 (XXV) GAOR, 25 Sess., Supp. No. 28, UN Doc. A/8028 (1971), reprinted in 9 I.L.M. 1292 [hereinafter Declaration on Friendly Relations], the General Assembly of the UN proclaimed, in the fourth and fifth principles, that "[s]tates shall co-operate in the promotion of universal respect for and observance of human rights and fundamental freedoms for all, and in the elimination of all forms of racial discrimination and all forms of religious intolerance" and that "[e]very state has *the duty to promote through joint and separate action* universal respect for and observance of human rights and fundamental freedoms *in accordance with the Charter"* [specifically referring here to the principle of international cooperation through the UN for the promotion and protection of all human rights under Article 56 of the UN Charter] [emphasis added]. See also W.M. Reisman and M. McDougal, "Humanitarian Intervention to Protect the Ibos" in R. Lillich, ed., *Humanitarian Intervention and the United Nations* (Charlotteville: University of Virginia Press, 1973) at 175; A. Petrenko, "The Human Rights Provisions of the United Nations Charter" (1978) 9 Man. L.J. 53 at 81-87; and J.-B. Marie and N. Questiaux, "Article 55: alinéa c" in J.-P. Cot and A. Pellet, *La Charte des Nations Unies: Commentaires Article par Article* (Paris: Economica, Bruylant, 1985) at 865-68; K.-J. Partsch, "Article 55(c)" in Simma, *supra* note 36 at 779-83.

[41] *Interpretation of Peace Treaties with Bulgaria, Hungary and Romania Case, Second Phase,* Advisory Opinion, [1950] I.C.J. Rep. 221 at 228-29 [hereinafter *Interpretation of Peace Treaties* case]; Lauterpacht, *supra* note 32 at 159.

[42] L.B. Sohn, "The New International Law: Protection of the Rights of Individuals Rather Than States" (1982) 32 Am. U. L. Rev. 1 at 13-17; T. Meron, *Human Rights*

The rights guaranteed by the Genocide Convention are non-derogable for they relate to the right to life, which is the most fundamental human right and an integral part of the irreducible core of the international human rights protection regime.[43] In the discussions on the protection of minorities as a right or an obligation for states and the UN to protect the existence of individuals belonging to these groups, it has often been overlooked that the prohibition against genocide is above all group-concerned.[44] In effect, genocide has been conceptualized as a coordinated plan of different actions aimed at the annihilation of the "essential foundations of life of national groups," which leads to the disintegration

---

and Humanitarian Norms as Customary Law (Clarendon: Oxford, 1989) at 81-85; P.C. Jessup, *A Modern Law of Nations*, 4ᵗʰ ed. (New York: Macmillan, 1952) at 87-93; J.-B. Marie and N. Questiaux, *supra* note 40 at 870. See also Proclamation of Teheran, Final Act of the International Conference on Human Rights, Teheran, April 22 to May 13, 1968, UN Doc. A/CONF. 32/41 at 3, which clearly refers to the relevant UN Charter provisions as constituting international obligations.

43 This right is specifically protected in a non-derogable form in many instruments. See Universal Declaration of Human Rights, *supra* note 13, Article 3; ICCPR, *supra* note 31; Convention for the Protection of Human Rights and Fundamental Freedoms, November 4, 1950, 213 U.N.T.S. 221, Eur. T.S. 5, art. 2; American Convention on Human Rights, November 22, 1969, 1144 U.N.T.S. 123, art. 27; and African Charter of Human and People's Rights, OUA Doc. CAB/LEG/67/3/Rev.5, (1982) 21 I.L.M. 58, art. 20. In his dissenting opinion in the *Case Concerning the Legality of the Threat and Use of Nuclear Weapons*, Advisory Opinion, [1996-I] I.C.J. Rep. 3 at 284 [hereinafter *Nuclear Weapons* case], Judge Weeramantry described this right as "one of the rights which constitute the irreducible core of human rights." See also T. Meron, "On a Hierarchy of International Human Rights" (1986) 80 A.J.I.L. 1 at 4, 11; B.G. Ramcharam, "The Concept and Dimensions of the Right to Life" in B.G. Ramcharam, ed., *The Right to Life in International Law*, Hague Academy of International Law, Center for Studies and Research (Dordrecht: Boston, Martinus Nijhoff, 1985) at 15; P.-M. Dupuy, *Droit International Public*, 3ʳᵈ ed. (Paris: Dalloz, 1995) at 172.

44 Declaration on the Rights of Persons Belonging to National and Ethnic Religious and Linguistic Minorities, GA Res. UN 47/135, annex, 47, UN GA OR, Supp. No. 49, 1993 UN Doc. A/47/49, 210; (1993), reprinted in 32 I.L.M. 911, Preamble; F. Ermacora, "The Protection of Minorities before the United Nations" (1983) 182 Rec. des Cours 247 at 312-13. See also United Nations, *Sub-Commission on Prevention of Discrimination and Protection of Minorities, Study of the Question of the Prevention and Punishment of the Crime of Genocide, prepared by Mr. Nicodème Ruhashyankiko (Rwanda), Special Rapporteur,* UN ESCOR, 31ˢᵗ Sess., Supp. No. 120, UN Doc. E/CN.4/Sub.2/416 (1978) at 121 ff. [hereinafter *Ruhashyankiko Report*], which concludes that there can be no doubt that the groups envisaged in the Genocide Convention can also be considered as minorities; Y. Ben Achour, "Souveraineté et Protection Internationale des Minorités" (1994) 245 Rec. des Cours 321 at 442-43.

of the "political and social institutions of culture, language, national feelings, religion, and the destruction of the personal security, liberty, health, dignity, and even lives of the individuals belonging to such groups."[45] The "group protection" mission of genocide prevention thus consists in the will of the international community and the UN to uphold the existence and autonomy of cultural, religious, national, and racial entities, which are in a given situation, non-dominant groups.[46] Therefore, it is evident that in creating a greatly strengthened human rights regime within the framework of the UN Charter, the principal responsibility and authority to prevent massive human rights violations such as genocide fell on the newly formed UN.

The view that the UN is authorized to take preventive action against impending genocide, even without the consent of the state on whose territory such acts are being committed, is further acknowledged through the doctrine of implied powers, which is an important aspect of the teleological interpretation of statutes of international organizations such as the UN Charter.[47] In effect, "[u]nder international law, the Organization must be deemed to have those powers which, though not expressly provided in the Charter, are conferred upon it *by necessary implication as being essential to the performance of its duties.*"[48] Since genocidal acts may sometimes be characterized as a "threat to international peace and security" and since the main responsibility for the maintenance of international peace and security lies with the Security Council under Article 24(1) of the UN Charter, the UN clearly has the necessary

---

[45] R. Lemkin, *Axis Rule in Occupied Europe* (Washington, DC: Washington Carnegie Endowment for International Peace, 1944) at 79-90; R. Lemkin, "Genocide as a Crime under International Law" (1947) 41 A.J.I.L. 145 at 145.

[46] *Case Concerning Reservations to the Convention on the Prevention and Punishment of the Crime of Genocide,* Advisory Opinion, [1951] I.C.J. Rep. 15 at 23; Ermacora, *supra* note 44 at 313-14; M.N. Shaw, "Genocide and International Law" in Y. Dinstein and M. Tabory, eds., *International Law at a Time of Perplexity: Essays in the Honor of S. Rosenne* (Dordrecht: Kluwer Academic Publishers, 1989) at 803-4.

[47] On the doctrine of implied powers, see A.I.L. Campbell, "The Limits of the Powers of International Organizations" (1983) 32 I.C.L.Q. 523 at 532; M. Rama-Montaldo, "International Legal Personality and Implied Powers of International Organizations" (1970) 44 Brit. Y.B. Int'l L. 111 at 147; R.L. Bindshedler, "La Délimitation des Compétences des Nations Unies" (1963) 108 Rec. des Cours 305 at 327-29.

[48] *Reparation* case, *supra* note 21 at 182; *Effects of Awards of Compensation Made by the United Nations Administrative Tribunal,* Advisory Opinion, [1954] I.C.J. Rep. 47 at 56-57.

authority to take appropriate action in cases of threatening geno-cide. Without such power, the council is left impotent if it becomes necessary to take military enforcement measures to prevent geno-cide, and, thus, the UN will not be able to perform the functions assigned to it by the member states.

Finally, pursuant to Article 89 of the Protocol Additional to the Geneva Conventions of 12 August 1949, and relating to the Protec-tion of Victims of International Armed Conflicts (Protocol I),[49] the high contracting parties undertook to act, jointly and separately, *in cooperation with* the United Nations in certain circumstances, namely when and wherever "serious violations" of international humanitarian law occurred.[50] The language of this provision paral-lels Article 56 of the UN Charter, whereby "all Members pledge themselves to take joint and separate action *in cooperation with* the Organization for the achievement of the purposes set forth in Article 55." The wording of these provisions clearly refers to the organization as a separate entity, functioning through its appropri-ate organs and mandated by the UN Charter to ensure the enforce-ment of humanitarian law.[51] I would suggest that Article 89 of

[49] Protocol Additional to the Geneva Conventions of 12 August 1949, and relating to the Protection of Victims of International Armed Conflicts (Protocol I), June 8, 1977, 1125 U.N.T.S. 3.

[50] In its Final Declaration, the International Conference for the Protection of War Victims, which was held in Geneva in 1993, took up the idea of Article 89 and stressed the obligation of the participating states "to act in cooperation with the UN and in conformity with the UN Charter to ensure full compliance with inter-national humanitarian law in the event of genocide and other serious violations of this law." See "International Conference for the Protection of War Victims (Geneva 1993), Final Declaration," reproduced in (1993) 294 Int'l Rev. Red Cross 377 at 378, para. I.6.

[51] See Wolfrum, *supra* note 36 at 794. Within the UN framework, the General Assembly, the Security Council, and the Commission on Human Rights have on various occasions condemned violations of humanitarian principles. Thus, for instance, regarding the implementation of international humanitarian law in Bosnia-Herzegovina, the Security Council, as the principal UN organ endowed with the responsibility for maintaining peace, has undertaken considerable efforts to demand that all parties "cease and desist from all breaches of interna-tional humanitarian law" (UN Doc. S/RES/780, 1992 at para. 2); to determine that certain acts constitute violations of that body of law; to condemn violations of some humanitarian laws; and to request that governments take specific actions in reaction to those violations. See on this point A. Roberts, "The Laws of War: Problems of Implementation in Contemporary Conflicts" (1995) 6 Duke J. Comp. & Int'l L. 11; L. Boisson de Chazournes, "The Collective Responsibility of States to Ensure Respect for Humanitarian Principles" in A. Bloed *et al.*, eds., *Monitoring Human Rights in Europe* (The Hague: Kluwer Academic Publishers, 1993) at 247-60.

Protocol I goes even further than Article 56 of the UN Charter because it does not limit itself to dealing with the promotion of universal respect for human rights but includes reacting to violations. The UN has indeed an important role in "ensuring respect" for humanitarian law in "all circumstances" since all states party to the 1949 Geneva Conventions[52] may act through and with the organization in fulfilling their obligation to ensure the implementation of this body of law whenever it is being violated by other states.[53] Although humanitarian law criminalizes genocidal acts committed in times of armed conflict,[54] it is now undisputed, both in theory

[52] 1949 Geneva Conventions, including Convention (I) for the Amelioration of the Condition of the Wounded and Sick in Armed Forces in the Field, August 12, 1949, 75 U.N.T.S. 31; Convention (II) for the Amelioration of the Condition of Wounded, Sick and Shipwrecked Members of Armed Forces at Sea, August 12, 1949, 75 U.N.T.S. 85; Convention (III) relative to the Treatment of Prisoners of War, August 12, 1949, 75 U.N.T.S. 135; Convention (IV) relative to the Protection of Civilian Persons in Time of War, August 12, 1949, 75 U.N.T.S. 287 [hereinafter Geneva Conventions]

[53] Common Article 1 of the Geneva Conventions, *supra* note 52.This provision is but an expression of the *erga omnes* character of humanitarian law and is often seen as providing the nucleus for a system of collective responsibility for international implementation of humanitarian law. The words "and ensure respect" have been widely interpreted as signifying that states, whether or not involved in a particular conflict, have a duty to ensure implementation of the conventions wherever and whenever they are being violated and should endeavour to bring the violating state back to an attitude of compliance with humanitarian law. On such an interpretation, see J. Pictet, *The Geneva Conventions of 12 August 1949: A Commentary*, vol. I (Geneva: International Committee of the Red Cross, 1952) at 26; L. Condorelli and L. Boisson de Chazournes, "Common Article 1 of the Geneva Conventions Revisited: Protecting Collective Interests" (March 31, 2000) 837 Int'l Rev. Red Cross 67, accessible at <http://www.icrc.org/eng/review-articles> (date accessed: July 21, 2003).

[54] In this author's view, there is no doubt that the UN Charter's notion of "human rights and fundamental freedoms for all" also encompasses what the United Nations itself has called "human rights in armed conflicts" and what is referred to as "humanitarian law" in this article. This is naturally based on the premise that humanitarian law and human rights law are not completely separate fields and sometimes overlap as both share the common basis of setting limits to violence against human life and dignity. The outbreak of violence within the territory of a state, which is the traditional and most common manifestation of genocidal acts, is thus the obvious example of the simultaneous applicability of rules upholding human rights and the humanitarian law governing non-international armed conflict. See on this point T. Meron, *Human Rights in Internal Strife: Their International Protection* (Cambridge: Grotius Publications, 1987) at 28; D. Schindler, "The International Committee of the Red Cross and Human Rights" (1979) 208 Int'l Rev. Red Cross 5; L. Doswald-Beck and S. Vité, "International Humanitarian Law and Human Rights Law" (1993) 800 Int'l Rev. Red Cross 99.

and practice, that the UN possesses the necessary authority to adopt appropriate measures to react to serious violations of international humanitarian law and, consequently, to prevent impending genocide.

COLLECTIVE HUMANITARIAN INTERVENTION EXEMPLIFIED:
THE SECURITY COUNCIL IN INTERNAL CRISIS SITUATIONS

As has become apparent in the preceding section, the UN may act in appropriate cases to prevent human rights abuses in internal conflicts.[55] However, the further "upstream" that international law may be prepared to go in preventing genocide, the more likely it will be that it will trench upon "matters which are essentially within the domestic jurisdiction of any state"[56] — the complementary principle of sovereignty and a foundational norm of the international legal order.[57] This primary legal impediment to the exercise of international jurisdiction by the UN in the domestic spheres of its member states has been articulated in many legal instruments[58] and is part of customary international law.[59] Preventive measures are taken in anticipation of, rather than in reaction to, events, and it is this aspect that creates a clash with national sovereignty.

Preventive measures do not normally operate as described in Article 2(7) of the UN Charter, which emphasizes that the international system should refrain from intervening where there is no

[55] L.F. Damrosch, "Introduction" in L.F. Damrosch, *Enforcing Restraint: Collective Intervention in Internal Conflicts* (New York: Council on Foreign Relations, 1993) at 6.

[56] This language is borrowed from Article 2(7) of the UN Charter, *supra* note 10.

[57] F. Ermacora, "Article 2(7)" in Simma et al, *supra* note 36 at 143; T. Opperman, "Intervention" in R. Bernhardt *et al.*, eds., *Encyclopedia of Public International Law*, Max Planck Institute of International Law, (Amsterdam: North-Holland, 1987), 233 at 235.

[58] The traditional Cold War view of the principle of non-intervention is reflected in the Declaration on Friendly Relations, *supra* note 40; see also Declaration on the Inadmissibility of Intervention in the Domestic Affairs of States and the Protection of Their Independence and Sovereignty, GA Resolution 2131 (XX), UN GAOR, Supp. (No. 24), UN Doc. A/6014, 1965. Unlike the UN Charter provision, these two documents prohibit intervention by states rather than the organization. It is to be noted that the former instrument, however unsatisfactory its provisions may be, remains the leading text reflecting the current state of general international law on the duty of non-intervention in internal affairs.

[59] *Case Concerning Military and Paramilitary Activities in and against Nicaragua, (Nicaragua v. United States of America)*, [1986] I.C.J. Rep. 14 at 102, paras 192-93 [hereinafter *Nicaragua* case].

conflict. Article 2(7), however, expressly exempts from the prohibition those cases where the organization is entitled to take coercive enforcement measures under Chapter VII of the UN Charter in order to maintain international peace and security. The question that now needs to be addressed is whether the scope of powers conveyed on the UN to respond effectively and in a timely manner to grave violations of human rights also comprises the authority to forcibly intervene to prevent impending genocide. This consideration requires an inquiry into the question of whether (1) systematic genocidal acts committed within the boundaries of a state without any transborder effects are purely an internal matter or a matter of international concern; and (2) there are any limits imposed on the Security Council's competence to determine threats to peace on the basis of internal humanitarian crises and to take action.

Unrestricted Sovereignty Is Incompatible with the Outlawing of Genocide

As was noted by Fernando Tesón as late as 1997, "international legal discourse suffers from a congenital tension between the concern for human rights and the notion of state sovereignty — two pillars of international law."[60] This tension, which has long been the subject of controversy under the League of Nations[61] and during the UN era, generates a major dilemma for all those concerned about the normative dimensions of international relations. On the one hand, it is contented that if intervention is prescribed to promote respect for human rights, then the floodgates will be opened to "unpredictable and serious undermining of world order."[62] This

---

[60] F. Tesón, *Humanitarian Intervention: An Inquiry into Law and Morality* (New York: Transnational Publishers, 1997) at 3.

[61] Article 15(8) of the Covenant of the League of Nations provided that the Council could take no action on a dispute arising out of a matter that, by international law, was solely within the domestic jurisdiction of the state concerned. However, under paragraph 12 of the Minorities Treaty between the Principal Allied and Associated Powers and Poland, the parties agreed that the minority provisions constituted "obligations of international concern," which were to be placed "under the guarantee of the League of Nations." This had the important effect of removing the protection of minority rights from the area of the exclusive domestic jurisdiction and putting it firmly within the jurisdiction of the League. For a thoughtful discussion, see P. Alston and H. Steiner, *International Human Rights in Context: Law, Politics, Morals* (Oxford: Clarendon Press, 1996) at 97; M.T. Kamminga, *Inter-State Accountability for Violations of Human Rights* (Philadelphia: University of Pennsylvania Press, 1992) at 64-66.

[62] This view was aptly favoured in the pre-United Nations and the Cold War era. See P. Szasz, "The Role of the United Nations in Internal Conflicts" (1983) 13

position is aptly defended by the proponents of the so-called *essentialist* view of domestic jurisdiction, who hold that the essence of sovereignty requires that certain matters broadly referred to as *domestic policy* be left outside the reach of international law.[63] This viewpoint refers particularly to the constitutional, political, and social organization of a state as well as the treatment of its subjects.[64] Such an unduly restrictive view of international affairs has led to such aberrations as a declaration by US Ambassador Henry Morgenthau in 1915, when he was encountered with Turkey's cold-blooded rulers, to the effect that "it is difficult for me to restrain myself from doing something to stop this attempt to exterminate a race, but I realize that I am here as Ambassador and must abide by the principles of non-interference with the internal affairs of another country."[65]

If intervention is prohibited altogether even to check gross human rights violations, then the principle of non-intervention involves a "morally intolerable proposition whereby the international community is impotent to combat massacres, acts of genocide, mass murder and widespread torture."[66] Although every state has an inalienable right to choose its political, economic, social,

---

Ga. J. Int'l. & Comp. L. 345 at 353; Ermacora, *supra* note 57 at 141, 151-52. It is to be noted that during the debates at the San Francisco conference, the actual substitution of the word "essentially" in lieu of "solely" was intended to serve as a limit on international rather than domestic jurisdiction. The Security Council's interpretation of this term, however, has not followed Article 2(7)'s intended meaning. See on this point D. Nincic, *The Problem of Sovereignty in the Charter and in the Practice of the United Nations* (The Hague: Martinus Nijhoff, 1970) at 159-160, 182.

[63] Tesón, *supra* note 60 at 137.

[64] See Nincic, *supra* note 62 at 186; Declaration on Friendly Relations, *supra* note 40. In the *Nicaragua* case, *supra* note 59 at 131, the International Court of Justice [hereinafter ICJ] has adopted a slightly different position. For the court, there is a presumption that a matter that is traditionally described as a matter or domestic policy falls within the exclusive domestic jurisdiction of the state. This presumption, however, can be rebutted by a showing that the state has bound itself internationally, through custom or treaty with respect to the issue.

[65] H. Morgenthau, *Ambassador Morgenthau's Story* (New York: Doubleday, Page and Company, 1918) at 326-63, quoted in Kamminga, *supra* note 61 at 16-17. During the Cold War, the Soviets particularly deplored UN human rights initiatives as impermissible intervention. See on this point T.M. Franck, "Soviet Initiatives: U.S. Responses New Opportunities for Reviving the United Nations System" (1989) 83 A.J.I.L. 531 at 533.

[66] Tesón, *supra* note 60 at 4.

and cultural systems without interference in any form by another state,[67] it can hardly be assumed that this right constitutes a license to commit genocide, massive human rights violations, and generally terrorize the population with impunity.[68] It is thus submitted that the question of whether a matter falls within a state's *domaine réservé* cannot be determined by appealing to a static notion of sovereignty, but rather is a relative matter that depends on the state of international law at any given time.[69] Further, where a treaty, customary or other rule of international law regulates an issue, the latter automatically ceases to be a matter of exclusive jurisdiction and becomes subject to international scrutiny for those states formally bound by this rule.[70]

---

[67] *Austro-German Customs Union Case,* Advisory Opinion (1931), P.C.I.J. (Ser. A/B) No. 41 [hereinafter *Austro-German Customs Union* case].

[68] In stressing the need for balancing the rights of states (as mentioned in the UN Charter) and the protection of individual human rights, then Secretary-General Javier Pérez de Cuellar challenged the traditional construction placed on Article 2(7): "It is now increasingly felt that the principle of non-interference with the essential domestic jurisdiction of States cannot be regarded as a protective barrier behind which human rights could be massively or systematically violated with impunity ... The case for impinging on the sovereignty, territorial integrity and political independence of States is by itself indubitably strong. But it would only be weakened if it were to carry the implication that sovereignty, even in this day and age, includes the right of mass slaughter or of launching systematic campaigns of decimation or forced exodus of civilian populations in the name of controlling civil strife or insurrection." See *Report of the Secretary General on the Work of the Organization,* UN Doc. GA/46/404, 1991, reprinted in (1991) 45 Y.B.U.N. 7 at 7-8.

[69] *Nationality Decrees in Tunis and Morocco Case* (1923), P.C.I.J. (Ser. B) No. 4 at 23-24. This approach was confirmed in a number of subsequent cases of the ICJ: *Anglo-Iranian Oil Co. Case (Interim Measures),* [1951] I.C.J. Rep. 89 at 93; *Interhandel Case (Switzerland* v. *United States of America),* [1959] I.C.J Rep. 6 at 24; *Interpretation of Peace Treaties* case, *supra* note 41; *Teheran Hostages* case, *supra* note 39 at 15-16; *Namibia* case, *supra* note 38 at 31. See also generally M.S. Rajan, *The Expanding Jurisdiction of the United Nations* (Bombay: Orient Longmans, 1982) at 168-69; J.E.S. Fawcett, "General Course on Public International Law" (1971) 132 Rec. des Cours 363 at 392; and G. Schwarzenberger and E. Brown, *A Manuel of International Law* (London: Stevens, 1960) at 60, where the authors state that "the totality of rules of international law can be explained as a constantly changing and dynamic interplay between the rules underlying the principles of sovereignty and those governing the other fundamental principles of international law."

[70] The Institut de Droit International addressed the question of the scope of the *domaine réservé* in 1954: "The reserved domain is the domain of state activities where the state is not bound by international law. The extent of this domain

It is now increasingly accepted that egregious human rights violations within sovereign states, which have traditionally been claimed by states as falling within their *domaine réservé*, will not preclude the taking of international action by international bodies such as the UN to redress those situations of abuse.[71] As states make commitments to a larger and more intrusive regime of international human rights treaties and as customary law expands its reach, the concept of exclusive domestic jurisdiction shrinks accordingly.[72] Although few states still object today to the overall process of the UN machinery based on some form of cultural relativism, governments singled out for human rights violations rarely claim that such actions of redress violate the principle of non-intervention.[73]

---

depends on international law and varies according to its developments." See Resolution of the Institut de Droit International, Session d'Aix-en-Provence, "La Détermination du Domaine Réservé et ses Effets" (1954-II) 45 Ann. instit. dr. int'l at 292 [my translation].

[71] Resolution of the Institut de Droit International, Session de Saint-Jacques-de-Compostelle, "The Protection of Human Rights and the Principle of Non-Intervention in Internal Affairs of States," Art. 2 (1990-II) 63 Ann. instit. dr. int'l, Paris, Pédone, 338 at 340, UN Doc. E/CN.4/1990/NGO/55. See the excellent analysis of the resolution and its earlier drafts in M. Ragazzi, *The Concept of International Obligations Erga Omnes* (Oxford: Clarendon Press, 1997) at 141-44. See also the special report submitted by Sir Gerald Fitzmaurice to the Institut de Droit International in 1973 where he refers to a "general duty to respect human rights," which every state has an interest to protect: G. Fitzmaurice, "The Future of Public International Law and of the International Legal System in the Circumstances of Today" in Institut de Droit International, *Livre du Centenaire 1873-1973: Évolution et perspectives du droit international* (Basel: Karger Publishers, 1973) at 323, para. 111(c). Although it would be impossible to render a full account of all the doctrinal proponents of this position, I would mention the following: R. Higgins, *The Development of International Law through the Political Organs of the United Nations* (New York: Oxford University Press, 1963) at 65-67; F. Ermacora, "Human Rights and Domestic Jurisdiction" (1968) 124 Rec. des Cours 371 at 436; W.M. Reisman, "Sovereignty and Human Rights in Contemporary International Law" (1990) 84 A.J.I.L. 866 at 869, 872-73; J.-P.L. Fonteyne, "The Customary International Law Doctrine of Humanitarian Intervention: Its Current Validity under the UN Charter" (1974) 4 Cal. W. Int'l L.J. 203 at 241; Lauterpacht, *supra* note 32 at 178. For the impact of the right to self-determination of peoples on the restriction of the notion of "domestic jurisdiction," see G. Arangio-Ruiz, "Le domaine réservé. L'organisation internationale et le rapport entre le droit international et le droit interne" (1990) 225 Rec. des Cours 9 at 320-27, 335-36.

[72] D. Scheffer, "Toward a Modern Doctrine of Humanitarian Intervention" (1992) 23 U. Toledo L. Rev. 253 at 260.

[73] K.K. Pease and D.P. Forsythe, "Human Rights, Humanitarian Intervention, and World Politics" (1993) 15 Hum. Rts. Q. 290 at 295. Some states have always

It should be borne in mind, however, that this article does not attempt to provide a definitive answer to this legal and jurisprudential dilemma. Rather, it will circumscribe the argument to the contention that massive and systematic human rights violations short of actual genocide are not a "matter falling essentially within the exclusive domestic jurisdiction" of states but rather one of international concern, regardless of any substantial international effects such acts may produce.[74] It is stressed that although human rights violations that *in fact* threaten peace do cease to be the sole concern of the offending state and give rise to accountability to the world organization,[75] the UN's authority to respond to these violations is by no means limited to such extreme situations.

This conclusion is buttressed by a review of the summary records of the Sixth Committee of the General Assembly, which is devoted to what became the non-interference provision of the Declaration on Principles of International Law Concerning Friendly Relations and Co-Operation among States in Accordance with the Charter of the United Nations.[76] During these debates, some delegates took the view that the principle of non-intervention "could not be construed to mean that a country could violate the fundamental

---

been disinclined to go along with international regimes that forcibly seek to prevent humanitarian disasters by promoting democracy. They see the UN as an instrument of the United States and other Northern countries — states dominating the organization — to meddle in their internal affairs. For example, these states may think that the UN overstepped its bounds by getting involved in Haiti (see discussion later in this article) and want to protect themselves from such interferences in the future. Philip Alston notes that one particular block of states, the signatories to the Bangkok Declaration, which was adopted at the World Conference Regional Preparatory Meeting for Asia in 1993, has been particularly reticent to extend the principles of human rights very far. See P. Alston, "The UN's Human Rights Record: From San Francisco to Vienna and Beyond" (1994) 16 Hum. Rts. Q. 375 at 382.

74 Some writers such as Rosalyn Higgins have argued that "states must be made responsible to the international community when their actions cause substantial international effects." See Higgins, *supra* note 71 at 62. However, as it has been rightly noted by Tesón, such a policy seems outmoded today in light of recent developments in UN law. See F. Tesón, "Collective Humanitarian Intervention" (1996) 17(2) Mich. J. Int'l L. 323 at 329 ff; B. Harff, *Genocide and Human Rights: International Legal and Political Issues* (Denver: Colorado, Graduate School of International Studies, University of Denver, 1984) at 42-43; Reisman and McDougal, *supra* note 40 at 189, 190-91. See also Judge Jessup's separate opinion in the *South West Africa* case, *supra* note 38 at 425-27.

75 See Rajan, *supra* note 69 at 133.

76 Declaration on Friendly Relations, *supra* note 40.

human rights of its citizens without that violation becoming the concern of the entire world community."[77] Others argued that only certain categories of human rights violations did not fall within the area of domestic jurisdiction, such as a denial of the right to self-determination, genocide, apartheid, and, more generally, violations threatening international peace and security.[78] Furthermore, the *travaux préparatoires* of the UN Charter reveal that some states, led by France, proposed an amendment to remove from the domestic jurisdiction clause of Article 2(7) large-scale and systematic human rights violations *that endangered inter-state relations*.[79] However, this proposal was widely rejected, and the Australian delegate observed that if UN members wanted to confer upon the organization powers to protect minorities, they would have to expressly declare that such a matter is of international concern and subsequently adopt a convention regulating it.[80] There appears however to be no valid support in these views for the proposition that fundamental rights and freedoms *only* cease to be the sole concern of a state if they are grievously outraged so as to create conditions that threaten the stability of the region.

This conclusion is further supported by the fact that the prohibition against genocide belongs to *jus cogens* — a rule that is recognized by the international community as being the concern of all states.[81] Furthermore, the General Assembly routinely adopts resolutions concerning human rights violations occurring within a state, and it seldom refers to the substantial international repercussions of these acts as a rationale for such soft intervention.[82] Finally,

---

[77] See statements in Kamminga, *supra* note 61 at 81, n. 57.

[78] *Ibid.* at n. 58. See also J.-P. Fonteyne, "Forcible Self-Help to Protect Human Rights: Recent Views from the United Nations" in Lillich, *supra* note 40 at 216.

[79] See the discussion on this point in G. Guillaume, "Article 2: paragraphe 7" in Cot and Pellet, *supra* note 40 at 144, 153-55.

[80] *Ibid.*

[81] See Vienna Convention, *supra* note 29, Article 53. During the codification of the law of treaties, the prohibition of genocide was in fact the most cited example of peremptory rule in the field of international human rights. See United Nations, *United Nations Conference on the Law of Treaties: Official Records, First Session*, vol. I (New York: United Nations, 1969) at 296-323. For support for the prohibition against genocide as a *jus cogens* rule, see L. Alexidze, "The Legal Nature of Jus Cogens in Contemporary International Law" (1981) 172 Rec. des Cours 219 at 262; Brownlie, *supra* note 37 at 513; Sinclair, *supra* note 29 at 216-17; *Ruhashyankiko Report*, *supra* note 44 at 799.

[82] See examples cited in Tesón, *supra* note 74 at 330-31.

the competence of the UN to respond to violations *not* representing a physical threat to international peace and security has been recognized in many resolutions adopted by the Economic and Social Council.[83] The UN Commission on Human Rights is authorized, for example, to investigate situations that reveal a "consistent pattern of gross and reliably attested violations of human rights,"[84] and it has further been held that "violations of human rights, wherever they exist, are of concern to the United Nations."[85] Under these resolutions, the legitimacy of UN involvement in investigating, discussing, and evaluating human rights abuses no longer depends on the question of whether the security of other states is being threatened but simply on the seriousness and scale of the violations being committed.[86]

Perhaps more explicit evidence of the authority of the UN to intervene to prevent massacres on the scale of genocide, without the fear of eroding sovereignty, is provided by the provisions of the UN Charter pertaining to the responsibility of the UN for the maintenance of international peace and security. These provisions are supplemented by Article VIII of the Genocide Convention, which provides that "[a]ny Contracting Party may call upon the competent organs of the United Nations to take such action under the Charter of the United Nations as they consider appropriate for the prevention and suppression of acts of Genocide." This article appears to play an important part in the prevention of genocide as it is arguably the only provision that deals expressly with *actual* "prevention and suppression" of this crime.[87] It has been suggested that the provision would have the effect of conferring upon the organs

[83] UN ECOSOC Resolution 1235 (XLII), UN ESCOR, 42nd Sess., Supp. No. 1 at 17, UN Doc. E/4393; *Procedure for Dealing with Communications Relating to Violations of Human Rights and Fundamental Freedoms,* May 27, 1970, ECOSOC Resolution 1503 (XLVIII), 48 UN ESCOR, Supp. (No. 1A) 8, UN Doc. E/4832/Add.1 (1970).

[84] UN ECOSOC Resolution 1235, *supra* note 83. Although it is not clear what should be understood by "a consistent pattern of gross violations," especially since the UN itself has not defined the concept, a precise definition is not needed since the political organs of the UN have on numerous occasions demonstrated that they do not consider themselves restricted by this category. For a tentative definition, see Kamminga, *supra* note 61 at 118, n. 216 and accompanying text.

[85] UN ECOSOC Resolution 37/200, UN Doc. A/RES/37/200 (December 18, 1982).

[86] Kamminga, *supra* note 61 at 117-19.

[87] *Ruhashyankiko Report, supra* note 44 at para. 304.

of the UN certain rights beyond those contained in the UN Charter.[88] However, the record of deliberations in the drafting of the Genocide Convention indicates that the latter provision did not enhance the existing powers of the organs of the UN,[89] and it was even suggested that it be deleted.[90] Thus, it did not add anything to the existing provisions contained in the UN Charter, which had already conferred general competence and responsibility to the organization to promote international peace and security and consequently to prevent threats to peace.[91]

While Article VIII of the Genocide Convention does not add anything to the substance of the powers of the organs of the UN,[92] it does remain highly important insofar as their competence is concerned with respect to member states that are non-party to the Genocide Convention and non-members of the UN who become parties to it. First, in regard to the former group, it has been contended that these states did not renounce their right to consider genocidal acts committed outside the territorial scope of the treaty as being essentially within their own jurisdiction. However, such an interpretation could hardly be sustained since genocide has been recognized unanimously and under customary law as a "crime

[88] For a thorough discussion of the debates in the Ad Hoc Committee and the Sixth Committee on Genocide on Article VIII, see W.A. Schabas, *Genocide and International Law: The Crime of Crimes* (Cambridge: Cambridge University Press, 2000) at 448-51.

[89] See N. Robinson, *Genocide Convention: A Commentary* (New York: Institute of Jewish Affairs, 1960) at 91; P.N. Drost, *The Crime of State II. Genocide* (Leyden: A.W. Sythoff, 1959) at 106; A. Cassese, "La Communauté Internationale et le Génocide" in D. Bardonnet, ed., *Le droit international au service de la paix, de la justice et du développement. Mélanges Michel Virally* (Paris: Pédone, 1991) at 185.

[90] See the declaration of the delegate of the United Kingdom, Gerald Fitzmaurice, UN GAOR 6ᵗʰ Comm., 3ʳᵈ Sess., pt.1, 101ˢᵗ Mtg. at 409, UN Doc. A/C.6/SR,61-140 (1948): "Under the provisions of the Charter ... Members were already entitled to appeal to organs of the United Nations in case of need and it was, therefore, unnecessary and undesirable to repeat those provisions in a new convention." In fact, the proposal of Belgium and the United Kingdom to delete the article was adopted (see respectively, UN Doc. A/C.6/236 and Corr. 1 and UN Doc. A/C.6/217), but the provision was reinstated by the Sixth Committee at the instigation of Australia for the sake of clarity.

[91] Robinson, *supra* note 89 at 90-91; J.L. Kunz, "The United Nations Convention on Genocide" (1949) 43 A.J.I.L. 738 at 745-46. According to Kunz, acts of genocide are at any rate violations of human rights that come within the purview of the UN Charter on the basis of Article 1(3), 13(1)b), 55(c), and 56. This view is also shared by Sir Hersch Lauterpacht, *supra* note 32 at para. 340.

[92] *Withaker Report, supra* note 8 at para. 66.

under international law."[93] Thus, the crime, which, if committed by a government in its own territory against its own citizens, has traditionally been of no concern to international law, is made expressly a matter of international concern and is therefore taken out of the matters essentially within the jurisdiction of any state of Article 2(7) of the UN Charter.[94] Although only contracting parties can invoke Article VIII, the UN is called to intervene in this sphere, and whether the targeted state is party or not to the Genocide Convention is, for the purpose of international law, irrelevant.

Second, it is well recognized that the powers of the organs of the UN are ordinarily restricted to members of the organization. By virtue of Article VIII of the Genocide Convention, non-members of the UN that are party to the treaty are granted the right to call upon these organs — a right that they generally would not have otherwise, except insofar as the Security Council is concerned. Thus, the organs of the UN have been granted the power of action, within UN Charter limits, also in the case of non-members of the UN that are parties to the treaty.[95] Nevertheless, the question of whether the organs of the UN may act only in instances of genocidal acts committed within the territory of a state party to the Genocide Convention or in any part of the world, particularly within the territory of states that are non-members of the UN, must be decided on the basis of the UN Charter.[96] According to Article 2(6), "the Organization shall ensure that States which are not Members of the United Nations act in accordance with these Principles [those contained in Article 2(1-4) of the UN Charter] so far as may be necessary for the

---

[93] *Ruhashyankiko Report, supra* note 44 at 799.

[94] R.W. Edwards, "Contributions of the Genocide Convention to the Development of International Law" (1981) 8 Ohio Northern U. L. Rev. 300 at 306-8; J. Verhoeven, "Le crime de génocide: originalité et ambiguité" (1991) 24 Rev. B.D.I. 5 at 12; Kunz, *supra* note 91 at 738; H.-H. Jescheck, "Genocide" in Bernhardt, *supra* note 57 at 256; Harff, *supra* note 74.

[95] Robinson, *supra* note 89 at 94.

[96] Drost, *supra* note 89 at 107-8. It is to be noted that Article 10 of the UN Charter is framed in terms so broad that no limitation whatsoever can be placed on the discussions and recommendations by the General Assembly on human rights issues. Thus, in the *Interpretation of Peace Treaties, supra* note 41 at 221-30, the ICJ rejected an objection that asserted that the General Assembly, by dealing with questions of human rights, was intervening in essentially domestic matters of (at that time) non-members states. The court concluded that, particularly in light of Article 55 of the UN Charter and the principle of promoting "universal respect for, and observance of, human rights," the latter were within the scope of the UN Charter.

maintenance of international peace and security." As is well known, the main responsibility for the maintenance of international peace and security lies within the Security Council, in accordance with the provisions of Chapters VI, VII, VIII, and XII of the UN Charter. The framers of the UN Charter proceeded upon the assumption that peace is one and indivisible, and they did not restrict the powers of the council to the territories under the authority of the members of the UN.[97]

The UN is thus *prima facie* authorized to intervene on the basis of the UN Charter and take decisions binding on all member states, which involve measures to prevent or suppress genocidal acts wherever they may occur.[98] This preventive action of the Security Council would not make the Genocide Convention binding as a whole upon non-parties, but would constitute a simple application of the general powers of the organs of the UN, as conferred by the UN Charter, to the specific case of genocide. The focus will now turn to the issue of the limits imposed on the exercise of coercive powers by the council in its determination of a threat to international peace and security. Before doing so, however, I wish to briefly address the claim that although the observance by a government of the human rights of its own citizens is now subject to international scrutiny, the international community acting through the UN should not be authorized to pass judgment on the internal political legitimacy of any government.[99]

Redefining Statehood: Genocidal Acts As an Abdication of Sovereignty and Legitimacy

Traditional international law recognizes that a government is the international representative of a people living in a territory if it has effective control over that people.[100] The independence of states is

---

[97] See *Certain Expenses* case, *supra* note 34 at 295 (dissenting opinion of Judge Bustamante).

[98] Drost, *supra* note 89 at 109. It is to be noted that the expression "*prima facie* authorized" refers to the ensuing discussion about the limits imposed by the UN Charter to the exercise of powers of the Security Council to prevent genocide wherever it occurs through coercive measures.

[99] This was the virtually unanimous view before 1948. See on this point G.H. Fox, "The Right to Political Participation in International Law" (1992) 17 Yale J. Int'l L. 539 at 549-69.

[100] See the Montevideo Convention on Rights and Duties of States, December 26, 1934, 165 L.N.T.S. 19, U.N.T.S. 881, which states at Article 1 that a state should

a particular attribute of their sovereignty and implies that a state has a right of decision in all matters economic, political, cultural, or other free from the authority of any other state.[101] This idea epitomizes the principle of non-intervention whereby the question of internal political legitimacy of a government is essentially a matter under the exclusive jurisdiction of the state, exempt from any type of intervention by international organizations or the international community as a whole. It is argued, however, that state sovereignty is contingent upon the respect for fundamental human rights or, more broadly, upon universal standards of moral conduct.[102] Failure by a state to protect the fundamental human rights of its citizens would constitute a temporary abdication of sovereignty for the particular purpose of protecting its population, thus creating a "vacuum" that the international community may fill by intervening and preventing large-scale human rights deprivations.[103]

The theory of "forfeiture" of sovereignty or legitimacy is not free from controversy and is premised upon the "Kantian" assumption that a sovereign ultimately derives its right to existence not from any supposed international order but from the effective protection

---

possess four qualifications: "(a) a permanent population; (b) a defined territory;(c) a government; and (d) capacity to enter into relations with other states." The convention has been described as basing recognition, as evidence of statehood, on effectiveness. Tesón also notes that "[w]hether political power has been consensually granted to the government or the usurpers rule instead through fear and terror is of little interest of the supporters of the doctrine of effectiveness." Tesón, *supra* note 60 at 141.

[101] *Austro-German Customs Union* case, *supra* note 67 (separate opinion of Judge Anzilotti); See also *Nicaragua* case, *supra* note 59 at 131.

[102] F.K. Abiew, *The Evolution of the Doctrine and Practice of Humanitarian Intervention* (The Hague: Kluwer Law International, 1999) at 58; Reisman and McDougal, *supra* note 40 at 167; B.S. Brown, "International Law. The Protection of Human Rights in Disintegrating States: A New Challenge" (1992) 68 Chi.-Kent. L. Rev. 203 at 224-25; M.L. Burton, "Legalizing the Sublegal A Proposal for Codifying a Doctrine of Unilateral Humanitarian Intervention" (1996) 85 Geo. L.J. 417 at 435-36

[103] According to Deng, "Where the government is not in control or the controlling authority is unable or unwilling to create the conditions necessary to ensure rights, and gross violations of the rights of masses of people result, sovereignty in the sense of responsible government is forfeited and the international community must provide the needed protection and assistance." See F. Deng, *Protecting the Dispossessed: A Challenge for the International Community* (Washington, DC: Brookings Institution, 1993) at 13,125; F. Deng, "Internally Displaced Persons" (1994) 6 Intern'l. J. Refugee L. 291 at 293, 301-2.

and enforcement of the rights of its citizens.[104] Modern international law requires changing the traditional definitions of sovereignty, domestic jurisdiction, human rights, and their relationships with one another.[105] Since sovereignty is derived from the popular will of the people, which is referred to as "popular sovereignty," and does not belong to the ruler who holds the power over the state, the ruler is included among those who can threaten and violate the sovereignty of the state by failing to protect the population from human rights abuses.[106]

Although willingness to respect international obligations is often seen as a criterion of statehood,[107] there has heretofore been little precedent in international legal discourse for the converse principle that failure to honour international obligations, particularly those pertaining to fundamental human rights, leads to a temporary surrender of firmly established sovereignty.[108] In the *Island of Palmas (Netherlands v. United States of America)* arbitration, Judge Max

---

104 Tesón, *supra* note 60 at 118-21. On an assessment of such a view through the perspective of international relations theory, see A.-M. Slaughter-Burley, "A Liberal Theory of International Law" (1998) 92 A.J.I.L. 1 at 14.

105 Reisman states that "by shifting the fulcrum of the system from the protection of sovereigns to the protection of people, it works qualitative changes in virtually every component ... Precisely because the human rights norms are constitutive, other norms must be reinterpreted in their light, lest anachronisms be produced." See Reisman, *supra* note 71 at 872-73.

106 *Ibid.* at 869-70; L. Wildhaber, "Sovereignty and International Law" in R. St. J. Macdonald and D.M. Johnston, eds., *The Structure and Process of International Law: Essays in Legal Philosophy, Doctrine and Theory* (The Hague: Martinus Nijhoff, 1983) at 4. For a discussion of the concept of "popular sovereignty" as supporting the emerging right to restore democracy, see L.E. Fielding, "Taking the Next Step in the Development of New Human Rights: The Emerging Right of Humanitarian Assistance to Restore Democracy" (1995) 5 Duke J. Comp. & Int'l L. 329 at 338-40. See also on this point K.A. Annan, "Two Concepts of Sovereignty," accessible at <http://www.un.org/Overview/SG/kaecon.htm> at 1-2.

107 J. Crawford, "The Criteria for Statehood in International Law" (1976-77) 48 Brit. Y.B. Int'l. L. 93 at 141-42; Brownlie, *supra* note 37 at 77.

108 Crawford does not seem to envisage such a hypothesis when enumerating the constituting elements of statehood. See J. Crawford, *The Creation of States in International Law* (Oxford: Clarendon Press, 1979) at 31 ff. Brownlie states that "once a state has been established, extensive civil strife or the breakdown of order through foreign invasion or natural disasters are not considered to affect personality." See Brownlie, *supra* note 37 at 73. Traditionally, the international law of recognition of statehood and of territorial acquisition has thus required far less for the maintenance of sovereignty than for its acquisition, perhaps out of legitimate concern about the destabilizing effects of easy allegations of forfeiture.

Huber articulated a definition of sovereignty, stating that modern international law has demanded with "growing insistence ... that occupation [of a territory] ... be effective" for a state to acquire or maintain sovereignty.[109] Moreover, under the inter-temporal principle, effective sovereignty is not static but instead must be measured according to the rules of international law that are applicable at the time relevant to the dispute,[110] particularly those rules that are relevant to the rights and duties of states in the field of human rights. In his decision, Huber articulated two attributes of sovereignty under modern international law that could lend support to the theory of temporary "forfeiture" of sovereignty and thus both legitimize and legalize intervention by the UN to prevent impending genocide. First, territorial sovereignty must be established and maintained by a continuous display of state activities.[111] Sovereignty also confers an exclusive right to display state activities but carries with it the corollary duty to protect the interests of other states within the territory from which they are thus excluded.[112] As it was previously discussed, the prohibition of genocide and the corresponding duty to respect the fundamental right to life of minority groups are by their very nature the concern of all states.[113] Therefore, it is submitted that maintaining absolute sovereignty in contemporary international law requires a state to respect at a minimum the fundamental human rights of its citizens. A government that engages in large-scale and systematic violations of human rights prohibited under principles that admit of no derogation betrays the very purpose for which it exists and so forfeits not only its domestic legitimacy but also its international legitimacy.[114]

---

[109] *Island of Palmas (Netherlands v. United States of America)* (1928), 2 R.I.A.A. 829 at 839.

[110] *Ibid.* at 845.

[111] *Ibid.* at 839.

[112] *Ibid.* This is similar to the "good neighbour principle" spelled out in the decision on the merits in the *Corfu Channel* case, *supra* note 9, where the ICJ stated at page 22 that it is "every state's obligation not to allow knowingly its territory to be used for acts contrary to the rights of other states." The latter proposition was not however articulated as an attribute of state sovereignty.

[113] A. Cassese, "*Ex iniuria ius oritur:* Are We Moving towards International Legitimation of Forcible Humanitarian Countermeasures in the World Community?" (1999) 10(1) Eur. J. Int'l L. 1 at 1-7. See also P. Thornberry, *International Law and the Rights of Minorities* (Oxford: Clarendon Press, 1991) at 48-52.

[114] Tesón, *supra* note 60 at 15-16; M.J. Levitin, "The Law of Force and the Force of Law: Grenada, The Falklands and Humanitarian Intervention" (1986) 27

Furthermore, while no particular governmental system is dictated by general international law and a state has the right to choose its own religion and political system without interference from other states,[115] it seems obvious that a state cannot "freely" choose to adopt a tyrannical and murderous regime, even though such a regime is a "political system."[116] This conclusion stems from the fact that the right to regional self-governance and the right to participate in the national decision-making process are both increasingly recognized today as forming part of a collective right to democratic rule — a necessary precondition for the enjoyment of other human rights.[117] To paraphrase John Rawls, all political entities meeting some basic functional requirements are entitled to be recognized

---

Harv. Int'l L.J. 621 at 652; R. Falk, "The Complexities of Humanitarian Intervention: A New World Challenge" (1996) 17 Mich. J. Int'l L. 491 at 503; Burton, *supra* note 102 at 436; See also M. Walzer, *Just and Unjust Wars: A Moral Argument with Historical Illustrations* (New York: Basic Books Publishers, 1977) at 53. Walzer acknowledges that state sovereignty and legitimacy derive ultimately from the rights of individuals, but cautions against the open-ended consequences of this viewpoint. According to this view, intervention can only be justified in extreme situations where massacres, genocide, or enslavement occur.

[115] *Competence of the General Assembly for the Admission of a State to the United Nations,* Advisory Opinion, [1950] I.C.J. Rep. 4 at 78 [hereinafter *Admissions* case] (individual opinion of judge Azevedo). See also the *Nicaragua* case, *supra* note 59 at 131-33 where the court stated that every state "is free to decide upon the principle and methods of popular consultation," this being part of a "fundamental right to choose and implement its own political, economic, and social systems." It stated further that "adherence by a State to any particular doctrine does not constitute a violation of customary international law; to hold otherwise would make nonsense of the principle of state sovereignty." This position of the World Court regarding the principle of democratic rule has been severely criticized by Tesón as entailing that states have the "freedom" to be undemocratic and even totalitarian. See Tesón, *supra* note 60 at 144.

[116] The Vienna Declaration and Programme of Action, World Conference on Human Rights, Vienna, June 14-25, 1993, UN Doc. A/CONF.157/24, July 12, 1993, art. 5, pt. 1, states: "All human rights are universal, indivisible, and interdependent and interrelated. The international community must treat human rights globally in a fair and equal manner, on the same footing, and with the same emphasis. While the significance of national and regional particularities and various historical, cultural and religious backgrounds must be borne in mind, *it is the duty of States, regardless of their political, economic and cultural systems, to promote and protect all human rights and fundamental freedoms*" [emphasis added].

[117] See Universal Declaration of Human Rights, *supra* note 13, Article 21; ICCPR, *supra* note 31, Article 25. See generally Fox, *supra* note 99; T.M. Franck, "The Emerging Right to Democratic Governance" (1992) 86 A.J.I.L. 46; Tesón, *supra* note 74 at 331-35. See also T.M. Franck, "Fairness in the International Legal and Institutional System" (1993) 240 Rec. des Cours 9 at 118-21.

and accepted as members of the international community. These are largely practical, non-ideological requirements and include the idea that legitimate rulers genuinely represent their people and the minority groups living within their territory.[118] This "true representativeness" requires governments, among other things, to enable ethnic groups and minorities to freely express their wishes in matters concerning their condition and destiny. Therefore, UN intervention does not seek to challenge the attributes of sovereignty, territorial integrity, or the political independence of a state. This fact holds true however in so far as the state can claim legitimacy in terms of respect for the fundamental human rights of ethnic groups living in its territory by virtue of a representative government.[119]

Genocide Prevention, Collective Security, and the Evolving Parameters of "Threats to Peace"

Even if one accepts that human rights violations of a genocidal nature within the borders of a sovereign nation are a subject of international concern, the ways in which the international community may legitimately prevent genocide through forcible measures remains to be assessed.[120] As noted earlier, the Security Council is empowered under Chapter VII of the UN Charter to authorize "collective security" military action in response to impending genocide upon a *bona fide* determination of a "threat to international peace and security" under Article 39. The founding fathers of the UN Charter intentionally declined to define this concept in order to vest the Security Council with very broad discretion in making this determination on a case-by-case basis and to decide what enforcement measures shall be taken to maintain and restore international peace and security.[121] This discretion, however, remains contingent

---

[118] J. Rawls, "The Law of Peoples" in S. Shute and S. Hurley, *On Human Rights: The Oxford Amnesty Lectures* (New York: Basic Books Publishers, 1993) at 53 ff., 82.

[119] Ermacora, *supra* note 57 at 152.

[120] As the International Law Commission has taken pains to point out, "it is one thing to state a rule and the content of the obligation it imposes, and another to determine ... what the consequences of ... [its] breach must be." See *Report of the International Law Commission on the Work of Its Thirty-Second Session*, UN GAOR, 35th Sess., Supp. No. 10, UN Doc. A/25/10, A/CN.4/SER.A/1980/Add.1 (81.V.4) (Part 2), reproduced in (1980) 2 Y.B. Int'l L. Comm. Part. 2 at para. 24.

[121] McDougal and Reisman, *supra* note 32 at 6; M. Virally, *L'Organisation Mondiale* (Paris: A. Colin, 1972) at 456-65; H. Kelsen, *The Law of the United Nations: A Critical Analysis of Its Fundamental Problems* (London: Stevens and Sons, 1951) at 727 ff, 737. Perhaps the most extreme view of the discretionary powers of the

on, and limited by, the purposes and principles of the UN Charter and *jus cogens* norms.[122]

One must inevitably rely on the subsequent practice of the Security Council as the most precise means of interpreting the relevant provisions of the UN Charter concerning international security and a "threat to the peace."[123] Until the Gulf War and its aftermath, the threatened use of the veto power effectively prevented the council from taking forcible action against states whose human rights violations took place primarily or exclusively within their borders.[124] However, recent UN practice in the post-Cold War era has shown an increasing willingness on the part of the Security Council to

---

Security Council with respect to this determination is defended by Jean Combacau, who states that "[a] threat to peace in the sense of article 39 of the Chapter is a situation which the organ, competent to impose sanctions, declares to be an actual threat to the peace" [my translation]. See J. Combacau, *Le pouvoir de sanction de l'ONU. Étude théorique de la coercition non militaire* (Paris: Pédone, 1974) at 100.

[122] *Case Concerning the Application of the Convention on the Prevention and Punishment of the Crime of Genocide (Bosnia and Herzegovina v. Yugoslavia (Serbia and Montenegro)) (Request for the Indication of Additional Provisional Measures)*, Order of September 13, 1993, [1993] I.C.J. Rep. 325 at 440, para. 100 (separate opinion of ad hoc judge Lauterpacht). See also the dissenting opinions of Judges Weeramantry and El-Kosheri in the *Case Concerning Questions of Interpretation and Application of the 1971 Montreal Convention Arising from the Aerial Incident at Lockerbie (Libya v. United States of America), Provisional Measures Order of April 14, 1992,* [1992] I.C.J. Rep. 114 at 174 and 206-7 (para. 23), 211-12 respectively [hereinafter *Lockerbie* case]; A. Pellet, "Peut-on et doit-on contrôler les actions du Conseil de Sécurité?" in Société Francaise de Droit International, ed., *Le Chapitre VII de la Charte des Nations-Unies: Colloque de Rennes* (Paris: Pédone, 1995) at 236-37.

[123] Vienna Convention on the Law of Treaties between States and International Organizations or between International Organizations, UN Doc. A/CONF. 129/15; (1986) 25 I.L.M. 543, art. 2(1)(j). On the principle of subsequent practice by an international organization as one of the most dependable tools for the interpretation of a treaty that is the constituent instrument of an international organization, see the *Admissions* case, *supra* note 115 at 9; Ress, "Interpretation" in Simma, *supra* note 36 at 39-42; E. Lauterpacht, "The Development of the Law of International Organizations by the Decisions of International Tribunals" (1976-IV) 152 Rec. des Cours 377 at 460. See also Judge Lachs's separate opinion joining the majority in the *Lockerbie* case, *supra* note 122 at 138, where he stated: "While the Court has the vocation of applying international law as a universal law, operating both within and outside the United Nations, *it is bound to respect, as part of that law, the binding decisions of the Security Council*" [emphasis added]. Thus, Security Council decisions are binding as to the current meaning of "threats to peace, breaches of peace, and acts of aggression."

[124] R. Lillich, "The Role of the UN Security Council in Protecting Human Rights in Crisis Situations: UN Humanitarian Intervention in the Post-Cold War World" (1994) 3 Tulane J. Int'l and Comp. L. 1 at 5.

intervene under Chapter VII to put an end to serious human rights violations within the borders of a sovereign state, by recognizing that the protection of human rights is vital and an essential precondition for the maintenance of international peace and security.[125] This new activism by the council has induced criticism for the manner in which it took shape and generated attempts to constrain it and strengthen its judicial control. On the whole, however, in this author's view, these fears prove to be unwarranted. Indeed, it seems that we may well have reached the high-water mark of such action in the aftermath of the crisis in Kosovo where the council gave a flimsy *ex post facto* seal of approval to the North Atlantic Treaty Organization's (NATO) air raids against the former Yugoslavia intended to put an end to the violations of humanitarian law.[126]

The view that future wars might be prevented by making states with minorities accountable to the international community was the underlying idea of the system for protection of minority rights under the League of Nations, whereby states were mandated to take positive steps to enable minorities to maintain their cultural, linguistic, religious, and other particularities.[127] It has been reflected in recent years within the United Nations, commencing with the resolutions condemning the system of apartheid in South Africa as threatening international peace and security.[128] Depending on the political will of states relating to international relations, this emerging body of UN practice may prove to be the most significant means of enforcement under the Genocide Convention.[129]

---

[125] D. Wippman, "Change and Continuity in Legal Justifications for Military Intervention in Internal Conflict" (1996) Col. H.R.L. Rev. 435 at 461-64; Y.K. Tyagi, "The Concept of Humanitarian Intervention Revisited" (1995) 16 Mich. J. Int'l L. 883 at 886-87 (stating that anticipatory breaches of human rights are being recognized by the international community as calls for UN intervention).

[126] UN SC Resolution 1244, UN SCOR, 4011th Mtg. at 1, UN Doc. S/RES/1244 (1999). The Security Council had also invoked its Chapter VII powers and retroactively legitimated the Economic Community of West African States [hereinafter ECOWAS] military operation in Liberia. See UN Security Council [hereinafter SC] Resolution 788, UN SCOR, 3138th Mtg. at 2, UN Doc. S/RES/788 (1992). See also J. Levitt, "Humanitarian Intervention by Regional Actors in Internal Conflicts: The Cases of ECOWAS in Liberia and Sierra Leone" (1998) 12 Temp. Int'l and Comp. L. J. 333 at 347.

[127] D. Wippman, "The Evolution and Implementation of Minority Rights" (1997) 66 Ford. L. R. 597 at 600, 604; Kamminga, *supra* note 61 at 116-17; Schachter, *supra* note 35 at 328-29.

[128] *Ibid.* See also *Special Commission on the Racial Situation in the Union of South Africa*, UN Doc. A/2505 at 16-22 (1953).

[129] Akhavan, *supra* note 11 at 237.

It has often been contended that massive human rights violations such as genocidal acts only constitute a threat to international
peace when they cause spillover effects, thus threatening regional
stability.[130] However, although a "threat" traditionally requires transnational effects in order to allow forcible UN intervention, the
Security Council has recognized a threat to *international* peace and
security to encompass internal factors such as economic, social,
and humanitarian conditions.[131] The council's intervention in internal crises acknowledges that such conflicts — the way they are
held today — constitute a source of human suffering of a degree
unknown to most inner-state conflicts of the past. The expansive and
at times porous interpretation by the council of what constitutes a
threat to peace, as evidenced through its numerous resolutions,
suggests that the substantive law of the UN Charter has evolved to
capture today large-scale human rights violations as situations that
may alone, depending on the attendant circumstances, warrant collective enforcement action.[132] Thus, it is argued that regardless
of the language in which the Security Council cloaks its decisions,
it authorizes collective humanitarian intervention *primarily* on the
basis of remedying extreme human rights abuses, whether or not
transborder effects impact on neighbouring states.[133] Through a

[130] N.S. Rodley, "Collective Intervention to Protect Human Rights and Civilian
Populations: The Legal Framework" in N.S. Rodley, ed., *To Loose the Bands of
Wickedness: International Intervention in Defence of Human Rights* (London:
Brassey's, 1992) at 14, 28, 40; V. Kartashkin, "Human Rights and Humanitar-
ian Intervention" in L. Fisler-Damrosch and D.J. Scheffer, *Law and Force in the
New International Order* (Boulder: Westview Press, 1991) at 218; Gordon, *supra*
note 18 at 569-70.

[131] See "Security Council Summit Declaration of 1992," quoted in Abiew, *supra*
note 102 at 143-44. See also *An Agenda for Peace: Preventive Diplomacy, Peacemaking and Peace-keeping, Report by the Secretary-General Pursuant to the Statement
Adopted by the Summit Meeting of the Security Council on 31 January 1992*, January
31, 1992, UN Doc. A/47/277-S/241 I 1 at paras. 16, 18 (1992).

[132] Franck, "Fairness," *supra* note 117 at 215 ff.

[133] M. Lailach, *Die Wahrung des Weltfriedens und der internationalen Sicherheit als Auf-
gabe des Sicherheitsrates des Vereinten Nationen* (Berlin: Duncker and Humblot,
1998) at 206, 237, 307; O. Corten and P. Klein, "L'Autorisation de Recourir à
la Force à des Fins Humanitaires: Droit d'"Ingérence ou Retour aux Sources?"
(1993) 4:4 Eur. J. Int'l L. 506 at 520-21and references therein; M. Bettati, "Un
Droit d'Ingérence" (1991) 95 Rev. D.I.P. 639 at 661 ff.; B.F. Burmester, "On
Humanitarian Intervention: The New World Order and Wars to Preserve
Human Rights" (1994) Utah L. Rev. 269 at 273-74; Tesón, *supra* note 74 at 341-
42; Abiew, *supra* note 102 at 153; C.E. Evans, "The Concept of 'Threat to Peace'
and Humanitarian Concerns: Probing the Limits of Chapter VII of the UN
Charter" (1995) 5 Transnat'l L. and Contemporary Problems 213 at 223 ff;

case study of Security Council action in southern Rhodesia and, more recently, in northern Iraq, Bosnia, Somalia, Haiti, and Rwanda, the following section will consider the limits imposed on the council's exercise of coercive powers in cases of impending genocide.

Southern Rhodesia

The fact that purely civil wars can trigger enforcement measures under Chapter VII was confirmed in 1966 when the Security Council enacted enforcement measures under Article 41 of the UN Charter after determining that the continued existence of southern Rhodesia's racist minority Smith regime constituted a threat to international peace and security.[134] The resolution focused on "the inalienable rights of the people of Southern Rhodesia to freedom and independence,"[135] and the Security Council's determination was not based on any tangible external consequences of southern Rhodesia's internal crisis, nor did the council attempt to articulate any evidentiary basis for its assessment.[136] Thus, the Rhodesian mandatory sanctions fully demonstrate the council's willingness to consider a secessionist regime denying a majority of its people fundamental human rights as creating peace-threatening circumstances that warrant the taking of collective measures under Chapter VII, even in the absence of manifest external consequences.

Northern Iraq

In early 1991, the Security Council adopted Resolution 688 to address the situation that had arisen in Iraq as a result of the Iraqi government's repression and abuse of its Kurdish population in

---

L.E. Fielding, "Taking a Closer Look at Threats to Peace: The Power of the Security Council to Address Humanitarian Crises" (1996) 73 U. Detroit Mercy L. Rev. 551 at 557 ff.

[134] UN SC Resolution 232, UN SCOR, 21st Sess., 1340th mtg. at 7, UN Doc. S/INF.21/Rev.1 (1966). On the question of southern Rhodesia, see generally V. Gowlland-Debbas, *Collective Responses to Illegal Acts in International Law — United Nations Action in the Question of Southern Rhodesia* (Dordrecht: M. Nijhoff, 1990).

[135] UN SC Resolution 232, *supra* note 134 at 3.

[136] P.H. Kooijmans, "The Enlargement of the Concept "Threat to the Peace" in R.-J. Dupuy, ed., *Peace-keeping and Peace-bulding: The Development of the Role of the Security Council*, Workshop at the Hague Academy of International Law (Dordrecht: Martinus Nijhoff, 1992) at 113. For a criticism of the Security Council's determination as constituting an interference in internal affairs, see C.G. Fenwick, "When Is There a Threat to the Peace? Rhodesia" (1967) 61 A.J.I.L. 753 at 753-55.

northern Iraq. After making a rare reference to both its responsibility for the maintenance of international peace and security and the principle of non-intervention, the council first condemned the "repression of the Iraqi civilian population in many parts of Iraq . . . the *consequences* of which threaten international peace and security in the region" and demanded that "Iraq . . . immediately end this repression."[137] The Security Council then added several provisos linking the resolution to the language and spirit of Article 39 to *reinforce* the legitimacy of this taking of jurisdiction, stressing that "a massive flow of refugees toward and across international frontiers and to cross-border incursions" caused by Iraqi repression *contributed* to the threat to peace and security in the region.[138] The council further emphasized that it was "deeply disturbed by the magnitude of human suffering involved"[139] and acquiesced to the stationing of foreign military forces within Iraq to protect an ethnic minority from impending genocide.[140]

It has been argued that such an internal crisis — the forcible repression of minorities in Iraq — constituted a threat to *international* peace and security only because of its consequences, that is, the refugee flow into Turkey and Iran and its potential escalation into an international conflict.[141] Under this rationale, "the

---

[137] UN SC Resolution 688, UN SCOR, 46th Sess., 2982nd mtg. at para. 1, UN Doc. S/Res/688 (1991).

[138] *Ibid.* at preamble. See also T.M. Franck, "The Security Council and 'Threats to the Peace': Some Remarks on Remarkable Recent Developments" in R.-J. Dupuy, *supra* note 136 at 102.

[139] UN SC Resolution 688, *supra* note 137.

[140] Resolution 688 did not explicitly refer to the Kurds as a people, nationality, group, or minority, but instead made reference to "the Iraqi population in many parts of Iraq, including most recently in Kurdish-populated areas." The observation has been made that in doing this, "the Security Council thus failed to highlight the measures of the Iraqi government aimed against the Kurds as peoples, measures which many considered were tantamount to genocidal actions." See on this point Abiew, *supra* note 102 at 149; Delbrück, *supra* note 32 at 895. See also Pease and Forsythe, *supra* note 73 at 290; O. Corten and P. Klein, "L'Assistance Humanitaire Face à la Souveraineté des États" (1992) Rev. Trim. Dr. H. 343; P. Akhavan, "Lessons from Iraqi Kurdistan: Self-determination and Humanitarian Intervention against Genocide" (1993) 11 N.Q.H.R. 41.

[141] Kooijmans, *supra* note 136 at 114; J. Delbrück, "A More Effective International Law or a New 'World Law?'— Some Aspects of the Development of International Law in a Changing International System" (1993) 68 Indiana L. J. 705 at 709; C. Bourloyannis, "The Security Council of the United Nations and the Implementation of International Humanitarian Law" (1992) 20 Denv. J. Int'l L. & Pol'y 335 at 352.

resolution cannot be cited as [binding] precedent for the proposition that the Security Council views a massive, but purely internal human rights violations as such, without tangible transboundary effects, as a direct threat to international peace and security."[142]

This author submits, however, along the same lines as Professor Tesón, that the relevant issue is not whether the Security Council can legally do what it wants so long as it is cloaked in the language of "threat to international peace and security."[143] The situation in northern Iraq was above all a human rights concern about Iraq's mistreatment of its own Kurdish minority and "the reference to the threat to peace and security was added for good measure."[144] This conclusion is further bolstered by the debates preceding the passage of Resolution 688, where it was asserted that the council was using the flow of refugees across borders as a cover to justify a threat to peace based solely on a matter essentially within Iraq's domestic jurisdiction.[145] Some members also discussed Iraq's mistreatment of its citizens and the refugee problem as humanitarian concerns rather than as threats to regional stability.[146] Thus, while no enforcement authority pursuant to Chapter VII was included in Resolution 688,[147] the latter has in fact proven to be quite revolutionary in that it represents a major shift in the way the council interprets Article 39 of the UN Charter by characterizing egregious human rights deprivations having indirect external effects as a threat to international peace and security.[148] The UN

---

[142] Malanczuk, *supra* note 32 at 17-18; R. Gordon, "Humanitarian Intervention by the United Nations: Iraq, Somalia and Haiti" (1996) 31(1) Tex. Int'l L.J. 43 at 49.

[143] Tesón, *supra* note 74 at 344.

[144] *Ibid.* See also Ben Achour, *supra* note 44 at 406-9.

[145] See, for example, the statements made by the representatives of Yemen, Zimbabwe, and Cuba to the Security Council. UN SCOR, 46th Sess., 2982th mtg., at 27-32, 13-15, UN Doc. S/PV.2982 (1991).

[146] See the statements made by the representatives of Yemen, Zimbabwe, and France, *ibid.* at 6-8, 13-15.

[147] Gordon, *supra* note 142 at 49; Malanczuk, *supra* note 32 at 18.

[148] According to Franck, the Security Council, in Resolution 688, endorsed the view that when human rights violations reach a certain threshold of ferocity, the crisis may be characterized as a threat to the peace and placed under UN supervision. See Franck, *supra* note 138 at 103; See also P.-M. Dupuy, "Après la Guerre du Golfe" (1991) 95 Rev. D.I.P. 621 at 628; P. Malanczuk, "The Kurdish Crisis and Allied Intervention in the Aftermath of the Second Gulf War" (1991) 2(2) Eur. J. Int'l L. 114; Bettati, *supra* note 133 at 662.

enforcement machinery remained however unused to prevent the repression.[149]

Bosnia

The notion that a lethal civil war and a rapidly deteriorating humanitarian situation, although primarily confined to one nation, could threaten international peace and security was evidenced through the numerous resolutions that addressed the fighting among parts of the former Yugoslavia. Upon a request made by the Yugoslav government, Resolution 713 was first adopted when the Security Council found that the continuation of the war constituted a threat to international peace and security and imposed an arms embargo under Chapter VII, despite the fact that the conflict involved parties *within* what was still a member state of the UN.[150] The resolution focused predominantly on the heavy loss of human life and material damage, but it also nodded to the consequences for the countries of the region, in particular, in the border areas of neighbouring countries.[151] The chaos and ethnic strife that followed from the unstable ethnic mix within Bosnia-Herzegovina's borders further resulted in widespread human rights violations involving a practice of "ethnic cleansing" and forced evacuations by the Serbs.[152]

In response to these concerns and acting under Chapter VII, the council adopted Resolution 770, which authorized the use of force by states to ensure the delivery of humanitarian assistance.[153] While it recognized that the situation in Bosnia constituted a threat to international peace and security, the Security Council was "deeply concerned" and made specific references to the egregious human

---

[149]   See R.C. Johansen, "Reforming the United Nations to Eliminate War" (1994) 4 Transnat'l L. Contemporary Problems 455 at 477-78 (suggesting that a preventive force might have been effective if one had been deployed on the Iraq-Kuwait border in 1990).

[150]   UN SC Resolution 713, UN SCOR, 46th Sess., 3009th mtg., UN Doc. S/RES/713 (1991).

[151]   Kooijmans, *supra* note 136 at 116; Franck, *supra* note 138 at 104.

[152]   See Tesón, *supra* note 74 at 366, and particularly n. 180 and references therein.

[153]   UN SC Resolution 770, UN SCOR, 47th Sess., 3106th mtg. at 2, UN Doc. S/RES/770 (1992), recognizing that "the situation in Bosnia and Herzegovina and the obstacles to the delivery of humanitarian assistance constitute a threat to international peace and security and that the provision of humanitarian assistance ... is an important element ... to restore international peace and security in the area."

rights abuses against Muslims imprisoned in camps and prisons who were being subjected to murders, ethnic cleansing, and widespread rape.[154] As evidenced by the debates preceding the passage of this resolution, the forcible intervention by NATO forces in 1995 was an action undertaken pursuant to authorization from the UN with the sole aim of ending the abhorrent human rights situation as a result of the conflict that shocked the international community.[155] It is also interesting to recall Resolution 808 whereby the council deplored the "widespread violations of humanitarian law occurring within the territory of the former Yugoslavia, including reports of mass killings and the continuance of the practice of "ethnic cleansing," prior to finding a situation that "constitutes a threat to international peace and security." This development further laid the foundations for the establishment of the International Criminal Tribunal for the Former Yugoslavia.[156] In short, although the impact of a massive exodus of refugees across borders was evident, the egregious human rights violations in the former Yugoslavia showed the preparedness of the Security Council to determine the existence of a threat to peace and authorize the use of force primarily for humanitarian concerns.

Somalia

The tragedy of Somalia represented perhaps the biggest challenge to the ability of the international community acting through the UN to intervene for humanitarian reasons. Following the eruption of civil war between the warring factions, the onset of mass starvation, and the collapse of Somali governmental institutions, the Security Council passed a series of resolutions under Chapter VII that were primarily motivated by the heavy loss of human life, with slight references to the consequences on the stability and

---

[154] Abiew, *supra* note 102 at 180, 186

[155] See, for example, the statements by the delegates of Zimbabwe, Ecuador, and India, *Provisional Verbatim Record of the Three Thousand One Hundred and Sixth Meeting*, UN SCOR, 47th Sess., plen. mtg., at 9-17, UN Doc. S/PV.3106 (1992), and *Provisional Verbatim Record of the Three Thousand One Hundred and Ninety-First Meeting*, UN SCOR, 48th Sess., plen. Mtg., at 19-21, UN Doc. S/PV.3191 (1993), referring to statements made by delegates from the US, France, Cape Verde, and Pakistan, which maintained that the Security Council must use its authority to authorize states to use force and put a stop to the tragedy of the Bosnian population. See on this point Abiew, *supra* note 102 at 186-89.

[156] UN SC Resolution 808, UN SCOR, 3175th mtg., at 2, UN Doc. S/RES/808 (1993).

peace in the region.[157] Resolution 794, however, went beyond a mere insistence on providing access to humanitarian relief agencies and authorized the use of force "to restore peace, stability and law and order" in Somalia.[158] The council determined that "the magnitude of the human rights tragedy caused by the conflict in Somalia, further exacerbated by the obstacles being created to the distribution of humanitarian assistance, constituted a threat to international peace and security,"[159] with no mention of then-existing or potential transborder effects on neighbouring states. While the debates preceding the resolution recognized that the situation in Somalia had external repercussions, "the main concern prompting enforcement action by the Security Council was the extreme situation created by the combination of famine, death, and disease caused by the civil war; the breach of humanitarian law by the warring factions; and the general situation of anarchy."[160]

It has been argued that although Resolution 794 was innovative in its acceptance that egregious human suffering can constitute a threat to international peace and security, its significance as a binding precedent for the legitimacy of collective humanitarian intervention was undermined by the "unique character" of the "deteriorating, complex, and extraordinary nature" of the situation in Somalia.[161] However, any unique situation and the solution that is adopted create of necessity a precedent against which future similar situations will be measured, which is exactly what happened shortly thereafter in Rwanda and Haiti. While it is true that the crisis in Somalia was indeed a unique and extraordinary case, it is one that was precisely covered by the principle according to which

---

[157] UN SC Resolution 733, UN SCOR, 47th Sess., 3039th mtg., UN Doc. S/RES/733 (1992). See on this point Evans, *supra* note 133 at 228-30; Kooijmans, *supra* note 136 at 115.

[158] UN SC Resolution 794, UN SCOR, 47th Sess., 3145 mtg. at 2-3, para. 10, UN Doc. S/Res/794 (1992). For a thoughtful analysis of this resolution, see H. Freudenschuß, "Between Unilateralism and Collective Security" (1994) 5 Eur. J. Int'l. L. 492 at 512-15.

[159] UN SC Resolution 794, *supra* note 158 at 1.

[160] Tesón, *supra* note 74 at 351; see also Lillich, *supra* note 124 at 7-8; S. M. Crawford, "UN Humanitarian Intervention in Somalia" (1993) 3 Transnat'l L. and Contemporary Problems 273 at 291.

[161] See discussions within the Security Council regarding Resolution 794, UN Doc. S/PV.3145 at 17 (China) and 51 (India); see also N. Wheeler and V. Morris, "Humanitarian Intervention and State Practice at the End of the Cold War" in R. Fawn, ed., *International Society after the Cold War: Anarchy and Order Reconsidered* (London: Macmillan Press, 1996) at 151.

the Security Council is indeed empowered to authorize forcible measures in such extreme cases of human rights abuses.[162] Thus, with respect to the "threat to international peace and security" requirement under Article 39 of the UN Charter, one may argue in a way that is similar to Judge Sir Percy Spender's opinion in the *Certain Expenses* case, where he stated that

[a] general rule is that words used in a treaty should be read as having the meaning they bore therein when they came into existence. But this meaning must be consistent with the purpose sought to be achieved. Where, as in the case of the Charter, the purposes are directed to saving succeeding generations in an indefinite future from the scourge of war ... the general rule above stated does not mean that the words in the Charter can only comprehend such situations and contingencies and manifestations of subject-matter as were within the minds of the framers of the Charter.[163]

It is true that the competence of the Security Council cannot be limited to activities traditionally contemplated under Chapter VII of the UN Charter. In the *Namibia* case, the ICJ endorsed a statement of the secretary-general to the effect that

the powers of the Council under Article 24 are not restricted to the specific grants of authority contained in Chapter VI, VII, VIII and XII ... The Members of the United Nations conferred upon the Security Council powers commensurate with its responsibility for the maintenance of peace and security. The only limitations are the fundamental principles and purposes found in Chapter I of the Charter.[164]

However, it would seem that "the Security Council runs afoul of the Charter if it determines that a situation is a threat to the peace when in reality it is not."[165] The council would therefore not have the authority to act arbitrarily and institute coercive measures to remedy *any* human rights problem occurring within the boundaries

---

[162] McDougal and Reisman, *supra* note 32 at 12-13.

[163] *Certain Expenses* case, *supra* note 34 at 182, 186 (separate opinion of Judge Sir Percy Spender).

[164] *Namibia* case, *supra* note 38 at 52. For a view that opposes this broad interpretation, see the dissenting opinion of Judge Fitzmaurice in the *Namibia* case, *ibid.* at 293. However, the court's position has found wide doctrinal support; see E. Jimenez de Aréchaga, "International Law in the Past Third of a Century" (1978) 159-I Rec. des Cours 1 at 124; R. Higgins, "The Advisory Opinion on Namibia: Which UN Resolutions Are Binding under Article 25 of the Charter?" (1972) 21 I.C.L.Q. at 270; G. Weissberg, "The Role of the International Court of Justice in the United Nations System: The First Quarter Century" in L. Gross, ed., *The Future of the International Court of Justice*, vol. I (Dobbs Ferry, NY: Oceana Publications, 1976) at 131, 142.

[165] Tesón, *supra* note 74 at 353-54.

of a state, so long as it pays lip service to the language of Article 39 of the UN Charter. The Somalia crisis, in contrast, clearly demonstrated that internal disorders producing severe and widespread human rights deprivations justify forceful action under the threat to the peace rationale.[166] It moved beyond what may have been expected by the framers of the UN Charter to place overwhelming human needs over and above the traditional paradigm of absolute state sovereignty. As such, it represented the first clear articulation of the principle of collective humanitarian intervention through the UN.

Haiti

The case of Haiti shares with the earlier ones the ingredient of massive human suffering in a situation involving egregious violations of human and political rights in the determination of a "threat to international peace and security" and represents undoubtedly the purest form of collective humanitarian intervention to date. As the pressures for international action continued to mount in the wake of the *de facto* government's brutal treatment of its people, which included the execution of children, the raping of women, and rampant killings, the Security Council passed Resolution 940 in 1994, which authorized member states "to form a multinational force [and] ... to use all necessary means to facilitate the departure from Haiti of the military leadership."[167] After expressing its grave concern with "significant further deterioration of the humanitarian situation in Haiti, in particular the continuing escalation by the illegal de facto regime of systematic violations of civil liberties," the council determined that "the situation in Haiti continues to constitute a threat to peace and security in the region."[168]

While there was a reference in passing to the "desperate plight of Haitian refugees" as an international element to further support the finding of a "threat to peace," this reference was clearly secondary to the almost exclusive concern of the council with the worsening human rights situation within the country and the removal

---

[166] R. Ramlogan, "Towards a New Vision of World Security: The United Nations Security Council and the Lessons of Somalia" (1993) 16 Houst. J. Int'l L. 213 at 236-38; Malanczuk, *supra* note 32 at 24; Gordon, *supra* note 142 at 52.

[167] UN SC Resolution 940, UN SCOR, 3413th mtg. at 2, UN Doc. S/RES/940 (1994).

[168] *Ibid.*

of the *de facto* government in Haiti as the operating reasons for authorizing military action.[169] Furthermore, the existence of mixed motives in regard to the United State's involvement, of which the concern for the continued mass exodus of Haitian refugees seeking asylum in the United States was accessory, should not affect the legitimacy of an otherwise justified intervention, since the humanitarian motive was overwhelmingly evident.[170] Thus, although the Haitian paradigm was, like the one in Somalia, of a "unique character and of a deteriorating, complex and extraordinary nature requiring an exceptional response," it further developed the legal framework for UN humanitarian intervention.[171] Yet above all, it greatly strengthened the interpretation of the UN Charter, according to which egregious violations of human rights that offend the international community may themselves constitute the basis for collective military action without the necessity of external consequences as a precondition to a Chapter VII determination.

Rwanda

Finally, the disgraceful UN response to the genocide and civil war in Rwanda suggests nevertheless that egregious internal conflicts producing massive human rights violations of a genocidal nature within a state *alone* may constitute a threat to the peace. Thus, in Resolution 918, the Security Council was deeply concerned "that the situation in Rwanda, which resulted in the deaths of many thousands of innocent civilians, including women and children, the internal displacement of a significant percentage of the Rwandan population, and the massive exodus of refugees to neighboring countries, constituted a humanitarian crisis of enormous proportions."[172] It also expressed its alarm over "continuing reports of systematic, widespread and flagrant violations of international humanitarian law in Rwanda, as well as other violations of rights to life and property" and further noted that "the killing of members of an ethnic group with the intention of destroying such a group,

[169] Lillich, *supra* note 124 at 10; Tesón, *supra* note 74 at 358.

[170] Tesón, *supra* note 74 at 359-60. For a criticism of this resolution, see R. Falk, "The Haiti Intervention: A Dangerous World Order Precedent for the United Nations" (1995) 36 Harv. Int'l L. J. 341.

[171] See generally, O. Corten, "La résolution 940 du Conseil de sécurité autorisant une intervention militaire en Haïti: L'émergence d'un principe de légitimité démocratique en droit international?" (1995) 6(1) Eur. J. Int'l L. 116.

[172] UN SC Resolution 918, UN SCOR, 49th Sess., 3377th mtg., UN Doc. S/RES/918 (1994).

in whole or in part, constitutes a crime punishable under international law." This statement led the council to find the continuation of this internal crisis to "constitute a threat to peace and security in the region" and to increase the authorized force level of the UN Assistance Mission for Rwanda (UNAMIR), although member states made no commitments to provide the requisite peacekeeping forces that could have prevented or reduced the enormity of the massacres.[173] It is to be noted that these pieces of evidence cited by the council were in support of its characterization of the Rwandan situation as a humanitarian crisis of unprecedented proportions rather than specifically in support of its threat to peace determination.[174] This fact suggests that the council was primarily concerned with putting an end to the atrocities taking place in Rwanda when acting under Chapter VII. Such an interpretation is fully consistent with the debates preceding the adoption of this resolution, which centered almost exclusively on the finding that genocide was being committed.[175]

Given the absence of multilateral action, the Security Council adopted Resolution 929 in June 1994, in which it authorized French forces to implement a "temporary operation under national command and control aimed at contributing ... to the security and protection of displaced persons, refugees and civilians"[176] and to conduct the operation "using all necessary means to achieve the humanitarian objectives." The resulting intervention, which became known as "Operation Turquoise," was thus an authorized and legitimate use of force but, nevertheless, a belated one that failed to prevent the impending carnage. It was grounded in the

---

[173] It is to be noted that, in its initial response to the potential genocide, the Security Council actually authorized a reduction in the forces of UNAMIR, in service in the country since late the previous year. See on this point UN Doc. S/RES/912 (1994) at para. 8 *in fine;* F. Ougergouz, "La tragédie rwandaise du printemps 1994: Quelques considérations sur les premières réactions de l'Organisation des Nations Unies" (1996) 100 Rev. D.I.P. 149.

[174] Evans, *supra* note 133 at 230, 234.

[175] See UN SCOR, 49th Sess., 3377th mtg., UN Doc. S/PV. 3377 (1994). At the time that the Security Council adopted Resolution 918 in May 1994, it was reported to the council that an estimated 250,000 to 500,000 Rwandan men, women, and children had already been killed. See United Nations, *Report of the Secretary-General on the Situation in Rwanda*, UN SCOR, 49th Sess., at 2, UN Doc. S/1994/640 (1994).

[176] See United Nations, *Draft Resolution Concerning the Deployment of a Temporary Multinational Humanitarian Operation in Rwanda*, UN SCOR, 49th Sess., UN Doc. S/1994/737 (1994); UN SC Resolution 929, UN SCOR, 49th Sess., 3392 mtg., UN Doc. S/RES/929 (1994).

characterization of the large-scale massacres in Rwanda, which
shocked the conscience of mankind, as a threat to international
peace and security and was motivated almost exclusively by the
desire of putting an end to such human suffering in the face of
which the international community could not remain passive.[177]
Regardless of the failure of the UN to take timely decisive action to
prevent genocide in Rwanda, this case builds on the other precedents and suggests that egregious human rights violations *themselves*
may amount to a threat to international peace and security and
lead to the authorization of Chapter VII enforcement measures,
irrespective of the consent of the affected parties.[178]

Summary Conclusion

As Michael Reisman reminds us, "[t]he United Nations system
was essentially designed to enable the Permanent Five, if all agree,
to use Charter obligations and the symbolic authority of the organization as they think appropriate to maintain or restore international peace, as they define it."[179] This wide margin of appreciation,
however, by no means entails that a decision by the Security Council to forcibly intervene to prevent impending genocide occurring
solely within the boundaries of a state, whether or not there is
any perceptible or realistic impact on neighbouring states, would
be *ultra vires* the UN Charter.[180] In fact, and as it was previously

[177] See also SC Resolution 955, UN SCOR, 49th Sess., UN Doc. S/1994/955
(1944), reprinted in 33 I.L.M. 1598, where the Security Council considered
that "genocide and other systematic, widespread and flagrant violations of international humanitarian law" constitute a threat to the peace and justified the
establishment of the International Tribunal for Rwanda for the purpose of
prosecuting persons responsible for these crimes.

[178] In 1996, the Security Council took an even more proactive step towards humanitarian intervention. In November 1996, a civil war in Zaire forced over one million Rwandan refugees and Zairian civilians into flight. The council responded
to the crisis by authorizing the formation of a military force to create "safe cor-
ridors" for the delivery of humanitarian aid to the refugees. The military force
was officially justified by the humanitarian crisis, rather than by the threat to
international peace portended by the predicted imminent disintegration of the
largest state in Central Africa. See UN SC Resolution 1078, UN SCOR, 49th
Sess., 3710th mtg., preamble and para. 7-8, UN Doc. S/RES/1078 (1996).

[179] W.M. Reisman, "Peacemaking" (1993) 18 Yale J. Int'l L. 415 at 418.

[180] In its advisory opinion concerning the *Certain Expenses* case, *supra* note 34 at
168, the ICJ stated that a presumption is seen to exist for actions appropriate for the fulfilment of one of the stated purposes of the United Nations not
being *ultra vires*. It is argued here that this statement is also applicable to those

argued, the council possesses the necessary competence to make threat-to-peace determinations based either primarily or exclusively on humanitarian concerns in the most extreme of cases.[181] In discharging its primary duty to maintain international peace and security, the Security Council would not be acting arbitrarily but rather in full accordance with the principles and purposes of the UN, as required under Article 24(2),[182] of which the prevention of genocide is arguably the most essential to its *raison d'être*.

It has further been contended that the unwillingness of the council to act consistently and efficiently in the face of other genocidal situations, such as in East Timor and Chechnya, and the inconsistency of the council in articulating the bases for its threat-to-peace determinations, undermine the credibility and legitimacy attached to the aforementioned precedents.[183] It has been suggested that the fact that all these cases also involved substantial collateral effects, particularly the exodus of a significant number of refugees into neighbouring countries, would further support the position that genocidal acts are beyond the reach of the council's powers to authorize collective humanitarian intervention when such acts are purely internal, without any detrimental effects jeopardizing international or regional stability. On this point, it is interesting to note the proposal made by the Soviet Union and France during the

---

situations where the organization takes action that warrants the assertion that it was appropriate for the fulfilment of the goal to prevent genocide which, although not expressly stated in the UN Charter, may be seen as fundamental to the *raison d'être* of the United Nations.

[181] B. Simma, "From Bilateralism to Community Interest in International Law" (1994) 250 Rec des Cours, 229 at 274-77; M. Bothe, "Les Limites du Pouvoir du Conseil de Sécurité" in R.-J. Dupuy, *supra* note 136 at 67 ff.

[182] See on this point J. Delbrück, "Article 24" in Simma, *supra* note 36 at 403-6; Tesón, *supra* note 74 at 354. According to Brownlie, a determination of a threat to the peace as a basis for action necessary to remove the threat cannot be used as a basis for action that (if the evidence so indicates) is for collateral and independent purposes, such as the overthrow of a government or the partition of a state. See I. Brownlie, "International Law at the Fiftieth Anniversary of the United Nations: General Course in Public International Law" (1995) 255 Rec. des Cours. 9 at 218. It is interesting to note that the Security Council has also been considered to possess the necessary powers under Article 24(1) of the UN Charter to fulfil its tasks in the maintenance of peace (and become active in cases of gross human rights violations) beyond the enumerated powers in Article 24(2), second sentence. See Delbrück, *ibid.* at 406.

[183] N.H.B. Jorgensen, *The Responsibility of States for International Crimes* (New York and Oxford: Oxford University Press, 2000) at 135-37.

drafting of the Genocide Convention. It was suggested that "the High Contracting Parties *undertake* to report to the Security Council *all cases of Genocide* and *all cases of a breach of the obligations imposed by the Convention* so that the necessary measures be taken in accordance with Chapter VII of the United Nations Charter."[184] This proposal was opposed, however, by some delegates and ultimately rejected on the grounds that it constituted an amendment of the UN Charter and an enlargement of the powers of the Security Council.[185] Thus, it was clear that proposing that *all cases* of genocide and violations of the convention be referred to the council and making it obligatory to bring to the attention of the council all violations was unacceptable since "it was possible that cases of genocide might occur which did not constitute any threat to peace."[186]

In this author's view, it would be equally untenable to hold outright that serious human rights violations, specifically genocidal acts, *never* constitute a threat to international peace if contained wholly within state borders, following a so-called "substantive notion

---

[184] United Nations, *General Assembly, 6th Committee, Genocide — Draft Convention and Report of the Economic and Social Council, Union of Soviet Socialist Republics: Amendments to the Draft Convention* (E/796) at 3, UN Doc. A/C.6/215/Rev.1 (1948) [emphasis added]. See also the response of the Soviet delegate Mr. Morozov to the explanation provided by the chair of the Ad Hoc Committee, the American John Maktos, regarding the rejection of the Soviet proposal requiring Security Council referral, to the effect that "[a]ny act of genocide was always a threat to international peace and security and as such should be dealt with under Chapters VI and VII of the Charter ... Chapters VI and VII of the Charter provided means for the prevention and punishment of genocide, means far more concrete and effective than anything possible in the sphere of international jurisdiction," UN Doc. A/C.6/SR.101. In the Ad Hoc Committee, Poland supported the Soviet Proposal, stating that "the convention should stipulate that the crime of genocide leads to international friction and endangers the maintenance of peace and security and that that could make the intervention of the Security Council necessary," UN Doc. E/AC.25/SR.8 at 17.

[185] See the statements of the US delegate, Mr. Maktos, and the Belgian delegate, Mr. Kaeckenbeeck: UN GAOR, 6th Comm., 3rd Sess., pt. 1, 101st mtg., at 410, 412-413, UN Doc. A/C.6/SR.61-140 (1948). It is to be noted that Article 99 of the UN Charter is itself worded in permissive terms and does not require the secretary-general to inform the Security Council of every potential conflict. Thus, under the present system, the council would not have the occasion to discuss many non-conventional threats to the peace, specifically those dealing with humanitarian disasters.

[186] M.C. Bassiouni, "International Crimes: *Jus Cogens* and *Obligatio Erga Omnes*" (1996) 59 Law & Contemp. Probs. 63 at 70; Robinson, *supra* note 89 at 90; Drost, *supra* note 89 at 105-6.

of what logically threatens the international peace."[187] Sadly, it does seem that the international community through the UN feels compelled to take concerted action in certain instances and not in others, giving rise to what Georges Abi-Saab has vividly condemned as "a shocking selectivity on the level of collective action."[188] However, it is important to draw a distinction between conscious and purposeful decision-making by UN organs and an act or omission that is not the result of a deliberate decision. The UN's failure to determine the case of Chechnya as a threat to international peace and security and to take appropriate action, therefore, is not necessarily equivalent to a statement that it does not constitute such a threat. Requirements of legitimacy do not call for the council's determinations of threats to peace to comport some fixed criteria or some commonality of understanding in the world community to govern collective humanitarian intervention in future cases. It would indeed be counterproductive and idle to expect the Security Council to follow "codified rules" since each crisis has its own configuration, and governments will always take account of their particular political, economic, and military interests as well as the unique features of the case.[189]

Granted, genocide generally has drastic effects outside the country where it occurs, and it is thus capable of placing an enormous strain on nearby countries.[190] International action through the UN to curb impending genocide before it actually spreads outside a state's national borders is thus justified by the reality of genocide's international consequences.[191] However, mass refugee flows and displaced persons are not inherently destabilizing factors of regional or international stability, and characterizing them as threats to peace

---

[187] For such a state-centric view, see M.E. O'Connell, "Continuing Limits on UN Intervention in Civil War" (1992) 67 Indiana L. J. 903 at 911.

[188] G.M. Abi-Saab, "Whither the International Community?" (1998) 9(2) Eur. J. Int'l L. 248 at 264.

[189] O. Schachter, "The United Nations Response to a Changing World: International Law Implications — Commentary" (1992) 86 Am. Soc. Int'l L. Proc. at 320.

[190] L.L. Bruun, "Beyond the 1948 Convention — Emerging Principles of Genocide in Customary International Law" (1993) 17 Maryland J. Internat'l L. and Trade 193 at 212-13.

[191] Rajan, *supra* note 69 at 142-60 (citing the example of the UN intervention in Congo as the only salient example of action taken on this premise). See also generally G. M. Abi-Saab, *The United Nations Operation in the Congo, 1960-1964* (Oxford: Oxford University Press, 1978).

and security without any real consideration of their actual transborder effects is a futile exercise that serves only to reduce the
precedential value of Security Council resolutions by disguising its
primary or exclusive humanitarian motives.[192] Genocide does not
occur in a vacuum — it never has and it never will.

It is thus submitted that impending genocide may, in appropriate circumstances to be scrutinized by the council at its discretion,
constitute a threat to the peace, whether or not there are direct
or immediate spillover effects, thus justifying the unleashing of
forcible preventive and enforcement measures through Chapter
VII. Genocide goes to the ultimate depths of human perversity and
has been listed among those aims designated as crimes "against
the peace and security of mankind,"[193] thereby illustrating the fact
that where transnational crimes require an extraterritorial element,

---

[192] D. Caron, "The Legitimacy of the Collective Authority of the Security Council"
(1993) 87 A.J.I.L. 552 at 559-60.

[193] *Draft Articles on the Draft Code of Crimes Against Peace and Security of Mankind*, International Law Commission [hereinafter ILC] Report, 1996, Chapter II, art. 17,
accessible at <http://www.un.org/law/ilc/reports/1996/chap02.htm> (date
accessed: April 18, 2001) [hereinafter *Draft Code of Crimes against Peace and Security of Mankind*]. In its commentary (3) to Article 17, the ILC noted that "the
tragic events in Rwanda clearly demonstrated that the crime of genocide, even
when committed primarily in the territory of a single State, could have serious
consequences for international peace and security and, thus, confirmed the
appropriateness of including this crime in the present Code." See *Report of the
International Law Commission on the Work of Its Forty-Eight Session*, UN Doc.
A/51/10, reprinted in *Yearbook of the International Law Commission 1996*, vol. 2,
Part 2, New York, 1998, UN Doc. A/CN.4/SER.A/1996/Add.1 (Part 2). It is
also interesting to note that according to the *Working Paper Submitted to the Commission on Human Rights by Stanislav Chernichenko on the Definition of Gross and
Large-Scale Violations of Human Rights as an International Crime*, UN Doc.
E/CN.4/Sub.2/1993/10 at 7, international crimes of states such as genocide
(not to be confused with "crimes under international law," which also comprise
genocide but refer to the responsibility of individuals) are defined as " the most
serious violations of international law ... constituting a *threat to the entire community*," without presupposing any specific transboundary element. See also
B.B. Ferencz, *New Legal Foundations for Global Survival: Security through the Security
Council* (New York: Oceana Publications, 1994) at 272-75. It is to be noted that
the term "international crimes" does not appear in the text of the second reading of Part 2 of the Draft Articles on State Responsibility of the International
Law Commission because of the many conceptual problems that arose and the
lack of general consensus among the members of the Commission on the subject. See on this point *First Report on State Responsibility by Mr. James Crawford, Special Rapporteur*, UN Doc. ILC, 50th Sess., UN Doc. A/CN.4/490/Add. 1 (1 May
1998), at 9-10, paras. 97 ff.

international crimes do not, although one or more may exist.[194] Of course, humanitarian intervention under Chapter VII is still an emerging norm, one that may be characterized as inconsistent. It remains to be seen whether the Security Council would consider a genocidal situation that in no way affects the interests of other states through, for example, the mass exodus of refugees as a threat to international peace and security. Its response to these problems in the future will dictate its role in the prevention of genocide and the maintenance of an adequate regime of collective security. However, considering the main purpose of the UN to maintain peace and security and particularly to prevent impending genocide when perceived at an early stage, it would fly in the face of common sense to expect the organization, merely as a matter of *legal* principle, to remain idle until potential threats arising under domestic jurisdiction expand across borders.[195]

CONCLUSION

In the post-Cold War era, the emphasis has clearly shifted from the necessity (and hence legality) of unilateral uses of force in certain circumstances to an institutionalized mechanism of collective response that would obviate such a need.[196] There has been, however, and still is, some controversy over the soundness of an overly

[194] J.J. Paust *et al.*, eds., *International Criminal Law: Cases and Materials* (Durham, NC: Carolina Academic Press, 1996) at 18 (citing M.C. Bassiouni, "An Appraisal of the Growth and Developing Trends of International Criminal Law" (1974) 45 Rev. I.D.P. 405 at 406). According to Byers, if states have accepted the idea of universal jurisdiction in respect of war crimes, crimes against humanity, and genocide, regardless of where they occur and the nationality of the perpetrators, they have done so because these activities pose a *threat to each and every state*, thus justifying a global extension of the principle of jurisdiction to all areas not covered by another state's jurisdiction. See M. Byers, *Custom, Power and the Power of Rules: International Relations and Customary International Law* (Cambridge: Cambridge University Press, 1999) at 64. It is submitted that a similar persuasive argument can be made with respect to the prevention of impending genocide. It is to be noted, however, that the argument made in this article is not to the effect that genocide must *always* be deemed a threat to international peace and security, within the meaning of Chapter VII of the UN Charter, but is rather a more nuanced one.

[195] Bruun, *supra* note 190 at 215.

[196] C.H.M. Waldock, "The Regulation of the Use of Force by Individual States in International Law" (1952-II) 81 Rec. des Cours 455 at 492; I. Brownlie, *International Law and the Use of Force by States* (Oxford: Clarendon Press, 1963); Scheffer, *supra* note 72 at 264.

permissive approach to Chapter VII powers and, in practice, humanitarian grounds are seldom invoked by the Security Council as a basis for Chapter VII enforcement action. In fact, while states may be endorsing broader responsibility for the UN to prevent genocide in principle, the actual practice of undertaking humanitarian activities suggests quite the opposite. This is due to the fact that the council has functioned in a primarily reactive and crisis-oriented manner — the tendency being to delay the implementation of effective measures until matters are boiling over, at which point it is often too late.[197] Had the Security Council been accustomed to acting preventively, various options would have been canvassed in Kuwait, Bosnia, Rwanda, Congo (Brazzaville), and Burundi, which would have arguably yielded a different outcome in each case.

Through a thorough analysis of the competence of the UN with respect to human rights matters, as exemplified in the UN Charter and illustrated in practice, this article has demonstrated that it is now a *fait accompli* that the organization holds the power to prevent the escalation of a situation involving massive, systematic, and murderous human rights violations into genocide through forcible measures. Thus, the so-called "controversy" over which humanitarian situations constitute a threat to international peace and security is a red herring. The particular use of preventive deployment of troops to prevent impending genocide clearly fits into the overall framework of UN early warning action and is an essential tool for promoting peace.

Despite significant developments in preventive measures, financial and political constraints in the UN have prevented military action from reaching its fullest potential in preventing impending genocide. In particular, the governments of some member states still oppose today UN involvement in conflict prevention, especially with respect to non-international conflicts in which genocide may potentially erupt. These member states can undermine the effectiveness of the UN collective security machinery in preventing genocide in a variety of ways, including a limitation on funding. Other shortcomings of the current system relate to information gathering and intelligence assessing as well as to structural problems, such as the veto power and the requirement of a prior determination of a "threat to peace," all of which widen the gap between

---

197 C. Peck, *The United Nations as a Dispute Settlement System: Improving Mechanisms for the Prevention and Resolution of Conflict* (The Hague: Kluwer Law International, 1996) at 16-17.

early warning and action. The difficulty in "predicting" an unprecedented genocide should also not be underestimated, even with the benefit of hindsight. Finally, despite various proposals to create stand-by forces or a volunteer force recruited in cases of impending genocide,[198] the failures of the UN to move in this direction has made preventive measures precarious. The result, as noted earlier in this article, has been the evaporation of any illusions about the effectiveness of UN collective measures in preventing mass murders.

The UN's capacity for preventive measures in cases of impending genocide could and must be improved, bridging the gap between early warning and responsive action. In considering ways in which to improve the organization's capacity to adequately respond to the challenge posed by threatening genocide, one must inevitably focus on the following factors: (1) the necessity of a comprehensive and holistic approach to genocide prevention; (2) the political will to act, both by the concerned parties and third states; (3) constitutional reform; and (4) the need to delegate preventive deployment powers to regional organizations and individual states in some cases. This article has attempted to highlight the obstacle posed by state sovereignty to UN-authorized military action to prevent genocide as well as the potential of such action. Certainly from a state's perspective, such measures may operate to prevent genocide in ways that involve a higher level of intrusiveness into its "domestic affairs" by international mechanisms and institutions than hitherto imagined. However, an averted genocide is likely to be cheaper in human, military, and fiscal terms than is a crisis resolved *post hoc* by military countermeasures.[199] Ultimately, the question of whether the benefits to be derived from coercive measures will outweigh a state's concerns about the considerable loss of their exercise of sovereignty will depend on how effectively such measures are deployed.

---

[198] See *Supplement to an Agenda for Peace*, UN Doc. A/50/60-S/1995/1 (1995) at para. 44, reprinted in B. Boutros-Ghali, *An Agenda For Peace*, 2nd ed. (New York: United Nations, 1995) at 5, 18. See also *Report of the Secretary-General on the Work of the Organization*, UN GAOR, 52nd Sess., Supp. No. 1, paras. 118-119, UN Doc. A/52/1 (1997).

[199] *Note by the Secretary-General, Joint Inspection Unit: Strengthening the United Nations System Capacity for Conflict Prevention*, UN GAOR, 52nd Sess., Agenda Items 10 and 120 at 3, UN Doc. A/52/184 (1997); B. Boutros-Ghali, "Beyond Peacekeeping" (1992) 25 N.Y.U. J. Int'l L. & Pol. 113 at 119.

Sommaire

Les mesures préventives du Conseil de sécurité des Nations Unies en cas de génocides imminents: une évaluation contemporaine

Au fil de l'augmentation des conflits civils entre les groupes ethniques et religieux, les Nations Unies ont développé une stratégie plus efficace d'intervention dans de tels conflits, mettant les mesures préventives au cœur de la planification et de l'activité dans le système onusien. Un obstacle à la mise en œuvre de mesures préventives est la souveraineté nationale. Cet article examine le potentiel encore partiellement exploité des Nations Unies de déployer des forces militaires afin de régler les crises importantes avant qu'elles ne s'enveniment et mènent au génocide, soulignant à la fois les difficultés que présente la souveraineté étatique et les chances de succès. L'article fait une étude exhaustive des dispositions de la Charte pour la protection des droits de la personne en cherchant à démontrer comment elles peuvent conférer aux Nations Unies l'autorité d'agir pour prévenir un génocide imminent. Un survol est fait de l'intervention du Conseil de sécurité en Rhodésie du Sud, en Iraq du Nord, en Bosnie, en Somalie, à Haïti et au Rwanda pour illustrer le potentiel de l'action militaire précoce et les questions qui se posent concernant le moment où il convient de prendre de telles mesures. L'article conclut que le défi le plus important auquel sont confrontées les Nations Unies est comment améliorer sa capacité de prévenir un génocide imminent. Le succès de l'intervention militaire comme mesure de prévention du génocide sera déterminant dans l'acceptation d'autres mesures préventives dans l'avenir, à mesure que les États peuvent évaluer si l'atteinte à leur souveraineté est raisonnable eu égard aux avantages qui en découlent.

Summary

Preventive Measures in Cases of Impending Genocide through the UN Security Council: A Contemporary Assessment

As civil conflicts between ethnic or religious groups have increased in number, the United Nations has developed greater effectiveness in intervening in such conflicts and has made preventive measures a focus of planning and undertakings of the UN system. One obstacle to implementing preventive measures is the problem of national sovereignty. This article looks at the still relatively unused potential of the UN to deploy military troops as a measure to deal with crises of serious magnitude before they erupt into genocide, highlighting both the obstacles posed by state sovereignty and the potential for success. The article offers a comprehensive study of the human rights provisions of the UN Charter to show how they can operate to authorize the UN to take action to prevent impending genocide. Further, Security Council action in southern Rhodesia, northern Iraq, Bosnia, Somalia, Haiti, and Rwanda is examined, both illustrating the potential of early military action and raising questions about the timing of preventive measures. The article concludes that the most important challenge facing the UN is how to improve its capacity to prevent impending genocide. The success of military action in preventing genocide will determine the acceptance of future preventive measures of this nature, as states weigh whether the cost to their sovereignty is reasonable in view of the benefits obtained.

Feature: The Macdonald Symposium Papers

Editorial Note

DONALD M. MCRAE

On May 10, 2002, a one-day symposium was held at Dalhousie University in honour of Judge Ronald St. J. Macdonald. The conference focused on the many areas of international law in which Macdonald has written, taught, and practised over the years. Each session was introduced by a short paper to focus discussion. The authors of these papers were then encouraged to expand their introductory remarks into articles that could be published in a special section of the *Yearbook*. The following articles attest to the range of Ronald St. J. Macdonald's interest and influence, to the profound impact he has had on scholars both in Canada and around the world, and to his legacy in the field of international law.

Judicial Notice and Reception Theory: Thoughts on the Contribution of Ronald St. John Macdonald

GIBRAN VAN ERT

When I decided, in 1998, to write a book on the application of international law in Canada, I was initially inspired by Allan Gotlieb's 1968 monograph *Canadian Treaty-Making*.[1] Later, I discovered

---

Gibran van Ert, BA (McGill), MA (Cantab.), LLM (Toronto).

[1] A.E. Gotlieb, *Canadian Treaty-Making* (Toronto: Butterworths, 1968).

Murray Hunt's *Using Human Rights Law in English Courts*[2] and
Herscht Lauterpacht's article "Is International Law a Part of the
Law of England?."[3] All of these texts were immensely influential
on me. However, it was Ronald St. John Macdonald's 1974 article
"The Relationship between International Law and Domestic Law
in Canada"[4] that determined the scope of what I wanted to do. The
article was only one of several important contributions to the
edited volume *Canadian Perspectives on International Law and Organization*, yet for me it has been the most significant. For at least twenty-
five years since it was written, Macdonald's article remained the
most complete account of how public international law took effect
in the domestic law of Canada. No one else had treated so fully and
so well the themes of the incorporation of customary international
law by Canadian common law, the implementation of treaties by
legislative enactment, and the judicial notice of international law by
common law courts. Nevertheless, much had happened in twenty-
five years, and there was more to say about this topic than could be
canvassed in a single article. Macdonald's themes deserved more
attention. My text, *Using International Law in Canadian Courts*,[5] was
my attempt to give them this attention.

I have often noticed copies of *Canadian Perspectives on International Law and Organization* on the bookshelves of Canadian international lawyers. I do not have one. My copy of "The Relationship
between International Law and Domestic Law in Canada" is a
dog-eared photocopy taken in the Bora Laskin Law Library, replete
with underscoring and margin notes in several shades of ink. The
earliest annotations are sometimes critical. Most of these, however,
have been amended in later, more informed readings with words to
the effect of, "No no, he's right." I still differ from Macdonald about
some things. I think he is too hesitant about the extent to which the
doctrine of incorporation is established in Canadian law.[6] Nevertheless, Macdonald's article stands out, to my mind, for its prescience

---

[2] M. Hunt, *Using Human Rights Law in English Courts* (Oxford: Hart Publishing,
1998).

[3] H. Lauterpacht, "Is International Law a Part of the Law of England?" (1939)
Transactions of the Grotius Society 51

[4] R. St. J. Macdonald, "The Relationship between Domestic Law and International
Law in Canada" in R. St. J. Macdonald et al., eds., *Canadian Perspectives on International Law and Organization* (Toronto: University of Toronto Press, 1974) 88.

[5] G. van Ert, *Using International Law in Canadian Courts* (The Hague: Kluwer Law
International, 2002).

[6] *Ibid.* at chapter 5.

and continuing relevance. A full exegesis of the piece would run far longer than space permits. I propose to take up two of the themes that have most influenced my own work, namely the judicial notice of international law by Canadian courts and the need for a theory of reception. First, a few words about the title of this opening session of the conference, "Canada and International Law."

CANADA AND INTERNATIONAL LAW

I suggest at the outset of my book that Canada's achievement of statehood is a fact to which Canadian law is still reconciling itself. If Canada can be said to have an independence day, it is not 1 July but rather 11 December — the anniversary of the proclamation of the Statute of Westminster 1931,[7] whereby Canada and other British dominions gained control over their external affairs. Yet each year, the anniversary goes largely unmarked. Likewise, the legal consequences of the statehood that this event brought Canada remain underappreciated by our bench and bar. Before Westminster, Canadian lawyers and politicians could afford to ignore international law. External affairs were a matter for the imperial authorities. This situation had prevailed since the earliest colonial times. It is no wonder, then, that early Canada produced so few international jurists. When at last Canada achieved independence, and assumed the responsibilities of statehood that came with it, our legal profession was (with important exceptions) rather unequipped. The uncertainty that marks the reasons of some of the learned judges of the Supreme Court of Canada in *Re Foreign Legations*[8] — but which is thankfully absent in the fine contribution of Chief Justice Sir Lyman Duff[9] — is perhaps a symptom of this. Canadian lawyers have been slow to adjust to Canada's international status. As late as 1967, one

---

[7] Statute of Westminster 1931, R.S.C. 1985 App. II No. 27.

[8] *Re Foreign Legations*, [1943] S.C.R. 209.

[9] See van Ert, *supra* note 5 at 142-44. Chief Justice Duff had gained some international legal experience as junior counsel for Canada in the Alaska boundary arbitration of 1903 (in which an Anglo-Russian boundary treaty of 1825 fell to be interpreted to determine the border between Alaska and British Columbia), and later in his role as joint commissioner on the report into the *I'm Alone* incident (in which an American navy vessel sunk a Canadian-registered rum runner in international waters off the coast of Louisiana). See D. Williams, *Duff: A Life in the Law* (Vancouver: UBC Press, 1984) at 44-52, 169-77; *Award of the Alaska Boundary Tribunal (UK v. USA)*, reported in External Affairs, *Treaties and Agreements Affecting Canada* (Ottawa: King's Printer, 1927) at 153; and *I'm Alone arbitration (USA v. Canada)* 3 R.I.A.A. 1609.

senses incredulity in the banal declaration of the Supreme Court of Canada that "[t]here can be no doubt now that Canada has become a sovereign state."[10] Even today, international law continues to be only an elective course in most Canadian law schools.

Ignorance of international law is a luxury that the Canadian legal profession can no longer afford. Confirmation of this fact is one of the many welcome consequences of the Supreme Court of Canada's important judgment in *Baker* v. *Canada*.[11] The question of the relationship between international law and the law of Canada is one that has grown only more pressing in the nearly thirty years since Macdonald addressed it. Now that Canadians can no longer ignore this question, where shall we look for its answer?

The answer, as Macdonald showed in 1974 and as I have attempted to demonstrate more recently, is to be found in the common law. While international law has come to prominence in Canada only relatively recently, it has been a matter of serious interest to English jurists since the eighteenth century. As the common law crossed the Atlantic, its rules for the reception of international law came with it. By reception, I mean the process by which public international law takes effect in domestic law. In the celebrated *Lotus* case, Judge Moore of the United States spoke of the "majestic stream of the common law, united with international law."[12] The stream's source is England, in whose jurisprudence the doctrines of the judicial notice of international law, the incorporation of customary international law, the implementation of conventional international law, and the presumption of international legality were first enunciated. In Canada, this stream still runs, with some diversions to meet our particular constitution. Yet for the most part, the reception of international law in Canada remains a question of common law. It is all the more important, then, that the common law's custodians — the judges and the counsel that appear before them — have a grasp of international law and the rules that govern its reception in this country.

JUDICIAL NOTICE OF INTERNATIONAL LAW[13]

That Canadian judges and counsel should have some grasp of international law is not simply desirable. It is required by the doctrine

---

[10]   *Re Offshore Mineral Rights of British Columbia*, [1967] S.C.R. 793.

[11]   *Baker* v. *Canada*, [1999] 2 S.C.R. 817 [hereinafter *Baker*].

[12]   *Lotus* case (1927) P.C.I.J. Series A No. 10 at 75.

[13]   See generally van Ert, *supra* note 5 at 30-40.

of judicial notice. By this doctrine, courts and other adjudicating bodies will accept the existence of certain laws or facts without requiring proof. Judges are required to take judicial notice of Acts of Parliament, rules of equity, and the common law. Furthermore, as Macdonald noted in 1974, judicial notice must also be taken of international law. Writing in 1939, Lauterpacht observed that while judicial practice supported the proposition that international law is judicially noticed by English courts and, therefore, need not be specifically proved before them, it was nevertheless difficult "to trace any judicial pronouncement bearing directly on the matter."[14] Lauterpacht was forced to dip into an American tributary of Judge Moore's "majestic stream of the common law" for judicial support of the notice rule. In *The Scotia*,[15] Justice Strong observed that "[f]oreign municipal laws must indeed be proved as facts, but it is not so with the law of nations." The best English authority for the rule today is not a case but *Halsbury's Laws of England*, which declares simply but forcefully that "[t]he courts take notice of every branch of English law, including the principles of international law."[16]

Similarly, Macdonald found that Canadian law provided few clear authorities for the rule that international law is judicially noticed by Canadian courts, though the practice of taking notice was clear. This practice is clearer still today, for judicial consultation of international authorities is increasingly frequent. Yet judicial pronouncements upon the appropriateness of such consultation remain rare. Macdonald's strongest authority was *The Ship "North"* v. *The King*, an early judgment of the Supreme Court of Canada.[17] The admiralty judge in the court below had quite correctly taken judicial notice of the customary law doctrine of hot pursuit and interpreted a federal statute in light of that doctrine. At the Supreme Court of Canada, Justice Louis Davies (Justice James MacLennan concurring) approved of this approach, declaring that "the Admiralty Court when exercising its jurisdiction is bound to take notice of the law of nations" and "the right of hot pursuit ... being part of the law of nations was properly judicially taken notice of and acted upon by the learned judge."[18] Macdonald admitted that this

---

[14] Lauterpacht, *supra* note 3 at 59, n. 1.

[15] *The Scotia*, (1871) 14 Wall 170 at 188.

[16] *Halsbury's Laws of England*, vol. 17, 4th ed. (London: Butterworths, 1977) at para. 100.

[17] *The Ship "North"* v. *The King* (1906), 37 S.C.R. 385.

[18] *Ibid.* at 394.

pronouncement might turn on the particularities of admiralty law and not apply to Canadian courts generally.[19] I do not believe this to be the case. Courts with admiralty jurisdiction are still Canadian courts,[20] and I see no reason why a court should have greater-powers of judicial notice of law when exercising one jurisdiction than when exercising another. Later cases (notably the recent jurisprudence of the Supreme Court of Canada) strongly support the proposition that Canadian courts take judicial notice of international law.

A 1997 judgment of the Federal Court is notable for its elucidation of the judicial notice rule from first principles. In *Jose Pereira E Hijos S.A.* v. *Canada (Attorney General),*[21] Justice W. Andrew MacKay faced several objections to the pleadings. The plaintiffs were the owner and operator of the Spanish fishing vessel *Estai.* The vessel was boarded (probably illegally) by Canadian officers in 1995.[22] In their pleadings, the plaintiffs invoked international law. MacKay J. rejected the attorney general's submission that the plaintiffs could not rely on international law in preference to Canadian law, but struck out parts of the pleadings on the ground that international law need not be specifically pleaded:

To the extent that international conventions or treaties are considered authority for international law principles, it is unnecessary to plead them specifically, in the same way that it is unnecessary to plead other authority, e.g., jurisprudence or legislation, and such pleading is not of facts, the essence of pleading, but of law, which is not to be pleaded.[23]

---

[19] Macdonald, *supra* note 4 at 100.

[20] There is a type of court that, while constituted by domestic judges, exercises a purely international jurisdiction, namely prize courts. (Prize is the law that allows belligerent states to seize and sell commercial vessels of the enemy.) In Canada, see the Canada Prize Act, R.S.C. 1970, c. P-24, which grants prize jurisdiction to the Federal Court of Canada and requires prize matters to be determined "according to the Course of Admiralty and the Law of Nations" (per s. 5(1)). Admiralty courts are not prize courts, however; they decide controversies by applying Canadian law (which, according to the judicial notice rules described above, includes international law).

[21] *Jose Pereira E Hijos S.A.* v. *Canada (Attorney General),* [1997] 2 F.C. 84 [hereinafter *Jose Pereira*].

[22] Spain brought Canada before the International Court of Justice over this matter. The court was forced to conclude that it lacked jurisdiction, given that Canada had conveniently amended its acceptance of the court's compulsory jurisdiction, adding a reservation concerning fisheries matters, only a year before. See *Fisheries Jurisdiction* case (*Spain* v. *Canada*) (*Jurisdiction*), [1998] I.C.J. 432.

[23] *Jose Pereira, supra* note 21 at para. 22; see also para. 25.

MacKay J. adverted to no authority on this point. He simply started from the principle that international law is law and proceeded to apply the ordinary rules of pleading. In this way, MacKay J. put the judicial notice doctrine into practice.

In his consideration of judicial notice, Macdonald pointedly distinguishes international law from foreign law (that is, the domestic laws of foreign countries). Common law courts do not take judicial notice of foreign law. Rather, foreign law is treated as a matter of fact to be ascertained by expert evidence.[24] As Lauterpacht observed, international law need not be proved in common law courts "apparently for the reason that it is not foreign law."[25] The importance of this distinction between international law and foreign law goes beyond the rules of evidence and pleading to the very foundation of Anglo-Canadian reception law. This body of law is predicated on the notion that international law is binding on Canada. It is binding on the Canadian state as a matter of international law. It may also be binding within Canada, where it is incorporated by the common law or implemented by statute. Furthermore, even unimplemented rules of conventional international law may gain a measure of bindingness through the application of the presumption of international legality.[26] Foreign law, by contrast, is not in any way binding on Canada. That was the great achievement of the Statute of Westminster — the laws of other countries do not bind us.[27] By drawing this clear distinction between international law and foreign law, the doctrine of judicial notice contributes to assuring compliance with Canada's international legal obligations and promotes an attitude of respect for international law within the Canadian legal community.[28]

[24] See generally J.-G. Castel, *Canadian Conflict of Laws*, 4th ed. (Toronto: Butterworths, 1997) at 155-62.

[25] Lauterpacht, *supra* note 3 at 59.

[26] *Baker, supra* note 11, is the leading example of this. See van Ert, *supra* note 5 at 207-27.

[27] Foreign laws and jurisprudence may of course be persuasive authority in the interpretation of Canadian laws.

[28] Karen Knop has argued that international law is similar to foreign law because both are "external sources of law" — the relevance of which "is not based on bindingness": K. Knop, "Here and There: International Law in Domestic Courts" (2000) 32 N.Y.U. J. Int'l L. & Pol. 501 at 520. Knop goes on to say that "the blurring of international law into comparative law" allows international lawyers "to develop a more complex and critical model of international law in domestic courts" (at 525). I disagree. In my view, this rule of judicial notice, and other rules of international law and Anglo-Canadian reception law, refute this approach.

The doctrine of judicial notice has other practical consequences for courts and litigants. It is the means by which courts apply the rule that customary international law is incorporated by the common law. If courts could not take judicial notice of custom, they could not give effect to the ancient common law rule that "whatever has received the common consent of civilized nations must have received the assent of our country."[29] Judicial notice is also the means by which our courts apply the presumption of international legality — that is, the interpretive presumption that legislation is not intended to violate rules of international law or comity.[30] If the courts could not inform themselves of the substance of international law, they could not apply this important rule of statutory interpretation.

Another practical consequence of the judicial notice doctrine is that expert testimony on international law (from law professors, for example) should not be admitted as evidence. The determination of international legal questions, like the determination of other questions of law, falls to the trial judge. Litigants wishing to employ international law experts at trial should not call them as witnesses but should instead instruct them as counsel. These matters have recently received very close attention from the Scottish High Court of Justiciary in *Lord Advocate's Reference No. 1 of 2000*.[31] Three people were acquitted of charges of malicious damage and theft in regard to a vessel associated with the United Kingdom's Trident nuclear missile program. At trial, the sheriff allowed evidence from international law experts on the legality of nuclear weapons in customary international law. Following the acquittals, the Crown referred the following question to the court: "In a trial under Scottish criminal procedure, is it competent to lead evidence as to the content of customary international law as it applies in the United Kingdom?" The court replied in part as follows:

[29] *West Rand Gold Mining* v. *The King*, [1905] 2 K.B. 391 (per Lord Alverstone). See, *inter alia*, *Saint John* v. *Fraser-Brace Overseas*, [1958] S.C.R. 263 at 268-9 (per Rand J.); *Re Regina and Palacios* (1984), 45 O.R. (2d) 269 (CA Ont); and *Re Canada Labour Code*, [1992] 2 S.C.R. 50 (per La Forest J.). See generally van Ert, *supra* note 5 at 137-70.

[30] See R. Sullivan, *Driedger on the Construction of Statutes*, 3rd ed. (Toronto: Butterworths, 1994) at 330. For a history of the presumption and recent case law applying it, see van Ert, *supra* note 5 at 99-136.

[31] *Lord Advocate's Reference No. 1 of 2000*, 2001 S.L.T. 507 (Scot. High Court of Justiciary Appeal Court) [hereinafter *Lord Advocate's Reference*]. Reported in Quicklaw under *HM Advocate* v. *Zelter*, [2001] Scot. J. No 84 (QL). Recall that the Appeal Court of the Scottish High Court of Justiciary is the supreme criminal court in Scotland; there is no appeal from it to the House of Lords.

We are in no doubt that in relation to evidence in the trial itself this Question must be answered in the negative. A rule of customary international law is a rule of Scots law. As such, in solemn proceedings it is a matter for the judge and not for the jury. The jury must be directed by the judge upon such a matter, and must accept any such direction. There can thus be no question of the jury requiring to hear or consider the evidence of a witness, however expert, as to what the law is.

It was pointed out to us that evidence as to foreign law may competently be led in Scottish proceedings. That is because the law in question is foreign, and in Scottish proceedings is a question of fact and not of law. Any analogy between such foreign law and customary international law is false . . .

Just as it is for the judge to direct the jury upon a point of law, it is important to remember that it is for the solicitor or counsel appearing on behalf of any party to present to the court any submission which is thought appropriate upon any issue of law . . .

We can see some initial attraction in the suggestion that if a court is willing to read what a particular expert has written in a general context, it might on occasion be sensible to hear what he has to say, in the particular context of the case in hand. We do not feel it appropriate to rule out that possibility, as a matter of law. Such argument as was addressed to us in relation to Question 1 was of course directed primarily to the question of evidence *in causa,* before the jury; and while the possible usefulness of such material to a judge was touched upon, having regard to what the sheriff had said, the point was not fully argued. At that level, we are inclined to think that the matter would be one for the judge's discretion, although we would wish to reserve our opinion on that point. We would, however, add that if in any particular situation it were thought necessary by those representing a party to have recourse to some specialist source of advice, the appropriate course would of course normally be to seek that advice, whether in writing or by consultation or both, so that the appropriate submissions could be made, by that party's representative, at the appropriate time . . . [W]e find it very hard to imagine any situation in which the appropriate material should be presented to the court in the form of evidence with examination and cross-examination, and perhaps counter-evidence for the other party.[32]

THE NEED FOR A THEORY

The second feature of Macdonald's important article that I wish to consider is his explanation of why we need a theoretical basis for understanding the relationship between international and Canadian law.[33] Macdonald's comments on this subject were directed towards custom in particular, but they can be applied to all sources of international law. Macdonald gave three reasons why Canadian

[32] *Lord Advocate's Reference, supra* note 31 at paras. 23-4, 26-7.

[33] Macdonald, *supra* note 4 at 88.

law needs a clear theoretical foundation for its interaction with international law.

The first reason that Macdonald gave has been especially influential on my work. We need to know how Canadian and international law interact, he said, because we need certainty in advising our clients. This rationale for clear reception rules will come as a surprise to those who see international law as a largely academic matter. For Macdonald, a theoretically sound reception system is not merely intellectually satisfying but also a matter of practical importance. The vision that Macdonald evokes of Canadian lawyers advising clients on the consequences of international law for their domestic affairs may once have seemed far-fetched. Yet it no longer appears that way. Immigration claimants,[34] town councils,[35] taxpayers,[36] secessionist provinces,[37] disappointed press barons,[38] employees of Canadian-based international organizations,[39] welfare recipients,[40] accused persons,[41] civil servants,[42] egg marketers,[43] estate claimants[44] — all have recently found their legal affairs to be bound up in Canadian reception law in various ways. Every indication is that international law will grow only more prevalent in future litigation. Like Macdonald, I view the relationship between international and Canadian law as chiefly a practical question.

Macdonald's second reason for elaborating a theoretical basis for using international law in Canadian courts is to ensure that Canadian domestic law conforms to the requirements of international law.[45] This conception has again been immensely influential

---

34 *Baker, supra* note 11; *Suresh* v. *Canada,* 2002 S.C.C. 1; and *Ahani* v. *Canada,* 2002 S.C.C. 2, [2002] O.J. No. 431 (Ont CA) (QL).

35 *114957 Canada Ltée (Spraytech, Société d'arrosage)* v. *Hudson (Town),* [2001] 2 S.C.R. 241.

36 *Chua* v. *Minister of National Revenue,* [2001] 1 F.C. 608 (FCTD), supplemental reasons [2001] 1 F.C. 641.

37 *Reference Re Secession of Quebec,* [1998] 2 S.C.R. 217.

38 *Black* v. *Chrétien* (2001), 54 O.R. (3d) 215 (Ont CA).

39 *Miller* v. *Canada,* [2001] 1 S.C.R. 407.

40 *Gosselin* v. *Quebec (Procureur général),* [1999] R.J.Q. 1033 (Que CA), and *M.B.* v. *British Columbia,* [2001] 5 W.W.R. 6.

41 *United States of America* v. *Burns,* [2001] 1 S.C.R. 283.

42 *Lavoie* v. *Canada (Public Service Commision),* 2002 S.C.C. 23.

43 *Canadian Egg Marketing Agency* v. *Richardson,* [1998] 3 S.C.R. 157.

44 *Ordon Estate* v. *Grail,* [1998] 3 S.C.R. 437.

45 Macdonald, *supra* note 4 at 89.

on my work. There is an understandable, but nonetheless regrettable, tendency to draw rigid distinctions between international and domestic (or "municipal") authorities and institutions. To paraphrase Rudyard Kipling, domestic law is domestic law, international law is international law, and never the twain shall meet. Macdonald's conception is different. Domestic courts have a role in the international legal system. Through their construction of legislation and their interpretation of decided cases, domestic courts seek to assure their states' compliance with international norms. This conception of the judicial role is, I suggest, implicit in the cardinal international legal principle that states must discharge their international obligations in good faith.[46] For a state's judiciary to ignore or decline to respect those obligations is inconsistent with the good faith requirement. It must be kept in mind that when we say that the Canadian state bears certain obligations at international law, the term "state" includes not only the executive but also the legislature and the judiciary. By assuring wherever possible that Canadian domestic law complies with Canada's international obligations, our courts are not just helping the government keep its commitments but discharging their own duties.

Macdonald's final justification for a theory of Canadian reception law is rather different. Writing as he was in an era where constitutional reform still seemed possible, Macdonald suggested that this sort of theorizing might prompt us to consider adding provisions about international law to our written constitution or making other institutional changes. There is a sense in which we did exactly that. The origin of the Canadian Charter of Rights and Freedoms in international human rights law are well documented.[47] While the

[46] See, for example, 1969 Vienna Convention on the Law of Treaties, (1980) Can. T.S. no. 37, arts. 26 and 31.

[47] Canadian Charter of Rights and Freedoms, Part 1 of the Constitution Act, 1982, being Schedule B to the Canada Act 1982 (U.K.), 1982, c. 11 [hereinafter Charter]. See: C. Heyns and F. Viljoen, eds., *The Impact of the United Nations Human Rights Treaties on the Domestic Level* (The Hague: Kluwer Law International, 2002) at 123, 132; B. Dickson, "The Canadian Charter of Rights and Freedoms: Context and Evolution" in G.-A. Beaudoin and E. Mendes, *The Canadian Charter of Rights and Freedoms*, 3rd ed. (Toronto: Carswell, 1996) at 1-4, 5; A.F. Bayefsky, *International Human Rights Law: Use in Canadian Charter of Rights and Freedoms Litigation* (Toronto: Butterworths, 1992) at 33-47; A.F. Bayefsky, *Canada's Constitution Act 1982 and Amendments: A Documentary History* (Toronto: McGraw-Hill Ryerson, 1989) at 150ff; D. Turp, "Le recours au droit international aux fins de l'interprétation de la Charte canadienne des droits et libertés: un bilan jurisprudentiel" (1984) 18 R.J.T. 353; G.V. La Forest, "The Canadian Charter of Rights

1982 constitution contains only one explicit reference to international law,[48] it is clear that the Charter is now the principal means by which Canada meets its obligations under international human rights law. Yet it remains the case that Canada's written constitution contains no important express provisions governing the application of international law in Canada. Stephen Toope has described the silence of our written constitution on this point as leaving a "constitutional vacuum."[49] But there is more to our constitution than its written provisions. The rules and principles according to which international law applies in Canadian jurisdictions are no less authoritative — and, indeed, no less constitutional — for being unwritten. Whatever omissions the written constitution has left in regard to international law are amply supplied by the unwritten constitution and common law adjudication.[50] My view is that there is probably little benefit to be gained from entrenching in our written constitution the common law rules of incorporation, implementation, judicial notice, and interpretation that together comprise Canadian reception law.

This is not to say, however, that there is no room for reform. Canadian parliamentary practice would benefit greatly from the reforms brought in Australia, New Zealand, and the United Kingdom

---

and Freedoms: An Overview" (1983) 61 Can. Bar Rev. 19 at 25; M. Cohen and A.F. Bayefsky, "The Canadian Charter of Rights and Freedoms and Public International Law" (1983) 61 Can. Bar Rev. 265; R. Elliott, "Interpreting the Charter: Using the Earlier Versions as an Aid" (1982) Charter Edition U.B.C. L. Rev. 110; and W.S. Tarnopolsky, "A Comparison between the Canadian Charter of Rights and Freedoms and the International Covenant on Civil and Political Rights" (1982) 8 Queen's L. J. 211.

[48] Charter, *supra* note 47, s 11(g): "Any person charged with an offence has the right ... not to be found guilty on account of any act or omission unless, at the time of the act or omission, it constituted an offence under Canadian or international law or was criminal according to the general principles of law recognized by the community of nations."

[49] S.J. Toope, "Keynote Address: Canada and International Law" in *The Impact of International Law on the Practice of Law in Canada. Proceedings of the 27th Annual Conference of the Canadian Council on International Law, Ottawa October 15-17, 1998* (The Hague: Kluwer Law International, 1999) 33 at 35.

[50] That this is so is not simply fortuitous or a case of necessity being the mother of invention. The written constitution explicitly contemplates that unwritten rules will determine such matters as are not addressed by it. Thus, the preamble to the Constitution Act 1867 (UK) 30 & 31 Vict. C. 3, reprinted in R.S.C. 1985 App. II No. 5 provides that Canada will have a constitution "similar in principle to that of the United Kingdom."

in the mid-1990s to inform Parliament of treaty action proposed by the government. The foreign affairs ministers of these countries now regularly table in Parliament (and publish on the Internet) simple, lucid summaries of treaties being considered for ratification by the government.[51] Interested members of parliament can use these summaries (known as "explanatory memoranda") to question the government, take soundings from constituents, and even initiate parliamentary debates. These reforms were brought in other Commonwealth countries to respond to popular feelings that governments had too much power to assume new international obligations without first considering their consequences in a democratic forum. At the root of these concerns, I suggest, is a growing unease about the continued existence, in its raw mediaeval form, of a royal prerogative over treaty-making. In an era when the excesses of executive power have been curbed by judicial review at almost every turn, and in a country whose English-derived constitutional history can be viewed as a steady erosion of prerogative power in favour of parliamentary democracy, it is incongruous that the Crown's power to make treaties remains so unchecked. I have come to this view, as Macdonald said one might, through the study of Canadian reception law. The only difference between us is that Macdonald envisioned amendments to written constitutional provisions, while I would like to see reform of our unwritten constitutional practices.

Sommaire

La connaissance d'office et la théorie de la réception du droit international en droit interne: Réflexions sur les contributions de Ronald St. J. Macdonald

À l'occasion d'une conférence en l'honneur du professeur Ronald St. John Macdonald, l'auteur considère à nouveau l'article de Macdonald, paru en 1974, intitulé "The Relationship between International Law and Domestic Law in Canada." L'auteur passe en revue, à la lumière de la jurisprudence récente, les propos de Macdonald quant à la connaissance d'office du droit international. Plus précisément, la pratique permettant aux spécialistes du

---

[51] See D. Turp, "Un nouveau défi démocratique: l'accentuation du rôle de parlement dans la conclusion et la mise en oeuvre des traités internationaux" in *The Impact of International Law on the Practice of Law in Canada* (Dordrecht: Kluwer Law International, 1999) 115; and van Ert, *supra* note 5 at 68-71.

droit international de témoigner à titre d'experts sur des questions de droit international est qualifié d'allant à l'encontre de la doctrine de la connaissance d'office. En terminant, l'auteur réfléchit sur l'opinion de Macdonald qu'il faut une base théorique pour expliquer la réception du droit international en droit interne au Canada.

Summary

Judicial Notice and Reception Theory: Thoughts on the Contribution of Ronald St. John Macdonald

On the occasion of a conference in honour of Ronald St. John Macdonald, the author revisits Macdonald's important 1974 article "The Relationship between International Law and Domestic Law in Canada." Macdonald's discussion of the judicial notice of international law by Canadian courts is considered in light of recent case law. In particular, the practice of international lawyers giving expert evidence on international law is criticized as inconsistent with the doctrine of judicial notice. Finally, the author reflects on Macdonald's view that a theoretical framework is needed to explain the reception of international law in the law of Canada.

The Continuing Contributions of Ronald St. J. Macdonald to UN Charter and Peace and Security Issues

JOHN H. CURRIE

INTRODUCTION

The Charter of the United Nations (UN Charter)[1] and peace and security issues are vast topics for such brief consideration, particularly when one considers the scope and volume of Ronald St. J. Macdonald's contributions in the area. I therefore thought it might be useful to isolate one particular strand of the UN Charter/ peace and security theme in order to provide a more tractable focus to this discussion. I have in mind the particularly thorny, but in my view never more important, issue of the relationship between the International Court of Justice (ICJ) and the UN Security Council on matters of international peace and security. This topic, of course, is particularly difficult for international lawyers because of the singular lack of guidance to be found in the UN Charter in terms of defining the respective roles of each organ — or, more precisely, the interaction between them — on peace and security matters.

One particularly memorable and important piece in which Macdonald addressed this topic was published in the 1993 volume of the *Canadian Yearbook of International Law* under the title "Changing Relations between the International Court of Justice and the Security Council of the United Nations."[2] This piece serves today's

John H. Currie, Associate Professor, Faculty of Law, Common Law Section, University of Ottawa. Adapted from introductory remarks to a roundtable discussion on the contributions of Ronald St. J. Macdonald to UN Charter and peace and security issues.

[1] Charter of the United Nations, June 26, 1945, Can. T.S. 1945 No. 7 (in force October 24, 1945) [hereinafter UN Charter].

[2] R. St. J. Macdonald, "Changing Relations between the International Court of Justice and the Security Council of the United Nations" (1993) 31 Can. Y.B. Int'l L. 3.

purposes particularly well not only because it raises for consideration various aspects of the relationship between the ICJ and the Security Council on peace and security matters but also because it illustrates very well certain elements of Macdonald's extensive work on the broader theme of constitutionalism in the international and UN systems.

In the next section, I review Macdonald's 1993 piece and briefly consider the continuing topicality and importance of the main issues it discussed. Then follows the main thrust of my comments, where I suggest another direction in which Macdonald's thinking about the relationship between the ICJ and the Security Council should be developed. Such further development is particularly urgent in my view in light of recent changes in the functioning of the Security Council on peace and security issues.

LOCKERBIE AND THE RELATIONSHIP BETWEEN THE
ICJ AND THE SECURITY COUNCIL

Macdonald's 1993 piece was a reaction to the 1992 case, *Questions of Interpretation and Application of the 1971 Montreal Convention Arising from the Aerial Incident at Lockerbie (Libyan Arab Jamahiriya v. United States of America; Libyan Arab Jamahiriya v. United Kingdom)* (*Lockerbie* case), in which the ICJ declined to order provisional measures, as requested by Libya, against the United States and the United Kingdom.[3] The United States and the United Kingdom had demanded that Libya extradite two Libyan nationals suspected of causing the explosion of Pan American Flight 103 on December 21, 1988, over Lockerbie, Scotland. Libya maintained that its obligation to extradite — or not — should be governed by the terms of the Convention for the Suppression of Unlawful Acts against the Safety of Civil Aviation (Montreal Convention),[4] and it sought an indication of provisional measures from the ICJ to protect its rights under that convention. The essential reason for the ICJ's refusal to order provisional measures was that, shortly after it heard argument from the parties but before it rendered its decision, the

---

[3] *Questions of Interpretation and Application of the 1971 Montreal Convention Arising from the Aerial Incident at Lockerbie (Libyan Arab Jamahiriya v. United States of America; Libyan Arab Jamahiriya v. United Kingdom), Provisional Measures, Order of April 14, 1992,* [1992] I.C.J. Rep. 114.

[4] Convention for the Suppression of Unlawful Acts against the Safety of Civil Aviation, done at Montreal on September 23, 1971, (1971) 10 I.L.M. 1151.

Security Council invoked Chapter VII and declared, in Resolution 748,[5] that Libya's continued failure to deliver the suspected terrorists constituted a threat to international peace and security. Resolution 748 accordingly decided that Libya must comply with the extradition requests of the United States and the United Kingdom. Thus, Resolution 748 essentially rendered Libya's invocation of its rights under the Montreal Convention moot.

What remained unclear in the order of the ICJ was whether it declined to indicate provisional measures because it considered the issue to be non-justiciable in light of Security Council Resolution 748; because Libya's rights under the Montreal Convention, or any order for provisional measures pursuant thereto, would in any case have to yield to Resolution 748 and could therefore have no effect; or because the ICJ simply chose not to exercise its full powers as a matter of "institutional comity" — that is, to avoid any conflict with a prior decision of the Security Council.

Macdonald took respectful issue with the ICJ for being so vague with respect to the underlying rationale for its decision.[6] In particular, he criticized the ICJ for not clearly upholding its many prior indications that it need not shy away from the "full exercise of its judicial power"[7] merely because the Security Council happens to be seized, in its own capacity, of the same matter. Thus, the major theme of his article was that the relationship between the ICJ and the Security Council, and even the potential for apparently conflicting decisions from the ICJ and the Security Council on peace and security issues, need not be an overriding concern. This argument was based on the ICJ's own view, oft-repeated in such decisions as *United States Diplomatic and Consular Staff in Tehran (United States of America v. Iran) (Tehran Hostages* case)[8] and the *Case Concerning Military and Paramilitary Activities in and against Nicaragua (Nicaragua v. United States of America) (Nicaragua* case),[9] that "the Security Council has functions of a political nature assigned to it, whereas the Court

---

[5] Security Council Resolution 748, adopted March 31, 1992, accessible at <http://www.un.org/documents/sc/res/1992/scres92.htm>.

[6] Macdonald, *supra* note 2 at 20-21.

[7] *Ibid.* at 5.

[8] *United States Diplomatic and Consular Staff in Tehran (United States of America v. Iran),* [1980] I.C.J. Rep. 3 [hereinafter *Tehran*].

[9] *Case Concerning Military and Paramilitary Activities in and against Nicaragua (Nicaragua v. United States of America), Jurisdiction and Admissibility,* [1984] I.C.J. Rep. 392 [hereinafter *Nicaragua*].

exercises purely judicial functions. Both organs can therefore perform their separate but complementary functions with respect to the same events."[10] Furthermore, the ICJ had indicated in its 1993 decision on the provisional measures sought by Bosnia-Herzegovina against Yugoslavia[11] that this complementary approach would be possible even where the Security Council had seized itself of a matter under Chapter VII of the UN Charter (as opposed to Chapter VI, which had been the case in the *Tehran Hostages* and *Nicaragua* cases).

In short, Macdonald's argument was that, given the different nature of the decision-making processes of the ICJ and the Security Council — judicial/legal versus political — any supposed conflict between their respective decisions on the same matter would be apparent only. That is, there would and possibly could be no *true* conflict because one organ would determine the existence of a threat to international peace and security on a legal standard, whereas the other would determine the same issue on a political standard.[12] In Macdonald's own words, "[i]n essence, it is misconceived to treat decisions of the Court and the Council as conflicting determinations."[13]

Of course, Macdonald was aware of the inherent difficulty in attempting to dissociate legal from political issues. While tentatively conceding that a rigid distinction between law and politics was philosophically unsustainable and that it would moreover be difficult to uphold such a distinction at the level of the content of rules or norms themselves, he nevertheless maintained that a distinction could still be made in terms of the process of reasoning and argument applicable in the legal and political contexts respectively.[14] As to which decision would carry the day in terms of enforcement or compliance, Macdonald considered that this would be governed by the UN Charter's stipulation that the Security Council had "primary responsibility for the maintenance of international peace

---

[10] *Tehran, supra* note 8 at 21-22; *Nicaragua, supra* note 9 at 433-35.

[11] *Application of the Convention on the Prevention and Punishment of the Crime of Genocide (Bosnia and Herzegovina v. Yugoslavia), Provisional Measures, Order of September 13, 1993,* [1993] I.C.J. Rep. 325.

[12] See especially Macdonald, *supra* note 2 at 18-20.

[13] *Ibid.* at 19.

[14] "Accepting for the moment that, perhaps, no meaningful philosophical distinction can be made between law and politics, our institutional experience tells us nevertheless that some matters are considered to be appropriate for judicial and others for political determination." *Ibid.* at 7.

and security."[15] Paradoxically, however, the non-exclusive nature of this hierarchical signal was taken as yet further support for the argument that such primary responsibility in no way renders legal issues of peace and security entirely non-justiciable before the ICJ.[16] The important point of the argument, in any case, was that if the Security Council's *political* determinations on peace and security issues conflict with a state's international *legal* position, it would be desirable that this be made clear.[17]

However, the article went further still and also raised the possibility that the relationship between the ICJ and the Security Council might in fact go beyond mere "complementary coexistence." Macdonald ventured into an even more controversial issue, which the ICJ had so studiously avoided in the 1992 *Lockerbie* decision and continued to sidestep in the 1998 *Lockerbie* case[18] — namely, the issue of whether the ICJ might not have some general role of superintendence to play over the powers exercised by various UN organs, including the Security Council itself. While acknowledging the absence of any express grant of such a power to the ICJ in the text of the UN Charter, Macdonald opined that "a powerful argument"[19] could be made for an inherent power of judicial review in the court, which could be supported by various textual indications in the UN Charter that the powers of the Security Council were limited and perhaps even constrained by principles of international law.[20] He did not purport, however, to prejudge the standard of review that might be applicable — whether for *vires,* procedural fairness, or compliance with substantive legal standards.[21]

When reviewing this article for today's purposes, one is struck by the continuing topicality and importance of the many issues, essentially of UN constitutionalism, that it raises. One is also struck by the intellectual vision and, indeed, the courage of Macdonald in challenging various organs of the United Nations to "grow up"

---

[15] UN Charter, *supra* note 1, Article 24(1).

[16] Macdonald, *supra* note 2 at 17-20.

[17] *Ibid.* at 31-32.

[18] *Questions of Interpretation and Application of the 1971 Montreal Convention Arising from the Aerial Incident at Lockerbie (Libyan Arab Jamahiriya* v. *United States of America; Libyan Arab Jamahiriya* v. *United Kingdom), Preliminary Objections,* [1998] I.C.J. Rep. 115.

[19] Macdonald, *supra* note 2 at 29.

[20] *Ibid.* at 29-30.

[21] *Ibid.* at 30.

(putting it in far more colloquial and much less diplomatic terms than he would have chosen) — that is, to move beyond facile characterizations of their respective "turf" and to accept that the proper functioning of the organization and, indeed, of international society might require that their interactions be complex, overlapping, and, perhaps even in some cases, conflicting.[22] It might require the multiplication of inputs into decision-making processes, rather than their neutralization, in order to produce more constructive long-term results. Certainly in democratic, domestic settings, we would not tolerate unchecked or unreviewable exercises of public power by lone institutions, other than in the most extraordinary of circumstances. There is recognition in such settings, and indeed it is implicit in the rule of law concept itself, that even official political action must itself conform to the law — if not substantively, then, in any event and at the very least, in terms of process and jurisdiction. What would lead us to expect that effective decision-making in the pluralistic world of international relations should require anything less?

Be that as it may, the more concrete questions raised in Macdonald's 1993 article continue to demand reasoned consideration, namely:

- Must the ICJ avoid making decisions conflicting with Security Council resolutions under Chapter VII? Or, if it must not, *ought* it, out of some sense of "institutional comity"?
- Should the ICJ avoid exercising its judicial power if in the end the effect of its orders will be annulled by contrary measures imposed by the Security Council?
- Are there limits to the decision-making powers of the Security Council and, if so, does the ICJ have a role in supervising the exercise of these powers?

These questions have of course attracted ongoing scholarly attention, both before and after Macdonald's important 1993 contribution.[23] And they are ever more urgent given that the number

---

[22] For example, "[i]f the Security Council is to be allowed to invoke its extensive powers under Chapter 7 of the Charter to override the legal rights of a state, this is a fact that should be openly recognized." *Ibid.* at 32.

[23] See, for example, E. Lauterpacht, "The Legal Effects of Illegal Acts of International Organisations" in *Cambridge Essays in International Law* (London: Stevens, 1965); T.M. Franck, "The 'Powers of Appreciation': Who Is the Ultimate Guardian of U.N. Legality?" (1992) 86 A.J.I.L. 519; V. Lowe, "Lockerbie — Changing the Rules During the Game" (1992) 51 Camb. L.J. 408; E. McWhinney, "The International Court as Emerging Constitutional Court and the Co-ordinate UN Institutions (Especially the Security Council): Implications of the Aerial Incident

of contentious cases before the ICJ that raise questions about the legality of the use of force continues to grow. The potential for conflict, real or apparent, between the roles of the ICJ and the Security Council on peace and security issues, therefore, continues to loom. Further, in the face of such potential conflict, the ICJ continues to adhere to the formal view, illustrated in its July 2000 decision ordering provisional measures in the *Case Concerning Armed Activities on the Territory of the Congo (Democratic Republic of the Congo v. Uganda)*,[24] that it can play a complementary role to that of the Security Council even when the latter has acted under Chapter VII. This continued stance might suggest a refinement to the first question posed above, namely whether the ICJ's insistence on its "complementary" Chapter VII role in fact signals that it must only avoid decisions that *directly* conflict with Security Council resolutions.

If further evidence is required of the ever-increasing importance of the interaction between judicial and political organs on matters of peace and security, one might also consider the peculiar relationship defined in the Statute of the International Criminal Court (Rome Statute) between the Security Council and the International Criminal Court (ICC).[25] In particular, is there merit to the American position that issues of aggression are inherently political rather than legal or justiciable — a position that has so far very effectively stymied efforts to include the crime of aggression in the ICC's operative jurisdiction?[26] Or, more broadly, is the distinction between

---

at Lockerbie" (1992) Can. Y.B. Int'l L. 261; W.M. Reisman, "The Constitutional Crisis in the United Nations" (1993) 87 A.J.I.L. 83; G.R. Watson, "Constitutionalism, Judicial Review, and the World Court" (1993) 34 Harv. Int'l L.J. 1; V. Gowlland-Debbas, "The Relationship between the International Court of Justice and the Security Council in Light of the Lockerbie Case" (1994) 88 A.J.I.L. 643; J.E. Alvarez, "Judging the Security Council" (1996) 90 A.J.I.L. 1; D. Akande, "The International Court of Justice and the Security Council: Is There Room for Judicial Control of Decisions of the Political Organs of the United Nations?" (1997) 46 I.C.L.Q. 309; and B. Fassbender, "*Quis Judicabit?* The Security Council, Its Powers and its Legal Control" (2000) 11 E.J.I.L. 219.

[24] *Case Concerning Armed Activities on the Territory of the Congo (Democratic Republic of the Congo v. Uganda), Provisional Measures,* July 1, 2000, accessible at <http://www.icj-cij.org/icjwww/idocket/ico/icoframe.htm>.

[25] Statute of the International Criminal Court, July 17, 1998, UN Doc. A/Conf. 183/9, accessible at <http://www.un.org/law/icc/statute/romefra.htm, articles 13, 16> [hereinafter Rome Statute].

[26] See, for example, Marc Grossman (American under-secretary for political affairs), "American Foreign Policy and the International Criminal Court: Remarks to the Center for Strategic and International Studies," May 6, 2002, accessible at

judicial and political decision-making an adequate answer to fears that the political effectiveness of Security Council action under Chapter VII would be undermined even by "apparently" conflicting judicial/legal decisions? Is there a sufficient distinction between the law and the politics of international peace and security determinations to be able to neatly compartmentalize the effects of decisions based on each set of considerations respectively?

However, beyond these pressing questions, it is to another disquieting trend in the functioning of the Security Council on peace and security issues that I wish to devote the remainder of these comments. I refer to the relatively recent emergence of so-called "implied" authorizations by the Security Council to use force under Chapter VII. I want to suggest that this trend amounts to a new crisis of constitutionalism in the UN system, one that demands that the complex relationship between the ICJ and the Security Council be further developed and one in which the ICJ must, again, not shrink from the "full exercise of its judicial power."[27]

FROM ANTAGONIST TO GUARDIAN: THE ICJ AS *DEFENDER* OF SECURITY COUNCIL AUTHORITY?

Even if it were considered unwise, untenable, or simply unrealistic for the ICJ to exercise a direct power of judicial review of Security Council peace and security decisions — even on some attenuated basis such as excess of jurisdiction or procedural fairness — there are other disturbing trends in Security Council peace and security practice that invite yet another, perhaps "activist," role for the ICJ. I refer to the recent proliferation of arguments that seek to support the legality of military interventions on the basis that these have been implicitly — rather than expressly or at least clearly — authorized by the Security Council pursuant to Chapter VII.

Craig Scott, in a feature article appearing in the last volume of this *Yearbook,* has documented the use of such arguments in the case of US and UK enforcement of no-fly zones and weapons inspection regimes in Iraq in the 1990s; the intervention of the Economic Community of West African States in Liberia in 1990; and the 1999 North Atlantic Treaty Organization (NATO) action

---

<http://www.state.gov/p/9949.htm>, in which Grossman announces the American government's decision to withdraw its signature of the Rome Statute on such grounds.

[27] Macdonald, *supra* note 2 at 5.

against the Federal Republic of Yugoslavia over the situation in Kosovo.[28] In essence, Scott's observation is that in each of these cases the relevant actors have not purported to sidestep the UN Charter's legal requirement of Security Council authorization for their use of force. Rather, they have argued that such authorization can be *inferred* from Security Council behaviours, usually but not exclusively[29] patterns of resolutions, which do not *explicitly* or clearly provide for such authorization. Scott characterizes this mode of argumentation as an "evolving re-interpretation" of Security Council resolutions and behaviours. Through this process, warnings of potential "serious consequences" are subsequently, in the absence of compliance by the target state, reinterpreted as implicitly authorizing the infliction of such serious consequences, in the specific form of armed action. Such implicit authorizations are placed, by those states advancing them, on an equal legal plane with the explicit authorizations more traditionally expected of the Security Council (and usually denoted by the expression "all necessary means"). Scott goes on to make the point that such a process of "evolving re-interpretation" of Security Council resolutions in turn implies an evolving re-interpretation of the UN Charter itself and, most particularly, of those provisions governing the process by which the Security Council exercises its extraordinary coercive powers under Chapter VII.[30]

While Scott's article was written prior to the September 11, 2001, terrorist attacks on the World Trade Center and the Pentagon, his observations have been borne out in legal justifications variously advanced, primarily but not exclusively by the United States and the United Kingdom, for their subsequent military actions in Afghanistan and most recently Iraq. For example, it has been argued that the wording of Security Council Resolution 1373, which was adopted on September 28, 2001, provided authorization for the American- and British-led actions in Afghanistan following the

---

[28] C. Scott, "Interpreting Intervention" (2001) 39 Can. Y.B. Int'l L. 333. On the emerging "doctrine of implied Security Council authorization," see also C. Gray, "From Unity to Polarization" (2002) 13 E.J.I.L. 1 at 8-13.

[29] Scott cites, as other elements relied upon to build the case for implicit authorization, statements made by the presidency of the Council, and even statements made by the Secretary-General. Scott, *supra* note 28 at 340-44.

[30] "As such, what we may be witnessing ... is a simultaneous re-interpretation of the Charter's premises through a Security Council practice that has begun to condone, even embrace, the possibility of treating Security Council resolutions as containing implicit authorizations to use force." *Ibid.* at 346.

September 11, 2001, attacks. In particular, the decision that "all States shall . . . [t]ake the necessary steps to prevent the commission of terrorist acts" has been said to constitute a potentially unlimited authorization to use force in combating terrorism, notwithstanding its partial departure from the usual "all necessary means" formulation.[31] It should be noted, however, that the United States has been reluctant to adopt this interpretation, preferring instead to rely on its inherent right of self defence, which was itself "recognized," "reaffirmed," and "reiterated" in Resolution 1373 and its predecessor, Resolution 1368.[32]

However, more recently and with respect to the forcible toppling of the Saddam Hussein regime in Iraq, Security Council Resolutions 678[33] and 687[34] have been resurrected, in combination with Resolution 1441,[35] in order to provide a mantle of implied Security Council legitimacy to military action that plainly could not have obtained explicit Security Council backing.[36] The argument, which was, in fact, well rehearsed by the Americans and the British as a justification for military action in Iraq throughout the 1990s, is that Resolution 678 authorized "all necessary means" to eject Iraq from Kuwait and to restore international peace and security in the area. Following the removal of Iraqi forces from Kuwait, Resolution 687 declared a cease-fire in the area and imposed comprehensive disarmament obligations on Iraq. The argument then proceeds

---

[31] Security Council [hereinafter SC] Resolution 1373, adopted September 28, 2001, accessible at <http://www.un.org/Docs/scres/2001/sc2001.htm>. See M. Byers, "Terrorism, the Use of Force and International Law after 11 September" (2002) 51 Int'l & Comp. L.Q. 401 at 401-3. Byers refers to several such interpretations given to Resolution 1373, including by British Prime Minister Tony Blair (at 402, note 8).

[32] SC Resolution 1368, adopted September 12, 2001, accessible at <http://www.un.org/Docs/scres/2001/sc2001.htm>. See also Byers, *supra* note 31 at 403.

[33] SC Resolution 678, adopted November 29, 1990, accessible at <http://www.un.org/Docs/scres/1990/scres90.htm>.

[34] SC Resolution 687, adopted April 3, 1991, accessible at <http://www.un.org/Docs/scres/1991/scres91.htm>.

[35] SC Resolution 1441, adopted November 8, 2002, accessible at <http://www.un.org/Docs/scres/2002/sc2002.htm>.

[36] "Plainly" because the required majority of votes endorsing such action could not be mustered by the sponsors of a resolution setting out such an explicit authorization — hence its withdrawal — and, in any event, because the French had made plain their intention of vetoing any such authorization. See, for example, "Chirac Says France Will Veto U.N. Resolution on Iraq," PBS Online Newshour, March 10, 2003, accessible at <http://www.pbs.org/newshour/updates/iraq_03-10-03.html>.

to reason that, if the disarmament obligations of Resolution 687 are not respected, the cease-fire imposed by the same resolution is automatically suspended and the authorization to use force in Resolution 678 is reactivated — albeit for radically different purposes than originally contemplated by the Security Council.[37]

There are many implausibilities in this argument, which Scott points out,[38] but, in my own view, the greatest of these stems from the explicit decision of the Security Council in Resolution 687 to "remain seized of the matter and to take such further steps as may be required for the implementation of the present resolution."[39] This explicit reservation of future remedial authority in case of a failure of implementation ousts the existence of, and at any rate the need for, any latent or implied authority to adapt prior express authorizations to wholly new purposes.[40] However, the proponents of such implied authorization further rely on Resolution 1441, which warns of "serious consequences" in the event that Iraq does not avail itself of its "final opportunity to comply with its disarmament obligations."[41] This additional warning, while again not explicitly authorizing any use of force, is thus pressed into service as a "further step" by the Security Council within the meaning of paragraph 34 of Resolution 687. And while Resolution 1441 itself provides for further *consideration* of the matter by the Security Council should Iraq continue to fail to honour its obligations, this, it is said, does not require further *authorization* before Resolution 678's permission to use all necessary means is revived. Hence, once again, despite the absence of any explicit authorization in Resolution 1441, conditional language is interpreted as a form of implicit permission to use force if certain conditions — not including, significantly, further Security Council authorization — are met.[42]

---

[37] For the clearest and most explicit articulation of this argument, see the legal opinion tabled by Lord Goldsmith, the UK Attorney General, in the British House of Commons on March 18, 2003, in answer to a question concerning the legality of military action in Iraq: (UK) Foreign and Commonwealth Office, "Iraq: Legal Basis for the Use of Force," March 17, 2003, accessible at <http://www.fco.gov.uk/servlet/Front?pagename=OpenMarket/Xcelerate/ShowPage&c=Page&cid=1007029394383&a=KArticle&aid=1047661460790>.

[38] Scott, *supra* note 28 at 339-40.

[39] SC Resolution 687, *supra* note 34 at para. 34.

[40] See M. Byers, "The Shifting Foundations of International Law: A Decade of Forceful Measures against Iraq" (2002) 13 E.J.I.L. 21 at 24.

[41] SC Resolution 1441, *supra* note 35 at paras. 2, 13.

[42] See the opinion given by the UK Foreign and Commonwealth Office, *supra* note 37.

Whatever view one may take of the value of such arguments (and, as suggested, my own view is that they are seriously flawed), the important point for present purposes is that this new mode of argumentation injects substantially greater uncertainty into the Security Council's peace and security practice. Whereas traditional practice, mindful of the profound legal and real-world ramifications of a Chapter VII authorization, has sensibly required that such authorization be clear and unambiguous — in a word, explicit — this relatively new practice, which shows signs of becoming endemic, is profoundly uncertain and therefore destabilizing.

First, it has the potential to move much of the debate as to the appropriate ultimate response to threats to international peace and security out of the Security Council altogether. While some people might perceive some potential benefit in such a development, in the sense of multiplying inputs into, and perhaps thereby "democratizing" to some degree[43] peace and security determinations, it is just as probable that the opposite will occur. As clearly illustrated in the latest series of events surrounding the American-and British-led invasion of Iraq, the "debate" over the meaning of extant Security Council resolutions was effectively dominated by very few states, indeed a minority of even the permanent members of the Security Council itself. Furthermore, such dominance was concretized by rapid and effective on-the-ground implementation of the implied authorization theory, even as the debate regarding the meaning of the relevant Security Council resolutions was ongoing. Force was in fact used to produce real-world effects, effects that, however perversely, bolster claims that they must therefore have been authorized. Opposition to the implied authorization argument thus loses its practical, immediate object and is relegated to the status of after-the-fact academic debate.

Second, all procedural guarantees — including a conclusive and readily ascertainable determination (an explicit resolution) reached through the participation of a defined set of participants

---

[43] For example, Scott envisions an enhanced role for the General Assembly in lending legitimacy to reinterpretations of SC resolutions, and to the overall process of articulating evolving understandings of the UN Charter's peace and security process itself, at least in the context of humanitarian interventions. Scott, *supra* note 28 at 362-68. However, Scott also acknowledges his own "profound misgivings about the process of Charter reinterpretation as it is currently evolving due to the overbearing role of the United States, and the West in general, and due to the relative lack of critical self-awareness of many states that their silence and pragmatic acquiescence is feeding into a normative realignment of Charter peace and security law" (at 336).

(the members of the Security Council wielding duly delegated authority) in a known and relatively transparent process (the voting requirements of Article 27 of the UN Charter) — are entirely lost. By moving the ultimate debate over the necessity, form, and timing of "serious consequences" out of the Security Council and into the foreign offices of a few powerful states, the indispensable constraint upon the powers of the Security Council — the need to achieve consensus among or at least acquiescence of a significant cross-section of states, including all of the Council's permanent members — is effectively evaded.

Third, and not least, this new practice is therefore a threat to the Security Council itself. If, notwithstanding a clear decision that the Security Council "remain[s] seized of the matter ... to take such further steps as may be required,"[44] individual states effectively arrogate to themselves the power to determine what "further steps" are in fact warranted, then the Security Council has indeed lost control of the situation. Words clearly designed by the Security Council to stop short of authorizing the use of force absent further consideration and action by the Council can suddenly be given precisely the opposite meaning by states acting alone or with others outside the Security Council chamber. The ultimate result is potentially to set loose upon the world a particularly virulent, indeed Orwellian, form of aggression — aggression masquerading as lawful enforcement of international peace and security, a role expressly delegated by the UN Charter to the Security Council and not to a few of its more powerful members.

The dangers of this development no doubt go beyond what I have suggested above, and a full exploration of them is not the purpose of the present discussion. My point is that, as the doctrine of implied authorization is unlikely to disappear anytime soon from Security Council practice, there is an urgent need for a forum in which such arguments of implied authorization can be authoritatively evaluated and either validated or rejected. I venture to suggest what strikes me as obvious, that there is no more qualified organ to carry out such evaluations than the ICJ.

It is certainly obvious that the Security Council is itself in no position to check self-serving interpretations of its decisions by states, at least not in the majority of cases in which the situation is likely to arise. If recent history is any guide, the states most likely to, and capable of, intervening militarily abroad in purported

---

[44] SC Resolution 687, *supra* note 34.

implementation of implied Security Council authorization are the permanent members of the Security Council themselves. Thus, the Council is constitutionally incapable of constraining the most likely sources of usurpation of its enforcement authority. Any attempt to do so would presumably be vetoed by the particular permanent member acting on its own or with others. This reality is clearly illustrated by the recent Iraq experience, where the requirement of permanent member concurrence would have made it effectively impossible for France or Russia to obtain a clarifying resolution decisively contradicting the American and British re-interpretations of Resolutions 678, 687, and 1441. It was similarly demonstrated in the Security Council's inability to clarify the implications of its warning of "severest consequences" in Resolution 1154, which was adopted in March 1998,[45] and on which the United States and the United Kingdom relied in part to justify their air strikes against Iraq in December of the same year.[46]

Scott urges that the General Assembly could have such a constraining interpretive role to play, at least in the context of implicit authorizations on humanitarian grounds.[47] The main attraction of this suggestion is that it fits within an overall program of reforming permanent-member domination of peace and security decisions and fostering a more inclusive and representative participation by states in such determinations. At the very least, it has the attraction of multiplying the number of players participating in the debate over the appropriate interpretation of Security Council resolutions and the degree to which authorizations to use force can be found to be implied in such resolutions. The main difficulty with this suggestion, however, is that General Assembly resolutions, declarations, or recommendations can only loosely be considered "authoritative" in the relevant sense. By this, I do not mean simply to rely on the well-worn mantra that General Assembly resolutions have no formal binding effect. There is no doubt that General Assembly concurrence or dissent could have an impact on the legitimacy and perhaps even legality of the implied authorization argument. However, it is doubtful that the views of such an inherently political organ (assuming any views could be formulated in such a way as to

---

[45] Security Council Resolution 1154, adopted March 2, 1998, accessible at <http://www.un.org/Docs/scres/1998/scres98.htm>.

[46] See B. Fassbender, "Uncertain Steps into a Post-Cold War World: The Role and Functioning of the UN Security Council after a Decade of Measures against Iraq" (2002) 13 E.J.I.L. 273 at 277.

[47] Scott, *supra* note 28 at 337-38.

command broad-based endorsement) could be satisfactorily *determinative* of what is, primarily, a legal issue: the correct interpretation of a legal text adopted pursuant to a legal procedure dictated by the UN Charter, which is itself obviously a legal instrument. While the participation of the General Assembly would certainly add to the symphony of political opinion on the legal matter under consideration, it is unlikely it would resolve it. I do not therefore suggest that the General Assembly would have no useful role to play nor do I take issue with Scott's proposal. I do believe, however, that when it comes to addressing the problems of *legal* uncertainty and indeterminacy raised by the "implied authorization" or "evolving interpretation" approaches, the participation of the General Assembly in the debate, without more, is unlikely to be equal to the task.

Which brings us back to the potential role of the ICJ and some of the observations made by Macdonald about the unique features of the judicial and legal process (as contrasted with the political processes of the Security Council or, for that matter, the General Assembly). It would appear that the only existing UN organ truly capable of authoritatively assessing differing legal interpretations of Security Council resolutions or evolving UN Charter requirements for Chapter VII authorization (at least those of a formal nature) is the ICJ, as the principal judicial organ of the organization. The task itself is an inherently judicial one. It requires the evaluation of legal arguments based on various legal texts and past practices, arguably having the force of law, all in the context of an overarching "constitutional" framework, namely that of the UN Charter and its evolving meaning as well as any legal rules of interpretation applicable to Security Council resolutions.[48]

---

[48] The International Court of Justice [hereinafter ICJ] has in fact articulated at least general legal standards for the interpretation of Security Council resolutions, albeit in a different context. In its Advisory Opinion in *Legal Consequences for States of the Continued Presence of South Africa in Namibia Notwithstanding Security Council Resolution 276 (1970)*, [1971] I.C.J. Rep. 16 at 53, the ICJ stated: "The language of a resolution of the Security Council should be carefully analysed before a conclusion can be made as to its binding effect. In view of the nature of the powers under Article 25, the question whether they have in fact been exercised is to be determined in each case, having regard to the terms of the resolution to be interpreted, the discussions leading to it, the Charter provisions invoked and, in general, all circumstances that might assist in determining the legal consequences of the resolution of the Security Council." On the interpretation of Security Council resolutions more generally, see Byers, *supra* note 40 at 23-27.

As a practical matter, the ICJ could in theory be seized of such issues at the behest of a state subjected to the use of force in purported but wrongful application of implied Security Council authorization. It is also probable that the General Assembly could seek an advisory opinion on the purported legality of an "implied authorization" interpretation advanced by a particular member state. Certainly, the General Assembly has the power to "discuss any questions or any matters within the scope of the present Charter or *relating to the powers and functions of any organs provided for in the present Charter.*"[49] A request for an advisory opinion would presumably circumvent the prohibition on General Assembly "recommendations" with respect to matters under consideration by the Security Council,[50] as the General Assembly's power to request such an opinion "on any legal question" is not so limited.[51] Further, the jurisdiction of the General Assembly to request advisory opinions on even broad legal questions was clearly upheld by the ICJ in its decision in the *Legality of the Threat or Use of Nuclear Weapons Case.*[52] Indeed, invoking the judicial mechanism could be an important device by which the role of the General Assembly, as envisioned by Scott,[53] would be significantly strengthened. By combining an authoritative legal opinion from the ICJ with the representative political legitimacy of a view expressed by the General Assembly, a powerful counterweight to unilateral and self-serving interpretations of Security Council authorizations would arise.

Moreover, there would be no question, in order to generate such a legal opinion, of the ICJ having to descend into the political arena and substitute its opinion as to the wisdom or desirability of any particular course of action, which is of course the main objection raised by opponents of a judicial review function for the Court. Even states purporting to advance implied authorization arguments do so in legal form and for a legal purpose.[54] Their objective is to

---

[49] UN Charter, *supra* note 1, Article 10 [emphasis added].

[50] *Ibid.*, Article 12(1).

[51] *Ibid.*, Article 96(1).

[52] *Legality of the Threat or Use of Nuclear Weapons Case, Advisory Opinion,* [1996] I.C.J. Rep. 226 at para. 16: "The General Assembly has the right to decide for itself on the usefulness of an opinion in the light of its own needs."

[53] See text accompanying note 48.

[54] See, for example, the opinion given by the UK Foreign and Commonwealth Office, *supra* note 37. The opinion is clearly structured as a legal argument and indeed is titled "Iraq: Legal Basis for the Use of Force."

demonstrate, through (admittedly complex) legal argument, that the legal requirement of a formal authorization for the use of force, as prescribed in the UN Charter, has in fact (however implicitly) been fulfilled. Their argument is not that authorization *ought* to be forthcoming, which would of course require the evaluation of various political as well as legal arguments. They argue rather that such authorization already exists in fact and law, even if implicitly. In short, their argument is the most straightforward type of all legal arguments, one based on the interpretation of legal texts, including the relevant Security Council resolutions and, implicitly, the UN Charter itself. The decision to be made is simply whether the admittedly political actor, the Security Council, has indeed and in law put all of the legal elements in place in order to carry out its political will. It can therefore be seen that the function to be carried out in evaluating such arguments is an eminently judicial one and not one that usurps powers of political decision-making at all.[55]

Similarly, there can be no suggestion of antagonism between the two organs as a result of the ICJ assuming such a duty either. This is because the object of the proceeding would be to determine, and thus uphold, the true intentions of the Security Council. In that sense, therefore, the ICJ's determination would be in defence of the Security Council's powers and responsibilities under the UN Charter. The only potential opposition would be between the ICJ and the party whose expansive interpretation of Security Council authorization is found to go beyond the Security Council's true intent. Indeed, the true danger to the Security Council's authority and effectiveness lies not in a potential interpretive role for the ICJ but rather in the unilateral acts of interpretation of some of the Council's own permanent members. The ICJ would in effect be acting as guardian, not antagonist, of the Security Council's role under Chapter VII.

Certainly some will object that, in the guise of interpreting Security Council resolutions, an overly activist ICJ would inevitably be

---

[55] Curiously, Scott dismisses rather summarily the potential role of the ICJ in filling the need for "authoritative new interpretations that are not necessarily consensus ones and that, indeed, can be argued to be legally correct in the face of resistance by powerful actors." Scott, *supra* note 28 at 353. He does so on the basis simply that the ICJ does not currently play such a role (at 353). The same might be said of the General Assembly. However, neither observation provides a compelling reason why such organs cannot and ought not take on such a role if appropriate opportunities arise within the governing framework of the UN Charter.

drawn into reshaping the meaning of such resolutions and therefore interfering in the political decisions of the Council. Aside
from Macdonald's forceful point that there is nothing inherently
problematic in judicial opinions that may state legal opinions inconsistent with Security Council policies,[56] there are at least three
further answers to this argument. The first is that the ICJ has historically shown no sustained penchant for judicial activism and there
is no reason to suppose such an inherently conservative body would
approach this particular task with any less circumspection. In fact,
precisely the opposite is likely, as illustrated by the extreme caution
shown by the ICJ in distinguishing between its functions and those
of the Security Council.[57] Second, the prospect of more frequent
judicial interpretation of Security Council resolutions might in fact
encourage the Security Council to use clearer language to convey
its intentions — a result that could only be considered salutary.
While some will argue that this effect would make consensus in the
Security Council harder to achieve, in fact and as we have seen
through recent events, consensus achieved through ambiguity can
ultimately only have destructive effects.[58] Third, the only alternative to the judicial process appears to be the much less transparent,
and much more readily manipulated, interference with the functioning of the Security Council by the unilateral and self-serving
interpretations of individual states. An open, structured legal debate
in a judicial forum, in which decisions on interpretation must be
justified through written reasons, strikes one as quite benign in
comparison.

Altogether aside from the appropriateness of such a role for
the ICJ, the process of adjudication would also have the obvious
benefit of bringing discipline and clarity to an otherwise uncertain and easily manipulated rhetorical exercise in self-justification.
Indeed, the whole area of international law governing the interpretation of Security Council resolutions cries out for clarification.[59]

---

[56] Macdonald, *supra* note 2 at 18-20.

[57] See text accompanying notes 6-13 and 24.

[58] The consensus achieved in adopting Resolution 1441, for example, masked fundamental differences of opinion, even among permanent members of the Security Council, as to the "automaticity" of the "serious consequences" threatened in
paragraph 13. The result was the diplomatic fiasco in the Security Council in the
weeks leading up to the March 2003 action by the United States and United
Kingdom in Iraq.

[59] See Byers, *supra* note 40 at 27: "The interpretation of Security Council resolutions presents even more scope for the advancement of differing views than does

Arms-length, third-party adjudication by a judicial body with acknowledged expertise in matters of interpretation and evaluation of legal argument would provide an authoritative and powerful counterweight to the otherwise dominant discourse of states seeking to enlarge their legal options in terms of the use of military power.

However, it is not necessary to my argument to assume that the ICJ would always favour conservative or formalistic interpretations of Security Council resolutions or of the UN Charter's requirements for Chapter VII authorizations or that it would always check expansive claims of Chapter VII authorization. It may well be, as suggested by Michael Byers,[60] Craig Scott,[61] Christine Gray,[62] and Bardo Fassbender,[63] among others, that the implied authorization practice of the past ten years or so has already had normative effects. Perhaps, in circumstances approximating those of the Kosovo crisis, a persuasive legal argument could be mounted for implicit Security Council authorization and dispensation with the historic preference for explicit language. The point is that if such a legal argument is to be mounted at all, it should be mounted before a body that is competent to assess it and has the authority to pronounce definitively upon it. The integrity of the peace and security mechanisms of the UN Charter can only be enhanced by such a process, if only in the sense that they will be more responsive to the true intent of the Security Council than to one of many, untested opinions as to that intent.

Such adjudication might even have the incidental beneficial effect, at least in some cases, of reversing the perverse neutering, by the permanent member veto power, of the Security Council's ability to act in its own defence. Rather than requiring the Security Council to adopt a resolution rejecting an implied authorization argument advanced by one of its permanent members, an authoritative declaration by the ICJ that the Council has not yet authorized, even implicitly, the use of force would clearly reverse the

---

the interpretation of treaties. Council resolutions are adopted by an executive organ rather than contractually agreed, the academic literature concerning their interpretation is extremely thin, and the Vienna Convention does not apply, at least not directly."

[60] Byers, *supra* note 31; and Byers, *supra* note 40.

[61] Scott, *supra* note 28.

[62] Gray, *supra* note 28.

[63] Fassbender, *supra* note 46.

legal (not to mention political) onus and require the relevant state to seek clear authorization in the Security Council. At the very least, it would force the relevant state to forego the comfort of legal justification for its actions based on implied Security Council authorization, with all the legal and political consequences that would entail.

Now, as the last sentence suggests, I am not so naïve as to believe that authoritative judicial pronouncement alone will always be sufficient to constrain the actions of states that are motivated to stretch and adapt Security Council authorizations to their own ends. It ought, however, to be at least as effective a rallying point as the General Assembly for those states, including perhaps even members of the Security Council themselves, who wish to oppose, in a concerted and constructive fashion, excessive claims of Security Council authorization. In part, this effect would be attributable to the profound institutional respect earned and enjoyed by the ICJ over the past six decades. Indeed, it is precisely this respect, evidenced by its overloaded docket, that adds to the ICJ's unique positioning as the most appropriate, and likely the most effective, new participant in the emerging dialogue over implied authorization. In short, the role falls squarely within the ICJ's power as principal judicial organ and squarely within its responsibilities as guardian not only of UN legality but also of the powers and privileges of all UN organs, including those of the Security Council.

CONCLUSION

This suggestion is really nothing more than an extension, to new circumstances, of what Macdonald suggested in 1993 and in much of his other work concerning the UN peace and security system. The ICJ must not be overly timid in defining its own powers, lest it undermine one of the key building blocks of an international rule of law — the notion that the single most potent actor in the UN system, the Security Council, must itself be considered a creature of the law. As a result, it is not only constrained by the law but also entitled to its protection, along with all other UN organs. The preservation, by the rule of law, of the integrity of the UN Charter's peace and security architecture could not be more important as Security Council decision-making and decision-interpretation drift from the practice of express authorization towards the murkier world of "evolving re-interpretation." It is precisely to contain potential abuse of this trend that increased activism by the ICJ in the sense described is not only desirable but crucial if the rules-based system of international relations envisioned in the UN Charter, with its affirmation of the sovereign equality of all states,[64] is to be preserved and enhanced.

Sommaire

Les contributions toujours pertinentes de Ronald St. J. Macdonald sur les questions de la Charte de l'ONU et de la paix et la sécurité internationales

Dans ce commentaire (une adaptation de remarques préliminaires lors d'une table ronde sur les contributions de Ronald St. J. Macdonald sur les questions de la Charte de l'ONU et la paix et la sécurité internationales), l'auteur vise en particulier les propos du professeur Macdonald quant aux rapports entre la Cour internationale de justice et le Conseil de sécurité de l'ONU. Après considération des incertitudes qui persistent dans ces rapports, l'auteur prétend que la pratique récente "d'interprétation évolutive" des résolutions du Conseil de sécurité en vertu du chapitre VII invite un autre rôle important pour la Cour: celui de gardien des compétences du Conseil de sécurité par moyen d'interprétations judiciaires définitives de voulues autorisations par le Conseil de sécurité du recours à la force.

Summary

The Continuing Contributions of Ronald St. J. Macdonald to UN Charter and Peace and Security Issues

In this article, the author focuses in particular on Macdonald's writings on the relationship between the International Court of Justice and the UN Security Council. After considering the continuing uncertainties in that relationship, the author argues that the emerging practice of "evolving reinterpretation" of Security Council Chapter VII resolutions suggests yet another important role for the court — that of guardian of Security Council authority through authoritative, judicial interpretation of purported Security Council authorizations to use force.

---

[64] UN Charter, *supra* note 1, Article 2(1).

Utopia without Apology:
Form and Imagination in the Work of
Ronald St. John Macdonald

KAREN KNOP

There is an unmistakable Ronald St. John Macdonald style of thought which is as hard to sum up as it is to miss. The style of thought includes an intellectual fizz, a commitment to imagination, a fearlessness about predictions and proposals that is informed by an insistence on a wide field of view, a promotion of bold vision. Yet these recognizable elements do not manage to do justice to the whole. In this article, I seek to show that Macdonald's embrace of the utopian form in his own and others' work and his fostering of such stylistic experimentation offer one way of theorizing this originality.

Ronald St. John Macdonald is undoubtedly a utopian in the familiar sense of seeing and wishing for the emergence of an international legal community unified by more than just the consent of states. In fact, he is unusual in his lack of preoccupation with the realist apologetics that such a stance necessarily entails.[1] Utopia in this sense means a substantive desideratum. Derived from *eu topos* — literally a "good place" — the term refers to an ideal society and its realization.

As readers of Thomas More's *Utopia* (1516)[2] know, however, "utopia" is a pun. More invented it from *ou topos* as well as *eu topos*.

Karen Knop is in the Faculty of Law at the University of Toronto. The author thanks Martti Koskenniemi for his comments and Kevin-Paul Deveau for his research assistance.

[1] See Martti Koskenniemi, *From Apology to Utopia: The Structure of International Legal Argument* (Helsinki: Finnish Lawyers' Publishing, 1989). See also David Kennedy, *International Legal Structures* (Baden-Baden: Nomos, 1987).

[2] Thomas More, *Utopia: Latin Text and English Translation,* translated by Robert M. Adams, edited by George M. Logan, Robert M. Adams, and Clarence H. Miller (Cambridge: Cambridge University Press, 1995).

The root *ou topos* gives utopia its other sense: *ou topos* means "no place," and hence ou-topia is a description of a society that does not exist.[3] The emphasis here is on a mode of narrative and not on a political goal. Utopia is a form: traditionally, a traveller's account of a visit to an imaginary country where the journey is either to a far-off land or to the distant future. For Northrop Frye, "[u]topian thought is imaginative, with its roots in literature, and the literary imagination is less concerned with achieving ends than with visualizing possibilities."[4]

If Macdonald is an unapologetic utopian in substance (eu-topia), I propose in this article that we see him as one also in form (ou-topia). I do so first by demonstrating Macdonald's own use of the form in the article "International Law and Society in the Year 2000,"[5] which he co-authored with Gerald Morris and Douglas Johnston in 1973, and his appreciation of the form as used by others in theory and practice. My intuition is that like Frye, Macdonald values the literary genre of the voyage to "no place" for its ability to open up possibilities, and I pursue this intuition in my discussion of Macdonald's writings in and on the genre. By possibilities, I mean not only that eu-topias confront us with a complete package of ideas for international law that would otherwise remain unimagined but also that ou-topia generally encourages comprehensive and radical thinking about international law's future and perhaps even jolts us into a heightened consciousness of our creativity and potential for change.[6] While I then touch on the corresponding disadvantages of utopias, I conclude by speculating that Macdonald reconciles the advantages and disadvantages partly through the fact that the power of the utopian form is available even to those who have been historically and unjustly excluded from international law. An example might be feminist utopian fiction,[7] one of the feminist methods used to overcome the mental and material limitations of

---

[3] *Ibid.* at 31, n. 2.

[4] Northrop Frye, "Varieties of Literary Utopias" in Frank E. Manuel, ed., *Utopias and Utopian Thought* (Boston: Houghton Mifflin, 1966) 25 at 31.

[5] Ronald St. John Macdonald, Gerald L. Morris, and Douglas M. Johnston, "International Law and Society in the Year 2000" (1973) 51 Can. Bar Rev. 316.

[6] On thinking outside the box in international law, compare David Kennedy, "When Renewal Repeats: Thinking against the Box" (2000) 32 N.Y.U. J. Int'l L. & Pol. 335 at 457-500 (discussing the New Approaches to International Law project).

[7] See, for example, Frances Bartkowski, *Feminist Utopias* (Lincoln, NB: University of Nebraska Press, 1989); Natalie M. Rosinsky, *Feminist Futures: Contemporary Women's Speculative Fiction* (Ann Arbor, MI: UMI Research Press, 1984).

a male-dominated society.[8] Accordingly, Macdonald's enthusiasm for utopias may reflect their potential to help develop and equalize the visions of outsiders and insiders in international law.

To differentiate between utopia as a desirable society and a style of exposition is only a beginning, and it is only one of the possible beginnings. There are many varieties and, hence, many typologies of utopia. In his praise for Philip Allott's *Euonomia*,[9] Macdonald himself implies that there are utopias and utopias: "Eunomia is not just another rambling account of a distant utopia."[10] Frank Manuel writes:

The "speaking picture" — to borrow Sir Philip Sydney's fortunate name for utopia — may resurrect a good historical society that has been in ages past and should be again. It may idealize or romanticize an existing polity, even one's own, project the vision far into space — to a distant island, a mountain-top, a hidden valley, another planet, into the bowels of the earth — or in time, into a future epoch. The vision may be borne of a mere wish, often a rather hopeless wish; or, at the other extreme, its actualization may be accepted on faith as inevitable in some historical or religious sense, in which event the separation of plain foretelling from dream becomes problematic.[11]

My reason for starting by separating form from substance is that the utopian form is a way to grasp a perceptible, yet elusive, dimension of Macdonald's individuality as a thinker and a significant figure in international life. From a substantive perspective, Macdonald's utopian focus on international law's transformation from a law of coordination to a law of cooperation that emphasizes common interests above sovereign will[12] aligns him with Columbia Law School professors Wolfgang Friedmann, Oscar Schachter, and

---

[8] See, for example, Angelika Bammer, *Partial Visions: Feminism and Utopianism in the 1970s* (New York: Routledge, 1991); Daphne Patai, "Beyond Defensiveness: Feminist Research Strategies" in Marleen Barr and Nicholas D. Smith, eds., *Women and Utopia: Critical Interpretations* (Lanham, MD: University Press of America, 1983) 148. In the context of feminist legal theory, see Nicola Lacey, "Normative Reconstruction in Socio-Legal Theory" in Nicola Lacey, *Unspeakable Subjects: Feminist Essays in Legal and Social Theory* (Oxford: Hart Publishing, 1998) 221.

[9] Philip Allott, *Eunomia: New Order for a New World,* paperback edition (Oxford: Oxford University Press, 2001).

[10] Ronald St. John Macdonald, "Book Review of *Eunomia: New Order for a New World* by Philip Allott" (1991) 70 Can. Bar Rev. 822 at 823.

[11] Frank E. Manuel, "Introduction" in Frank E. Manuel, ed., *Utopias and Utopian Thought* (Boston: Houghton Mifflin, 1966) vii at viii.

[12] Ronald St. John Macdonald, "Solidarity in the Practice and Discourse of Public International Law" (1996) 8 Pace Int'l L. Rev. 259; Ronald St. John Macdonald,

Louis Henkin,[13] as do his concern for international distributive justice through economic development assistance,[14] social welfare policies,[15] and human rights,[16] and his initiatives reaching out to international law scholars in socialist countries.[17] Macdonald also shares with a number of European authors[18] an attention to the

---

"The Principle of Solidarity in Public International Law" in Christian Dominicé, Robert Patry, and Claude Reymond, eds., *Études de droit international en l'honneur de Pierre Lalive* (Bâle: Helbing and Lichtenhahn, 1993) 275.

[13] See Wolfgang Friedmann, *The Changing Structure of International Law* (New York: Columbia University Press, 1964) at 60-71. On the Columbia school of thought in international law, see Martti Koskenniemi, *The Gentle Civilizer of Nations: The Rise and Fall of International Law, 1870-1960* (Cambridge: Cambridge University Press, 2001) at 477-78; and Kennedy, *supra* note 6 at 380-87.

[14] Macdonald, "Solidarity in Practice and Discourse," *supra* note 12.

[15] Ronald St. John Macdonald, Douglas M. Johnston, and Gerald L. Morris, eds., *The International Law and Policy of Human Welfare* (Alphen aan den Rijn, The Netherlands: Sijthoff and Noordhoff, 1978); Ronald St. John Macdonald, Douglas M. Johnston, and Gerald L. Morris, "International Law of Human Welfare: Concept, Experience, and Priorities" in Ronald St. John Macdonald, Douglas M. Johnston, and Gerald L. Morris, eds., *The International Law and Policy of Human Welfare* (Alphen aan den Rijn, The Netherlands: Sijthoff and Noordhoff, 1978) 3.

[16] Ronald St. John Macdonald, "The United Nations and the Promotion of Human Rights" in Macdonald, Johnston, and Morris, *Human Welfare, supra* note 15 at 203.

[17] See, for example, Craig Scott, "Ronald St. John Macdonald and International Legal Education" (2002) 4 Int'l Law Forum 215 at 216-17.

[18] These authors include Alfred Verdross, Hermann Mosler, Christian Tomuschat, and Bardo Fassbender. See generally Bardo Fassbender, "The United Nation Charter as Constitution of the International Community" (1998) 36 Colum. J. Transnat'l L. 529. While at the University of Toronto in the early 1990s, Macdonald taught a course called "The International Community as a Legal Community," which the calendar describes as follows:

> This seminar is devoted to an intensive examination and evaluation of the fundamental norms of contemporary international law. In particular, it will explore the extent to which a hierarchy of norms exists in international law and the interrelationship between superior and subordinate principles and rules. The impact of the Covenant of the League of Nations, the Charter of the United Nations, the doctrine of *jus cogens*, and the *erga omnes* doctrine will be examined with a view to identifying and analyzing the significance of basic constitutional features of the international legal order.

Faculty of Law, University of Toronto, "Calendar, 1990-91" at 42-43; Faculty of Law, University of Toronto, "Calendar, 1991-92" at 46; Faculty of Law, University of Toronto, "Calendar, 1992-93" at 47; Faculty of Law, University of Toronto, "Calendar, 1993-94" at 43. *Towards a Constitutional International Law*, Craig Scott's choice of title for his forthcoming edited collection of Macdonald's work, also signals Macdonald's interest in this quality of international law.

components of an emerging international constitutional law, with writings on the status of the Charter of the United Nations,[19] the hierarchy of international legal norms,[20] the domestic application of international law,[21] the force of interim measures by the European Court of Human Rights,[22] and the margin of appreciation in European human rights law.[23] In addition, Macdonald's commitment to developing a Canadian approach to international law,[24]

[19] Charter of the United Nations, June 26, 1945, Can. T.S. 1945 No. 7 (in force October 24, 1945). Ronald St. John Macdonald, "The United Nations Charter: Constitution or Contract?" in Ronald St. John Macdonald and Douglas M. Johnston, eds., *The Structure and Process of International Law: Essays in Legal Philosophy, Doctrine, and Theory* (The Hague: Martinus Nijhoff, 1983) 889; Ronald St. John Macdonald, "Reflections on the Charter of the United Nations" in Jürgen Jekewitz *et al.*, eds., *Des Menschen Recht zwischen Freiheit und Verantwortung: Festschrift für Karl Josef Partsch zum 75. Geburtstag* (Berlin: Duncker and Humblot, 1989) 29.

[20] Ronald St. John Macdonald, "Fundamental Norms in Contemporary International Law" (1987) 25 Can. Y.B. Int'l Law 115.

[21] Ronald St. John Macdonald, "Public International Law Problems Arising in Canadian Courts" (1956) 11 U.T.L.J. 224; Ronald St. John Macdonald, "International Treaty Law and the Domestic Law of Canada" (1975) 2 Dal. L.J. 307; Ronald St. John Macdonald, "The Relationship between International Law and Domestic Law in Canada" in Ronald St. John Macdonald, Gerald L. Morris, and Douglas M. Johnston, eds., *Canadian Perspectives on International Law and Organization* (Toronto: University of Toronto Press, 1974) 88.

[22] Ronald St. John Macdonald, "Interim Measures in International Law, with Special Reference to the European System for the Protection of Human Rights" (1992) 52 Heidelberg J. Int'l L. 703.

[23] Ronald St. John Macdonald, "The Margin of Appreciation" in Ronald St. John Macdonald, Franz Matscher, and Herbert Petzold, eds., *The European System for the Protection of Human Rights* (Dordrecht: Martinus Nijhoff, 1993) 83; Ronald St. John Macdonald, "The Margin of Appreciation in the Jurisprudence of the European Court of Human Rights" in Andrew Clapham and Frank Emmert, eds., *Collected Courses of the Academy of European Law: 1990, The Protection of Human Rights in Europe*, vol. 1, book 2 (Dordrecht: Martinus Nijhoff, 1992) 95; and Ronald St. John Macdonald, "The Margin of Appreciation in the Jurisprudence of the European Court of Human Rights" in *Le droit international à l'heure de sa codification: études en l'honneur de Roberto Ago: les differends entre les états et la résponsabilité*, tome 3 (Milan: Giuffrè, 1987) 187. On European human rights law generally, see Ronald St. John Macdonald, Franz Matscher, and Herbert Petzold, eds., *The European System for the Protection of Human Rights* (Dordrecht: Martinus Nijhoff, 1993).

[24] Macdonald, Morris, and Johnston, *Canadian Perspectives, supra* note 21; Ronald St. John Macdonald, Gerald L. Morris, and Douglas M. Johnston, "Canadian Approaches to International Law" in Macdonald, Morris, and Johnston, *Canadian Perspectives, supra* note 21 at 940; Ronald St. John Macdonald, "Highlights of CCIL Activities (1972-76)" in Canadian Council on International Law, eds.,

which would further some of these objectives, is common to other
prominent Trudeau-era Canadian nationalists-as-internationalists
such as Ivan Head,[25] Maxwell Cohen,[26] and John Humphrey.[27]
Finally, of course, the substance of Macdonald's scholarship owes
much to his long collaboration with Canadians Douglas Johnston
and Gerald Morris.[28] In comparison to Macdonald's presence in
the vanguard of humanist thinking about the international legal
community, his monumental joint editorial projects, and his leadership in building a Canadian community of international lawyers,
his sense of the relationship between form and imagination in
international law is among his singular and highly personal contributions to scholarship and to the profession.

Ronald St. John Macdonald's most obvious embrace of the utopian form is in "International Law and Society in the Year 2000,"[29]
an article that he, Morris, and Johnston contributed to a 1973
Canadian Bar Review series on law and the legal profession in the

---

Compendium: The First Twenty-Five Years (Ottawa: Canadian Council on International Law, 1998) 106 at 106-7; Craig Scott, "1972: New Approaches to International Law" in Canadian Council on International Law, *supra* note 24 at 128,
129.

[25] See Ivan L. Head and Pierre Elliot Trudeau, *The Canadian Way: Shaping Canada's
Foreign Policy 1968-1984* (Toronto: McClelland and Stewart, 1995).

[26] See, for example, Ronald St. John Macdonald, "Maxwell Cohen at Eighty: International Lawyer, Educator, and Judge" (1989) 27 Can. Y.B. Int'l Law 3 at 16-22.

[27] See, for example, Ronald St. John Macdonald, "Leadership in Law: John P.
Humphrey and the Development of the International Law of Human Rights"
(1991) 29 Can. Y.B. Int'l Law 3 at 15-17, 23-32, 82-90.

[28] Macdonald, Morris, and Johnston, "International Law and Society," *supra*
note 5; Macdonald, Morris, and Johnston, *Canadian Perspectives, supra* note 21;
Macdonald, Morris, and Johnston, "Canadian Approaches," *supra* note 24;
Ronald St. John Macdonald, Gerald L. Morris, and Douglas M. Johnston, "The
New Lawyer in a Transnational World" (1975) 25 U.T.L.J. 343; Macdonald,
Johnston, and Morris, eds., *Human Welfare, supra* note 15; Macdonald, Johnston,
and Morris, "International Law of Human Welfare," *supra* note 15; Ronald St.
John Macdonald and Douglas M. Johnston, eds., *The Structure and Process of Inter-
national Law: Essays in Legal Philosophy, Doctrine, and Theory* (The Hague: Marti-
nus Nijhoff, 1983); Ronald St. John Macdonald and Douglas M. Johnston,
"International Legal Theory: New Frontiers of the Discipline" in Ronald St. John
Macdonald and Douglas M. Johnston, eds., *The Structure and Process of International Law: Essays in Legal Philosophy, Doctrine, and Theory* (The Hague: Martinus
Nijhoff, 1983) 1.

[29] Macdonald, Morris, and Johnston, "International Law and Society," *supra* note 5.

twenty-first century.[30] Written over twenty-five years before the year 2000, it interprets that date as symbolic of the near, but still distant, future,[31] akin to George Orwell's choice of an exact year as the time in which his utopian satire *1984* is set.[32]

The international law and society that Macdonald, Morris, and Johnston forecast is not eu-topia, More's "place of felicity."[33] Instead, it is an imaginary future where a titanic struggle has already occurred between technology and democracy, between power as knowledge and power as the will of the people.[34] By 2000, the authors speculate, this confrontation will have resolved into an uneasy coexistence between the international technocratic super-elites, perhaps the sinister end-game of the current scholarly interest in government networks as the "real new world order,"[35] and the Peoples' Assembly, a system of global popular representation that institutionalizes the moral authority now already achieved by international civil society. The article's introduction vividly depicts the dynamic:

International society will become increasingly complex, burdened with colossal bureaucracies subject to elites with control over critical areas of technology. Gradually this will engender an atmosphere of aggressiveness which will be felt in varying degrees of acuteness by diverse groups and individuals in many parts of the world. By a gradual coalescing of talents, hastened perhaps by cataclysmic intervention, such as an eco-disaster,

[30] J.-G. Castel, ed., "The Law and the Legal Profession in the Twenty-First Century" (1973) 51 (1, 2) Can. Bar Rev. 1.

[31] Macdonald, Morris, and Johnston, "International Law and Society," *supra* note 5 at 317.

[32] George Orwell, *Nineteen Eighty-Four* (London: Penguin Books, 1989). The importance of a date that balances the near and distant future is nicely illustrated by the fact that as the writing of Orwell's novel dragged on, he changed its settting from 1980 to 1982 and, eventually, from 1982 to 1984. Peter Davison, "A Note on the Text" in Orwell, *ibid.* at v.

[33] Quoted in Bertrand de Jouvenel, "Utopia for Practical Purposes" in Frank E. Manuel, ed., *Utopias and Utopian Thought* (Boston: Houghton Mifflin, 1966) 219 at 219.

[34] While the article's principal narrative is the *modus vivendi* between technology and democracy in the international legal system of the future, the article also describes other changes. For a comprehensive treatment, see Chi Carmody, "A Look Back at Looking Forward: Ronald St. John Macdonald and the Future of International Law" in this volume of the *Yearbook*.

[35] Anne-Marie Slaughter, "The Real New World Order" (1997) 76(5) *Foreign Affairs* 183.

there will come into existence a "Peoples' Assembly" heavily influenced by anti-statist, counter-elitist sentiment.[36]

Technology has its upbeat sci-fi moments in "International Law and Society in the Year 2000." In a throw-away line about new participants in the international policy-making process, Macdonald, Morris, and Johnston note, "[t]echnology will be ready to create new communities in underwater and lunar resettlement centres, whose interests will have to be represented in still another form."[37] Overwhelmingly, however, technology is a dark force.[38] The authors foresee a multitude of intergovernmental agencies, each depleted of democratic accountability by its dependence on scientific method and the new information technology. "By virtue of their technical mastery of research procedures and data retrieval techniques, technocratic super-elites will have acquired control over the process of implementing decisions taken in the name of each agency and considerable influence on the process of identifying problems."[39] In turn, these elites will compete with similar elites serving other interests; specifically, the transnational entrepreneurial elites and the national bureaucratic elites of the super states (America, Russia, Japan, and China) and the European Community.[40]

Increasingly recognized as "a statist, bureaucracy-ridden, computer-bound, growth-minded and majority oriented organization,"[41] the United Nations will not be able to satisfy the growing popular demand for limits on the powers of the intergovernmental agencies. Hope will lie with the neo-humanism of the Peoples' Assembly, an annual transnational forum that will have come to assume greater legitimacy than the UN General Assembly but will have chosen to work through the UN rather than develop a large bureaucratic infrastructure that would compromise its voluntarist tradition.[42] The Peoples' Assembly will represent the individual

---

[36] Macdonald, Morris, and Johnston, "International Law and Society," *supra* note 5 at 316.

[37] *Ibid.* at 317.

[38] While Macdonald, Morris, and Johnston predicted the power of information technology in the year 2000, they did not anticipate its democratization through the personal computer revolution and the Internet.

[39] Macdonald, Morris, and Johnston, "International Law and Society," *supra* note 5 at 321.

[40] *Ibid.*

[41] *Ibid.* at 322.

[42] *Ibid.* at 323.

world "citizen" directly and will formulate general policy guidelines for the international community. As a result of the Peoples' Assembly's democratic legitimacy, there will be political pressure on the UN General Assembly to debate and implement the policies that the Peoples' Assembly adopts. The non-technocratic character of the Peoples' Assembly will also make it more hospitable to the initiatives of developing states, which will lack the training and expertise to participate effectively in the system of interstate specialized agencies.[43]

Using the pictorial style of utopias,[44] Macdonald and his co-authors contrast the employees of the intergovernmental agencies with the delegates of the Peoples' Assembly. Whereas the intergovernmental agencies will be staffed most successfully by ambitious male techno-wonks between the ages of thirty-five and fifty with highly developed information-processing skills and an emotional make-up and minimal personal life adapted to their stressful and extremely mobile professions, the Peoples' Assembly delegates will include distinguished scientists, scholars, and poets. Although there will be disagreement among socialists, formerly colonized peoples, and environmentalists over the correct basis for representation in the Peoples' Assembly, certain features of its composition are clear. Over half of the delegates will be women — who will otherwise continue to be discriminated against in the sciences, the legal profession, governmental politics, professional diplomacy, and within bureaucratic hierarchies in general — and the under-thirty-five and over-fifty age groups will be robustly represented.[45]

As is typical of utopias,[46] the authors of "International Law and Society in the Year 2000" do not tell us directly how to respond to their portrayal of the future.[47] Should we equip ourselves for it

---

[43] *Ibid.* at 329-30.

[44] See Frye, *supra* note 4 at 26. See also Fredric Jameson, "Of Islands and Trenches: Naturalization and the Production of Utopian Discourse" (1977) 7(2) Diacritics 2 at 6 (referring to "tours and interminable guide-book explanations" and "static descriptions of institutions and geographical and architectural layouts" as typical of utopian texts).

[45] Macdonald, Morris, and Johnston, "International Law and Society," *supra* note 5 at 323-24.

[46] See Frye, *supra* note 4 at 27.

[47] Although the article makes the case for the right of every individual to equal living space, it does so to illustrate how the issue of population and living space would arise and be negotiated in the complex world ordering system of the twenty-first century. Macdonald, Morris, and Johnston, "International Law and Society," *supra* note 5 at 325.

professionally? Should we concentrate our efforts on forestalling it bit by bit? Should we seek to stave it off more radically? Macdonald, Morris, and Johnston do not say, but all three options appear elsewhere in their work. In a follow-up article, published two years later, they develop the comparatively benign implications of their forecast for the training of lawyers.[48] In his writing in the early 1990s on the International Court of Justice's power to review the legality of the Security Council's actions, Macdonald implicitly pursues the gradualist option of safeguarding the integrity of the United Nations.[49] The boldest strategy is contained in Johnston's 1988 formulation of a functionalist approach to international law, which resurrects the prediction of a World People's Assembly as a proposal.[50]

Like "International Law and Society in the Year 2000," Macdonald's 1998 chapter "Rummaging in the Ruins"[51] is utopian without apparently being his eu-topia. "Rummaging in the Ruins" is a complex lament for the evanescence of the Soviet international law and policy of the USSR's early years. "Is anything left?"[52] asks Macdonald, "Is there guidance, not to mention inspiration, to be derived from the opinions and practical efforts of so many Soviet lawyers who worked for so many years in their own isolated vineyard with the aim of leading 'legal scientists' into the New Jerusalem?"[53] There is a palpable sense of loss in his conclusion that next to nothing remains.[54]

This disappointment is certainly not nostalgia for the Soviet regime. Macdonald describes it as oppressive and barbarous in his very first sentence, and its cruel hypocrisy is a central theme of the chapter. Nor does Macdonald ignore the subservience of Soviet theories of international law to the Communist party line, whatever

48 Macdonald, Morris, and Johnston, "New Lawyer," *supra* note 28; Macdonald, Morris, and Johnston, "International Law and Society," *supra* note 5 at 317.

49 See, for example, Ronald St. John Macdonald, "Changing Relations between the International Court of Justice and the Security Council of the United Nations" (1993) 31 Can. Y.B. Int'l Law 3.

50 Douglas M. Johnston, "Functionalism in the Theory of International Law" (1988) 26 Can. Y.B. Int'l Law 3 at 29, n. 91.

51 Ronald St. John Macdonald, "Rummaging in the Ruins: Soviet International Law and Policy in the Early Years: Is Anything Left?" in Karel Wellens, ed., *International Law: Theory and Practice: Essays in Honour of Eric Suy* (The Hague: Martinus Nijhoff, 1998) 61.

52 *Ibid.* at 61 (subtitle of chapter).

53 *Ibid.* at 81.

54 *Ibid.* at 82.

that happened to be. He includes, for example, the denouncement of Vladimir Emmanuilovich Grabar, Iurii Veniaminovich Kliuchnikov, Evgenii Aleksandrovich Korovin, and Andrei Vladimirovich Sabanin as bourgeois thinkers in 1929-30 and the execution of the well-known Soviet international lawyer and legal theorist Evgenii Bronislavovich Pashukanis[55] in 1937. On the substance of Soviet attempts to create a new doctrine of international law and to change radically some of the main institutional features of international law, Macdonald expresses little opinion other than to describe their newness and to conclude that virtually all were compromised, exploited, or abandoned by the Soviet Union in practice.

Why, then, does the chapter convey a feeling of regret? The answer may lie in what Paul Tillich has called the fruitfulness of utopia: "[U]topia opens up possibilities which would have remained lost if not seen by utopian anticipation."[56] Macdonald frames his search for guidance from the Soviet experience with international law as rummaging for things that would be of use in the ongoing imagination and construction of a just world order.[57] Any eu-topia is a repository of possibilities. But Macdonald's allusion to inspiration as well as guidance[58] suggests that he also seeks to summon the soup-to-nuts creativity that is characteristic of the utopian form. In his study of utopias, Chris Ferns notes that "[d]etail ... is a recurrent preoccupation of utopian fiction. Not only are the broad outlines of the utopian social system provided, but also all manner of minutiae."[59] Even if not recommending itself or its aims, the Soviet vision of international law might help to provoke that order of radical thought.

Accordingly, "Rummaging in the Ruins" gives an impression both of the different world order envisaged by the early Soviet international lawyers and of the scale of the changes that they considered.

---

[55] *Ibid.* at 71-72. See also Ronald St. John Macdonald, "Introduction: Wang Tieya: Persevering in Adversity and Shaping the Future of Public International Law in China" in Ronald St. John Macdonald, ed., *Essays in Honour of Wang Tieya* (Dordrecht: Martinus Nijhoff, 1994) 1 at 15-21 (giving an affecting account of the distinguished Chinese international lawyer's suffering under the successive ideological purges of the Anti-Rightist Movement and Cultural Revolution).

[56] Paul Tillich, "Critique and Justification of Utopia" in Frank E. Manuel, ed., *Utopias and Utopian Thought* (Boston: Houghton Mifflin, 1966) 296 at 297.

[57] Macdonald, "Rummaging in the Ruins," *supra* note 51 at 81.

[58] See note 53 and accompanying text.

[59] Chris Ferns, *Narrating Utopia: Ideology, Gender, Form in Utopian Literature* (Liverpool: Liverpool University Press, 1999) at 24.

Macdonald's description of the initial Soviet efforts to make the conduct of foreign policy more transparent and egalitarian is particularly effective at conveying this range and *esprit*. The example most likely to be familiar is Lenin's abolition of secret diplomacy in his 1917 Decree on Peace. Although the new Russian Socialist Federative Soviet Republic (RSFSR), and later the USSR, notoriously resumed the practice, the RSFSR first managed to publish more than one hundred secret diplomatic documents.[60] Macdonald also discusses the RSFSR's cancellation of unequal treaties between Russia and Turkey, Iran, and China,[61] and the USSR's establishment of high-level diplomatic relations with China at a time when the exchange of ambassadors was a privilege extended only among Western states.[62] Another early benchmark of reform that Macdonald highlights is the composition of the RSFSR's delegation to the 1917 peace negotiations with Germany, Austro-Hungary, Bulgaria, and Turkey. Instead of professional diplomats, the delegates were representatives of the Bolshevik party and another leftist party, together with a peasant, a worker, a sailor, and a soldier as voices for the social classes that had come to power.[63] At a somewhat more symbolic level, Macdonald cites the RSFSR's repeal of the traditional diplomatic ranks of ambassador, envoy, and chargé d'affaires for its diplomats stationed abroad and for foreign diplomats posted to the RSFSR. As he describes, this departure from the regulations on diplomatic agents in use since the 1815 Congress of Vienna initially played havoc with established diplomatic protocol in foreign capitals.[64] In a similar symbolic vein, indignation at home over photographs of Soviet delegates to the Genoa Conference of 1922 attired in traditional tail-coats led briefly to the adoption of a less bourgeois form of Soviet diplomatic dress.[65]

Macdonald's admiration for Philip Allott's *Eunomia: New Order for a New World*[66] reflects the importance that Macdonald places on the comprehensiveness of the utopian vision. (Sharing a prefix with eu-topia, Allott's title means a good social order.)[67] In an article on nuclear weapon-free zones in international law — an idea already

[60] Macdonald, "Rummaging in the Ruins," *supra* note 51 at 77-79.

[61] *Ibid.* at 77-78.

[62] *Ibid.* at 75.

[63] *Ibid.* at 74.

[64] *Ibid.* at 74-75.

[65] *Ibid.* at 76.

[66] Macdonald, Review of *Eunomia, supra* note 10.

[67] On the history of the word "eunomia," see Allott, *supra* note 9 at xxvii, n. 1.

tinged with idealism for many — Macdonald cautions against stopping with the consideration of such isolated interim reforms:

[I]n public international law, as in physics, and indeed in the other social sciences as well, the parts are so interconnected that some of their very attributes arise from their connections: things are what they are mainly by virtue of their relationships to other things. An adequate view of the complexity of the international control system can only come from studying it as a whole.[68]

His view that the parts of international law do not exist separately and must therefore be reformed relative to one another is of a piece with his enthusiasm for Allott's book, which sees the reconception of ourselves and then the societies to which we belong as necessary before we can reconceive the society of societies, the international society of humanity.[69]

Macdonald also endorses the relationship of form to imagination in *Euonomia*. Early in his review, he registers the book's total absence of footnotes or endnotes and its lack of any references to treaties, cases, statutes, or scholarly writings.[70] Macdonald further records Allott's explanation that such a break with convention is essential to the book's general ambition of proposing a theory for a new and better ordering of international society.[71] Attentive to Allott's style of writing as well, Macdonald says of *Eunomia*'s prose: "Within a rigid structure, the writing itself is at times almost poetic; there is an internal rhythm to the work, a sense of cycle and process. Devices of repetition and reiteration are used, creating a rather liturgical effect."[72] While he observes that this style may be disturbing and, at first, confounding to "longtime readers of straightforward legal writing," he defends it as integral to the book.[73]

---

[68] Ronald St. John Macdonald, "Nuclear Weapon-Free Zones and Principles of International Law" in Wybo P. Heere, ed., *International Law and Its Sources: Liber Amicorum Maarten Bos* (Deventer, The Netherlands: Kluwer, 1989) 47 at 75. In a number of his writings, Macdonald directly or indirectly advocates the systemic examination of international law or the study of its theoretical foundations. See especially Ronald St. John Macdonald, "An Historical Introduction to the Teaching of International Law in Canada, Part III" (1976) 14 Can. Y.B. Int'l Law 224 at 247-56. See also Macdonald, "Leadership in Law," *supra* note 27 at 19-23; Macdonald and Johnston, "International Legal Theory," *supra* note 28.

[69] Macdonald, "Review of *Eunomia*," *supra* note 10 at 822.

[70] *Ibid.* at 822

[71] *Ibid.*

[72] *Ibid.* at 823.

[73] *Ibid.*

Although Fredric Jameson has a more specific set of mental operations in mind, Macdonald's description of *Euonomia*'s effect as "liturgical" is reminiscent of the approach to utopias that Jameson sets forth. For Jameson, it is less illuminating to treat utopian discourse as a mode of narrative than to appreciate it as "an object of meditation, analogous to the riddles or *koan* of the various mystical traditions, or the aporias of classical philosophy, whose function is to ... jar the mind into some heightened but unconceptualizable consciousness of its own powers, functions, aims and structural limits."[74] Macdonald's response to *Eunomia* seems similarly to recognize that form opens minds and that experimentation with style and genre is therefore worthwhile in international law. Such a view would be consistent with his interest in two public law scholars who expressed themselves also through literature: the noted Canadian law professor, political activist, and poet F.R. Scott (1899-1985), and the intriguing figure of the British international lawyer and little-known novelist Thomas Baty (1869-1954). Macdonald co-edited *On F.R. Scott: Essays on His Contributions to Law, Literature, and Politics*,[75] a 1983 collection of essays that brings together reflections on the different dimensions of Scott's influence on Canadian culture. And Macdonald was fascinated to discover that Thomas Baty, author of the extraordinary[76] *The Canons of International Law*[77] and *International Law in Twilight*,[78] had also penned feminist utopian fiction in obscurity under the pseudonym of Irene Clyde.[79]

If Macdonald sees *Eunomia* as fruitful in the way of utopias,[80] he is equally sensitive to the contrary potential that Tillich terms their

---

[74] Jameson, *supra* note 44 at 11.

[75] Sandra Djwa and Ronald St. John Macdonald, eds., *On F.R. Scott: Essays on His Contributions to Law, Literature, and Politics* (Kingston: McGill-Queen's University Press, 1983).

[76] See J.A. Carty, "Changing Models of the International System" in William E. Butler, ed., *Perestroika and International Law* (Dordrecht: Martinus Nijhoff, 1990) 13 at 22 (describing Baty as "a rather unusual Englishman" and these two works as brilliant).

[77] Thomas Baty, *The Canons of International Law* (London: Murray, 1930).

[78] Thomas Baty, *International Law in Twilight* (Tokyo: Maruzen, 1954).

[79] See Daphne Patai and Angela Ingram, "Fantasy and Identity: The Double Life of a Victorian Sexual Radical" in Angela Ingram and Daphne Patai, eds., *Rediscovering Forgotten Radicals: British Women Writers, 1889-1939* (Chapel Hill, NC: University of North Carolina Press, 1993) 265.

[80] See, for example, Macdonald, "Review of *Eunomia*," *supra* note 10 at 831 ("The great merit of Allott's timely and imaginative vision is that it stimulates debate on the transcending purposes of a single, sharing, society").

unfruitfulness.[81] One of the benefits of utopia is "its discovery of possibilities which can be realized only by pushing forward into the unlimitedness of possibility."[82] But this can tip over into the pursuit of the impossible. The activist strain of utopia writers typical of the nineteenth century condemned the tendency to naïve or wishful thinking in utopianism. Utopias were located firmly in the future, and they were calls to action.[83] Marx and other political philosophers therefore rejected the inclination to unrealism in the utopian imagination and made utopia dependent on what they showed were real possibilities.[84] Macdonald's criticisms of *Eunomia* seem to reflect this preference for the dynamic utopia or utopia of action.[85] While Macdonald is fully aligned with the *Eunomian* project of invoking "the power of the future,"[86] he is frustrated with what he speculates is Allott's failure to ground his anticipation in the workings of international society, contrasting Allott's vision with Macdonald's own in "International Law and Society in the Year 2000."[87] Relatedly, he is disappointed at the briefness of Allott's treatment of "the visible pathways that could in fact lead to the Golden City."[88]

Macdonald's preferred form of the dynamic utopia also addresses the concern that, whether or not a particular utopia is achievable, its picture of static, completed perfection will unintentionally reinforce the status quo either by inspiring resignation rather than

---

[81] Tillich, *supra* note 56 at 300.

[82] *Ibid.*

[83] See Judith Shklar, "The Political Theory of Utopia: From Melancholy to Nostalgia" in Frank E. Manuel, ed., *Utopias and Utopian Thought* (Boston: Houghton Mifflin, 1966) 101 at 109 (distinguishing nineteenth-century utopias from the earlier classical utopias aimed at contemplation or critique).

[84] Tillich, *supra* note 56 at 300. A number of authors consider Marx to be utopian and read his attack on utopian socialism as a disagreement about the process of transition only. See Ruth Levitas, *The Concept of Utopia* (Syracuse, NY: Syracuse University Press, 1990) at 35-58 (on Marx, Engels, and utopian socialism), 102-4 (on Tillich).

[85] Such a preference is consistent with the penchant for historical periodization found elsewhere in Macdonald's work. See, for example, Macdonald, Johnston, and Morris, "International Law of Human Welfare," *supra* note 15.

[86] Allott, *supra* note 9 at xxvi. In this respect, Macdonald differs from many of *Eunomia*'s readers. See *ibid.* at xxvii.

[87] Macdonald, "Review of *Eunomia*," *supra* note 10 at 828.

[88] *Ibid.* at 830. For Allott's response to these criticisms, see Allott, *supra* note 9 at xxx-xxxiv.

action or by distracting from the needs of the present.[89] Although the dynamic utopia may avoid these difficulties, it leaves another concern; namely, that it stifles the imagination. Such a utopia may tell us the road to the Golden City and convince us that we can get there, but the Golden City is a fixed ideal. It is already fully described and therefore already fully built.[90] Our only choice is to take it or leave it.

While utopian fiction may have the potential to open up wider horizons, to suggest the sheer extent of the possible, its *effect* is often impoverishing rather than enriching: instead of opening up space for the imagination, the utopian vision merely fills it with a construct, to use Ernst Bloch's phrase, "made banal by the fulfilment."[91]

There is evidently a great deal more that could be said about the utopian form in international law and Ronald St. John Macdonald's approach to it. Because I have chosen to focus on the relationship of form to the intellectual imagination, I have not dwelled on the oppressive power of utopias historically, a point that Macdonald's look back at the Soviet Union illustrates all too well, or on their psychological projection of desire. My aim in this article was to introduce the distinction between the substance and the form of utopia as a way to appreciate one dimension of Macdonald's originality and thereby to return the tribute that he pays to the Québec international lawyer Maximilien Bibaud (1823-87), whom he praises as "energetic, vitalizing, and exhilaratingly new" in both ideas and techniques.[92]

To conclude, I offer the suggestion that Macdonald has not only a eu-topia and a belief in the importance of ou-topias, but an un-articulated theory of the genre that he acts on and that enables him to negotiate the dilemmas of utopias. Although we have seen that Macdonald favours the utopia of action, he is undoubtedly cognizant of its deficiencies. Related to the form's potential to colonize rather than liberate the imagination is the problem of the "partial vision" of utopias. Utopias are "partial" in the double sense that

---

[89] See Levitas, *supra* note 84 at 57.

[90] Ferns, *supra* note 59 at 20.

[91] *Ibid.* at 4 [emphasis in original], quoting Ernst Bloch, *The Utopian Function of Art and Literature: Selected Essays*, translated by Jack Zipes and Franck Mecklenburg (Cambridge, MA: MIT Press, 1988) at 2 (Bloch's actual phrase is "made banal through the fulfillment").

[92] Ronald St. John Macdonald, "Maximilien Bibaud, 1823-1887: The Pioneer Teacher of International Law in Canada" (1988) 11 Dal. L.J. 721 at 721, 740.

any substantive utopia is partisan and thus achieves only limited insight into the perfect society.[93] The deficiencies of the dynamic utopia also include the all-too-real dangers of fanaticism and coercion. The response of many has therefore been to announce the End of Utopia. Among some theorists, an alternative response has been to reconceive the idea of utopia yet again; in particular, to shift from prescriptive utopias to experimental, predictive to speculative, a politics of change cast not in the imperative mode but in the subjunctive.[94]

While Macdonald would presumably accept the underlying criticisms of utopias, his actions imply that he would probably not be prepared to modify the idea and recast utopias as internally dialogic or open-ended, or as hope or desire rather than action. Instead, the events that he organized during the United Nations Decade of International Law,[95] the mandate of the new *Journal of the History of International Law* that he established and edits,[96] and his indefatigable one-on-one encouragement of fresh ideas and aspirations for international law, point to a different response on his part to the trouble with utopias. That response is to retain the idea of the dynamic utopia and to use the form to advantage in a way that also seeks to remedy its defects.

[93] Bammer, *supra* note 8 at 4.

[94] *Ibid.* at 51. Among the overviews of such efforts are *ibid.* at 48-66; Ferns, *supra* note 59 at 8-9; Levitas, *supra* note 84.

[95] On the Decade of International Law generally, see Ronald St. John Macdonald, "The United Nations Decade of International Law" (1990) 28 Can. Y.B. Int'l Law 417. Macdonald served as the first chair of the United Nations Decade Interest Group [hereinafter UNDIG] of the American Society of International Law. For an indication of UNDIG's activities, see "UN Decade Newsletter #1" (December 1992), accessible at <http://www.asil.org>; "UN Decade Newsletter #3" (May 1993), accessible at <http://www.asil.org>. He has been applauded for his part in "organizing activities and roundtables under the aegis of the Decade, which have provided outstanding opportunities for information-sharing and informal exchanges among various constituencies, including exchanges of points of view between the Sixth Committee and ICJ members." UNDIG-Sponsored Panel, "Goals of the United Nations Decade of International Law: Law Reform and National Programs" (1993) 87 Proc. Am. Soc. Int'l L. 357 at 373 (Abraham Montes de Oca, Permanent Mission of Mexico to the United Nations). In an echo of the Peoples' Assembly of "International Law and Society in the Year 2000," Macdonald maintained that the activities of the national committees established to promote the decade should include the constituencies of education, journalism, religion, trade unionism, youth movements, and senior citizens' groups. *Ibid.* at 357-58.

[96] Ronald St. John Macdonald, "Editorial" (1999) 1 J. Hist. Int'l L. v.

In serving as a roving ambassador for the utopian form, Macdonald implicitly seeks to harness equality to the energy of outopia. He has long publicized and fostered what might be called subaltern utopias, the future visions of groups outside the mainstream of international law.[97] Among other things, he has argued for a distinct Canadian approach to international law as Canada came of age as an independent state in matters of foreign policy,[98] he has introduced a range of socialist approaches to the West through his scholarship,[99] he has built Third World approaches into his work,[100] and he has pushed for feminist approaches to international law.[101]

Macdonald's commitment to promoting subaltern utopias may also be read in his statement of the aims of the *Journal of the History of International Law*: "[T]o open new fields of inquiry, to enable new questions to be asked, to be awake to and always aware of the plurality of human civilizations and cultures, past and present, and an appreciation of patterns of cultural flow and interaction that centrally affect international law and development."[102] Although we associate utopias most often with the future, historical writing too can be utopian. Manuel's description of the types of utopias, quoted earlier, includes those utopias that "resurrect a good society

---

[97] See Nancy Fraser, "Rethinking the Public Sphere: A Contribution to the Critique of Actually Existing Democracy" in Nancy Fraser, *Justice Interruptus: Critical Reflections on the "Postsocialist" Condition* (New York: Routledge, 1997) 69 at 80-83 (theorizing "subaltern counterpublics").

[98] See especially Ronald St. John Macdonald, "An Historical Introduction to the Teaching of International Law in Canada" (1974) 12 Can. Y.B. Int'l Law 67; Ronald St. John Macdonald, "An Historical Introduction to the Teaching of International Law in Canada, Part II" (1975) 13 Can. Y.B. Int'l Law 255; Macdonald, "Historical Introduction, III," *supra* note 68. See also sources cited in note 24.

[99] See, for example, V. Kartashkin, "The Marxist-Leninist Approach: The Theory of Class Struggle and Contemporary International Law" in Macdonald and Johnston, *Structure and Process, supra* note 28 at 79; Ronald St. John Macdonald, ed., *Essays in Honour of Wang Tieya* (Dordrecht: Martinus Nijhoff, 1994); Macdonald, "United Nations Charter," *supra* note 19; Macdonald, "Rummaging in the Ruins," *supra* note 51.

[100] Macdonald, "Solidarity in Practice and Discourse," *supra* note 12.

[101] An early instance is the inclusion of Annemarie Jacomy-Millette, "La Femme Nouvelle dans la vie sociale internationale des années 1970" in Macdonald, Johnston, and Morris, *Human Welfare, supra* note 15 at 291.

[102] Macdonald, "Editorial," *supra* note 96 at v.

that has been in ages past and should be again."[103] In her discussion of the classical utopias that predate the activist utopias of the nineteenth century, Judith Shklar refers to "an anguished recollection of antiquity, of the polis and of the Roman Republic of virtuous memory."[104] Similarly, the *Journal's* invitation to study the international legal past in all its variety and eccentricity may be understood as including a call for the utopian as well as for the subaltern. Macdonald's first editorial speaks of the "pasts" and not simply the "past" of international law.[105]

Macdonald's motivation seems to be a recognition that in a stratified international society, it is not enough simply to merge the viewpoints of historically excluded groups into the discussion of issues already identified without their input and in terms shaped without their involvement.[106] To begin to counter the participatory privileges enjoyed by the dominant groups in international society, there must also be opportunities for subordinated groups to break the frame of international law. Utopias are valuable for this reason; they enable subordinated groups to formulate a radical total vision that may startle and even mobilize us with its justness. Subaltern utopias thus have the potential to improve the equality as well as the diversity of the discussion in international law.

Moreover, the resulting variety of utopias suggests how Macdonald may navigate the advantages and disadvantages of utopias. Each utopia will have the comprehensiveness and the intensified sense of creativity and change that recommend the form. In addition, the contemplation of many different "speaking pictures" of the ideal world will help to prevent the monopoly on imagination that the comprehensiveness of ou-topia might otherwise produce. It will also assist in overcoming the partial vision of a single substantive utopia because one eu-topia can always be tested against another, and they can be combined to improve on both. And the hope is too, presumably, that this process will lessen utopia's risk of zealotry. This, at least, would be one possible interpretation of how Macdonald reconceives the praxis of utopianism to both capitalize on its strengths and compensate for its weaknesses.

---

[103] Manuel, *supra* note 11.

[104] Shklar, *supra* note 83 at 105.

[105] Macdonald, "Editorial," *supra* note 96 at v.

[106] In "International Legal Theory: New Frontiers of the Discipline," Macdonald and Johnston lament the European dominance of the philosophy and doctrine of international law. Macdonald and Johnston, "International Legal Theory," *supra* note 28 at 9.

In a utilitarian society, Frank and Fritzie Manuel have written, there is a tendency to reduce the value of utopians to the accuracy of their predictions. For the Manuels, this is a mistake: "The short-term prognosticator can be a bore. He is merely a meteorologist, useful in planning an outing or a military invasion."[107] As a practitioner, presenter, and promoter of the utopian form, Ronald St. John Macdonald is anything but boring. But, then, even if we haven't had a theory to explain why, we've been celebrating that all along.

Sommaire

L'utopie sans apologie: la forme et l'imagination dans l'œuvre de Ronald St. John Macdonald

Le mot "utopie" est un jeu d'esprit entre eu topos (un endroit agréable) et ou topos (un endroit fictif). Alors que le mot utopie dans le sens de eu topos fait référence à la société idéale et à sa réalisation, le mot utopie dans le sens de ou topos décrit davantage un mode narratif qu'un but politique. Traditionnellement, l'utopie est le récit que fait un voyageur de sa visite à un pays imaginaire, soit vers une terre lointaine soit dans un avenir éloigné. Cet article examine l'œuvre de Ronald St. John Macdonald en tant que praticien, conférencier et promoteur d'une forme utopique de droit international. Si une eu-topie particulière peut nous proposer toute une série d'idées sur le droit international que nous pourrions difficilement imaginer autrement, en général l'ou-topie encourage une analyse approfondie et radicale concernant l'avenir du droit international qui peut même stimuler une prise de conscience plus grande de notre créativité et des possibilités de changement. L'article souligne aussi les désavantages propres à ces utopies et spécule que Macdonald réconcilie les avantages et les désavantages en partie du fait que le pouvoir de l'utopie est accessible même aux personnes qui historiquement ont été injustement exclues du droit international.

---

[107] Frank E. Manuel and Fritzie P. Manuel, *Utopian Thought in the Western World* (Oxford: Basil Blackwell, 1979) at 28.

Summary

Utopia without Apology: Form and Imagination in the Work of Ronald St. John Macdonald

The word "utopia" is a pun on eu topos (a good place) and ou topos (no place). While utopia in the sense of eu topos refers to an ideal society and its realization, utopia in the sense of ou topos emphasizes a mode of narrative rather than a political goal. Traditionally, the utopian form is a traveller's account of a visit to an imaginary country where the journey is either to a far-off land or to the distant future. This article offers an appreciation of Ronald St. John Macdonald as a practitioner, presenter, and promoter of the utopian form in international law. Beyond the ability of a particular eu-topia to confront us with a complete package of ideas for international law that would otherwise remain unimagined, ou-topia generally encourages comprehensive and radical thinking about international law's future and perhaps even jolts us into a heightened consciousness of our creativity and potential for change. The article also touches on the corresponding disadvantages of utopias and speculates that Macdonald reconciles the advantages and disadvantages partly through the fact that the power of the utopian form is available even to those who have been historically and unjustly excluded from international law.

European Court of Human Rights

LUZIUS WILDHABER

INTRODUCTION

It is a great pleasure to pay tribute to my colleague and dear friend from the former, part-time European Court of Human Rights (ECHR), Ronald St. J. Macdonald, by describing the court's present-day reality and work. The principal and overriding aim of the system set up by the Convention for the Protection of Human Rights and Fundamental Freedoms (Human Rights Convention)[1] is to bring about a situation in which in each and every contracting state the rights and freedoms are effectively protected. This mandate primarily means ensuring that the relevant structures and procedures are in place to allow individual citizens to vindicate those rights and to assert those freedoms in the national courts.

As the European Court of Human Rights has recently emphasized, "the object and purpose underlying the Convention, as set out in Article 1, is that the rights and freedoms should be secured by the Contracting State within its jurisdiction. It is fundamental to the machinery of protection established by the Convention that the national systems themselves provide redress for breaches of its provisions, the Court (exercising) its supervisory role subject to the principle of subsidiarity."[2] This purpose was confirmed in the

---

Luzius Wildhaber is president of the European Court of Human Rights [hereinafter ECHR].

[1] Convention for the Protection of Human Rights and Fundamental Freedoms, November 4, 1950, E.T.S. No.005 (entered into force September 3, 1953) [hereinafter Human Rights Convention].

[2] *Z. and Others* v. *United Kingdom*, October 5, 2001, Eur. Ct. H.R. at para. 103 (2001-V).

context of Article 13 (which requires contracting states to provide an effective remedy for violations of the convention). The ECHR held that the obligation to provide a remedy extended also to problems of length of proceedings in breach of Article 6. As the court noted,

the [exhaustion of domestic remedies] rule in Article 35 § 1 is based on the assumption, reflected in Article 13 (with which it has a close affinity), that there is an effective domestic remedy available in respect of the alleged breach of an individual's Convention rights. In that way, Article 13, giving direct expression to the States' obligation to protect human rights first and foremost within their own legal system, establishes an additional guarantee for an individual in order to ensure that he or she effectively enjoys those rights. The object of Article 13, as emerges from the *travaux préparatoires*,[3] is to provide a means whereby individuals can obtain relief at national level for violations of their Convention rights before having to set in motion the international machinery of complaint before the Court.[4]

This then is the framework for the ECHR's judicial activity. I should like now to consider some recent cases under three headings: evolutive interpretation, separation of powers, and human dignity. If these themes provide only a glimpse of the court's work last year, they are each fundamental to the effectiveness of the convention system and the ECHR's authority.

EVOLUTIVE INTERPRETATION

On the question of evolutive interpretation, it is precisely the genius of the Human Rights Convention that it is indeed a dynamic and a living instrument. It has shown a capacity to evolve in light of social and technological developments that its drafters, however far-sighted, could never have imagined. It has shown that it is capable of growing with society, and, in this respect, its formulations have proved their worth over five decades. The convention has remained a live and modern instrument. The "living instrument" doctrine is one of the best-known principles of Strasbourg case law. It expresses the principle that the Human Rights Convention is interpreted "in the light of present day conditions," that it evolves through the interpretation of the ECHR.

---

[3] See the *Collected Edition of the "Travaux Préparatoires" of the European Convention on Human Rights*, vol. 2 (The Hague: Martinus Nijhoff, 1975) at 485 and 490; and vol. 3 (The Hague: Martinus Nijhoff, 1976) at 651.

[4] *Kudła v. Poland*, October 26, 2000, Eur. Ct. H.R. at para. 152 (2000-XI).

This principle of dynamic interpretation was first enounced in relation to corporal punishment following criminal proceedings.[5] Yet it has received its most frequent expression in relation to Article 8. This fact is hardly surprising not only because of the breadth of the interests covered by Article 8, which are private and family life as well as correspondence and home, but also because it is precisely those interests that are most likely to be affected by changes in society. In a dynamic instrument, Article 8 has proved to be the most elastic provision. Thus, it has embraced such matters as the taking of children into care, nuisance caused by a waste treatment plant, planning issues, aircraft noise, transsexuals' rights, corporal punishment in schools, access to confidential documents relating to an applicant's past in the care of the public authorities, the choice of a child's first name, the application of immigration rules, the disclosure of medical records, and many other situations — the list is a long one.

The breadth of the potential scope of the interests protected by Article 8 has thus been an advantage in allowing the development of the ECHR's case law in this area to keep pace with the modern world. It is, however, something of a disadvantage when governments are seeking to establish exactly what is expected of them under the Human Rights Convention. This is all the more so, because in one of its earliest judgments concerning Article 8,[6] the court made it clear that in addition to the obligation to abstain from arbitrary interference with the protected interests, the state authorities could be under a positive obligation to ensure effective "respect" for those interests. This case concerned the status of a child born out of wedlock. The ECHR noted that respect for family life implied in particular "the existence in domestic law of legal safeguards that render possible as from the moment of birth the child's integration in his [or her] family."[7] Moreover, such positive obligations may involve the adoption of measures designed to secure respect for private life even in the sphere of the relations of individuals between themselves.[8]

A line of cases on transsexuals' rights sheds light on the evolutive process of interpretation of the Human Rights Convention. The essence of the applicants' complaints has been that the respondent

[5] *Tyrer* v. *United Kingdom*, April 25, 1978, Eur. Ct. H.R. (Series A No. 26) at 31.

[6] *Marckx* v. *Belgium*, June 13, 1979, Eur. Ct. H.R. (Series A No. 31).

[7] *Ibid.* at para. 31.

[8] *X and Y* v. *Netherlands*, March 26, 2000, Eur. Ct. H.R. (Series A No. 91) at para. 23.

states in question have failed to take positive steps to modify a system that operates to their detriment — the system being that of birth registration. The court carried out its usual exercise of seeking a fair balance between the general interest and the interests of the individual. It had until last year, by a small and dwindling majority and with one exception distinguished on the facts,[9] found that there was no positive obligation for the respondent state to modify its system of birth registration so as to have the register of births updated or annotated to record changed sexual identity.[10]

However, the ECHR never closed the door on the possibility of requiring legal recognition of new sexual identity.[11] It reiterated the need for contracting states to keep the question under review. In the case of *Sheffield and Horsham* v. *United Kingdom*, which was decided in 1998, the court acknowledged the increased social acceptance of transsexualism and the increased recognition of the problems that post-operative transsexuals encounter. In order to determine whether it should revise its case law, the court looked at two aspects: scientific developments and legal developments. With respect to scientific developments, it confirmed its view that there remains uncertainty as to the essential nature of transsexualism and observed that the legitimacy of surgical intervention was sometimes questioned. There had not been any findings in the area of medical science that settled conclusively the doubts concerning the causes of the condition of transsexualism. The non-acceptance by the respondent state of the sex of the brain as being the crucial determinant of gender could not be criticized as being unreasonable.[12] Looking at the legal development, the ECHR examined the comparative study that had been submitted by a human rights organization. It was not satisfied that this study established the existence of any common European approach to the problems created by the recognition in law of post-operative gender status. In particular, there was no common approach as to how to address the repercussions that such recognition might entail for other areas of the law such as marriage, filiation, privacy, or data protection.

---

[9] *B.* v. *France*, March 25, 1992, Eur. Ct. H.R. (Series A No. 232-C).

[10] *Rees* v. *United Kingdom*, October 17, 1986, Eur. Ct. H.R. (Series A No. 106); *Cossey* v. *United Kingdom*, September 27, 1990, Eur. Ct. H.R. (Series A No. 184); *Sheffield and Horsham* v. *United Kingdom*, July 30, 1998, Eur. Ct. H.R. (1998-V) [hereinafter *Sheffield*].

[11] See dissenting opinion of Judge van Dijk in *Sheffield, supra* note 10.

[12] *Sheffield, supra* note 10 at para. 55.

In the case of *Goodwin* v. *United Kingdom,* however, which was decided last year, the court finally reached the conclusion that the fair balance now tilted in favour of the legal recognition of transsexuals.[13] It recalled that it had to have regard to the changing conditions within the respondent state and within contracting states generally and to respond to any evolving convergence as to the standards to be achieved. A failure by the court to maintain a dynamic and evolutive approach would risk rendering it a bar to reform or improvement. In this case, the ECHR attached less importance to the lack of evidence of a common European approach to the resolution of the legal and practical problems posed by transsexualism. Rather, it stressed the clear and uncontested evidence of a continuing international trend in favour not only of the increased social acceptance of transsexuals but also of the legal recognition of the new sexual identity of post-operative transsexuals. No concrete or substantial hardship or detriment to the public interest had been demonstrated as being likely to flow from the changes to the status of transsexuals. Society could reasonably be expected to tolerate a certain inconvenience to enable individuals to live in dignity and worth in accordance with sexual identity chosen by them at great personal cost. In other words, the individual interest asserted did not impose an excessive burden on the community as a whole.

The ECHR is understandably wary of extending its case law on positive obligations. It has first to be convinced not only that there has been a clear evolution of morals but also that this evolution, where appropriate substantiated by an accompanying evolution of scientific knowledge, is reflected in the law and practice of a majority of the contracting states. The court will then interpret the terms of the Human Rights Convention in light of this evolution. It is not, I would say, the court's role to engineer changes in society or to impose moral choices.

SEPARATION OF POWERS

Another, rather different, example of the living instrument approach can be seen in the case of *Stafford* v. *the United Kingdom,* which was also decided last year.[14] In this case, the ECHR revisited its earlier finding that mandatory life sentences for murder in the United Kingdom constituted punishment for life and therefore

---

[13] *Goodwin* v. *United Kingdom,* July 11, 2002, Eur. Ct. H.R. at 447 (2002).

[14] *Stafford* v. *United Kingdom,* May 28, 2002, Eur. Ct. H.R. (2002-IV).

that re-detention after release on licence could be justified on the basis of the original conviction and need not be the subject of new judicial proceedings. The court took judicial notice of the evolving position of the British courts as to the nature of life sentences in an interesting example of a two-way process. In this process, developments in the domestic legal system influenced Strasbourg to change its case law, which, in turn, resulted in the consolidation of the evolution at national level — what one might call jurisprudential osmosis.

The applicant Stafford had been convicted of murder and released on licence after completing the punitive element or tariff of his sentence. He was subsequently convicted and sentenced for an unconnected, non-violent offence. His continued detention after completing the second sentence under the first mandatory life sentence was found to be in breach of Article 5, paragraph 1, of the Human Rights Convention. Admittedly, the court found that there was no material distinction on the facts between *Stafford* and the earlier case.[15] However, having regard to the significant developments in the domestic sphere, the court proposed to re-assess "in the light of present-day conditions" what was now the appropriate interpretation and application of the convention. This was necessary to render the convention rights practical and effective, not theoretical and illusory. Thus, the ECHR had regard to the changing conditions and any emerging consensus discernible within the domestic legal order of the respondent contracting state. It found that there was not a sufficient causal connection between the applicant's continued detention and his original sentence for murder. The court also held that there had been a breach of Article 5, paragraph 4, in that the power of decision concerning the applicant's release lay with a member of the executive, the home secretary, who could reject the parole board's recommendation. In other words, the lawfulness of the applicant's continued detention was not reviewed by a body with the power to order his release or with a procedure containing the necessary judicial safeguards.

The ECHR thus drew attention to another issue raised by the *Stafford* case. This issue involved the separation of powers and the difficulty of reconciling the power of a member of the executive to fix the punitive element of a prison sentence and to decide on a prisoner's release with that notion, which had assumed a growing importance in the Strasbourg case law. In another British case,

15 *Wynne* v. *United Kingdom,* July 18, 1994, Eur. Ct. H.R. (Series A No. 294-A).

which concerned the release of persons detained in a mental hospital,[16] the power to order release lay with the secretary of state. The decision to release would therefore be taken by a member of the executive and not by the competent tribunal. This was not a matter of form but rather impinged on the fundamental principle of separation of powers and detracted from a necessary guarantee against the possibility of abuse.

The separation of powers is a crucial element in the Human Rights Convention system as one of the fundamental pillars of the rule of law. At the same time, it is a principle that also has to apply, admittedly in a rather different way, to the functioning of the Strasbourg court. There is no room for even the slightest perception of external interference or of any lack of independence on the part of the ECHR. In this respect, it has to be recognized that there are still unresolved questions about the court's status as well as its true position within the Council of Europe architecture. I should also say that we in Strasbourg have ourselves on occasion had to remind governments of the special character of the court's judicial function, which should command the same respect owed to a national judiciary.

The issue of the practical independence of the judiciary has also arisen in other circumstances. Last year, the ECHR found a violation of the fair trial guarantee in the Ukrainian case of *Sovtransavto v. Ukraine,* in which there had been in the domestic proceedings numerous interventions by the Ukrainian authorities at the highest political level. Such interventions disclosed a lack of respect for the very function of the judiciary.[17]

HUMAN DIGNITY

My third theme is a recurring one in the ECHR's case law, namely the notion of human dignity, which lies at the heart of the Human Rights Convention. The court held last year that a state must ensure that a person is imprisoned in conditions that are compatible with respect for his human dignity. The manner and execution of the measure should not subject him to distress and hardship of an intensity exceeding the unavoidable level of suffering inherent in detention. In the case of *Kalashnikov v. Russia,* the court found that at any given time the overcrowding was such that each inmate in the

---

[16] *Benjamin and Wilson* v. *United Kingdom,* September 9, 2002.

[17] *Sovtransavto* v. *Ukraine,* July 25, 2002, no 48553/99, Eur. Ct. H.R. (2002-VII).

applicant's cell had between 0.9 and 1.9 square metres of space; that the inmates in the applicant's cell had to sleep taking turns, on the basis of eight-hour shifts; that the cell was infested with pests; that the toilet facilities in the cell were filthy and dilapidated with no privacy; and that some prison inmates suffered from contagious diseases. The absence of any positive intention to humiliate or debase the detainee, although a factor to be taken into account, could not exclude a finding of inhuman and degrading treatment and thus of a violation of Article 3 of the Human Rights Convention.[18]

Human dignity was at issue in other contexts in 2002. Early in the year, the ECHR had a particularly poignant case to decide called *Pretty* v. *United Kingdom*.[19] The applicant was a British national in the terminal stages of motor neurone disease. She had unsuccessfully sought an undertaking from the director of public prosecutions that her husband would not be criminally prosecuted if he assisted her to commit suicide. The applicant claimed that this refusal infringed, among other things, her right to life under Article 2 of the Human Rights Convention, the prohibition of inhuman or degrading treatment under Article 3, and the right to respect for private life under Article 8.

The court looked primarily at the plain meaning of the convention terms. Thus, it could not read into the "the right to life" guaranteed in Article 2 a right to die. Nor could the notion of inhuman and degrading treatment prohibited under Article 3 of the Human Rights Convention be extended to cover the refusal to give the undertaking that the applicant sought. The positive obligation on the part of the state that was invoked would require that the state sanction actions intended to terminate life, an obligation that could not be derived from Article 3 of the convention. The ECHR nevertheless reiterated, in its consideration of the complaint under Article 8, that the very essence of the convention was respect for human dignity and human freedom. Without negating the principle of sanctity of life protected under the Human Rights Convention, it was under Article 8 that notions of the quality of life took on significance. In an era of growing medical sophistication combined with longer life expectancy, many people were concerned that they should not be forced to linger on in old age or in states of advanced physical or mental decrepitude, which conflicted with strongly held

---

[18] *Kalashnikov* v. *Russia*, July 15 2002, no. 47095/99, Eur. Ct. H.R. (2001-VI) [hereinafter *Kalashnikov*].

[19] *Pretty* v. *United Kingdom*, July 29, 2002, no. 2346/02, Eur. Ct. H.R. (2002-VII).

ideas of self and personal identity. The circumstances of the case could therefore give rise to an interference with the right to respect for private life.

This finding meant that under the second paragraph of Article 8, the court had to determine the necessity of such interference. It found that states were entitled to regulate through the operation of the general criminal law activities that were detrimental to the life and safety of other individuals. The law in issue was designed to safeguard life by protecting the weak and vulnerable and especially those who were not in a condition to take informed decisions against acts intended to end life or to assist in ending life. It was primarily for each state to assess the risk and the likely incidence of abuse within its society if the general prohibition on assisted suicides were relaxed or if exceptions were to be created. The contested measure came within the spectrum of those laws that could be considered "necessary in a democratic society."

This sensitive and difficult case provides a further example of the ECHR's cautious approach to the living instrument doctrine in areas that are still a matter of intense legal, moral, and scientific debate. Moreover, it reminds us that there are areas of action within which states should retain a degree of discretion both as the local authorities best placed to carry out certain assessments and also in accordance with the principles of a democratic society.

GROWING CASE LOAD AND REFORM

The main challenge facing the ECHR is now its ever-growing caseload.[20] The court has currently some 34,000 applications pending before its decision bodies. Applications allocated to a decision body have increased by around 470 per cent since the present court took office in November 1998, by about 2,800 per cent since 1988. The potential for growth is almost unlimited as a result of the massive expansion of the Council of Europe over the last decade. Moreover, the evolution of the court's caseload is not merely quantitative. The nature of the cases coming before the court inevitably reflects the changed composition of the Council of Europe, with a significant number of states still being in many respects, particularly in regard to their judicial systems, in transition, even if considerable progress has been made in several of them. In such states,

---

[20] See Luzius Wildhaber, "A Constitutional Future for the European Court of Human Rights?" (2002) 23 H.R.L.J. 161-65.

there are likely to be structural problems, which cannot be resolved overnight. The understandable political imperatives of the heady days since 1989 have, it must be said, left the court with a major headache, just because it is a court and must decide issues of law, without reference to political expediency.

I am convinced that only four-and-a-half years after the radical reform of the Human Rights Convention mechanism implemented by Protocol no. 11, which replaced the two original institutions with a single judicial body, the system is in further need of a major overhaul. This is why we should now be looking for a mechanism, first, for the expeditious and cheap disposal of applications that do not satisfy the admissibility requirements. Since the ECHR at present declares 92 per cent of all applications inadmissible, it is imperative that the introduction of a filtering mechanism in the early stages of the procedure should be studied closely. Second, such a mechanism should also relieve the court of routine, manifestly well-founded cases and particularly repetitive cases where a structural violation in the state concerned has already been identified. The obligation for a respondent state arising from a finding of a violation of the Human Rights Convention is the elimination of the causes of the violation in order to prevent its repetition. Therefore, subsequent applications whose complaint derives from the same circumstances should be seen as a problem of execution. This is particularly true of violations of a "structural" nature.[21] Once the ECHR has established the existence of a structural violation or an administrative practice, is the general purpose of raising the level of human rights protection in the state concerned really served by continuing to issue judgments establishing the same violation? In this case, we see the conflict between general interest and individual justice at its clearest. If individual justice is the primary objective of the convention system, then in the situation described earlier the court must obviously continue to give judgments so as to be able to award compensation to the individual victim. Yet if we look at the scheme for just satisfaction set up by the Human Rights Convention under Article 41, we can see that it hardly supports the individual justice theory. To begin with, it is discretionary since the court is to award satisfaction "if necessary." The court's case law shows that it is indeed not the automatic consequence of a finding of violation. Hence, the court's well-established practice of holding in appropriate cases that a finding of a violation constitutes in itself

---

[21] See *Botazzi* v. *Italy*, July 28, 1999, Eur. Ct. H.R. (1999-V).

sufficient just satisfaction.[22] This is surely also an indication of the "public-policy" nature of the system.

Let us take a concrete example. The ECHR found, as I have said, a violation of Article 3 prohibiting inhuman and degrading treatment with respect to prison conditions in Russia.[23] The evidence adduced by the government itself indicated that this situation was widespread throughout the state concerned. It has to be asked whether there would be a great deal of sense in the court's processing the potentially tens of thousands of applications brought by detainees in similar conditions? Would the award of substantial compensation on an individual basis, always supposing that the court was able to deal with the cases concerned, hasten the resolution of the problem or contribute to the elimination of the causes of the original violation? Very probably not, particularly if one of the causes of the problem in the first place was a lack of funding. At the same time, it would undermine the credibility of the ECHR if it were to continue to issue findings of violations with no apparent effect. The inflow of thousands of same-issue cases would clog up the system almost irremediably. This state of affairs might lead to judgments delivered five or more years after the lodging of the application. Not only is this sort of delay hardly acceptable, it also complicates the execution process because governments can claim that the situation represented in the judgment no longer reflects the reality. I cite prison conditions, but the same problem could, indeed undoubtedly will, arise in relation to structural dysfunction in the operation of legal systems in some contracting states. We have already had a foretaste of this situation with the length of proceedings in Italy. We now realise that about half the contracting states have problems with the length of judicial proceedings. We also know that in many of them there are grave difficulties with respect to the non-execution of final and binding judicial decisions.

It follows that this type of problem should be regarded as part of the process of execution. The ECHR should hand down a few "pilot" judgments and should transmit these judgments to the Committee of Ministers of the Council of Europe. The committee should then ask the respective state or states not only to proceed to make the legislative changes in order to resolve the structural

---

[22] The first time this formula was used was in *Golder* v. *United Kingdom*, February 21, 1975, Eur. Ct. H.R. (Series A No. 18) It was recently confirmed in *Kingsley* v. *United Kingdom*, May 28, 2002, Eur. Ct. H.R. at 177 (2002), no. 36605/97 Eur. Ct. H.R. (2000-IV).

[23] *Kalashnikov, supra* note 18.

problem but also to introduce effective remedies in domestic law in favour of the victims of the structural deficiencies found by the court. The process of execution of the ECHR's judgments in such cases should moreover not be solely "condemnatory." Once a structural problem has been identified, if the governments are serious about raising the standard of human rights throughout Europe, then they must ensure that the Council of Europe is in a position to assist the state concerned to resolve it, in particular, by providing expert advice as well as judicial or police training schemes. In other words, I believe that we need to look again not just at the way the court operates but also at the whole Human Rights Convention system, particularly the approach to execution. The emphasis should be not only on the pressure to be exerted on the respondent state but also, where appropriate, on the necessary assistance to deal with the problem raised by the judgment.

It therefore seems to me that the way forward is to make it possible for the ECHR to concentrate its efforts on decisions of "principle" — decisions that create jurisprudence. This would also be the best means of ensuring that the common minimum standards are maintained across Europe. The lowering of standards is often cited in European Union circles as a potential consequence of the enlargement of the Council of Europe. An examination of the cases decided over the last four years belies this fear. Yet there is a risk in the longer term — a risk that can be avoided if the court adheres to a more "constitutional" role, as I have advocated. With many thousands of applications being brought annually before the court, the right of individual application will in practice be in any event endangered by the material impossibility of processing them in anything like a reasonable timeframe. Will we really be able to claim that with 38,000 cases a year, full, effective access can be guaranteed? Is it not better to take a more realistic approach to the problem and preserve the essence of the system, in conformity with its fundamental objective? The individual application would then be seen as a means to an end rather than as an end in itself — as a magnifying glass that reveals the imperfections in national legal systems and as the thermometer that tests the democratic temperature of the states. Is it not better for there to be fewer judgments, yet ones that are promptly delivered and extensively reasoned and that establish the jurisprudential principles with a compelling clarity that will render them *de facto* binding *erga omnes*? At the same time, they would reveal the structural problems that undermine democracy and the rule of law in parts of Europe.

GOAL OF THE CONVENTION SYSTEM

The latter remarks bring me back to my opening comment about the fundamental goal of the Human Rights Convention system. This system will never provide an adequate substitute for effective human rights protection at the national level — it has to be complementary to such protection. It should come into play where the national protection breaks down. However, it cannot wholly replace national protection or even one area of national protection. While it is true that the convention is primarily concerned with individuals, it is not only concerned with the tiny proportion of the individuals subject to its jurisdiction who actually bring their cases to Strasbourg (and it will never be more than a tiny proportion). As long as we remain too wedded to the idea of purely individual justice, we actually make it more difficult for the system to protect a greater number.

It is a privilege to preside over a court that is perhaps the most successful emanation of international justice so far. It is important for the international community as a whole that it remains a model for a truly effective international system of human rights protection, which is why all those concerned must work towards ensuring that it can face up to the challenges of the new century.

Sommaire

La Cour européenne des droits de l'homme

La Cour européenne des droits de l'homme a pour but de créer une situation qui permette aux individus d'obtenir la protection réelle de leurs droits dans leurs systèmes juridiques nationaux. Partant de là, l'auteur passe en revue l'évolution du droit dans la jurisprudence récente de cette Cour en matière de l'interprétation des dispositions de la Convention, du rôle du partage des pouvoirs en matière de la protection des libertés garanties par la Convention et de la notion de la dignité humaine dans le cadre de la Convention. L'auteur constate le volume croissant de dossiers devant la Cour et le besoin d'une réforme, puis conclut que le système européen est le système international le plus efficace à ce jour pour assurer la protection des droits de la personne.

Summary

European Court of Human Rights

The aim of the European Court of Human Rights is to bring about a situation in which individuals are able to get effective guarantees of their rights within their national legal systems. With this in mind, the author reviews some of the recent developments in cases before the court relating to evolutionary interpretation of the provisions of the convention, the role of the separation of powers in ensuring the protection of freedoms under the Convention for the Protection of Human Rights and Fundamental Freedoms, and the notion of human dignity within the convention framework. The author also considers the growing case load before the court and the need for reform and concludes by pointing out that the European system is the most effective international system yet for securing human rights protection.

A Look Back at Looking Forward: Ronald St. John Macdonald and the Future of International Law

CHI CARMODY

INTRODUCTION

In May 1973, an article entitled "International Law and Society in the Year 2000" appeared in the *Canadian Bar Review*.[1] The article was written by Ronald St. John Macdonald, Gerald Morris, and Douglas Johnson and was published in a two-part series devoted to law and the legal profession in the twenty-first century. It attempted to paint a portrait of what international law would look like three decades into the future.

In sum, Macdonald and his collaborators forecasted with remarkable accuracy the course of future trends and identified many of the tensions that would underlie the international law of the future. "International Law and Society in the Year 2000" grapples with some important issues that continue to confront international law today: who are its actors, what role do they play, and what is the cumulative impact of these developments on the theory and practice of international law? The authors correctly foresaw that international law would evolve in a more complex and contested world, one where international law had reached "a stage of parametric stress" and where "fundamental concepts could no longer accommodate the dynamics of change inherent in the problems they purported to treat."[2] It would be a world where the collision

Chi Carmody is an assistant professor in the Faculty of Law at the University of Western Ontario in London, Ontario. The author would like to thank the University of Western Ontario Faculty of Law for making attendance at the Halifax symposium possible, and Robert Druzeta and Marianne Welch for their research assistance.

[1] Ronald St. John Macdonald, Gerald Morris et al., "International Law and Society in the Year 2000" (1973) 51 Can. Bar Rev. 316.

[2] *Ibid.* at 332.

of actors, interests, and resources would have to be adjusted and reconciled.

The underlying tone of the article is grim and antagonistic, one that is more reminiscent of revolutionary Europe in the 1840s than of a comfortable Canada in the 1970s. Macdonald and his co-authors did not say exactly what the ultimate source of conflict would be, but in an almost Malthusian way they predicted that environmental depletion would play a major role in hastening change in international law. In this challenging milieu, "[i]t will be demanded of international law ... that it divest itself of its empty abstractions" and that "polemical debates will be waged over the relative utility of statist fictions."[3]

As unsettling as these observations may be, they are perhaps more a reflection on the general state of affairs in the world in 1973 than of humanity's ability to solve diverse problems through international law. In later work, Macdonald took a sunnier view, but he and his co-authors never recanted what was set out in "International Law and Society in the Year 2000." Looking around us today we can say that if Macdonald and his co-authors were mistaken about some of the particulars, they were definitely right to predict the multiplication of actors, the growing diversity of sources, and the expanded coverage of international law. More particularly, they were correct in their assessment that environmental concerns — as opposed to the more evident military, humanitarian, or criminal ones — would be the principal catalyst for change in times to come. A look back at Macdonald's article therefore offers a valuable retrospective on current developments in international law and helps to frame his question in our time: how will international law evolve from here?

It is worthwhile observing that "International Law and Society in the Year 2000" is far from the only place where Ronald St. John Macdonald cast an eye to the future. The future is, in fact, an abiding theme throughout his work.[4] While the broad range of

---

[3] *Ibid.*

[4] Even in efforts that were essentially retrospective in nature, such as an article from about the same time entitled "An Historical Introduction to the Teaching of International Law in Canada," there is evidence of a Janus-like gaze simultaneously backwards and forward. In this instance, Macdonald examined the way in which international law as a subject was transmitted in Canada. He provided careful detail about teaching curricula, the backgrounds of those who taught international law and their intellectual commitment to the subject as evidenced from their writings, all as if to pose the implicit question: "How was it done in the past so that we can do it better in the future?" *See* R. St J. Macdonald,

Macdonald's own writings reveal him to be a person deeply committed to international law in all of its temporal dimensions, his return again and again to visions of the future distinguish him as a theorist and guide. "International Law and Society in the Year 2000" is perhaps his most direct vision of international law's future and, in this sense, is a useful place to begin an assessment of his views and of our own.

CANADA AND THE WORLD IN 1973

To be interested in international law is to be interested in the world, and so it is useful to recall something of the world in which "International Law and Society in the Year 2000" first appeared.[5] Canada in the early 1970s was a country of twenty-two million people, with a per capita annual income of about $17,000, nearing the end of its Trudeauvian summer of love. The invocation of the War Measures Act[6] lay behind, wage and price controls were ahead. A bestselling Canadian single of the time was *Seasons in the Sun* by Terry Jacks, but there were also the provocative ideas of Northrop Frye and Marshall McLuhan, the compelling fiction of Antonine Maillet and Margaret Atwood, and the arresting forms of Arthur Erickson, Moshe Safdie, and Douglas Cardinal, all to be proud of. Together they offered an array of new and distinct possibilities — of many cultures in a different voice.

It may be hard to believe in our own era of globalization, but in 1973 Canada's federal government was preparing for a foreign investment review and the nationalization of key resource industries. It had also enunciated a "Third Option" in trade relations to wean Canada away from its dependence upon the United States. Likewise in external affairs, the government had conducted a

---

An Historical Introduction to the Teaching of International Law in Canada (1974) 12 Can. Y.B. Int'l L. 67. For other references to the future in his work, see R. St. J. Macdonald, "Future Generations: Searching for a System of Protection" in Emmanuel Agius and Salvino Busuttil, eds., Future Generations and International Law (1998) 149.

[5] Although 1973 was not so very long ago, it was a different time. It was still an era when a federal deputy minister had the luxury of time to write an article for the *Canadian Bar Review*'s pages and when the typical contributor was often white and usually male. See A.E. Gottlieb, "Some Social and Legal Implications of New Technology: The Impact of Communications and Computers" (1973) 51 Can. Bar Rev. 246.

[6] War Measures Act, R.S.C. 1970, c. W-2, repealed R.S.C. 1985, c. 22 (4th Supp.), s. 80.

review of Canada's foreign relations and decided that new international realities demanded an independent foreign policy. Canadian leadership in the Commonwealth facilitated good relations with many newly independent countries and there was still talk of an "Ottawa-Delhi Axis."

A purely domestic perspective might have suggested that all was well, but, in fact, there were serious problems abroad. To any observer of international affairs, the greatest threat at that time was the ongoing confrontation between capitalism and Communism. Today, it is difficult to recall or take seriously the perception in many Western countries at that time that Communism was advancing and might soon make serious gains. Yet from the perspective of 1973, Communism seemed to be on the move.[7] A revolution in Lisbon in April of the following year would lead to the collapse of Portugal's centuries-old empire and to apparent victories for communists in Mozambique and Angola. Ethiopia followed a few months later, and Cambodia and South Vietnam soon thereafter.

A number of countries were working at the time to diffuse tensions between East and West. President Richard Nixon himself had visited Beijing in December 1972. The members of the Non-Aligned Movement were particularly active. In October 1970, they worked to secure passage in the United Nations General Assembly of the Declaration on Principles of International Law Concerning Friendly Relations and Co-operation among States[8] and, in December 1974, the Resolution on the Definition of Aggression.[9] In light of these efforts, it would not be unnatural for a person like Ronald St. John Macdonald to see international law at that time as the product of a global confrontation between polar opposites and as a balance of power wherein existing rights were jealously guarded and carefully preserved.

However, another, and in many ways more profound, confrontation was then brewing that was to inform Macdonald's thinking.

[7] From the vantage point of 1973, it would have been hard to tell that socialism in its ideologic and political sense would be virtually eliminated as a source of international law and reduced in practice to a few outposts. See Gregory I. Tunkin, ed., *International Law: A Textbook* (1986).

[8] Declaration on Principles of International Law Concerning Friendly Relations and Co-operation among States, UN General Assembly [hereinafter GA] Resolution 2625 (XXV), UN GAOR, 25th Sess., Supp. No. 28, at 121, UN Doc. A/8028 (1971).

[9] Resolution on the Definition of Aggression, UNGA Resolution 3314 (XXXIX), UN GAOR, 29th Sess., Supp. No. 31, at 142, UN Doc. A/0631 (1975).

Through the still-new medium of television the world had come face-to-face for the first time with a large-scale humanitarian emergency during the Biafran War. In 1971, a similar emergency occurred during the Indo-Pakistani War that led to the independence of Bangladesh. Out of these horrifying circumstances, Thomas Franck and others debated the merits of humanitarian intervention — not a new idea, but one that provoked renewed controversy and remains very much alive today.[10] The emergencies in Biafra and Bangladesh were closely linked to resource depletion and underscored the fragility of the natural environment to sustain human life. They helped put into question the quality of human life, not so much in material, as in environmental, terms. This understanding was broadly consonant with the nascent eco-consciousness of the era, as evident in the Club of Rome's conclusions on the limits to growth and the Stockholm Declaration's reference to the then-new concept of sustainable development.[11]

INTERNATIONAL LAW AND SOCIETY IN THE YEAR 2000

Into this world of tranquility at home and turmoil abroad came Ronald St. John Macdonald's article. The authors made clear that their reference to the year 2000 was approximate. In no way did they claim absolute accuracy, although they described many developments that have since come to pass. The article predicted, for instance, that

[t]he year 2000 will see extraordinary variety in form and substance among the participants in the international policy-making process. Decentralized

---

[10] Thomas M. Franck and Nigel S. Rodley, "After Bangladesh: The Law of Humanitarian Intervention by Military Force" (1973) 67 Am. J. Int'l L. 275. For more recent commentary, see Louis Henkin, "Kosovo and the Law of 'Humanitarian Intervention'" (1999) 93 Am. J. Int'l. L. 824; Richard A. Falk, "Kosovo, World Order, and the Future of International Law" (1999) 93 Am. J. Int'l L. 847; Thomas M. Franck, "Lessons of Kosovo" (1999) 93 Am. J. Int'l L. 857; and Bruno Simma, "NATO, the UN and the Use of Force: Legal Aspects" (1999) 10 Eur. J. Int'l L. 1.

[11] The Club of Rome's conclusions in *The Limits to Growth* (1972) were to stress the importance of the environment and its essential links with population and energy. In June 1972, the first UN Conference on the Environment adopted the Stockholm Declaration on the Human Environment, UN Doc. A/Conf.48/14/rev.1 (UN Pub. E 73, IIA. 14) (1973), which referred to humanity's "solemn responsibility to protect and improve the environment for present and future generations" — a phrase commonly regarded as the first multilateral expression of the concept of sustainable development.

states, centralized states, blocs of states, mini-states, shell states, international organizations, land-based cities, off-shore cities, international recreation and conservation zones, and various associations of individuals and groups of individuals will be familiar actors in a system that will be characterized by the complexity and diversity of its sub-systems.[12]

One could take a considerable portion of what was said in this quotation to be a reasonably accurate description of current conditions. The authors offer no explanation about *why* this explosion of actors would take place, but it is logical to assume that they believed that technology would empower individuals with a new sense of possibility — the same sense of possibility that Macdonald and his colleagues must have seen as they looked around themselves at Canadian society in 1973. The article went on to forecast that

[t]echnology will be ready to create new communities in underwater and lunar resettlement centers, whose interests will have to be represented in still another form. There will be an extensive network of overlapping jurisdictions, each of which will be recognized as vested with prescriptive or contractual rights of its own. The heterogeneity of the participants will bring about a fundamental incoherence in the present system.[13]

For Macdonald and his co-authors, the outcome of this florescence of actors would be a state that would "speak with many voices."[14] There would be endemic conflict between higher and lower authority, with the outcome often decided "more frequently in favour of the latter."[15] Central governments would be reduced "to the role of mediators between semi-independent sectors of the political process."[16] Furthermore, "sentiments of loyalty will not coincide with national boundaries and the nation state will resemble more closely the incipient nation of the late middle ages instead of the developed state of the nineteenth century."[17] The complexity of the evolving scene forced Macdonald and his co-writers to conclude tentatively that

[i]n our view the increased erosion of state authority, the rise of diverse new actors, and the proliferation of inter-connected principles, regulations and procedures will mean that the inter-state system will be inadequate to the dynamics of the tasks at hand. We foresee a world so diversified

[12] Macdonald et al., *supra* note 1 at 317.

[13] *Ibid.*

[14] *Ibid.* at 318.

[15] *Ibid.*

[16] *Ibid.*

[17] *Ibid.*

as regards actors and activities as to make it unreasonable to expect the emergence of a single, universal, all-purpose, ordering system. We believe that there will emerge a variety of ordering systems, some more special-ized than others, each with its own built-in techniques for correcting disturbances, ironing out deviations, and keeping the system operationally normal. The speciality of these systems will make the task of coordination exceedingly difficult.[18]

When we consider the many sub-systems of international law today — the revived Central American Court of Justice, the International Criminal Court, the Court of Justice of the Common Market for Eastern and Southern Africa to name a few recent ones — we real-ize that the astonishing array of actors that Macdonald and his col-leagues foresaw has, in fact, come true.

But how would all of this diversity be handled? How would it be guided and shaped? This important managerial question, which Macdonald and his co-authors considered, would be answered in part by the development of an international technocracy and counter-development of what they termed "inter-populism." By the year 2000, they foresaw that a bewildering number of intergovern-mental agencies would have come into existence, "each striving for super-efficiency not so much in terms of larger budgetary allocations as in terms of easier access to the most sophisticated computers in regional and global data centers."[19] These agencies would be staffed by a highly trained cadre of international lawyers skilled in "tech-nologic areas of international law," whose chief function would be to argue legal issues against government and corporate advocates.

Of course, to argue presumes a forum, but Macdonald and his colleagues did not stop to speculate about *where* the disputes of the future would be heard. Instead, they went on to describe the counter trend of "inter-populism." This development would take the form of a "new coalition of anti-statist, anti-bureaucratic, anti-technological, environmental and minority groups" who come to "a consensus ... that the concept of the 'supremacy of the people' should be translated transnationally into institutional form." Mac-donald and his colleagues foresaw this would lead to the crea-tion of a "People's Assembly." In theory, this body "would have a higher order of authority than the General Assembly of the United Nations."[20]

---

[18] *Ibid.* at 320.

[19] Macdonald et al., *supra* note 1 at 321.

[20] *Ibid.* at 322.

The article gave no details about how the People's Assembly would trump the General Assembly. Yet what we are witnessing today in the phenomenon of "instant treaties" — that is, international arrangements in which the participation of civil society is motivating and sustaining and where action is relatively swift[21] — is the coming together of diverse coalitions on leading international issues that governments are evidently struggling to manage. There is a new popular energy and dynamism that is changing the landscape of international law in profound, and from the viewpoint of only a few years ago, astonishing, ways that are broadly consonant with the mass activism that Macdonald predicted.

At the same time, it remains clear that the establishment of a true "People's Assembly" is some ways off. Civil society does not yet seek to subsume the nation state. It remains instigative and additive, giving direction and helping to shape international negotiations. Beyond a few, very tentative, steps in the direction of a "People's Assembly," there is little to show in the nature of such an institution right now. The United Nations is not a world government and other initiatives, such as the Porto Alegre counter-summit to the annual World Economic Forum in Davos or proposals to establish an oversight body of parliamentarians to supervise the World Trade Organization (WTO), have yet to mature.

Macdonald also mistook the United Nations of the future, which he foresaw would be the subject of general criticism "as a statist, bureaucracy-ridden, computer-bound, growth-minded and majority-oriented organization."[22] While the UN may have tended in that direction in 1973, today there is a cautious sense that it is remaking itself into a more nimble, focused organization even if it cannot do all that the words Charter of the United Nations (UN Charter) imply that it should.[23] As we look back, indeed, the more considered view must be to appreciate the immensely useful work that the UN has accomplished or encouraged in so many fields. There have been some mistakes in its operations, but the general trend of the

---

[21] One could think of the following examples: the Convention on the Prohibition of the Use, Stockpiling, Production and Transfer of Anti-Personnel Mines and on Their Destruction, 36 I.L.M. 1507 (1997), the Rome Statute of the International Criminal Court, 37 I.L.M. 999 (1998), the Cartagena Protocol on Biosafety to the Convention on Biological Diversity, 39 I.L.M. 1027 (2000), and the Framework Convention for Tobacco Control, 42 I.L.M. 518 (2003).

[22] Macdonald et al., *supra* note 1 at 322.

[23] Charter of the United Nations, June, 26 1945, Can. T.S. 1945 No. 7 (in force October, 24, 1945) [hereinafter UN Charter].

UN's work has been highly positive. One needs only to contrast the worldwide depression in the 1930s with the coordinated institutional response to the economic "meltdown" that occurred in several countries in the late 1990s to realize just how much the UN and its affiliates have achieved.[24]

However, if Macdonald and his colleagues saw the UN differently than we do, they did so, in part, because they did not forecast the demise of Communism, the end of the Soviet empire, and the pressures and possibilities for the UN that have arisen as a result. Undoubtedly, such a prediction would have been difficult to make in 1973.

What Macdonald did foresee most presciently was the threat of environmental degradation. He and his colleagues forecasted that "[a]s the year 2000 approaches, a radical, novel claim to living space will become a major source of stress between traditional concepts of the sovereign nation state and the growing concept of transnationalism."[25] They predicted that this claim would be prompted by the ever-expanding notions of equity and egalitarianism. Macdonald and his co-authors reasoned as follows:

The logic of the right to equal living space follows from existing general acceptance (in theory, if not always in practice) that discrimination based on race or place of origin is unacceptable; that individuals everywhere should be entitled to comparable economic and social opportunities; and, more recently, that everyone can reasonably expect to live his life in an adequate environment.[26]

Macdonald and his colleagues also foresaw that there would be claims for space:

[T]he equal space concept is a separate principle which emphasizes the right of an over-crowded state to thin out its population through transnational migration and the corresponding obligation of states with demonstrable absorbtive capacity to accept such migrants with only minimal selective restrictions.[27]

---

[24] The collapse of the Thai currency in July 1997 provoked a financial crisis in several countries in southeast Asia, Russia, and South America that prompted the International Monetary Fund [hereinafter IMF] to provide substantial assistance to countries in trouble in the form of reserve lending and to propose the creation of a new financial architecture. Later, coordinated IMF and World Bank action is generally credited with staving off the worst effects of monetary collapse. See Joseph J. Norton, "A 'New International Financial Architecture?' — Reflections on the Possible Law-Based Dimension" (1999) 33 Int'l Law 891.

[25] Macdonald et al., *supra* note 1 at 325.

[26] *Ibid.* at 325.

[27] *Ibid.* at 326.

While it is true that living space has given rise to international conflict in a few selected instances — Rwanda and several island states being examples[28] — it is the broader phenomenon of environmental stress that more immediately faces human beings everywhere today. In retrospect, the error of Macdonald and his co-authors was to equate rights that are based on inherent characteristics, namely that of race and place of origin, with the right to living space, which is more abstract. So far we have not witnessed the pressure that Macdonald and his colleagues foresaw in any generalized degree. True, there have been selected instances of foreigners crammed aboard "mystery ships" running aground on Canada's shores, the antagonistic relationship of the Australian government with detained migrants, and the horrific event of illegal Chinese immigrants being found dead in a refrigerated container in Britain in June 2000. All of these might appear to confirm Macdonald's views. But to date, population pressure is a more limited problem than he predicted. What Macdonald did foretell with great accuracy was that the real locus of new concerns generally would be with an "adequate environment." In the first decade of the twenty-first century, this preoccupation is more central and pressing, particularly since we live in and share a carbon-constrained environment.

THE FUTURE OF INTERNATIONAL LAW: FOUR ISSUES

With this background in mind, we can now consider how what was said in 1973 is relevant to the future of international law today. One can infer much from the scenarios that Macdonald and his colleagues described, but they offered little substantive detail. For reasons of space, Macdonald and his colleagues were forced to be highly selective in anticipating the impact of developments on legal theory and practice. They did, however, recognize that the future would pose "basic questions ... respecting the concepts of sovereignty and territorial jurisdiction when the world community is no longer controlled by an exclusive club of nations and when the horizontal flow of transnational activity (including migration) challenges the meaning of national boundaries."[29]

---

[28] William A. Plummer, "The Big Push: Emigration in the Age of Environmental Catastrophe" (1996) 4 Ind. J. Global Legal Stud. 231; Jessica B. Cooper, "Environmental Refugees: Meeting the Requirements of the Refugee Definition" (1998) 6 N.Y.U. Envt'l L.J. 480; and RoseMary Reed, "Rising Seas and Disappearing Islands: Can Island Inhabitants Seek Redress under the Alien Tort Claims Act?" (2002) 11 Pac. Rim L. & Pol'y J. 399.

[29] *Ibid.* at 330.

It is useful to compare Macdonald's view on the future of international law with others who have written closer to our own time. What is interesting about commentators such as Edith Brown Weiss and Philippe Sands is that their views are very similar to Macdonald's. All refer to globalization, technologic innovation, democracy, and market forces as features shaping international law.[30] What we must address are the underlying substantive questions. How will the parts of this new, and increasingly varied, international regime interact? What sort of law will they produce together? In this connection, we can ask what will be the nature and texture of international law in the future? What are the substantive ramifications of the changes that are occurring? It is important to point out that Macdonald and his colleagues were not blind to these questions. For instance, they too predicted that the task of coordination would be "exceedingly difficult."[31] However, such issues were less proximate to them, and the foregoing queries would have appeared less immediate and compelling. For us, on the other hand, they are the important questions and the ones that we must attempt to answer in discerning the future of international law.

For us, a central issue must be the problem of coherence. The growing number of actors has created a "proliferation" of systems and institutions of international law with the possibility of conflict.[32] At the same time, the mechanism of international law does not yet work so smoothly as Macdonald might have foreseen. After all, his article refers to "interlocking bureaucracies" of technocrats,[33] but it is clear that the various systems of international law are not yet wholly integrated. The disparate parts may create conflict and place a premium on principles of coherence. Traditional

---

[30] See Edith Brown Weiss, "The Rise of the Fall of International Law" (2000) 69 Fordham L. Rev. 345; and Philippe Sands, "Turtles and Torturers: The Transformation of International Law" (2001) 33 N.Y.U. J. Int'l L. & Pol. 527.

[31] "We believe that there will emerge a variety of ordering systems, some more specialized than others, each with its own built-in techniques for correcting disturbances, ironing out deviations, and keeping the system operationally normal. The speciality of these systems will make the task of coordination exceedingly difficult." MacDonald et al., *supra* note 1 at 320. The lack of attention to these issues may also be due, in part, to Macdonald's vision of a People's Assembly, which might have provided an apparatus for resolving issues of conflict between different subsystems of international law.

[32] Laurence Boisson de Chazournes, *Implications of the Proliferation of International Adjudicatory Bodies for Dispute Resolution* (1995); and Niels Blokker and Henry G. Schermers, eds., *Proliferation of International Organizations: Legal Issues* (2001).

[33] Macdonald et al., *supra* note 1 at 321.

thinking would appear to accord the UN Charter a kind of foundational or entrenched status, with the ability of the Security Council or the General Assembly to override decisions of other institutions in some instances.[34] However, this is not always the case, and, moreover, it runs counter to the practice of international law as coordinate and essentially non-hierarchical in nature. For instance, there remains the delicate question raised in the International Court of Justice's (ICJ) *Questions of Interpretation and Application of the 1971 Montreal Convention Arising from the Aerial Incident at Lockerbie (Libyan Arab Jamahiriya* v. *United States of America; Libyan Arab Jamahiriya* v. *United Kingdom)*[35] decision regarding the Security Council's relationship with the Court: which is primate?[36]

Conflict elsewhere in the expanding galaxy of international law also puts a certain emphasis on questions of characterization. If the jurisdiction of international institutions is founded on constitutive instruments and self-determinations of their own competence, does it not then become supremely important to take account of the optic through which one sees a problem? Is it economic, or environmental, or human rights-based in some degree? In short, the preliminary question of jurisdiction — which we refer to in Canadian constitutional law as "pith and substance" — becomes key. Take, for instance, the request by Ireland in December 2001 for provisional measures from the International Tribunal for the Law of the Sea to stop Britain from operating a mixed oxide plant at Sellafield in Cumbria.[37] Ireland's contention was that the transport

---

34 See, for instance, Article 103 of the UN Charter, *supra* note 23, which states that "[i]n the event of a conflict between the obligations of the Members of the United Nations under the present Charter and their obligations under any other international agreement, their obligations under the present Charter shall prevail."

35 *Questions of Interpretation and Application of the 1971 Montreal Convention Arising from the Aerial Incident at Lockerbie (Libyan Arab Jamahiriya* v. *United States of America; Libyan Arab Jamahiriya* v. *United Kingdom), Provisional Measures, Order of April 14, 1992,* [1992] I.C.J. Rep. 114.

36 Thomas M. Franck, "The 'Powers of Appreciation': Who Is the Ultimate Guardian of U.N. Legality?" (1992) 86 Am. J. Int'l L. 519.

37 *The MOX Plant Case (Ireland* v. *United Kingdom), Provisional Measures,* ITLOS Case no. 10 (2001) [hereinafter *MOX Plant* case]. The case involves the transportation to Sellafield of spent uranium fuel rods, which are reprocessed in order to separate the useful fuel for recycling from the waste. Recovered plutonium can be combined with uranium and turned into a mixed-oxide fuel referred to as "MOX" for use in certain reactors. The owner of the Sellafield plant, British Nuclear Fuels, estimates that each six-gram MOX pellet holds the equivalent energy of

of spent uranium to the plant would raise the risk of marine collision and the plant's eventual operation would irrevocably pollute
the Irish Sea. The counter-argument asserted by the United Kingdom was that the Tribunal lacked jurisdiction since certain aspects
of the Irish complaint were governed by the Treaty of Rome (EC
Treaty)[38] relating to the movement of goods, by the Euratom
Treaty[39] regarding the treatment and disposal of nuclear waste, and
by Ireland's prior submission of a complaint to arbitration under
the Convention for the Protection of the Marine Environment of
the North-East Atlantic.[40] The Tribunal ultimately decided that
because the parties had agreed to arbitration under the 1982 Convention on the Law of the Sea[41] it had sufficient jurisdiction to grant
provisional relief.[42]

There are many other examples that one could think of to illustrate the potential "collision" of international tribunals. In the
future, decisions with disparate elements — of trade and the environment, of sovereignty and human rights — will have to be adjudicated. Equally problematic is the muscular assertion of jurisdiction
at the national level, which was attempted with notoriety in *R.* v. *Bow
Street Metropolitan Stipendiary Magistrate ex parte Pinochet Ugartge*[43]

---

one ton of coal. Three pellets can provide a family's domestic energy needs for
a year. See *Q&A: Sellafield's Mox Plant* BBC (November 8, 2001), available at
<http://news.bbc.co.uk/hi/english/uk/newsid_1643000/1643435.stm>.

[38] Treaty of Rome (renamed the Treaty Establishing the European Community),
1992 O.J. (C 224) 1 (1992), [1992] 1 C.M.L.R. 573 (1992).

[39] Treaty Establishing the European Atomic Community, March 25, 1957, 298
U.N.T.S. 167.

[40] Convention for the Protection of the Marine Environment of the North-East
Atlantic, 32 I.L.M. 1069 (1993).

[41] Convention on the Law of the Sea, 21 I.L.M. 1261 (1982) [hereinafter LOSC].

[42] The Tribunal decided that "since the dispute before the Annex VII arbitral tribunal concerns the interpretation or application of the Convention and no
other agreement, only the dispute settlement procedures under the Convention
are relevant to that dispute" (*MOX Plant* case, *supra* note 37, Order of December
3, 2001, para. 52). The Tribunal did not find that the urgency of the situation
required the prescription of the provisional measures requested by Ireland
(principally, prevention of the operation of the plant), but went on to indicate
that prudence and caution required the two countries to cooperate in exchang-
ing information concerning risks or effects of the operation of the MOX plant
and in devising ways to deal with them.

[43] *R.* v. *Bow Street Metropolitan Stipendiary Magistrate ex parte Pinochet Ugarte*, [1999] 2
W.L.R. 827.

and which was dealt with more recently by the ICJ in *Arrest Warrant of 11 April 2000 (Democratic Republic of the Congo v. Belgium).*[44]

Current affairs therefore make clear that international law does not yet work with the instrumental coherence that Macdonald in some cases assumed. Secondary rules will have to be developed to ensure integrity and consistency in decision-making. It may also be that institutions will be forced to develop self-definitions of their own expertise that tie them squarely to a particular competence. The Appellate Body of the WTO has already made clear, for example, that WTO dispute settlement focuses on the interpretation of the Marrakesh Agreement Establishing the World Trade Organization and that other sources of international law are supplementary interpretative aids to that dominant task.[45] Nevertheless, all of the care invested in circumscribing jurisdiction will still not insulate international tribunals from the charge that they are adjudicating matters that are in reality often multi-faceted and beyond their competence.[46] The development of theories of deference now featured

---

44 *Case Concerning the Arrest Warrant of 11 April 2000 (Democratic Republic of the Congo v. Belgium)*, February 14, 2002 (Judgment), (2000) 41 I.L.M. 536, accessible at <http://www.icj-cij.org/icjwww/idocket/iCOBE/iCOBEframe.htm>.

45 Marrakesh Agreement Establishing the World Trade Organization, 33 I.L.M. 15 (1994) [hereinafter WTO Agreement]. Thus, Article 3.2 of the WTO Dispute Settlement Understanding, 33 I.L.M. 1125 (1994), describes the role of the WTO dispute settlement as being "to preserve the rights and obligations of [WTO] Members under the covered agreements, and to *clarify* the existing provisions of those agreements in accordance with customary rules of interpretation of public international law" [emphasis added]. An example of this treaty-specific focus arose in *United States – Import Prohibition of Shrimp and Shrimp Products*, WTO Doc. WT/DS58/AB/R (1998), where the Appellate Body interpreted the treaty term "exhaustible natural resources" found in Article XX(g) of the WTO Agreement "in the light of contemporary concerns of the community of nations about the protection and conservation of the environment," citing to the LOSC, *supra* note 41, the Convention on Biological Diversity, 31 I.L.M. 818 (1992), and the Convention on the Conservation of Migratory Species of Wild Animals, 19 I.L.M. 15 (1980).

46 In this respect, it is interesting to note party arguments about the limits of party jurisdiction. In the *MOX Plant* case, for instance, *supra* note 37, Ireland argued that a reason for the tribunal's appropriateness was that "neither the OSPAR arbitral tribunal nor the Court of Justice of the European Communities would have jurisdiction that extends to all of the matters in the dispute before the Annex VII arbitral tribunal [under the LOSC, *supra* note 41]" (*Mox Plant* case, Order of December 3, 2001, para. 46). In other words, the extent of jurisdiction was pre-determined by the breadth of jurisdiction. Ireland also argued that other jurisdictions were cumulative, supplementary to the 1982 LOSC, and invoked the principle that "the application of international law rules on interpretation of

in the administrative law of domestic systems may provide a possible response to this criticism.[47]

In the global search for coherence and consistency, a second issue will be the role of precedent. We know that Article 59 of the Statute of the International Court of Justice provides that "the decision of the Court has no binding force except between the parties and in respect of that particular case."[48] We are also aware that, despite this and other iterations, international decisions *do* have an inevitable tendency to create legitimate expectations, if not for judges and lawyers who deal with international law, then for the global public that will be dissatisfied with perennial rationalizations of reasoning on a "case-by-case" basis. Moreover, in the future there will be growing pressure for tribunals in similar situations to come to the same results — for the Inter-American Court of Human Rights, for instance, to follow the lead of its European counterpart, and vice versa[49] — and with it like pressure on judges and advocates to demonstrate why this precedent may, or may not, be appropriate.

A third issue, and one that is directly related to technological advances and the ease of communication today, is the impact of the rapid dissemination of information on international law. The Internet has become the medium of choice, and, with it, there has been a rallying around international issues that gain almost instant prominence. One can think of the Millenial Debt Relief campaign[50]

---

treaties to identical or similar provisions of different treaties may not yield the same results, having regard to, *inter alia*, differences in the respective contexts, objects and purposes, subsequent practice of parties and *travaux préparatoires*" (*ibid.* at paras. 45-52).

[47] In the Canadian context, this is developed in *C.U.P.E., Local 963* v. *New Brunswick Liquor Corp.*, [1979] 2 S.C.R. 227, as well as in later cases. There is also the possibility that over time a spectrum of standards might develop on which to base deference by other tribunals or the exercise of supervisory jurisdiction: *Alberta (Workers' Compensation Board Appeals Commission)* v. *Penny* (1993), 106 D.L.R. (4th) 707 (Alta C.A.).

[48] Statute of the International Court of Justice, June 26, 1945, 59 Stat. 1055, 3 Bevans 1179.

[49] For an example of a case where reference to inter-American jurisprudence was made before the European Court of Human Rights, see *Kurt* v. *Turkey*, 27 Eur. Ct. H.R. 373 (1998).

[50] Millennial Debt Relief — a coalition of non-governmental organizations, churches, and aid agencies has championed a program with respect to the debt relief for heavily indebted poor states, known as Jubilee 2000. See more in, *inter alia*, Sean D. Murphy, ed., "Contemporary Practice of the United States Relating to International Law" (2000) 94 Am. J. Int'l L. 102, 133 *ff.*

or the demise of the Multilateral Agreement on Investment[51] as evidence of this development. This trend stands in sharp contrast to some earlier organizing efforts, such as the original plans for the creation of an International Trade Organization in the late 1940s, the multi-year effort to ratify the statute of the International Center for the Settlement of Investment Disputes,[52] or the dozen or more years that it took the 1982 LOSC[53] to enter into force. Today, new popular campaigns can create a groundswell for change on a long-standing issue almost immediately.

Yet one can also wonder whether the episodic nature of modern efforts in international law means that they will just as quickly become outdated? We often say that what goes up must come down. Will the rush to do justice introduce error? Will we look back in a decade or two in disillusion at what is being done? Some commentators have contended, for instance, that the spectacle of Slobodan Milosevic in the dock of the International Criminal Tribunal for the Former Yugoslavia — cameras and all — has led to a show trial. Will the future agree with them? Will the future look back at the US $50 million used to secure the conviction of a Libyan terrorist by Scottish judges at Camp Geest and say that it was well spent?[54] We must take care to recall the high hopes behind any number of international undertakings and recognize that results may fall short.

From a substantive perspective, the abridgement of the temporal element in international law may have other profound consquences as well. It may, for instance, point to a change in the concept of custom. The ICJ in the *North Sea Continental Shelf (Federal Republic of Germany* v. *Denmark; Federal Republic of Germany* v. *Netherlands)* cases stated that custom could evolve rapidly,[55] but just how rapidly is now in issue given that conception, incubation, and birth of conventional instruments said to embody custom are moreand more often close together. Time still does play a role in the generality

---

[51] Multilateral Agreement on Investment, text available at <http://www.oecd.org>.

[52] Statute of the International Centre for the Settlement of Investment Disputes, contained within the Convention on the Settlement of Investment Disputes between States and Nationals of Other States, March 18, 1965, 4 I.L.M. 532 (1965) (entered into force on October 14, 1966).

[53] LOSC, *supra* note 41.

[54] John R. Grant, "The Background" (1999) 11 Int'l Legal Perspectives 3.

[55] *North Sea Continental Shelf (Federal Republic of Germany* v. *Denmark; Federal Republic of Germany* v. *Netherlands)*, I.C.J. Rep. 3 (1969).

and consistency of custom.[56] Yet does the radical collapsing of the temporal dimension presage something new in the creation of international law? Time also undoubtedly features in the emergence of *jus cogens*, the fundamental norms of international law from which no country can derogate. Will the abbreviation of time for the creation of international law somehow alter the emergence of *jus cogens*?

Given the multiplicity of treaties, a fourth, and parallel, issue in the future of international law will be the question of the relationship between the sources of international law — that is, between treaties, custom, and *jus cogens*. In particular, new treaty systems raise the question of their interplay with custom. The generally accepted position appears to be that custom continues alongside treaties and is a source of law independent from it.[57] Yet can a treaty in some cases arrest the evolution of custom or perhaps eclipse it altogther? In *Military Activities in and against Nicaragua (Nicaragua v. United States of America)*, the ICJ indicated that it would not, but in a landscape increasingly dotted with treaties we must wonder when a given treaty will crystallize norms and when they will continue to evolve?[58] Additionally, what primacy will be given to treaty interpretations of a norm, to iterations of this same norm in the customary context, and to the mutual reflections that treaties and custom will cast upon each other in the future? It is plausible that some interpretations will be more definitive than others, but how will we tell?[59] Similarly, with respect to *jus cogens*, the Vienna Convention on the Law of Treaties makes clear that treaties are trumped by *jus cogens* and emerging *jus cogens* to the extent of any inconsistency.[60] The same rules would suggest that careful efforts will have to be made in the future to

[56] Ian Brownlie, *Principles of Public Internatiional Law* (5ᵗʰ ed., 1998) at 5.

[57] "In any event, even if norms of treaty origin crystallize as new principles or rules of customary law, the customary norms retain separate identity even if the two norms appear identical in content." *Ibid.* at 13.

[58] *Military Activities in and against Nicaragua (Nicaragua v. United States of America)*, [1986] I.C.J. Rep. 95-96 (paras. 178-79).

[59] In this context, the interpretive method will be critical. Bruno Simma has observed that "if one takes modern philosophy of language into account, a dynamic understanding of legal rules becomes simply inevitable." It is, he says, an "environment in which the meaning of legal rules is continuously being shaped and reshaped." See Bruno Simma, "Editorial" (1992) 3(2) Eur. J. Int'l L. 1.

[60] See Vienna Convention on the Law of Treaties, 8 I.L.M. 679 (1969), Articles 53 (treaties conflicting with a preemptory norm of general international law) and 64 (emergence of a new preemptory norm of general international law).

distinguish between *jus cogens* and other sources of international law, perhaps through the development of margins of appreciation.[61]

THE RIGHT(S) SOCIETY AND THE WRONG(S) SOCIETY

Each of the foregoing questions leads to a fifth, and for present purposes, a final, issue in the future of international law. There is a tendency — even an unexpressed desire — of international law to look more and more like domestic law, with provisional measures, burdens of proof, rules of evidence, remedies, and so forth. This development, sometimes referred to in French law as *jurisdictionnalisation*, has been long predicted by commentators and, in its logical progression, is oddly reassuring to most of us who have had our first exposure to law as students in domestic systems. The development will undoubtedly place greater stress on precision and enforcement and more emphasis on the rights of winners and the obligations of losers. In so doing, it will ensure that greater attention is paid to the tangible results of international law.

Ronald St. John Macdonald dealt with this development in a 1998 work entitled "Future Generations: Searching for a System of Protection."[62] In this instance, he was proposing a guardian for future generations and counseled against the confrontation or desire for quick results that is so evident in domestic law. The future he foresaw was not that of "instant treaties" nor of the brash assertions of rights. Instead, it was one of pragmatism and conciliation. Macdonald's earlier predictions of a world without an "adequate environment" had come to pass. He described this as being

[t]he global losses of arable land, desertification, destruction of tropical rainforests, the extinction of genetic resources, overpopulation, accumulation of greenhouse gases, air and water pollution and mismanagement of non-renewable and renewable energy resources.[63]

---

[61] For instance, although several human rights norms are commonly considered to be *jus cogens,* governments have been considered by international tribunals as retaining a margin of appreciation as to how many rights are implemented in the domestic order.

[62] R. St. J. Macdonald, "Future Generations: Searching for a System of Protection" in Emmanuel Agius and Salvino Busuttil, eds., *Future Generations and International Law* (1998) 149. Macdonald sets out to examine the UN high commissioner for human rights, the UN high commissioner for refugees, and UNESCO as "procedural models for the establishment and operation of a guardian for future generations."

[63] *Ibid.* at 158.

Despite this pessimistic landscape, Macdonald recognized that "[d]iscreet diplomacy in many instances remains the most effective tool."[64] He also recognized that while "rights can be based on a non-specific and undefined ... group ... [and] there are duties that exist separately from any parallel right." For this reason, he suggested an incremental approach to the creation of a guardian for future generations, as follows

persuasive access to sovereign decision-making authorities will be instrumental to the effectiveness of a guardian for future generations. Once firmly established, opportunities will exist for expansion and deepening of the role and authority of the guardian as well as for setting norms which may become codified into binding law. A carefully proscribed mandate will facilitate the establishment of the office of guardian for future generations and will provide the best means for achieving success in a formidable but necessary undertaking.[65]

This passage is of interest, for it echoes a statement found in "International Law and Society in the Year 2000," in which the assertion of claims internationally is also described in shades of persistence and incrementalism. In that earlier work, the co-authors wrote:

[T]he issue would not be couched in such stark, unalloyed terms in the early stages. It would be presented in carefully selected, limited contexts in combination with other factors designed to evoke sympathy and to make some form of affirmative reaction both easy and desirable. The process of obtaining gradual, progressive acceptance by this "meat-slicer" technique is well-known to diplomatists and political tacticians. It is surprisingly successful. Even when put forward in blunt, unvarnished phrases, the principle may sound less ominous and alien when years of tireless repetition and persuasive argument have worn down mental defences. This mode of blunting resistance to "unthinkable" ideas through a blend of mesmerizing repetition, prolonged pressure and sheer mental fatigue has sometimes achieved striking success in changing public attitudes towards major international questions, especially where, as here, the proposition contains elements of equity and appears generally consonant with the broad trend of history.[66]

This stance commands attention. In it, Macdonald does not assert a single position or the strident maintenance of claims, nor does he evidently believe that any single system of law provides all of the answers. Rather, his view is evolutionary and almost organic in

---

[64] *Ibid.*

[65] *Ibid.* at 159.

[66] Macdonald et al., *supra* note 1 at 327.

nature. In his 1998 piece, he likewise says that it is "clear that concepts based on separate systems of international law and municipal
law must yield to a realization that law is more akin to a continuum
... of how do we want to live, as internal regulation of society is
increasingly brought into conjunction and conformity with global
regulatory administrative regimes."[67] In this quotation, Macdonald
reveals himself as a gradualist. He is careful, and he counsels the
patient accumulation of successes in the advancement of international law. His sources are many: domestic law is only one of them.

From this conclusion we may take the view that there is reason to
be wary of jurisdictionalization. International law has often been
thought of as a "law of cooperation."[68] Its most consistent theme
is a harmony between the vigourous assertion of rights and the
more insistent reminder of obligations. It would be unfortunate,
Macdonald appears to suggest, to lose sight of this tradition in
the name of a rigidly corrective model of international law. While
a rights-driven approach is necessary and appropriate in many
instances, there must remain opportunities for distributive justice
where common sense dictates. We must learn to achieve peaceful
transitions from the wrong society to a progressive vision of the
right one.

CONCLUSION

Three decades after it was written, "International Law and Society in the Year 2000" continues to be of interest. In it we are given
Ronald St. John Macdonald's vision of the future that is very much
our present. It is not always a comfortable or attractive vision, but
it is a generally accurate one. Like him, we have to consider the
issues in our own future of international law — issues of conflict
and coherence, of precedent and the radical abridgement of time,
of sources of international law and pressures for jurisdictionalization — in order to foresee the future. And we must do so with the
same commitment to reason and principle, as well as to equality
and internationalism, that so evidently motivated Ronald St. John
Macdonald. His work, then, is ours to continue.

[67] Abraham and Antonia Handler Chayes referred to the fundamental instrument
for maintaining compliance with treaties as an "iterative process of discourse" —
that is, one where a conversation takes place among parties, the treaty organization, and the wider public. *See* Abraham Chayes and Antonia Handler Chayes,
The New Sovereignty (1995) at 25.

[68] Georg Schwarzenberger, *The Frontiers of International Law* (1962) at 13.

Sommaire

Retour sur une vision d'avenir: Ronald St. John Macdonald et l'avenir du droit international

En mai 1973, Ronald St. John Macdonald, Gerald Morris et Douglas Johnson publiaient un article sur le droit international et la société de l'an 2000 dans la Revue du barreau canadien. L'article cherchait à décrire leur vision de ce que serait le droit international trois décennies plus tard. Si Macdonald et ses collaborateurs ont fait erreur au niveau de certains détails, leurs prédictions étaient certainement très justes en ce qui a trait à la multiplication des acteurs en droit international, à la diversité croissante des sources du droit international et à l'expansion importante de la portée du droit international. En particulier, les auteurs ont bien évalué la situation en déclarant que les préoccupations environnementales — par opposition aux préoccupations militaires, humanitaires et pénales plus évidentes — seraient le principal catalyseur de changement dans l'avenir. Un retour sur l'article "International Law and Society in the Year 2000" nous fait prendre conscience en rétrospective de la contribution valable de Macdonald au droit international et nous aide à formuler la question clé que nous devons à notre tour nous poser à notre époque : comment évoluera le droit international à partir de maintenant?

Summary

A Look Back at Looking Forward: Ronald St. John Macdonald and the Future of International Law

In May 1973, an article entitled "International Law and Society in the Year 2000" written by Ronald St. John Macdonald, Gerald Morris, and Douglas Johnson, appeared in the Canadian Bar Review. *The article attempted to provide a vision of what international law would look like three decades in the future. If Macdonald and his co-authors were mistaken about some of the details they forecasted, they were definitely right about the multiplication of actors, the growing diversity of sources, and the expanded coverage of international law. More particularly, they were correct in their assessment that environmental concerns — as opposed to the more evident military, humanitarian, or criminal ones — would be the principal catalyst for change in times to come. A look back at "International Law and Society in the Year 2000" therefore offers a valuable retrospective on Macdonald's contribution to international law and helps to frame the central question that we must take up in our own time: how will international law evolve from here?*

Notes and Comments / Notes et commentaires

———

L'importance de l'opinion publique: L'homoparentalité et la décision de la Cour européenne des droits de l'Homme dans l'affaire *Fretté* c. *France*

I Introduction

Récemment, dans l'affaire *Fretté* c. *France*,[1] l'État français a échappé d'extrême justesse à une condamnation de la Cour européenne des droits de l'Homme (ci-après la Cour) pour discrimination fondée sur l'orientation sexuelle. La décision, rendue le 26 février 2002, concerne un homme gai français qui s'est vu refuser la possibilité d'adopter un enfant en raison de son orientation sexuelle. La Cour a décidé, par quatre voix contre trois, que la France n'avait pas porté atteinte aux droits de la personne.[2] En effet, la Cour a estimé qu'il n'y avait pas eu violation de l'article 14

Nicole LaViolette tient à exprimer sa reconnaissance à Marie Lasnier pour son assistance à la recherche. L'auteure remercie aussi Pacifique Manirakiza et Michel Morin pour leur révision du texte.

[1] *Fretté* c. *France*, Cour européenne des droits de l'Homme, 26 février 2002, req. n° 36515/97, en ligne: Cour européenne des droits de l'homme <http://hudoc.echr.coe.int/hudoc> [ci-après *Fretté*].

[2] Cependant, sur un point subsidiaire, ils ont admis, à l'unanimité, qu'il y avait eu violation de l'art. 6 (droit à un procès équitable), déclarant ainsi la requête de Philippe Fretté partiellement recevable. Il faut souligner que l'arrêt est maintenant définitif. Les deux parties disposaient de trois mois pour soumettre un renvoi devant la Grande Chambre de la Cour européenne des droits de l'Homme: *Convention de sauvegarde des droits de l'Homme et des libertés fondamentales* 4 novembre 1950, (1955), 213 R.T.N.U. 221, S.T.E. n° 5 (entrée en vigueur: 3 septembre 1953) art. 43, § 1 et art. 44, § 2. Aucune des deux parties ne s'est prévalue de cette possibilité avant l'écoulement du délai de trois mois.

(interdiction de la discrimination)[3] de la *Convention européenne des Droits de l'Homme* (ci-après Convention) combiné avec l'article 8 (droit au respect de la vie privée et familiale).[4]

Dans ce commentaire, nous espérons vous convaincre que la décision de la Cour est mal fondée. Nous chercherons à démontrer que le raisonnement suivi par la Cour est aussi suspect que sa conclusion, et que cette conclusion est le résultat d'une interprétation manifestement conservatrice, voire même homophobe, des droits que protège la Convention. Cette affaire doit être qualifiée de recul inquiétant pour la défense des droits des minorités sexuelles en Europe.[5]

II   LES FAITS DE L'AFFAIRE FRETTÉ

C'est en octobre 1991 que Philippe Fretté, un professeur de physique, célibataire et homosexuel, a présenté à la Direction départementale de l'action sanitaire et sociale (la "Ddass") de Paris une demande d'agrément préalable en vue d'adopter un enfant.[6] Selon

---

[3] Article 14 — Interdiction de discrimination

> La jouissance des droits et libertés reconnus dans la présente Convention doit être assurée, sans distinction aucune, fondée notamment sur le sexe, la race, la couleur, la langue, la religion, les opinions politiques ou toutes autres opinions, l'origine nationale ou sociale, l'appartenance à une minorité nationale, la fortune, la naissance ou toute autre situation.

[4] Article 8 — Droit au respect de la vie privée et familiale

> 1. Toute personne a droit au respect de sa vie privée et familiale, de son domicile et de sa correspondance.
>
> 2. Il ne peut y avoir ingérence d'une autorité publique dans l'exercice de ce droit que pour autant que cette ingérence est prévue par la loi et qu'elle constitue une mesure qui, dans une société démocratique, est nécessaire à la sécurité nationale, à la sûreté publique, au bien-être économique du pays, à la défense de l'ordre et à la prévention des infractions pénales, à la protection de la santé ou de la morale, ou à la protection des droits et libertés d'autrui.

[5] Cette qualification de la décision *Fretté* est partagée par La Ligue des droits de l'homme: "Les juges de la Cour marquent un recul inquiétant dans la lutte contre les discriminations, pourtant fortement engagée par le Conseil." Agence France Presse, "La Ligue des droits de l'homme dénonce un recul inquiétant" (6 mars 2002), en ligne: Cyberpresse.ca, <http://www.cyberpresse.ca/reseau/monde/0203/mon_102030073800.html> (date d'accès: 6 mars 2002) [ci-après La Ligue].

[6] La demande d'agrément est suivie d'enquêtes par des travailleurs sociaux sur l'adoptant potentiel ainsi que des entrevues avec un psychiatre et un psychologue: Robert Wintemute, "European Court of Human Rights, 4-3, Permits France

le Code de la famille et de l'aide sociale français,[7] toute personne qui souhaite accueillir un enfant en vue de son adoption doit demander un agrément auprès des services départementaux de protection de l'enfance, qui diligentent alors une enquête sociale.[8] En vertu de l'article 343 du code civil, l'adoption est ouverte à toute personne célibataire, quel que soit son sexe.[9] Dès son premier entretien avec un membre du personnel de l'agence sociale, Fretté dévoile son homosexualité.

Après la conclusion de différentes enquêtes et la rédaction de rapports sociaux et psychologiques, la demande d'agrément en vue d'adoption est refusée au requérant par la direction de la Ddass. L'enquête sociale s'était pourtant avérée "élogieuse sur ses qualités humaines et éducatives," relevant notamment le fait que Fretté était déjà tuteur du fils d'un ami décédé.[10] Dans un rapport social, on ajoute la conclusion suivante:

Monsieur Fretté possède des qualités humaines et éducatives certaines. Un enfant serait probablement heureux avec lui. Ses particularités, homme célibataire homosexuel, permettent-elles de lui confier un enfant?[11]

La décision de la direction, en date du 3 mai 1993, rejette la demande en se fondant tout particulièrement sur "l'absence de référence maternelle constante" et "sur les difficultés de [M. Fretté] à projeter dans le concret les bouleversements occasionnés par l'arrivée d'un enfant."[12] Cinq mois plus tard, dans une décision subséquente suite au recours gracieux de Fretté, la direction de la Ddass invoque aussi le "choix de vie" du requérant pour motiver le refus. Ce choix de vie ne présente pas, selon l'administration, des "garanties suffisantes quant aux conditions d'accueil d'un enfant sur les plans familial, éducatif et psychologique," et soulève

---

to Ban Adoptions by Lesbian and Gay Individuals" dans Arthur Leonard, dir., *Lesbian/Gay Law Notes* (Avril 2002), en ligne: Lesbian/Gay Law Notes, <http://www.qrd.org/qrd/usa/legal/lgln/04.02> (date d'accès: 24 mai 2002).

[7] Articles 343 à 370 C. civ., relatifs à l'adoption sont issues de la loi 66-550 du 11 juillet 1966 modifiée par la loi 76-1179 du 22 décembre1976 et la loi 96-604 du 5 juillet 1996.

[8] Gérard Bach-Ignasse, "'Familles' et homosexualités" dans Daniel Borillo, dir., *Homosexualités et droit*, Paris, P.U.F., 1998, 122 à la p. 133.

[9] *Supra* note 7.

[10] Bach-Ignasse, *supra* note 8 à la p. 134.

[11] *Fretté, supra* note 1 au § 10.

[12] *Ibid.*

par conséquent des risques importants pour l'épanouissement de l'enfant adopté.[13]

Monsieur Fretté entreprend alors une série de procédures judiciaires pour tenter d'obtenir le renversement de cette décision. Le tribunal administratif de Paris lui donne raison en 1995,[14] mais ce jugement est annulé par le Conseil d'État. En effet, statuant sur le fond, celui-ci valide la position de la Ddass et rejette la demande d'agrément de M. Fretté.[15] Ayant épuisé ses recours internes, M. Fretté dépose en 1997 un recours devant la Cour européenne des droits de l'Homme pour "discrimination fondée sur l'orientation sexuelle," invoquant l'article 14, combiné à l'article 8, de la *Convention européenne des Droits de l'Homme*. Comme nous le constaterons plus loin dans l'analyse, la Cour dans sa décision avalise l'interdiction d'adoption opposée par l'administration française aux personnes homosexuelles.

III   LES PRÉTENTIONS DU REQUÉRANT

Devant la Cour, Philippe Fretté se plaint d'une ingérence arbitraire dans sa vie privée et familiale.[16] Il invoque donc la violation de deux articles de la Convention à l'appui de ses prétentions. L'article 8 de la Convention prévoit le respect de la vie privée et familiale, libre de toute ingérence arbitraire d'une autorité publique. L'article 14 garantit la jouissance des droits et libertés reconnus dans la Convention sans distinction discriminatoire. Comme l'exige la jurisprudence dominante de la Cour, le requérant se prétend

---

[13] *Fretté, supra* note 1 au § 11.

[14] Le tribunal administratif considéra "qu'en se référant aux "choix de vie" de [Fretté] l'administration visait son homosexualité et que cet aspect de sa personnalité ne pouvait justifier à elle seule un refus d'agrément...": Bach-Ignasse, *supra* note 8 à la p. 134.

[15] *N° 22766* (1997) 2 J.C.P. 34. (Cons. d'État). Pour une analyse de l'arrêt du Conseil d'État, voir Daniel Borillo et Thierry Pitois, "Adoption et homosexualité: analyse critique de l'arrêt du Conseil d'État du 9 octobre 1996" dans D. Borillo, *supra* note 8, aux pp. 141–51.

[16] M. Fretté invoque aussi la méconnaissance du droit à un procès équitable garanti par l'article 6(1) de la Convention. En effet, il allègue ne pas avoir été convoqué à l'audience devant le Conseil d'État et, par ce fait, de ne pas avoir eu accès aux conclusions du commissaire du Gouvernement avant l'audience. Sur ce point subsidiaire, la Cour a admis, à l'unanimité, qu'il y avait eu violation de l'art. 6, déclarant ainsi la requête de Philippe Fretté partiellement recevable et ordonnant à l'État français de lui verser une réparation de 3 500 euros à titre de réparation: *Fretté, supra* note 1 aux § 44–55.

victime d'une discrimination prohibée par la combinaison des deux articles.[17]

À l'appui de ses prétentions, le requérant soutient que le "refus d'agrément a violé son droit à la jouissance du droit au respect de la vie privée sans discrimination fondée sur son orientation sexuelle."[18] Bien qu'il admette "que le droit au respect de la vie privé[e] et familiale ne comprend pas le droit de tout célibataire d'adopter un enfant,"[19] Fretté soutient que l'adoption constitue une vie familiale projetée, et peut de ce fait tomber sous les droits garantis par la combinaison des articles 8 et 14.[20]

Fretté plaide que le seul motif du refus d'agrément est le fait qu'il est homosexuel. Cette "différence de traitement ne saurait reposer sur une justification objective et raisonnable."[21] Il soutient que le rejet de sa demande

revient à exclure de façon absolue toute possibilité d'adoption pour une catégorie de personnes définies par leur orientation sexuelle ... sans prendre d'aucune façon en considération leurs qualités humaines et éducatives individuelles.[22]

Le requérant fait donc valoir que "toute différence de traitement fondé sur l'orientation sexuelle constitue une ingérence dans la vie privée d'un homosexuel" dans la mesure où cette différence de traitement force une personne homosexuelle ou bisexuelle soit à nier son orientation sexuelle, soit à renoncer à la possibilité de devenir parent adoptif.[23]

Le requérant conteste également un autre argument invoqué par le gouvernement pour motiver le refus de lui accorder l'agrément, celui de l'intérêt de l'enfant, puisqu'aucun enfant spécifique n'est identifié dans la procédure d'agrément. Le rejet de la demande de

---

[17] Voir *Abdulaziz, Cabales et Balkandi* (1985), 94 (Sér. A) Cor. Eur. D.H. 71 [ci-après *Abdulaziz*].

[18] *Fretté, supra* note 1 au § 28.

[19] *Ibid.* Dans l'affaire *Di Lazzaro* de 1997, la Commission européenne des droits de l'Homme avait déclaré irrecevable la requête d'une femme qui contestait une loi italienne qui ne reconnaissait pas aux célibataires le droit d'adoption. La Commission rappelle dans cette décision que le droit d'adopter ne figure pas au nombre des droits garantis dans la Convention: *Di Lazzaro c. Italie*, (1996) 90 C.E.D.H. D.R. à la p. 134.

[20] *Fretté, supra* note 1 au § 28.

[21] *Ibid.* au § 35.

[22] *Ibid.* au § 26.

[23] *Ibid.* au § 28.

Fretté démontre selon lui que l'État entendait "exclure de l'adoption tout célibataire homosexuel,"[24] et révèle un *a priori* défavorable aux personnes gaies et lesbiennes.[25] Philippe Fretté soutient en effet que la présomption qu'aucune personne homosexuelle ne possède les qualités nécessaires pour accueillir un enfant "reflète en réalité un préjugé social et une peur irrationnelle."[26]

IV   LES PRÉTENTIONS DE L'ÉTAT FRANÇAIS

L'État français soutient que l'article 8 ne trouve aucune application aux faits de l'affaire, et qu'il "n'y a dès lors pas d'atteinte à l'article 14, qui n'a pas d'existence autonome."[27] Le gouvernement allègue à l'appui que la Convention ne garantit pas un droit à développer une vie familiale par l'adoption. Selon la défense,

[c]e que revendique le requérant, ce n'est pas la reconnaissance — et la protection — d'un droit entrant dans la sphère de sa vie privée, mais la reconnaissance d'une simple potentialité, une virtualité de paternité adoptive.[28]

Par ailleurs, le gouvernement français affirme que le refus d'agrément n'est pas seulement motivé par l'orientation sexuelle du requérant, mais également par des incertitudes sur la mise en oeuvre de son projet d'adoption et par "un mode de vie quotidien qui a laissé penser qu'il n'était pas prêt à accueillir un enfant."[29] Même si les décisions des instances inférieures utilisent l'expression "choix de vie." le gouvernement soutient que cette expression ne vise pas exclusivement l'orientation sexuelle du requérant, mais d'autres circonstances laissant à penser que le requérant ne répondrait pas à toutes les exigences requises chez un parent adoptif.[30]

Même si l'orientation sexuelle du requérant a revêtu un caractère déterminant dans la décision de lui refuser l'agrément, le gouvernement prétend que ceci ne peut être considéré comme une différence de traitement discriminatoire puisque la "décision prise trouve sa justification dans l'intérêt supérieur de l'enfant."[31] S'il y

[24] *Ibid.* au § 28.

[25] *Ibid.* au § 2.

[26] *Ibid.* au §35.

[27] *Ibid.* au § 29.

[28] *Ibid.* au § 29.

[29] *Ibid.* au § 36.

[30] *Ibid.* aux § 29 et 36.

[31] *Ibid.* au § 36.

a eu ingérence dans la vie privée et familiale du requérant, cette ingérence sert à protéger le bien-être psychologique de l'enfant susceptible d'être adopté. On ajoute à ces arguments le manque de consensus au sein des États membres du Conseil de l'Europe sur la question de l'homoparentalité. Ce manque d'uniformité conduit traditionnellement la Cour, selon le gouvernement français, à reconnaître aux États membres une marge d'appréciation importante sur la question pour éviter "de se substituer aux autorités nationales pour trancher de manière équivoque une controverse aussi délicate."[32]

V LA DÉCISION

A JUGEMENT DE LA COUR

La Cour, par quatre voix contre trois, a donné à la France le droit d'interdire l'adoption d'enfants par des homosexuels. Cependant, les motifs des sept juges révèlent une division importante. Les juges Costa (France), Jungwiert (République tchèque) et Traja (Albanie) ont rejeté les deux principaux points de la plainte de Philippe Fretté. Ils ont estimé que le droit du requérant au respect de sa vie privée et familiale et l'interdiction de la discrimination en raison de l'orientation sexuelle n'ont pas été violés. Le Juge Kuris (Lituanie) en arrive au même résultat, mais ses motifs ne concordent pas avec les trois autres. Il accepte l'applicabilité des articles 8 et 14, mais trouve objective et raisonnable la justification présentée par les autorités françaises pour fonder la différence de traitement dont a été victime Phillipe Fretté. Les juges Bratza (Royaume-Uni), Fuhrman (Autriche), et Tulkens (Belgique) ont tranché en faveur de Fretté, affirmant que l'article 14 s'applique en l'espèce, et que la différence de traitement constituait une discrimination interdite par la Convention. Ces opinions mitigées font que, de manière exceptionnelle, les motifs de la Cour regroupent les motifs des trois juges minoritaires sur l'applicabilité des articles 8 et 14 combinés, et les motifs du Juge Kuris sur la justification de la différence de traitement.[33] Nous examinerons donc le regroupement de ces motifs qui constituent effectivement la décision de la Cour.

Dans un premier temps, la Cour devait se prononcer sur l'applicabilité des articles 8 et 14 sur lesquels le requérant fondait son allégation de violation de la Convention. La jurisprudence sur l'article

---

[32] *Ibid.* au § 36.

[33] Wintemute, *supra* note 6.

14 est constante et elle souligne que cette disposition n'a pas d'existence indépendante des autres dispositions de la Convention, puisqu'elle vise uniquement la "jouissance des droits et libertés" qu'elles garantissent."[34] Il faut donc que les faits d'un litige tombent sous l'emprise de l'une au moins des dispositions de la Convention.

La Cour conclut que le droit de toute personne célibataire à faire une demande d'adoption, prévu par le droit interne français, tombe sous l'empire de l'article 8 de la Convention, sans toutefois préciser si ce droit relève de la vie privé ou de la vie familiale.[35] En outre, la Cour a accepté l'applicabilité de l'article 8 combiné avec l'article 14 de la Convention, déclarant que le requérant a été victime d'une différence de traitement reposant sur son orientation sexuelle, un motif de discrimination interdit par l'article 14. La Cour est d'avis que l'homosexualité du requérant a revêtu un caractère déterminant dans la décision de l'administration, ajoutant que si "les autorités compétentes ont également eu égard à d'autres circonstances, elles apparaissent comme secondaires."[36]

Toutefois, la jurisprudence de la Cour admet le principe de discriminations "légitimes." Selon la jurisprudence européenne, même en présence d'une différence de traitement relative à l'exercice d'un droit reconnu, il n'y a discrimination au sens de l'article 14 que si cette différence de traitement est accompagnée d'un manque de justification objective et raisonnable. En effet, comme le constate J.L. Charrier, la Cour accepte toute discrimination qui poursuit un but légitime, quand il existe un rapport de proportionnalité entre le but visé et les moyens employés.[37] La Cour s'est donc penchée sur la question de savoir si la différence de traitement dont a fait l'objet Phillipe Fretté constitue ou non une discrimination prohibée.

---

[34] *Abdulaziz, supra* note 17.

[35] Adeline Gouttenoire-Cornut et Frédéric Sudre critiquent fortement cette partie de l'analyse de la Cour, la considérant incohérente avec la jurisprudence existante: "La volonté du juge européen de permettre dans cette affaire l'application du principe de non-discrimination ... conduit inéluctablement à étendre la champ d'application de ce droit à la question de l'adoption. Se marque ici l'ambiguïté fondamentale de l'arrêt *Fretté*: la vie privé et familiale, au sens de l'article 8, inclut désormais — sans que l'on sache précisément à quel titre — le droit d'accès à l'adoption." Adeline Gouttenoire-Cornut et Frédéric Sudre, "La réponse de la CEDH à la question de l'adoption par un parent homosexuel," *La Semaine Juridique Édition Générale* n°s 19–20 (8 mai 2002) 885 à la p. 887.

[36] *Fretté, supra* note 1 au § 37.

[37] J.L. Charrier, *Code de la Convention européenne des droits de l'Homme,* Paris, Litec, 2000 à la p. 212.

En l'espèce, la Cour conclut que la justification avancée par le Gouvernement paraît objective et raisonnable. En effet, pour la Cour, le refus d'agrément opposé aux homosexuels n'est pas une discrimination interdite par l'article 14, mais une distinction légitime et raisonnable car elle est effectuée "dans l'intérêt des enfants susceptibles d'être adoptés."[38] On explique que "les décisions de rejet de la demande d'agrément poursuivaient un but légitime: protéger la santé et les droits des enfants."[39] À l'appui de ces arguments, la Cour soutient que la différence de traitement "résulte, en l'état actuel des connaissances, des incertitudes pesant sur le développement d'un enfant élevé par une personne homosexuelle."[40] Les arguments du gouvernement remplissent donc la première condition nécessaire pour justifier une mesure discriminatoire, soit la poursuite d'un but légitime.

Mais une différence de traitement ne doit pas seulement poursuivre un but légitime. Le gouvernement doit démontrer qu'il existe un rapport raisonnable et proportionnel entre les moyens et le but visé. Or, la Cour reconnaît aux États une "certaine marge d'appréciation pour déterminer si et dans quelle mesure des différences entre des situations à d'autres égards analogues justifient des distinctions de traitement juridique."[41] Un des facteurs pertinents dans l'évaluation de l'étendue de la marge d'appréciation est la "présence ou absence d'un dénominateur commun aux systèmes juridiques des États contractants."[42] En matière d'adoption par des parents homosexuels, la Cour soutient que la situation européenne manque d'uniformité. Admettant que la majorité des États ne prévoient aucune exclusion explicite des adoptants homosexuels, la Cour insiste sur le fait "qu'il n'existe pas de principes uniformes sur ces questions de société sur lesquelles de profondes divergences d'opinions peuvent raisonnablement régner dans un État démocratique."[43] La Cour estime que les "autorités nationales sont en principe mieux placées qu'une juridiction internationale pour évaluer les sensibilités et le contexte locaux."[44] Ceci est d'autant

---

[38] *Fretté, supra* note 1 au § 42.

[39] *Ibid.* au § 38.

[40] *Ibid.* au § 36.

[41] *Ibid.* au § 40.

[42] *Ibid.*

[43] *Ibid.* au § 41.

[44] *Ibid.*

plus vrai, selon la Cour, pour les "questions délicates qui touchent à des domaines où il n'y a guère de communauté de vues entre les États."[45]

Les autorités françaises ont donc, selon la Cour, légitimement évalué les intérêts concurrents dans l'affaire, soit ceux du requérant et ceux des enfants pouvant être adoptés. Avant de choisir les individus comme adoptants, l'État doit s'assurer que les enfants adoptifs pourront être les bénéficiaires des conditions d'accueil les plus favorables. La Cour dénote l'impossibilité d'évaluer les effets néfastes ou positifs de l'homoparentalité pour les enfants, faute de preuve.[46] La Cour prétend donc que "les autorités nationales ont légitimement et raisonnablement pu considérer que le droit de pouvoir adopter trouvait sa limite dans l'intérêt des enfants susceptibles d'être adoptés."[47] Le refus d'agrément n'ayant donc pas transgressé le principe de proportionnalité, la Cour conclut que la "justification avancée par le Gouvernement paraît objective et raisonnable et la différence de traitement litigieuse n'est pas discriminatoire au sens de l'article 14 de la Convention."[48]

B   OPINION PARTIELLEMENT CONCORDANTE DES JUGES COSTA,
       JUNGWIERT ET TRAJA[49]

C'est sur la question du champ d'application matériel de la Convention que les Juges Costa, Jungwiert et Traja ont rejeté les prétentions du requérant. Statuant sur l'applicabilité des articles 8 et 14, les trois juges ont estimé que le droit du requérant au respect de sa vie privée et familiale et l'interdiction de la discrimination en raison de l'orientation sexuelle n'ont pas été violés. Les juges sont d'avis que si la Convention ne prévoit pas un droit ou une liberté d'adopter, il ne peut y avoir d'atteinte à la vie privée ou familiale du requérant en vertu de l'article 8.[50] Cette conclusion conduit inéluctablement à une conclusion de non violation de la Convention puisqu'une demande en vertu de l'article 14 doit être combinée avec un droit reconnu ailleurs dans l'instrument international. Quant

---

[45] *Ibid.*

[46] *Ibid.* au § 42.

[47] *Ibid.*

[48] *Ibid.*

[49] "Opinion partiellement concordante de M. le Juge Costa, à laquelle les Juges Jungwiert et Traja déclarent se rallier," *Fretté, supra* note 1.

[50] *Ibid.*

au résultat donc, soit la déclaration d'irrecevabilité, les trois juges forment une majorité avec le Juge Kuris.

C   OPINION PARTIELLEMENT DISSIDENTE DES JUGES BRATZA,
    FUHRMAN ET TULKENS[51]

Pour l'essentiel, l'analyse de la Cour sur l'applicabilité de l'article 14 lu en conjonction avec l'article 8 est en fait l'approche prônée par les juges Bratza, Fuhrman et Tulkens.[52] Les motifs de leur opinion partiellement dissidente concordent avec les motifs de la Cour sur ce point. En effet, ils ont statué que le droit de faire une demande d'agrément tombait sous le champ du droit à la vie privée et familiale et que le refus d'un agrément fondé sur l'orientation sexuelle constituait une violation de l'article 14. Cependant, sur la question de la légitimité de la discrimination, les trois juges ne retiennent pas la justification du gouvernement et estiment au contraire que la différence de traitement dont a été l'objet Philippe Fretté est discriminatoire au sens de l'article 14.

L'opinion dissidente rejette l'argument de la défense selon lequel la discrimination peut être justifiée car le gouvernement poursuivait un but légitime et a employé des moyens proportionnels au but poursuivi. Selon les trois juges, le gouvernement ne peut se fonder sur la protection de l'enfant puisque aucun élément précis du dossier de Philippe Fretté n'est de nature à faire naître des craintes pour l'intérêt de l'enfant.[53] Le refus d'agrément repose uniquement sur l'orientation sexuelle du requérant, et les autorités nationales n'ont pas justifié que "ce choix mettait concrètement en péril l'intérêt d'un enfant."[54] Le gouvernement a plutôt considéré l'homosexualité "comme constituant en soi une contre-indication,"[55] et les juges dissidents sont d'avis que ceci ne peut justifier une différence de traitement interdite à l'article 14.[56]

Sur la question de la proportionnalité, ils soulignent l'absence de rapport raisonnable entre les moyens employés — l'exclusion

---

[51] "Opinion partiellement dissidente commune à Sir Nicolas Bratza, M. Fuhrmann et Mme Tulkens, Juges," *Fretté, supra* note 1.

[52] Les trois juges ont apporté des éléments complémentaires à l'analyse de la Cour sur la question de l'applicabilité de l'art. 8, par. 1.

[53] *Ibid.*

[54] *Ibid.*

[55] *Ibid.*

[56] *Ibid.*

absolue de tout parent adoptif homosexuel — et le but visé — la protection des enfants.[57] Estimant que ce manque de proportionnalité dissimulait en réalité un préjugé contre les minorités sexuelles, les juges Bratza, Fuhrman et Tulkens on refusé de se joindre à l'avis de la majorité de la Cour.

VI ANALYSE CRITIQUE

L'affaire *Fretté* procurait une excellente occasion à la Cour européenne des droits de l'Homme d'examiner l'hésitation actuelle des autorités européennes à étendre aux homosexuels hommes et femmes des droits de parentalité. C'était en effet la première fois que la Cour se penchait de manière explicite sur une question d'adoption les concernant. Auparavant, la Cour avait seulement abordé la question du droit de visite et de garde d'un père homosexuel.[58] De manière regrettable, l'arrêt de la Cour européenne des droits de l'Homme semble entériner le fait que les hommes gais et les lesbiennes sont exclus de certains droits à la parentalité. Comme nous l'avons constaté, la Cour reconnaît que la décision française mise en cause repose de manière déterminante sur l'homosexualité.[59] Or, la majorité conclut que l'intérêt que possède Philippe Fretté à ne pas subir une discrimination fondée sur son homosexualité ne peut écarter les intérêts des enfants adoptables. Tout ceci présume que les intérêts des enfants ne sont pas compatibles avec l'homoparentalité.

Pour en arriver à sa conclusion que l'État français pouvait refuser aux personnes homosexuelles toute possibilité d'adoption, la Cour a été obligée d'adopter une stratégie suspecte. Elle a dû invoquer l'opinion publique pour fonder sa décision, argument utilisé depuis longtemps pour justifier le refus de reconnaître des droits aux minorités sexuelles. À plusieurs reprises, la Cour qualifie la question de l'adoption par des homosexuels comment étant "une

---

[57] Voici les propos des juges dissidents sur cette question: "En fait, la décision du Conseil d'État a constitué une décision de principe, sans se livrer précisément, concrètement, au test de proportionnalité et sans prendre en compte la situation des personnes concernées. Le refus est *absolu* et il a été prononcé sans autre explication que le choix de vie du requérant, envisagé de manière générale et *in abstracto,* qui devient en lui-même une présomption irréfragable de contre-indication à tout projet adoptif, quel qu'il soit." *Ibid.*

[58] *Salgueiro da Silva Mouta* c. *Portugal,* Cour européenne des droits de l'Homme, 21 décembre 1999, req. n° 33290/96, en ligne: Cour européenne des droits de l'homme, *supra* note 1 [ci-après *da Silva*].

[59] *Fretté, supra* note 1 au § 37.

controverse délicate,"[60] une question de société sur laquelle de "profondes divergences d'opinions peuvent raisonnablement régner,"[61] un domaine "où il n'y a guère de communauté de vues."[62] Face à ses divergences d'opinions et de législations, la Cour a conclu à un manque de "dénominateur commun" aux systèmes juridiques européens, et s'est donc permise de laisser une large marge d'appréciation aux autorités de chaque État.

Cependant, dans sa jurisprudence, la Cour avait auparavant indiqué que "seules de très fortes raisons" peuvent justifier des différences de traitement selon d'autres motifs de discrimination.[63] Comme le constatent les professeurs Gouttenoire-Cornut et Sudre, la décision de la Cour, "c'est signifier qu'en l'état présent de la société européenne il n'y a lieu d'avoir des exigences identiques" pour des différences de traitement fondée sur l'orientation sexuelle. La latitude de la marge d'appréciation laissée aux autorités étatiques en matière d'orientation sexuelle "est telle que la Cour pratique en l'espèce un contrôle purement formel."[64] En effet, en reconnaissant le déni de justice sur la forme, mais en se défaussant sur l'opinion publique et sur le pouvoir discrétionnaire de l'État quant au fond, la Cour abdique son rôle avant-gardiste en matière de droits fondamentaux et fortifie de nombreux préjugés contre les personnes gaies et lesbiennes.

La Cour a pourtant raison de signaler que c'est dans le domaine de la filiation que les débats sur l'homosexualité demeurent les plus défavorables. Dans plusieurs juridictions européennes, la reconnaissance des couples de même sexe s'est faite sans pour autant permettre l'adoption, la procréation médicalement assistée ou le droit de garde. Seules les lois des Pays-Bas et de la Suède permettent aux couples de même sexe d'adopter des enfants.[65] Au Danemark

---

[60] *Fretté, supra* note 1 au § 37.

[61] *Ibid* au § 41.

[62] *Ibid*.

[63] Gouttenoire-Cornut et Sudre citent les cas de distinctions fondées sur la naissance ou sur le sexe: Gouttenoire-Cornut et Sudre, *supra* note 35 à la p. 889.

[64] *Ibid*. à la p. 890.

[65] La Suède a légalisé l'adoption pour les personnes gaies au mois de juin 2002: Agence France Presse, "La Suède légalise l'adoption pour les homosexuels," en ligne: Cyberpresse.ca, <http://www.cyberpresse.ca/admin/article/imprime. php?page=/reseau/monde/0206/mon_102060105754.html> [ci-après Suède]. Aux Pays-Bas, la loi prévoit que seuls les enfants de nationalité néerlandaise peuvent faire l'objet d'une adoption par un couple de même sexe: Services des Affaires européennes, Division des Études de législation comparée, Les

et aux Pays Bas, on donne à l'un des partenaires d'un couple homosexuel le droit d'adopter l'enfant de l'autre, mais cette possibilité
est exclue dans tous les autres pays européens.[66] Par ailleurs, très
peu de juridictions européennes reconnaissent à une personne
homosexuelle le droit d'exercer l'autorité parentale sur un enfant.[67]
En Allemagne et au Danemark, on réserve explicitement l'accès
à l'assistance médicale à la procréation aux femmes qui vivent au
sein d'un couple hétérosexuel.[68] Comme le constate Benoît Moore,
l'argument le plus régulièrement soulevé pour contester le mariage
homosexuel est la question de la procréation.[69] Il appert en effet
que, de façon générale, lorsque que l'on discute des droits des gais
et lesbiennes, la protection de l'enfant demeure le domaine où les
préjugés et les réticences restent les plus forts.

Le bien-être des enfants est une préoccupation légitime de toute
société responsable. La réalité des familles dans lesquelles des enfants sont conçus ou élevés par des parents homosexuels et l'affirmation par des personnes gaies et lesbiennes de leur désir d'enfant
ne vont pas sans poser des questions, voire susciter certaines craintes.
L'exposé du Commissaire du gouvernement[70] devant le Conseil
d'État est, à cet égard, instructive. Madame Christine Maugüe
s'exprime comme suit: "l'administration n'a pas motivé son refus
d'agrément par l'homosexualité de monsieur F. en tant que tel mais
par les risques qui lui ont paru en résulter pour l'enfant."[71] Si certains acceptent que ce questionnement est légitime, les réponses
apportées par la Cour européenne témoignent d'un manque de
réflexion et de connaissance.

---

documents de travail du Sénat, Série Législation Comparée, "L'homoparentalité" n°· LC 100, Janvier 2002 à la p. 2.

[66] *Ibid.*

[67] *Ibid.* aux p. 3-4.

[68] *Ibid.* à la p. 4.

[69] Benoît Moore, "L'union homosexuelle et le Code civil du Québec: de l'ignorance à la reconnaissance?" 2002, 81:1 R. du B. can. 121 à la p. 147.

[70] Précisons par souci de clarté que, contrairement à ce que pourrait laisser penser
l'intitulé de sa fonction, le Commissaire du gouvernement ne représente pas
l'administration dans les procès se déroulant devant les juridictions administratives françaises. Ce magistrat est un membre à part entière de la formation de
jugement, son rôle étant de proposer à ses collègues une solution pour le litige
qu'ils sont appelés à trancher.

[71] Caroline Mécary, *Droit et homosexualité*, Paris, Dalloz, 2000 à la p. 88.

Un argument traditionnel contre l'homoparentalité est que les enfants ont besoin d'une mère et d'un père.[72] Dans la première décision refusant à Philippe Fretté l'agrément, la Ddass invoquait "l'absence de référence maternelle constante."[73] Pour Daniel Borillo, il s'agit d'une attaque non seulement contre les parents homosexuels, mais aussi contre les familles alternatives en général. Il estime que "[c]onsidérer qu'un adulte avec un enfant n'est pas une famille porte un coup à l'homoparentalité et à la monoparentalité."[74]

Dans ce même ordre d'idée, il faut souligner que si les autorités françaises veulent donner effet aux dispositions du Code civil octroyant aux personnes célibataires la possibilité d'adopter, il est difficile de comprendre l'imposition d'une condition, la combinaison d'une référence maternelle et paternelle, qui ne peut être remplie que par la présence d'un deuxième parent. En effet, cette absence d'influence maternelle ou paternelle ne semble pas gêner lorsque l'on est en présence de célibataires hétérosexuels. Un courant jurisprudentiel français a déjà censuré les refus d'agrément fondés sur le seul fait que l'adoptant était célibataire.[75] Or, en confirmant la décision des instances nationales dans l'affaire *Fretté*, la Cour européenne des droits de l'Homme a choisi d'exclure les homosexuels de l'application de ce principe estimable. En effet, bien que l'adoption soit un procédé juridique et non biologique,[76] la Cour maintient la tendance traditionnelle qui veut que l'adoption soit "calquée sur le modèle biologique," c'est à dire fasse référence nécessairement à deux parents de sexe différents.[77]

Plusieurs soucis additionnels jaillissent lorsque l'on discute de l'homoparentalité, notamment l'amalgame erroné souvent fait entre

---

[72] Pour un examen plus détaillé de cet argument, voir E.J. Graff, *What is Marriage For? The Strange Social History of Our Most Intimate Institution*, Boston, Beacon Press, 1999 aux pp. 117–25.

[73] *Fretté, supra* note 1 au § 10.

[74] Judith Silberfeld, "Réactions politiques et associatives," en ligne: Têtu.com <http://infos.tetu.com/lire/2186> (date d'accès: 25 mai 2002).

[75] Mécary, *supra* note 71 à la p. 85. La cour administrative d'appel de Bordeaux a statué que si "le statut de célibataire rendrait difficile pour l'enfant la question de la représentation paternelle, cette situation commune à toutes les familles monoparentales, ne peut légalement être opposé à l'intéressé": *ibid.* aux pp. 85–86.

[76] "L'adoption est une fiction qui permet l'établissement d'un lien de filiation ne correspondant pas à une réalité biologique mais à une réalité affective ou élective: c'est donc un lien artificiel créé et fondé par et sur le droit." *Ibid.* à la p. 81.

[77] Moore, *supra* note 69 à la p. 134.

homosexualité et pédophilie,[78] et la peur de voir l'enfant adopté devenir homosexuel.[79] La Cour ne mentionne pas explicitement ces préoccupations, mais en qualifiant la question de l'adoption d'enfants par des personnes homosexuelles de "question délicate et controversée," il y a lieu de se demander si la Cour ne contribue pas implicitement à la confusion culturelle qui règne universellement relativement à ces questions. Ceci est d'autant plus incompréhensible en l'espèce, que le gouvernement admet que Philippe Fretté présente les qualités humaines et éducatives requises d'un candidat à l'adoption. Au minimum, la Cour aurait pu contester la validité de ces préjugés les plus extrêmes dans le cas particulier de Philippe Fretté, ce qui semblerait être le rôle premier d'une institution internationale vouée en partie à la défense des droits des minorités. Elle a préféré confirmer un traitement discriminatoire qui nous semble être essentiellement fondé sur des préjugés répandus dans la majorité hétérosexuelle.

Nous sommes d'avis que la Cour cautionne carrément une certaine homophobie. Les professeurs Gouttenoire-Cornut et Sudre qualifient la décision de la Cour avec les propos suivants:

Cette décision imprévisible au regard de la jurisprudence antérieure se caractérise par la faiblesse insigne de sa motivation qui témoigne sans doute du malaise des juges européens face à une question particulièrement délicate.[80]

Compte tenu des qualités intellectuelles et humaines incontestables de Philippe Fretté, identifiées par les enquêtes effectuées, il semble que "derrière l'apparente neutralité des motifs de la Cour, se profile en réalité le refus de voir un homme célibataire homosexuel adopter un enfant."[81] Comme le déclare Philippe Fretté lui-même, la décision permet au gouvernement français de "sélectionner des catégories de parents au regard d'un modèle parental estimé socialement correct."[82]

---

[78] Voir Graff, *supra* note 72 aux pp. 135-39.

[79] Il n'y a pas de "déterminisme dans l'orientation sexuelle de l'enfant lié à la sexualité des parents alors qu'à de rares exceptions, les homosexuel/les sont issus de familles composées d'un homme et d'une femme." Mécary, *supra* note 71 à la p. 87.

[80] Gouttenoire-Cornut et Sudre, *supra* note 35 à la p. 887.

[81] Mécary, *supra* note 71 à la p. 88.

[82] Pascale Kremer, "La France se voit reconnaître le droit de refuser l'adoption aux homosexuels" *Le Monde*, 27 février 2002, en ligne: LeMonde.fr <http://www.lemonde.fr/article/0,5987,3226—264514-,00.html> (date d'accès: 28 février 2002).

Nous estimons qu'il n'appartient décidément pas à la Cour de renforcer les préjugés homophobes encore présents dans la société européenne. De fait, la Cour avait refusé de le faire dans le cas de la révocation de membres homosexuels des forces armées britannique.[83] Le gouvernement dans ces affaires avait justifié ces mesures discriminatoires en invoquant les attitudes négatives des militaires hétérosexuels envers leurs collègues homosexuels. Selon la Cour:

> Dans la mesure où ces attitudes négatives correspondent aux préjugés d'une majorité hétérosexuelle envers une minorité homosexuelle, la Cour ne saurait les considérer en soi comme une justification suffisante aux ingérences dans l'exercice des droits susmentionnés des requérants, pas plus qu'elle ne le ferait pour des attitudes négatives analogues envers les personnes de race, origine ou couleur différentes.[84]

Or, confrontée implicitement aux préjugés les plus tenaces et extrêmes contre les minorités sexuelles, la Cour a préféré démontrer une grande déférence envers les autorités nationales et avaliser l'exclusion des adoptants homosexuels au seul motif de leur orientation sexuelle.

La Cour défend sa prise de position en soulevant une division de la communauté scientifique sur les conséquences de l'homoparentalité:

> Force est de constater que la communauté scientifique — et plus particulièrement les spécialistes de l'enfance, les psychiatres et les psychologues — est divisée sur les conséquences éventuelles de l'accueil d'un enfant par un ou des parents homosexuels, compte tenu notamment du nombre restreint d'études scientifiques réalisées sur la question à ce jour.[85]

Pourtant, de plus en plus d'études sont réalisées sur le thème de l'homoparentalité, surtout depuis le début des années 1990.[86] Bien que ces études soient dans leur immense majorité nord-américaines,

---

[83] *Lustig-Prean et Beckett* c. *Royaume-Uni,* 27 septembre 1999, en ligne: Cour européenne des droits de l'homme, *supra* note 1.

[84] *Ibid.* au § 90.

[85] *Fretté, supra* note 1 au § 42.

[86] Voir par exemple Judith Stacey et Timothy J. Biblarz, "(How) does the Sexual Orientation of Parents Matter?" 2001, 66 A.S.R. 159 à la p.166. Stacey et Biblarz ont étudié les résultats de 21 études psychologiques publiées entre 1988 et 1998. Voir également Charlotte J. Patterson, "Summary of research findings" dans *Lesbian and Gay Parenting: A Resource for Psychologists,* Washington, A.P.A., 1995 aux pp. 1–12. Patterson estime que les premières études sur les enfants de parents gais ou lesbiens datent de 1978, et que la plupart ont été publiées plus récemment. Elle liste en notes plus d'une cinquantaine d'études. Ces études sont dans leur immense majorité nord-américaines.

l'étude récente faite en France par le Dr Stéphane Nadaud dans le cadre d'une thèse de médecine ne fait pas état de résultats discordants avec ceux des études nord-américaines.[87] Les études s'accordent pour dire que les enfants élevés par des parents homosexuels ne souffrent pas de l'identité sexuelle de leurs parents pour ce qui concerne leur développement.[88] En effet, le Dr Nadaud, se basant sur les conclusions tirées de son étude scientifique, déclare sans équivoque: "L'homoparentalité ne semble pas constituer, en soi, un facteur de risque pour les enfants."[89]

Il est vrai que les recherches ne sont apparemment pas à l'abri de toute critique, celle de la Cour concernant le nombre encore restreint des études en étant une.[90] Cependant, on ne peut nier le fait que les études existantes révèlent que les enfants de parents gais et lesbiennes jouissent d'un développement normal. Les résultats obtenus à ce jour ne peuvent soutenir l'affirmation du gouvernement français selon laquelle l'homosexualité d'un adoptant pourrait faire courir des risques aux enfants adoptés. Comme le soutient l'organisation SOS Homophobie:

> Les arguments avancés par la Cour, relatifs à l'absence de consensus des scientifiques sur les effets de l'homoparentalité sur les enfants sont manifestement spécieux: l'hétérosexualité n'a jamais été un gage de bonne conduite parentale à en voir les bien tristes statistiques sur la maltraitance des enfants ou les carences éducatives de nombreux parents. Pour autant ne s'applique pas un principe de précaution interdisant l'adoption aux hétérosexuels![91]

Il faut ajouter que la Cour n'a pas seulement décidé de ne pas tenir compte des données révélées par les études scientifiques: elle n'a

---

[87] Stéphane Nadaud, "Homoparentalité: Une nouvelle chance pour la famille?" Paris, Éditions Fayard, 2002; Pascale Kremer "La vie ordinaire des enfants de parents homosexuels" *Le Monde,* 28 octobre 2000, en ligne: LeMonde.fr <http://www.lemonde.fr/article/0,2320,110835,00.html> (date d'accès: 31 mai 2002).

[88] Voir Stacey et Biblarz, *supra* note 86; Patterson, *supra* note 86.

[89] Kremer, *supra* note 87.

[90] Certaines études ont été critiquées pour la faiblesse des échantillons, la surreprésentation des mères lesbiennes par rapport aux pères homosexuels, le fait que les parents étudiés sont quasi uniformément de race blanche, majoritairement urbains, et socialement favorisés. La majorité des études sont faites à partir d'adultes recrutés non pas au hasard mais dans la communauté homosexuelle grâce à un réseau de publications et d'associations. Voir Stacey et Biblarz, *supra* note 86 aux pp. 164 et s. Voir également Patterson, *supra* note 86 aux pp. 1–2.

[91] Silberfeld, *supra* note 74.

pas non plus exigé du gouvernement qu'il établisse la preuve que l'intérêt des enfants s'opposait à l'homoparentalité en général, ou plus spécifiquement, à l'accueil par Phillipe Fretté d'un enfant adoptif éventuel. La Cour avait à sa disposition d'une part des études majoritairement positives envers l'homoparentalité, et d'autre part le dossier soumis par le gouvernement d'où il ne ressort "aucun élément précis de nature à faire craindre pour l'intérêt de l'enfant."[92] La Cour a malgré tout tranché en faveur des autorités nationales françaises.

La décision *Fretté* définit certainement une orientation de principe, en ce sens que la Cour a adopté une "position délibérée de ne pas accorder l'agrément aux célibataires qui ne cachent pas leur homosexualité."[93] C'est de fait la décision que les autorités françaises recherchaient, une décision de principe, et non d'espèce.[94] Seules les qualités humaines et éducatives de l'adoptant, véritables garantes du bien-être et du développement de l'enfant, devraient être examinées par les services d'adoption. Gouttenoire et Sudre s'expriment ainsi:

Le raisonnement, confinant au dogme, qui consiste à définir par avance et abstraitement l'intérêt de l'enfant au regard de l'homosexualité de l'adoptant ne peut cependant être admis ... Pour qu'elle justifie le refus d'agrément, il faudrait expliquer en quoi cette homosexualité, telle qu'elle est vécue par le candidat à l'adoption, est susceptible de nuire à l'intérêt de l'enfant. En l'espèce l'agrément en vue de l'adoption a été refusé au

---

[92] "Conclusions de Mme Christine Maugüé, Commissaire du gouvernement" *La Semaine Juridique Édition Générale* n° 4, 1997, 34 à la p. 35 [ci-après Conclusions].

[93] Mécary, *supra* note 71 à la p. 90.

[94] Rejoignant cette position, le Commissaire du gouvernement, avait tenu les propos suivants devant le Conseil d'État:

Compte tenu des éléments du dossier, cette interrogation revêt le rang d'une question de principe. En effet, il n'est pas possible de régler cette affaire par une décision d'espèce car nous n'avons pas de doute, au vu des pièces qui figurent au dossier, sur le fait que M. F. possède à bien des égards de réelles aptitudes pour l'éducation d'un enfant. Le seul élément qui a conduit l'administration à refuser l'agrément est le fait que M. F. est homosexuel et qu'elle a estimé que de ce fait il ne présentait pas des garanties suffisantes quant aux conditions d'accueil d'un enfant sur les plans familial, éducatif et psychologique ... Admettre la légalité du refus d'agrément dans le présent cas revient à condamner implicitement mais nécessairement à l'échec toute demande d'agrément en vue de l'adoption émanant d'un homosexuel.

Conclusions, *supra* note 92 à la p. 35.

requérant sans justifier que son "choix de vie" mettait concrètement en péril l'intérêt d'un enfant.[95]

La Cour a consacré l'exclusion de tous les membres d'une minorité européenne d'un droit reconnu aux membres de la majorité hétérosexuelle, et ce sur la base de préjugés décidément bien tenaces, mais sans fondements scientifiques. Comme nous l'avons soulevé dans ce commentaire, cette position est critiquable et mérite d'évoluer et ce d'autant plus que certaines juridictions européennes et ailleurs reconnaissent progressivement l'homoparentalité.[96]

La conclusion de la majorité de la Cour surprend moins lorsque l'on situe la décision *Fretté* dans la perspective de l'évolution de la reconnaissance des droits des gais et lesbiennes. En effet, l'affaire confirme que la jurisprudence de la Cour quant à la reconnaissance des droits des minorités sexuelles suit un processus par étape, semblable à celui que semble adopter la grande majorité des États démocratiques. Nous nous tournons vers le modèle tracé par Kurt Waaldijk pour situer l'approche de la Cour.

Waaldijk présente l'évolution de la reconnaissance des droits des minorités sexuelles comme un ensemble à plusieurs étapes, se succédant dans le temps.[97] La première étape serait celle de la dépénalisation des actes homosexuels, qui se manifeste par la disparition du crime d'homosexualité et de lesbianisme dans les

[95] Gouttenoire et Sudre, *supra* note 35 à la p. 890.

[96] Voir Suède, *supra* note 65; "Denmark May Allow Homosexuals to Adopt Partners' Kids" *Agence France Presse*, 17 janvier 1999, en ligne: LEXIS (International news). American Civil Liberties Union, "ACLU Fact Sheet: Overview of Lesbian and Gay Parenting, Adoption and Foster Care" 6 avril 1999, en ligne: American Civil Liberties Union <http://www.aclu.org/issues/gay/parent.html> (date d'accès: 24 juin 2002); Nicole LaViolette, "Family Affair: Providing Joint Custody for Same-Sex Parents" *Capita Xtra!*, 27 janvier 1995, 13; Jeff Lindstrom, "Limited Adoption Rights Granted Ontario Lesbians" *Xtra West*, 1er juin 1995; Cindy Filipenko "Adoption Act for Gay Couples" *Xtra West*, 24 juin 1995; D. Lessard, "Québec reconnaîtra les marriages civils homosexuels" *La Presse*, 8 décembre 2001, en ligne: Cyberpresse.ca <http://www.cyberpresse.ca/reseau/politique/0112/pol_101120044266.html> (date d'accès: 17 janvier 2002); Kees Waaldijk, "Text of Dutch Law on Adoption by Persons of the Same Sex: Summary Translation" janvier 2001, en ligne: <http://ruljis.leidenuniv.nl./user/cwaaldij/www/NHR/transl-adop.html> (date d'accès: 24 juin 2002).

[97] Voir K. Waaldijk, "Civil Developments: Patterns of Reform in the Legal Position of Same-Sex Partners in Europe" 2000, 17 Can. J. Fam. L. 62 à la p. 66; K. Waaldijk, "Small Changes: How the Road to Same-Sex Marriage Got Paved in the Netherlands" dans R. Wintemute et M. Andenæs, dir., *Legal Recognition of Same-Sex Partnership. A Study of National, European and International Law*, Oxford: Hart Publishing, 2001 à la p. 437.

dispositions pénales d'un pays, une étape déjà accomplie dans de nombreuses juridictions à travers le monde. La seconde étape, qui serait en train de s'accomplir aujourd'hui dans bien des endroits, effectuerait le passage de la dépénalisation à l'interdiction de discrimination. L'État offrirait alors une protection juridique contre la discrimination dans les secteurs public et privé, au moyen par exemple de dispositions législatives interdisant le licenciement fondé sur l'orientation sexuelle ou garantissant un accès équitable au logement. Viendrait ensuite l'étape de la reconnaissance des relations de couple de même sexe, cette étape impliquant nécessairement le dépassement de la dépénalisation et de l'interdiction de discrimination pour atteindre l'octroi, par l'État, d'un statut d'égalité entre le couple homosexuel et hétérosexuel.

Il nous semble qu'il faut ajouter une dernière étape au modèle de Waaldijk avant qu'une société puisse atteindre la pleine reconnaissance des minorités sexuelles. Cette étape, complémentaire à la troisième, serait la reconnaissance par l'État des rapports familiaux entre enfants et parents homosexuels. Car les homosexuels, hommes et femmes, sont parfois parents; ils peuvent en effet être parents biologiques d'un enfant issu d'une relation hétérosexuelle, ou d'une insémination alternative. Ils peuvent d'autre part exercer un rôle de parent envers les enfants d'un conjoint ou d'une conjointe, ou même se retrouver tuteur ou tutrice d'un enfant dont les parents sont décédés.[98] Finalement, ils peuvent se retrouver dans la situation de Philippe Fretté, à la recherche d'un enfant adoptif. Dans le cas de l'adoption, une personne homosexuelle désire peut-être adopter l'enfant de son conjoint ou de sa conjointe, ou obtenir l'adoption d'un enfant à charge de l'État ou d'un enfant étranger. Malgré la présence de l'homoparentalité sous toutes ces facettes, peu d'États se sont engagés à ce jour à étendre explicitement des droits de parentalité aux homosexuels.[99]

La Cour européenne des droits de l'homme et les autres institutions européennes semblent avoir suivi l'évolution tracée par Waaldijk.[100] En effet, les premières revendications juridiques des

---

[98] Bach-Ignasse, *supra* note 8 à la p. 133.

[99] Cependant, certaines juridictions ont accordé des droits de parentalité aux hommes gais et lesbiennes. C'est le cas de plusieurs provinces canadiennes et états américains, ainsi que certains États européens dont les Pays-Bas et la Suède: *supra* note 96.

[100] Pour un examen plus détaillé de la jurisprudence de la Cour européenne en matière d'orientation sexuelle, voir Daniel Borillo, "Pluralisme conjugal ou hiérarchie des sexualités: la reconnaissance juridique des couples homosexuels

minorités sexuelles qui ont été déclarées légitimes par la Cour portaient sur des dispositions pénales interdisant les relations sexuelles entre personnes de même sexe. La Cour a reconnu à partir de 1981 que le droit de toute personne à mener la vie sexuelle de son choix est une composante fondamentale du droit au respect de la vie privée.[101] La Cour a, par la suite, condamné certaines mesures discriminatoires prises contre des individus homosexuels.[102] Par ailleurs, dans une résolution de février 1994, le Parlement européen a recommandé à tous les États membres de l'Union européenne d'abolir toute forme de discrimination juridique, administrative et sociale à l'égard des homosexuels.[103] La Charte des droits fondamentaux adoptée en 2000 et le Conseil des ministres du Conseil de l'Europe dans une déclaration de 2001 ont posé le principe de la prohibition de toutes discriminations fondées sur l'orientation sexuelle.[104]

Cependant, la jurisprudence de la Cour est mitigée en ce qui a trait à la reconnaissance des couples de mêmes sexe. En 1986, la Commission européenne des droits de l'Homme a statué qu'une relation intime entre deux femmes ne constituait pas une "vie familiale" au sens de l'article 8 de la Convention.[105] La Cour, pour sa part, a soutenu en 1998 le refus d'un employeur britannique d'accorder aux couples de même sexe les mêmes avantages sociaux offerts aux employés hétérosexuels.[106] Comme le constate Daniel Borillo, "la Cour continue à scinder la vie privée des homosexuels de leur vie familiale."[107] Finalement, une discrimination perdure

---

dans l'Union européenne" 2001, 46 R.D. McGill 875 [ci-après Pluralisme conjugal].

[101] Voir *Dudgeon* c. *Royaume-Uni* (1981), 45 Cour Eur. D.H. (Sér. A) 1, 4 E.H.R.R. 149; *Norris* c. *Irlande* (1988), 142 Cour Eur. D.H. (Sér. A) 1; *Modinos* c.*Chypre* (1993), 259 C.E.D.H. (Sér. A) 1, 16 E.H.R.R. 485.

[102] *Lustig-Prean et Beckett* c. *Royaume-Uni*, 27 septembre 1999, *supra* note 83; *Smith et Grady* c. *Royaume-Uni*, 27 septembre 1999, en ligne: Cour européenne des droits de l'homme, *supra* note 1.

[103] De telles législations non-discriminatoires sont d'ores et déjà en vigueur dans plusieurs pays de l'Europe du Nord: voir Robert Wintemute et Mads Andenaes, *Legal Recognition of Same-Sex Partnerships: A Study of National, European and International Law*, Oxford, Hart Publishing, 2001.

[104] La Ligue, *supra* note 5.

[105] *S.* c. *Royaume-Uni* (1986), 47 DR 274.

[106] *Grant* c. *South West Trains*, [1998] Rec. C.E. I-621 à la p. I-622.

[107] Pluralisme conjugal, *supra* note 100 à la p. 883.

dans la jurisprudence pour les questions qui touchent l'homo-parentalité, comme en témoigne l'affaire *Fretté*.

La Cour se trouve donc à mi-chemin dans la troisième étape de Waaldjik, et comme le démontre l'affaire *Fretté*, elle est encore plus réticente à toucher à la toute dernière étape que nous avons rajoutée au modèle, celle de l'homoparentalité. Bien que la Cour ait auparavant tranché en faveur d'un père homosexuel qui revendiquait la garde de son enfant dans l'affaire *da Silva*,[108] elle refuse d'étendre cette ouverture au contexte de l'adoption dans l'affaire *Fretté*.

Face à la réticence de la Cour à étendre certains droits aux gais et lesbiennes, il faut souligner l'importance que revêt maintenant, pour les minorités sexuelles, la ratification du *Protocole n° 12 à la Convention de sauvegarde des Droits de l'Homme et des Libertés fondamentales*. Ce traité a vocation pour les États signataires à s'ajouter aux obligations qui découlent de la Convention et des autres protocoles ratifiés. Il a pour objet d'introduire une interdiction générale de discrimination au moyen d'une énumération non limitative de motifs interdits de discrimination. Le traité est ouvert à la signature depuis le 4 décembre 2000, mais plusieurs États, notamment la France, ne l'ont pas signé à ce jour.[109]

L'importance du Protocole se situe au niveau de la réforme qu'il introduit relativement à l'article 14 de la Convention. Cette disposition est actuellement de portée limitée du fait qu'elle ne garantit pas un droit autonome et indépendant à l'égalité, contrairement à ce qui est le cas pour l'article 26 du *Pacte international relatif aux droits civils et politiques*[110] qui prévoit une protection dans toutes

---

[108] Dans l'affaire *da Silva*, une vie familiale établie existait déjà entre le père gai et sa fille et la Cour n'a pas eu de difficultés à conclure que la perte d'autorité parentale constituait une nette interférence dans le droit au respect de la vie familial du père: *da Silva, supra* note 58.

[109] Le Protocole entrera en vigueur après 10 ratifications, et pour le moment il n'y en a que deux: Chypre et la Géorgie. Voir en ligne: Conseil de l'Europe, <http://conventions.coe.int/treaty/FR/cadreprincipal.htm> (date d'accès: 24 juin 2002).

[110] Article 26:

Toutes les personnes sont égales devant la loi et ont droit sans discrimination à une égale protection de la loi. À cet égard, la loi doit interdire toute discrimination et garantir à toutes les personnes une protection égale et efficace contre toute discrimination, notamment de race, de couleur, de sexe, de langue, de religion, d'opinion politique et de toute autre opinion, d'origine nationale ou sociale, de fortune, de naissance ou de toute autre situation.

Pacte international relatif aux droits civils et politiques 1976, 999 R.T.N.U. 171.

les sphères d'activités de l'État. En effet, comme nous l'avons dit plus haut, l'article 14 ne peut être invoqué qu'à titre accessoire et seulement si la discrimination en cause s'applique à l'un des droits reconnus par la Convention. L'article 14 est donc une disposition subordonnée au lieu d'être une interdiction générale de toute mesure discriminatoire.[111] En outre, l'article 14 "se contente d'interdire des traitements inégaux dans l'exercice des droits et libertés."[112] La Convention ne garantit pas un droit à l'égalité, bien que ce principe constitue un élément fondamental du droit international en matière de droits de l'homme.[113]

Le texte du nouveau protocole supprime ces limitations et "garantit que personne ne doit faire l'objet d'une quelconque forme de discrimination par aucune autorité publique et sous quelque motif que ce soit."[114] Nous pouvons espérer que l'effet du Protocole 12 sera de promouvoir un réel principe d'égalité de traitement dans l'exercice des droits et libertés garantis par la Convention, l'approche restrictive actuelle visant plutôt, elle, l'interdiction des discriminations. Il nous semble en effet qu'une garantie d'égalité porte plus aisément la notion d'engagements positifs que celle de la non-discrimination.[115] Il faut ajouter que les trois juges de la Cour qui ont rejeté l'applicabilité de l'article 14 dans sa forme actuelle ont indiqué que le Protocole 12 pourrait, une fois ratifié, constituer un meilleur fondement pour les contestations du type de celles présentées par Philippe Fretté.[116]

---

[111] D.J. Harris, M. Boyle et C. Warbrick, *Law of the European Convention on Human Rights,* London, Butterworths, 1995 à la p. 463.

[112] Charrier, *supra* note 37 à la p. 207.

[113] P. van Dijk et G.J.H. van Hoof, *Theory and Practice of the European Court on Human Rights,* Deventer, The Netherlands, Kluwer, 1990 aux pp. 532–33. Le principe d'égalité est consacré dans plusieurs traités internationaux: *Convention internationale sur l'élimination de toutes les formes de discrimination raciale* 1969, 660 R.T.N.U. 195, art. 5; *Convention sur l'élimination de toutes les formes de discrimination à l'égard des femmes* 1981, 1249 R.T.N.U. 13, art. 2; *Pacte international relatif aux droits économiques, sociaux et culturels* 1976, 999 R.T.N.U. 171, art 2, § 2; *Convention relative aux droits de l'enfant* 1992, R.T. Can. n° 3, art.2.

[114] Conseil des ministres du Conseil de l'Europe, Communiqué "Convention européenne des Droits de l'Homme: une meilleure proctection contre la discrimination" 27 juin 2000, en ligne: <http://press.coe.int/cp/2000/473f (2000)htm>.

[115] Harris, Boyle et Warbrick, *supra* note 111 à la p. 463.

[116] *Fretté, supra* note 1.

VII CONCLUSION

Dans l'affaire *Fretté*, la Cour européenne des droits de l'homme a avalisé une différence de traitement discriminatoire et absolue envers les personnes homosexuelles. Même si des adoptants homosexuels présentent des conditions de stabilité et des capacités éducatives au même titre que des personnes hétérosexuelles, la Cour a déclaré acceptable le refus par les autorités nationales de leur accorder des droits de parentalité en matière d'adoption. Nous l'avons démontré, la Cour ne fonde aucunement sa décision sur une preuve explicite et concluante quant au préjudice que peut présenter l'homosexualité d'un parent pour l'enfant adopté. La Cour invoque plutôt la controverse publique pour motiver la déclaration d'inadmissibilité de la demande de Philippe Fretté.

En France, la décision a déjà des répercussions importantes. Ainsi, l'interdiction de l'adoption d'enfants par des homosexuels a été confirmée au mois de juin 2002 dans un autre litige, concernant cette fois-ci une institutrice lesbienne. Le Conseil d'État a confirmé la validité du refus d'agrément qui lui a été opposé, alors que celui-ci était uniquement motivé par son orientation sexuelle.[117] Pourtant, la France n'entretient pas que des rapports de répression avec l'homosexualité. Depuis 1999, a été mis en place un type de partenariat enregistré ouvert aux couples de même sexe, communément appelé le Pacs.[118] Or, dans la toute récente affaire, la personne souhaitant adopter avait pourtant signé un Pacs. Comme le déclare Borillo, "des espaces de répression, des aires de tolérance et des dispositifs de reconnaissance des homosexualités" peuvent coexister dans une même société.[119] La Cour européenne a garanti la survie de ces "espaces de répression" avec la décision dans l'affaire *Fretté*. Les minorités sexuelles européennes devront dorénavant

[117] Cons. d'État, 5 juin 2002, *Emmanuelle Berthet* (à paraître dans le Recueil Lebon). L'administration françaises avait reconnu à la requérante "ses qualités d'écoute, d'ouverture d'esprit et de disponibilité nécessaires à l'adoption": Collectif Pacs, et cætera, Communiqué, "Décision manifestement homophobe et pacsophobe" 21 décembre 2000, en ligne: <http://www.club-internet.fr/perso/ccucs> (date d'accès 6 mars 2002).

[118] Ce type d'union civil permet à deux personnes majeures, de sexe différent ou de même sexe, d'organiser leur vie commune en octroyant droits et responsabilités dans différents domaines, tel le soutien matérielle, les dettes contractées, et la division des biens meubles. Le Pacs fut introduit en droit français par la *Loi no. 99-944 du 15 novembre 1999, relative au pacte civil de solidarité,* J.O. 15 et 16 novembre 1999, p. 16959, D. 1999, Lég.515.

[119] Daniel Borillo, "Introduction" dans Borillo, *supra* note 8 à la p. 1.

miser sur des réformes politiques pour pouvoir jouir des droits de parentalité, car la plus importante institution juridique vouée à la défense des droits des minorités européennes, la Cour européenne des droits de l'Homme, est actuellement en défaut de son mandat humanitaire et de protection pour ce qui concerne les minorités sexuelles européennes.

NICOLE LAVIOLETTE
Professeure agrégée, Faculté de droit, Université d'Ottawa

Summary

The Importance of Public Opinion: Lesbigay Parents and the Decision of the European Court of Human Rights in *Fretté* v. *France*

Recently, in Fretté *v.* France, *France narrowly escaped condemnation by the European Court of Human Rights for discrimination based on sexual orientation. In* Fretté, *the European Court upheld a French decision that denied a gay man the right to adopt. The author argues that despite the fact that many gay men and lesbians possess the educational and social qualities required of adoptive parents, the European Court endorsed discriminatory treatment towards sexual minorities. In the author's view, the court failed to require explicit and conclusive proof that children are at greater risk if placed with gay or lesbian adoptive parents. Rather, the court pointed to public controversy over the issue to justify its refusal to overturn the French ban on gay and lesbian adoptions. In doing so, the European Court of Human Rights abdicated its leadership role on pivotal human rights issues.*

Sommaire

L'importance de l'opinion publique: L'homoparentalité et la décision de la Cour européenne des droits de l'Homme dans l'affaire *Fretté* c. *France*

Récemment, dans l'affaire Fretté *c.* France, *l'État français a échappé d'extrême justesse à une condamnation de la Cour européenne des droits de l'Homme pour discrimination fondée sur l'orientation sexuelle. Dans l'affaire* Fretté, *la Cour européenne confirme que l'interdiction d'adoption opposée par l'administration française aux personnes homosexuelles ne porte pas atteinte aux droits de la personne. Selon l'auteure, la Cour a négligé le fait qu'un grand nombre d'hommes gais et de lesbiennes présentent les qualités humaines et éducatives requises d'un candidat à l'adoption, et elle a préféré avaliser une différence de traitement discriminatoire et absolue envers les personnes homosexuelles. La Cour ne fonde aucunement ses motifs sur une preuve explicite et concluante quant au préjudice que peut présenter l'homosexualité d'un parent pour l'enfant adopté. Elle invoque plutôt la controverse publique pour motiver sa décision en faveur de l'interdiction d'adoption par les gais.*

Nova Scotia-Newfoundland Dispute over Offshore Areas: The Delimitation Phase

INTRODUCTION

On March 26, 2002, an ad hoc arbitration tribunal, established by the federal minister of natural resources under the Canada-Newfoundland Accord and the Canada-Nova Scotia Accord,[1] determined the line of delimitation dividing the respective offshore areas of the province of Newfoundland and Labrador[2] and the province of Nova Scotia.[3] The tribunal did not adopt the boundary proposed by either party in its pleadings and drew its own delimitation line. However, the result was closer to the position urged by Newfoundland and Labrador than the outcome sought by Nova Scotia.

This unanimous decision, which is binding on both provinces, is the only interprovincial boundary established through arbitration applying the principles of international law governing maritime boundary delimitation. The decision is important for its practical impact because the jurisdictional certainty provided by the tribunal's decision paved the way for the commencement of hydrocarbon

---

This note is written in the writer's personal capacity.

[1] Memorandum of Agreement between the Government of Canada and the Government of the Province of Newfoundland on Offshore Petroleum Resource Management and Revenue Sharing, dated February 11, 1985; Canada-Nova Scotia Offshore Petroleum Resources Accord, dated August 26, 1986.

[2] The province of Newfoundland and Labrador will, for the remainder of the comment, be referred to as the province of Newfoundland or as Newfoundland.

[3] Arbitration between Newfoundland and Labrador and Nova Scotia Concerning Portions of the Limits of Their Offshore Areas as Defined in the Canada-Nova Scotia Offshore Petroleum Resources Accord Implementation Act and the Canada-Newfoundland Atlantic Accord Implementation Act, Award of the Tribunal in the Second Phase, March 26, 2002 [hereinafter Award, Second Phase]. The award may be found at <www.boundary-dispute.ca>.

exploration in the formerly disputed area as well as for its legal implications, including its contribution to the development of international law governing maritime boundary delimitation.

The March 2002 "award of the tribunal" is the second decision under the arbitration process. In May 2001, the same arbitration tribunal decided, contrary to the position advanced by Nova Scotia but in agreement with the one urged by Newfoundland, that the line dividing the respective offshore areas of Newfoundland and Nova Scotia had not been resolved previously by agreement between the two provinces.[4] Having determined that there was no agreement on the location of the maritime boundary in the offshore area between the two provinces, the tribunal embarked on the delimitation phase of the arbitration. This note describes the arguments of the parties and the decision of the arbitration tribunal in the delimitation phase of the arbitration process.

BACKGROUND

HISTORY OF THE DISPUTE

The arbitration tribunal was established pursuant to the dispute settlement provisions found in the federal and provincial legislation[5] implementing the Canada-Newfoundland Accord and the Canada-Nova Scotia Accord. The accords established administrative regimes governing the management of oil and gas exploration in the offshore area, as defined in the legislation. The legislation stipulates that, where a dispute arises between the provinces in relation to the description of the limits of the offshore area and the

---

[4] Arbitration between Newfoundland and Labrador and Nova Scotia Concerning Portions of the Limits of Their Offshore Areas as Defined in the Canada-Nova Scotia Offshore Petroleum Resources Accord Implementation Act and the Canada-Newfoundland Atlantic Accord Implementation Act, Award of the Tribunal in the First Phase, May 17, 2001 [hereinafter Award, First Phase]. The first phase of the arbitration and the tribunal's first award are described in Valerie Hughes, "The Nova Scotia-Newfoundland Dispute over the Limits of Their Respective Offshore Areas" (2000) 38 Can. Y.B. Int'l L. 189. The award of the tribunal in the first phase may be found at <www.boundary-dispute.ca>.

[5] Canada-Newfoundland Atlantic Accord Implementation Act, S.C. 1987, c. 3; Canada-Newfoundland Atlantic Accord Implementation (Newfoundland) Act, S.N. 1986, c. 37; Canada-Nova Scotia Offshore Petroleum Resources Accord Implementation Act, S.C. 1987, c. 28; and Canada-Nova Scotia Offshore Petroleum Resources Accord Implementation (Nova Scotia) Act, S.N.S., 1987, c. 3 [hereinafter Accord Acts].

government of Canada is unable by means of negotiation to bring about a resolution within a reasonable period of time, the dispute is to be referred to an impartial person or tribunal whose membership and procedures would be determined by the federal minister of natural resources.[6] The legislation also prescribes the applicable law for such arbitration as "the principles of international law governing maritime boundary delimitation, with such modifications as the circumstances require."[7]

In January 1998, the federal minister of natural resources notified Nova Scotia and Newfoundland that he was exercising the authority granted to him under the dispute settlement provisions to refer the dispute to arbitration. Terms of Reference[8] for the arbitration were developed by the minister following consultations with the provinces. Article 2 prescribes the composition of the arbitration tribunal as the Honourable Gérard La Forest,[9] to serve as chairperson, and Leonard Legault[10] and James Richard Crawford,[11] to serve as members. Article 3 of the Terms of Reference sets out the tribunal's mandate as follows:

3.1 Applying the principles of international law governing maritime boundary delimitation with such modification as the circumstances require, the Tribunal shall determine the line dividing the respective offshore areas of the Province of Newfoundland and Labrador and the Province of Nova Scotia, as if the parties were states subject to the same rights and obligations as the Government of Canada at all relevant times.

3.2 The Tribunal shall, in accordance with Article 3.1 above, determine the line dividing the respective offshore areas of the Province of

---

[6] Canada-Nova Scotia Offshore Petroleum Resources Accord Implementation Act, *supra* note 5 at s. 48; and Canada-Newfoundland Atlantic Accord Implementation Act, *supra* note 5 at s. 6.

[7] Canada-Nova Scotia Offshore Petroleum Resources Accord Implementation Act, *supra* note 5 at s. 48; Canada-Newfoundland Atlantic Accord Implementation Act, *supra* note 5 at s. 6.

[8] The Terms of Reference may be found in Appendix A of the Award, First Phase, *supra* note 4.

[9] Justice La Forest served on the Supreme Court of Canada from 1985 to 1997.

[10] Leonard Legault is a former legal adviser in the Department of Foreign Affairs and International Trade. He served as agent for Canada and counsel in maritime boundary disputes.

[11] James Richard Crawford is Whewell Professor of International Law at the University of Cambridge. He has appeared as counsel before the International Court of Justice.

Newfoundland and Labrador and the Province of Nova Scotia in two phases.

(i) In the first phase, the Tribunal shall determine whether the line dividing the respective offshore areas of the Province of Newfoundland and Labrador and the Province of Nova Scotia has been resolved by agreement.

(ii) In the second phase, the Tribunal shall determine how in the absence of any agreement the line dividing the respective offshore areas of the Province of Newfoundland and Labrador and the Province of Nova Scotia shall be determined.

FIRST PHASE OF THE ARBITRATION: THE BOUNDARY
HAS NOT BEEN RESOLVED BY AGREEMENT

In the first phase of the arbitration, Nova Scotia argued that the line dividing the offshore areas of Nova Scotia and Newfoundland had been resolved by agreement in 1964 and subsequently applied both by Nova Scotia and Newfoundland (as well as by the other East Coast provinces). Nova Scotia sought to prove the existence of the agreement by relying on interprovincial and federal-provincial negotiations dating from as early as 1958 as well as on documents, maps, oil and gas permitting activity, and federal-provincial legislation. In Nova Scotia's view, as the boundary had been resolved by agreement in 1964, there was no need to proceed to the second phase — the delimitation phase — of the arbitration. Newfoundland denied the existence of any agreement resolving the boundary, noting that the negotiations referred to by Nova Scotia resulted in conditional proposals that eventually lapsed when the conditions, including federal acceptance and recognition of provincial offshore jurisdiction, failed to materialize.

The tribunal, applying "the principles of international law governing maritime boundary delimitation with such modification as the circumstances require,"[12] explained that it would be sufficient to establish an agreement resolving the boundary if it could be shown that the provinces "definitively agreed on a boundary separating their respective offshore areas."[13] To establish a "definitive" agreement, the tribunal said it would be necessary to show that the provinces agreed on the boundary:

(a) for all purposes, and not only for the purpose of presenting to the Federal Government a proposal which was ultimately rejected;

[12] Terms of Reference, *supra* note 8 at Article 3.1.

[13] Award, First Phase, *supra* note 4 at para. 3.30.

(b) by an agreement which was not subject to any subsequent process of confirmation or ratification or any analogous process in order to be considered binding; and

(c) which was sufficiently clear, so as to allow the boundary to be determined by a process of legal interpretation of the agreement.[14]

According to the tribunal, "[o]nly if these conditions were met could it be said that the boundary was 'resolved by agreement' for the purposes of the Terms of Reference."[15] The tribunal found that these conditions had not been met and, consequently, that the boundary had not been resolved by agreement:

> In the Tribunal's view, the documentary record looked at as a whole does not disclose the existence of an agreement resolving the offshore boundaries of Newfoundland and Labrador and Nova Scotia, within the meaning of the Terms of Reference ... In particular, the Tribunal concludes that the parties at no stage reached a definitive agreement resolving their offshore boundary, in the sense explained in paragraph 3.30 above.[16]

The tribunal was of the view that the interprovincial boundary agreement was predicated on the federal acceptance of the provinces' proposal regarding provincial ownership of the offshore, and this acceptance had not been obtained. Moreover, the tribunal was not persuaded that the subsequent conduct of the parties, be it in negotiations or in oil and gas permit activity, was sufficiently clear and unequivocal to permit determination of an agreed boundary line.

SECOND PHASE: THE DELIMITATION

Having determined that the line delimiting the offshore areas between Newfoundland and Nova Scotia had not been resolved by agreement, the tribunal proceeded to the second phase, where it was requested to determine "how ... the line dividing the respective offshore areas of [Newfoundland and Nova Scotia] shall be determined."[17] In accordance with Article 6 of the Terms of Reference, the second phase of the arbitration proceeded with the simultaneous filing of memorials on August 17, 2002, and counter-memorials on October 17, 2001. The tribunal heard oral argument on November 19, 20, 22, 23, 26, and 28, 2001. The seat of the tribunal

[14] *Ibid.* at para. 3.30.

[15] *Ibid.* at para. 3.30.

[16] *Ibid.* at para. 7.1.

[17] Terms of Reference, *supra* note 8 at Article 3.2 (ii).

was Ottawa,[18] but the hearings took place in Fredericton, New Brunswick.[19]

APPLICABLE LAW

International Law or Domestic Law?

As in the first phase, the question of applicable law was also an issue in the second phase. In the first phase, Nova Scotia had argued that it was clear from Article 3.1 of the Terms of Reference that the tribunal was required to apply international law and, in particular, international law governing the conclusion and interpretation of international agreements. According to Nova Scotia, the "principles of law governing maritime boundary delimitation" set out in the Terms of Reference[20] called for delimitation by agreement first, to be followed by arbitration when agreement could not be reached. Thus, Nova Scotia called on the tribunal in the first phase to determine whether the provinces would be found to have concluded a binding agreement at international law regarding the boundary dividing the offshore area.

Newfoundland argued that the Terms of Reference provided no guidance on the applicable law for the first phase. Newfoundland suggested that no rules of international law addressed whether two provinces had concluded a binding agreement and that only domestic Canadian law could provide a response to this question. According to Newfoundland, the words "with such modifications as the circumstances require" in Article 3.1 of the Terms of Reference permitted the tribunal to rely on domestic Canadian law for the purposes of answering the first question put to it by the parties.

The tribunal determined in the first phase that the Terms of Reference required the application of international law in deciding the first phase of the arbitration, noting that rules of international law on maritime boundary delimitation refer to agreement as the primary mode of delimitation. The tribunal also pointed out that the legislation underlying the Terms of Reference also refers to international law as the applicable law.[21] The reference to the words "with such modifications as the circumstances require" in

---

[18] *Ibid.* at Article 2.3.

[19] As in the first phase, Newfoundland appointed Donald McRae as agent for the arbitration. Nova Scotia appointed L. Yves Fortier as agent for the arbitration.

[20] Terms of Reference, *supra* note 8 at Article 3.1.

[21] Award, First Phase, *supra* note 4 at para. 3.24.

the dispute settlement provisions provide the necessary flexibility to apply international law to a provincial agreement on an offshore maritime boundary.[22]

In the second phase, in what the tribunal described as a "curious transposition,"[23] Newfoundland argued for the application of international law to the delimitation phase, while Nova Scotia pleaded for a resolution that took into account domestic law and, in particular, the Accord Acts. Newfoundland asserted that "[t]he law applicable to Phase Two of this arbitration is ... the customary international law respecting the delimitation of the continental shelf."[24] It contended that the expression "principles of international law" in the Terms of Reference "refers *prima facie* to generally applicable principles of law and not to the *lex specialis* created by particular treaties"[25] — notably Article 6 of the 1958 Geneva Convention on the Continental Shelf.[26] Newfoundland was nevertheless of the view that "nothing turns on whether the applicable law is Article 6 or customary international law" because the "result and process of delimitation would be the same" since the two sources of law are identical.[27] Newfoundland relied on the fundamental norm of maritime boundary delimitation articulated in the *Case Concerning Delimitation of the Maritime Boundary in the Gulf of Maine Area (Canada v. United States of America) (Gulf of Maine* case),[28] which provides that "delimitation is to be effected by the application of equitable criteria and by the use of practical methods capable of ensuring, with regard to the geographic configuration of the area and other relevant circumstances, an equitable result."[29] In the final analysis, according to Newfoundland, the law governing maritime boundary delimitation dictates that the equity of the result is of paramount importance and that "it is above all the controlling

---

[22] *Ibid.* at paras. 3.25-3.29.

[23] Award, Second Phase, *supra* note 3 at para. 2.3.

[24] Memorial of Newfoundland and Labrador at para. 72 [on file with the author] [hereinafter Newfoundland Memorial].

[25] *Ibid.* at para. 72.

[26] Geneva Convention on the Continental Shelf, 499 U.N.T.S. 311, 1970 C.T.S. 4 (entered into force June 10, 1964; ratified by Canada on February 2, 1970).

[27] Newfoundland Memorial, *supra* note 24 at para. 73.

[28] *Case Concerning Delimitation of the Maritime Boundary in the Gulf of Maine Area (Canada v. United States of America),* [1984] I.C.J. Rep. 246 [hereinafter *Gulf of Maine* case].

[29] *Ibid.,* quoted in Newfoundland Memorial, *supra* note 24 at para. 79.

importance of the coastal geography that gives the principles governing maritime boundary delimitation a truly legal character."[30] Newfoundland stressed that continental shelf rights are inherent and need not be claimed or exercised. Consequently, according to Newfoundland, the conduct of the parties is only a "secondary consideration, and never the primary basis for establishing a line" and "[w]hat counts, instead, is the inherent title emerging from the facts of geography."[31]

Nova Scotia argued that the "conventional law of maritime boundary delimitation ... is of limited utility in the present case."[32] According to Nova Scotia, the delimitation provisions of the 1958 Geneva Convention on the Continental Shelf "are not directly applicable in this arbitration ... because the continental shelf regime to which the [Geneva Convention] applies is inherently different from the regime of joint management and revenue sharing that is the object of this arbitration."[33] For Nova Scotia, because the provinces would acquire only limited, shared entitlements as set out in the Accord Acts, the "rights enjoyed by the parties to this dispute are fundamentally at odds, as regards both their nature and scope, with the 'exclusive' and 'sovereign' rights to explore and exploit the natural resources of the continental shelf."[34] Nova Scotia also pointed out that the "substantive scope of the interests is different"[35] because the offshore regime does not apply to non-hydrocarbon minerals, sedentary species, or the regulation of seabed activities such as the laying of submarine cables or pipelines. Moreover, the geographic area covered by the offshore areas under the Accord Acts covered areas not within the continental shelf. For many of the same reasons, Nova Scotia also denied the applicability of the 1982 Convention on the Law of the Sea (LOSC).[36]

Thus, for Nova Scotia, the tribunal was bound to turn to the customary law of maritime boundary delimitation as articulated in the

[30] Newfoundland Memorial, *supra* note 24 at para. 82.

[31] *Ibid.* at para. 83.

[32] Memorial of Nova Scotia at Part III, para. 2 [on file with the author] [hereinafter Nova Scotia Memorial].

[33] *Ibid.* at Part III, para. 6.

[34] *Ibid.* at Part III, para. 12.

[35] *Ibid.*

[36] United Nations Convention on the Law of the Sea, December 10, 1982, 450 U.N.T.S. 11 (entered into force November 16, 1994; Canada has not ratified the convention) [hereinafter LOSC].

jurisprudence of the International Court of Justice (ICJ) and other tribunals. Nova Scotia understood this jurisprudence as providing that "the fundamental norm governing maritime boundary delimitation at customary international law ... requires that delimitation be effected by the application of equitable principles, taking into account all the relevant circumstances, in order to achieve an equitable result."[37] In addition, Nova Scotia contended that the legal basis of title (or entitlement in the case at hand, for title was not in issue), which is emphasized repeatedly in the jurisprudence, is critical for the determination of relevant circumstances, the choice of equitable criteria, and the definition of the relevant area. Nova Scotia described the legal entitlement in this arbitration as "truly *sui generis* to the Accord legislation"[38] and that this unique nature and origin of the zone to be delimited "must underlie all aspects of the delimitation."[39] In particular, Nova Scotia argued that "this aspect of the case distinguishes the delimitation from all those previously adjudicated."[40]

In its counter-memorial, Newfoundland characterized Nova Scotia's position on the applicable law as an "attempt to divorce the delimitation from accepted legal principles,"[41] with a view to relegating geographic considerations to a "mere afterthought" and giving pride of place to a failed negotiating process.[42] According to Newfoundland, Nova Scotia's approach "literally turns the law of maritime boundary delimitation on its head,"[43] for geographic considerations are always "centre stage."[44] Newfoundland was untroubled by the differences in the nature and subject matter of the zones to which Nova Scotia referred, arguing that the requirement in the Terms of Reference to apply the international law of maritime boundary delimitation required the adoption of a legal fiction — that the parties are the subjects of international law — and a legal assumption — that the subject matter of the dispute is

---

[37] Nova Scotia Memorial, *supra* note 32 at Part III, para. 19.

[38] *Ibid.* at Part III, para. 6.

[39] *Ibid.* at Part III, para. 7.

[40] *Ibid.*

[41] Counter-Memorial of Newfoundland and Labrador at para. 154 [on file with the author] [hereinafter Newfoundland Counter-Memorial].

[42] *Ibid.* at para. 164.

[43] *Ibid.* at para. 157.

[44] *Ibid.* at para. 158.

within the scope of international law of maritime delimitation.[45] Indeed, this was what was intended by the words "as if the parties were states" in Article 3.1 of the Terms of Reference. Otherwise, the arbitration would be a "logical impossibility." The Nova Scotia approach would lead to a *non liquet*, and the result would be a "total frustration of the statutory adoption of international law, and of this arbitration."[46]

Nova Scotia argued in its counter-memorial that the "entire thrust of Newfoundland's case is to limit the range of circumstances to be taken into account by the Tribunal in effecting the delimitation," which, according to Nova Scotia, is "the opposite of what the law requires."[47] Nova Scotia also criticized Newfoundland for "ignoring" the basis of legal entitlement involved in the arbitration, with the result that "Newfoundland justifies its virtually exclusive focus on geography in the construction of its proposed line by reference to a fictitious basis of entitlement to the offshore areas, one drawn from the institution of the continental shelf."[48]

Decision of the Tribunal on the Applicable Law

The tribunal was "not persuaded" that the origin of the parties' rights in the Accord Acts "makes any relevant difference to the process of delimitation."[49] The tribunal said that it was bound by the Terms of Reference and the Accord Acts and that these dictated that the tribunal was to apply the principles of international law governing maritime boundary delimitation. Although the provinces were not subjects of international law and the principles governing maritime boundary delimitation would not normally apply to offshore zones described in the Accord Acts — that is, a domestic federal-provincial arrangement on the management and revenue sharing relative to offshore hydrocarbon resources — Article 3.1 of the Terms of Reference required the tribunal to effect the delimitation "as if the parties were states subject to the same rights and obligations as the Government of Canada." In other words, all of the attributes of states, including territorial sovereignty and

---

[45]   *Ibid.* at para. 160.

[46]   *Ibid.* at para. 162.

[47]   Counter-Memorial of Nova Scotia at Part, II, para. 4 [on file with the author] [hereinafter Nova Scotia Counter-Memorial].

[48]   *Ibid.* at Part II, para. 34.

[49]   Award, Second Phase, *supra* note 3 at para. 2.14.

exclusive sovereign rights with respect to the resources of the continental shelf adjacent to their coats were conferred on the provinces for the limited purpose of the delimitation arbitration. Moreover, having the same rights and obligations as the government of Canada meant that the provinces' rights were not those derived from domestic law but rather those derived from Canada's legal basis of title under international law.[50]

The tribunal was of the view that none of the differences between the regime of negotiated entitlements and the regime of the continental shelf "conflict with or impede the application of the Terms of Reference."[51] Moreover, according to the tribunal, the history of the inter-provincial and federal-provincial negotiations regarding the offshore made it clear that Nova Scotia and Newfoundland "always looked upon [the offshore] as being governed by the same principles of delimitation as the continental shelf."[52]

The tribunal pointed out that the government of Canada was not required to set out in the Accord Acts that international law principles of delimitation would be used to allocate interest between the provinces — it could have laid down some other applicable law. Noting, however, that the Accord Acts "expressly stipulated that, in the absence of agreement, disputed offshore areas of the two provinces were to be delimited according to the principles of international law," the tribunal asserted that "the Canadian Parliament was seeking to resolve a difficulty, not to create one."[53] According to the tribunal, "[i]t was entirely appropriate to apply the international law principles of delimitation to this task"[54] and "[t]he Parliament of Canada having done so, there is no reason to treat the legislative mandate and the Terms of Reference as saying anything else than their words provide."[55] The tribunal concluded that, in any event, "the purpose for which the offshore areas are created are key purposes of the continental shelf — the administration of and benefit from exploitation of oil and gas resources."[56]

[50] *Ibid.* at para. 2.15.

[51] *Ibid.* at para. 2.16.

[52] *Ibid.* at para. 2.17.

[53] *Ibid.* at para. 2.18.

[54] *Ibid.*

[55] *Ibid.*

[56] *Ibid.*

Turning to the applicability of the 1958 Geneva Convention on the Continental Shelf, which both provinces dismissed as not applicable in the delimitation (albeit for different reasons), the tribunal disagreed with both parties and found that the convention and, in particular, Article 6 did apply to the delimitation. The tribunal dismissed Nova Scotia's concern that the offshore regime covered areas that fall outside the area covered by the continental shelf, namely the area landward of the continental shelf (since the offshore zones begin at the low water mark) and the seaward extent (since the offshore zones extend to the outer edge of the continental margin as defined in the 1982 LOSC[57]). The tribunal noted that "the line will at no point represent a territorial sea boundary."[58] In addition, the tribunal thought the contrast that Nova Scotia sought to draw between the 1958 convention and the 1982 convention was "too stark" and said that the definitions in the conventions of the seaward extent of the zones were "essentially compatible."[59] The tribunal pointed out that it was not aware of any delimitation out to 200 nautical miles "that required adjustment in terms of its direction beyond that limit."[60]

The tribunal also rejected Newfoundland's thesis that the Terms of Reference referred to general principles of law and not to the *lex specialis* of a particular treaty such as the 1958 Geneva Convention on the Continental Shelf, ruling that it did not accept such a narrow construction of the Terms of Reference. In the tribunal's view, it was appropriate to apply the 1958 Geneva Convention on the Continental Shelf, which is binding on Canada and, by virtue of Article 3.1 of the Terms of Reference, is also binding on Newfoundland and Nova Scotia. The tribunal thus concluded that the applicable law for the second phase of the arbitration "include[d] the provisions of Article 6 of the 1958 Geneva Convention and the developments under customary international law that have been associated with the interpretation and application of Article 6."[61]

---

[57] The outer edge of the continental margin is defined in the Oceans Act (S.C. 1996, c. 31), which prescribes the limits of Canadian jurisdiction using the terms found in Article 76 of the 1982 LOSC, *supra* note 36.

[58] Award, Second Phase, *supra* note 3 at para. 2.21.

[59] *Ibid.* at para. 2.22.

[60] *Ibid.*

[61] *Ibid.* at 2.35.

PROCESS OF DELIMITATION

Parties' Arguments: Relevant Circumstances, Equitable Criteria, and Choice of Method

As noted earlier in this comment, both provinces claimed to rely on the "fundamental norm of maritime boundary delimitation" — that "the delimitation is to be effected by the application of equitable criteria and by the use of practical methods capable of ensuring, with regard to the geographic configuration of the area and other relevant circumstances, an equitable result."[62] Their legal positions, however, in the words of the tribunal, were "radically opposed."[63]

Newfoundland: Coastal Geography First and Foremost

Newfoundland's appreciation of the delimitation exercise was founded on its view that "when the law refers to the 'relevant circumstances,' what is meant is first and foremost the coastal geography and its relationship to the delimitation area,"[64] and it opined

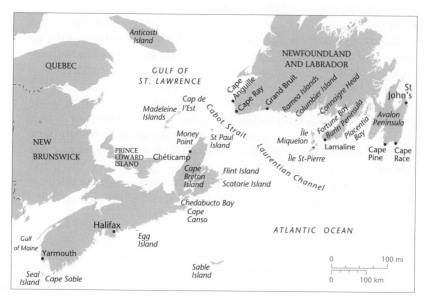

Figure 1. Geographical setting

---

[62] *Gulf of Maine* case, *supra* note 28 at 299-300.

[63] Award, Second Phase, *supra* note 3 at para. 1.26.

[64] Newfoundland Memorial, *supra* note 24 at para. 90.

that "the present dispute can and should be resolved exclusively on the basis of the coastal geography of the delimitation area."[65] The fundamental importance of coastal geography, according to Newfoundland, is founded in the principle that the land dominates the sea, which was enunciated in *North Sea Continental Shelf (Federal Republic of Germany* v. *Denmark; Federal Republic of Germany* v. *Netherlands) (North Sea Continental Shelf* cases).[66] In other words, sovereignty over the coastline enables a state to claim title to continental shelf areas situated in front of its coasts. Newfoundland asserted that "[a]ll the leading cases delimiting the continental shelf have been based primarily or exclusively on the coastal geography."[67] Thus, geography is "overwhelmingly the most important factor, and most often it is the only relevant factor."[68] Newfoundland contended that according to customary law as it has evolved, the distance principle provides that states are entitled to continental shelf rights out to 200 miles regardless of geology or geomorphology considerations. To Newfoundland, the distance principle implied that "spatial factors — in other words geography — have become more than ever the principal consideration."[69]

Newfoundland conceded that non-geographical considerations could be relevant in some cases, provided they were "demonstrably relevant"[70] to the legal institution of the continental shelf. It noted that economic factors generally had been given short shrift in the cases and were only considered at all as an *ex post facto* test of the method chosen on other (notably, geographic) grounds and, then, only in relation to pre-existing and established dependence on known resources. The conduct of the parties could be relevant only if it met the "very stringent test"[71] of being "mutual, sustained, consistent and unequivocal in indicating acceptance"[72] of a proposed line as an equitable basis of delimitation. If the conduct does not meet that test, it must be disregarded.

---

[65] *Ibid.* at para. 84.

[66] *North Sea Continental Shelf (Federal Republic of Germany* v. *Denmark; Federal Republic of Germany* v. *Netherlands),* [1969] I.C.J. Rep. 3 [hereinafter *North Sea Continental Shelf* cases].

[67] Newfoundland Memorial, *supra* note 24 at para. 89.

[68] *Ibid.* at para. 90.

[69] *Ibid.* at para. 95.

[70] *Ibid.* at para. 90.

[71] *Ibid.* at para. 105.

[72] *Ibid.*

In terms of equitable criteria (or principles, as Newfoundland called them), Newfoundland asserted that the first step in delimitation is to determine the seaward extensions of the coasts, or their natural prolongations, and it affirmed that coasts project frontally. Newfoundland referred to the notion of frontal projection as a "pervasive theme"[73] in the jurisprudence. It controlled the selection of the relevant coasts, is reflected in the use of particular methods (such as perpendicular lines), and has been the basis of the analysis of the coastal relationship, notably in the boundary arbitration in *Case Concerning the Delimitation of the Maritime Areas between Canada and France*.[74] Newfoundland underscored the importance of the principle of non-encroachment, which requires the avoidance of any cut-off effect of a party's natural prolongation. Finally, Newfoundland called attention to the need to give proportionate effects to the coastal geography, which could be achieved in different ways. It pointed to "two situations where the concern for proportionate effects typically arises": the potentially distorting effect of incidental features such as islands and the need to take into account "significant disparities in coastal lengths so that the areas resulting from the delimitation correspond broadly to the coastal frontage that constitutes the basis of title."[75] In terms of islands, Newfoundland urged that it was not only size that had to be considered but also position (such as whether the island forms part of the general configuration of the coast or deviates from it), which was critical. As to disparities in the lengths of coasts, Newfoundland posited that proportionality — the relationship between coastal length and maritime entitlement — was a "critical factor,"[76] and it contended that proportionality could play a role as a contributing factor in the selection of a line or as an *ex post facto* test of the equitable character of the delimitation line.

As to the choice of method, Newfoundland asserted that there "are no legally mandatory methods."[77] The only requirement is that the choice of method leads to an equitable result. It also referred to the practice of using different methods in different sectors of the delimitation area as dictated by different geographic

---

[73] *Ibid.* at para. 108.

[74] *Case Concerning the Delimitation of the Maritime Areas between Canada and France* (1992), 31 I.L.M. 1145 [hereinafter *Maritime Areas between Canada and France*].

[75] Newfoundland Memorial, *supra* note 24 at para. 112.

[76] *Ibid.* at para. 117.

[77] *Ibid.* at para. 122.

circumstances. Newfoundland characterized equidistance as "a method of exemplary utility"[78] in the case of opposite coasts where the seaward extensions of the coasts converge and overlap, but it considered this method "less reliable"[79] where coasts are adjacent and the convergence is different. Moreover, with adjacent coasts, the median line would be controlled by a single pair of basepoints, instead of in the case of opposite coasts where the basepoints are constantly shifting in response to the continuous changes in the contours of the coasts. Newfoundland referred to a number of instances where international courts and tribunals have used a median line as a provisional first step in the determination of the delimitation line but noted that this procedure had by no means "any character of legal necessity."[80] Newfoundland pointed out that equidistance "is *par excellence* the method that reflects micro-geography rather than macro-geography,"[81] and it referred to the "dramatic effects"[82] that off-lying islands could have on the position of the line. Newfoundland explained that, with the equidistance method where each basepoint is given the same weight and value, "an island detached from the mainland, however small the dimensions and however distant from the coast, has exactly the same effect as a hypothetical extension of the mainland to wherever the island may happen to be."[83] Thus, the method itself can cause "an effective refashioning of geography," which "in the name of equity is inadmissible" in maritime boundary delimitation.[84]

Newfoundland characterized islands as "the classic instance of special circumstances."[85] It explained the various techniques used to address the potential source of inequity, including enclaving, reduced or no effect, and using straight lines (perpendiculars and bisectors) uninfluenced by islands. It emphasized that both size and position of the island would determine the appropriate effect to be given to an island in a delimitation exercise. Newfoundland referred to the geometrical methods of delimitation, notably bisectors and perpendiculars, to the general direction of the coast or

---

[78] *Ibid.* at para. 126.

[79] *Ibid.* at para. 128.

[80] *Ibid.* at para. 131.

[81] *Ibid.* at para. 137.

[82] *Ibid.* at para. 138.

[83] *Ibid.*

[84] *Ibid.*

[85] *Ibid.* at para. 140.

to a closing line of a concavity. According to Newfoundland, these methods avoid the "distortions that are inherent in the equidistance method"[86] and have the advantages of flexibility, simplicity, and clarity.

Newfoundland's Line

Newfoundland's line is composed of bisectors and perpendiculars and is divided into four segments (see Figure 2 at the end of this comment). Its choice of methods was determined by its conclusion that an equidistance line, which it drew on a provisional basis as a starting point, could not lead to an equitable result in the circumstances of this case, even if it were adjusted with a view to taking into account those circumstances. Newfoundland explained that the prevalence of incidental features, including St. Paul Island and Sable Island, the marked disparity in coastal lengths, and the cutoff effect produced by the protruding coasts of Cape Breton Island and Saint-Pierre and Miquelon, together with the recessed coast of Newfoundland at the back of the concavity, combined to render the equidistance method inappropriate for this case.

Newfoundland stressed that the incidental features would distort the course of an equidistance line to such an extent that the use of equidistance was inappropriate "on this ground alone."[87] In particular, it claimed that utilizing equidistance would be tantamount to shifting the mainland coast of Nova Scotia eighty-eight nautical miles to sea, to the eastern tip of Sable Island — a result that Newfoundland described as "disproportionate, inequitable and illogical."[88] Newfoundland also claimed that the constitutional status of Sable Island, which is under the jurisdiction of the federal government, gave Nova Scotia only a "nominal interest" in the island and "[o]n that ground alone"[89] should not be used as a source of entitlement for Nova Scotia to the continental shelf.

Regarding coastal lengths, Newfoundland pointed out that it was self-evident — as observed by the Court of Arbitration in the *Canada* v. *France* case — that the most extensive coasts fronting on the delimitation area are those of Newfoundland and that the marked disparity of coastal lengths ruled out "in the most unequivocal terms" a method that is based on a half-way line between two

---

[86] *Ibid.* at para. 161.

[87] *Ibid.* at para. 176.

[88] *Ibid.* at para. 182.

[89] *Ibid.* at para. 184.

coastal fronts that "are not of similar orders of magnitude."[90] New-foundland also pointed out that the equidistance method would create an inequitable cut-off of the Newfoundland coast due to the concavity of the Newfoundland coast coupled with the convexity of Cape Breton Island. Moreover, according to Newfoundland, per-mitting such a cut-off would "contradict the whole thrust of the decision"[91] in the *Maritime Areas between Canada and France* case, which sought to minimize the cut-off of the seaward projection of the south coast of Newfoundland by awarding a narrow corridor to the French islands. Newfoundland opined that it would be a "strange twist of fate"[92] if this tribunal reintroduced the cut-off by applying equidistance in this case.

Newfoundland further objected to equidistance based on the view that it would result in encroachment on Newfoundland's nat-ural prolongation, particularly in the outer area of the delimitation zone where, according to the Court of Arbitration in the *Maritime Areas between Canada and France* case, there was no competing pro-jection from Nova Scotia. Indeed, according to Newfoundland, in the area outside the concavity, "it is hardly meaningful to speak of a coastal relationship at all."[93] Finally, Newfoundland pointed to the "unique political geography" where a continuos equidistant line "is patently an impossibility" due to the need to "leap-frog" the corri-dor awarded to the French islands of Saint-Pierre and Miquelon — a situation that would be "more than anomalous" and "would not be countenanced by international law or practice."[94]

In light of these considerations, Newfoundland proposed a line starting from the mid-point of the closing line in Cabot Strait between Money Point on Cape Breton Island and Cape Ray on New-foundland, disregarding the "incidental feature" of St. Paul Island for the purposes of determining the mid-point. Proceeding east-ward, the first segment of the line is a bisector of the angle formed by the two coastal fronts facing this "inner concavity,"[95] which is "inherently equitable in that it averages the general direction of the two coastal fronts"[96] and will effect an equal division of the areas

[90] *Ibid.* at para. 192.

[91] Newfoundland Memorial, *supra* note 24 at para. 200.

[92] *Ibid.*

[93] *Ibid.* at para. 201.

[94] *Ibid.* at para. 206

[95] *Ibid.* at para. 214.

[96] *Ibid.* at para. 217.

of overlap and convergence of seaward extensions "as required by the *Gulf of Maine* case."[97]

The second segment of the line is also a bisector, but the controlling coastal front of Newfoundland has changed to take account of the change in direction of the Newfoundland coast at Connaigre Head and Fortune Bay, with the result that the line is more southward in its bearing. The "unmistakable analogy" to the situation in the *Gulf of Maine* case,[98] where the chamber shifted the line to take into account the marked disparity in coastal lengths suggested the shifting of the line in this case. The line was thus shifted towards Nova Scotia so that it intersects the closing line between Scatarie Island (Nova Scotia) and Lamaline Shag Rock (Newfoundland) at a point along the line that reflects the coastal ratio.[99] The closing line defines the inner concavity. The third segment of Newfoundland's line responds to the "shift in the predominant coastal relationship from one of opposite coasts to one of adjacency"[100] at the closing line of the inner concavity. According to Newfoundland, "practice and precedent immediately suggest[ed]"[101] a line running perpendicular to the closing line of the inner concavity, starting from the point where the second segment of the line intersects the closing line to the inner concavity. This line, according to Newfoundland, avoids potential distortion that might be caused by Sable Island, takes account of the "dominant position"[102] of the Newfoundland coasts in the outer area, and avoids any tendency to swing towards either coast, thus avoiding encroachment on the seaward projections of the coasts. Newfoundland indicated that it was not appropriate for the tribunal to define the terminal point of the line "in view of the policies that Canada may wish to adopt [regarding the location of the outer limit of the continental shelf] in the event of the ratification of the 1982 Convention on the Law of the Sea."[103]

Newfoundland turned finally to the segment of the line inside the Gulf of St. Lawrence, which Newfoundland considered should

---

[97] *Ibid.* at para. 217.

[98] *Gulf of Maine* case, *supra* note 28.

[99] Newfoundland asserted that the coastal ratio was 2.42 to 1.00, so it shifted the bisector line towards Nova Scotia a distance of 34.6 nautical miles from the midpoint of the 166.3 nautical-mile line.

[100] Newfoundland Memorial, *supra* note 24 at para. 229.

[101] *Ibid.* at para. 238.

[102] *Ibid.* at para. 242.

[103] *Ibid.* at para. 240.

be determined only after determining the segments related to the "principle focus"[104] of the dispute. Arguing that this segment should "conform to, rather than influence" the principles and methods applied in the seaward areas, Newfoundland proposed a perpendicular to the Cabot Strait closing line starting at the mid-point identified earlier, which it argued would reflect the general direction of the coasts and would avoid any tendency to swing towards the territory of either party. Newfoundland suggested that the award should not prescribe a terminal point given the potential third party interests in the Gulf of St. Lawrence. It proposed instead that the tribunal simply determine that the perpendicular shall extend to the limit of the offshore areas of Newfoundland and Nova Scotia respectively within the gulf.

Newfoundland asserted that there were no non-geographical considerations that were relevant to determining the equity of the result. Economic factors have no relevance, it said, because past dependence is impossible in an area where resource exploitation is potential rather than actual. Given that the conduct of the parties did not meet the "exacting standards of consistency, mutuality and longevity" and there was no evidence of "real activity on the ground," conduct can have no role in the delimitation.[105] Thus, left with geographic considerations alone, Newfoundland concluded that the perpendicular to the closing line was logical and equitable because it "reflects ... the basic structure of the coastal geography."[106] Moreover, Newfoundland contended that the line as a whole produces a proportionate result. The application of the proportionality test to an area defined by perpendiculars reflecting the seaward extensions of the relevant coastal fronts results in a ratio of coastal lengths (69.4 per cent for Newfoundland to 30.6 per cent for Nova Scotia) that is almost identical to the ratio of offshore areas (69.6 per cent for Newfoundland to 30.4 per cent for Nova Scotia).

Nova Scotia: The Predominance of Legal Title

Nova Scotia's case began with the premise that the legal nature of the zone "constituted, in effect, the starting-point for the application of the fundamental norm of maritime boundary delimitation

---

[104] *Ibid.* at para. 172.

[105] *Ibid.* at para. 252.

[106] *Ibid.* at para. 255.

in any given case."[107] According to Nova Scotia, "the significance of the juridical nature of the zone is such that it affects all aspects of a delimitation,"[108] and the "predominance"[109] of legal title as a factor "to be given special weight in the delimitation exercise cannot be overstated."[110] Nova Scotia claimed that the legal basis of entitlement "had been found to have direct significance"[111] for the determination of relevant circumstances, the choice of an equitable method, and the definition of the relevant area.

Nova Scotia asserted that the arbitration involved a maritime zone that is "truly *sui generis*,"[112] and therefore it must be "distinguishe[d] ... from all those previously adjudicated."[113] The tribunal was not concerned with a continental shelf claim or with jurisdiction over the water column but rather with offshore areas defined in the Accord Acts that involved entitlements that were "entirely the creation of negotiated arrangements implemented in Canadian law"[114] and that were limited in nature and scope. Hence, the determination of the relevant area did not require any analysis of relevant coasts or coastal projections, for the "straightforward"[115] answer was already set out in the Accord Acts. The provinces have no *ab initio* entitlements, and their maximum entitlements are set out in the Accord Acts. According to Nova Scotia, it is the area where the provinces' respective entitlements converge and overlap that "forms the area of primary relevance for purposes both of effecting the delimitation and testing the equitableness of the result."[116]

In terms of relevant circumstances, Nova Scotia argued that the conduct of the parties was "highly relevant" for "effecting an equitable delimitation."[117] According to Nova Scotia, although the tribunal found in the first phase that the conduct of the parties was

[107] Nova Scotia Memorial, *supra* note 32 at Part III, para. 60.

[108] *Ibid.*

[109] *Ibid.* at Part III, para. 49.

[110] *Ibid.*

[111] *Ibid.*

[112] *Ibid.* at Part IV, para. 6.

[113] *Ibid.* at Part IV, para. 7.

[114] *Ibid.* at Part IV, para. 6.

[115] *Ibid.* at Part IV, para. 20.

[116] *Ibid.* at Part IV, para. 24.

[117] *Ibid.* at Part IV, para. 30.

insufficient to demonstrate that the parties had concluded a binding agreement on the line dividing their respective offshore areas, this finding was not dispositive of the relevance of conduct for the second phase of the arbitration.[118] Nova Scotia maintained that the relevance of prior conduct had been consistently recognized in previous adjudications. Based on the jurisprudence, Nova Scotia cited three types of conduct that could be found to be relevant: mutual actions by which parties agree upon some line; independent and concordant actions establishing a *de facto* line; and unilateral actions accompanied by acquiescence of the other party. Nova Scotia contended that all three types of conduct existed in the present case. First, in 1964, the parties came to a political, albeit not binding, agreement on the line, which lapsed only because the federal government refused to recognize provincial rights in the offshore — a matter beyond the parties' control. This agreement, according to Nova Scotia, "constituted evidence of the most compelling kind of what the parties themselves believed to be ... an equitable delimitation of their respective claims."[119] Second, the concordant actions of the parties in issuing oil and gas permits along the line leads to the "inescapable conclusion that the parties, during the 1960s and 1970s, acted on the understanding that there was at least a *de facto* boundary in place between their respective offshore areas."[120] Third, Newfoundland never protested Nova Scotia's permit issuance along the line, nor did it object to depictions of the line on maps used in interprovincial and federal-provincial negotiations. Nor did Newfoundland object to the use of the line in certain federal provincial agreements or in the legislation implementing such agreements.[121] Thus, Nova Scotia argued that, by their conduct, the parties established a *de facto* boundary. It further contended that the conduct in this case was far stronger than the conduct that

---

[118] Indeed, the tribunal said as much in its award in the first phase. See Award, First Phase, *supra* note 4 at para. 7.8.

[119] Nova Scotia Memorial, *supra* note 32 at Part IV, para. 37.

[120] *Ibid.* at Part IV, para. 98.

[121] Nova Scotia referred to the Federal-Provincial Memorandum of Understanding in Respect of the Administration and Management of Mineral Resources Offshore of the Maritime Provinces (February 1, 1977), which was set up between Canada and Nova Scotia, Prince Edward Island, and New Brunswick, and to the Canada-Nova Scotia Agreement on Offshore Oil and Gas Resources Management and Revenue Sharing (March 2, 1982). See Nova Scotia Memorial, *supra* note 32 at Part IV, para. 74.

was accepted by the ICJ in the *Case Concerning the Continental Shelf (Tunisia v. Libyan Arab Jamahiriya) (Tunisia v. Libya* case)[122] as an indicator of what the parties themselves believed to be an equitable line.

Nova Scotia also argued that the location of resources "insofar as it relates to access to those resources by parties to maritime boundary disputes"[123] could be a relevant circumstance in effecting a delimitation, depending on the facts of the case.[124] For Nova Scotia, given the facts of this case — that access to the benefits of hydrocarbon resources is the only objective of the delimitation and that the location of the hydrocarbon resources was a factor in the creation of the offshore areas themselves — it was clear that this factor had to be considered to the extent that pertinent information was available. Nova Scotia claimed that Newfoundland enjoyed a considerable advantage over Nova Scotia in terms of access to resources, and, thus, any movement of the boundary to the detriment of Nova Scotia would add to the "already disproportionate advantage"[125] enjoyed by Newfoundland.

Nova Scotia referred to other delimitations in the region (with the United States in the Gulf of Maine and with France off the islands of Saint-Pierre and Miquelon) as a relevant circumstance to be borne in mind. According to Nova Scotia, there were a number of existing or prospective delimitations that affected or could affect the overall equitableness of the result, because Nova Scotia's offshore entitlement was or could be curtailed as a result of these delimitations.

Finally, Nova Scotia turned to geographic circumstances. It acknowledged that geographic factors "have tended to dominate the selection of equitable criteria in the cases"[126] but said that this was because they were related to the nature of the title involved in those cases. As for the present case, Nova Scotia contended that geographic circumstances "can be expected ... to be less relevant to the present delimitation, in which the nature of the zone and

---

[122] *Case Concerning the Continental Shelf (Tunisia v. Libyan Arab Jamahiriya)*, [1982] I.C.J. Rep. 18 [hereinafter *Tunisia v. Libya* case].

[123] Nova Scotia Memorial, *supra* note 32 at Part IV, para. 109.

[124] Nova Scotia declared that by this argument it was not referring to questions of relative wealth between the parties or degree of dependence on the resources, acknowledging that such matters are irrelevant to maritime delimitation.

[125] Nova Scotia Memorial, *supra* note 32 at Part IV, para. 123.

[126] *Ibid.* at Part III, para. 55.

the source of legal entitlement ... are based neither on distance (as with the exclusive economic zone), or the seaward extension of land sovereignty (as with the continental shelf), but on negotiated entitlements to certain restricted rights within a single zone falling under the jurisdiction of a third party."[127]

In terms of equitable criteria, Nova Scotia recalled the distinction made by the chamber of the ICJ in the *Gulf of Maine* case between primary and auxiliary criteria — the former being those applicable to the drawing of the boundary line and the latter being those used for correcting a provisional line or testing the result. Nova Scotia contended that there were two primary criteria in this case, the application of which would lead to a result that requires no adjustment. First, that the delimitation should give effect to the line that the parties, as demonstrated through their prior conduct, may have considered equitable, and, second, that the delimitation should reflect the equal division of the overlapping legal entitlements of the parties to the zone in question. With respect to conduct, Nova Scotia claimed that the "single most dominant feature" of the case was the "overwhelming record of both mutual and 'matching' conduct that effectively establishes a line" that the parties themselves, "in good faith negotiations and subsequent practice," considered to be equitable.[128] Nova Scotia referred to what it called "an extensive pattern of conduct" in concluding a mutually agreed line for purposes of negotiations with the federal government, matching permit issuance along the line and acquiescence in the use of the line. Nova Scotia claimed that the evidence of conduct demonstrating the parties' acceptance of a boundary line "is stronger here than in any other recorded maritime boundary case."[129] In Nova Scotia's view, a line established by the parties' conduct would reflect more genuinely what the parties consider to be equitable than would a line established for the purposes of adjudication.

In regard to the equal division of overlapping entitlements, Nova Scotia asserted that the concept of overlapping entitlements was rooted in the principle of non-encroachment. The definition of the extent of the offshore areas set out in the Accord Acts, which relies on criteria related to distance, geophysical, and geomorphological factors, provided, in Nova Scotia's view, an "objective" means of

---

[127]   *Ibid.* at Part IV, para. 137.

[128]   *Ibid.* at Part V, para. 8.

[129]   *Ibid.* at Part V, para. 14.

determining the area of overlapping entitlements. Nova Scotia also cited three auxiliary criteria: proportionality between relevant coastal lengths and maritime areas; equitable division of access to resources; and avoidance of cut-off and consideration of macro-geography, including other delimitations. It referred to these criteria when testing the result of its claimed line and found that its line met the tests of these criteria so that no adjustment was sought on the basis of these or the primary criteria.

Finally, Nova Scotia argued that the conduct of the parties demonstrates acquiescence in the "existing" line by Newfoundland and the creation of an estoppel regarding that line in favour of Nova Scotia. Thus, not only does the existing line match the result of the application of the fundamental norm of maritime boundary delimitation but it is also indicated by the application of the principles of acquiescence and estoppel.

Nova Scotia's Line

Nova Scotia's line is "the line drawn by the parties"[130] (see Figure 2 at the end of this comment). Nova Scotia indicated that the practical method for drawing the line "can be, *prima facie,* determined by reference to the conduct of the parties" given the "extraordinary continuity and relevance" of this conduct.[131] The method employed is a series of straight line segments starting from a tri-junction point in the Gulf of St. Lawrence joining the points defined in the 1964 "unratified" agreement and later delineated with coordinates in 1972[132] — effectively a simplified median line. From the last mid-point between Flint Island (Nova Scotia) and Grand Bruit (Newfoundland), which is known as Point 2017, the line extends as a 135-degree azimuth to the outer edge of the continental margin. This line "arises from the 1964 agreement" and is "confirmed precisely" by all of Nova Scotia's permits as well as one of Newfoundland's.[133] The method was also followed in subsequent conduct.

Nova Scotia also provided an alternative method of drawing the line in the outer segment. Instead of direct reference to the parties'

---

[130] *Ibid.* at Part V, para. 22.

[131] *Ibid.*

[132] These were mid-points between opposing coastal features. For a description of the 1964 agreement and the 1972 delineation, see Award, First Phase, *supra* note 4 at sections 4 and 5 as well as Hughes, *supra* note 4 at 195-97.

[133] Nova Scotia Memorial, *supra* note 32 at Part V, para. 24.

conduct, reference could be made to the methods set out in the
1964 agreement, which provided that "[i]slands lying between the
Provinces ... are considered as if they were peninsulas" and
"[m]ineral right boundaries are so drawn as to join median points
between prominent landmarks ... along parallel shores."[134] Nova
Scotia claimed Sable Island to be the only relevant "prominent
landmark" on the Nova Scotia side and considered it "as if it were
a peninsula." It indicated Cape St. Mary's (on the Avalon Peninsula
in Newfoundland) as the nearest opposite point to Sable Island.
The mid-point of the closing line between these two points falls on
the boundary defined by the 135-degree azimuth. Thus, according
to Nova Scotia, both methods — one referring to the conduct of
the parties and one referring to the methods stipulated in the 1964
agreement — lead to the identical result in the outer segment,
namely the 135-dgree azimuth. Nova Scotia noted that the boundary determined by these methods is precisely defined in Schedule I
of the Canada-Nova Scotia Accord Act.[135]

Nova Scotia pointed out that, as with the first primary criterion
of conduct of the parties, both practical methods were equally
consistent with the implementation of the second primary criteria
upon which it relied, namely the equal division of overlapping
entitlements. It noted, relying on reasoning in the *North Sea Continental Shelf* cases and the *Gulf of Maine* case, that in circumstances
of opposition the median line "can be expected to effect the equal
division of the overlapping areas of entitlements ... between opposite states."[136] For the outer area, Nova Scotia asserted that no
particular method is dictated where the coastal relationship was
primarily one of adjacency.[137] Overall, the line composed of the
simplified median line and the 135-degree azimuth resulted in
"quite close to an equal division" of the areas, although Newfoundland received the larger share.

In testing the equitableness of the line, Nova Scotia also examined the proportionality of the result, although it contended that
the "overall relevance" of proportionality was "somewhat less" in

---

[134] *Ibid.* at Part V, para. 25.

[135] *Ibid.* at Part V, para. 30.

[136] *Ibid.* at Part V, para. 33.

[137] Nova Scotia also argued that the appropriate technical method was a loxo-
drome instead of a geodesic because the former would facilitate management
of permit areas and would not require a precise end-point for the seaward
extent of the line.

this case because the source of title is not based on coastlines but on negotiated arrangements. In any event, defining the relevant area with reference to the Accord Acts and the relevant coasts by taking into account larger bays and indentations rather than using general direction lines, the application of the proportionality test resulted in the following ratio: relevant coats of 52 per cent for Nova Scotia and 48 per cent for Newfoundland to a relevant area of 47 per cent for Nova Scotia and 53 per cent for Newfoundland. Despite the slight disproportion in Newfoundland's favour, Nova Scotia characterized the result as being overall proportional.

Nova Scotia asserted that its line avoided any cut-off and equitably distributed the impact of other delimitations in the area. Nova Scotia accepted that Newfoundland would retain the lion's share of hydrocarbon resources, but it sought only an equitable, rather than an equal, division of resources. On balance, Nova Scotia was of the view that its line, the "*de facto* line established by the conduct of the parties, and consistently respected by them for many years, was not only regarded by the parties as a fair and reasonable division of the offshore, it was, and remains, a fully equitable delimitation in all the circumstances of this case."[138]

Parties' Rebuttals

In its counter-memorial, Newfoundland described the parties' memorials as "ships passing in the night," noting, in particular, the "overarching divergence" in the approach to the basis of title.[139] Newfoundland rejected Nova Scotia's approach that the basis of title is a negotiated entitlement implemented in Canadian law, arguing that it would not be possible to apply the international law of maritime delimitation as required by the Terms of Reference under Nova Scotia's theory. Newfoundland asserted that the legal framework proposed by Nova Scotia leads to an inversion of the proper hierarchy of relevant circumstances, such that geography is relegated to a very low rank, and a failed negotiating process is declared legally determinative.

Newfoundland denied the relevance of the 1964 "statement,"[140] arguing that its conditional nature, as confirmed by the tribunal in the first phase of the arbitration, was also relevant in the second

---

[138] Nova Scotia Memorial, *supra* note 32 at Part V, para. 66.

[139] Newfoundland Counter-Memorial, *supra* note 41 at para. 6.

[140] Newfoundland Memorial, *supra* note 24 at para. 32.

phase. In Newfoundland's view, it was only "wishful thinking"[141] on the part of Nova Scotia that would accord any weight to this conditional understanding in the context of the delimitation.

With respect to Nova Scotia's geography arguments, Newfoundland described Nova Scotia's posited area of overlapping entitlements as "mystifying"[142] and "absurd,"[143] given their breadth (from the Gulf of Maine to the Hibernia oil field), and as divorced from any basis in international law, given their disregard of the concept of geographical adjacency. Nova Scotia was accused of relying on a rule that does not exist in international law in espousing the equal division of overlapping entitlements. In addition, Newfoundland criticized Nova Scotia's selection of relevant coasts, arguing that some of them do not face the delimitation area. Newfoundland observed that the relevant coasts had already been identified in the substantially similar delimitation area involved in the *Maritime Areas between Canada and France* case. Newfoundland also complained of Nova Scotia's disregard for the significant disparity in the overall coastal frontage.

Newfoundland marvelled at Nova Scotia's treatment of Sable Island, alleging that Nova Scotia gave this incidental feature "prominence that overshadows the entire landmass"[144] of Nova Scotia. Hence it is accorded "far more that than the full weight it would have received in a 'strict equidistance' scenario."[145] Newfoundland also mocked Nova Scotia's claim of general concavity for the Nova Scotia coastline, calling it a "flight of fancy based on features that are remote from the delimitation area, including ... a location somewhere in the vicinity of the Bahamas."[146] Newfoundland dismissed Nova Scotia's arguments based on the conduct of the parties, asserting that the conduct is too brief, is remote in time, and that the permits have long-since expired. In regard to access to resources, Newfoundland maintained that this factor was not only irrelevant legally but was also factually distorted and was based on estimates that are far from reliable.

Nova Scotia, for its part, rejected Newfoundland's "stunningly narrow interpretation of the law"[147] and considered that Newfoundland's approach of a delimitation based solely on geography was

---

[141] Newfoundland Counter-Memorial, *supra* note 41 at para. 33.

[142] *Ibid.* at para. 13.

[143] *Ibid.* at para. 14.

[144] *Ibid.* at para. 20.

[145] *Ibid.* at para. 22.

[146] *Ibid.* at para. 24.

[147] Nova Scotia Counter-Memorial, *supra* note 47 at Part II, para. 13.

flawed. Nova Scotia criticized Newfoundland for ignoring the long pattern of conduct of the parties with respect to their mutual boundary, the macro-geographical situation including existing and prospective delimitations, and the distribution of resources effected by Newfoundland's proposed boundary. Nova Scotia asserted that Newfoundland's approach "violated" the fundamental norm of maritime boundary delimitation, "which requires a delimitation to be effected in the light of all, not some, of the relevant circumstances."[148] According to Nova Scotia, Newfoundland's "single-minded focus on geography"[149] led to a failure to engage in a "balancing-up"[150] of all the relevant considerations, as required by the jurisprudence in order to achieve an equitable result. Nova Scotia also denounced Newfoundland for failing to consider the true nature and origin of the offshore areas to be delimited, which Newfoundland incorrectly assumed was a juridical continental shelf. Nova Scotia was also critical of Newfoundland's "artificial"[151] relevant area, which ended at 200 nautical miles, rather than at the outer limit of the continental shelf.

Nova Scotia took issue with the role that Newfoundland accorded to previous decisions, arguing that Newfoundland blindly applied conclusions from previous cases while failing to take into account the different factual circumstances present in these cases, including the different nature of the zones being delimited. Nova Scotia condemned Newfoundland's application of factual findings from the *Maritime Areas between Canada and France* case with respect to the coastal geography, as if they were directly applicable in this case where the circumstances are "entirely different."[152]

Nova Scotia found fault with Newfoundland's appreciation of maritime delimitation jurisprudence. It claimed that coasts project radially and argued that there is no legal authority for Newfoundland's frontal projection theory. Nova Scotia denied that access to resources was relevant only with respect to an established dependency on those resources, as argued by Newfoundland, and claimed that the jurisprudence supported its view that resource location is

---

[148] Nova Scotia Memorial, *supra* note 32 at Part V, para. 5.

[149] Nova Scotia Counter-Memorial, *supra* note 47 at Part II, para. 13.

[150] *Ibid.* at Part II, para. 139, quoting *North Sea Continental Shelf* cases, *supra* note 66 at 50-51.

[151] Nova Scotia Counter-Memorial, *supra* note 47 at Part V, para. 8.

[152] *Ibid.* at Part II, para. 44.

relevant "so far as known or readily ascertainable"[153] as a circumstance relevant to the assessment of a particular result. Nova Scotia accused Newfoundland of misapplying the legal test for acquiescence and estoppel to the role of conduct as a relevant circumstance in a delimitation or as an indicator of what the parties believed to be equitable. Nova Scotia maintained that the cases address conduct going to acquiescence and estoppel differently from conduct as an *indicia* of what parties consider to be equitable.

TRIBUNAL'S DELIMITATION

The tribunal approached the delimitation aspect of its decision by looking first at what it called the "preliminary issues" of the conduct of the parties and the issue of access to resources.

Conduct of the Parties

The tribunal recalled that it ruled in the first phase that the conduct of the parties was insufficient to establish an agreement between them resolving the boundary. This was because the conduct was not considered sufficiently clear and unequivocal to establish such an agreement, and because the conduct was conditional on the federal acceptance of provincial jurisdiction in the offshore, which never came about. For the same reasons, the tribunal was not persuaded in the second phase that the subsequent conduct of the parties, be it in negotiations or in oil and gas permit activity, was sufficient to create an estoppel in favour of Nova Scotia, such that Newfoundland was estopped from denying the existence of a political, if not legally binding, agreement on the boundary. The tribunal ruled that there was "no distinct statement or representation by Newfoundland and Labrador after 1972 that it accepted the boundary, and no statement before or after 1972 that it accepted the boundary 'for all purposes.'"[154]

The tribunal nevertheless acknowledged that, "although more often than not rejected" for a variety of reasons, arguments that the parties have by conduct established or consolidated a particular line or part of one "have been carefully considered" in the cases.[155] The tribunal, relying on the *Case Concerning the Continental Shelf*

---

[153] *Ibid.* at Part II, para 110, quoting *North Sea Continental Shelf* cases, *supra* note 66 at 53-54.

[154] Award, Second Phase, *supra* note 3 at para. 3.2.

[155] *Ibid.* at para. 3.5.

(Libyan Arab Jamahiriya v. *Malta)* (*Libya* v. *Malta* case),[156] explained what it considered to be necessary to establish that a boundary has been established by agreement: "[I]t is necessary to show an unequivocal pattern of conduct as between the two parties concerned, relating to the area and supporting the boundary, or the aspect of the boundary, which is in dispute."[157] The tribunal said that it "fail[ed] to see how conduct which was equivocal or uncertain could be considered decisive" and "accordingly [saw] no reason to depart from the standard laid down by the International Court in *Libya/Malta,* namely whether there is 'any pattern of conduct on either side sufficiently unequivocal to constitute either acquiescence or any helpful indication of any view of either Party as to what would be equitable.'"[158]

The tribunal examined the parties' conduct separately for the "inner area" and the "outer area" of the delimitation area. For the inner area, the tribunal concluded that Newfoundland "never expressly accepted" the 1964 boundary for all purposes, although Newfoundland "did not expressly query the use of the turning points as a basis for a delimitation based on an adjusted equidistance line."[159] The tribunal also noted that permits were issued and that there was limited seismic exploration, albeit no wells were drilled, but it reasoned that "it is difficult to accept that seismic activity, of itself, could give rise to a situation analogous to that in *Tunisia/Libya.*" In any event, the tribunal found that "there is no evidence that there was seismic activity in the critical areas close to the equidistance line."[160] The tribunal criticized Newfoundland for its failure to protest claims and actions, but only in relation to the period after 1992, and opined that "[o]il activity pursuant to the Atlantic Accord in the 1990s, had it conformed to the 1964 line, could very well have led to the conclusion that the boundary was now settled."[161] However, this was not the case because "no such activity [had] been drawn to the Tribunal's attention and it may be inferred that there was none."[162] Thus, the tribunal ruled that

---

[156]   *Case Concerning the Continental Shelf (Libyan Arab Jamahiriya* v. *Malta),* [1985] I.C.J. Rep. 13 [hereinafter the *Libya* v. *Malta* case].

[157]   Award, Second Phase, *supra* note 3 at para. 3.5.

[158]   *Ibid.* at para. 3.7.

[159]   *Ibid.* at para. 3.9.

[160]   *Ibid.*

[161]   *Ibid.* at para. 3.10.

[162]   *Ibid.*

Newfoundland had not, by its conduct, accepted "the 1964 line" in the inner sector: "In the circumstances, the Tribunal concludes that there was no 'sufficiently clear, sustained and consistent' conduct on the part of Newfoundland and Labrador to justify holding that it accepted the line in the inner sector."[163]

However, the tribunal did not dismiss the parties' conduct entirely. Indeed, the tribunal considered it relevant that Newfoundland had not protested the methodology used for the inner sector. In particular, the tribunal pointed out that Newfoundland had not disputed the use of St. Paul Island as a basepoint but had "expressly accepted" it in 1972. Nor was there any indication, according to the tribunal, that Newfoundland "found [the use of St. Paul Island as a basepoint] inequitable."[164] Thus, the tribunal concluded that "these are factors to be taken into account ... in the determination of an eventual line in the inner area."[165]

For the outer area, the tribunal analyzed the conduct in two stages: first, in relation to the pre-October 1972 period and, second, in relation to the post-1972 conduct when Nova Scotia was on notice that Newfoundland disagreed with the 135-degree line.[166] In regard to the pre-October 1972 conduct, the tribunal emphasized that the oil practice was more substantial than it was in the inner area but that, nevertheless, there was no drilling activity and "no evidence whatsoever of reliance on provincial permits as the legal basis for actual expenditure in the disputed area."[167] It pointed out that this consideration was important in the *Tunisia* v. *Libya* case and concluded that "there was, it is true, a degree of concordant practice associated with the line ... but this conformity was neither complete nor, in its context, did it reflect a clear consensus of the Parties as to where any boundary should be drawn."[168] Thus, the tribunal dismissed the permitting conduct in the outer area as "little more than a paper trail."[169]

---

[163] *Ibid.*

[164] *Ibid.*

[165] *Ibid.*

[166] This notice was provided in a letter dated October 6, 1972, from C.W. Doody, Minister of Mines, Agriculture and Resources for Newfoundland, to the Principal Secretary to the Premier of Nova Scotia. See Award, Second Phase, *supra* note 3 at para. 1.10.

[167] *Ibid.* at para. 3.14.

[168] *Ibid.* at para. 3.13.

[169] *Ibid.* at para. 3.14.

The tribunal was also dismissive of Nova Scotia's claim based on the conduct of the parties because of the short period involved, namely 1965 to 1972. It recalled the ICJ's decision in the *Gulf of Maine* case, where the court rejected Canada's claims based on the United States's conduct because, *inter alia*, the period 1965-72 was considered "too brief."[170] Finally, the tribunal referred to the failed common front of the provinces in seeking to persuade the federal government to recognize provincial claims in the offshore. The tribunal explained that "that front having failed ... the Tribunal does not think that the limited conduct of Newfoundland and Labrador up to that point — even if it were to be considered unequivocal — can be converted into the all purposes acceptance of a boundary."[171]

Thus, the tribunal found nothing relevant with respect to the pre-October 1972 conduct for purposes of determining the boundary in the outer area. For the post-October 1972 period, the position was "even clearer," in the tribunal's view, because Newfoundland had given notice that it did not accept the claim and, as a result, "strong evidence [was] needed [to show] that it [had] thereafter abandoned its position."[172] The tribunal found that "there was no indication from any Newfoundland and Labrador source that the line was considered equitable."[173] Nor, in the tribunal's view, was there any "sufficient adherence to the 135° line on the part of Newfoundland and Labrador after 1972."[174] The tribunal considered that there were "indications that all parties were aware of the existence of a disagreement about the line in the period after 1972."[175] In the circumstances, the tribunal said that Newfoundland "could not be regarded as having somehow acquiesced in Nova Scotia's position without the clearest evidence" and ruled that "there is no such evidence."[176]

Moreover, the tribunal did not regard the line as equitable. In the tribunal's view, there was no justification for a line "drawn on the Newfoundland side of the strict or full-effect equidistance line," given that Newfoundland had the longer coastline and having regard to the potentially serious impact of the French claims around

[170] *Gulf of Maine* case, *supra* note 28 at 307-8.

[171] Award, Second Phase, *supra* note 3 at para. 3.14.

[172] *Ibid.* at para. 3.15.

[173] *Ibid.*

[174] *Ibid.* at para. 3.17.

[175] *Ibid.*

[176] *Ibid.*

Saint-Pierre and Miquelon. "In such circumstances," opined the tribunal, "it cannot seriously be argued that a full-effect equidistance line required further adjustment at the expense of Newfoundland and Labrador."[177] The tribunal referred to "the lack of any articulated justification for the 135° line," and said that "[t]hat factor must ... affect [the tribunal's] appreciation of the situation."[178] Thus, the tribunal held that post-1972 conduct was irrelevant for the outer area, concluding that "Newfoundland and Labrador's practice in relation to the supposed 135° boundary southeast of turning point 2017 does not sustain a claim of acquiescence, or support the view that the Parties regarded that line as equitable.[179]

Access to Resources

Moving to its second "preliminary issue," access to resources, the tribunal observed that neither party was asking the tribunal to take into account the relative wealth or natural resources of the parties, for these are, under maritime delimitation law, "wholly extraneous."[180] However, the tribunal did "not think that this factor [access to specific resources of the zone in question] was irrelevant."[181] The tribunal, relying on the jurisprudence,[182] indicated that access to resources may be relevant in two ways: first, if the result would have "catastrophic repercussions for the livelihood and well-being of the population of the countries concerned,"[183] which the tribunal excluded for the present case; and, second, there was the possibility of having regard to the natural resources of the area "so far as known or readily ascertainable"[184] to determine the effect of any proposed line on the allocation of the resources.

The tribunal made it clear that it was "not the Tribunal's function to share out equitably any offshore resource, actual or hypothetical,

177 *Ibid.* at para. 3.16.

178 *Ibid.*

179 *Ibid.* at para. 3.18.

180 *Ibid.* at para. 3.21.

181 *Ibid.*

182 The tribunal referred to the *Gulf of Maine* case, *supra* note 28; the *North Sea Continental Shelf* cases, *supra* note 66; and the *Case Concerning Maritime Delimitation in the Area between Greenland and Jan Mayen (Denmark* v. *Norway)*, [1993] I.C.J. Rep. 38 [hereinafter *Jan Mayen* case].

183 *Gulf of Maine* case, *supra* note 28 at 342.

184 *North Sea Continental Shelf* cases, *supra* note 66 at 53-54.

irrespective of its location." However, the tribunal did consider that it could "properly take into account," along with other factors, the "effect of any proposed line on the allocation of resources."[185] The tribunal noted that "officials of both sides have referred to an area of potential resources as being at stake" and said that, in such a situation, it did not believe that the "*North Sea* formula ('known or readily ascertainable') should be restrictively applied."[186] Accordingly, the tribunal concluded that "the impact of any delimitation on access to that resource is a potentially relevant factor in the present case."[187] The tribunal then pointed out that "no information is available to it which would suggest that the line it will award is inequitable to either party on this ground — and certainly not to the extent of justifying any further adjustment."[188]

Geographic Context: Coasts, Areas, and Islands

The tribunal made some preliminary observations with respect to the geographic context of the delimitation. It described the delimitation area as being composed of an inner area and an outer area — these areas being separated by a closing line drawn between Cormorandière Rocks (near Scatarie Island, Nova Scotia) and Lamaline Shag Rock (Newfoundland). Despite the two-area approach, the tribunal noted that the geographic situation was distinct from that in the *Gulf of Maine* case, thereby rejecting Newfoundland's approach of adopting the methodology of that decision for the present case. The tribunal explained that the distinction between the inner and outer areas corresponded to the transition from a relationship of oppositeness (in the inner area) to one of adjacency (in the outer area).

In terms of the seaward extent of the boundary, the tribunal's mandate required it to determine the line dividing the respective offshore areas of the provinces, which areas were defined in the Accord Acts as extending to the outer edge of the continental margin. The tribunal noted that "no international tribunal has yet had to delimit to the outer edge of the continental shelf as between adjacent states."[189] The tribunal observed that Canada had not yet

[185] Award, Second Phase, *supra* note 3 at para. 3.21.

[186] *Ibid.* at para. 3.22.

[187] *Ibid.*

[188] *Ibid.* at para. 3.23.

[189] *Ibid.* at para. 2.29.

prescribed the precise geographical coordinates of points defining the outer edge of its continental margin[190] and said the tribunal
was not competent or mandated to delimit that outer limit. The
tribunal "simply note[d] that a continental shelf wider than 200
nautical miles from the territorial sea baselines probably exists
through most, if not all, of the area seaward" of Newfoundland and
Nova Scotia.[191] In drawing its boundary, the tribunal did not specify the end point of the line other than to say "to the point where
the delimitation line intersects the outer limit of the continental
margin of Canada as it may be determined in accordance with
international law."[192]

Turning to the parties' submissions, the tribunal dismissed the
parties' definitions of relevant coasts as "restrictive" on the part of
Newfoundland and "greatly extended" on the part of Nova Scotia.[193]
The tribunal sought to define for itself the relevant coasts by reference to "those coasts which may affect the actual delimitation" and
described the process as one that "involves a practical judgement,
not merely a geometrical concept."[194] It rejected Newfoundland's
and Nova Scotia's versions as having "an unmistakable odour of
the pre-cooked."[195]

The tribunal accepted Newfoundland's definition of the Newfoundland coast but took issue with Newfoundland's *a priori*
assumption that Sable Island was irrelevant to the delimitation,
especially given its possible role in defining the area of Canadian
continental shelf to be delimited. The tribunal added eighty-eight
nautical miles to Newfoundland's description of the Nova Scotia
coast, extending it southwest from Cape Canso to Egg Island, just
east of Halifax, noting that this coast also contributed to the area
of potential convergence and overlap. The result is a coastal ratio
of 1 to 1.38 in favour of Newfoundland.

In terms of the relevant area, the tribunal said that the area proposed by Nova Scotia provided the tribunal with "no assistance
whatsoever in carrying out its task."[196] It noted that the "Nova Scotia
concept of potential overlapping entitlements has been applied

190 See Ocean's Act, *supra* note 57.

191 Award, Second Phase, *supra* note 3 at para. 2.30.

192 *Ibid.* at para. 6.4.

193 *Ibid.* at para. 4.20.

194 *Ibid.*

195 *Ibid.*.

196 *Ibid.* at para. 4.22.

only once" — in the *Case Concerning Maritime Delimitation in the Area between Greenland and Jan Mayen (Denmark v. Norway)*[197] — where "the circumstances . . . were very different from the present case."[198] In any event, the tribunal decided not to define a relevant area in this case for three reasons. First, it did not consider it appropriate to apply a proportionality test of coastal lengths to maritime areas.[199] Second, no existing or potential delimitations were present that would require the tribunal to confine the delimitation to certain defined lateral limits. Third, the "area where the delimitation takes place will be self-evident and requires no further definition."[200]

With respect to the islands, the tribunal looked first to the French islands of Saint-Pierre and Miquelon. The tribunal rejected the arguments put forward by both parties that they had paid for, or would pay for, any maritime area lost to these islands in previous or potential delimitations. The tribunal said that it was "aware of no principle whereby [the parties] should be 'compensated' in this delimitation for what [the parties] 'lost' or might hypothetically lose, in another."[201]

The tribunal looked next to St. Paul Island, which was discussed earlier in this comment in the section on the relevance of the conduct of the parties. The tribunal mentioned that the island, which was the site of numerous shipwrecks with an area less than five square kilometres, had "never supported human habitation."[202] It noted Newfoundland's view that, because the island was uninhabited and was located in enclosed waters more than twelve miles from the coast, it should have no effect. However, the tribunal was of the view that "[i]n the context of a provisional equidistance line drawn from opposite coasts, it is unusual for no effect to be given to an island (not merely a rock or other minor feature), even where other delimitation methods are used." The tribunal admitted that it "would have been inclined to give half effect to St. Paul Island" were it not for the past conduct of Newfoundland. The fact that "Newfoundland expressly accepted St. Paul Island as a basepoint for the purposes of delimitation" during the earlier inter-provincial discussions and that it "did not object to this at the time (1972)

[197] *Jan Mayen* case, *supra* note 182.
[198] Award, Second Phase, *supra* note 3 at para. 4.23.
[199] This point is discussed further later in this comment.
[200] Award, Second Phase, *supra* note 3 at para. 4.24.
[201] *Ibid.* at para. 4.28.
[202] *Ibid.* at para. 4.30.

when it made clear it did not accept any line eastwards of turning-point 2017, or for that matter at any subsequent time before 1997"[203] led the tribunal to accord full effect to St. Paul Island.

Sable Island, by contrast, was given no effect. The tribunal observed that, unlike St. Paul Island, Sable Island was not expressly referred to in the 1964 statement or in the other inter-provincial documents, nor was there any "unequivocal indication that New-foundland and Labrador ever accepted its use as a basepoint for the purposes of maritime delimitation with Nova Scotia."[204] The tribunal also pointed out that "in the context of a delimitation between adjacent coasts and a line proceeding out to the open sea, a relatively minor feature such as Sable Island is capable of hav-ing major effects."[205] The tribunal relied on the precedent in the *Case Concerning Maritime Delimitation and Territorial Questions between Qatar and Bahrain (Qatar v. Bahrain)* (*Qatar v. Bahrain* case),[206] where the ICJ gave no effect to Fasht al Jarim Island, which was described by the court as a "a maritime feature located well out to sea and of which at most a minute part is above water at high tide."[207] The tribunal conceded that Sable Island is "considerably more sub-stantial" than Fasht al Jarim but said that "in the context of the pre-sent delimitation, [Sable Island] is clearly a 'special' or 'relevant' circumstance which needs to be taken into account."[208]

Delimitation Process

The tribunal did not accept either party's proposed boundary lines. It drew its own, starting with a provisional equidistance line

---

[203] *Ibid.* at para. 4.31. The tribunal recalled that French conduct in accepting Eddy-stone Rock as a basepoint was treated as relevant in the *Arbitration between the United Kingdom of Great Britain and Northern Ireland and the French Republic on the Delimitation of the Continental Shelf,* Decisions of the Court of Arbitration, dated June 30, 1977 and March 14, 1978, London, H.M.S.O., Cmnd. 7438 [here-inafter *Anglo-French Channel Islands* case].

[204] Award, Second Phase, *supra* note 3 at para. 4.35.

[205] *Anglo-French Channel Islands* case, *supra* note 203 at para. 4.35.

[206] *Case Concerning Maritime Delimitation and Territorial Questions between Qatar and Bahrain (Qatar v. Bahrain),* [1994] I.C.J. Rep. 112 [hereinafter *Qatar v. Bahrain* case].

[207] Quoted in Award, Second Phase, *supra* note 3 at para. 4.35.

[208] *Ibid.* at para. 4.36. The tribunal described Sable Island as twenty-two nautical miles long and less than one nautical mile wide, with an area of thirty-three square kilometres. (*Ibid.* at para. 4.32.)

and then adjusting it as required. The tribunal stated that "the choice of practical method that will assure an equitable result in the particular circumstances of this case ... is not difficult to determine."[209] As the parties are bound by Article 6 of the 1958 Geneva Convention on the Continental Shelf, the tribunal decided that it "was appropriate to begin with the construction of a provisional equidistance line and to determine whether it requires adjustment in the light of special circumstances."[210] The tribunal opined that the approach "would have been precisely the same" had it applied customary international law or Article 83 of the 1982 LOSC, for, in its view, the "law governing maritime boundary delimitation [had] attained a basic unity" and noted that "the overarching objective of all maritime boundary delimitations, whether under customary or conventional international law," is to achieve an equitable result.[211]

The tribunal proceeded to delimit the boundary in three stages, starting with the inner area, then moving to the outer area, and concluding with the portion in the Gulf of St. Lawrence (see Figure 2 at the end of this comment). For the inner area, the tribunal began its provisional equidistance line at the closing line of the Gulf of St. Lawrence, a point that "substantially coincides" with point 2016 as defined in 1969 by the inter-provincial group of experts and approved by the premiers in 1972.[212] The tribunal found no inequitable effect, as alleged by Newfoundland, resulting from "the so-called protrusion of the Cape Breton coast, together with the so-called recessiveness of the Newfoundland coast."[213] The tribunal also rejected Newfoundland's assertion of cut-off due to its being "squeezed" between Saint-Pierre and Miquelon and Nova Scotia, which the tribunal said was belied by "a glance at the map — without the illusory perceptions created by colour tinting."[214] Finally, the tribunal disagreed with Newfoundland that there was any inherent inequity in using equidistance in the inner area based on differences in coastal lengths and noted that the westward shift of 34.6 nautical miles from the mid-point on the closing line as proposed by Newfoundland "would be excessive and unreasonable"

[209] *Ibid.* at para. 5.2.

[210] *Ibid.*

[211] *Ibid.*

[212] These points are depicted and their origins described in Award, First Phase, *supra* note 4, and are discussed in Hughes, *supra* note 4.

[213] Award, Second Phase, *supra* note 3 at para. 5.5.

[214] *Ibid.*

and "would amount to the dividing up of offshore areas on a strict mathematical basis, a procedure which the International Court has consistently denied is required by equitable principles."[215]

Reviewing its provisional equidistance line in the inner area in light of the conduct of the parties, the tribunal recalled that Newfoundland "never raised any objection or difficulty" with the "dividing line conditionally drawn in 1964, and conditionally affirmed in 1972 ... up to turning-point 2017 [located in the inner area]," which the tribunal described as "essentially a simplified median line." The tribunal then decided as follows:

For this reason, and to a lesser extent for reasons of administrative convenience, the Tribunal considers that it would be both equitable and appropriate to simplify its strict equidistance line by drawing a straight line between turning points 2016 and 2017.[216]

The tribunal then extended the last segment of the inner line, reasoning as follows:

The tribunal has already explained why it does not consider the conduct of the parties to be relevant beyond turning point 2017. Nevertheless, the Tribunal is of the view that it would be appropriate, for reasons of convenience and consistency, to simplify the last segment of the inner equidistance line by drawing a straight line between turning point 2017 and the point where the equidistance line meets the closing line of the inner area.[217]

The tribunal observed that "it is clear that the simplified equidistance line reflects and responds to the relevant circumstances of geography" and noted that its line "is not significantly different from ... the lines respectively proposed by Nova Scotia and Newfoundland and Labrador."[218]

Turning to the delimitation in the outer area, the tribunal described the relationship as one of "increasing adjacency rather than oppositeness as the eye moves seaward from the closing line of the inner area."[219] Nevertheless, despite this different geographic situation, the tribunal, in relying on precedent in the *Qatar* v. *Bahrain* case and the *Arbitration between the United Kingdom of Great Britain and Northern Ireland and the French Republic on the Delimitation of the*

---

[215] *Ibid.* at para. 5.6

[216] *Ibid.* at para. 5.7.

[217] *Ibid.*

[218] *Ibid.* at para. 5.6.

[219] *Ibid.* at para. 5.9.

Continental Shelf[220] once again drew a provisional equidistance line, to be adjusted as appropriate. Thus, the line started from the point of intersection of the simplified equidistance line in the inner area and the closing line of the inner area and continued to the outer edge of the continental margin. The tribunal stressed that the intersection point on the closing line was 11.8 nautical miles west of the mid-point of the line. The tribunal recalled its finding that there was no requirement to adjust the line on the basis of the conduct of the parties in the area eastward of the closing line. Noting again the equivocal and limited nature of the conduct, the lack of evidence of reliance on provincial permits, and the specific rejection by Newfoundland of the existence of a line in the outer sector in 1972, the tribunal concluded that "[n]one of this amounts to the clear, substantial and unequivocal practice required to establish a distinct *de facto* line."[221] The tribunal accordingly: "agree[d] with Newfoundland and Labrador that beyond the Scatarie-Lamaline Shag Rock closing line, this case is to be decided exclusively on grounds of the relevant coastal geography."[222]

At this point in its decision, the tribunal addressed the effect of Sable Island. It first examined what the result would be if the island were given half effect, "[h]aving regard to its remote location and to the very substantial disproportionate effect this small, unpopulated island would have on the delimitation if it were given full effect."[223] It adjusted the provisional equidistance line accordingly. However, the adjustment proved insufficient, for, as noted earlier, the tribunal eventually decided to accord Sable Island no effect. The tribunal reasoned that "[i]n outer shelf areas where large spaces are at stake, the question is not so much one of strict proportionality as a manifest lack of disproportion."[224] It also looked to the cut-off effect on the south coast of Newfoundland, another "significant concern," and rejected Nova Scotia's position that "the cut-off necessarily becomes irrelevant as the distance from the coast increases."[225] The tribunal then considered the further adjustment of the provisional line, which, by giving no effect to Sable Island, "would accommodate in a reasonable way the disparity in

---

[220] *Anglo-French Channel Islands* case, *supra* note 203.

[221] Award, Second Phase, *supra* note 3 at para. 5.11.

[222] *Ibid.* at para. 5.12.

[223] *Ibid.* at para. 5.13.

[224] *Ibid.* at para. 5.14.

[225] *Ibid.* at para. 5.15.

the lengths of the Parties' coasts (as determined by the Tribunal) in both the inner and outer areas."[226] Finally, the tribunal drew the line in the Gulf of St. Lawrence: "[H]aving regard to the conduct of the Parties in this sector, [the tribunal] considers it appropriate to delimit this small, innermost area by a straight line joining turning points 2026 and 2015."[227]

Confirming the Equity of the Result

As noted earlier in this comment, the tribunal decided not to apply a proportionality test comparing the ratios of the parties' respective coastal lengths with respective areas awarded to the parties, referring to the "pitfalls inherent in this exercise" and the "imprecision and impressionism" found in the parties' arguments regarding the identification of the relevant area.[228] The tribunal acknowledged that its decision not to apply a proportionality test was due in large measure to the fact that this case was the first to involve the delimitation of the continental shelf beyond 200 nautical miles. It also mentioned that the test "may be more contrived than constructive in some instances," noting that each party, despite the radically different approaches adopted by them, was able to satisfy the test "down to almost the last decimal point."[229]

The tribunal nevertheless applied a "hypothetical proportionality test" using the line determined by the tribunal and the relevant areas defined by the parties. Using the Nova Scotia relevant area, the result was a coastal ratio of 52 per cent for Nova Scotia and 48 per cent for Newfoundland, compared with an area ratio of 39 per cent for Nova Scotia and 61 per cent for Newfoundland. Using the area defined by Newfoundland but adjusted to add the area beyond the 200-mile limit, the coastal area was 33 per cent for Nova Scotia and 67 per cent for Newfoundland, compared with an area ratio of 38 per cent for Nova Scotia and 62 per cent for Newfoundland. The tribunal noted that "such results would reveal no shocking disproportionality" over such vast areas "even if the Parties' relevant areas

---

[226] *Ibid.*

[227] *Ibid.* at para. 5.16. The tribunal emphasized that its decision was binding only on the parties to the dispute and that it could not prejudice the rights of any other party that may be concerned. Thus, the provinces of New Brunswick, Prince Edward Island, and Québec are not affected by this boundary line in the Gulf.

[228] *Ibid.* at para. 5.18.

[229] *Ibid.*

were appropriately defined — which they have been held not to be." In the end, the tribunal drew "no conclusions from them beyond the fact that they demonstrate the vagaries associated with the definition of relevant areas and the use of a proportionality test."[230] The tribunal concluded its award with a technical description of the line of delimitation, setting out its geographic coordinates, and appended to its decision the technical report, which was prepared by David Gray, the tribunal's technical expert.

CONCLUSION

The issuance of the award of the tribunal for the second phase completed the tribunal's tasks set out in the Terms of Reference. Following the issuance of this award, Newfoundland announced that it was "extremely pleased" with the line established by the tribunal, pointing out that it provided Newfoundland with "almost 70 per cent of the area that was in dispute."[231] Newfoundland also noted that the "tribunal's decision provides both provinces and industry with jurisdictional certainty" and signalled that it would now "move forward with the business of opening up this area to advanced exploration [that] will provide substantial benefits to both provinces."[232] Nova Scotia reacted by noting that the decision "gives the clarity and certainty industry needs to search for oil and gas in the eastern area offshore Nova Scotia."[233] Nova Scotia put the best light on the result, noting that "Nova Scotia has retained the overwhelming majority of exploration activity on its side of the new boundary line," asserting that "the new line will affect only a small portion of one active licence offshore."[234] By virtue of Article 15 of the Terms of Reference, the tribunal's decision is final and binding on both provinces and is implemented by way of regulations made pursuant to the Accord Acts.

VALERIE HUGHES
Director, Appellate Body Secretariat, World Trade Organization, Geneva

---

[230] *Ibid.* at para. 5.19.

[231] News Release, "Government Reacts to Decision in Newfoundland and Labrador/ Nova Scotia Offshore Boundary Dispute," April 2, 2002, accessible at <www.gov.nf.ca>.

[232] *Ibid.*

[233] News Release, "Nova Scotia Says Boundary Decision Paves Way for Oil and Gas Activity," April 2, 2002, accessible at <www.gov.ns.ca>.

[234] *Ibid.*

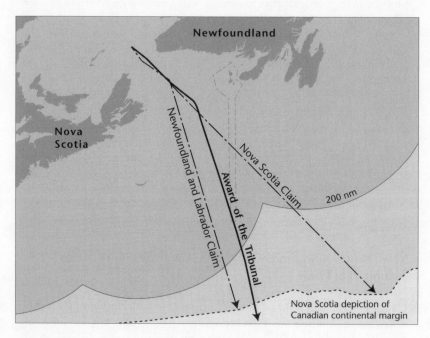

Figure 2. Claims of Nova Scotia and Newfoundland and the award of the tribunal

Sommaire

Le différend Nouvelle Écosse–Terre-Neuve et Labrador sur leurs zones extra-côtières: La phase de la délimitation

Le 26 mars 2002, un tribunal d'arbitrage ad hoc a déterminé de la frontière délimitant les zones extra-côtières respectives des provinces de Terre-Neuve et Labrador et de la Nouvelle Écosse. Dans sa décision, le tribunal, établi par le Ministre fédéral des ressources naturelles, s'est fondé sur les principes de droit international régissant la délimitation des frontières maritimes et, selon son mandat, a traité les deux provinces d'États sujets aux mêmes droits et obligations que le gouvernement du Canada. Le tribunal avait rendu une première décision en mai 2001, statuant qu'une frontière maritime n'avait pas encore été établie par l'accord des deux provinces, contraire aux prétentions de la Nouvelle Écosse. La décision du tribunal sur la frontière maritime est finale et obligatoire pour les deux provinces. La décision accorde à la province de Terre-Neuve et Labrador la plus grande partie de la zone extra-côtière contestée. La décision du tribunal met fin à l'incertitude engendrée par le différend entre les provinces et crée les conditions nécessaires pour l'amorce de l'exploration d'hydrocarbures dans la zone autrefois contestée.

Summary

Nova Scotia-Newfoundland Dispute over Offshore Areas: The Delimitation Phase

On March 26, 2002, an ad hoc arbitration tribunal determined the line of delimitation dividing the respective offshore areas of the province of Newfoundland and Labrador and the province of Nova Scotia. In making its decision, the tribunal, which was established by the federal minister of natural resources, applied the principles of international law governing maritime boundary delimitation and, pursuant to its terms of reference, treated the two provinces as if they were states subject to the same rights and obligations as the government of Canada. The tribunal had issued a first decision in May 2001, ruling that the delimitation line had not already been established by agreement between the provinces, as Nova Scotia had contended. The tribunal's decision on the boundary line is final and binding on the two provinces. It awards to Newfoundland and Labrador the greater part of the offshore area that had been in dispute. The tribunal's decision marked the end of the uncertainty created by the provincial disagreement and paved the way for the commencement of hydrocarbon exploration in the formerly disputed area.

Chronique de Droit international économique en 2001 / Digest of International Economic Law in 2001

I Commerce

préparé par
RICHARD OUELLET

I INTRODUCTION

En matière de commerce international, l'année 2001 en fut une d'espoir et de relance, autant au plan hémisphérique qu'au plan multilatéral.

Le Canada fut l'hôte en avril à Québec du Troisième Sommet des Amériques qui a, avec d'autres événements, permis de raviver les discussions devant mener à la création d'une zone de libre-échange des Amériques (ZLÉA). En novembre, la tenue de la Conférence ministérielle de l'OMC à Doha au Qatar a été quant à elle l'occasion d'accueillir au sein de cette organisation un membre de taille, la Chine, et de relancer les négociations commerciales multilatérales sur de nouvelles bases recueillant un appui neuf et accru chez bon nombre de Membres de l'OMC, notamment les pays en développement.

Le Canada est très actif dans ces deux grands chantiers de négociations qui doivent tous deux aboutir en 2005. Le Canada a aussi été impliqué dans bon nombre de différends liés à l'application de l'ALÉNA et des accords de l'OMC.

Pour bien rendre compte de l'activité commerciale internationale touchant le Canada pour l'année 2001, il nous est apparu opportun de diviser la présentation en deux grandes parties, l'une touchant le commerce canadien aux plans bilatéral et régional,

Richard Ouellet, Faculté de droit, Université Laval.

419

la seconde touchant le commerce canadien au plan multilatéral. Dans chaque partie, nous rapportons d'abord les développements des négociations commerciales et relatons ensuite les faits saillants des principaux litiges touchant de près ou de loin le Canada.

II   LE COMMERCE CANADIEN AUX PLANS BILATÉRAL ET RÉGIONAL

A   LES NÉGOCIATIONS COMMERCIALES AUX PLANS BILATÉRAL ET RÉGIONAL

1   *Le projet de la ZLÉA*

Le projet de création de la Zone de libre-échange des Amériques a connu des avancées importantes en 2001. Lors de la Sixième Réunion des Ministres du commerce de l'hémisphère, tenue le 7 avril à Buenos Aires en Argentine, les groupes de négociation de la ZLÉA ont présenté un avant-projet de texte qui a permis aux Ministres du commerce de constater et dire l'importance des progrès réalisés dans le processus de négociation. À l'initiative du Canada, les Ministres ont convenu de rendre public cet avant-projet de texte dans les quatre langues officielles, après le Troisième Sommet des Amériques.[1] Dans la déclaration ministérielle publiée à l'issue de la Réunion, les Ministres ont également insisté sur l'importance d'accroître la participation de la société civile à l'initiative hémisphérique.[2] Ils ont assigné des tâches précises à chacun des groupes de négociation,[3] convenu que le Comité des négociations commerciales se réunirait au moins trois fois avant le 31 octobre 2002[4] et considéré que le Troisième Sommet des Amériques constituait "une occasion pour continuer ... à appuyer les efforts de chaque pays concernant les aspects importants à leur pleine participation aux négociations et aux bénéfices de la ZLÉA."[5] Les Ministres du

---

[1] Le texte a finalement été rendu public le 3 juillet, une fois les traductions en langues française et portugaise achevées. On peut trouver le texte de l'avant-projet de ZLÉA sur le site Web de la ZLÉA à l'adresse <http://www.alca-ftaa.org> (dernière visite le 27 mai 2003).

[2] *Zone de libre-échange des Amériques, Sixième réunion des Ministres du commerce de l'hémisphère, Déclaration ministérielle,* Buenos Aires, Argentine, le 7 avril 2001, disponible sur le site Web de la ZLÉA à l'adresse <http://www.alca-ftaa.org/ministerials/Bamin_f.asp> (dernière visite le 27 mai 2003).

[3] *Ibid.,* annexe I.

[4] *Ibid.* au par. 15.

[5] *Ibid.* au par. 8.

commerce ont également recommandé à leurs leaders de fournir, lors du Troisième Sommet des Amériques, "les lignes directrices pour assurer que les négociations de l'accord de la ZLÉA soient conclues au plus tard en janvier 2005, et pour tâcher qu'il entre en vigueur le plus tôt possible ou au plus tard en décembre 2005."[6]

Du 20 au 22 avril, les trente-quatre chefs d'État et de gouvernement démocratiquement élus des Amériques se sont réunis à Québec pour le Troisième Sommet des Amériques. Ils ont notamment entériné et réaffirmé les principes énoncés deux semaines plus tôt par les Ministres du commerce. Ils ont insisté sur leur engagement collectif à l'égard de la transparence et d'une communication accrue et soutenue avec la société civile.[7] Ils ont rappelé l'échéance des négociations prévue pour 2005 et le principe voulant que l'accord de la ZLÉA devra être conforme aux principes et disciplines de l'OMC et constituera un engagement unique.[8]

L'ébauche du texte de négociation de la ZLÉA a été rendu public le 3 juillet 2001. On peut donc désormais le consulter aisément sur le Web.[9] De larges parties de ce texte sont entre crochets pour signifier que les pays qui participent aux négociations n'ont pas encore convenu de leur contenu. Le juriste averti constatera sans difficulté la parenté évidente entre ce texte et plusieurs chapitres de l'ALÉNA.

2   *Les autres développements aux plans bilatéral et régional*

En plus des négociations hémisphériques, le Canada a mené de front des négociations bilatérales qui ont porté leurs fruits pendant l'année 2001. Le 23 avril, une cérémonie de signature d'un *Accord de libre-échange entre le Canada et le Costa Rica*[10] s'est tenue à Ottawa. À l'instar du *Pacte de libre-échange Canada-Chili*, cet accord

---

[6] *Ibid.* au par. 2.

[7] Troisième Sommet des Amériques, Déclaration de Québec, le 22 avril 2001, disponible sur le site Web de la ZLÉA à l'adresse <http://www.alca-ftaa.org/ministerials/Quebec/declara_f.asp> (dernière visite le 27 mai 2003).

[8] *Ibid.*

[9] *Supra* note 1.

[10] On peut trouver le texte intégral de l'*Accord de libre-échange entre le Canada et le Costa Rica* sur le site Internet du Ministère des Affaires étrangères et du Commerce international à l'adresse <http://www.dfait-maeci.gc.ca/tna-nac/Costa_Rica-f.asp> (dernière visite le 27 mai 2003).

s'accompagne de deux accords parallèles soit un *Accord de coopération environnementale*[11] et un *Accord de coopération de la main-d'œuvre.*[12]

L'*Accord de libre-échange entre le Canada et le Costa Rica* se distingue du fait qu'il est le premier accord bilatéral de libéralisation des échanges signé par le Canada qui contienne tout un chapitre consacré spécifiquement à la facilitation du commerce.[13] En plus de ces dispositions innovatrices, l'Accord contient des engagements classiques par lesquels les pays signataires consentent d'importantes réductions des tarifs douaniers exigibles. Aux termes de l'Accord, le Costa Rica éliminera immédiatement les droits demandés sur 67 % de ses secteurs de tarification et éliminera progressivement, sur une période maximale de quatorze ans, les droits touchant les autres secteurs. Le Canada, quant à lui, accordera immédiatement, sur 86 % de ses secteurs de tarification, l'admission en franchise aux marchandises costariciennes. Il éliminera sur une période pouvant aller jusqu'à huit ans les autres tarifs.[14] L'Accord devrait donc contribuer à l'augmentation du commerce bilatéral de marchandises entre les deux pays qui s'élevait en 2000 à 269 millions de dollars.[15] La loi canadienne de mise en œuvre de l'Accord a reçu la sanction royale en décembre 2001 et l'Accord devrait entrer en vigueur au cours de l'année 2002 quand le Costa Rica aura complété son processus législatif de mise en œuvre.

Toujours avec des partenaires de l'hémisphère américain, le gouvernement canadien a annoncé en fin d'année le lancement de négociations en vue d'un accord de libre-échange avec quatre pays d'Amérique centrale[16] et l'amorce de consultations publiques sur

---

[11] On peut trouver le texte intégral de l'*Accord de coopération environnementale entre le Canada et le Costa Rica* à l'adresse <http://www.ec.gc.ca/international/costarica/index_f.htm> (dernière visite le 27 mai 2003).

[12] On peut trouver le texte intégral de l'*Accord de coopération de la main-d'oeuvre entre le Canada et le Costa Rica* à l'adresse <http://labour.hdrc-drhc.gc.ca/psait_psila/aicdt_ialc/documentation> (dernière visite le 27 mai 2003).

[13] Voir le chapitre IX de l'Accord, *supra* note 10. On trouve aujourd'hui des dispositions de ce type dans les projets de texte de la ZLÉA.

[14] Voir les annexes à l'Accord, *supra* note 10. Pour une consultation rapide de quelques données sur les termes de l'Accord, voir aussi *Document d'information, Accord de libre-échange entre le Canada et le Costa Rica,* disponible sur le site Web du Premier ministre du Canada à l'adresse <http://pm.gc.ca> (dernière visite le 27 mai 2003).

[15] *Ibid.*

[16] Le Guatemala, le Salvador, le Honduras et le Nicaragua

un éventuel accord de libre-échange avec les pays membres de la Communauté des Caraïbes (CARICOM).[17]

Enfin, dans un tout autre contexte, celui de la réunion des dirigeants de l'APEC tenue en octobre à Shanghai, les premiers ministres canadien et singapourien ont annoncé le lancement de négociations devant mener à la conclusion d'un accord bilatéral de libre-échange entre leurs pays.

B   LES DÉCISIONS ET RAPPORTS LIÉS À L'ALÉNA

Deux rapports de groupes spéciaux rendus en vertu de procédures de règlement des différends prévues à l'ALÉNA ont retenu notre attention pendant l'année 2001.[18]

Le premier de ces rapports a été rendu le 6 février par le Groupe spécial arbitral institué conformément au chapitre 20 de l'ALÉNA et chargé d'examiner l'*Affaire des services transfrontières de camionnage*.[19] Dans cette affaire, le Mexique reprochait aux États-Unis de ne pas avoir éliminé progressivement, comme ils s'étaient engagés à le faire à l'annexe I de l'ALÉNA, les restrictions frappant les services transfrontières de camionnage et l'investissement par des personnes du Mexique dans l'industrie américaine du camionnage, alors qu'ils accordent à cet égard le traitement national au Canada.[20] Le Mexique prétendait donc que les États-Unis avaient enfreint les articles 1202 et 1203 de l'ALÉNA relatifs aux services transfrontières et les articles 1102 et 1103 relatifs à l'investissement.[21]

---

[17] À la fin 2001, les Membres de la CARICOM étaient Antigua-et-Barbuda, les Bahamas, la Barbade, le Belize, la Dominique, la Grenade, le Guyana, la Jamaïque, Sainte-Lucie, Saint-Kitts-et-Nevis, Saint-Vincent et les Grenadines, le Suriname, Trinité-et-Tobago, Montserrat (territoire indépendant du Royaume-Uni).

[18] En plus des deux rapports que nous relatons ici, un autre rapport a été rendu en 2001, le 3 août, dans l'affaire MEX-USA-98-1904-01 *Importations de sirop de maïs élevé en fructose originaires des États-Unis d'Amérique (dumping)*. Le contenu de ce rapport, bien qu'intéressant, ne nous a pas apparu justifier de commentaires dans la présente chronique.

[19] Accord de libre-échange nord-américain, Groupe spécial arbitral institué conformément au chapitre 20 dans l'Affaire des services transfrontières de camionnage, Dossier du Secrétariat n° USA-MEX-98-2008-01, Rapport final du Groupe spécial, 6 février 2001. Le texte intégral du rapport est disponible sur le site du Secrétariat de l'ALÉNA à l'adresse <http://www.nafta-sec-alena.org/french/decisions/nafta/index.htm> (dernière visite le 27 mai 2003).

[20] *Ibid.* aux par. 1 et 2.

[21] *Ibid.* Aux dires du groupe spécial, au par. 287, les États-Unis n'ont pas déployé d'efforts notables pour justifier leur position en matière d'investissement. De ce

Le Mexique dénonçait le fait que les demandes de permis d'exploitation présentées par les entreprises mexicaines de camionnage faisaient l'objet d'un refus "général" alors que les transporteurs américains et canadiens avaient le droit d'être évalués en fonction de leurs dossiers individuels et disposaient d'un droit de recours sans réserves contre le rejet de leurs demandes de permis.[22]

Les États-Unis justifiaient leur façon de faire en expliquant que la réglementation mexicaine du camionnage n'est pas aussi rigoureuse que les réglementations américaine et canadienne. Ainsi, d'après les États-Unis, les entreprises mexicaines de camionnage ne se trouvent pas, au sens des articles 1202 et 1203, "dans ces circonstances analogues"[23] à celles des entreprises américaines et canadiennes.[24] Suivant cet argument américain, le Mexique ne peut donc pas prétendre qu'il y a infraction à ces deux articles. Ce sont donc des raisons de sécurité qui motivaient l'inaction américaine. Dans la foulée, les États-Unis invoquaient l'article 2101 de l'ALÉNA qui prévoit notamment que l'ALÉNA ne doit pas être interprété comme empêchant l'application de mesures nécessaires pour assurer le respect de lois qui ont trait à la sécurité.[25]

Le Groupe spécial a procédé à l'analyse des points en litige en quatre parties bien distinctes. Il a d'abord rappelé les textes et principes qui doivent guider son interprétation de l'ALÉNA. Il a référé abondamment au préambule et à l'article 102 de l'ALÉNA ainsi qu'aux articles 27, 31 et 32 de la Convention de Vienne sur le droit des traités et conclu qu'"il ne devrait pas être fait appel ni au droit interne des États-Unis ni aux lois mexicaines pour interpréter l'ALÉNA."[26]

Le Groupe spécial a ensuite vérifié le sens de l'engagement de libéralisation pris par les États-Unis en matière de transport terrestre à l'annexe I de l'ALÉNA. Guidé par l'alinéa 3b) de la Note interprétative qui se trouve au début de l'annexe, guidé aussi par le texte de la réserve en matière de transport terrestre qui se trouve

---

fait, le rapport ne traite que brièvement de cette question. Nous nous attarderons ici aux questions touchant plus spécifiquement le commerce des services.

[22] *Ibid.* au par. 3.

[23] Dans le texte français de l'ALÉNA, on trouve aussi l'expression "dans des circonstances similaires."

[24] *Supra* note 19 aux par. 7 et 8.

[25] *Ibid.* au par. 9.

[26] *Ibid.* au par. 224.

aux pages I-U-22 et suivantes,[27] le Groupe spécial a jugé que les engagements de libéralisation progressive comme celui contenu dans la réserve américaine en matière de transport terrestre doivent avoir l'entière primauté sur les autres éléments de l'annexe I.[28] Il a également établi que les engagements de libéralisation pris à l'annexe I sont inconditionnels[29] et que les États-Unis n'ont démontré aucun motif valable de non-respect de ces engagements.[30] Il a conclu en indiquant qu'il revenait aux États-Unis de trouver dans l'ALÉNA d'autres dispositions qui permettent de déroger aux engagements de libéralisation du transport terrestre qu'ils ont pris à l'annexe I.[31]

Le Groupe spécial a subséquemment analysé les articles 1202 et 1203 relatifs au commerce transfrontières des services. Le Groupe spécial a constaté que les transporteurs mexicains jouissaient effectivement d'un traitement moins favorable que les transporteurs américains et canadiens. Il s'est ensuite intéressé au sens de l'expression "dans des circonstances analogues"[32] que l'on trouve aux articles 1202 et 1203 et au sens de l'article 2101. Le Groupe spécial a d'abord estimé "peu vraisemblable qu'on puisse s'autoriser de l'expression 'dans des circonstances analogues' des articles 1202 et 1203 pour maintenir au commerce entre des Parties à l'ALÉNA un obstacle aussi important qu'une prohibition à la prestation de services transfrontières de camionnage."[33] En s'inspirant de la jurisprudence découlant de l'article XX du GATT, le groupe spécial a ensuite jugé que les États-Unis auraient dû démontrer qu'il n'existait pas pour eux des moyens d'atteindre leurs objectifs de sécurité qui seraient plus compatibles avec l'ALÉNA que le traitement que les États-Unis réservaient aux demandes mexicaines de permis d'exploitation.[34]

---

[27] Dans la version papier de l'ALÉNA en langue française publiée par le Gouvernement du Canada, les mêmes annexes se trouvent aux pages I-U-15 et s. Dans la version papier en langue anglaise, ces annexes se trouvent aux pages I-U-18 et s.

[28] *Supra* note 19 au par. 238.

[29] *Ibid.* au par. 235.

[30] *Ibid.* au par. 239.

[31] *Ibid.* au par. 240.

[32] Ou "dans des circonstances similaires" selon les paragraphes.

[33] *Supra* note 19 au par. 258.

[34] *Ibid.* aux par. 268-70.

Dans la dernière partie de son analyse, le Groupe spécial a indiqué qu'il n'existait pas de circonstances qui justifiaient que les investisseurs et les investissements mexicains dans le secteur du transport terrestre aux États-Unis fassent l'objet d'un traitement différent de celui de leurs homologues américains ou canadiens au titre des dispositions du chapitre 11 de l'ALÉNA.[35] Le groupe spécial a donc constaté que le refus par les États-Unis d'examiner les demandes de permis d'exploitation pour la prestation de services de camionnage transfrontières présentées par les transporteurs mexicains était un manquement aux obligations des États-Unis aux termes de l'ALÉNA.[36]

Le deuxième rapport qui a retenu notre attention est celui qui fut rendu le 20 mars 2001 par le Groupe spécial binational institué en application de l'article 1904 de l'ALÉNA dans l'*Affaire des produits en tôle d'acier non allié inoxydable en provenance du Canada*.[37] L'intérêt de ce rapport réside dans le fait que le Groupe spécial binational y énonce et y rappelle quelques principes importants qui doivent guider les déterminations qu'établissent les autorités américaines en matière de dumping ainsi que quelques principes applicables à l'examen des déterminations par les groupes spéciaux binationaux établis en application du chapitre 19 de l'ALÉNA.

Dans cette affaire, le Groupe spécial binational était appelé à examiner l'évaluation faite par l'Administration du commerce international au Département du commerce des États-Unis (DOC) des prix des intrants de Stelco inc., fabricant et exportateur canadien de produits en tôle d'acier non allié inoxydable. Stelco contestait la détermination du DOC pour trois motifs dont le plus important, et le plus longuement discuté dans la décision, était que le DOC avait surévalué les coûts réels de production de Stelco au titre des services rendus par ses fournisseurs affiliés Baycoat et Z-Ligne.[38]

---

[35] *Ibid.* au par. 294.

[36] *Ibid.* aux par. 295 et s.

[37] Accord de libre-échange nord-américain, Examen par un groupe spécial binational institué en application de l'article 1904 de l'Accord de libre-échange nord-américain dans l'Affaire des produits en tôle d'acier non allié inoxydable en provenance du Canada, Dossier du Secrétariat n° USA-CDA-98-1904-01, Décision du Groupe spécial et renvoi, 20 mars 2001. Le texte intégral du rapport est disponible sur le site du Secrétariat de l'ALÉNA à l'adresse <http://www.nafta-sec-alena.org/french/decisions/nafta/index.htm> (dernière visite le 27 mai 2003).

[38] *Ibid.* à la p.1.

Cette décision du Groupe spécial binational n'est pas la première décision portant sur les déterminations établies par le DOC à l'égard des produits exportés par Stelco aux États-Unis. Elle s'inscrit dans un contexte particulier qu'il faut connaître pour bien comprendre l'analyse faite par le groupe spécial et l'impact de la décision rendue. Stelco et son fournisseur Baycoat sont des parties liées.[39] Baycoat appartient en partie à Stelco et fonctionne comme une de ses divisions.[40] Quand Baycoat fournit des services de peinture à Stelco, elle lui facture un prix appelé prix de cession interne. Baycoat consigne aussi sur les factures les bénéfices qu'elle fait sur chaque transaction passée avec Stelco. Périodiquement, soit à la fin de ses exercices financiers, Baycoat verse ces bénéfices à Stelco.[41] Stelco prétend ainsi que son véritable coût de production est composé des prix de cession interne facturés auxquels doivent être soustraits les bénéfices que lui verse Baycoat.

En avril 1997, quelques temps après l'entrée en vigueur aux États-Unis de modifications au Tariff Act,[42] le DOC a procédé à un examen administratif d'une ordonnance rendue à la suite d'une enquête en dumping couvrant la période s'étendant du 1er août 1994 au 31 juillet 1995. Le DOC a alors estimé que le droit américain prescrivait, pour établir le coût de production de Stelco, de tenir compte des prix de cession interne sans tenir compte des remboursements faits par Baycoat à Stelco.[43] Deux décisions d'un groupe spécial binational[44] ont décidé que le DOC est tenu de prendre en considération le versement des bénéfices de Baycoat à Stelco, qu'il a l'obligation de déduire les bénéfices des prix de cession interne et que le fait que le DOC s'y soit dérobé n'est pas conforme aux dispositions de la loi américaine. Le 14 juin 1999,

---

[39] Le Groupe spécial constate qu'on ne discute pas de Z-Ligne dans son analyse.

[40] *Ibid.* à la p. 30.

[41] *Ibid.* à la p. 3.

[42] *Tariff Act of 1930* ou Loi de 1930 sur les traifs douaniers. Les modifications dont il est question ici étaient amenées par l'adoption de l'*Uruguay Round Agreements Act.*

[43] *Supra* note 37 à la p.3.

[44] Dans l'affaire des produits en tôle d'acier non allié inoxydable en provenance du Canada, Décision du Groupe spécial, USA-97-1904-03, 4 juin 1998 (décision I); Dans l'affaire des produits en tôle d'acier non allié inoxydable en provenance du Canada, Deuxième examen par un groupe spécial binational institué en application de l'article 1904 de l'ALÉNA, USA-97-1904-03, 20 janvier 1999 (décision II)

le DOC a effectivement recalculé les coûts de production de Stelco en prenant en compte le versements de bénéfices par Baycoat mais en continuant d'affirmer que, selon son interprétation de la législation, il n'était pas tenu de le faire.[45] Parallèlement à ces événements, une autre enquête couvrant cette fois la période s'étendant du 1er août 1995 au 31 juillet 1996 était menée. Le 17 septembre 1996, le DOC a engagé un examen administratif de l'ordonnance instituant des droits antidumping pour cette nouvelle période. Dans la détermination rendue à l'issue de son examen, en 1998, le DOC a établi les coûts de production de Stelco en se fondant sur les prix de cession interne sans tenir compte des bénéfices versés plus tard par ses fournisseurs. C'est cette dernière détermination qui a fait l'objet de la demande d'examen par le Groupe spécial dont nous relatons ici la décision.

En se penchant d'abord sur les critères qui doivent guider l'examen qu'il fait de la détermination du DOC, le Groupe spécial binational a insisté sur l'idée que: "Les paragraphes 1904(2) et 1904(3) et l'annexe 1911 de l'ALÉNA disposent qu'un groupe spécial binational est tenu de décider si la détermination antidumping contestée a été rendue conformément à la législation sur les droits antidumping ou sur les droits compensateurs du pays importateur."[46] Dans cette optique, le Groupe spécial binational a procédé à une revue de la jurisprudence américaine portant sur la prise en compte des éléments de preuve pertinents et sur l'interprétation que peut faire un tribunal ou un organisme administratif de la loi. À la lumière des arrêts Chevron[47] et *National Railroad Passenger Corp.*,[48] le Groupe spécial binational a conclu que:

... si les déterminations du DOC pouvaient être confirmées au seul motif de leur plausibilité par opposition à leur caractère raisonnable, les pouvoirs du DOC dépasseraient considérablement ceux que lui confère l'ALÉNA. La procédure d'examen de l'ALÉNA s'en trouverait aussi privée d'une grande partie de son sens. Le groups spécial estime préférable, conformément au contexte législatif et à la pratique administrative, y compris à la procédure d'examen des groupes spéciaux, d'appliquer le critère du caractère raisonnable aux mesures du DOC.[49]

---

[45] Voir *supra* note 37 à la p.4.

[46] *Ibid.* à la p. 10.

[47] *Chevron U.S.A., Inc.* v. *Natural Resources Defense Council, Inc.*, 467 U.S 837 (1984), cité à la p. 12 de la décision du groupe spécial binational.

[48] *National Railroad Passenger Corp.* v. *Boston Maine Corp.*, 503 U.S. 407 (1992).

[49] *Supra* note 44 à la p.12.

Guidé par ces principes, le Groupe spécial a ensuite procédé à l'analyse des points en litige à l'aune des dispositions législatives américaines pertinentes. Il a étudié l'interprétation et l'application qu'a faites le DOC des différents alinéas de l'article pertinent, soit l'article 1677 du 19 U.S.C. Il a indiqué que la détermination rendue par le DOC était mal fondée et ne justifiait pas la retenue dont font ordinairement l'objet les déterminations du DOC.[50] Il a rappelé les termes de la loi américaine qui prévoit que l'administration compétente doit prendre en compte tous les éléments disponibles concernant la juste répartition des coûts, y compris ceux qui sont mis à sa disposition par l'exportateur ou le producteur.[51] Il a estimé que Stelco a effectivement produit des renseignements que le DOC aurait dû utiliser pour sa détermination. Il a rappelé le principe enchâssé dans le droit international et incorporé dans la législation américaine qui veut que l'on prévienne le gonflement des coûts de production et l'élargissement qui s'ensuivrait des marges de dumping.[52] Il a ajouté que le DOC n'avait pas la faculté de ne pas prendre en compte tous les éléments disponibles et qu'il aurait dû tenir compte des bénéfices versés dans le calcul du coût réel de production.[53] Étant donné aussi que le DOC n'a pas établi à partir du dossier que les coûts des transactions considérées ne représentaient pas fidèlement le montant d'ordinaire associé à de telles ventes, il ne pouvait pas ne pas tenir compte de toutes les données fournies par Stelco.[54] Le groupe spécial binational a donc renvoyé l'affaire au DOC en lui ordonnant de recalculer les coûts de production de Stelco en tenant compte des bénéfices versés par celui-ci par Baycoat en fin d'exercice.[55] Le groupe spécial a aussi ordonné au DOC de communiquer sa méthode de calcul et de l'expliquer à la lumière des dispositions légales applicables telles qu'interprétées par le groupe spécial.[56]

Cette décision dans l'affaire Stelco, la troisième rendue par un Groupe spécial sur la même question, constitue dans une certaine mesure une rebuffade pour le DOC qui devra se résoudre à modifier pour de bon son interprétation de l'article 1677 du 19 U.S.C et à renoncer à certaines méthodes de calcul des coûts de production.

[50] *Ibid.* à la p. 18.

[51] *Ibid.*

[52] *Ibid.*, à la p. 20; voir aussi la p.15.

[53] *Ibid.* à la p. p.20.

[54] *Ibid.* à la p. 26.

[55] *Ibid.* à la p.34.

[56] *Ibid.*

II LE COMMERCE CANADIEN ET L'OMC

A LES NÉGOCIATIONS COMMERCIALES MULTILATÉRALES: LA CONFÉRENCE MINISTÉRIELLE DE DOHA

C'est certainement la quatrième session de la Conférence ministérielle de l'OMC tenue à Doha au Qatar en novembre qui fut en 2001 le point culminant de l'activité commerciale multilatérale. Comme l'a dit lui-même le directeur général de l'OMC, Mike Moore, la Conférence de Doha fut peut-être la plus importante de l'histoire de l'OMC. Parmi les événements marquants de la Conférence, on songe évidemment d'emblée à l'entrée de la Chine à l'OMC. Le pays le plus populeux de la planète et l'un de ceux connaissant depuis quelques années l'une des croissances économiques les plus rapides a finalement achevé après presque quinze ans les négociations relatives à son protocole d'accession. Mais les résultats de la Conférence de Doha sont aussi remarquables à d'autres égards, notamment par la place qui fut faite aux discours et aux intérêts des pays en voie de développement. Sous de nombreux aspects, la Déclaration ministérielle publiée à l'issue de la Conférence traduit une préoccupation des Membres de l'OMC pour les moins favorisés d'entre eux que l'on ne retrouvait pas fréquemment avec cette acuité dans les déclarations émanant des Membres.[57]

La Déclaration de Doha énumère vingt et un sujets à propos desquels les Membres souhaitent lancer ou poursuivre leurs pourparlers. Parmi ces sujets, on remarque évidemment l'agriculture et les services pour lesquels les négociations avaient déjà commencé en 2000. Pour le premier de ces sujets, on ne s'étonnera pas de constater que les Membres se sont donnés comme objectif d'améliorer substantiellement l'accès aux marchés, de réduire les subventions à l'exportation et de réduire substantiellement les soutiens internes ayant des effets de distorsion des échanges. Le traitement spécial et différencié des PVD fait aussi intégrante de l'ensemble des négociations. En matière de services, les négociations visent à augmenter les engagements des Membres. Parmi les autres sujets ciblés dans la Déclaration de Doha, mentionnons en vrac l'accès au marché

---

[57] Déclaration ministérielle, Conférence ministérielle, Quatrième session, Doha, 9-14 novembre 2001, WT/MIN(01)/DEC/1, 20 novembre 2001. Comme l'ensemble des autres textes et documents émanant de l'OMC, il est facile de consulter la déclaration sur le site Web de l'OMC à l'adresse <http://ww.wto.org>.

pour les produits non agricoles, les aspects de droit de propriété intellectuelle qui touchent au commerce, l'interaction du commerce et de la politique de la concurrence, la transparence des marchés publics, la facilitation des échanges, le Mémorandum d'accord sur le règlement des différends, le commerce et l'environnement, le commerce électronique, les petites économies, les pays les moins avancés et le traitement spécial et différencié.

La Déclaration ministérielle n'est pas la seule décision prise à Doha allant dans le sens d'une préoccupation plus grande à l'égard des PVD. La *Déclaration sur l'Accord sur les ADPIC et la santé publique*[58] revêt aussi une grande importance à cet égard. Dans cette déclaration, les Membres reconnaissent la gravité des problèmes de santé publique qui touchent de nombreux pays en développement et les pays les moins avancés, en particulier ceux qui résultent du VIH/SIDA, de la tuberculose, du paludisme et d'autres épidémies. Ils réaffirment le droit des Membres de l'OMC de recourir pleinement aux dispositions de l'Accord de l'OMC sur les aspects de droit de propriété intellectuelle qui touchent au commerce (Accord sur les ADPIC) qui ménagent une flexibilité permettant aux Membres de l'OMC de protéger la santé publique et de promouvoir l'accès de tous aux médicaments. Les Membres reconnaissent ainsi que l'application de l'Accord sur les ADPIC ne doit pas avoir pour effet d'entraver l'accès aux médicaments aux populations qui en ont besoin. Une autre décision prise à Doha, intitulée celle-là *Questions et préoccupations liées à la mise en œuvre*[59] va aussi dans le sens des préoccupations des PVD. Cette décision renferme essentiellement des principes, des mesures et des mandats qui faciliteront la mise en œuvre des accords de l'OMC par les PVD Membres.

La relance des négociations commerciales multilatérales amenée par la Conférence de Doha, de par une meilleure participation des PVD et de par une meilleure prise en considération de leurs intérêts, est présage de négociations commerciales fructueuses dont on espère pouvoir récolter les fruits au début de l'année 2005.

---

[58] Déclaration sur l'Accord sur les ADPIC et la santé publique adoptée le 14 novembre 2001, Conférence ministérielle, Quatrième session, Doha, 9-14 novembre 2001, WT/MIN(01)/DEC/2, 20 novembre 2001.

[59] Questions et préoccupations liées à la mise en œuvre, adoptée le 14 novembre 2001, Conférence ministérielle, Quatrième session, Doha, 9-14 novembre 2001, WT/MIN(01)/17, 20 novembre 2001.

B   LES DIFFÉRENDS DEVANT L'OMC IMPLIQUANT LE CANADA

1   Communautés européennes: Mesures affectant l'amiante et les produits en contenant

On se rappellera que, dans son rapport de septembre 2000, le Groupe spécial chargé d'examiner cette affaire avait jugé que le décret français n° 96-1133 était justifié par l'exception de l'article XXb) du GATT de 1994 et que de ce fait la mesure française n'était pas incompatible avec le GATT. Le 12 mars 2001,[60] l'Organe d'appel a confirmé cette constatation mais a aussi et surtout constaté que les fibres d'amiante chrysotile et les autres produits de substitution qui ne présentaient pas le même degré de dangerosité pour la santé n'étaient pas des produits similaires au sens de l'article III:4 du GATT. Dans une longue étude de la preuve de dangerosité des produits d'amiante et de l'usage qui peut être fait de cette preuve dans l'examen de la similarité de deux produits au sens de l'article III:4, l'Organe d'appel énonce plusieurs principes importants relatifs à la prise en compte de l'effet d'un produit sur la santé, tant dans le contexte de l'article III:4 que dans le contexte de l'article XXb) du GATT. Le Canada n'a donc pas eu gain de cause dans cette affaire.

2   États-Unis: Loi de 2000 sur la compensation pour continuation du dumping et maintien de la subvention

Dans une communication datée du 21 mai 2001, le Canada et le Mexique ont demandé la tenue de consultations à propos d'une loi des États-Unis intitulée "Loi de 2000 sur la compensation pour continuation du dumping et maintien de la subvention."[61] Cette loi, qui est un amendement à la Loi douanière de 1930 et qui a été signée par le Président américain et pris force de loi le 28 octobre 2000, fait obligation aux autorités douanières des États-Unis de distribuer chaque année "aux producteurs nationaux affectés" le produit des droits de douane perçus conformément à une ordonnance instituant un droit compensateur, à une ordonnance antidumping ou à une constatation de l'existence d'un dumping en vertu de la Loi antidumping de 1921.

[60] Communautés européennes — Mesures affectant l'amiante et les produits en contenant, Rapport de l'Organe d'appel, OMC/WT/DS135/AB/R, le 12 mars 2001.

[61] États-Unis — Loi de 2000 sur la compensation pour continuation du dumping et maintien de la subvention, Demande de consultations présentée par le Canada et le Mexique, OMC/WT/DS234/1, le 1er juin 2001.

Le Canada et le Mexique considèrent que ces "compensations" incitent fortement les producteurs nationaux à déposer des demandes de mesures antidumping ou compensatoires. Ils estiment aussi que la nouvelle Loi crée un contexte qui ne permet pas une application impartiale des lois et règlements des États-Unis qui portent mise en œuvre de plusieurs dispositions des accords de l'OMC. Le Canada et le Mexique considèrent que la Loi semble incompatible avec l'article XVI:4 de l'Accord de Marrakech, avec les articles VI:2, VI:3 et X 3)a) du GATT, avec les articles premier, 5.4, 8, 18, 18.1, 18.4 de l'Accord antidumping et avec les articles 5, 10, 11.4, 18, 32.1 de l'Accord SMC. De nombreux Membres ont demandé à participer aux consultations.

Le 10 août, le Canada a demandé la constitution d'un Groupe spécial. L'Organe de règlement des différends (ORD) a décidé qu'un Groupe spécial unique entendrait cette plainte ainsi qu'une plainte de la Thaïlande se rapportant aux mêmes questions. Le rapport de ce Groupe spécial est attendu au cours de l'année 2002.

3   Canada: Mesures visant l'importation de lait et l'exportation de produits laitiers

Ce qu'il est maintenant convenu d'appeler l'affaire du lait a connu quelques rebondissements au cours de l'année 2001. À la fin de 1999, l'ORD avait constaté que le Canada exportait des produits laitiers subventionnés contrairement aux engagements de réduction des subventions à l'exportation contractés dans le cadre de l'*Accord sur l'agriculture*. L'ORD avait alors recommandé au Canada de rendre ses mesures conformes à cet accord. Par entente entre les États-Unis, la Nouvelle-Zélande et le Canada, il avait été convenu que ce dernier achèverait la mise en œuvre des recommandations et décisions de l'ORD au plus tard le 31 janvier 2001. En février 2001, le Canada n'ayant pas procédé à la mise en œuvre prévue, les États-Unis et la Nouvelle-Zélande ont demandé des consultations puis ont demandé que l'affaire soit portée devant un Groupe spécial, conformément à l'article 21:5 du Mémorandum d'accord sur le règlement des différends. Dans son rapport présenté le 5 juillet, le Groupe spécial a conclu que le Canada avait continué d'agir d'une manière incompatible avec ses obligations au titre des articles 3:3 et 8 de l'*Accord sur l'agriculture*, en octroyant des subventions à l'exportation au sens de l'article 9:1c) dudit accord excédant les niveaux d'engagement en matière de quantités spécifiés dans sa *Liste pour les exportations de fromage*, pour la campagne de commercialisation 2000/2001. Le Canada a fait appel de cette décision. Dans son rapport du 3 décembre 2001, l'Organe d'appel a infirmé la constatation du Groupe spécial et indiqué qu'il n'était pas possible de conclure que la fourniture de lait d'exportation commerciale par les producteurs de lait canadiens aux transformateurs de lait canadiens donnait lieu à des "versements" à l'exportation de lait "qui étaient financés en vertu d'une mesure des pouvoirs publics" au sens de l'article 9:1c) de l'*Accord sur l'agriculture*.[62] L'Organe d'appel a aussi indiqué qu'à la lumière des constatations factuelles faites par le Groupe spécial et des faits incontestés figurant dans le dossier du Groupe spécial, il n'était pas en mesure d'achever l'analyse des allégations formulées par la Nouvelle-Zélande et les États-Unis au titre des articles 9:1c) ou 10:1 de l'*Accord sur l'agriculture,* ni l'allégation formulée par les États-Unis au titre de l'article 3.1 de l'*Accord SMC.* Ce qui apparaissait comme une victoire au moins partielle pour le Canada n'était en fait qu'une bref délai dans la poursuite d'une lutte à finir entre les parties au différend. Le 6 décembre, les États-Unis ont demandé, en s'appuyant sur l'article 21:5 du Mémorandum d'accord que la question soit ramenée devant le Groupe spécial initial. Les divergences entre le Canada d'une part et les États-Unis et la Nouvelle-Zélande d'autre part, quant à la mise en œuvre des recommandations et décisions de l'ORD du 27 octobre 1999 ne sont apparemment pas près de s'aplanir.

4   *États-Unis: Article 129 C) 1) de la Loi sur les accords du Cycle d'Uruguay*

Dans une communication datée du 17 janvier, le Canada a demandé l'ouverture de consultations avec les États-Unis au sujet de l'article 129c)1) de la Loi sur Accords du Cycle d'Uruguay et de l'Énoncé des mesures administratives accompagnant cette loi.[63] Les mesures attaquées concernent la mise en œuvre des recommandations ou décisions adoptées par l'ORD pour lesquelles il a été constaté que les États-Unis ont agi d'une manière incompatible avec leurs obligations au titre de l'Accord antidumping ou de l'Accord

---

[62] Canada — Mesures visant l'importation de lait et l'exportation de produits laitiers, Recours des États-Unis et de la Nouvelle-Zélande à l'art. 21:5 du Mémorandum d'accord, Rapport de l'Organe d'appel, OMC/WT/DS103/AB/RW et OMC/WT/DS113/AB/RW, 3 décembre 2001.

[63] États-Unis — Article 129c)1) de la Loi sur les Accords du Cycle d'Uruguay, Demande de consultation présentée par le Canada, OMC/WT/DS221/1, le 22 janvier 2001.

SMC. D'après le Canada, les mesures américaines en cause obligent dans certains cas les autorités des États-Unis à procéder à des déterminations en matière de dumping ou de droits compensateurs sans attendre voire sans tenir compte des décisions de l'ORD. Le Canada estime donc que les mesures américaines sont incompatibles avec plusieurs dispositions du Mémorandum d'Accord sur le règlement des différends, de l'Accord de l'OMC, du GATT de 1994, de l'Accord SMC et de l'Accord antidumping. À la demande du Canada, un Groupe spécial a été constitué le 31 octobre. Son rapport est attendu au cours de l'année 2002.

5   *États-Unis: Mesures traitant les restrictions à l'exportation comme des subventions*

Dans une autre affaire reliée au conflit sur le bois d'œuvre, le Groupe spécial chargé d'examiner ce différend a rendu son rapport le 29 juin 2001.[64] Le Groupe spécial a confirmé la position prise par le Canada dans sa demande d'établissement d'un groupe spécial faite un an plus tôt. Le Groupe spécial a en effet confirmé que les restrictions à l'exportation telles qu'appliquées par le Canada ne peuvent pas constituer une fourniture de biens à laquelle les pouvoirs publics ont chargé ou ordonné de procéder et par conséquent, ne constituent pas une contribution financière au sens de l'article 1.1a) de l'Accord SMC. Elles ne sauraient donc être considérées comme des subventions pouvant donner lieu à des mesures compensatoires. Les États-Unis n'ont pas appelé de ce rapport du Groupe spécial. Cet aspect du dossier du bois d'œuvre est donc clos pour l'heure.

6   *États-Unis: Déterminations préliminaires concernant certains bois d'œuvre résineux en provenance du Canada*

Le 21 août, le Canada a demandé l'ouverture de consultations avec les États-Unis au sujet de la détermination préliminaire en matière de droits compensateurs et de la détermination préliminaire de l'existence de circonstances critiques établies par le Département du commerce des États-Unis le 9 août 2001 en ce qui concerne certains bois d'œuvre résineux en provenance du Canada.[65]

---

[64] États-Unis — Mesures traitant les restrictions à l'exportation comme des subventions, Rapport du groupe spécial, OMC/WT/DS194/R, le 29 juin 2001.

[65] États-Unis — Déterminations préliminaires concernant certains bois d'œuvre résineux en provenance du Canada, Demande de consultations présentées par le Canada, OMC/WT/DS236/1, le 27 août 2001.

Ces déterminations ont été établies à la suite d'enquêtes démarrées dès après l'extinction de l'Accord sur le bois d'œuvre entre le Canada et les États-Unis.

À propos de la détermination préliminaire en matière de droits compensateurs, le Canada est d'avis qu'elle est incompatible avec l'Accord SMC et avec le GATT pour plusieurs raisons. Elle serait incompatible du fait que, dans la détermination, la coupe de bois est considérée comme une contribution financière; la coupe est considérée comme spécifique au sens de l'Accord SMC; on présume qu'un avantage serait transféré de la coupe à un bénéficiaire en aval; l'"adéquation de la rémunération" est jugée par rapport aux conditions existant dans un autre pays et non par rapport aux conditions existant au Canada; et le fait que la subvention dont l'existence a été constatée a été gonflée.

À propos de la détermination préliminaire de l'existence de circonstances critiques, le Canada considère qu'elle est incompatible avec l'Accord SMC parce qu'elle est fondée sur une prétendue subvention à l'exportation qui a été jugée *de minimis;* qu'elle vise à appliquer un taux supérieur au taux déterminé pour les subventions jugées avoir été accordées d'une manière incompatible avec le GATT de 1994 et avec l'Accord SMC; qu'elle a été établie sans qu'ait été constatée l'existence d'un dommage causé par des importations massives de bois d'œuvre résineux bénéficiant de cette prétendue subvention à l'exportation; et qu'elle était fondée sur une constatation erronée de l'existence d'importations massives.

Le Canada a également demandé des consultations au sujet de certaines mesures des États-Unis qui ne permettent pas de procéder à des réexamens accélérés dans les affaires de droits compensateurs dans lesquelles l'enquête a été menée sur une base globale ou au niveau national et dans lesquelles il a été prescrit qu'un taux de droit national unique remplace tous les taux individuels précédemment déterminés.

Au moment de la demande de consultations, les mesures américaines attaquées affectaient des échanges de bois d'œuvre résineux en provenance du Canada d'un montant d'environ 26 millions de dollars par jour. Compte tenu de l'importance des impacts des mesures américaines, le Canada a demandé la tenue de consultations d'urgence. Ces consultations ont été vaines. La constitution d'un Groupe spécial a été demandée par le Canada. Ce Groupe devrait être constitué tôt en 2002. On peut craindre que le différend sur le bois d'œuvre qui, sous différentes formes, oppose le

Canada et les États-Unis depuis près d'un quart de siècle donne lieu à quelques rebondissements en 2002 et en 2003.

7   *Le différend canado-brésilien sur les aéronefs civils*

Un peu comme le conflit canado-américain sur le bois d'œuvre, le conflit canado-brésilien sur les aéronefs civils a donné lieu à de multiples recours au Mémorandum d'Accord sur le règlement des différends de l'OMC.[66] En 2001, deux dossiers liés à ce conflit ont notablement progressé. Le 22 janvier, le gouvernement brésilien a demandé l'ouverture de consultations avec le Canada.[67] Le Brésil estime que des crédits à l'exportation et des garanties de prêts prohibés par l'article 3 de l'Accord SMC ont été accordés à l'industrie canadienne des aéronefs de transport régional. Ces mesures ont été prises au bénéfice de Bombardier en vue de faciliter une importante transaction avec un acheteur américain, Air Wisconsin, et de préserver à l'avionneur canadien ses parts de marché. Un Groupe spécial a été constitué et une décision est attendue au début de 2002. Par ailleurs, le 26 juillet, le Groupe spécial chargé aux termes de l'article 21:5 d'examiner la mise en œuvre des décisions et recommandations de l'ORD dans l'affaire *Brésil — Programme de financement des exportations pour les aéronefs* a rendu son rapport.[68] Le Groupe spécial a alors conclu que le programme de financement en cours au Brésil, ProEx III, n'était pas en soi incompatible avec l'article 3 de l'Accord SMC mais a soumis son application à toute une gamme de conditions financières techniques et laissé au Canada la possibilité de contester éventuellement cette application aux termes du Mémorandum d'Accord sur le règlement des différends.

III   CONCLUSION

Des conflits commerciaux tels que ceux du lait, du bois d'œuvre et des aéronefs civils ont mis le système de règlement des différends

---

[66] Les dossiers WT/DS46, WT/DS70, WT/DS71 et WT/DS222 découlent en effet directement de ce conflit. Les dossiers WT/DS70 et WT/DS71 sont maintenant inactifs.

[67] Canada — Crédits à l'exportation et garanties de prêts accordés pour les aéronefs régionaux, Demande de consultations présentée par le Brésil, OMC/WTDS222/1, le 25 janvier 2001.

[68] Brésil — Programme de financement des exportations pour les aéronefs, Deuxième recours du Canada à l'article 21:5 du Mémorandum d'Accord sur le règlement des différends, Rapport du Groupe spécial, OMC/WT/DS46/RW/2, le 26 juillet 2001.

à rude épreuve au cours de l'année 2001. On constate en effet que la mise en œuvre des décisions et recommandations de l'ORD sont de plus en plus ardues, longues et sources de tension. Peut-être le *Mémorandum d'accord sur les règles et procédures régissant le règlement des différends* est-il victime de son succès. Peut-être aussi le droit international économique change-t-il lentement de nature. Les disciplines qui affectaient essentiellement les tarifs douaniers et exigeaient le respect des principes de traitement national et de nation la plus favorisée ne sont plus au cœur des litiges comme auparavant. C'est aujourd'hui des questions touchant différemment la souveraineté, l'intervention voire la mission de l'État que les accords économiques et les conflits qui en découlent touchent. Le droit international économique est probablement, de ce point de vue, en pleine phase de transition. Et l'année 2001, avec le lancement d'ambitieuses négociations à l'OMC et sur l'hémisphère américain, a amené la preuve que la communauté des États souhaite voir jusqu'où et comment peut être améliorée et poussée cette intégration économique.

II Le Canada et le système financier international en 2001

préparé par
BERNARD COLAS

L'histoire retiendra de l'année 2001 la perpétration des attentats du 11 septembre et le ralentissement marqué de l'économie mondiale. Dans ce contexte, la communauté internationale a naturellement consacré une part de ses travaux à la consolidation du système financier international et une autre part à l'intensification de la lutte contre le terrorisme et le blanchiment d'argent. Cette consolidation du système financier international et cette lutte contre le terrorisme ont été menées de concert par le Groupe des vingt (I), les institutions internationales (II) et les organismes de contrôle des établissements financiers (III), le Groupe d'action financière (IV) et le Forum de stabilité financière (V).

I Le Groupe des vingt

A l'occasion de leur réunion annuelle tenue à Ottawa les 16 et 17 novembre 2001, le Groupe des vingt (G-20) a relevé, avec satisfaction, que de nombreux membres du G-20 s'étaient soumis de manière volontaire aux évaluations menées aux termes du Programme d'évaluation du secteur financier de la Banque mondiale et du FMI.[1]

Les membres du G-20 ont, par ailleurs, rappelé l'importance des normes et des codes internationaux en tant qu'instrument propre à

Bernard Colas, Avocat de l'étude Gottlieb et Pearson (Montréal), Docteur en droit, Commissaire, Commission du droit du Canada, Président de la Société de droit international économique (SDIE). L'auteur remercie Xavier Mageau, LL.M., de la même étude pour son importante contribution à la préparation de cet article.

[1] *Communiqué des Ministres des Finances et gouverneurs des banques centrales des pays du G-20*, 17 novembre 2001 [ci-après *Communiqué du G-20*].

favoriser la croissance économique et à réduire les crises financières. Outre l'importance des normes et des codes internationaux, les membres du G-20 ont réaffirmé leur attachement au libre-échange et à l'ouverture des marchés internationaux. Les membres du G-20 ont cependant souhaité que la mondialisation profite à l'ensemble des citoyens de la planète et particulièrement aux pays les plus pauvres.

En réaction aux crises financières des années précédentes et aux attentats du 11 septembre, le G-20 a adopté une série de mesures stratégiques fortes telles que le renforcement des mesures de sécurité, le gel des avoirs des terroristes dans le but d'assurer la stabilisation des marchés et le maintien des liquidités. Même si les membres du G-20 se sont déclarés convaincus que ces mesures suffiraient, les membres ont néanmoins précisé que des mesures additionnelles pourraient être prises le cas échéant.

Outre ces mesures stratégiques, les membres du G-20 ont adopté un plan d'action pour pallier les conséquences économiques des attentats et pour lutter contre le terrorisme.[2] Ce plan d'action repose sur trois axes: le renforcement de la coopération des diverses organisations internationales, l'adoption de normes internationales efficaces en matière de lutte contre le terrorisme, l'application concrète de la réglementation internationale existante en la matière. Il a notamment été question d'appliquer les résolutions du Conseil de sécurité des Nations Unies relatives au gel des avoirs de façon à permettre, entre autre, le gel des avoirs visés par la résolution.[3] Les normes internationales existantes telles que la Convention des Nations Unies pour la répression du financement du terrorisme ou encore la Convention contre la criminalité transnationale organisée seront également appliquées. La collaboration entre les organisations internationales, entre les États et l'échange de renseignements entre les États seront intensifiés. Par ailleurs, une aide technique sera apportée aux États la requérant pour leur permettre d'élaborer et de mettre en œuvre des lois, des règlements et des politiques nécessaires pour combattre le financement du terrorisme et le blanchiment de capitaux.

---

[2] *Communiqué du G-20, supra* note 1.

[3] Parmi les autres mesures permises en application des résolutions du Conseil de sécurité des Nations Unies relatives au gel des avoirs, il faut mentionner la publication du nom des groupes terroristes dont les avoirs ont été gelés ainsi que la publication du montant des avoirs ainsi gelés.

La mise en œuvre de ce plan d'action sera suivie annuellement par le G-20. À cet égard, la première évaluation aura lieu à l'occasion de la réunion annuelle du G-20 en 2002 à New Delhi (Inde).

II   Les institutions internationales

A   fonds monétaire international (fmi)

Le ralentissement de l'économie mondiale de 2001 n'a pas permis à l'Argentine et à la Turquie de sortir définitivement de la crise que ces pays rencontrent depuis plusieurs années. Comme il l'avait fait au cours de l'année précédente, le FMI est à nouveau intervenu pour soutenir ces pays.[4] Dans ce contexte économique morose, le FMI a donc poursuivi ses travaux sur la réforme du FMI en matière de renforcement de la surveillance, de mise en œuvre des normes et des codes internationaux, des mécanismes du FMI et du renforcement de la régie du FMI.

Tout d'abord, sur le plan de la prévention des crises financières, le FMI a créé, en 2001, le département des marchés financiers internationaux dont le rôle consiste essentiellement à accroître la capacité du FMI à déceler les symptômes de crise pour y apporter rapidement les correctifs nécessaires.[5] Les crises financières des années précédentes ont mis en évidence l'importance fondamentale que revêt la libéralisation progressive et ordonnée du compte capital des pays. Sur la base de constat, le FMI a amorcé, en 2001, des discussions sur les principes généraux de nature à aider les pays dont les marchés financiers sont peu solides, sous-développés ou mal réglementés à ordonner et à coordonner la libéralisation du compte capital.[6]

Depuis plusieurs années, de nombreux pays insistent sur le rôle essentiel qui peut être dévolu au secteur privé en matière de prévention et de règlement des crises. S'agissant de cette participation du secteur privé, le FMI a reçu, en novembre 2001, une proposition relative à l'implantation d'un mécanisme de rééchelonnement de

---

[4] L'Argentine et la Turquie ont, à nouveau, bénéficié du soutien du FMI. S'agissant de l'Argentine, le FMI a approuvé une bonification de 8 milliards de dollars américains de l'Accord de confirmation de trois années et de la Facilité de réserve supplémentaire de l'Argentine. Quant à la Turquie, le FMI a approuvé un soutien financier additionnel de 8 milliards de dollars américains en mai 2001. *Rapport sur les opérations effectuées en vertu de la Loi sur les accords de Bretton Woods et des accords connexes 2001* à la p. 11 [ci-après *Bretton Woods 2001*].

[5] *Bretton Woods 2001*, *supra* note 4 à la p. 15.

[6] *Ibid.*

la dette publique des pays.[7] Le mécanisme proposé est semblable à celui des régimes nationaux de règlements de faillites. Cette initiative, dont le FMI a souligné l'intérêt, sera étudiée de manière plus approfondie au cours de l'exercice 2002.

Au cours de l'année, le FMI a fait le point sur les progrès relatifs à la norme spéciale de diffusion des données (NSDD) adoptée en 1996. Pour compléter la NSDD, le FMI a approuvé l'intégration d'une méthode cadre d'évaluation de la qualité des données à la structure des modules de données des rapports sur l'observation des normes et des codes.[8]

En ce qui concerne la régie interne, le FMI a procédé à la révision de ses règles de régie. Suite à cette révision, il est apparu que les règles de régie élaborées en 1997 demeuraient pertinentes.[9] Néanmoins, ces règles ont été complétées par de nouvelles règles destinées à accroître la transparence du système telle la mise en place du programme initial d'évaluation des activités, des politiques et des programmes du FMI par le Bureau d'évaluation indépendant. Par ailleurs, le FMI a, au cours des dernières années, manifesté la volonté de réformer le système de quotes-parts afin que les quotes-parts du FMI reflètent mieux l'évolution de l'économie mondiale et que les mécanismes de régie du FMI soient davantage représentatifs des membres.[10]

Les attentats du 11 septembre 2001 ont contraint le FMI à donner une nouvelle orientation aux travaux du FMI. En effet, suite à ces événements, le FMI a mis au point un plan d'action pour intensifier la lutte contre le blanchiment de capitaux et le financement du terrorisme. La mise en œuvre du plan d'action sera assurée tantôt par le FMI seul et tantôt par le FMI en étroite collaboration avec d'autres organisations internationales tels que le Groupe d'action financière sur le blanchiment de capitaux (GAFI).

Le Comité monétaire et financier international du FMI a également participé à l'identification des mesures de nature à lutter contre le blanchiment de capitaux. À cet égard, le Comité a proposé la création de nouvelles mesures dont les plus importantes sont d'une part la création de services de renseignements financiers pour recueillir les rapports d'opérations douteuses en provenance du secteur financier et d'autre part la mise en place de stratégies

---

[7] *Ibid.* à la p. 20.

[8] *Ibid.* à la p. 18.

[9] *Ibid.* à la p. 23.

[10] *Ibid.*

pour assurer le partage de l'information et la collaboration entre ces services de renseignements financiers.

B   BANQUE MONDIALE

Au cours de l'année 2001, les activités de la Banque mondiale ont été axées sur trois thèmes principaux: la lutte contre la pauvreté, l'aide technique aux pays les plus vulnérables et la définition d'un plan d'actions pour palier les conséquences financières découlant des attentats du 11 septembre 2001.

1   La lutte contre la pauvreté

Dans le cadre de ses activités de lutte contre la pauvreté, la Banque mondiale a procédé à un examen exhaustif du processus des Cadres stratégiques de lutte contre la pauvreté (CSLP).[11] Les CSLP ont été mis en place en 1999 et sont conçus depuis leur origine comme un mécanisme exhaustif établissant un lien étroit entre l'allègement de la dette des pays pauvres très endettés et les initiatives de réduction de la pauvreté. Cette révision entamée en 2001 devrait être achevée au cours de l'année 2002.

La Banque mondiale a apporté son soutien aux stratégies nationales de développement et de réduction de la pauvreté.[12] Ce soutien a pris la forme de prêts structurels destinés à soutenir les réformes sociales et structurelles mises en œuvre par les pays en développement. Par ailleurs, le Conseil d'administration de la Banque mondiale a approuvé l'instauration d'un crédit de soutien contre la pauvreté, lequel ne sera cependant offert qu'aux États s'engageant résolument dans l'application d'un processus budgétaire et fiduciaire transparent et de stratégies dynamiques de réduction de la pauvreté.[13]

En dépit des progrès importants enregistrés au cours de l'année 2001 en matière de réduction de la dette multilatérale des pays pauvres très endettés (PPTE), ces pays restent très vulnérables aux chocs extérieurs comme la chute des prix des produits de base. C'est pourquoi, les gouverneurs de la Banque mondiale et du FMI ont, en novembre 2001, convenu de l'adoption de mesures additionnelles d'allègement de la dette dans des cas tout à fait exceptionnels.[14]

---

[11] *Ibid.* à la p. 39.

[12] *Ibid.* à la p. 40.

[13] *Ibid.* à la p. 41.

[14] *Ibid.* à la p. 75

De son côté, le Canada a décidé d'appliquer un moratoire sur le recouvrement de la dette de onze PPTE occupés à instaurer des réformes.

Pour venir en aide aux plus démunis, la Banque mondiale a augmenté, à hauteur de 30 millions de dollars américains, le financement apporté au Groupe consultatif d'assistance aux plus défavorisés (GAPD). Le GAPD cherche à renforcer la capacité des institutions de micro-financement ayant fait leurs preuves et à aider les pauvres. Ce renforcement apparaît essentiel face à l'augmentation des opérations de micro-crédits constatées en 2001.[15] Ces opérations consistent en des prêts de montant relativement peu élevé consentis aux démunis par des organismes communautaires locaux. Le GAPD a, en 2001, consacré une somme de 6,7 millions de dollars américains à l'élargissement des opérations de micro-crédits dans les pays les plus pauvres du monde. Le Canada a appuyé fortement les efforts du GAPD pour élargir la portée du micro-crédit et a contribué à son financement par l'intermédiaire de l'Agence canadienne de développement international à hauteur de 1,5 millions de dollars canadiens.

En juin 2001, le Groupe de la Banque mondiale a préparé un document intitulé *Stratégie de développement du secteur privé — Questions et options à des fins de consultations auprès des gouvernements, du secteur privé, des ONG et des organismes multilatéraux.*[16] Cette stratégie de développement du Groupe de la Banque mondiale est fondée sur deux grands thèmes: l'élargissement de la portée des marchés et l'amélioration de la prestation des services de base.[17]

Toujours sur le plan du développement, le Comité du développement de la Banque a procédé, en 2001, à l'analyse du document stratégique de la Banque intitulé *Leveraging Trade for Development.*[18] Ce document stratégique définit le rôle de la Banque au regard de l'aide qu'elle peut apporter aux pays en développement en vue de leur assurer une meilleure intégration et participation au

---

[15] *Ibid.* à la p. 54.

[16] *Ibid.* à la p. 53.

[17] Pour que cette stratégie soit mise en œuvre, plusieurs facteurs doivent être réunis parmi lesquels la création d'un climat propice à l'investissement, la prestation d'un soutien direct aux sociétés privées, l'appui à la participation du secteur privé à l'infrastructure, le renforcement du rôle du secteur privé pour soutenir les efforts publics déployés pour offrir un accès universel et abordable aux services sociaux ou encore l'adoption d'une nouvelle approche ciblant mieux les subventions destinées aux démunis et améliorant la prestation des services

[18] *Bretton Woods 2001, supra* note 4 aux pp. 57-58.

commerce international. Pour se faire, la Banque collabore avec cinq institutions dans le contexte du Cadre intégré de l'aide technique liée au commerce.[19] Le Canada a versé une contribution de 1 million de dollars canadiens au fonds fiduciaire du Cadre intégré.

Au cours de l'année 2000, l'Afrique avait été placée au centre des activités du FMI et de la Banque mondiale à l'occasion de l'année 2000. Cet engagement s'est traduit en 2001 par la visite des dirigeants du FMI et de la Banque mondiale dans la région pour s'entretenir des principaux enjeux du développement avec les dirigeants de vingt-deux pays d'Afrique.[20] Suite à cette visite, cinquante-trois chefs d'États africains ont, à l'occasion du sommet de l'Organisation de l'unité africaine, adopté un Nouveau partenariat pour le développement de l'Afrique.

En matière de santé publique, la Banque mondiale a, par l'intermédiaire de l'IDA, accru son soutien à la lutte contre la pandémie du VIH/SIDA. Au cours de l'année 2001, le conseil des administrateurs a approuvé la première étape d'un projet multinational de prévention et de surveillance du VIH/SIDA pour les Caraïbes dont le montant est de 155 millions de dollars américains dont 40 millions sont réservés à la Barbade et à la République Dominicaine où le nombre de personnes porteuses du VIH/SIDA est d'environ 390 000.[21]

La Banque mondiale avait, en 2000, créé le Fonds prototype pour le carbone[22] destiné à la protection de l'environnement. En 2001, ce Fonds, doté de 145 millions de dollars américains, a financé un projet de gestion des déchets solide à Liepaja en Lettonie. Les administrateurs de la Banque mondiale ont approuvé une stratégie révisée en matière d'environnement afin d'assurer l'observation des politiques de protection de l'environnement de la Banque mondiale. Pour ce faire, la Banque a nommé des coordonnateurs régionaux de la protection, mis sur pied des guichets

---

[19] Ce Cadre est devenu le principal véhicule permettant d'intégrer de manière cohérente le commerce aux stratégies d'aide aux pays dans la mesure où la Banque mondiale assume le rôle de chef de file.

[20] *Bretton Woods 2001*, *supra* note 4 à la p. 42.

[21] *Ibid.* à la p. 43.

[22] Ce fonds, qui constitue le premier mécanisme d'échange commercial des émissions de carbone, finance plusieurs projets destinés à réduire de manière substantielle les émissions de gaz à effet de serre. *Rapport sur les opérations effectuées en vertu de la Loi sur les accords de Bretton Woods et des accords connexes 2000* aux pp. 58-59 [ci-après *Bretton Woods 2000*].

d'aide à l'intention du personnel et mis à niveau sa formation interne dans le domaine.[23]

2   *L'atténuation des répercussions financières des attentats du 11 septembre 2001*

Après la perpétration des attentats du 11 septembre 2001, la Banque mondiale a consacré une partie de ses travaux à l'élaboration de mesures palliant les conséquences économiques des attentats. C'est dans ce contexte que la Banque mondiale a, en collaboration avec le FMI et d'autres banques régionales de développement, entrepris d'accroître les prêts et d'intensifier l'aide technique en faveur des pays en développement pour les aider dans la lutte contre le blanchiment de capitaux et le financement du terrorisme. Pour venir en aide aux pays à faible revenu, la Banque s'est engagée à apporter un soutien accru, que ce soit sous la forme d'aide technique, d'une augmentation des prêts d'urgence et des prêts à l'ajustement, de décaissement rapide des prêts, d'une analyse plus ciblée de la pauvreté, des finances et de l'économie des pays, de la part du personnel de la Banque. Dans ce contexte, la Banque mondiale collaborera de manière plus étroite avec les Nations Unies, les banques régionales de développement et les organismes bilatéraux. L'évaluation des besoins en Afghanistan est le premier exemple de coopération concrète entre le Programme des Nations Unies pour le développement et la Banque asiatique de développement.[24] Par ailleurs, cette évaluation constituera la base de l'aide future apportée à ce pays par la communauté internationale.

3   *La régie interne de la Banque mondiale*

Depuis plusieurs années, le Canada souhaite un accroissement de la transparence de la part de la Banque mondiale. C'est à cette demande qu'ont accédé les administrateurs de la Banque en approuvant les révisions à la politique en matière de communication des renseignements. Au terme de ces révisions, la Banque s'engage à communiquer au public l'ensemble des documents relatifs aux activités de la Banque de manière beaucoup plus large qu'auparavant.[25]

---

[23] *Bretton Woods 2001*, *supra* note 4 aux pp. 56-57.

[24] D'ailleurs, l'Afghanistan deviendra admissible aux prêts concessionels de la Banque mondiale dès que le pays aura réglé l'arriéré dû à l'IDA. *Bretton Woods 2001*, *supra* note 4 aux pp. 33 et 38.

[25] *Bretton Woods 2001*, *supra* note 4 aux pp. 58-59.

III   ORGANISMES DE CONTRÔLE DES ÉTABLISSEMENTS FINANCIERS

Les travaux des organismes de contrôle des établissements financiers ont été assez peu affectés par les attentats du 11 septembre 2001. En effet, leurs travaux restent profondément liés au développement et à la mise en œuvre de normes prudentielles ainsi qu'à la consolidation du système financier international. Cette affirmation vaut tant pour les actions du Comité de Bâle sur le contrôle bancaire, de l'Organisation internationale des commissions de valeur (OICV) que pour celles du Forum de stabilité financière (FSF) mais également dans une moindre mesure pour le Groupe d'action financière sur le blanchiment de capitaux (GAFI) dont le mandat est précisément de lutter contre le blanchiment de capitaux.

A   COMITÉ DE BÂLE SUR LE CONTRÔLE BANCAIRE

En 2001, le Comité de Bâle sur le contrôle bancaire a poursuivi ses travaux portant sur la révision de l'Accord de Bâle sur les fonds propres qui sert maintenant de fondement à la réglementation d'une centaine de pays. Cette révision a pour objet de définir des exigences de solvabilité correspondant mieux au profil de risque réel des établissements de crédit.[26] Cette année, une deuxième version du projet a été mise en consultation. Suite à ces consultations, les positions écrites de plusieurs institutions financières ont mis en évidence la complexité des nouvelles méthodes d'assujettissement aux fonds propres et la difficulté de calibrer les exigences relatives aux risques notamment de crédit et opérationnels. Il a donc été convenu de procéder à une troisième procédure de consultation, laquelle sera amorcée au début de l'année 2002. Le recours à une troisième procédure de consultation entraînera un report de l'entrée en vigueur de cet accord à l'année 2005 alors qu'elle était initialement prévue pour 2004. En outre, le délai octroyé pour procéder à la transposition nationale du nouvel accord sur les fonds propres pourrait être prolongé jusqu'en 2006. Les autres modifications apportées suite à la seconde consultation portent sur l'aplatissement des courbes de pondération du risque relatives à la méthode des ratings internes utilisée pour l'assujettissement des risques de crédit. Cet aplatissement affectera les crédits aux entreprises et les affaires de détails.[27]

[26] La révision menée en vue d'un nouvel Accord prend appui sur trois piliers, à savoir le ratio minimal de fonds propres, le processus de surveillance prudentielle et les exigences en matière de communication financière.

[27] *Rapport de gestion, Commission fédérale des banques 2001* aux pp. 156 et 249-56 [ci-après *Commission fédérale*].

En février 2001, le Comité de Bâle a publié en collaboration avec l'*International Auditing Practices Committee l'Exposure Draft "The Relationship Between Banking Supervisors and the Bank's External Auditors."*[28] Ce document, dont la publication finale est prévue en 2002, traite des responsabilités du Conseil d'administration et de la direction lorsqu'un organe de révision externe et une autorité de surveillance sont présents au sein de l'établissement de crédit. Le rapport souligne clairement que la présence de l'organe de révision externe et de l'autorité de surveillance ne réduit en aucun cas les responsabilités des membres du Conseil d'administration et de la direction. Ce document définit le rôle de la révision externe comme celui consistant à permettre au réviseur externe indépendant de rendre une opinion sur la conformité des états financiers publiés sous tous les aspects matériels avec les normes comptables en vigueur.

Au cours de l'année 2001, l'*"Electronic Banking Group"* du Comité de Bâle sur le "E-Banking"[29] a réduit ses activités. Ce comité a consacré ses travaux à la gestion des risques liés à l'*Electronic Banking* et à la surveillance des activités e-banking. Dans le cadre de ses travaux, le comité a publié le document *"Risk Management Principles for Electronic Banking."* Ce rapport, bien que dépourvu de recommandation contraignante, fournit néanmoins des indications pour la gestion des risques liés à l'*Electronic Banking* afin d'atteindre dans ce domaine un fonctionnement plus sûr. Le document conclut que les principes traditionnellement admis en matière de gestion des risques doivent s'appliquer à l'*Electronic Banking*. Toutefois, le document complète ces principes traditionnels par quatorze principes spécifiques à la gestion des risques liés à l'*Electronic Banking*, lesquels sont répartis en trois catégories: la surveillance par les organes supérieurs de la banque, les mesures de sécurité et les mesures visant à limiter les risques juridiques et le risque de réputation.

En matière d'identification des clients, le Comité de Bâle a, cette année, franchi un pas décisif en publiant en octobre 2001 la version définitive des standards minimaux en matière d'identification des clients.[30] Ces *"Customer due diligence for banks"* comprennent d'une part les standards applicables à toutes les relations bancaires

---

[28] *Ibid.* à la p. 257.

[29] *Ibid.* aux pp. 257-58.

[30] *Ibid.* aux pp. 260-61. L'origine de ces *"Customer due diligence for banks"* remonte à l'année 1999. Au cours de l'année 1999, le Comité de Bâle a constaté la disparité des règles relatives à l'identification des clients en matière internationale. Ce constat a convaincu le Comité de Bâle qu'il devait élaborer des standards minimaux en matière d'identification.

et d'autre part les règles relatives à des clients comportant un risque réputationnel élevé que ce soit en raison de leur position politique ou de leur fortune. Ce document, qui constitue le nouveau standard international en matière d'identification des clients des établissements bancaires, n'a cependant aucune force obligatoire.

B   ORGANISATION INTERNATIONALE DES COMMISSIONS
     DE VALEURS (OICV)

La conférence annuelle de l'OICV a été placée sous la devise *"Securities Markets in the Information Age."*[31] L'influence d'Internet sur les marchés et leur régulation, l'accès au marché et à l'information pour les investisseurs à l'ère d'Internet, la stabilité des marchés, l'indépendance des réviseurs et la transparence du processus de régulation sont les thèmes qui ont été abordés au cours de cette réunion annuelle.[32]

Fort du succès rencontré lors du premier "Internet Surf Day," l'OICV a réitéré l'expérience. Le thème retenu pour ce deuxième "Internet Surf Day" a été le renforcement de la protection des investisseurs et de la confiance des marchés.[33]

En 1998, l'assemblée annuelle de l'OICV a adopté les buts et les principes relatifs à la surveillance des marchés des valeurs mobilières. Dans le but de vérifier le caractère obligatoire et la transposition des buts et des principes dans les pays membres de l'OICV, l'OICV a, en 2001, mis en place un comité dont le rôle sera d'effectuer un contrôle rapide de la situation actuelle dans chaque pays.[34]

Suite aux événements du 11 septembre 2001, l'OICV a entamé un examen concernant l'implication des attentats en matière de surveillance. Pour ce faire, l'OICV a mis sur pied un groupe de projet spécifique dont la tâche a consisté à analyser trois aspects précis. Le premier aspect a trait aux dispositifs d'urgence concernant les marchés, leurs participants, les autorités de surveillance et la nécessité d'adapter la réglementation pour agir en cas de perturbation des marchés. Le second aspect a concerné l'intensification de la coopération et de l'échange d'informations sur le plan international nécessaires à la lutte contre la criminalité dans le domaine financier. Le troisième aspect a porté sur les bases nécessaires à

---

[31]   L'OICV a organisé sa conférence annuelle à Stockholm du 23 au 29 juin 2001.

[32]   *Commission fédérale, supra* note 27 à la p. 262.

[33]   *Ibid.* à la p. 263.

[34]   *Ibid.* à la p. 263.

l'établissement d'un système sévère d'identification des clients et des négociants en valeurs mobilières pour lutter contre la criminalité dans le domaine financier.[35]

IV GROUPE D'ACTION FINANCIÈRE SUR LE BLANCHIMENT DE CAPITAUX (GAFI)

Au cours de l'année 2001, le GAFI a poursuivi ses travaux d'identification des juridictions dont le dispositif de lutte contre le blanchiment de capitaux présente de graves défaillances. La liste des pays considérés comme non-coopératifs dans la lutte contre le blanchiment de capitaux a été fixée à 17 au 22 juin 2001.[36] Parallèlement à cette identification, le GAFI a étudié les mesures possibles qui pourraient être prises contre les pays non-coopératifs.[37]

Le GAFI a poursuivi la révision de ses quarante recommandations.[38] Quatre groupes ont été constitués pour accélérer cette révision. Un groupe se penchera sur les questions relatives à l'identification et à la divulgation des transactions suspectes. Un second groupe étudiera les *"corporate vehicles"* et en particulier les sociétés anonymes qui émettent des titres au porteur et d'autres formes sociales permettant de protéger l'ayant droit économique véritable de fonds telles que les trust ou les fondations. Un troisième groupe analysera la question de l'application intégrale ou seulement partielle des recommandations à certaines professions et activités non-financières. Le quatrième et dernier groupe tentera de mettre au point une méthodologie pour le FMI tendant à vérifier l'application des recommandations du GAFI en adéquation avec les principes développés par le FMI pour ses examens relatifs à l'observation des standards et des codes.[39]

---

[35] *Ibid.* à la p. 264.

[36] *Deuxième rapport visant à identifier les territoires ou pays non coopératifs: Améliorer au plan mondial les mesures de lutte contre le blanchiment,* 22 juin 2001 [ci-après *Rapport GAFI*]. Parmi les territoires ou pays considérés comme non coopératifs à cette date: Îles Cook, Dominique, Égypte, Guatemala, Hongrie, Indonésie, Israel, Liban, Îles Marshall, Myanmar, Nauru, Nigeria, Niue, Philippines, Russie, Saint-Christophe-et-Niévès et Saint-Vincent et les Grenadines. Lors de la réunion du 7 septembre 2001, la Grenade et l'Ukraine ont été ajoutés à cette liste.

[37] *Commission fédérale, supra* note 27 à la p. 269. Le GAFI a recommandé le 22 juin 2001 d'appliquer des contre-mesures à Nauru, les Philippines et la Russie à compter du 30 septembre 2001. *Rapport GAFI, supra* note 36.

[38] B. Colas, "Le Canada et le système financier international en 2000," A.C.D.I., 2001.

[39] *Commission fédérale, supra* note 27 à la p. 269.

Après les attentats du 11 septembre 2001, le GAFI a décidé d'élargir la portée de l'examen des juridictions non-coopératives à la lutte contre le financement du terrorisme. Ce nouvel examen débutera en juin 2002.

V LE FORUM DE STABILITÉ FINANCIÈRE

Au cours de l'année 2001, le Forum de stabilité financière a porté une attention particulière à la détérioration de la croissance économique en cherchant notamment à évaluer les sources de faiblesse du système financier international, ce qui inclut en particulier l'analyse des canaux par lesquels une crise financière limitée peut s'étendre à l'ensemble du système.[40]

En 2001, le FSF a examiné le rapport des groupes d'experts sur la mise en œuvre des recommandations adoptées en 2000 à l'intention des institutions à fort effet de levier. Le FSF a approuvé le rapport final du groupe de suivi de l'application des standards internationaux. Ces standards internationaux comprennent les standards rédigés par le FMI, la Banque mondiale, l'OCDE, l'OICV, le Comité de Bâle, l'*International Association of Insurance Supervisors, l'International Auditing Practices Committee, l'International Federation of Accountants* et le *Committee on Payment and Settlement Systems*. Le groupe de suivi a constaté une meilleure connaissance des standards de la part des acteurs des marchés ainsi qu'une meilleure communication entre les institutions chargées d'élaborer ces standards et les institutions financières internationales chargées d'en vérifier l'application.[41]

L'année 2001 aura donc été marquée par la perpétration des attentats du 11 septembre 2001 et par le ralentissement de l'économie mondiale. En réponse à ces attentats, les organismes financiers internationaux ont consacré une part importante de leurs travaux à la lutte contre le terrorisme et contre le blanchiment de capitaux. Au-delà de la lutte contre le terrorisme et le blanchiment d'argent, ce sont la consolidation du système financier international et l'élaboration de mesures destinées à limiter les répercussions financières négatives des attentats qui ont retenu l'attention des divers organismes financiers internationaux.

---

[40] *Rapport annuel 2001 de la Commission des Opérations de Bourse* à la p. 196.
[41] *Rapport annuel 2001 de la Commission des Opérations de Bourse* à la p. 197.

III   Investissement

préparé par
CÉLINE LÉVESQUE

I   INTRODUCTION

Au cours de l'année 2001, deux événements ont retenu notre attention: l'annonce du lancement prévu de négociations multilatérales sur l'investissement à l'Organisation mondiale du commerce (OMC), et la publication du texte de négociation de la Zone de libre-échange des Amériques (ZLÉA), qui comprend un chapitre sur l'investissement. En eux-mêmes, ces événements sont dignes de mention. En effet, rappelons l'absence de tout accord multilatéral de portée générale sur l'investissement. Aussi, la diffusion au public d'un projet d'accord international — en cours de négociation — est exceptionnelle.

De surcroît, une comparaison entre les approches révèle des divergences significatives. À l'OMC, on semble s'éloigner du modèle bilatéral de traités de promotion et de protection des investissements, en adoptant un programme de libéralisation conforme aux principes du GATT-OMC (II). Dans le cadre de la ZLÉA, on semble plutôt en voie de procéder à la régionalisation et à la consolidation du modèle bilatéral nord-américain (III).

II   NÉGOCIATIONS (PRÉVUES) À L'OMC

En novembre 2001, à Qatar, les membres de l'OMC se sont entendus pour lancer un nouveau cycle de négociations commerciales multilatérales sous le thème du développement. La Déclaration ministérielle de Doha comporte une section intitulée "liens entre commerce et investissement," dont il est utile de citer le premier paragraphe:

Céline Lévesque, professeure à la Faculté de droit, Section de droit civil, de l'Université d'Ottawa.

Reconnaissant les arguments en faveur d'un cadre multilatéral destiné à assurer des conditions transparentes, stables et prévisibles pour l'investissement transfrontières à long terme, en particulier l'investissement étranger direct, qui contribuera à l'expansion du commerce, et la nécessité d'une assistance technique et d'un renforcement des capacités accrus dans ce domaine ... nous convenons que des négociations auront lieu *après la cinquième session de la Conférence ministérielle sur la base d'une décision qui sera prise, par consensus explicite, à cette session sur les modalités des négociations.*[1]

Pour le moins, la voie des négociations est sinueuse. La cinquième Conférence ministérielle de l'OMC doit se dérouler au Mexique à l'automne 2003. Une décision serait alors prise sur les "modalités" des négociations portant sur l'investissement. Si ce terme n'est pas particulièrement limpide dans le contexte, que faut-il penser de l'exigence du consensus explicite? Suffit-il, comme certains pays l'ont suggéré, qu'un seul pays membre s'oppose pour faire échec à ces négociations?[2] Rien n'est moins sûr.

Par ailleurs, la Déclaration révèle certaines orientations qui sont en apparence claires et soigneusement choisies (A). Cela étant, la réalité promet un parcours difficile à l'OMC (B).

A   APPARENCE

L'extrait de la Déclaration de Doha, cité plus haut, laisse entendre que le temps est venu de négocier un accord multilatéral portant sur l'investissement international. À cet égard, deux interrogations sont soulevées. D'une part, on peut se demander: pourquoi maintenant? Et d'autre part, on peut se questionner sur les objectifs qui seront poursuivis dans ces négociations.

Afin de répondre à la première question, il faut tenir compte de données historiques, économiques et politiques. D'abord, la conclusion d'un accord multilatéral portant sur l'investissement est un objectif de longue date. Plusieurs tentatives de conclure un tel accord ont échoué. La Charte de la Havane, négociée dans les années 1940 et d'ailleurs fort timide en ce qui concerne l'investissement, a connu ce sort.[3] Plus récemment, au cours des années

---

[1] Déclaration ministérielle de Doha (OMC Doc. WT/MIN(01)/DEC/1, en date de novembre 2001), au para. 20, en ligne: <http://www.wto.org/french/thewto_f/minist_f/min01_f/mindecl_f.htm> [nos italiques].

[2] Voir R. Bachand, "Les investissements: le conflit Nord-Sud" dans *L'Organisation mondiale du commerce — Où s'en va la mondialisation?* (2002) sous la direction de C. Deblock, Fides, La Presse, Québec, à la p. 158.

[3] Cette Charte n'est jamais entrée en vigueur. Pour un bref historique, voir M. Robert et T. Wetter, "Towards an Investment Agreement in the Americas: Building

1990, l'OCDE a été le forum de négociations du défunt Accord multilatéral sur l'investissement (AMI).[4] Par ailleurs, ce vide juridique a été en partie comblé, à partir des années 1960, par un réseau de traités bilatéraux qui comptait à la fin de 1999 plus de 1800 accords.[5]

Ensuite, il faut noter que, durant les dernières années, l'investissement étranger a connu une croissance plus rapide que les échanges commerciaux internationaux. En l'an 2000, l'investissement étranger direct a atteint un montant record de 1 300 milliards de dollars (US), montant qui a toutefois diminué par la suite.[6]

Finalement, l'annonce du lancement prévu (possible?) de négociations est le résultat d'un compromis politique. La rencontre ministérielle de 1999 à Seattle avait été un échec, dans la mesure où le nouveau cycle de négociations n'avait pu y être lancé. Déjà à ce moment, il était question de négocier un accord sur l'investissement, ce qui aurait en partie contribué à l'échec de cette rencontre.[7] À Doha, en 2001, les membres voulaient éviter un second échec. Un compromis a donc été atteint, qui a fait en sorte que l'investissement se trouve maintenant — en apparence — à l'ordre du jour.

Avant de répondre à la deuxième question, il est utile de faire un bref rappel des liens entre le GATT-OMC et la réglementation de l'investissement international. D'entrée de jeu, il faut noter qu'avant les années 1980, la réglementation des investissements ne faisait pas partie des priorités du système *commercial* international. La réglementation des investissements est toutefois devenue un sujet

---

on Existing Consensus" dans *Trade Rules in the Making — Challenges in Regional and Multilatéral Négotiations* (1999), M.R. Mendonza, P. Low et B. Kotschwar, dir., OAS, Brookings Institution Press, Washington, DC.

[4] La documentation officielle sur les négociations de l'AMI est archivée sur le site de l'OCDE en ligne à: <http://www.oecd.org/daf/investment/fdi/reports-fr. htm> (date d'accès: 6 février 2001). D'autres tentatives existent dans différents forum. Voir P. Juillard, "À Propos du décès de l'AMI" (1998) XLIV, A.F.D.I. aux pp. 599-601.

[5] Voir UNCTAD, *Bilateral Investment Treaties, 1959-1999* (2000), Internet Edition Only à la p. 1. Ce document est disponible à: <http://www.unctad.org/en/pub/ poiteiiad2.en.htm> (date d'accès: 19 juin 2001).

[6] Sur ces données, voir Conférence des Nations Unies sur le commerce et le développement, *Rapport sur l'investissement dans le monde 2001: Vers de nouvelles relations interentreprises*, Nations Unies, New York, 2001 à la p.1.

[7] Voir M. Koulen, "Foreign Investment in the WTO" dans *Multilateral Regulation of Investment* (2001) E.C. Nieuwenhuys et M.M.T.A. Brus, dir., Kluwer Law International, La Haye aux pp. 196-99.

de préoccupation notamment sous la forme d'un obstacle non-tarifaire au commerce.[8] Cette préoccupation a finalement mené à l'adoption de l'Accord sur les mesures concernant les investissement et liées au commerce (MIC), dans le cadre du cycle d'Uruguay. D'autres accords de l'OMC traitent de l'investissement de façon plus ou moins accessoire. Il s'agit notamment de l'Accord général sur le commerce des services (AGCS), de l'Accord sur les aspects des droits de propriété intellectuelle qui touchent au commerce (ADPIC), et de l'Accord sur les subventions et les mesures compensatoires.[9] Somme toute, il n'existe, dans le cadre de l'OMC, aucun accord de portée générale visant la réglementation de l'investissement étranger.

Ce constat nous permet de revenir aux objectifs des négociations prévues à Doha. L'annonce de négociations à venir a fourni l'occasion de revoir le mandat du Groupe de travail sur les liens entre commerce et investissement qui avait été créé en 1996.[10] Ce Groupe a été chargé de clarifier un certain nombre de questions, dont la Déclaration fait la liste, en préparation de la tenue de la prochaine Conférence ministérielle. Évidemment, il faut faire preuve de prudence dans notre analyse basée sur le texte d'une Déclaration, résultant d'un compromis délicat, dans un contexte où l'OMC cherche encore la voie à suivre. Toutefois, celle-ci révèle d'ores et déjà certaines orientations qui paraissent établies.

Dans l'extrait cité plus haut de la Déclaration, on souligne l'opportunité d'un cadre multilatéral répondant à certaines exigences. Dans le contexte de l'OMC, il s'agit manifestement de règles contraignantes. Au sujet de la portée de l'accord, on vise l'investissement à long terme, et en particulier l'investissement *direct* étranger, ce qui semblerait exclure l'investissement spéculatif, à court terme.

---

[8] *Ibid.* aux pp. 184-85.

[9] Voir ces Accords reproduits dans GATT, *Résultats des négociations commerciales multilatérales du cycle d'Uruguay — Textes juridiques*, Genève, Secrétariat du GATT, 1994. L'Accord sur les MIC vise principalement les prescriptions de résultats imposées aux investisseurs qui constituent des obstacles au commerce des marchandises. Dans l'AGCS, le commerce des services comprend "la présence commerciale" sur le territoire d'un autre membre, ce qui a pour conséquence que certains investissements vont être touchés par les règles de cet Accord. Voir Koulen, *ibid.* aux pp. 185-91.

[10] Ce Groupe de travail a été créé lors de la réunion ministérielle de l'OMC tenue à Singapour en 1996. Voir le par. 20 de la Déclaration ministérielle de Singapour à l'annexe 1 du Rapport du Groupe de travail (OMC doc. WT/WGTI/3 en date du 22 octobre 99), en ligne: <http://docsonline.wto.org/gen_search. asp> (date d'accès:12 février 2001).

Les principes retenus sont caractéristiques d'un instrument de mobilité plutôt que d'un instrument de sécurité. Premièrement, il est question d'un "cadre ... qui contribuera à l'expansion du commerce." Deuxièmement, on retrouve dans le texte des références aux principes charnières du système commercial international, dont la non-discrimination et la transparence. Enfin, on demande que soient clarifiées les "modalités pour des engagements avant établissement reposant sur une approche fondée sur des listes positives de type AGCS."[11] Ce dernier élément est particulièrement révélateur, car il renvoie à la méthode de libéralisation utilisée pour le commerce des services. Appliquée à l'investissement, cette méthode implique une renonciation par les États membres au droit souverain de contrôler l'admission sur leur territoire,[12] pour les investissements étrangers dans les secteurs qu'ils auront choisi de libéraliser ("listes positives"). En revanche, aucune mention n'est faite de principes de protection des investissements. D'ailleurs, les travaux du Groupe de travail qui ont suivi confirment que les questions de norme minimale de traitement et d'expropriation ne font pas partie du mandat du Groupe.[13]

En harmonie avec l'approche préconisée par l'OMC, la Déclaration souligne également l'importance du respect des intérêts des différentes parties prenantes à la relation d'investissement international, et en particulier de ceux des pays en voie de développement. En outre, l'accent n'est pas uniquement placé sur le soutien accru d'assistance technique requis pour les pays en développement. L'objectif d'adaptabilité devrait se refléter, à travers l'accord, de façon horizontale.[14]

---

[11] Déclaration de Doha, *supra* note 1 au par. 22.

[12] Voir D. Carreau et P. Juillard, *Droit international économique* (1998) 4ᵉ éd., L.G.D.J., Paris aux pp. 419 et s.

[13] Rapport (2002) du Groupe de travail des liens entre commerce et investissement au Conseil Général (OMC doc. WT/WGTI/6 en date du 9 décembre 2002), en ligne: <http://www.wto.org/french/tratop_f/invest_f/invest_f.htm>.

[14] Voir Déclaration de Doha, *supra* note 1 au par. 22: "Tout cadre devrait refléter de manière équilibrée les intérêts des pays d'origine et des pays d'accueil, et tenir dûment compte des politiques et objectifs de développement des gouvernements d'accueil ainsi que de leur droit de réglementer dans l'intérêt général. Les besoins spéciaux des pays en développement et des pays les moins avancés en matière de développement, de commerce et de finances devraient être pris en compte en tant que *partie intégrante* de tout cadre, qui devrait permettre aux Membres de contracter des obligations et des engagements qui correspondent à leurs besoins et circonstances propres" [nos italiques].

Du point de vue systémique, la Déclaration donne le mandat au Groupe de travail de clarifier le règlement des différends *entre les Membres*. Aucune mention n'est faite de la procédure de règlement des différends entre investisseurs et États. Enfin, elle déclare qu'il faudra tenir compte des autres dispositions pertinentes de l'OMC, ainsi que des accords bilatéraux et régionaux existants, dans la mesure appropriée.[15]

Malgré une certaine incertitude, la négociation semble engagée dans une voie dont les balises sont assez déterminées. Les apparences, en l'espèce, dissimulent une réalité plus troublante.

B   RÉALITÉ

La réalité politique est au centre du succès des négociations sur l'investissement à l'OMC, mais aussi de leur lancement effectif à l'automne 2003. Cette réalité, par contre, de par sa nature changeante et imprévisible, est difficile à cerner. Selon la mouvance des négociations portant sur d'autres domaines, tels que l'agriculture ou les brevets pharmaceutiques, le climat pourrait être favorable ou non à des négociations sur l'investissement. Cela étant dit, il existe une autre réalité, celle-ci plus palpable, qui promet un parcours difficile à l'OMC. Elle a sa source dans le projet de libéralisation de l'OMC et dans son intégrité systémique.

Afin d'atteindre les objectifs énoncés de libéralisation des investissements, les négociateurs auront à surmonter plusieurs difficultés. À titre d'illustration, nous soulignerons ici deux domaines problématiques: la définition de l'investissement et l'application du principe de traitement national.

Le débat quant à la *définition de l'investissement* nous est familier. Faut-il retenir une définition étroite, basée sur l'entreprise ou la transaction, et axée sur l'investissement direct étranger (à l'exclusion de l'investissement de portefeuille), ou plutôt adopter une définition large, basée sur la notion d'actifs, qui englobe l'investissement direct tout comme l'investissement de portefeuille? Les travaux du Groupe de travail révèlent que certains pays craignent "qu'une définition large de l'investissement ne provoque la libéralisation de toutes les formes de mouvement de capitaux et n'accroisse le risque de déstabilisation due à des mouvements spéculatifs."[16] De surcroît, selon eux, c'est l'investissement direct étranger, de par sa

---

[15] *Ibid.*

[16] Rapport (2002) du Groupe de travail, *supra* note 13 au par. 19.

nature, qui contribue le plus à l'économie du pays d'accueil et à la croissance des échanges. Certains autres pays, par contre, ne croient pas de nos jours qu'il soit possible, ou souhaitable, de faire la distinction entre l'investissement direct et indirect. Selon eux, on doit assurer une protection globale à l'investissement, quitte à traiter, dans l'accord, de ces deux types d'investissement de façon différente afin de maintenir une certaine flexibilité.[17]

La définition de l'investissement donnée dans l'AMI, qui était large, a fait l'objet de nombreuses critiques. Notamment, on a souligné qu'il s'agissait moins d'un accord sur l'investissement que d'un accord sur "les biens de toute nature, et même si ceux-ci ne présentent en aucune façon le caractère d'investissement."[18] C'est ce *caractère* que les négociateurs à l'OMC auront à saisir.

À en croire les travaux du Groupe de travail, il apparaît que la Déclaration, malgré son penchant pour l'investissement direct étranger, laisse la porte ouverte à toutes les possibilités.

En matière d'investissement étranger, la question clé quant à *l'application du principe de traitement national* est de savoir si ce dernier sera applicable aussi bien avant qu'après l'établissement de l'investissement. Plusieurs pays sont réticents à voir le principe du traitement national s'appliquer *avant* l'établissement, car cela équivaut pour eux à la négation de leur droit souverain de contrôler l'admission des investissements étrangers sur leur territoire. En revanche, d'autres pays ne manquent pas de souligner que sans certains engagements de cette nature, on pourra difficilement atteindre l'objectif de mobilité des investissements.[19]

La Déclaration suggère une piste de compromis lorsqu'elle se réfère aux "modalités pour des engagements avant établissement reposant sur une approche fondée sur des listes positives de type AGCS." Selon cette méthode, dite de l'inclusion, chaque pays s'engage uniquement pour les secteurs inscrits dans une liste à cet effet. Elle s'oppose à la méthode des listes négatives ou de l'exclusion, qui est plus exigeante pour l'État.[20] Appliquée au traitement national, cette méthode exige des États qu'ils énoncent les secteurs où ce principe ne jouera pas, la conséquence étant, évidemment, que ce principe s'applique autrement à tous les secteurs restants.

---

[17] Sur ce paragraphe, voir *ibid.* aux par. 17-27.

[18] Voir P. Juillard, *supra* note 4 aux pp. 606-07.

[19] Sur ce paragraphe, voir Rapport (2002) du Groupe de travail, *supra* note 13 aux par. 84-93.

[20] Voir *ibid.* au par. 68. Voir aussi Juillard, *supra* note 4 à la p. 609.

Ce compromis, toutefois, ne sera peut-être pas acceptable pour certains pays, dont, en premier lieu, les États-Unis. Les conventions bilatérales de promotion et de protection des investissements conclues par les États-Unis appliquent le principe du traitement national aux phases pré- et post-investissement (en vertu de la méthode de l'exclusion). Aussi, ce n'est pas par hasard que dans l'AMI on a retenu un principe similaire. En effet, quel est l'intérêt pour un pays comme les États-Unis de négocier un accord multilatéral lui offrant une protection moindre que celle de son réseau de traités bilatéraux?[21] La difficulté demeure entière, car l'objectif de la libre-circulation des investissements ne peut véritablement être atteint que sur une base multilatérale.

Afin de traiter des obstacles liés à l'intégrité systémique de l'OMC, il est utile de situer cette question dans le contexte des différences de perspectives, du moins à l'origine, entre le régime international de l'investissement étranger et celui du commerce international. Le droit international public portant sur la *protection* des étrangers, et éventuellement de leurs biens, est à l'origine de la pratique des traités bilatéraux de promotion et de protection des investissements étrangers. Ce droit est animé par des considérations éthiques. Le système commercial international, pour sa part, vise la *libéralisation* des marchés à la poursuite d'objectifs d'ordre économique.[22]

De ces différences traditionnelles découlent certaines conséquences. Comme le signale D. Price, si les biens ont une origine, les investissements ont une nationalité. Alors que le système commercial international protège les flux commerciaux, le droit international

---

[21] Voir Juillard, *ibid.* aux pp. 596-97.

[22] Voir D. Carreau et P. Juillard, *supra* note 12 à la p. 391. Le droit international des investissements est décrit comme un prolongement du droit de la condition des étrangers. De source ancienne, ce droit est fondé sur des considérations éthiques: "Parce que le Souverain est l'élu de Dieu, il doit protection au chrétien, dans la personne de l'étranger. Le droit international lui fait donc obligation de respecter certains droits fondamentaux de l'étranger, dès lors que celui-ci se trouve en séjour sur ses États." (*Ibid.*) Longtemps limités aux droits de la personne, ces droits fondamentaux ont finalement été étendus aux *biens* des étrangers. En cas de violation, la protection de ces droits s'exerce par le biais de la protection diplomatique des étrangers. Dans ce cadre, un dommage causé à l'investisseur, ou à son investissement, est un dommage causé à l'État et demande réparation. Sur l'exercice de la protection diplomatique, voir E.M. Borchard, *Les principes de la protection diplomatique des nationaux à l'étranger,* T. 3, Lvgdvni Batavorvm Apvd, E.J. Brill (1924).

des investissements a traditionnellement protégé les droits individuels d'un investisseur à l'étranger. Le but d'une procédure de règlement des différends en matière d'investissement est la compensation du dommage subi par l'investisseur. En matière commerciale, il s'agit plutôt d'un recours prospectif: la priorité est donnée à la modification de la mesure décriée, et non pas à une compensation rétrospective d'un dommage.[23]

De prime abord, on pourrait penser que ces différences de perspectives n'ont plus d'importance de nos jours, dans la mesure où plusieurs accords bilatéraux, régionaux et sectoriels sont arrivés à marier des objectifs de protection (visant la sécurité) et de libéralisation (visant la mobilité) plus ou moins sans heurts.[24] Qui plus est, la Déclaration ignore toutes questions de protection. Ainsi, peut-on penser, suivant un programme de "pure" libéralisation, on arrive à éviter les antécédents lourds de la protection traditionnelle des droits des étrangers. Deux arguments nous permettent de mettre en question ces conclusions.

Premièrement, les accords internationaux dont il est question comportent un mécanisme de règlement des différends investisseur-État en plus du mécanisme de règlement des différends entre États membres. Cette procédure permet à un investisseur lésé de porter plainte directement contre un État, et éventuellement d'obtenir une compensation monétaire pour le dommage subi. Avec le temps, on s'est en effet éloigné de l'exercice de la protection diplomatique au profit d'une procédure "dépolitisée" permettant au véritable plaignant de faire face au défendeur.[25] En bref, ces accords respectent la perspective originelle du droit international des investissements. Dans ce contexte, si une convergence des valeurs — de sécurité et de mobilité — a eu lieu, elle s'est faite en faveur de ce régime.

Deuxièmement, on peut remettre en question l'opportunité de conclure un accord multilatéral qui vise à libéraliser l'investissement sans chercher à offrir à ce dernier, une fois fait, une protection adéquate. En effet, est-il possible d'assurer "des conditions transparentes, stables et prévisibles pour l'investissement" sans

---

[23] Sur ce paragraphe, voir D. Price, "Chapter 11 — Private Party vs. Government, Investor-State Dispute Settlement: Frankenstein or Safety Valve?" Can.-U.S. L.J., vol. 26 (2000) à la p. 108.

[24] Voir les Traités bilatéraux signés par les États-Unis et le Canada, l'ALÉNA ainsi que la Charte de l'Énergie.

[25] Voir Price, *supra* note 23 à la p. 112.

dispositions visant sa protection? Peut-être avons-nous exagéré la portée de cette Déclaration sommaire, qui demande uniquement au Groupe de travail de clarifier certaines questions? Ou, au contraire, a-t-on voulu à l'OMC éviter le choc des cultures entre le régime commercial international et le régime international des investissements étrangers?

En toute hypothèse, l'intégrité systémique de l'OMC risque d'être bouleversée par ces négociations. À titre d'illustration, on peut se demander si les procédures de règlement des différends ainsi que les recours offerts à l'OMC sont adaptés à l'investissement étranger. Sous un autre angle, il faut noter que la question de l'interaction entre les différends Accords de l'OMC pose aussi des problèmes systémiques. Par exemple, est-ce que l'Accord sur les MIC ou encore la partie de l'AGSC couvrant l'investissement devraient demeurer intacts? Les liens entre un tel accord et les accords bilatéraux et régionaux existants qui se chevaucheront bien souvent présentent aussi des défis pour l'OMC.[26]

En conclusion, il est évident que les membres de l'OMC veulent à tout prix éviter une répétition de l'AMI. Dans cette voie, les membres semblent avoir essayé de circonscrire leur négociation à des disciplines "classiques" du GATT-OMC. Ce faisant, on risque de négliger la culture propre de la réglementation de l'investissement étranger, sa réalité.

III   Négociations de la ZLÉA

Depuis 1998, les négociations visant la conclusion de la ZLÉA, avant la date fixée de 2005, ont fait des progrès. Le Groupe de négociations sur l'investissement a été chargé du mandat suivant: "[é]tablir un cadre juridique juste et transparent qui crée un environnement stable et prévisible qui protège les investisseurs, leurs investissements et les flux respectifs sans créer des obstacles aux investissements extra-hémisphériques."[27] D'un schéma annoté en 1999, on est passé à un avant-projet du chapitre en 2000.

Il existe davantage de renseignements sur ces négociations pour la raison évidente qu'elles sont en cours depuis quelques années,

---

[26] Sur ces différentes préoccupations, voir Rapport (2002) du Groupe de travail, *supra* note 13 aux par. 141-57.

[27] Zone de libre-échange des Amériques, Quatrième réunion ministérielle, San José, Costa Rica, *Déclaration conjointe*, 19 mars 1998, à l'Annexe II: Objectifs par sujet de négociation, en ligne: <http://www.ftaa-alca.org/ministerials/costa_f.asp> (date d'accès: 26 février 2001).

mais aussi pour la raison moins évidente que l'avant-projet d'accord a été diffusé en juillet 2001.[28] En apparence, donc, cette ouverture permet aux intéressés de connaître la nature et la portée des discussions en cours (A). Dans la réalité, cet avant-projet révèle aux yeux de tous des points de vue divergents ainsi que des omissions surprenantes (B).

A APPARENCE

La publication d'un avant-projet d'accord international en cours de négociations est exceptionnelle. Ce développement mérite qu'on s'y arrête, avant d'étudier les grandes lignes du contenu du chapitre portant sur l'investissement.

Dans le cadre de ses travaux, le Groupe de négociations sur l'investissement s'est réuni plusieurs fois par année.[29] Lors des différentes réunions ministérielles, on a donné des consignes aux groupes de négociations visant à faire avancer le processus. Lors de la cinquième réunion ministérielle tenue à Toronto en 1999, les Ministres ont demandé aux groupes de préparer un avant-projet de leurs chapitres respectifs. En particulier, on leur a demandé de "préparer un texte qui soit le plus complet possible et qui contiendra les textes qui ont fait l'unanimité et, entre crochets, ceux à l'égard desquels il n'aura pas été possible de parvenir à un consensus."[30] Cela étant, ce texte ne devait pas être considéré comme une ébauche définitive ou exclusive d'un accord éventuel, mais bien comme un outil visant à faciliter les travaux des groupes.[31]

Tout semblait se dérouler comme prévu, du moins jusqu'au Sommet des Amériques tenu à Québec en avril 2001. La ZLÉA, malgré des efforts de diversion, suscit de vives réactions de la part des foules réunies à Québec. Notamment, des manifestants ont souligné le manque d'adéquation entre le discours officiel baigné de valeurs démocratiques et de transparence et la réalité du processus de négociations en cours. Le Canada, et le ministre Pettigrew

---

[28] Voir ZLÉA — Avant-Projet d'Accord, Chapitre sur l'investissement (Doc. no. FTAA.TNC/w/133/Rev.1) 3 juillet 2001, en ligne: <http://www.alca-ftaa.org>.

[29] Voir ZLÉA, Groupe de négociation sur l'Investissement, en ligne: <http://www.ftaa-alca.org/ngroups/nginve_f.asp>.

[30] Zone de libre-échange des Amériques, Cinquième réunion ministérielle, Toronto, Canada, *Déclaration des Ministres,* 4 novembre 1999, en ligne: <http://www.ftaa-alca.org/ministerials/minis_f.asp> (date d'accès: 26 février 2001).

[31] Pour de l'information additionnelle, voir site de la ZLÉA, en ligne: <http://www.ftaa-alca.org>.

personnellement, ont choisi de relever le défi et ont pris l'initiative d'une démarche qui allait mener à la publication de l'ébauche du texte après que les membres de la ZLÉA eurent appuyé par consensus l'initiative canadienne.[32]

Ni la structure de l'ébauche, ni ses grandes lignes, n'offrent de grandes surprises. En effet, ce chapitre contient des dispositions qu'on retrouve dans le modèle nord-américain de traités bilatéraux sur l'investissement et notamment dans l'ALÉNA. Les dix-neuf articles contenus dans l'ébauche portent sur les sujets suivants: champ d'application, traitement national, traitement de la nation la plus favorisée, exceptions au traitement national et au traitement de la nation la plus favorisée, norme de traitement, traitement juste et équitable, prescriptions de résultats, personnel clé, transferts, expropriation et indemnisation, indemnisation des pertes, réserves et exceptions générales, règlement des différends, règlement des différends entre États, différends entre États et investisseurs, définitions de base, transparence, engagement de ne pas assouplir les lois nationales sur le travail en vue d'attirer l'investissement, engagement de ne pas assouplir les lois nationales sur l'environnement en vue d'attirer l'investissement. Il est à noter que l'intitulé des trois derniers articles (portant sur la transparence, les normes de travail, et l'environnement) apparaît entre crochets dans le texte. Cela laisse entendre que les autres dispositions font l'unanimité.

En 2001, le Canada a aussi rendu publique sa position dans le cadre des négociations de la ZLÉA sur l'investissement.[33] Celle-ci est conforme aux orientations de l'ALÉNA, à une exception près: elle rejette l'inclusion dans la ZLÉA d'une procédure de règlement des différends investisseur-État. L'insatisfaction du gouvernement canadien à l'égard de la procédure de règlement des différends investisseur-État au Chapitre 11 de l'ALÉNA est connue et inspire cette prise de position.

Dans ses grandes lignes, la négociation de ce chapitre n'apparaît pas comporter de difficultés majeures. Elle semble faire oeuvre de consolidation. Toutefois, les crochets multiples trouvés dans l'ébauche présentent une réalité autre.

---

[32] Voir Ministère des Affaires étrangères et du Commerce international, en ligne: <http://www.dfait-maeci.gc.ca/tna-nac/ftaa_min_decl-fr.asp>. Il a fallu quelques mois pour que le texte soit traduit dans les quatre langues officielles de la ZLÉA: l'anglais, l'espagnol, le français et le portugais.

[33] Voir Ministère des Affaires étrangères et du Commerce international, en ligne <http://www.dfait-maeci.gc.ca/tna-nac/I-P&P-f.asp> (date d'accès: 13 décembre 2001).

B RÉALITÉ

Tout comme dans le cas de l'OMC, le succès des négociations de la ZLÉA est tributaire des réalités politiques et économiques dans la région. Des événements comme des élections, des changements de partis au pouvoir ou des crises financières, risquent de faire dérailler la conclusion d'un accord. Toutefois, d'autres incertitudes existent. Elles sont révélées non pas dans les grandes lignes de l'ébauche, mais dans son détail. Il sera question de trois pôles de l'oeuvre de consolidation entreprise: les dispositions visant la mobilité des investissements, la sécurité des investissements et les procédures de règlement des différends.

Quant à la *mobilité* des investissements, nous verrons que si on semblait s'entendre sur l'objectif de libéralisation, les moyens d'y arriver ne font pas l'unanimité. À titre d'illustration, nous traiterons de la définition de l'investissement ainsi que de l'application du principe de traitement national. Sur une ébauche qui compte quarante-huit pages, cinq d'entre elles sont consacrées à la définition de l'investissement. On y retrouve donc des définitions multiples, des plus larges jusqu'aux étroites. Certaines excluent l'investissement de portefeuille, d'autres pas. Certaines tentent de donner des caractéristiques objectives à l'investissement, d'autres sont générales.[34] Somme toute, la portée de cet accord pourrait encore varier de façon substantielle.

Pour ce qui est du traitement national, il n'est pas clair notamment si ce dernier sera applicable aux phases pré- et post-établissement ou seulement après l'admission de l'investissement. Comme on l'a vu dans la première partie de cette chronique, il s'agit d'une question fondamentale. Afin de donner un aperçu plus concret de cette ébauche, il est utile de citer un extrait tiré de l'article 2 portant sur le traitement national. Il s'agit de la troisième version du paragraphe premier de cet article:

[1. [Chacune des Parties contractantes, une fois qu'elle a permis à des investisseurs de l'autre Partie contractante d'investir sur son territoire,] [leur] accordera [aux investissements de l'autre Partie contractante, établis ou exécutés sur son territoire] [aux investissements faits par les investisseurs des autres Parties contractantes sur leur territoires respectifs] un traitement non moins favorable que celui accordé aux investissements de [ses propres investisseurs] [ses investisseurs nationaux, dans l'établissement, l'acquisition, l'expansion, la gestion, la direction, l'exploitation, la vente ou autre aliénation d'un investissement] [ou aux investisseurs d'un

---

[34] Voir ZLÉA — Avant-Projet d'Accord, *supra* note 28 aux pp. 3.38-3.42.

État tiers, s'il est plus favorable dans ce dernier cas]. [Le traitement national sera accordé conformément aux lois du pays hôte.]][35]

C'est en raison de ce type de facture qu'on a qualifié dans les journaux cette ébauche de "fromage suisse."[36] Il faut avouer que la transparence est toute relative dans ce contexte.

Quant à la *sécurité* des investissements, on peut s'étonner du fait que certaines dispositions visant la protection n'aient pas fait l'objet d'une attention plus particulière (du moins en date de l'avant-projet). En effet, compte tenu des difficultés d'interprétation de certaines de ces dispositions dans le cadre du règlement des différends investisseur-État du Chapitre 11 de l'ALÉNA, on aurait pu s'attendre à ce que les articles sur le traitement juste et équitable et sur l'expropriation soient plus détaillés.

L'article 6 de l'ébauche est intitulé "traitement juste et équitable." On reconnaît là une facture différente de celle de "norme minimale de traitement" retenue dans le Chapitre 11 de l'ALÉNA. Toutefois, le teneur de cette norme de traitement n'est pas plus intelligible, car la référence au droit international est non seulement entre crochets, mais générale. S'agit-il de la norme de droit international coutumier ou d'une norme générale d'équité? En août 2001, le Canada a soumis une proposition au Groupe de négociation sur l'investissement visant à clarifier cette question en faveur de l'application de la norme minimale de droit international coutumier.[37]

L'article 10 de l'ébauche prohibe l'expropriation ne répondant pas à certaines conditions. Dans les quatre versions du premier paragraphe de cet article, on trouve des références aux "mesures équivalant" à l'expropriation ou "autre mesure ayant le même effet," sans efforts, semble-t-il, de clarifier ces concepts. Pourtant, on sait que l'article de l'ALÉNA qui traite de la même question a suscité la controverse en raison de la difficulté de faire la distinction entre l'expropriation (donnant ouverture à indemnisation) et la réglementation (ne donnant pas droit à indemnisation). La complexité de la tâche pourrait expliquer ce vide. Toutefois, il demeure surprenant de ne trouver dans l'ébauche aucune tentative

---

[35] *Ibid.* à la p. 3.4.

[36] Voir Mark MacKinnon, *Globe and Mail*, lundi le 5 mars 2001.

[37] Voir Ministère des Affaires étrangères et du Commerce international, en ligne: <http://www.dfait-maeci.gc.ca/tna-nac/inv-augo1-fr.asp>. Voir aussi les notes d'interprétation de la Commission du libre-échange, 31 juillet 2001, en ligne: <http://www.dfait-maeci.gc.ca/tna-nac/NAFTA-Interpr-fr.asp>.

de solution à ce problème. Selon la position canadienne, "il est important de préciser de façon plus claire le lien entre cette disposition et le rôle des gouvernements en ce qui concerne des questions telles la protection de la santé, de la sécurité et de l'environnement."[38] Cette position, par ailleurs, ne semble pas accompagnée d'une proposition.

Quant aux *procédures de règlement des différends* investisseur-État, elles font l'objet de près de 40 % de l'ébauche.[39] Malgré cette attention particulière, certaines questions et problèmes soulevés dans le cadre du Chapitre 11 de l'ALÉNA ne semblent pas trouver réponse dans l'ébauche, notamment les questions de transparence, de confidentialité et d'accès.

Ces faiblesses ne justifient toutefois pas le refus du Canada d'appuyer l'introduction dans l'accord d'un tel mécanisme de règlement des différends. Ce refus est d'autant plus surprenant que le Canada reconnaît investir beaucoup plus dans les pays d'Amérique centrale, d'Amérique du Sud, et des caraibes que ceux-ci n'investissent au Canada.[40] Qui, en réalité, est susceptible de profiter davantage de ces dispositions?

IV CONCLUSION

Comme on a pu le constater, l'année 2001 était davantage une année charnière qu'une année d'aboutissement sur la scène multilatérale de la réglementation de l'investissement étranger. Seul l'avenir nous dira si l'OMC est mûre pour entreprendre et mener à bien les négociations d'un accord multilatéral de portée (plus ou moins) générale sur l'investissement. Du côté de la ZLÉA, les travaux sont plus avancés, et à certains égards, plus prometteurs. Il semble en effet que la consolidation du modèle bilatéral, à l'échelle des Amériques, est une tâche plus aisée que la libéralisation des investissements à l'échelle mondiale, du moins en apparence.

---

[38] ZLÉA — Position du Canada, *supra* note 32 à la p. 3.

[39] Voir ZLÉA — Avant-Projet d'Accord, *supra* note 28 aux pp. 3-20-3-38.

[40] ZLÉA — Position du Canada, *supra* note 32 à la p. 1.

Canadian Practice in International Law / Pratique canadienne en matière de droit international

At the Department of Foreign Affairs in 2001-2 / Au ministère des Affaires étrangères en 2001-2

compiled by / préparé par
COLLEEN SWORDS

INTERNATIONAL HUMANITARIAN LAW

Attack on the United States of September 11, 2001

In September 2001, the Legal Bureau wrote:

The attack on the United States of September 11, 2001 can be characterized as a "crime against humanity."

I. Definition of the Crime

The most recent codification of crimes against humanity is found in article 7 of the 1998 Rome Statute of the International Criminal Court:

1. For the purpose of this Statute, "crime against humanity" means any of the following acts when committed as part of a widespread or systematic attack directed against any civilian population, with knowledge of the attack:

(a) Murder; ...

Colleen Swords, Legal Adviser, Department of Foreign Affairs and International Trade, Ottawa. The extracts from official correspondence contained in this survey have been made available by courtesy of the Department of Foreign Affairs and International Trade. Some of the correspondence from which the extracts are given was provided for the general guidance of the enquirer in relation to specific facts that are often not described in full in the extracts within this compilation. The statements of law and practice should not necessarily be regarded as a definitive.

(e) Imprisonment or other severe deprivation of physical liberty in violation of fundamental rules of international law; ...

(k) Other inhumane acts of a similar character intentionally causing great suffering, or serious injury to body or to mental or physical health.

The term "attack directed against any civilian population" is defined in Art.7(2)(a) as follows:

2. For the purpose of paragraph 1:

(a) "Attack directed against any civilian population" means a course of conduct involving the multiple commission of acts referred to in paragraph 1 against any civilian population, pursuant to or in furtherance of a State or organizational policy to commit such attack.

The evidence made publically available to date appears to support the conclusion that all four elements could successfully be proven.

II. The Elements of the Crime

Commission of Specific Acts

In order to prosecute a person for the events of September 11, a prosecutor would need to prove the commission of one or more of the specific acts listed under the Rome Statute's definition of crimes against humanity. A prosecutor would not likely have difficulty proving the commission of murder, severe deprivation of physical liberty (due to the hijackings) and/or inhumane acts intentionally causing great suffering or serious injury to body or to mental or physical health (for those who survived the World Trade Center and Pentagon events).

Widespread or Systematic Attack

A prosecutor need only prove that the attack was widespread *or* that it was systematic.

The *Nuremberg Judgement* linked "organized" and "systematic." Due to the extremely detailed level of the planning and logistical support required and the number of hijackers involved in the attack, the four September 11 acts on their own likely qualify as "systematic" in nature. The September 11 attack involved four virtually simultaneous hijackings from different airports by different teams, all designed to bring the planes to specifically-targeted buildings within a one-half to one hour period. At least some of the hijackers had undergone pilot training in the months prior to the attack. In addition, if other attacks are also considered, such as those on the US embassies in 1998, then the September 11 acts may be seen as part of a larger systematic plan to target US citizens, interests and buildings.

In the *Blaskic* decision [International Criminal Tribunal for the Former Yugoslavia (ICTY)], the Trial Chamber noted that the following may provide evidence of a systematic attack:

a) the existence of a plan, ideology or political objective to destroy, persecute or weaken a community. The plan does not need to be declared expressly or stated clearly or precisely, and it may be inferred from the occurrence of a series of events;

b) very large scale criminal act or repeated and continuous inhumane acts linked to one another;

c) the preparation and use of significant public or private resources, military or other; or

d) the implication of high-level authorities in the definition and establishment of the methodical plan.

The *Blaskic* decision states that this refers to authorities within States, organizations or groups.

The September 11 attack would likely meet this test as: (a) a plan was needed to carry out the virtually simultaneous hijackings; (b) the destruction of the World Trade Center would likely qualify as "very large scale" and the four hijackings would likely qualify as "repeated inhumane acts linked to one another"; (c) significant human and financial resources were needed to plan and carry out the hijackings; and (d) the UK document indicates that evidence is available linking the highest levels of Al Qaida (one of bin Laden's closest and most senior associates) to the detailed planning of the September 11 attack. The ICTY's *Kupreskic* decision held that inherent in the term "systematic" is the requirement that the crimes may not be committed by an individual acting independently. The term also logically excludes spontaneous crimes committed by individuals acting without coordination. The four September 11 acts, taken together, could also be considered to be widespread. There is some debate as to whether "widespread" refers to the number of victims, the geographical space over which the crimes took place, or a combination of the two.

The *Blaskic* Trial Chamber decision, relying on the *Tadic* case [International Criminal Tribunal for the Former Yugoslavia] and the International Law Commission's draft Code, states rather confusingly: the "widespread characteristic refers to the scale of the acts perpetrated *and* to the number of victims," demonstrated by the "cumulative effect of a series of inhumane acts *or* the singular effect of an inhumane act of extraordinary magnitude" [emphasis added]. There is a strong argument that the September 11 attack was numerically widespread, as thousands of people died. Geographically, the attack was spread over three cities. Therefore, whether the test separates or combines number of victims and geographical space, it s likely that a prosecutor could meet it. If earlier attacks (for example, on the US embassies) are taken into account, then both the numerical and geographical arguments are strengthened.

The term "attack" is defined in the Rome Statute as "a course of conduct involving the multiple commission of acts . . . pursuant to or in furtherance of a State or organizational policy to commit such attack." Some have argued that the term "attack" and the definition of attack found in the Rome Statute are not indicative of customary international law. They refer to the fact that "attack" is not included in the crimes against humanity provisions of the Statute of the International Criminal Tribunal for the

Former Yugoslavia or the Nuremberg Charter. However, the term "attack" is used in the crimes against humanity provision of the Statute of the International Criminal Tribunal for Rwanda.

The process of codifying crimes against humanity in the Rome Statute led to agreement among States that an attack was required and that it should be defined by referring to multiple acts that were pursuant to some kind of policy. The word "multiple" was used to indicate that more than one act was required to amount to an attack. The September 11 events clearly comprised thousands of acts of murder, and more of severe deprivation of physical liberty and serious injury to body, mental or physical health. The term "policy" was meant to measure a degree of instigation, direction or planning. The ICC's Elements of Crime recognize that a policy can be the result of either action or a failure to take action and therefore need not be formalized, and can be inferred from the relevant facts and circumstances. Clearly, planning — and therefore action — can be inferred from the four virtually simultaneous hijackings on September 11, and the "policy" element could be met.

Delegates to the Elements of Crimes discussions were careful not to conflate "widespread" with "multiple" or "systematic" with "policy," as both "multiple" and "policy" have lower thresholds than "widespread" or "systematic." The terms "multiple" and "policy" were considered necessary, however, in order to clearly exclude those cases where the attack was only widespread and there was no unifying reason behind the attack, or there was a well-organized policy, but completely insubstantial acts.

Other aspects of the term "attack" are the commission of these acts against any civilian population (which will be dealt with below) and the link to a State or organization (discussed above). The fact that thousands of civilians died in the World Trade Center would likely satisfy the link required to civilian population. In addition, the planning of the September 11 events by one of bin Laden's closest and most senior associates would likely satisfy the link required to an organizational policy. Therefore, a prosecutor could prove that the events of September 11 amounted to an "attack."

Directed against any Civilian Population

The attack on the World Trade Center would clearly qualify as "directed against any civilian population." The ICTY indicated in the *Kupreskic* and *Blaskic* cases that the words "civilian" and "population" are intended to be defined broadly. In particular, "civilian" not only refers to the term in the strict sense (those who take no active part in hostilities), but also to those who were members of a resistance movement and former combatants — regardless of whether they wear or wore uniforms or not — as long as they were no longer taking part in hostilities when the crimes were perpetrated (for example, they had left the armed forces, were no longer bearing arms, or had been placed *hors de combat* due to their wounds or being detained). The *Blaskic* case further noted that the presence of soldiers within a civilian population does not alter the civilian nature of that population. The World Trade Center victims, like the US embassy bombing victims, were clearly civilians who were not involved in a conflict.

The question arises as to whether the Pentagon staff killed in the September 11 attack could also be considered civilians. If a court considered that the attack took place in peacetime, an argument could be made that they should be considered civilians. Under international humanitarian law, protections and exclusions of soldiers and other fighting forces only apply in times of armed conflict. In addition, the *Blaskic* case rejected the notion that a crime does not amount to a crime against humanity because the victims were soldiers. It held that what is most important is the specific situation of the victim at the moment the crimes were committed, rather than his or her status. As the situation of the victims at the time of the crimes was perhaps more similar to a civilian than a combatant, it could be argued that the Pentagon staff (military and otherwise) killed on September 11 should be treated as civilians. However, this argument may not be available as the United States has consistently referred to the events of September 11 as acts of war, which could lead to the assumption that the situation of the Pentagon victims at the time of the crimes was that of a combatant.

Knowledge of the Attack

A prosecutor will need to prove that a perpetrator had knowledge of the wider context in which his or her acts occurred. Whether a prosecutor could prove that the perpetrator knew that his or her acts were performed in the context of a widespread or systematic attack directed against any civilian population would depend on the evidence collected against the person being prosecuted. The ICTY's *Kupreskic* and *Blaskic* decisions and the International Criminal Tribunal for Rwanda (ICTR) *Kayishema* judgement accept that:

[p]art of what transforms an individual's act(s) into a crime against humanity is the inclusion of the act within the greater dimension of criminal conduct; therefore an accused should be aware of this greater dimension in order to be culpable thereof. Accordingly, actual or constructive knowledge of the broader context of the attack, meaning that the accused must know that his act(s) is part of a widespread or systematic attack on a civilian population and pursuant to some sort of policy or plan, is necessary to satisfy the requisite *mens rea* element of the accused.

The ICTY Appeals Chamber in *Tadic* specifically stated that the motives of the accused are not relevant in this context. In other words, if the accused had purely personal motives over and above his knowledge of the context of the crime, these motives are irrelevant.

In the case of the events of September 11, a prosecutor could not try those who directly carried out the attack, since the hijackers died on September 11. However, a prosecutor could try those who aided, abetted or otherwise assisted the September 11 hijackers (including financially), or were involved in the conspiracy. In addition, those who gave orders to commit the attack could be held responsible as far up the chain of command as the orders originated, provided that the order could be proven. As well, those who did not order, but knew or should have known of the attack and failed to prevent the attack, could be held liable under the doctrine of command responsibility. In all cases, a prosecutor would need to demonstrate that an accused assisted in the knowledge that his or her assistance was taking place in the wider context of planning for or carrying out a widespread or systematic attack directed against any civilian population.

There have been reports that Al Qaida uses a structure involving many cells in different countries. Some of these cells may use so-called "sleeper agents" that carry out tasks as directed. If a "sleeper agent" carries out a task with no idea that his or her task is assisting in a wider context of a widespread or systematic attack, then this agent would not possess the requisite *mens rea* for crimes against humanity. However, it is more likely that the "sleeper agent" would be able to be prosecuted. The ICC's Elements of Crimes clarified that, while the accused must know that something was planned, he or she need not be aware of all characteristics of the attack or the precise details of the plan or policy of the State or organization. Therefore, the "sleeper agent" would not need to know of the magnitude or extent of the plan or the attack as a whole. In addition, if the "sleeper agent" joined the cell in order to support its overall goals, and if it can be shown that these goals are terrorist in nature and directed against any civilian population, then it could be inferred that the agent supported those goals. Therefore, it could also be inferred that, when the agent was carrying out instructions given by his or her handler, the agent would know that action was in furtherance of the cell's terrorist goals.

While it is more difficult to conclude that the *mens rea* aspect of crimes against humanity could be met by a prosecutor, a prosecutor would not likely bring a case without at least some evidence in hand about the link between an accused and the September 11 attack through which the *mens rea* could be demonstrated.

III. Implications of Characterizing the Events as
    Crimes against Humanity

The conclusion that the September 11 terrorist attack falls within the definition of crimes against humanity does not mean that all terrorist (or similar type) acts can be characterized as crimes against humanity. The acts would need to fall within the list of specific acts, such as murder or inhumane acts, and form part of a widespread or systematic attack undertaken pursuant to a State or organizational policy and directed against a civilian population (and therefore meet the definitions of "widespread" or "systematic," "attack" and "civilian population"). In order to prosecute an individual for crimes against humanity, a prosecutor must demonstrate that the perpetrator committed the specific acts with knowledge that they were part of a widespread or systematic attack. The facts of each terrorist act will need to be examined in order to determine if the act meets the high threshold of crimes against humanity.

Under customary international law, all States have the option of exercising jurisdiction to prosecute or extradite individuals suspected of crimes against humanity. This is often referred to as exercising universal jurisdiction. Therefore, the main implication of recognizing the events of

September 11 as crimes against humanity is that Canada could exercise its universal jurisdiction and try suspects found in Canada for these crimes. These prosecutions would take place pursuant to the *Crimes Against Humanity and War Crimes Act*, with the consent of the Attorney General of Canada.

UN Security Council Resolution 1422: Exemption from ICC Prosecution for UN Peacekeepers

In a statement to the UN Security Council on July 10, 2002, the Ambassador and Permanent Representative of Canada to the United Nations said:

Mr. President,

I am grateful to Council members for agreeing to an open debate on an issue of profound interest not only to most United Nations members but also to the organization itself. My government is deeply worried by the discussions that have been taking place in the Security Council concerning sweeping exemptions for peacekeepers from prosecution for the most serious crimes known to humanity. Issues of such potentially far-reaching consequences need to be debated openly, not in closed door consultations, if their conclusions are to carry the conviction of the membership as a whole.

I would like to make three basic points today, on which I will elaborate.

1. The issue is larger than the International Criminal Court; fundamental principles of international law are in question.
2. The Council is not empowered to re-write treaties; the resolutions that are circulating contain elements that exceed the Council's mandate and passage of them would undermine the credibility of the Security Council.
3. The issue is not a choice between peacekeeping and the ICC; options exist to resolve this issue that provide for the continuation of UN peacekeeping and that preserve the integrity of the international legal system and of the Rome Statute.

We respectively submit that those options should be used.

The United States has clearly voiced its concerns about the International Criminal Court. We respectfully disagree with the US on those concerns, because of the numerous safeguards written into the Rome statute, including through extensive US input into devising checks and balances, precisely in order to preclude politically-motivated prosecutions.

None of the States parties wants a political court. The crimes were meticulously defined in a manner acceptable to US negotiators and all states, with thresholds that exclude the random and isolated acts that a peacekeeper might conceivably commit. For example, Article 8 requires the Court to focus on war crimes "committed as part of a plan or policy or as part of a large-scale commission of such crimes." In addition, the Court is obliged to defer to genuine national legal proceedings.

No one in this room believes that the US government and the highly reputable American legal system would turn a blind eye to allegations of such grievous crimes. And when the US discharged its obligations to investigate alleged perpetrators, and if necessary to prosecute them, as it would, intervention by the International Criminal Court would be precluded. Nonetheless, we respect the US decision not to ratify the Rome Statute. No one could, or would want to try, to force the United States or any other UN member to become a party to the International Criminal Court. Acceding to a treaty is a sovereign decision. The US government clearly has no obligations to the Court. That is not the issue.

At stake today are entirely different issues that raise questions whether all people are equal and accountable before the law. Whether everyone on the territory of a sovereign state is subject to that state's laws, including international laws binding on that state. And whether states may collectively exercise their sovereignty to prosecute perpetrators of grievous crimes. These principles were affirmed at Nuremberg.

As a country with extensive experience in peacekeeping — having participated in almost all of the UN peacekeeping missions and having lost 106 servicemen and women in peacekeeping missions, more than any other country — Canada has no doubt that peacekeeping and peacebuilding are critical to the maintenance of international peace and security.

The current debate has been mischaracterized as a choice between peacekeeping and the ICC. In fact, the stakes are actually different and even higher. Fundamental principles of international law and the place of those principles in the conduct of global affairs are in question.

First, in the absence of a threat to international peace and security, the Council's passing a Chapter VII resolution of the kind currently circulating would be ultra vires.

Second, acting beyond its mandate would undermine the standing and credibility of the Council in the eyes of the membership.

Third, the proposed resolutions currently circulating would set a negative precedent under which the Security Council could change the negotiated terms of any treaty it wished, e.g. the nuclear Non-Proliferation Treaty, through a Security Council resolution. The proposed resolution would thereby undermine the treaty-making process. The UN Security Council has no such mandate.

Fourth, the proposals now circulating would have the Council, Lewis Carroll-like, stand Article 16 of the Rome Statute on its head. The negotiating history makes clear that recourse to Article 16 is on a case-by-case basis only, where a particular situation — for example the dynamic of a peace negotiation — would warrant a twelve-month deferral. The Council should not purport to alter that fundamental provision. Those states that have pledged to uphold the integrity of the Statute, especially the six States Party in the Council, have a special responsibility in this regard.

Fifth, passage of the proposed resolutions currently circulating would send an unacceptable message that some people — peacekeepers — are above the law. It would, thus, entrench an unacceptable double standard in international law.

Sixth, it is worth recalling that the ICC may only exercise jurisdiction where impunity would otherwise result. Let me emphasize what the effect of this resolution would be. Where sending states declined to prosecute peacekeepers alleged to have perpetrated crimes, the proposals now circulating would guarantee the alleged perpetrators impunity from prosecution for genocide, crimes against humanity and war crimes.

For these reasons, adoption of the resolutions currently circulating could place Canada and, we expect, others in the unprecedented position of having to examine the legality of a Security Council resolution. The Council does not have to pursue this fraught course of action. Solutions exit outside the ambit of Council responsibility.

The United States, as do all countries, has several options to protect its interests without vetoing United Nations peacekeeping missions, which are so vital to millions of people around the world. In considering these options, it is perhaps helpful to recall the point made by the Secretary-General that for the missions in the Balkans, the ICTY already has primacy over the ICC. Also, no mandate renewal beyond the Balkans is foreseen for UN mission operating on the territory of a State party in which the USA has stationed personnel.

The first option, therefore, is to do nothing now because the ICC does not have jurisdiction over any US personnel on UN peacekeeping missions. Second, and the absence of ICC jurisdiction notwithstanding, the USA could simply withdraw its forces from current missions. Their doing so would be regrettable and would not be without consequence, even significant consequence to those missions but, as the US contributes, 704 of 45,159 UN peacekeeping personnel, all told, adjustments could be made. Third, the USA could decline to participate in future UN missions. Fourth, for all UN or coalition missions, the United States could negotiate appropriate bilateral agreements with receiving states. Doing so would be consistent with article 98 of the Rome Statute.

Recently, I sent a letter to all members of the Security Council urging them not to endorse a blanket immunity for these most serious of crimes. I respectfully repeat that plea again today.

The proposed resolutions circulating avoid the word "immunity" but in fact have precisely the same effect as the proposal that the Security Council members would not entertain June 30.

We appeal to members of the UN Security Council to ensure that essential principles of international law, and the spirit and letter of the Rome Statute, not be compromised. That a solution to this problem be found that preserves the indispensable instrument of UN peacekeeping. And, that the unique authority of the Council not be undermined by over-reaching.

We have just emerged from a century that witnessed the evils of Hitler, Stalin, Pol Pot, and Idi Amin, and the Holocaust, the Rwandan genocide, and ethnic cleansing in the former Yugoslavia. Surely, we have all learned the fundamental lesson of this bloodiest of centuries, which is that impunity from prosecution for grievous crimes must end.

We remain convinced that the concerns expressed by the United States can be addressed in ways that do not compromise the Court or international law, or place the UN Security Council in the untenable position of permitting the possibility of impunity for genocide, crimes against humanity and war crimes.

INTERNATIONAL ECONOMIC LAW

Authority of NAFTA Chapter 11 Tribunals to Review Free Trade Commission Interpretations

In a submission to a North American Free Trade Agreement (NAFTA) tribunal dated July 19, 2002, the Legal Bureau wrote:

Nothing in the NAFTA grants Chapter Eleven tribunals the authority to review interpretations issued by the Free Trade Commission ("FTC" or "Commission"). Article 1131(2) is unequivocal:

[a]n interpretation by the Commission of a provision of this Agreement shall be binding on a Tribunal established under this Section.

Despite the clear wording of Article 1131(2), the Tribunal in *Pope & Talbot, Inc.* v. *Government of Canada* (*Pope & Talbot*) determined that a Chapter Eleven tribunal should question whether it is bound by a Note of Interpretation. In its view:

[i]f a question is raised whether, in issuing an interpretation, the Commission has acted in accordance with Article 2001, an arbitral tribunal has a duty to consider and decide that question and not simply to accept that whatever the Commission has stated to be an interpretation is one for the purposes of Article 1131(2).

The Tribunal's analysis reflects a misunderstanding of the respective roles of Chapter Eleven tribunals and of the Free Trade Commission. It is the Parties to the NAFTA acting collectively as the Commission, and not an *ad hoc* tribunal established under a chapter of NAFTA, that is the final authority with respect to the interpretation of the Agreement.

The FTC is vested with the prime and final authority as the interpreter of the NAFTA. Article 2001(2) unambiguously states that the "Commission shall (a) supervise the implementation of the Agreement; (b) oversee its further elaboration; [and] (c) resolve disputes that may arise regarding its implementation and application." Acting in their plenary capacity as the Commission, the Parties act as the guardians of the Agreement.

By contrast, a tribunal established under Section B of Chapter Eleven is established on an *ad hoc* basis for the sole purpose of arbitrating a particular investment dispute. The jurisdiction of a Chapter Eleven tribunal is confined to the subject matter set out in Articles 1116 and 1117. That is the full extent of its jurisdiction *ratione materiae*. Nowhere is there any suggestion that Chapter Eleven tribunals should adjudicate an interpretation by the Commission, even where it is contested by an investor.

The *Pope & Talbot* Tribunal ignored the relevant context of the word "interpretation" in Article 1131(2), which includes 1131(2) itself, Article 1132(2), and Article 2001.

Article 1131(2) provides that interpretations by the Commission "shall be binding" on Chapter Eleven tribunals. In order to give full effect to term "binding," the term "interpretation" cannot be understood to mean an "interpretation with which a tribunal agrees."

Article 1132(1), entitled "Interpretation of Annexes," provides that a tribunal must request the interpretation of the Commission on the scope of Annexes I through IV where an issue arises concerning the interpretation of these Annexes. Article 1132(2) states that "[f]urther to Article 1131(2), a Commission interpretation submitted under paragraph 1 shall be binding on the Tribunal," and then goes on to state that "If the Commission fails to submit an interpretation within 60 days, the Tribunal shall decide the issue." Thus, Article 1132(2) makes it clear that where the Commission does submit an interpretation on an issue, a tribunal is not entitled to decide the issue.

Article 2001(2)(c) states that the Commission shall "resolve" disputes that may arise regarding the interpretation of the Agreement. If the Commission's interpretations are subject to review by Chapter Eleven tribunals, then the Commission will be rendered incapable of "resolving" disputes over the interpretation of the Agreement. Moreover, Article 2001(3)(c) states that the Commission has unlimited power to take "such other action in the exercise of its functions as the Parties may agree."

The Tribunal also ignored the purpose of Article 1131(2), which is to ensure that NAFTA Chapter Eleven is applied in a consistent and uniform manner and that the Parties could clarify matters where necessary. That purpose would be undermined if each *ad hoc* Chapter Eleven tribunal could assess and decide whether to reject or accept an interpretation issued by the Commission.

Interpretation of the First Sentence of GATT 1994, Article III:2

In a memorandum dated January 8, 2002, the Legal Bureau wrote:

If the tax burden on imported products is found to be "in excess" of the tax burden on like domestic products, there is a *prima facie* infringement of Article III:2 of the *General Agreement on Tariffs and Trade 1994* ("GATT 1994").

In examining the tax burdens, the panel in *Argentina – Measures Affecting the Export of Bovine Hides and the Import of Finished Leather* ("*Argentine Leather*") held:

it is necessary to recall the purpose of Article III:2, first sentence, which is to ensure "equality of competitive conditions between imported and like domestic products." Accordingly, Article III:2, first sentence, is not concerned with taxes or charges as such but with their economic impact on the competitive opportunities of imported and like domestic products. It follows, in our view, that what must be compared are the tax burdens imposed on the taxed products.

We consider that Article III:2, first sentence, requires a comparison of actual tax burden rather than merely of nominal tax burdens. Were it otherwise, Members could easily evade its disciplines. Thus, even where imported and like domestic products are subject to identical tax rates, the actual tax burden can still be heavier on imported products.

It may thus be stated, in more general terms, that the determination of whether an infringement of Article III:2, first sentence, exists must be made on the basis of an overall assessment of the actual tax burdens imposed on imported products on the one hand and like domestic products on the other hand.

The Panel in *Argentine Leather,* recognizing that there was no difference in the tax rates to which the imported and domestic goods were ultimately subject, nevertheless held as a factual matter that there was a difference in the actual tax burden as between imported and domestic goods as a result of the differing tax collection mechanisms. Argentina claimed, for example, that as the amounts pre-paid were to be credited against the definitive tax liability, there was no "in excess" net tax payment and hence no infringement of Article III:2. The panel held, however, that this did not mean that no tax burden was being imposed. Indeed, it found that an actual tax burden did arise, not as a result of any difference in the tax rates but as a result of the incidental financial burden that could be attributed to the measures at issue. In the case of Argentina, the panel made a finding of "in excess" attributable solely to the interest that was either foregone or paid in order to comply with the requirement to pre-pay the tax at the point of importation (i.e., lost opportunity costs, financing costs).

In the event that it can be shown that the "actual tax burden" borne by the importer at the time of importation is greater than that which is borne by the purchaser of like goods as a result of a domestic transaction, there is a violation of Article III:2, first sentence. The actual tax burden was interpreted in *Argentine Leather* to require a more detailed economic analysis than a simple comparison of nominal tax rates. It was further made clear that the comparison could include any factors that might impose additional financial costs (e.g., lost opportunity costs, debt financing costs, compliance costs, etc.) that may be attributable or incidental to the measure in question.

Article 10 of the Customs Valuation Agreement

In a memorandum dated January 18, 2002, the Legal Bureau wrote:

> Article 10 of the *Agreement on Implementation of Article VII of the General Agreement on Tariffs and Trade 1994* ("Customs Valuation Agreement" or "CVA") provides as follows:
>
> > All information which is by nature confidential or which is provided on a confidential basis for the purposes of customs valuation shall be treated as strictly confidential by the authorities concerned who shall not disclose it without the *specific permission* of the person or government providing such information, except to the extent that it may be required to be disclosed in the context of judicial proceedings. [Emphasis added]
>
> Article 10 is therefore concerned with all information that is provided for the purposes of customs valuation. In the light of the information that is provided, and the express purpose for which it is provided, "specific permission" is "an act of permitting, formal consent, authorization, leave,

license or liberty granted" that is "precisely formulated or restricted" to customs valuation information.

One of the corollaries of the "general rule of interpretation" in Article 31 of the *Vienna Convention on the Law of Treaties* is that interpretation must give meaning and effect to all the terms of a treaty. This is known as the principle of effectiveness. Applying this principle of interpretation to the term "specific permission" means that the word "specific" must be given some meaning. It restricts the scope of the word "permission" to something that is "precisely formulated or restricted." In any event, "specific permission" cannot be the same thing as a "general permission," which is more like what a blanket statement would be.

It is also noteworthy that the word "permission" is used rather than simply "consent" or some other word. "Consent" may imply in some situations "acquiescence." The word "permission," on the other hand, does not appear to carry a connotation of "acquiescence." "Permission" involves "an act of permitting, formal consent, authorization, leave, license or liberty granted."

The overall object and purpose of the CVA would prefer an interpretation of "specific permission" as "an act of permitting, formal consent, authorization, leave, license or liberty granted" that is "precisely formulated or restricted" to customs valuation information. The main thrust of the CVA is to provide "for a fair, uniform and neutral system for the valuation of goods for custom purposes that precludes the use of arbitrary or fictitious customs values." The CVA drafters intended to create an agreement specifically for customs valuation purposes. Viewed in this light, the term "specific permission" can mean only "an act of permitting, formal consent, authorization, leave, license or liberty granted" that is "precisely formulated or restricted" to the customs valuation information required to be provided.

Article 10 reflects the balanced nature of the CVA. In situations where highly sensitive business confidential information (such as valuation information) of private parties — parties that are not Member governments — is required to be produced, the CVA provides a particularly high threshold, or safeguard, before that information may be disclosed. The World Trade Organization ("WTO") Appellate Body has commented on how WTO provisions involve "'carefully negotiated language — which reflects an equally carefully drawn balance of rights and obligations of Members — that balance must be respected." Therefore, it is important to the balance of rights and obligations that valuation information that is provided for the purposes of customs valuation be treated as "strictly confidential" and that it not be disclosed without "specific permission," "except to the extent that [the information] may be required to be disclosed in the context of judicial proceedings."

Interpretation of "Serious Prejudice" in the Agreement on Subsidies and Countervailing Measures

In a memorandum dated October 7, 2002, the Legal Bureau wrote:

To be actionable a subsidy must, among other things, be shown to cause "adverse effects." One form of "adverse effects" is "serious prejudice."

"Serious prejudice" is defined in Article 6.3(a) of the *Agreement on Subsidies and Countervailing Measures* ("SCM Agreement"). It provides four circumstances, one or more of which, if established, is sufficient to constitute "serious prejudice."

Footnote 13 to Article 5(c) clarifies that the term "serious prejudice to the interests of another Member" in the SCM Agreement is used in the same sense as it is used in paragraph 1 of Article XVI of the *General Agreement on Tariffs and Trade 1994* ("GATT 1994"), and includes threat of serious prejudice. Paragraph 1 of GATT 1994 Article XVI provides that

> If any contracting party grants or maintains any subsidy, including any form of income or price support, which operates directly or indirectly to increase exports of any product from, or to reduce imports of any product into, its territory, it shall notify the CONTRACTING PARTIES in writing of the extent and nature of the subsidization, of the estimated effect of the subsidization on the quantity of the affected product or products imported into or exported from its territory and of the circumstances making the subsidization necessary. In any case in which it is determined that serious prejudice to the interests of any other contracting party is caused or threatened by any such subsidization, the contracting party granting the subsidy shall, upon request, discuss with the other contracting party or parties concerned, or with the CONTRACTING PARTIES, the possibility of limiting the subsidization.

It adds that serious prejudice or threat of serious prejudice may be found where it can be shown that any subsidy "including any form of income or price support ... operates directly or indirectly to ... reduce imports of any product into" the territory of the Member maintaining the subsidy. In *Indonesia — Certain Measures Affecting the Automobile Industry* the panel held that the "text of Article XVI and of Part III [Articles 5-7] of the SCM Agreement makes clear that serious prejudice may arise where a Member's trade interests have been affected by subsidization."

Article 6 discusses the type of evidence necessary to establish serious prejudice. Article 6.5, concerning price undercutting, provides in part that "price undercutting shall include any case in which such price undercutting has been demonstrated through a comparison of prices of the subsidized product with prices of a non-subsidized like product supplied to the same market." Article 6.6 notes that "[e]ach Member in the market of which serious prejudice is alleged to have arisen shall ... make available to the parties ... and to the panel ... all relevant information that can be obtained as to the changes in market shares of the parties to the dispute as well as concerning prices of the products involved." Finally, Article 6.8 of the SCM Agreement states that "the existence of serious prejudice should be determined on the basis of the information submitted to or obtained by the panel, including information submitted in accordance with the provisions of Annex V."

Annex V to the SCM Agreement is entitled "Procedures for Developing Information Concerning Serious Prejudice." As its name states, it provides for procedures for gathering information regarding serious prejudice.

Paragraph 2 provides that information to be gathered should be "as necessary to establish the existence and amount of subsidization, the value of total sales of the subsidized firms, as well as information necessary to analyze the adverse effects caused by the subsidized product. Paragraph 5 notes: "[t]his information should include, *inter alia*, data concerning the amount of the subsidy in question (and, where appropriate, the value of total sales of the subsidized firms), prices of the subsidized product, prices of the non-subsidized product, prices of other suppliers to the market, changes in the supply of the subsidized product to the market in question and changes in market shares."

One World Trade Oranization ("WTO") panel report and a few GATT cases address claims of serious prejudice or threat of serious prejudice and offer some guidance on the standard for establishing adverse effects in this form. In *Indonesian — Autos*, the European Communities ("EC") and the United States argued that they suffered serious prejudice as a result of displacement/impedance or of price undercutting as provided in Articles 6.3(a) and (c) by Indonesian subsidies to its domestic model car, the Timor. The case established the high evidentiary burden the complainant bears in proving its claims. The panel found no violation based on displacement or impedance. However, it did find price undercutting of two models of cars.

The panel also held that the complainants had the burden to demonstrate serious prejudice on the basis of positive evidence. The panel rejected the displacement/impedance argument based on the fact that the evidence before it was highly speculative. EC market share data had indicated that there was a close correlation between the decline in relative market shares for its models and the introduction of the subsidized Timor but the panel found that was not enough and looked for clear causation. The panel held that the EC "must demonstrate that the 'effect of the subsidy is to displace or impede the imports' of an EC-origin 'like product' into the Indonesian market, i.e., that some imports that would have occurred did not occur as a result of the subsidies. While declining market share may be relevant to establishing such a situation, we consider that we must proceed further with the analysis and look at actual sales figures for the products in question." It found that the absolute volume of sales for EC models did not decline after the introduction of the Timor but that the size of the Indonesian market had expanded and that this expansion was caused by the introduction of the Timor itself. The EC submitted some evidence to show that its market share had in fact been increasing prior to the introduction of the Timor but the panel found that the data were inconclusive and showed no clear upward trends.

With respect to the argument that, absent the Indonesian subsidies, the EC and the United States would have introduced new cars into Indonesia (including building new assembly plants for this purpose) and increased sales, the panel found that the information provided was not properly developed and documented, and that it was far too general. The information included company letters and newspaper reports on the basis of which it was difficult for the panel to assess the degree of commitment of the companies to the plans or the reasons why those plans were abandoned. It said:

We do not mean to suggest that in WTO dispute settlement there are any rigid evidentiary rules regarding the admissibility of newspaper reports or the need to demonstrate factual assertions through contemporaneous source information. However, we are concerned that the complainants are asking us to resolve core issues relating to adverse trade effects on the basis of little more than general assertions.

The panel noted that it may have been persuaded by actual business plans relating to the new models, government documentation indicating approval for such plans and corporate minutes or internal decision memoranda relating both to the initial approval and the subsequent abandonment of the plans in question. The panel also noted that if Ford and Chrysler had in fact abandoned their plans to introduce the Escort and Neon after determining that Timor would undercut the prices of those models by US$5000, contemporaneous company documents reflecting this assessment could have been submitted and might have been highly probative.

The alternative to arguing actual serious prejudice is showing "threat" of serious prejudice. Threat of serious prejudice is not defined in the SCM Agreement. As noted, footnote 13 states that the "[t]he term 'serious prejudice to the interests of another Member' is used in this Agreement in the same sense as it is used in paragraph 1 of Article XVI of GATT 1994, and includes threat of serious prejudice." It has also not been discussed by any panels. In the *EEC — Sugar* panels (*European Economic Community – Refunds on Exports of Sugar,* Complaints by Brazil and Australia), the panels found that the potential of the EEC's sugar programme to cause uncertainty and price depression in the world market created a threat of serious prejudice. However, neither panel elaborated on this standard.

In interpreting "threat of serious prejudice," a future panel may draw guidance from the interpretation of "threat of material injury" and "threat of serious injury" in the WTO Agreements. The Appellate Body, in interpreting the concept of "threat of serious injury" in the *Agreement on Safeguards* (the Safeguards Agreement), looked to the interpretation of "threat of material injury" in the *Agreement on Implementation of Article VI of the General Agreement on Tariffs and Trade 1994* (the Anti-Dumping Agreement) and Part V of the SCM Agreement for guidance.

Article 15.7 of the SCM Agreement sets out the requirements for "threat of material injury" and provides in pertinent part:

> A determination of a threat of material injury shall be based on facts and not merely on allegation, conjecture or remote possibility. The change in circumstances, which would create a situation in which the subsidy would cause injury, must be clearly foreseen and imminent.

Article 15.8 includes a cautionary note: "[w]ith respect to cases where injury is threatened by subsidized imports, the application of countervailing measures shall be considered and decided with special care." These provisions parallel Articles 3.7 and 3.8 of the Anti-Dumping Agreement.

A WTO panel may interpret threat of serious prejudice similarly to the interpretation of threat of material injury or serious injury. Past decisions indicate that the "threat" standard is a lower threshold to meet than showing actual prejudice although the evidentiary burden for establishing threat remains high. The decisions, GATT reports and the terms of material injury and serious injury in the Agreements indicate that threat must be established with "special care" and "particular care." Threat of serious prejudice would deal with the potential effects of an *actual* subsidy rather than the possible effects of a *potential* subsidy, as with threat of serious injury and threat of material injury. Those standards clarify that the threat analysis must be based on objective and factual evidence and not on mere speculation. They also indicate that the same factors that are used to determine serious prejudice must be examined to determine threat. However, when it comes to "threat," all elements need not have come to pass. "Threat" requires a future-oriented analysis of the present situation to determine whether a change in circumstances is "clearly imminent." The temporal dimension is important. Projections and forecasts must be carefully developed and be susceptible to revision. The more remote in time, the less reliable data will be seen to be a current indicator of future developments. Moreover, there must be clear and substantial evidence of causation.

Article XIV of the General Agreement on Trade in Services

In a memorandum dated August 8, 2002, the Legal Bureau wrote:

An analysis of Article XIV of the *General Agreement on Trade in Services* ("GATS") must proceed from the understanding that this is an exception and thus its application will only arise after the panel examining the matter has reached the conclusion that, absent the consideration of the potential exception, the measure at issue is in breach of an obligation of a Member. That is, where the measure of a Member is found to contravene an obligation of that Member under the GATS, for instance one of the obligations referred to above, it can still be "saved" through the application of a particular exception. Article XIV of the GATS contains a number of general exceptions that apply in respect of any obligation under the GATS. It provides:

> Subject to the requirement that such measures are not applied in a manner which would constitute a means of arbitrary or unjustifiable discrimination between countries where like conditions prevail, or a disguised restriction on trade in services, nothing in this Agreement shall be construed to prevent the adoption or enforcement by any Member of measures:
>
> (a) necessary to protect public morals or to maintain public order;
> (b) necessary to protect human, animal or plant life or health;
> (c) necessary to secure compliance with laws or regulations which are not inconsistent with the provisions of this Agreement including those relating to:
>> (i) the prevention of deceptive and fraudulent practices or to deal with the effects of a default on services contracts;

    (ii) the protection of the privacy of individuals in relation
to the processing and dissemination of personal data and
the protection of confidentiality of individual records and
accounts;

    (iii) safety;

(d) inconsistent with Article XVII, provided that the difference in
treatment is aimed at ensuring the equitable or effective imposition or collection of direct taxes in respect of services or service suppliers of other Members;

(e) inconsistent with Article II, provided that the difference in
treatment is the result of an agreement on the avoidance of
double taxation or provisions on the avoidance of double taxation in any other international agreement or arrangement by
which the Member is bound. [footnotes omitted]

    Like the exceptions of Article XX of the *General Agreement on Tariffs and
Trade* (GATT), the exceptions of Article XIV of the GATS reflect policy
objectives that Members recognize as legitimate and that, upon meeting
certain conditions, can be implemented without giving rise to a breach of
the Agreement. Although Article XIV has yet to be interpreted and applied
by a panel or the Appellate Body, its structure is identical to that of Article
XX of the GATT. It is also very similar to Article XX of the GATT in terms
of substance. One can thus expect Article XIV of the GATS to be applied
in a similar fashion as Article XX of the GATT and, where appropriate,
take guidance from the existing case law concerning the latter provision.

    In accordance with what panels and the Appellate Body do in the con-
text of Article XX of the GATT, one must first determine whether the measure at issue falls within the ambit of paragraphs (a) through (e) of Article
XIV. If it does, one must then determine whether the measure also meets
the requirements of the chapeau, that is, whether it is applied in a manner
which constitutes a means of arbitrary or unjustifiable discrimination
between countries where like conditions prevail, or a disguised restriction
on trade in services. It must be emphasized that under the chapeau, what
is at stake is not so much the questioned measure or its specific content, but
rather the manner in which it is applied. The purpose and object of the
chapeau is essentially to prevent the abuse of the specific exceptions set
out in paragraphs (a) through (e).

Interpretation of GATT 1994, Article XXIV:3(a)

In a memorandum dated August 16, 2002, the Legal Bureau wrote:

    Article XXIV:3(a) has not received substantive consideration in any
General Agreement on Tariffs and Trade (GATT) or World Trade Organization (WTO) report.

(i) Ordinary Meaning of Article XXIV:3(a)

The starting point for interpreting a treaty provision is its text. Article
XXIV:3(a) provides that,

3. The provisions of this Agreement shall not be construed to prevent:

(a) *Advantages* accorded by any contracting party to adjacent countries in order to *facilitate frontier traffic* [emphasis added]

The chapeau of this provision creates an exception to the application of GATT 1994 for the measures listed in the sub-paragraphs. There are three terms in Article XXIV:3(a) that defines the scope of the exception: "advantages" granted to "adjacent countries," and "in order to facilitate frontier traffic."

Under the GATT and WTO, the term "advantage" has been considered in the context of the most-favoured nation principle in Article I:1. These decisions have interpreted "advantage" broadly. In *European Communities — Regime for the Importation, Sale and Distribution of Bananas,* for example, the Appellate Body found that,

Also a broad definition has been given to the term "advantage" in Article I:1 of the GATT 1994 by the panel in United States — Non Rubber Footwear... For these reasons, we agree with the Panel that the activity function rules are an "advantage" granted to bananas imported from traditional ACP States ... within the meaning of Article I:1. [Emphasis added]

The term "advantage" was also considered by the panel in *Indonesia — Certain Measures Affecting the Automobile Industry.* In this instance, the Indonesian motor vehicle program provided import duty reductions based on the amount of local content and the type of vehicle in which the parts were used. In addition, the program also reduced the sales taxes on motor vehicles with specified local content rates. In its report the panel concluded that these reduced import duties and sales taxes were "advantages" under Article I:1.

Not all advantages, however, fall within the scope of Article XXIV:3(a); the scope of the exception is defined by the language of the remainder of the provision. The exception provided in Article XXIV:3(a) applies to, "advantages accorded ... adjacent countries *in order to* facilitate frontier traffic" [emphasis added]. The limiting phrases in Article XXIV:3(a) have three consequences.

First, the advantage in question must be granted to adjacent countries. The second limiting element is the connecting term "in order to." This indicates that the country providing the "advantage" must demonstrate a causal relationship between the advantage in question and the facilitation of frontier traffic. Third, the advantages in question must have as their object and effect the facilitation of frontier traffic. It is not clear, from the text of Article XXIV:3(a), what this phrase means. "Facilitation" could refer to administrative measures; it could equally contain a substantive element such as a tariff or tax reduction. Nor is it evident from the text of Article XXIV:3(a) what the scope of "frontier traffic" might be — whether, for example, it refers to cross-border shopping, or includes a frontier-region trade liberalisation element. In such circumstances, the negotiating history of the treaty may provide guidance.

(ii) Supplementary Means of Interpretation of Article XXIV:3(a)

A limited amount of information is available concerning the preparatory work for Article XXIV:3(a). The provision appears to have originated with a U.S. proposal that was almost identical to Article XXIV:3(a). In the London session of the Preparatory Committee of the International Conference on Trade and Employment, Mr. Hawkins, the U.S. delegate explained the meaning of Article 33(2)(a) [XXIV:3(a)]. He stated that,

> Paragraph 2(a) referred to *facilities for frontier traffic, in cases where a frontier ran through a city, etc.; but sub-paragraph (a) did not relate to regional preference arrangements.* The area affected by this provision was usually limited to a distance of 15 kilometres from the frontiers. [Emphasis added]

At first glance, the statement by the U.S. delegate confirms what common sense would dictate: the provisions relating to frontier traffic were intended to exist independently of those relating to customs unions or free trade areas. This means the provisions of Article XXIV:3 were not intended to duplicate the regimes relating to free trade areas and customs unions. The reference to "cases where a frontier ran through a city" is further illustration of the potential scope of this provision. At a minimum, frontier traffic is facilitated by simplified customs procedures. In certain cases (such a divided city or a highly economically integrated frontier region), advantages captured by Article XXIV:3(a) might also include duty exemptions for individuals and small businesses. It would be irrational to expect citizens of a divided city to pay customs duty on their daily cross-border purchases.

(iii) The Principle of Effectiveness

A fundamental tenet of treaty interpretation is the principle of effectiveness. If the exception for frontier traffic permitted members to lower tariffs and the taxes payable on land borders in any designated frontier region this would reduce the effectiveness of the most-favoured nation principle under Article I:1. This provision states that,

> 1. *With respect to customs duties and charges of any kind* imposed on or in connection with importation or exportation ... and with respect to all rules and formalities in connection with importation and exportation, and with respect to all matters referred to in *paragraphs 2 and 4 of Article III, any advantage,* favour, privilege or immunity granted by any contracting party to any product originating in ... any other country shall be accorded immediately and unconditionally to the like product originating in ... the territories of all other contracting parties. [Emphasis added]

The panel in *Indonesia — Autos* indicated that reduced duties and tax rates will fall under the provisions of Article I:1. In its decision the panel stated that,

The customs duty benefits of the various Indonesian car programmes are explicitly covered by the wording of Article I. As to the tax benefits of these programmes, we note that Article I:1 refers explicitly to "all matters referred to in paragraphs 2 and 4 of Article III." We have already decided that the tax discrimination aspects of the National Car programme were matters covered by Article III:2 of GATT.

Tariff reductions fall under the ambit of Article I:1. Similarly, in some situations taxes would also be subject to this provision. The purpose of Article I:1 is to ensure that all WTO members are entitled to receive the most favourable treatment given by any member. If a member were permitted to effect general tariff and VAT reductions in respect of imports through specific border crossings at any time this would undermine Article I:1.

(iv) Working Party Reports

Under GATT 1947 the Working Parties made numerous reports that were frequently adopted by the contracting parties. In 1955 the Review Working Party II on Tariffs, Schedules and Customs Administration considered a German proposal to amend Article XXIV:3(a). Although the amendment was rejected the Working Party stated that,

> While the CONTRACTING PARTIES would no doubt wish to examine the terms of any particular treaty in the event of a dispute, the Working Party understands that traffic in zones designated in treaties between adjacent countries, designed *solely to facilitate clearance at the frontier,* would normally be covered by the phrase "frontier traffic." [Emphasis added]

While the Working Party did not arrive at a conclusion as to the general scope of Article XXIV:3(a), the interpretation above supports the analysis that this exception at least includes streamlined customs procedures, but does not extend to general tariff or VAT reductions that do not have as their object and effect the facilitation of frontier traffic.

It is clear from the foregoing that, Article XXIV:3(a) provides an exception for frontier traffic to the application of GATT 1994. This provision permits "advantages" that are intended to facilitate "frontier traffic." Article XXIV:3(a) is distinct from the other exceptions in Article XXIV that relate to free trade areas and customs unions.

The frontier traffic exception is limited to advantages that have the effect of making frontier traffic easier. This conclusion is supported by a textual analysis and the negotiating history of this provision. A GATT Working Party report also supports this view.

Article XXIV:3(a) was intended to permit advantages that facilitate frontier traffic that might otherwise violate GATT 1994. These advantages might include reduced duties on the import of goods for individuals or for small businesses. Measures that were designed to streamline or simplify customs procedures would also fall under the ambit of this exception.

TREATIES

Canadian Ratification Practice

In April 2002, the Legal Bureau wrote:

Ratification is defined by the *Vienna Convention on the Law of Treaties* as "the international act ... whereby a State establishes on the international plane its consent to be bound by a treaty." The most common misconception about ratification is that it is a constitutional process. While parliamentary approval of a treaty or the implementation of a treaty in domestic law may be required under a country's constitution — and may be referred to as ratification — the two are distinct processes. Ratification on the international plane normally consists of the execution of an instrument of ratification by the executive of one state and either its exchange for the instrument of ratification of another state (bilateral treaty) or its lodging with the treaty depositary (multilateral).

In *Modern Treaty Law and Practice,* Anthony Aust gives the usual reason for requiring ratification as the fact that, following adoption and signature of a treaty, one of more of the negotiating states will need time before it can give its consent to be bound. Generally, this is because the treaty will require national legislation to implement. According to Aust, this should be done before the treaty enters into force for the state, otherwise the state risks being in breach of its treaty obligations. Sometimes a state will ratify internationally before necessary legislation has been enacted, to allow it to say, for example, that it has been one of the first to ratify. Although this stratagem may encourage other states to ratify early, Aust terms it "inherently risky" since the treaty might enter into force before the ratifying state has enacted implementing legislation. Signature of a treaty imposes no obligation to ratify although, as a matter of international practice, commentators generally indicate that a state should refrain from signing a treaty it has little intention of ratifying.

Article 26 of the Vienna Convention contains the fundamental principle of the law of treaties, *pacta sunt servanda:* every treaty in force is binding upon the parties to it and must be performed in good faith. The corollary principle is contained in Article 27: a party may not invoke the provisions of its internal law as justification for its failure to perform a treaty.

Canadian Treaty Practices

Canada's constitutional practices with regard to international treaties reflect the British dualist tradition. Under the dualist approach, the *Constitution Act, 1867* accords no special status to treaties: rights and obligations created thereunder have no effect in domestic law unless legislation has been enacted to give effect to them. When legislation is specifically made for this purpose, the rights and obligations are then said to be "incorporated" into domestic law. In this model, the conduct of foreign affairs and the conclusion of treaties is a matter of royal prerogative, i.e. an area in which the Crown can act without the consent of Parliament, exercisable in Canada by the Governor General in Council.

(I) Procedure

In terms of procedure, the first step involved in gaining Cabinet approval for ratification of an international treaty, in this case the Kyoto Protocol, is the development of a policy memorandum (Memorandum to Cabinet, MC) which will be put before Cabinet by the Minister of Foreign Affairs and his colleagues involved in the issue (in this case, the Ministers of Environment, Natural Resources and International Cooperation) for a decision approving domestic implementation and international ratification. The MC will then be considered by the relevant Cabinet Committee.

A positive decision to proceed with implementation and ratification will next require submission to Privy Council Office (PCO) of a request for an Order in Council to be considered by the Special Committee of Council (SCC). Once the SCC has reviewed the request and made a positive recommendation, the Governor General will sign an Order in Council authorizing international ratification. Once the Order in Council is signed, DFAIT will prepare an instrument of ratification, signed by the Minister of Foreign Affairs, and the instrument will be deposited with the Secretary-General of the United Nations, the depository of the Kyoto Protocol, at UN Headquarters in New York.

If the criteria for coming into force of the Protocol, contained in its Article 25, have been met when Canada deposits its instrument of ratification, the Protocol will come into force for Canada ninety days after deposit. If the Protocol is not yet in force internationally when Canada ratifies, it will enter into force on the ninetieth day after the fifty-fifth instrument of ratification is deposited, as long as the (at least) fifty-five ratifications include Annex I Parties (Parties with greenhouse gas limitation or reduction targets) that accounted for at least fifty-five percent of Annex I greenhouse gas emissions in 1990.

Role of Parliament

It is the legislative implementation of treaties that affords Parliament its main role in the treaty process: if new legislation must be passed, or existing legislation amended, it is Parliament that must pass or amend the legislation according to usual parliamentary practices. A practice has developed for the federal government to table annually in Parliament international treaties that have come into force for Canada in the previous year. The practice fell into disuse for a number of years, but has resumed since 1999 in accordance with a Standing Order of the Parliament. This practice is voluntary: it is not required by any statute or constitutional provision.

There is no legal requirement for Parliamentary approval prior to international ratification of a treaty. On occasion, international agreements were brought to the attention of Parliament before ratification, and their approval sought by joint resolution. The decision on whether to seek Parliamentary approval was made, in each instance, by the Government of the day. This practice has now fallen into disuse: the last Parliamentary resolution approving an international treaty was passed in 1966. Still, treaties that are considered of national importance and that require new or amended legislation will often be approved by Parliament within the provisions of the implementing legislation: article 10 of the *North American Free Trade Agreement Implementation Act* approves the NAFTA, for example. In some cases, the text of the treaty is incorporated *in toto* into the implementing legislation, as well as approved by Parliament in that legislation: see article 2 and schedules I to VI of the *Geneva Conventions Act;* this is also the usual practice in statutes implementing double taxation agreements, see, for example, the *Income Tax Conventions Implementation Act, 1999.*

INTERNATIONAL ORGANIZATIONS

Privileges and Immunities

En novembre 2002, le Bureau juridique a écrit:

Au sens de la loi canadienne, une organisation internationale est définie comme "une organisation intergouvernementale formée de plusieurs États, constituée ou non par traité ... " (art. 2(1) de la *Loi sur les missions étrangères et les organisations internationales*). D'après les différents éléments d'information en notre possession et suite à une analyse préliminaire des documents constitutifs de l'organisation, il apparaît que cette dernière pourrait potentiellement être considérée comme une organisation intergouvernementale non-constituée par traité mais qu'elle n'aurait pas de personnalité juridique en droit international. Toutefois, nous devons déterminer si elle a été incorporée sous une loi du pays où ses locaux se trouvent présentement, ce qui créerait une situation différente.

Dans la situation où l'organisation est considérée comme une organisation internationale aux termes de la loi canadienne, nous pourrions potentiellement négocier et conclure un type d'arrangement approprié entre le Gouvernement du Canada et celle-ci tel un protocole d'entente. Nous ne pourrions toutefois conclure un accord de siège avec l'organisation puisque, comme nous l'avons déjà mentionné, elle ne semble pas avoir une personnalité juridique en droit international et, donc, n'a pas la capacité de conclure un traité. La décision d'entreprendre des négociations en vue de conclure un mémoire d'entente devrait avoir été autorisée au préalable par le Ministre des Affaires étrangères. Suite à la conclusion dudit document, le Gouvernement du Canada pourrait par la suite disposer par un décret du gouverneur en conseil pris en vertu de la *Loi sur les missions étrangères et les organisations internationales* que l'organisation a la capacité juridique d'une personne morale et qu'elle bénéficie, dans la mesure spécifiée au décret et conformément au protocole d'entente, de privilèges et immunités.

Les hauts fonctionnaires de l'organisation, son personnel et les représentants des Parties pourraient également, dans la mesure prévue au décret, bénéficier de certains privilèges et immunités. Il faut prévoir que les hauts fonctionnaires et le personnel qui sont citoyens canadiens ne pourraient bénéficier que d'immunités limitées et, dans le cas de l'exonération fiscale, que dans la mesure où Revenu Canada et l'organisation en seraient venus à une entente quant au régime applicable.

L'étendue des privilèges et immunités dont pourraient potentiellement bénéficier respectivement l'organisation, les représentants des États étrangers qui en sont membres, les hauts fonctionnaires et les membres de son personnel peut être variable et aller jusqu'à l'octroi de privilèges et immunités similaires à ceux prévus par la *Convention internationale sur les privilèges et immunités des Nations Unies* et par la *Convention de Vienne sur les relations diplomatiques* dans le cas des représentants des États étrangers membres de l'organisation.

L'étendue et la nature exacte des privilèges et immunités devraient cependant faire l'objet de discussions et de négociations entre le Gouvernement du Canada et l'organisation. De plus la décision finale en ce domaine relève de la compétence du Ministre des Affaires étrangères qui devrait faire une recommandation à cet effet au gouverneur en conseil. Cette recommandation devrait être présentée conjointement à celle du Ministre des Finances si le décret confère une exonération fiscale ou douanière.

Dans la situation où l'organisation a été incorporée sous la loi du pays où ses locaux sont situés, nous ne serions pas en mesure de lui conférer une personnalité juridique et des privilèges et immunités aux termes de la *Loi sur les missions étrangères et les organisations internationales* puisqu'elle ne serait pas une organisation internationale au sens de la loi.

JURISDICTION AND TERRITORIAL SOVEREIGNTY

Extraterritorial Evidence Gathering

In October 2002, the Legal Bureau wrote:

An examination whether ... [foreign] ... officials may undertake sampling activities [for evidentiary purposes] in Canada is inevitably linked to the issues of territorial sovereignty and jurisdiction under international law. Professor Ian Brownlie describes "sovereignty" as the "normal complement of state rights, the typical case of legal competence" and "jurisdiction" as "particular rights, or accumulations of rights quantitatively less than the norm." Sovereignty stands for the legal personality of statehood and jurisdiction for particular aspects of it, especially rights, liberties and powers. The sovereignty and equality of states represent the basic constitutional doctrines of international law. The principal corollaries are a jurisdiction over a territory and the permanent population living there and a duty of non-intervention in the area of exclusive jurisdiction of other states. The presumption is that jurisdiction is territorial.

When discussing jurisdiction and territory, a distinction needs to be made between "an attempt to give effect in domestic law to actions, people or things outside the territory governed by domestic law (jurisdiction to prescribe)" and "a purported enforcement of domestic law in the territory of a foreign state (jurisdiction to enforce)."[R. v. Cook [1998] 2 S.C.R. 597 (S.C.C.) at para. 131] The purpose of this memorandum is ... to look at the issue of extraterritorial evidence gathering by foreign officials or by private persons in the absence of extraterritorial foreign legislation or a foreign court order. Therefore, the issue of prescriptive jurisdiction will merely be introduced to provide some context. The focus of discussion will then be on extraterritorial evidence gathering and enforcement jurisdiction.

Prescriptive Jurisdiction

The starting point is the proposition that prescriptive jurisdiction is territorial. However, this area of the law is still unsettled and the territorial theory has been refined to accommodate some of the modern jurisdictional conflicts. While the territorial theory remains the best foundation for the law, it has been accepted that states may exercise extraterritorial prescriptive jurisdiction under certain circumstances. An important element for the exercise of jurisdiction is that a significant portion of an activity take place in the territory of the state claiming jurisdiction. There should be a "real and substantial link" between the subject matter of jurisdiction and the territorial base.

Since commentators still disagree on the appropriateness of various principles underlying extraterritorial prescriptive jurisdiction, their categorizations of principles often differ from each other but usually include at least variants of the following:

- *Nationality:* It is generally recognized that a state may exercise jurisdiction over its nationals, wherever they are located.

- *Effects:* The "effects doctrine," or "objective territoriality principle," holds that a state may have jurisdiction in respect to conduct outside its territory that has an effect inside its territory. The principle has been used extensively in the area of antitrust and competition policy enforcement, with the result that there is considerable, if not always consistent, commentary and domestic jurisprudence on the limits of this doctrine.

- *Universality:* Some crimes are considered so heinous as to justify universal jurisdiction by states over the perpetrators. These include crimes such as piracy, slavery, war crimes, air hijacking, etc. In the post-war era, the international community has generally identified such crimes by adoption of international conventions.

- *Passive Personality:* This is still controversial, but some states assert jurisdiction over non-nationals when the victim is a national outside the territory of the state.

- *Protective:* It is accepted that states may exercise jurisdiction over non-nationals outside the state if their conduct constitutes a threat to the security of the state. This principle is rarely used by common law jurisdictions.

The federal government of Canada can and does exercise extraterritorial prescriptive jurisdiction. Accordingly, Canada does not object to the assertion of extraterritorial jurisdiction *per se.* Indeed, Canada asserted extraterritorial jurisdiction in several statutes, including the Criminal Code (aircraft highjacking, hostage taking, crimes against humanity, etc.), the Arctic Waters Pollution Act of 1970, the Coastal Fisheries Protection Act (1995 seizure of the Spanish fishing trawler Estai), the Competition Act, the United Nations Act, and the Special Economic Measures Act. What Canada does oppose is conflict created by such assertions of jurisdiction. More specifically, Canada opposes extraterritorial measures that contradict or undermine the laws or clearly enunciated policies of another state exercising concurrent jurisdiction on a territorial basis over the same conduct. As a corollary, Canadian policy is not to impose extraterritorial jurisdiction which could create such conflict with the laws or policies of states exercising territorial jurisdiction.

Enforcement Jurisdiction

The basic principle in relation to enforcement jurisdiction is that states cannot act within the territory of another state without consent. Professor Ian Brownlie expressed this principle as follows:

> The governing principle is that a state cannot take measures on the territory of another state by way of enforcement of national laws without the consent of the latter. Persons may not be arrested, a summons may not be served, police or tax investigation may not be mounted, orders for production of documents may not be executed, on the territory of another state, except under the terms of a treaty or other consent given.

Brownlie cites as authority the decision of the Permanent Court of International Justice in the *Lotus* case, where the Court stated:

> Now, the first and foremost restriction imposed by international law upon a State is that — failing the existence of a permissive rule to the contrary — it may not exercise its power in any form in the territory of another State. In this sense jurisdiction is certainly territorial; it cannot be exercised by a State outside its territory except by virtue of a permissive rule derived from international custom or from a convention.

It seems fair to say [evidence gathering] ... activities by foreign officials in their official capacity in Canada can be viewed in terms of the exercise of investigatory state powers by another country on Canadian territory. If these activities were to be undertaken without consent by Canadian authorities, they would not be compatible with the principles of national sovereignty and territorial jurisdiction.

Treaties

The evidence gathering under discussion does not involve compulsion or a criminal offence and there are no treaties to which Canada is a party which would apply to the fact scenario under discussion. However, the Treaty between the Government of Canada and the Government of the United States of America Regarding the Application of their Competition and Deceptive Marketing Practices Laws, and the Hague Convention on the Taking of Evidence Abroad in Civil or Commercial Matters (Hague Convention — Canada is not a party), among other examples, contain some principles which underline the importance of the principles of sovereignty and territorial jurisdiction in matters of extraterritorial evidence gathering.

Canadian Law

While there may be no statutory authority prohibiting the taking of [evidence] ... in Canada, Canadian courts have recognized the basic principle that states generally do not have the jurisdiction to act in the territory of other states. In *R. v. Cook,* the Supreme Court of Canada recognized that limitations are imposed on Canadian law by the principles of state sovereignty and international comity. The Court restated the principle found in *Daniels v. White* that "... Parliament is not presumed to legislate in breach of a treaty or in any manner inconsistent with the comity of nations and the established rules of international law ..." After noting the difference between enforcement jurisdiction and prescriptive jurisdiction the Court stated that "[a]ttempts to enforce domestic law directly in the territory of a foreign state are prohibited in all but the most exceptional circumstances" and quoted with favour the citations by Professor Ian Brownlie and the Permanent Court of International Justice reproduced above.

Canadian Policy

The Department stated in the *International Judicial Co-operation* manual [1987] ... that even when evidence is provided on a voluntary basis, "the conduct of the hearing in Canada remains subject to the consent of the Government of Canada when it is presided by a foreign official." Before approving such a hearing, the practice of the Government of Canada generally seeks the following assurances from a foreign administrative agency or tribunal:

   (a) the fact that the person to be examined is willing to do so voluntarily;
   (b) that the testimony to be taken is entirely voluntary, and that the person's failure to appear or respond will carry no liability in any subsequent foreign proceeding;
   (c) that the person's consent to testify carries no liability or obligation in addition to the testimony itself, apart from perjury or false statements;
   (d) the date, time, and location of the deposition, and the persons involved, including whether the person to be examined will be represented by counsel.

While extraterritorial evidence gathering may not be prohibited under any Canadian law or regulation, it is Canadian policy to insist that foreign officials seek permission before undertaking such activities in Canada.

Conclusion

While there may be no Canadian legislation explicitly prohibiting ... [foreign] officials from gathering [evidence] ... in Canada, principles of public international law, recognized in treaty practice and by the Supreme Court of Canada, and Canadian policy militate against such exercise of foreign authority without consent from the appropriate Canadian authorities.

OCEANS LAW

Global Warming and Sovereignty over Waters in the Canadian Arctic Archipelago

In conjunction with a January 2002 conference in Ottawa entitled "On Thinning Ice," a member of the Legal Bureau wrote:

Increasing evidence that global warming is reducing ice cover in Canada's north has raised questions about how this might affect international acceptance of Canada's ownership over the waters in the Canadian archipelago. It is Canada's position that straight baselines drawn around the perimeter of the Arctic archipelago constitute the outer limits of its internal waters.[1] Canada's full sovereignty over these waters, including the Northwest Passage, is based on historic title[2] and no right of passage is therefore recognized.[3] Further strengthening Canada's sovereignty position is the ongoing use and occupation of the covering ice by its Inuit people "*from time immemorial.*"[4] However, with the gradual melting of covering ice in the Northwest Passage, commentators have questioned whether Canada's position might be severely undermined with the removal of this legal underpinning.[5]

Advocates of Canada's position respond that it would not because "Canada has never embraced the 'ice-is-land' view of Arctic sovereignty."[6] Assuming for a moment that Canada's position is not supportable on grounds of historic title alone, the question then arises whether the Northwest Passage constitutes a strait used for international navigation and by extension a right of transit passage exists. Determining whether a waterway constitutes a strait used for international navigation is a complicated question of fact dependent, among other things, on whether the waterway has been used for international shipping.[7] Most observers would be hardpressed to make such an assertion, notwithstanding sporadic voyages by United States vessels through the Passage. In this regard, the controversial 1969-1970 passage of the American tanker *Manhattan* and the 1985 voyage of the United States Coast Guard icebreaker *Polar Sea* sparked a public debate over whether the federal government was doing enough to prevent internationalization of the Northwest Passage and preserve Canada's sovereignty in the Canadian Arctic.

The Agreement[8] reached between the Canadian and United States governments in the aftermath of the *Polar Sea's* transit seeks to preserve each

[1] Territorial Sea Geographical Co-ordinates (Area 7) Order (Privy Council 1985-2739).

[2] D. Johnston, "The Northwest Passage Revisited," manuscript, at 4-5, subsequently published in (2002) 33(2) Ocean Development and International Law 145-64.

[3] L. Legault, "Climate Change and the Law of the Sea in the Canadian Arctic, (unpublished paper presented to the Canadian Maritime Seminar on Global Warming and Canada's Shipping Lanes, Montreal, June 16, 2001) at 3.

[4] External Affairs Canada, Statements and Speeches, "Policy on Canadian Sovereignty," September 10, 1985.

[5] R. Huebert, "The Impact of Climate Change on the Northwest Passage" (2001) 2(4) Isuma: Canadian Journal of Policy Research.

[6] Legault, *supra* note 3 at 6.

[7] *Corfu Channel Case*, Merits, Judgment, I.C.J. Reports 1949.

[8] Agreement between Canada and the United States of America, signed and in force January 11, 1988, C.T.S. 1988, no 29.

sides' position on the status of the Northwest Passage — namely the Canadian position that it is not a strait used for international navigation and the United States' position that it is — while providing a practical way for United States ship traffic to utilize the Passage.[9] Whether this agreement would suffice in the face of significantly reduced ice cover combined with increased pressure by private United States entities judging the Passage's use to be economically advantageous is a question being asked by legal scholars and other experts. Moreover, other foreign governments' treatment and characterization of vessel traffic in the Passage may be even more pressing where there are fewer overriding bilateral considerations tempering the policy approach that they might pursue.

Beyond the issue of sovereignty, the most obvious practical significance of whether the Passage is internal waters or a strait used for international navigation is what means are employed to protect the Arctic marine environment. As internal waters, there is no question that Canadian environmental law, including the *Arctic Waters Pollution Prevention Act*[10] and associated regulations, would apply to vessels utilizing the Passage, whether or not it is ice covered. As a strait used for international navigation, it is quite likely that this legislation and consequential regulations would govern vessel traffic transiting the Passage as long as ice cover remains most of the year. Article 234 of the *United Nations Law of the Sea Convention* [11] gives coastal states the right to protect areas within their exclusive economic zones that are ice covered for most of the year, where the climactic conditions are particularly severe, there are navigational hazards created by the ice, and pollution would cause irreversible environmental damage.[12] Should there be melting such that there is no longer ice coverage most of the year, then proper protection of the marine environment may become linked that much more closely with Canada's position that the Passage constitutes internal waters by virtue of historic title.

---

[9] Pursuant to section 3 of the agreement, the United States government requests the Canadian government's consent for its vessels to conduct scientific research during voyages of icebreakers and the Canadian Government grants its consent to the transit. For a succinct analysis of the Agreement, see R.G. Purver, "Aspects of Sovereignty and Security in the Arctic" in D. McRae, and G. Munroe, ed., *Canadian Oceans Policy: National Strategies and the New Law of the Sea* (Vancouver: UBC Press, 1989).

[10] Arctic Waters Pollution Prevention Act, R.S.C. 1985, c. A-12.

[11] United Nations Convention on the Law of the Sea, done at Montego Bay, December 10, 1982, entered into force November 16, 1994, 34 I.L.M. 1547 (1995) [hereinafter LOSC].

[12] Some commentators have argued that because Canada is not yet a party to LOSC, this basis of authority if this provision is questionable (see Huebert, *supra* note 5 at 7.) and express doubt about assertions of other commentators that Article 234, like much of the LOSC, has now achieved the status of customary international law owing to the almost universal adherence to its provisions.

Parliamentary Declarations in 2001-2 / Déclarations parlementaires en 2001-2

compiled by / préparé par
ALIAKSANDRA LOGVIN

A   STATEMENTS MADE ON THE INTRODUCTION OF LEGISLATION /
DÉCLARATIONS SUR L'INTRODUCTION DE LA LÉGISLATION

1   *Bill S-23: An Act to Amend the Customs Act and to Make Related Amendments to Other Acts / Loi S-23: Loi modifiant la Loi sur les douanes et d'autres lois en conséquence*

Hon. Martin Cauchon (Minister of National Revenue and Secretary of State (Economic Development Agency of Canada for the Regions of Quebec)):

Les organismes douaniers dans le monde doivent continuer à moderniser leurs procédures s'ils veulent suivre le rythme du perfectionnement et de l'évolution des tactiques et des priorités des terroristes et des autres groupes qui constituent une menace pour les citoyens honnêtes. C'est pourquoi, en avril de l'année dernière, j'ai lancé une réforme des douanes dans le but de renforcer notre aptitude à gérer la frontière canadienne.

Our new approach to border management is outlined in Bill S-23. It provides the logistical framework for the customs action plan which would give us the tools to protect Canadians by focusing on high risks. At the same time it would strengthen our economy by facilitating the movement of low risk people and goods. For example, the new system would give us advance critical information on passengers and flight crews so that customs officers could make decisions on admissibility prior to their arrival.

On the commercial side, the same concepts would be implemented for goods entering Canada by enhancing the ability of custom officers to target, identify and examine high risk shipments. We are in the process of rolling out all these action plan initiatives over the next four years.

Toutefois, étant donné les événements au cours des dernières journées, j'ai donné instruction à l'ensemble de l'équipe des douanes de faire ce qui suit. Premièrement, d'évaluer la faisabilité d'une accélération de la mise en oeuvre des initiatives du plan d'action.

Aliaksandra Logvin is in the Faculty of Law at the University of Ottawa.

Deuxièmement, de concentrer nos nouvelles initiatives de protection sur le périmètre, là où le risque est le plus grand.

Troisièmement, à compter d'aujourd'hui, toutes nos procédures, tant du côté des voyageurs que du secteur commercial, seront examinées dans le but de nous assurer que les leçons tirées des événements de la dernière semaine puissent servir à identifier et intercepter les personnes à risques élevés et à traiter les marchandises avec plus d'efficacité.

(House of Commons Debates, September 17, 2001, p. 5147)

(Débats de la Chambre des Communes, le 17 septembre 2001, p. 5147)

Hon. Martin Cauchon (Minister of National Revenue and Secretary of State):

Le projet de loi S-23 favorisera la compétitivité et la prospérité des Canadiennes et des Canadiens sur les marchés internationaux. Il permettra à l'Agence [canadienne des douanes et du revenu] de faciliter le plus possible la circulation des expéditions commerciales et des voyageurs en règle. Il nous donnera aussi les outils dont nous avons besoin pour mieux protéger nos frontières et notre pays et pour mieux assurer la sécurité de nos collectivités et de nos familles. Je suis sûr que l'on conviendra que les Canadiennes et les Canadiens n'attendent rien de moins.

(House of Commons Debates, September 21, 2001, p. 5421)

(Débats de la Chambre des Communes, le 21 septembre 2001, p. 5421)

Ms. Sophia Leung (Parliamentary Secretary to the Minister of National Revenue):

Bill S-23 proposes to modernize the management of our border, to further encourage trade and tourism, all this without jeopardizing safety and the security of Canadians ... Bill S-23 includes a range of enforcement initiatives and services that support the protection of Canadians and the competitiveness of business. It is important not to lose sight of the fact that the great majority of travellers comply with our laws and regulations. However there are those who cross our border illegally, some with the intent to undermine the safety of Canadians. The amendments in Bill S-23 can help stop this threat ...

Bill S-23 will also enable CCRA to better channel its efforts and resources by concentrating its attention on high risk people or goods trying to enter Canada. Bill S-23 will clarify current laws to allow the CCRA to effectively administrate and enforce its mandate. For this reason the purpose of the changes proposed in Bill S-23 will help Canada customs do a better job of keeping undesirable people and illegal drugs out of this country.

Furthermore the proposed changes in Bill S-23 will give Canada customs more authority in controlled areas of airports and other border points. Those controlled areas not only support the business goals of the Canadian air industry but they will also create seamless connection processes for travellers in a secured and protected environment.

It is important to note that Canada customs will continue to work closely with enforcement agencies and other government departments to address illegal activities and the threats to health, safety and the security at our borders.

(House of Commons Debates, September 24, 2001, pp. 5468-69)
(Débats de la Chambre des Communes, le 24 septembre 2001, pp. 5468-69)

2   *Bill S-31: An Act to Implement Agreements, Conventions and Protocols Concluded between Canada and Slovenia, Ecuador, Venezuela, Peru, Senegal, the Czech Republic, the Slovak Republic and Germany for the Avoidance of Double Taxation and the Prevention of Fiscal Evasion with Respect to Taxes on Income /*
   Loi S-31, Loi mettant en oeuvre des accords, des conventions et des protocoles conclus entre le Canada et la Slovénie, l'Équateur, le Venezuela, le Pérou, le Sénégal, la République tchèque, la République slovaque et l'Allemagne, en vue d'éviter les doubles impositions et de prévenir l'évasion fiscale en matière d'impôts sur le revenu

Mr. John McCallum (Parliamentary Secretary to the Minister of Finance):

One of the principal disadvantages of not having a tax treaty is double taxation. Double taxation is something that citizens and companies do not relish. Double taxation is to be avoided because it represents a very important potential impediment to international transactions which are becoming increasingly important . . .
   Bill S-31 is not something radical. It is not rocket science. It is standard, routine legislation to increase our stable of countries with which we have tax treaties and to improve the tax treaties from some of the existing cases. In general, these tax treaties are modelled on a standard OECD model . . .
   There are three basic advantages to adopting these tax treaties: first, it would avoid double taxation, which is good for corporate and private citizens and good from the point of view of the national interest; second, it would lead to a simplified tax system; and third, it would enhance the degree of certainty and provide a more stable environment for international transactions. Given that the global scene is becoming more important for Canada, this increased ability to conduct foreign transactions is definitely in the national interest.

(House of Commons Debates, November 9, 2001, pp. 7199-200)
(Débats de la Chambre des Communes, le 9 novembre 2001, pp. 7199-200)

3   *Bill C-11: An Act Respecting Immigration to Canada and the*
     Granting of Refugee Protection to Persons Who Are Displaced,
     Persecuted or in Danger / Loi C-11: Loi concernant l'immigration
     au Canada et l'asile conféré aux personnes déplacées, persécutées ou
     en danger

Hon. Elinor Caplan (Minister of Citizenship and Immigration):

In Bill C-11 we are streamlining the refugee determination procedures because we all recognize that it takes too long ... [W]henever we have evidence that someone poses a national security risk we have the powers to detain and argue for continued detention, and we do that.

In the new Bill C-11 we will also have the ability to deny access to the refugee determination system for those who are inadmissible to Canada. For those who need our protection, we will continue to do that.

(House of Commons Debates, September 20, 2001, p. 5350)
(Débats de la Chambre des Communes, le 20 septembre 2001, p. 5350)

Hon. Elinor Caplan (Minister of Citizenship and Immigration):

Bill C-11 ... contains comprehensive measures that would further strengthen national security, which is of course a priority not only for the government but for my department.

The new immigration and refugee protection act would add new grounds of inadmissibility. It would strengthen the authority to arrest criminals and individuals who present a threat to security. It would eliminate appeal rights in these cases and streamline the removal process for persons who are security threats.

Bill C-11 would provide our immigration officers with a set of up to date tools, the tools they need to bar entry to those who pose a threat to national security or engage in acts of terrorism or are part of a terrorist organization. Bill C-11 would bar entry to those who have committed human rights violations such as war crimes or crimes against humanity. It would also bar entry to those who have been convicted for serious criminality in or outside Canada.

(House of Commons Debates, October 23, 2001, p. 6446)
(Débats de la Chambre des Communes, le 23 octobre 2001, p. 6446)

4   *Bill C-31: An Act to Amend the Export Development Act and to Make*
     Consequential Amendments to Other Acts / Loi C-31: Loi modifiant
     la Loi sur l'expansion des exportations et d'autres lois en conséquence

Mr. Pat O'Brien (Parliamentary Secretary to the Minister for International Trade):

The bill contains specific amendments that flow from a comprehensive review process which began in 1998 and brings a balanced approach to change at EDC [Export Development Corporation]. This legislation also complements other policy direction from government, as well as changes that have been initiated by EDC since the review process got under way.

It is fair to say that the period leading up to this legislation has seen the most thorough review of Canada's export financing activities that has ever been undertaken. The broad based review included public consultations, parliamentary committee recommendations, and advice and recommendations from many other experts, stakeholders and independent observers.

The bill ... is a product of a focused discussion on what is best for Canada in the intensely competitive world of international trade as well as a thorough examination of how best to reflect Canadian values in our dealings with other countries.

A key feature of the bill is a new statutory requirement for the environmental review of projects being considered for EDC support. This is a significant change that positions Canada in the forefront of the international community in efforts to more closely link export credit activities and environmental impacts. The bill also includes other statutory changes that provide the necessary legal basis for a number of operational changes at EDC.

Bill C-31 fulfills a commitment made by the Minister for International Trade last June. At that time the minister announced important policy changes for Canada's export credit agency ...

Those changes include a significant expansion of the commercial mandate of the Export Development Corporation so that it could fill perceived gaps in the private sector financial services market or more actively support the international financing needs of Canadian exporters ...

It is clear that the Export Development Corporation is a key part of our country's success in export markets. The EDC has demonstrated its value to Canada by filling gaps in the private sector's financial services, by reaching out to bring more small and medium size businesses into the export marketplace, by providing needed financial support to Canada's customers in developing countries, and overall by ensuring that Canadian exporters have access to the kind of financing that will keep them competitive with exporters from other countries.

Due to the fact that the EDC plays such a key role in our country's trade development strategy, we must ensure that it will continue to meet the competitive financing needs of Canadian exporters, and especially the small and medium size businesses that are the backbone of our economy and the main creators of jobs throughout Canada ... [O]ur public policy challenge is to find a balance between the twin priorities of international business competitiveness and corporate social responsibility. Bill C-31 helps to do just that.

(House of Commons Debates, October 1, 2001, pp. 5759-60)
(Débats de la Chambre des Communes, le 1er octobre 2001, pp. 5759-60)

5   *Bill C-32: An Act to Implement the Free Trade Agreement between the
    Government of Canada and the Government of the Republic of Costa
    Rica / Loi C-32: Loi portant mise en oeuvre de l'Accord de libre-
    échange entre le gouvernement du Canada et le gouvernement de la
    République du Costa Rica*

Mr. Pat O'Brien (Parliamentary Secretary to the Minister of International Trade):

[The Canada-Costa Rica] agreement is an important step forward on several levels. To begin with, the success of this endeavour clearly demonstrates that free trade agreements can be negotiated between larger and smaller economies. That bodes well for the future of the free trade area of the Americas.

At the same time, this agreement will open up a new market with exciting potential for Canadian exporters. It also includes precedent setting chapters in the areas of trade facilitation and competition policy ...

Formal trade relations between our two countries date back more than 50 years to a bilateral commercial agreement concluded in 1950. Since then our relationship has developed steadily. A free trade agreement will only make it stronger ...

The agreement will include immediate elimination of Costa Rican tariffs on most Canadian industrial exports. It is expected that over 90% of Canada's current agriculture and agri-food exports to Costa Rica will realize market access benefits.

Canada and Costa Rica believe that a commitment to environmental and labour co-operation along with the effective enforcement of domestic laws should go hand in hand with trade liberalization. That is why, in addition to the FTA, two complementary co-operation agreements on the environment and labour were negotiated in parallel.

These parallel agreements are practical and reflect the scope of our relationship with Costa Rica. They are also designed to promote values shared by both countries, such as the rule of law and sustainable development ...

The Canada-Costa Rica free trade agreement is a symbol of our long term commitment to the hemisphere. It will help advance negotiations leading to the free trade area of the Americas. The agreement will provide much needed insight into how to address the needs of smaller and more vulnerable regional economies ...

Canada is a free trading nation. We stand by that and support Bill C-32.

(House of Commons Debates, September 28, 2001, pp. 5703-05)
(Débats de la Chambre des Communes, le 28 septembre 2001, pp. 5703-05)

6   *Bill C-35: An Act to Amend the Foreign Missions and International Organizations Act/ Loi C-35: Loi modifiant la Loi sur les missions étrangères et les organisations internationales*

Ms. Aileen Carroll (Parliamentary Secretary to the Minister of Foreign Affairs):

[T]he Foreign Missions and International Organizations Act provides the statutory basis for the privileges and immunities of diplomats in Canada. It also provides the government with the ability to deal by order in council with the privileges, immunities and legal status of international organizations and their events or summits in Canada ...

The bill's core amendment is key to providing privileges and immunities to foreign officials who attend intergovernmental conferences or summits in Canada. The amendment broadens the definition of "international organization" to include international organizations and meetings that are presently excluded such as the Organization for Security and Cooperation in Europe and the G-8 ... This amendment would ensure that these meetings and foreign officials involved obtain protection and treatment under Canadian law.

The second amendment in the bill ... concerns the police authority to provide security and protection for intergovernmental conferences held in Canada ... The legislation would provide that the Royal Canadian Mounted Police has the primary responsibility to ensure the security for the proper function or a meeting of an international organization attended by persons granted privileges and immunities under the Foreign Missions and International Organizations Act and for which an order has been passed under that act ...

The bill would allow the government to extend privileges and immunities to international inspectors who come to Canada on temporary duty in order to carry out inspections under the chemical weapons convention and the agreement with the preparatory commission for the Comprehensive Nuclear Test-Ban Treaty Organization.

Under the chemical weapons convention, a treaty ratified by Canada in 1999, a verification regime was established providing for both reporting via declarations and on site inspection by inspectors from the Organization for the Prohibition of Chemical Weapons. The chemical weapons convention requires that inspectors be granted diplomatic privileges and immunities similar to those accorded to diplomatic agents under the Vienna convention on diplomatic relations. The problem is that neither the implementing legislation nor any other Canadian legal instrument can at present provide the privileges and immunities up to this level for these inspectors. As a temporary arrangement, privileges and immunities have been provided by an order in council, which invokes less extensive privileges and immunities. This means that Canada could be criticized as not being in full compliance with the treaty. Therefore it is the government's obligation to resolve this situation as soon as possible, and the bill does just that.

The bill also broadens privileges and immunities to permanent missions accredited to international organizations, such as the International Civil

Aviation Organization, ICAO, located in Montreal. ICAO is presently the largest international organization operating its headquarters in Canada.

By enhancing our relationship with ICAO, the amendment would improve the ability of Montreal and other Canadian cities to service the headquarters of international organizations operating their headquarters in Canada.

The amended legislation would also help Canada compete with other countries to attract these headquarters of other international organizations.

In summary . . . [t]he amendments would enable Canada to continue to safely host important international events and summits in Canada and thereby fulfill our treaty responsibilities.

(House of Commons Debates, October 5, 2001, pp. 6011-12)
(Débats de la Chambre des Communes, le 5 octobre 2001, pp. 6011-12)

7   *Bill C-36: An Act to Amend the Criminal Code, the Official Secrets Act, the Canada Evidence Act, the Proceeds of Crime (Money Laundering) Act and Other Acts, and to Enact Measures Respecting the Registration of Charities, in Order to Combat Terrorism / Loi C-36: Loi modifiant le Code criminel, la Loi sur les secrets officiels, la Loi sur la preuve au Canada, la Loi sur le recyclage des produits de la criminalité et d'autres lois, et édictant des mesures à l'égard de l'enregistrement des organismes de bienfaisance, en vue de combattre le terrorisme*

Hon. Anne McLellan (Minister of Justice and Attorney General of Canada):

The horrific terrorist acts of September 11 created suffering, fear and uncertainty. These events challenged Canadians' sense of safety and security and it is this that we must address as our first priority.

Terrorism seeks to undermine the rule of law and human rights. Terrorism seeks to undermine our values and way of life. Terrorism tries to turn one community against another, religion against religion, and race against race. Terrorism seeks all these things but it will achieve none of them, not here in Canada. This government has been clear but it is worth repeating over and over again: this is not a war against any one group or ethnicity but a war against terrorism.

Les mesures contenues dans ce projet de loi [C-36] ciblent les personnes et les activités qui portent atteinte à la sécurité et au bien-être des Canadiens et des Canadiennes. Nos efforts sont dirigés contre les actes terroristes et non pas contre les membres d'une communauté ou d'un groupe ethnique ou religieux particulier. La diversité constitue l'une des plus grandes forces du Canada et nous prenons des mesures pour la protéger . . .

Bill C-36 is one element of the Government of Canada's comprehensive action plan on Canadian security, a plan whose objectives are to stop terrorists from getting into Canada and protect Canadian citizens from terrorist acts, to bring forward tools to identify, prosecute, convict and punish terrorists, to keep our borders secure and to work with the international community to bring terrorists to justice and address the root causes of hatred.

In developing this legislation we have paid close attention to what other democratic countries are doing in their fight against terrorism. It is important that we act in a way that is consistent with the approach of other democratic nations and in conformity with international law ...

The proposed legislative package focuses on three elements. Bill C-36 targets terrorist activity and those who would carry out or support such activity. The three main objectives of the new measures are as follows: first, to suppress the very existence of terrorist groups; second, to provide new investigative tools; and, third, to provide a tougher sentencing regime to incapacitate terrorists and terrorist groups.

The bill seeks to identify, dismantle, prosecute and punish terrorist activity. Bill C-36 includes criminal code amendments to ratify the remaining two United Nations conventions and protocols related to terrorism. The suppression of terrorist financing convention concerns the freezing of terrorist property.

It would prohibit dealing in any property of an individual involved in terrorist activities and it would prohibit making available funds and financial means or services to terrorists. These measures would allow a federal court judge to order the seizure and forfeiture of property used in or related to terrorist activity ...

The legislation ... would provide a definition of terrorist activity for the first time. This definition is critical, as many of the legal implications under the bill are tied to the concept of terrorist activity. The first element of the definition outlines the offences that are established in the 12 international conventions related to terrorism, all of which we have signed.

Equally important, however, is a general definition that refers to acts or omissions undertaken for political, religious or ideological purposes and which are intended to intimidate the public, force governments to act and cause serious harm.

We have carefully restricted the definition to make it clear that property damage and disruption of an essential service are not in and of themselves sufficient to constitute a terrorist activity. The action taken must also endanger lives or cause serious risks to the health and safety of the public ...

Bill C-36 represents an appropriate legislative balance to reflect Canadian values. Though our allies may have designed different legislative means to suit their legislative and constitutional frameworks, we nevertheless share a collective goal: to provide our citizens with security for themselves, their families and their communities.

(House of Commons Debates, October 16, 2001, pp. 6164-67)
(Débats de la Chambre des Communes, le 16 octobre 2001, pp. 6164-67)

8   *Bill C-41: An Act to Amend the Canadian Commercial Corporation
     Act / Loi C-41: Loi modifiant la Loi sur la Corporation commerciale
     canadienne*

Hon. Pierre Pettigrew (Minister for International Trade):

[I]n Doha, Qatar last week ... WTO partners agreed to start a process
that will lead to an effective integrated rules based trading system and
greater market access for citizens, not just of Canada but of all member
countries ...

[T]he Canadian government believes that contributing to greater
equity in the world provides stability for long term and lasting peace.
Moreover, the launch of the new round of negotiations at the World Trade
Organization is good news for Canada, for our farmers and for agriculture
producing countries around the world ...

La Corporation commerciale canadienne a la capacité unique de nous
faire accéder aux marchés publics internationaux et de les cibler. Elle a les
contacts et les compétences dont les exportateurs canadiens ont besoin
pour mener leur activité commerciale sur le marché international. Ces
contacts et ces compétences donnent à nos exportateurs un avantage
important pour trouver de nouveaux contrats, respecter leurs critères et
les remporter dans ce marché concurrentiel et spécialisé. C'est une bonne
activité commerciale, d'un type qui débouche sur des emplois de grande
qualité et sur une création de richesse, partout à travers le Canada.

La Corporation commerciale canadienne met l'accent sur trois domaines uniques en leur genre de soutien aux exportateurs canadiens: des
services spécialisés de ventes internationales et de passation de contrats;
une garantie d'exécution du marché, appuyée par le gouvernement au
nom des fournisseurs canadiens d'acheteurs étrangers; enfin, l'accès à
un financement commercial à l'intention des entreprises canadiennes
qui ont besoin d'un fonds de roulement, avant expédition, pour financer
les exportations ...

Bill C-41 is meant to update the act and provide for necessary changes
to the corporation's governance and operating procedures, so that the
corporation can serve the needs of Canadian exporters in a commercially
responsible way and assist Canadian exporters to exploit the significant
opportunities that exist in the huge public procurement market.

Bill C-41 proposes three changes. First, it creates separate job descriptions for the offices of chair and president of the corporation, bringing
CCC's governance structure in line with treasury board guidelines. This is
also consistent with modern corporate management practices.

Second, it allows the corporation to charge a fee for service that will
balance the cost of providing the services with the value to client. The fee
structures will be fair and will balance the price of service and the value
received by clients.

Third, it expands CCC's borrowing authority which will strengthen the
corporation's capacity to service large scale international contracts and
make timely progress payments to Canadian suppliers ...

Overall, these amendments will strengthen the Canadian Commercial

Corporation's capacity to deliver the specialized services that contribute to the success of thousands of Canadian companies in export markets and that have helped produce high quality employment for Canadians throughout the country.

(House of Commons Debates, November 19, 2001, pp. 7272-73)
(Débats de la Chambre des Communes, le 19 novembre 2001, pp. 7272-73)

9 *Bill C-42: An Act to Amend Certain Acts of Canada, and to Enact Measures for Implementing the Biological and Toxin Weapons Convention, in Order to Enhance Public Safety / Loi C-42: Loi modifiant certaines lois fédérales et édictant des mesures de mise en oeuvre de la convention sur les armes biologiques ou à toxines, en vue de renforcer la sécurité publique*

Hon. David Collenette (Minister of Transport):

The bill [C-42] would be known as the public safety act and would promote and protect public safety and strengthen the government's ability to improve the safety of Canadians...
    The public safety act adds features to much of the legislation which may be needed to prevent or respond to security issues. For example, those things that are being added include the clarification and, in some cases, the strengthening of existing aviation security authorities.

- The act would discourage unruly passengers, more commonly known as air rage, by making it an offence to engage in any behaviour that endangers the safety or security of a flight or persons on board an aircraft.
- The act would require air carriers or those operating aviation reservation systems to provide basic information on specific passengers on flights when it is needed for security purposes.
- The act would speed implementation of various security amendments already made to the Immigration Act.
- The act would require licences for activities related to dangerous biological substances such as anthrax.
- The act would deter irresponsible hoaxes that endanger the public or heighten public anxiety.
- The act would establish tighter controls over explosives.
- The act would provide for control over the export and transfer of sensitive technology.
- The act would prevent unauthorized use or interference with national defence computer systems and the act would deter the proliferation of biological weapons...

(House of Commons Debates, November 22, 2001, pp. 7411-12)
(Débats de la Chambre des Communes, le 22 novembre 2001, pp. 7411-12)

10   *Bill C-44: An Act to Amend the Aeronautics Act / Loi C-44:*
      Loi modifiant la Loi sur l'aéronautique

Hon. David Collenette (Minister of Transport):

Bill C-44 ... is another important step in the government's fight against terrorism.

The basic objective of Bill C-44 is to ensure the Government of Canada has the proper authority to establish and maintain an appropriate security program for the protection of Canadians ...

The particular amendment contained in C-44 addresses the provision of passenger and crew member data to our international partners in the interest of transportation security. I believe the proposed amendment allows for the capture of just enough of the data held by Canadian carriers to provide for increased passenger safety through the intelligent use of modern information technology ...

By advancing, as Bill C-44 ... we will be able to prepare regulations that will allow Canadian air carriers to provide approved information to approved countries.

(House of Commons Debates, November 30, 2001, pp. 7695-96)
(Débats de la Chambre des Communes, le 30 novembre 2001, pp. 7695-96)

11   *Bill C-50: An Act to Amend Certain Acts As a Result of the Accession*
      of the People's Republic of China to the Agreement Establishing the
      World Trade Organization / Loi C-50: Loi modifiant certaines lois
      en conséquence de l'accession de la République populaire de Chine à
      l'Accord instituant l'Organisation mondiale du commerce

Hon. Pierre Pettigrew (Minister for International Trade):

Bill C-50 [is] the legislation that will allow Canada to enjoy all of the advantages of China's accession to the World Trade Organization ...

On a broad level, China's membership in the WTO confirms Canada's important position in both Canadian and international trade. China has officially accepted the WTO's internationally negotiated rights and obligations concerning the administration of international trade, including the fundamental principles of national and most favoured nation treatment, the settlement of trade disputes, and the continued liberalization of international trade ...

Normally negotiations to join the WTO usually affect only the acceding country, requiring it to make concessions and changes to its domestic laws and regulations. Amendments of Canadian legislation are normally not required. However, in the negotiations Canada and other countries sought and obtained the right to invoke China specific safeguards and to apply appropriate non-market economy rules in anti-dumping investigations on Chinese goods. The China safeguards differ from safeguards in other trade agreements in that they will be applicable only to imports from China, they will have a lower injury threshold and they will be temporary.

Legislative changes are necessary to integrate these provisions into the existing legislative framework. Amendments are also necessary so that while China makes the transition to a market economy Canada can continue to apply special price comparability rules to China in anti-dumping investigations. These amendments will allow Canada to implement fully the rights it obtained during the China accession negotiations. They are fully supported by industry and all the provinces of our country. All WTO members have the right to implement such measures.

(House of Commons Debates, February 27, 2002, pp. 9305-7)

(Débats de la Chambre des Communes, le 27 février 2002, pp. 9305-7)

12 *Bill C-55: An Act to Amend Certain Acts of Canada, and to Enact Measures for Implementing the Biological and Toxin Weapons Convention, in Order to Enhance Public Safety / Loi C-55: Loi modifiant certaines lois fédérales et édictant des mesures de mise en oeuvre de la convention sur les armes biologiques ou à toxines, en vue de renforcer la sécurité publique*[1]

Hon. David Collenette (Minister of Transport):

Suite aux événements tragiques et atroces du 11 septembre, nous sommes intervenus immédiatement pour mettre en place des outils stratégiques, opérationnels, financiers et législatifs nécessaires pour renforcer notre capacité d'assurer la protection du Canada et des Canadiens contre le terrorisme ... Dans le cadre de ce processus initial, nous avons élaboré le projet de loi C-42 qui représentait notre cadre législatif original pour assurer la sécurité publique ...

The government ... has withdrawn the original bill and has brought forward a new bill which is improved and would deal with the criticisms that were levelled. While the new bill contains many of the important elements of Bill C-42, it also incorporates many significant improvements.

First, we have revised the provisions concerning the government's ability to issue interim orders when they are essential to combat an immediate and serious threat or risk to health, safety, security or to the environment ...

Dans un deuxième temps ... [l]es nouvelles dispositions ont pour effet de réduire considérablement les dimensions des ["zone[s] militaire d'accès contrôlé"] ... en limitant leur utilisation à la protection de la sécurité et de la sûreté des établissements de défense ainsi que du personnel des Forces canadiennes et d'une force étrangère et des biens situés à l'extérieur des établissements de défense. Nous avons également ajouté des limites de temps et des exigences plus rigoureuses concernant l'établissement et l'approbation d'une zone ...

Third, we ... have added an amendment to the Aeronautics Act that would provide the solicitor general with access to airline passenger information for transportation security, anti-terrorism and other limited law enforcement purposes ...

[1] Bill C-55 replaces Bill C-42, the Public Safety Act, introduced in November 2001.

We believe it is essential to protect the privacy of personal information. For this reason we have built in numerous privacy safeguards ...

In tabling this new bill the government has signalled its openness to improve the legislative framework that would enhance our ability to respond quickly and effectively should a significant threat arise and to provide Canadians with a safe and secure environment. It will continue to be flexible as we move forward in the legislative process, and we will continue to work in the interests of all Canadians as we strive to protect Canada from the tragedy of war or terrorism.

(House of Commons Debates, May 1, 2002, pp. 11060-62)
(Débats de la Chambre des Communes, le 1ᵉʳ mai 2002, pp. 11060-62)

B   STATEMENTS IN RESPONSE TO QUESTIONS / DÉCLARATIONS EN RÉPONSE AUX QUESTIONS

1   *Environment / Environnement*

(a)   Kyoto Protocol / Le Protocole De Kyoto

Mr. Bill Blaikie (Winnipeg—Transcona):

[Y]esterday the Minister of Industry seemed to suggest that Canada is not going to keep its commitments on the Kyoto accord. I ask the Prime Minister, was the Minister of Industry speaking for the government when he made the suggestion that Canada might not keep its Kyoto commitments?

Right Hon. Jean Chrétien (Prime Minister):

[T]he government has one policy that we all agree on. We want to and we hope that we will be able to sign the Kyoto agreement. The negotiations are not yet terminated. At the meeting in Bonn we made progress on some elements of it. We made more progress at the meeting in Marrakesh last week.

The question of the export of clean energy has not been concluded yet. We have to consult with the provinces too, but we intend to go through the process. The goal is to sign the Kyoto agreement.

(House of Commons Debates, November 21, 2001, pp. 7371-72)
(Débats de la Chambre des Communes, le 2¹ novembre 2001, pp. 7371-72)

M. Bernard Bigras (Rosemont — Petite-Patrie):

Est-ce que le ministre a l'intention de ... mettre à l'ordre du jour [de la quatrième rencontre intergouvernementale sur la gouvernance internationale de l'environnement] l'importance de réintégrer les Américains dans les pourparlers sur le protocole de Kyoto?

Mrs. Karen Redman (Parliamentary Secretary to the Minister of the Environment):

[W]e have had many triumphs through the Bonn negotiation as well as the ones at Marrakesh keeping alive the Kyoto protocol. In the main that has been largely because of the leadership of the Minister of the Environment in Canada and part of the umbrella group.

We have maintained all along that it is very important to continue to invite Americans to the table because this is a global problem and they will continue to be a positive force for us in reaching this worthy goal.

(House of Commons Debates, November 30, 2001, p. 7712)
(Débats de la Chambre des Communes, le 30 novembre 2001, p. 7712)

(b)   Nuclear Waste / Déchets nucléaires

Mr. Joe Comartin (Windsor — St. Clair):

[W]hen the G-8 foreign ministers meet in Whistler tomorrow they will discuss a U.S. proposal to fund a plutonium disposition program. The proposal to pursue the so-called MOX option is unsafe for the environment, extremely costly and could increase the potential of plutonium falling into the hands of terrorists ... [W]ill [the Prime Minister] oppose the MOX option.?

Right Hon. Jean Chrétien (Prime Minister):

[T]his is an extremely important problem. We have to ensure that nuclear waste is not circulated across the world. Any positive contribution Canada could make would be very good for the security of the Canadian people and very good for the protection of the environment.

(House of Commons Debates, June 11, 2002, pp. 12531-32)
(Débats de la Chambre des Communes, le 11 juin 2002, pp. 12531-32)

(c)   Oil Dumping/ Déversements de pétrole

Mr. Bob Mills (Red Deer):

Foreign tankers and cargo vessels passing through our waters actually have an incentive to dump their oil because our fines are so ridiculously low. When will the Minister of Transport increase his department's charges and fines for oil dumping so that we can stop this sabotage of our waters?

Hon. David Collenette (Minister of Transport):

Canada is a signatory to the Paris MOU and the Tokyo MOU to ensure that standards are maintained and improved and that they are enforced around the world. With respect to individual fines, these are matters under constant review.

(House of Commons Debates, February 4, 2002, p. 8645)
(Débats de la Chambre des Communes, le 4 février 2002, p. 8645)

2   Foreign Affairs / Affaires étrangères

(a)   Armenia / Arménie

Mr. Sarkis Assadourian (Brampton Centre):

On April 24, next week, Canadian Armenian communities and people from around the world will remember and commemorate the Armenian genocide that took place over 87 years ago in 1915. What is the position of the Canadian government on this very tragic moment in the history of mankind?

Hon. Bill Graham (Minister of Foreign Affairs):

[T]he government and the Prime Minister on many occasions have expressed the sympathy of our government and our people for the tragedy that occurred to the Armenian people with the collapse of the Ottoman Empire. In specific terms, in 1996 we in the House dedicated the week of April 20 to 27 in memory of the Armenian people and the suffering they had. In 1999 we remembered specifically the tremendous tragic fate that occurred in that country. We still urge that we should consider these tragic events in their historical context and remember that we must move forward and try to ensure peace and harmony among all people.

(House of Commons Debates, April 18, 2002, p. 10564)
(Débats de la Chambre des Communes, le 18 avril 2002, p. 10564)

(b)   Afghanistan / Afghanistan

Mr. Sarkis Assadourian (Brampton Centre):

The basic framework for an interim government for the war ravaged Afghanistan has been established by delegates in Bonn, Germany. Could the minister tell the House the views of the Canadian government in regard to this very historic agreement?

Hon. John Manley (Minister of Foreign Affairs):

[T]he agreement reached last week in Bonn involving various Afghan parties is a very important one. It opens the way for a transition to a new government that is representative in nature. It includes women which is one of the issues that members of the House have been raising with concern. There is a lot more to do. There are many more challenges to face in Afghanistan, including a major humanitarian problem.

(House of Commons Debates, December 10, 2001, pp. 8062-63)
(Débats de la Chambre des Communes, le 10 décembre 2001, pp. 8062-63)

(c)   Burma / Birmanie

Mr. Bryon Wilfert (Oak Ridges):

The [Burmese] regime has allowed some of its offices to re-open and has released 200 political prisoners but human rights abuses are still prevalent in that country. Would the Minister of Foreign Affairs comment on Canada's position regarding relations with this regime and give an assessment of the current situation?

Hon. John Manley (Minister of Foreign Affairs):

Canada certainly welcomes the positive, if somewhat limited, developments that have been occurring in Burma ... On the other hand, we note that there are continuing very serious human rights abuses that are occurring, in particular political repression and harsh treatment of those in ethnic and border regions. In the meantime, as we observe developments, Canada's position on our relationship with Burma will not change from that which was introduced in 1997.

(House of Commons Debates, November 28, 2001, p. 7610)
(Débats de la Chambre des Communes, le 28 novembre 2001, p. 7610)

(d)   China / Chine

Mr. Bryon Wilfert (Oak Ridges):

[O]n Monday, September 17 negotiators agreed to terms allowing the People's Republic of China to join the World Trade Organization. [What is] the significance of China's WTO accession[?]

Hon. Rey Pagtakhan (Secretary of State (Asia-Pacific)):

Mr. Speaker, Canada welcomes this historic event. As the agreement is fully ratified, China, our fourth largest trading partner, becomes a member of the rules based international trading system and therefore is bound by the provisions on transparency and the rule of law.

As the Minister for International Trade earlier indicated in another avenue, it means more enhanced business between Canada and China and also more opportunities, and therefore economic and social benefits for all Canadians.

(House of Commons Debates, September 19, 2001, p. 5295)
(Débats de la Chambre des Communes, le 19 septembre 2001, p. 5295)

(e)   Diplomatic Immunity / Immunité diplomatique

Mr. Bill Casey (Cumberland — Colchester):

Bill C-35 is expanding immunity to foreigners. Will the minister put into legislation a requirement to report to the House on who claims civil immunity and criminal immunity under this new legislation?

Hon. John Manley (Minister of Foreign Affairs):

[W]e have debated this at some length in the committee ...
    The fact is that a very small proportion of those who are here representing their countries ever make a claim of diplomatic immunity and these obligations are ones we have taken on under the Vienna convention.

(House of Commons Debates, November 19, 2001, pp. 7263-64)
(Débats de la Chambre des Communes, le 19 novembre 2001, pp. 7263-64)

(f)   International Exchanges / Échanges internationaux

M. Dan McTeague (Pickering — Ajax — Uxbridge):

[L]e secrétaire d'État aux Sciences, à la Recherche et au Développement est de retour d'Allemagne où il a pris part aux célébrations du 30ᵉ anniversaire de la signature de l'Accord germano-canadien de coopération scientifique et technique. Le secrétaire d'État peut-il dire à la Chambre en quoi cette entente sera avantageuse pour notre pays?

L'hon. Gilbert Normand (secrétaire d'État (Sciences, Recherche et Développement)):

[E]n effet, le 25 octobre dernier, à Bonn, en Allemagne, nous avons célébré le 30ᵉ anniversaire d'échanges technologiques entre nos deux pays. J'ai signé une nouvelle entente avec ma collègue, la ministre des Sciences de l'Allemagne, Mme Bulmahn. Pour concrétiser cette entente, le Conseil national de recherche du Canada et le Conseil national de recherche allemand fourniront 720 000 $ par année. Les échanges porteront principalement sur la télé-médecine, l'opto-électronique, l'agriculture et les bio-technologies. C'est encore un signe que le Canada est capable de faire des échanges internationaux.

(House of Commons Debates, October 30, 2001, p. 6734)
(Débats de la Chambre des Communes, le 30 octobre 2001, p. 6734)

(g)   Iran / Iran

Ms. Colleen Beaumier (Brampton West — Mississauga):

[T]he Minister of Foreign Affairs is currently in the Middle East, with a visit to Iran. Given the events of the past six and a half weeks, could the parliamentary secretary to the minister please inform us of the purpose of this trip?

Ms. Aileen Carroll (Parliamentary Secretary to the Minister of Foreign Affairs, Liberal):

Mr. Speaker, the visit of the Minister of Foreign Affairs aims at seeking the widest possible coalition in the effort to fight terrorism and to increase world security. The best way to do that is by direct engagement of key middle eastern regional states such as Iran. This is the first time a Canadian minister of foreign affairs has visited Iran in almost a decade.

As an important regional country, Iran will be key as a major contributor to the effort to combat terrorism.

(House of Commons Debates, October 29, 2001, pp. 6664-65)
(Débats de la Chambre des Communes, le 29 octobre 2001, pp. 6664-65)

(h)   Iraq / Irak

Mr. John Reynolds (Leader of the Opposition):

What exactly is our government's position on Iraq?

Hon. Bill Graham (Minister of Foreign Affairs):

We have clearly supported the position at the United Nations of bringing sanctions to bear against a person or a regime which we find detestable. We will continue to support that and to support UN actions against Iraq. We will continue to make sure we are free to act to constrain Saddam Hussein.

(House of Commons Debates, February 19, 2002, p. 8991)
(Débats de la Chambre des Communes, le 19 février 2002, p. 8991)

Hon. Bill Graham (Minister of Foreign Affairs):

We will continue to operate within the confines of international law and international relations in a way that is in the best interests of Canada.

(House of Commons Debates, February 26, 2002, p. 9258)
(Débats de la Chambre des Communes, le 26 février 2002, p. 9258)

(i)   Israel / Israël

Mme Francine Lalonde (Mercier):

[H]ier, le ministre des Affaires étrangères du Canada a rencontré le premier ministre israélien. Il doit rencontrer aujourd'hui ... l'autorité palestinienne. Le vice-premier ministre peut-il confirmer que l'objectif du Canada consiste à obtenir de l'État israélien qu'il reconnaisse le droit du peuple palestinien à un État viable et qu'il se retire des territoires occupés, et à obtenir de l'autorité palestinienne la reconnaissance du droit à l'existence de l'État d'Israël et au respect de sa sécurité?

L'hon. Herb Gray (vice-premier ministre):

[L]e but du ministre est d'encourager les deux parties à retourner à la table de négociations et de cesser la violence, surtout contre les civils, en Israël et ailleurs. J'espère qu'il aura du succès dans ses efforts.

(House of Commons Debates, November 1, 2001, p. 6840)
(Débats de la Chambre des Communes, le 1er novembre 2001, p. 6840)

M. Pierre Paquette (Joliette):

[V]endredi dernier, Shimon Peres acceptait qu'une mission d'information de l'ONU se rende en Israël pour faire la lumière sur l'intervention militaire dans le camp de réfugiés de Jénine. Nous apprenions hier la volte-face du gouvernement israélien qui veut maintenant retarder l'arrivée des enquêteurs de l'ONU. Le Canada va-t-il joindre sa voix à celle du secrétaire général des Nations Unies et signifier clairement aux autorités israéliennes qu'il estime nécessaire et urgente l'arrivée à Jénine de la mission d'information de l'ONU?

L'hon. Bill Graham (ministre des Affaires étrangères):

[L]e Canada soutient les efforts du secrétaire général de l'ONU d'avoir une mission d'enquête en Israël et dans les pays palestiniens. Nous soutenons cet effort et nous l'avons dit clairement aux autorités israéliennes, aussi bien qu'à l'ONU. Nous continuerons de soutenir cela et nous sommes confiants que M. Kofi Annan, d'ici la fin de la semaine, aura mis en place une telle enquête.

(House of Commons Debates, April 24, 2002, p. 10769)
(Débats de la Chambre des Communes, le 24 avril 2002, p. 10769)

(j)   Madagascar / Madagascar

Mme Diane St-Jacques (Shefford):

[N]ous suivons depuis quelques semaines le déroulement des élections à Madagascar ... Aux dernières nouvelles, il y a maintenant deux gouvernements parallèles et deux capitales. Le secrétaire d'État pour l'Amérique latine, l'Afrique et la Francophonie pourrait-il nous dire ce que le Canada fait pour essayer de résoudre la situation?

L'hon. Denis Paradis (secrétaire d'État (Amérique latine et Afrique) (Francophonie)):

[L]a situation à Madagascar est très préoccupante. Toutefois, nous apprenions que l'Organisation de l'Unité africaine propose, dans un rapport déposé hier, un gouvernement de réconciliation nationale. J'ai rencontré, hier, l'ambassadeur de Madagascar. Ce matin, je me suis entretenu avec notre ambassadeur de la Francophonie et je lui ai demandé de solliciter l'appui de la Francophonie, notamment du secrétaire général Boutros Boutros-Ghali qu'il va rencontrer demain à Paris, pour continuer à faire pression sur les parties pour un règlement pacifique de la situation.

(House of Commons Debates, March 13, 2002, p. 9588)
(Débats de la Chambre des Communes, le 13 mars 2002, p. 9588)

(k) Middle East / Moyen-Orient

Mme Francine Lalonde (Mercier):

[A]u Moyen-Orient, on assiste à une inqualifiable escalade de la violence qui peut mettre en cause la paix dans le monde. Aussi, de plus en plus d'observateurs constatent qu'il faudra aller plus loin que ne le proposent les rapports Mitchell et Tennet qui n'ont pu nous ramener ni la paix ni le retour aux négociations. Est-ce que la mise en place d'un processus politique plus large n'est pas la seule solution qui puisse s'avérer intéressante et qui ait des chances de porter fruit et de ramener la paix et une solution?

L'hon. Bill Graham (ministre des Affaires étrangères):

La politique du Canada est d'essayer de calmer les esprits et de persuader les parties impliquées dans le conflit de cesser la violence et de permettre à la communauté internationale de travailler avec elles pour rétablir la paix dans cette région très troublée ... Cette année, nous avons la chance d'avoir la présidence du G-8, et je vous promets que le premier ministre et moi-même ferons de notre mieux pour persuader nos collègues du G-8 de participer à un processus de paix au Moyen-Orient.

(House of Commons Debates, February 21, 2002, p. 9100)
(Débats de la Chambre des Communes, le 21 février 2002, p. 9100)

(l)   Nuclear Disarmament / Désarmement nucléaire

Mr. Svend Robinson (Burnaby — Douglas):

Today's decision by George Bush to scrap the 1972 ABM treaty is a body blow to nuclear disarmament ... Will Canada condemn this decision?

Hon. John Manley (Minister of Foreign Affairs):

I think it is important to recognize that the ABM treaty is a bilateral agreement between the United States and the Russian federation, formerly the Soviet Union and that the United States has acted within the terms of that treaty in giving six months notice.

It is the hope of our government that during the process of the six months notice period the parties will be able to agree on a new strategic framework which will include not only the basis for arms control and disarmament between them, but also provide a verifiable and transparent system to supervise the reduction in offensive weapons that both parties have promised to initiate.

(House of Commons Debates, December 13, 2001, p. 8250)
(Débats de la Chambre des Communes, le 13 décembre 2001, p. 8250)

(m)   Peru / Pérou

M. Bernard Patry (Pierrefonds — Dollard):

Lors de violentes manifestations qui ont éclaté dans les rues d'Arequipa au Pérou au cours de la fin de semaine dernière, de nombreux Canadiens se sont vus coincés à Arequipa. Que fait le Canada pour assurer la sécurité de ces Canadiens?

L'hon. Denis Paradis (secrétaire d'État (Amérique latine et Afrique) (Francophonie)):

[L]a sécurité des Canadiens à l'étranger est une priorité pour le Canada. Nous avons recensé quelque 33 Canadiens qui se trouvaient dans cette région trouble. Ils ont pu sortir de la région grâce à l'aide du Canada. J'ai moi-même parlé à des étudiants du Cégep de Montmagny ainsi qu'à leurs parents. Ils sont maintenant en sécurité.

(House of Commons Debates, June 20, 2002, p. 12959)
(Débats de la Chambre des Communes, le 20 juin 2002, p. 12959)

(n)   Somalia / Somalie

Mr. Roy Cullen (Etobicoke North):

The people of Somalia are most anxious for peace and stability in the Horn of Africa. What is our government doing to support the peace process in Somalia and how can the large Somali diaspora in Canada contribute to this dialogue?

Hon. Bill Graham (Minister of Foreign Affairs):

[T]here are obviously tremendous problems in Somalia but we can take some comfort in the fact that there have been positive results in Eritrea and Ethiopia next door ... We have been providing substantial humanitarian aid to enable a better environment to deal with the drought and to deal with the humanitarian crisis and we urge our Somalian-Canadian citizens of whom many are represented here in the House ... to tell their colleagues in Somalia to work for a peaceful solution to this.

(House of Commons Debates, April 17, 2002, p. 10499)
(Débats de la Chambre des Communes, le 17 avril 2002, p. 10499)

(o)   Sri Lanka / Sri Lanka

Mr. John McKay (Scarborough East):

For over 20 years Sri Lanka has been racked by a bloody civil war pitting the government of Sri Lanka against the Tamil Tigers of Tamil Eelam. On Friday, the government of Norway announced that the leader of the Tamil Tigers and the Prime Minister of Sri Lanka had signed a formal cessation of hostilities, paving the way for face to face peace talks. What are the views of the Minister of Foreign Affairs on this breakthrough? Is Canada willing to offer any assistance to the parties?

Hon. Bill Graham (Minister of Foreign Affairs):

We welcome the peace initiative in Sri Lanka and we welcome the initiative of the government of Norway ... I am proud of the fact that CIDA has engaged in a program in Sri Lanka over the last couple of years searching to find solutions to conflict resolution, solutions to federalism. In fact, the Secretary of State for Western Economic Diversification was made a part of that team. We are proud of our efforts to date and we will continue those efforts.

(House of Commons Debates, February 25, 2002, p. 9200)
(Débats de la Chambre des Communes, le 25 février 2002, p. 9200)

(p)   Sudan / Soudan

Mr. Joe Fontana (London North Centre):

What steps is Canada taking to facilitate, in co-operation with our allies, a lasting peace with the aim of creating humanitarian economic stability in Sudan?

Hon. Denis Paradis (Secretary of State (Latin America and Africa) (Francophonie)):

[W]e are encouraged by the recent agreement among the government of Sudan, the Sudanese People's Liberation Army, SPLA, and the United States on ending of attacks against civilian targets by both the government and the opposition forces.

The agreement has the potential to allow the safe and secure delivery of humanitarian assistance by the international community.

Cet accord entre les deux parties pourrait contribuer à réunir les conditions menant à des négociations de paix officielles.

(House of Commons Debates, March 18, 2002, p. 9758)

(Débats de la Chambre des Communes, le 18 mars 2002, p. 9758)

(q)   Syria / Syrie

Mr. Brian Pallister (Portage — Lisgar):

The United Nations will vote very soon on whether or not to make Syria, a state with a long record of sponsoring terrorist groups, a member of the United Nations Security Council. Will the government oppose terrorism by opposing Syria?

Hon. John Manley (Minister of Foreign Affairs):

[W]e do not generally announce who we are voting for or against before Security Council elections, but ... to this point in time the group within which that country belongs has not nominated any other countries to the Security Council ...

[T]he efforts of the United States to build a broader coalition have resulted in a clear denunciation by Syria of the acts that occurred last week.

(House of Commons Debates, September 19, 2001, p. 5293)

(Débats de la Chambre des Communes, le 19 septembre 2001, p. 5293)

(r) Ukraine / Ukraine

Mr. Stan Dromisky (Thunder Bay — Atikokan):

In light of his recent visit to Ukraine, could the secretary of state [for Central and Eastern Europe and the Middle East] inform the House of Commons regarding the present status of Canada-Ukraine relations?

Hon. Gar Knutson (Secretary of State (Central and Eastern Europe and Middle East)):

I was warmly welcomed on the tenth anniversary of the establishment of diplomatic relations between Canada and the Ukraine. As my hon. colleague knows, there are one million Canadians of Ukraine heritage who call Canada home and they form a vital and valued part of Canadian society. I met with foreign minister Zlenko and other senior members of the Ukrainian government where I strongly emphasized Canada's commitment to the conduct of free and fair parliamentary elections and I strongly reiterated Canada's support for Ukraine's efforts in the area of political and economic reform. The federal government will continue to call for closer ties with Ukraine.

(House of Commons Debates, February 21, 2002, p. 9101)
(Débats de la Chambre des Communes, le 21 février 2002, p. 9101)

(s)   United Arab Emirates / Émirats arabes unis

Mr. Walt Lastewka (St. Catharines):

Canada has always enjoyed an excellent trade relationship with the United Arab Emirates, especially Dubai ... [Has] the present situation in the Middle East ... adversely affected our trade relationship and, if so, what is he doing to overcome this and increase trade with the UAE?

Hon. Gar Knutson (Secretary of State (Central and Eastern Europe and Middle East)):

[H]aving just returned from the region, I learned that while the Israel-Palestine conflict is a major preoccupation throughout the Arab world, countries on the Arabian peninsula are determined to expand trade and commercial links with Canada. More specifically, my visit highlighted opportunities for Canada in health care, tourism, housing and education which can augment major investments made to date in the oil and gas sectors.

(House of Commons Debates, April 22, 2002, p. 10652)
(Débats de la Chambre des Communes, le 22 avril 2002, p. 10652)

(t)   United States / États-Unis

Mr. Bill Graham (Toronto Centre — Rosedale):

Two weeks ago the permanent joint board of defence held its 208th meeting in Ottawa to discuss continental security. Could the defence minister explain the nature of this important Canada-U.S. institution and brief the House as to what was accomplished at that meeting?

Hon. Art Eggleton (Minister of National Defence):

[T]he permanent joint board of defence is the senior bilateral advisory group between Canada and the United States on continental defence matters. It reports directly to the Prime Minister of Canada and to the president of the United States.

The board existed since the Second World War. It is not a policy setting device but it is an opportunity for broad ranging discussion on defence and security issues. It has both military and civilian personnel. It is co-chaired by someone from each side of the border. The member of parliament for Brossard — La Prairie ably represents Canada on the board. It recently had discussions about September 11 and its fallout, which of course is the current issue.

(House of Commons Debates, November 1, 2001, p. 6843)
(Débats de la Chambre des Communes, le 1er novembre 2001, p. 6843)

(u)   Zimbabwe / Zimbabwe

Mr. Bryon Wilfert (Oak Ridges):

[W]hat steps Canada has taken in conjunction with other states to ensure fair, free and open elections in Zimbabwe?

Hon. Bill Graham (Minister of Foreign Affairs):

[T]he government has been making strong representations to the government of Mr. Mugabe to ensure fair and free elections will be held in that country.

Last week on behalf of the government I attended the ministerial meeting of the Commonwealth. We proposed to send Commonwealth observers and I am proud to report that Canada agreed to send three. We made it clear to the Zimbabwean government that unless observers are accepted, our group will recommend that action be taken against Zimbabwe at the leaders' meeting in Australia at the beginning of March which would probably mean the removal of Zimbabwe from the Commonwealth.

(House of Commons Debates, February 4, 2002, p. 8645)
(Débats de la Chambre des Communes, le 4 février 2002, p. 8645)

3   *Health / Santé*

Mr. Tony Tirabassi (Niagara Centre):

Yesterday the minister [of Health] hosted a meeting of his counterparts from the G-7 and the OECD countries on health security and bioterrorism. The minister has agreed to co-operate and forge a new partnership to address the critical issue of protecting public health and security ... [W]hat role Canada will play in this new global action?

Hon. Allan Rock (Minister of Health):

[I]t is clear that defeating terrorism and bioterrorism will take an international effort. It is for that reason I was delighted yesterday to host the G-7 and OECD health ministers in Ottawa ... At the request of those ministers, Canada will take the lead in co-ordinating international efforts to link laboratories, to share information, to have surveillance systems work together, and on pharmaceutical and vaccine stockpiling and other issues. Canada will lead this effort because we believe strongly in protecting public health.

(House of Commons Debates, November 8, 2001, pp. 7163-64)
(Débats de la Chambre des Communes, le 8 novembre 2001, pp. 7163-64)

4   Human Rights / Droits de la personne

Mr. Derek Lee (Scarborough — Rouge River):

[L]ast week we witnessed a 36 hour fast and a peaceful demonstration on Parliament Hill by Canadian Falun Gong practitioners attempting to bring attention to the alleged abuse of fellow practitioners in China ... [W]hat actions [the Canadian] government has taken to encourage and promote greater respect for human rights in all parts of China?

Hon. David Kilgour (Secretary of State (Asia-Pacific)):

Canada has spoken out about the human rights situation, both at the UN human rights commission and in Beijing, and will continue to do so. On many occasions we have raised our concerns directly with senior Chinese officials, both in Beijing and here in Ottawa.

Canada would very much like China to end the suppression of freedom of religious expression and spiritual practice and to ratify the two human rights conventions that China has already ratified at the UN.

(House of Commons Debates, March 20, 2002, p. 9889)
(Débats de la Chambre des Communes, le 20 mars 2002, p. 9889)

(a)   Discrimination against Women / Discrimination à l'égard des femmes

Mᵐᵉ Diane Bourgeois (Terrebonne — Blainville):

Safiya Husseini, une jeune Nigérianne, est en ce moment accusée dans son pays d'avoir eu des relations sexuelles hors mariage. Selon la charia ... la sentence à une telle offense est la lapidation. Cette situation est tout à fait inacceptable. Devant l'imminence d'un geste aussi barbare, le ministre des Affaires étrangères a-t-il fait des représentations auprès du gouvernement du Nigeria pour empêcher qu'un acte d'une telle atrocité soit perpétré?

L'hon. Denis Paradis (secrétaire d'État (Amérique latine et Afrique) (Francophonie)):

[L]e gouvernement canadien est très préoccupé par ces sentences de mort par lapidation. Tout le monde connaît la position du gouvernement canadien sur la peine de mort.

Nous continuons, par l'entremise de l'ONU, à faire pression sur l'ensemble des pays pour l'abolition de la peine de mort dans le monde entier.

C'est tout à fait contraire au Traité sur les droits humains dont le Nigeria lui-même est un des signataires. Nous allons donc continuer à faire pression sur le Nigeria pour leur faire comprendre le bon sens.

(House of Commons Debates, February 20, 2002, p. 9026)
(Débats de la Chambre des Communes, le 20 février 2002, p. 9026)

(b)   Self-Determination / Autodétermination

Mr. Svend Robinson (Burnaby — Douglas):

In 1948 and 1949 the United Nations supported a referendum to allow the people of Kashmir to determine their own future. Does Canada continue to support the principle of self-determination for the Kashmiri people and will we call on India to finally accept this political solution to avoid a disastrous war with Pakistan [over Kashmir]?

Hon. Bill Graham (Minister of Foreign Affairs):

The Prime Minister personally spoke to President Musharraf on the weekend. He also spoke to the prime minister of India. We are doing everything we can along with our colleagues at the NATO meeting, which we were at yesterday, and in the international community to ask these two parties to draw back from the brink of what could be a nuclear war. I do not think it would be appropriate for us now to interfere in the fight between them. What we need to do is stop the rhetoric and stop the potential of this tremendous violence.

(House of Commons Debates, May 29, 2002, p. 11881)

(Débats de la Chambre des Communes, le 29 mai 2002, p. 11881)

5   *International Humanitarian Law / Droit international humanitaire*

(a)   Geneva Conventions / Conventions de Genève

Mme Francine Lalonde (Mercier):

[T]out combattant qui offre de se rendre n'est plus une cible militaire légitime. C'est là un concept de base du droit international humanitaire. Malheureusement, selon le Comité international de la Croix-Rouge, il y aurait certaines parties de l'Afghanistan où il ne serait fait aucun prisonnier ... Est-ce que le Canada entend dénoncer ces violations à la Convention de Genève sur les prisonniers de guerre?

L'hon. John Manley (ministre des Affaires étrangères):

[N]ous ne sommes pas en faveur de tels actes. Nous croyons qu'il faut non seulement respecter les principes de la Convention de Genève, mais également les principes des règles de droit.

(House of Commons Debates, November 26, 2001, p. 7498)

(Débats de la Chambre des Communes, le 26 novembre 2001, p. 7498)

M. Claude Bachand (Saint-Jean):

[L]e Canada s'est placé en situation de non-respect des ententes internationales en remettant les prisonniers faits en Afghanistan aux États-Unis, sans avoir conclu une entente claire quant au statut de ces prisonniers. Le ministre de la Défense peut-il nous informer des conséquences [de cet incident]?

Hon. Art Eggleton (Minister of National Defence):

[T]he fact is that we do respect international law. That is the cornerstone of how we are conducting ourselves in this campaign. We respect international law and we respect Canadian law. The United States, to whom we have turned over these prisoners, has given us assurances that it respects international law and will operate consistent with the Geneva conventions.

(House of Commons Debates, February 4, 2002, pp. 8642-43)
(Débats de la Chambre des Communes, le 4 février 2002, pp. 8642-43)

(b)   Humanitarian Aid / Aide humanitaire

Mr. David Pratt (Nepean — Carleton,):

The headline on the front page of the Ottawa *Citizen* today claims that "1 million flee Afghanistan" and that officials are predicting a major disaster. What is Canada doing to avert a human catastrophe in Pakistan and Iran?

Mrs. Marlene Jennings (Parliamentary Secretary to the Minister for International Cooperation):

[J]ust today the Minister for International Cooperation announced $1 million in humanitarian assistance to aid the millions of Afghani refugees who have fled to Pakistan and Iran. Our assistance will provide basic health care needs, shelter and water to these displaced people in Pakistan and Iran and it will be done through the UN agencies and their staff on the ground.

(House of Commons Debates, September 19, 2001, p. 5294)
(Débats de la Chambre des Communes, le 19 septembre 2001, p. 5294)

Mrs. Marlene Jennings (Parliamentary Secretary to the Minister for International Cooperation):

Canada has been helping Afghanistan for over 10 years. We have given over $120 million to Afghanistan. We do not recognize the Taliban, that is clear. Our money is funneled through the UN agencies and the NGOs. We are working closely with both to ensure that we are there to help the refugees who are there now and those who may become refugees in the future. We will be there.

(House of Commons Debates, September 28, 2001, pp. 5714-15)
(Débats de la Chambre des Communes, le 19 septembre 2001, pp. 5714-15)

M. Michel Gauthier (Roberval):

Comment le ministre des Finances peut-il exprimer de bonnes intentions avec ses collègues du G-20 quant à la nécessité d'accroître l'aide internationale?

L'hon. Paul Martin (Ministre des Finances):

[D]ans le dernier budget, on a augmenté l'aide à l'étranger. Dans le précédent budget avant celui-là, on a augmenté l'aide à l'étranger; et dans le budget avant cela, on a augmenté l'aide à l'étranger.

D'ailleurs, on est un des rares pays, lorsqu'on regarde le G-7, qui, année après année, a augmenté sa dette et, en même temps, on a occupé une position de leadership en étendant le moratoire sur l'endettement des pays les plus pauvres. C'est le Canada qui a pris le leadership ...

[À] la réunion de la Banque mondiale à Prague, il y a un an et demi ... [et] [l]ors de la dernière fin de semaine ici, à Ottawa, encore une fois, c'est le Canada qui, au G-20, au FMI et à la Banque mondiale, a pris le leadership dans tout ce domaine de la baisse de la dette des pays les plus pauvres. Cela a été accepté par les autres pays, et on va continuer de lutter pour cela.

(House of Commons Debates, November 19, 2001, p. 7260)
(Débats de la Chambre des Communes, le 19 novembre 2001, p. 7260)

Ms. Beth Phinney (Hamilton Mountain):

[A]n estimated 60 million people in the southern African region are suffering from political upheaval and what has been described as the worst regional drought since 1992 ... [H]ow [does] the Government of Canada intend to address this urgent situation?

Hon. Susan Whelan (Minister for International Cooperation):

We are deeply concerned about the worsening conditions in southern Africa. Due to the urgent nature of this humanitarian crisis, Canada, through the Canadian International Development Agency, has pledged $34.2 million to provide much needed food, medicine and other assistance to the region. This contribution will allow us to build on our history of providing assistance to countries in southern Africa and to help those in need.

(House of Commons Debates, June 19, 2002, p. 12881)
(Débats de la Chambre des Communes, le 19 juin 2002, p. 12881)

5   *International Criminal Law / Droit pénal international*

(a)   Extradition / Extradition

Mr. Kevin Sorenson (Crowfoot):

If the evidence pointed that a terrorist, not in this past terrorist attack [committed on Sept. 11, 2001], carried out an attack in the United States where there were multiple deaths and where the mastermind of such an activity had found safe haven in Canada, would the Minister of Justice extradite that mastermind of terrorism back to the United States on a capital offence?

Hon. Anne McLellan (Minister of Justice):

I do not accept the reference to Canada as a safe haven. By working domestically and with our allies across the world, we have ensured that no country is a safe haven for those who would commit such heinous acts.

[E]xtradition requires a request. If that request is made, procedures as outlined in the Extradition Act would be followed ...

The Supreme Court of Canada made it absolutely clear [in the decision in *Burns and Rafay*] that the Minister of Justice does not have to seek assurances from a requesting state in exceptional circumstances.

It is my obligation on a case by case basis to determine whether exceptional circumstances exist and therefore assurance is not sought.

(House of Commons Debates, September 18, 2001, p. 5221)
(Débats de la Chambre des Communes, le 18 septembre 2001, p. 5221)

(b)   International Criminal Court and Ad Hoc International Criminal Tribunals / Cour pénale internationale et tribunaux pénaux internationaux ad hoc

Ms. Alexa McDonough (Halifax):

Will ... Canada ... lead the way in fighting terrorism through multilateral democratic institutions such as the International Criminal Court?

Right Hon. Jean Chrétien (Prime Minister):

[S]peaking of the Statute of Rome, Canada has been a leading force to develop this new system of international justice that has been quite effective so far in the Netherlands at this time, where criminals of war in the Balkans are facing international justice.

If there is a need to amend the treaty, Canada will always be a participant, because at the beginning of this system Canada was one of the initiators.

(House of Commons Debates, September 17, 2001, p. 5141)
(Débats de la Chambre des Communes, le 17 septembre 2001, p. 5141)

Mme Francine Lalonde (Mercier):

[A]ujourd'hui, le terrorisme, par sa nature comme par son ampleur, revêt un caractère international. Pourtant, contrairement aux crimes de guerre, de génocide ou aux crimes contre l'humanité, le terrorisme n'est pas un crime en droit international.

Le gouvernement appuie-t-il l'idée de faire du terrorisme un crime en droit international et d'inclure le crime de terrorisme à la compétence de la Cour pénale internationale?

L'hon. John Manley (ministre des Affaires étrangères):

[N]ous allons continuer d'appuyer l'établissement de la Cour pénale internationale. C'est un objectif de la politique étrangère du Canada. Toutefois, à ce moment-ci, nous avons également une obligation d'essayer d'assurer que les peuples puissent vivre en sécurité.

Pour le moment, notre priorité est de trouver les meilleurs moyens disponibles pour accomplir cette tâche...

[N]ous sommes d'accord qu'il est nécessaire de trouver des moyens de composer avec des situations internationales de crimes et même de crimes de terrorisme.

Mais c'est peut-être un crime un peu plus compliqué et, dans le contexte des discussions dans la communauté internationale, il faut déterminer les moyens disponibles pour mettre en vigueur un système pour associer à un acte terroriste le statut de crime contre l'humanité.

(House of Commons Debates, September 18, 2001, p. 5251)
(Débats de la Chambre des Communes, le 18 septembre 2001, p. 5251)

Mme Francine Lalonde (Mercier):

S'il s'avérait que la culpabilité d'Oussama ben Laden soit établie et que l'impasse survenait quant à son extradition aux États-Unis, le ministre est-il prêt à proposer au Conseil de sécurité la création d'un tribunal pénal international ad hoc pour dénouer la situation et permettre d'élargir la coalition?

L'hon. John Manley (Ministre des Affaires étrangères):

[T]out d'abord, il faut souligner que les événements du mardi 11 septembre sont un crime qui a été commis aux États-Unis.

Je ne pense pas que les États-Unis vont accepter l'idée que quelqu'un qui est responsable d'un tel crime soit traduit devant des tribunaux qui ne sont pas situés aux États-Unis.

Mais de toute façon, nous sommes certainement en faveur de continuer notre travail, en faveur du Traité de Rome, qui créera une cour internationale criminelle.

(House of Commons Debates, September 20, 2001, p. 5348)
(Débats de la Chambre des Communes, le 20 septembre 2001, p. 5348)

M. Antoine Dubé (Lévis-et-Chutes-de-la-Chaudière):

[L]es États-Unis s'opposent à ce que l'autorité de la future Cour pénale internationale s'étende au personnel américain en mission de paix. Cette attitude ne met pas seulement en péril le rôle de la cour, mais aussi l'existence même des futures missions de paix qui pourraient voir le jour sous l'égide de l'ONU. Le premier ministre ... entend-il lui faire part de son opposition et l'inviter fermement à modifier son attitude?

Le très hon. Jean Chrétien (premier ministre):

Nous aimerions évidemment que les Américains y participent mais ils ne le veulent pas. Nous le déplorons et j'ai déjà eu l'occasion de le dire aux autorités américaines.

(House of Commons Debates, June 21, 2002, p. 13001)
(Débats de la Chambre des Communes, le 21 juin 2002, p. 13001)

(c) Terrorism / Terrorisme

Mr. John Reynolds (West Vancouver — Sunshine Coast):

[T]here are profound implications for Canada in what happened last week [Attack on the United States on September 11, 2001]. [What is] the government ... planning in the weeks to come? What type of legislation or laws are we looking at to protect all Canadians? What is our involvement in the whole situation?

Hon. John Manley (Minister of Foreign Affairs):

[I]t is undeniable that the events of last Tuesday force us to review all our practices and policies and consider whether a response is necessary. I do not think it should be hasty. I do not think it should be ill-considered. However it needs to be firm and resolute. We will take the action that is required.
[I]f I were to offer a set of options today they would not be well thought out. They would be too hasty. The government will need to take time ... to consider what responses need to be given to the threat which now becomes more evident to us than it was before.

(House of Commons Debates, September 17, 2001, pp. 5127-28)
(Débats de la Chambre des Communes, le 17 septembre 2001, pp. 5127-28)

Mr. Svend Robinson (Burnaby — Douglas):

[Will] Canada, in any response to a request for assistance militarily from the United States ... insist that the response fully respects international law and avoids any further loss of civilian lives?

Right Hon. Jean Chrétien (Prime Minister):

Canada will stand by our neighbour and friend, the United States. We are a member of NATO and will be discussing with our allies to make sure that an appropriate response is prepared.

There is no rush. We have to do it deliberately, with calm, and with the clear goal of destroying terrorism. When there is an adequate plan we will join our friends and allies, the Americans and the other nations of the world, to make sure we work effectively against terrorism ...

[N]o one can guarantee to anyone that there will be no civilians who unfortunately might lose their lives in any operation. It would be naive to think so. When we are in a war we have to make sure that those who are guilty face the consequences of their acts.

We cannot promise that not a single life will be lost. Some soldiers and some civilians might be affected, but sometimes that is the price we pay to have peace and destroy the evil of terrorism.

(House of Commons Debates, September 17, 2001, p. 5143)
(Débats de la Chambre des Communes, le 17 septembre 2001, p. 5143)

Mr. Vic Toews (Provencher):

[A]lthough Britain and the United States have passed strict anti-terrorist laws, it is an international disgrace that Canada has none. Why has the minister [of Justice] failed to take the essential steps to protect the security of Canadians?

Hon. Anne McLellan (Minister of Justice):

Canada has signed all 12 UN counterterrorism conventions, has ratified 10 of them and in fact is in the process of taking steps to ratify and implement the remaining two.

(House of Commons Debates, September 17, 2001, p. 5145)
(Débats de la Chambre des Communes, le 17 septembre 2001, p. 5145)

Mr. Stockwell Day (Leader of the Opposition):

U.S. President George Bush announced that he is launching a financial offensive in the fight against terrorism ... [Is] the [Canadian] government ... prepared to join [the USA] ... [and size] the financial assets of ... terrorist groups and organizations in Canada [?]

Hon. Jim Peterson (Secretary of State (International Financial Institutions)):

[O]n the issue of being able to seize these assets, we are looking at the possible legal routes that might be taken. We have already undertaken those investigations, but I would remind ... that we have already acted on the Afghan resolutions of the security council when we passed regulations in parliament on February 22 of this year allowing the seizure of all assets related to Osama bin Laden and any of his entities or associates.

(House of Commons Debates, September 24, 2001, p. 5481)
(Débats de la Chambre des Communes, le 24 septembre 2001, p. 5481)

Ms. Alexa McDonough (Halifax):

[E]vidence against alleged perpetrators of the criminal terrorist attacks in the U.S. has been presented to NATO members in Brussels. UN Secretary General Kofi Annan has said that only the United Nations could give legitimacy to global action.

In light of that, will the Prime Minister show some international leadership here? Will he use Canada's voice in NATO to urge that this evidence be placed now before the United Nations?

Right Hon. Jean Chrétien (Prime Minister):

The security council faced a problem on September 12 and it voted on a resolution at that time authorizing actions against those who perpetrated the crime in New York City and Washington.

Already the United Nations has been very much involved. I was discussing what can be done with the secretary general of the United Nations yesterday. So far the actions of the United Nations are adequate.

(House of Commons Debates, September 26, 2001, p. 5592)
(Débats de la Chambre des Communes, le 26 septembre 2001, p. 5592)

6   *Law of the Sea / Droit de la mer*

(a)   Fisheries / Pêches

Mr. Loyola Hearn (St. John's West):

The inshore shrimp fishery in Newfoundland is in a state of crisis. Fishers cannot afford to fish and processors cannot afford to operate their plants. One of the main reasons is the 20% tariff charged for Canadian shrimp going into European markets.

What steps has the minister taken to make sure that this inequity is corrected?

Hon. Herb Dhaliwal (Minister of Fisheries and Oceans):

We have allocated a quota on shrimp so we can continue to be competitive in the European Union. The government is doing everything it possibly can to have the European's look at that again so they can get rid of the 20% tariff that our producers have to face.

(House of Commons Debates, September 24, 2001, p. 5489)
(Débats de la Chambre des Communes, le 24 septembre 2001, p. 5489)

Mr. Shawn Murphy (Hillsborough):

[W]ith respect to the conservation and management of highly migratory fish stocks in the high seas, [w]hat is the[ir] status? I am speaking about both ratification and implementation of the United Nations fisheries agreement on these issues.

Hon. Herb Dhaliwal (Minister of Fisheries and Oceans):

I am happy to report to the House on something that we have been working on since 1995. We have learned that the 30th country has signed the United Nations fisheries agreement to make it effective December 11.

Those of us who worked on this know what a tremendous achievement this is for Canada and the international community to ensure that we can manage our fish stocks in international waters with conservation and rules and regulations that we can abide by. This is a great success for all Canadians.

(House of Commons Debates, November 22, 2001, p. 7451)
(Débats de la Chambre des Communes, le 22 novembre 2001, p. 7451)

Mr. Loyola Hearn (St. John's West):

Yesterday a Russian vessel, the *Olga,* under Icelandic control, was arrested for polluting Canadian waters. The boat, according to confirmed reports, has 70 to 80 tonnes of mature breeding cod in its hold. This species is under moratorium. Has the minister asked his officials to deal with this blatant abuse of regulations?

A sister ship, the *Otto,* which was also headed for Newfoundland, has now suspiciously changed direction and is headed for Iceland. Will the minister see that this vessel is boarded and checked, because if he does not do it soon we know what is going to happen to the catch?

Hon. Robert Thibault (Minister of Fisheries and Oceans):

[T]his government ... takes matters of overfishing and unregulated harvesting on the nose and the tail of the Banks very seriously. We will work with the provinces concerned, with the industry and with the international community to bring all fisheries under proper, good jurisdiction and management ...

If those countries and vessels do not want to follow the regulations of NAFO and the Canadian regulations, then we are happy to have them turned away.

(House of Commons Debates, March 20, 2002, p. 9887)
(Débats de la Chambre des Communes, le 20 mars 2002, p. 9887)

(b)   Protection of the Marine Environment / Protection de
l'environnement marin

Mr. Lawrence O'Brien (Labrador):

[I]n November 1995 Canada joined 108 other countries in adopting the global program of action for protection of the marine environment from land based activities, which recognized the need for concerted actions by every coastal state to protect the marine environment from the negative impacts of land based pollution. [What is] the progress of meetings of the United Nations environment program being held in Montreal this week?

Hon. Herb Dhaliwal (Minister of Fisheries and Oceans):

I had the honour of being in Montreal to open the conference on the global program and action on how we deal with land based activities that cause pollution in our waters ...
  Canada is working very hard to make sure that we play our part. We have three oceans that touch our country. Protecting our oceans is a priority. We will be there fully supporting the conference. A hundred countries have come together to see how, as a global community, we can do a better job of protecting our oceans and marine environment.

(House of Commons Debates, November 27, 2001, p. 7565)
(Débats de la Chambre des Communes, le 27 novembre 2001, p. 7565)

7   *Trade and Economy / Commerce et économie*

(a)   APEC / L'APEC

Mr. John Harvard (Charleswood St. James — Assiniboia):

[O]n October 20 and 21 Asia-Pacific leaders met in Shanghai to attend the Asia Pacific Economic Cooperation summit. Some media reports characterized the APEC statement on counterterrorism as weak. Would the Secretary of State for Asia-Pacific please tell the House what was achieved at the summit?

Hon. Rey Pagtakhan (Secretary of State (Asia-Pacific)):

[T]he APEC leaders in fact issued a strong and unprecedented political statement unanimously condemning the terrorist attacks in the United

States. They committed themselves to enhanced co-operation on counterterrorism in very specific ways under the UN charter and other international laws. They in fact indicated in the statement that the APEC leaders are very much against terrorism.

(House of Commons Debates, October 25, 2001, p. 6594)
(Débats de la Chambre des Communes, le 25 octobre 2001, p. 6594)

Mr. John McKay (Scarborough East):

[R]ecently the Secretary of State for Asia-Pacific attended the APEC conference. A number of important trade initiatives were discussed which will affect Canadian companies. Could the minister outline to the House specific initiatives which will be of assistance to Canadian companies?

Hon. Rey Pagtakhan (Secretary of State (Asia-Pacific)):

[W]e market Canada's strengths through team Canada, trade missions and other programs, speaking about Canada as a high tech country and a country with first class products in goods and services and business people with integrity. We participate in political and economic fora. We launch free trade negotiations, as with Singapore. We encourage trading countries to join the WTO so that they can participate in an internationally known, rules based system. We offer our business people support like the Export Development Corporation. Indeed, we have a lot of initiatives.

(House of Commons Debates, November 7, 2001, pp. 7097-98)
(Débats de la Chambre des Communes, le 7 novembre 2001, pp. 7097-98)

(b)   Central America / Amérique centrale

Mr. Walt Lastewka (St. Catharines):

[L]ast week the Minister for International Trade announced the launch of bilateral free trade negotiations with El Salvador, Guatemala, Honduras and Nicaragua. Could the minister's parliamentary secretary explain what Canadians can expect from new bilateral agreements with these countries?

Mr. Pat O'Brien (Parliamentary Secretary to the Minister for International Trade):

[L]ast Thursday the Minister for International Trade and his counterparts from El Salvador, Guatemala, Nicaragua and Honduras announced the launch of free trade talks. This agreement would give our exporters advantaged access to the important central American market. It would also help us to further our foreign policy objectives in the region of the alleviation of poverty, promotion of peace and democracy, and economic stability and growth.

(House of Commons Debates, November 27, 2001, p. 7563)
(Débats de la Chambre des Communes, le 27 novembre 2001, p. 7563)

Ms. Nancy Karetak-Lindell (Nunavut):

[T]he Minister of Natural Resources led a trade mission of energy companies to Mexico last week. Why did the minister choose Mexico, why now and what was accomplished?

Hon. Ralph Goodale (Minister of Natural Resources):

[I]t was my honour to lead a very positive Canadian energy business mission to Mexico last week ...
    Canadian energy business activity already exceeds $1 billion in Mexico. There is great potential for more. To position ourselves well in that market we need to be present in person, persistent and patient to establish the lasting foundations upon which future business opportunities will be built. I believe we did that last week.

(House of Commons Debates, October 22, 2001, p. 6423)
(Débats de la Chambre des Communes, le 22 octobre 2001, p. 6423)

Mr. Mac Harb (Ottawa Centre):

[W]hat [is] the government ... doing in order to ensure that Canadian entrepreneurs have access to the market in Mexico?

Hon. Pierre Pettigrew (Minister for International Trade, Lib.):

[S]ince NAFTA was signed by our government in 1994, Canadian exports to Mexico have more than doubled and Canadian investments in Mexico have more than tripled.
    This very week we have worked very hard at further deepening our relationship with Mexico. This week I led a very successful trade mission ... to Mexico. I met with President Fox and his economy minister, Mr. Derbez, to discuss bilateral relations and ways to enhance our trade and investments.

(House of Commons Debates, June 6, 2002, p. 12264)
(Débats de la Chambre des Communes, le 6 juin 2002, p. 12264)

(c)   Dairy Exports / Exportation des produits laitiers

M. Serge Marcil (Beauharnois — Salaberry):

Les producteurs et les transformateurs laitiers de partout au pays attendaient avec impatience la décision de l'Organe d'appel de l'OMC sur l'approche du Canada en matière d'établissement des prix pour les produits laitiers d'exportation. Quelle est la décision de l'Organe d'appel et quelles en seront les conséquences au pays?

Hon. Lyle Vanclief (Minister of Agriculture and Agri-Food):

I am pleased to inform dairy producers, processors and exporters that New Zealand and the United States failed to prove that our programs for commercial export of milk were inconsistent. We won the appeal. The dairy industry will continue with business as usual. It is another example of a partnership between industry and government for a strong proposal and a strong case, and we won.

(House of Commons Debates, December 3, 2001, p. 7766)
(Débats de la Chambre des Communes, le 3 décembre 2001, p. 7766)

(d) Economic Consequences of the Attack on the United States of America on September 11, 2001 / Conséquences économiques de l'attaque contre les Etats-Unis le 11 septembre 2001

Mr. Jason Kenney (Calgary Southeast):

What, if anything, is the finance minister doing to react to the economic and fiscal consequences [of Sept.11, 2001]?

Hon. Paul Martin (Minister of Finance, Liberal):

[I]t is important to understand that we are in the middle of a global slow-down. When one is in the middle of a global slowdown, one should compare how Canada has reacted to the other countries.

Since we last met, in the middle of this global slowdown we have paid down more debt than any other OECD country. We have cut our taxes more than any other G-7 country. Our dollar has been one of the strongest currencies in the world, albeit weaker than the United States. The fact is we have done better than most other countries.

(House of Commons Debates, September 18, 2001, pp. 5254-55)
(Débats de la Chambre des Communes, le 18 septembre 2001, pp. 5254-55)

Mr. Charlie Penson (Peace River):

What specifically is the government doing to develop a new border protocol that will satisfy American security requirements while maintaining the free flow of goods across that border?

Hon. Martin Cauchon (Minister of National Revenue and Secretary of State (Economic Development Agency of Canada for the Regions of Quebec)):

First ... since the tragic event we have heightened security at the border, which is to say more interviews, as well as using the technology we have such as passport and palm readers.

While facing this situation, we have to recognize that most of our economic interests are within North America. Therefore, we have to recognize that it has to keep going that way as well.

We need a balanced approach and we need to focus more on the question of perimeter, working of course with Transport Canada and the RCMP, but working as well in co-operation with the United States.

(House of Commons Debates, September 18, 2001, p. 5255)
(Débats de la Chambre des Communes, le 18 septembre 2001, p. 5255)

(e) EFTA

Mr. Rodger Cuzner (Bras d'Or — Cape Breton):

[T]he offshore supply and marine fabrication industry is starting to boom in Atlantic Canada. This is an industry that provides great promise, but a trade deal with the EFTA potentially could harm this emerging sector. Will the Minister for International Trade ensure that in any trade talks the benefits of this offshore sector will be preserved so that we can realize its maximum impact for all Canadians?

Hon. Pierre Pettigrew (Minister for International Trade):

[W]e will use due diligence. We have been considering the EFTA trade agreement for three years now. Trade is the lifeblood of Canada, but we are preoccupied with what the member has been bringing to our attention. We are continuing to consult with the shipbuilding industry and we will continue those consultations to make sure that any agreement reflects the interests of all Canadians.

(House of Commons Debates, January 28, 2002, pp. 8330-31)
(Débats de la Chambre des Communes, le 28 janvier 2002, pp. 8330-31)

(f) Inter-American Development Bank / La Banque interaméricaine de développement

Mr. Stan Dromisky (Thunder Bay — Atikokan):

[T]he Minister for International Cooperation represented Canada at the 43rd annual meeting at the Inter-American Development Bank earlier this week in Fortaleza, Brazil. Could the minister inform the House what was discussed and achieved at the meeting?

Hon. Susan Whelan (Minister for International Cooperation):

[T]he Inter-American Development Bank plays a very important role in the social and economic development for both Latin America and the Caribbean. I was very pleased earlier this week to meet with the president, Mr. Iglesias, to sign a formal agreement between Canada and the Inter-American Development Bank. Hopefully it will deepen our longstanding partnership and allow CIDA to have better investments to collaborate on specific projects and works in the Americas.

(House of Commons Debates, March 15, 2002, p. 9711)
(Débats de la Chambre des Communes, le 15 mars 2002, p. 9711)

(g)   Softwood Lumber / Bois d'œuvre

Mr. Dominic LeBlanc (Beauséjour — Petitcodiac):

[W]hat has the [Canadian] government done to defend Canada's softwood lumber industry from U.S. trade actions and protectionist American lumber industries?

Mr. Pat O'Brien (Parliamentary Secretary to the Minister of International Trade):

The government has been very active on three specific fronts relevant to softwood lumber. First, we are committed to trade action. We are now in the process of requesting a WTO panel and the government will take six measures to the WTO for adjudication regarding the U.S. trade action. We continue to hold official discussions. Last week in Toronto there was enough progress made that there will be discussions next week in Washington to look at the root causes.

   In light of the tragedy in the United States, the government is advocating quietly but persistently for our lumber industry.

(House of Commons Debates, September 28, 2001, p. 5717)
(Débats de la Chambre des Communes, le 28 septembre 2001, p. 5717)

Mr. David Pratt (Nepean — Carleton):

A recent CBC news program highlighted the connection between the timber trade in Liberia and the brutal and destabilizing regime of the country's president, Charles Taylor. It also drew attention to the fact that Liberian timber processed in a third country is sold in Canada ... [W]hat Canada is doing to break the link between natural resources and conflict with particular reference to Liberian timber?

Hon. Denis Paradis (Secretary of State (Latin America and Africa) (Francophonie)):

Canada is working with its G-8 partners to combat the wrongful use of timber resources.

Le Canada est favorable à inclure le bois dans le régime de sanctions des Nations Unies à l'encontre du Liberia. Le bois ne doit pas devenir un instrument et un moyen de financer la guerre.

Unfortunately, there has been no consensus at this time on this issue at the United Nations Security Council, but Canada will continue to push to support the inclusion of timber in the sanction regime, just like we did with diamonds.

(House of Commons Debates, June 12, 2002, pp. 12606-07)
(Débats de la Chambre des Communes, le 12 juin 2002, pp. 12606-07)

(h) WTO / OMC

Mr. Bryon Wilfert (Oak Ridges):

Canada believes that the WTO growth and development round will address the objectives and concerns of developing countries. Canada, along with other WTO members, has been working hard to demonstrate to developing countries that the new round will assist their development efforts ... [W]hat specific steps or proposals is the government prepared to make with regard to this round?

Hon. Pierre Pettigrew (Minister for International Trade):

[I]ndeed Canada has been very active ... in efforts to accommodate the developing countries. We want them to be in a position to benefit fully from their partnership in the WTO. There needs to be some capacity building there.

We need to make sure that they can get the full benefits of their membership. We need to do further work on implementation measures. We need to give them some better market access. We need to make sure that we do agricultural reform trade because that is what the south needs. We want these countries fully engaged in the WTO.

(House of Commons Debates, November 5, 2001, pp. 6934-35)
(Débats de la Chambre des Communes, le 5 novembre 2001, pp. 6934-35)

Ms. Beth Phinney (Hamilton Mountain):

[T]he Minister for International Trade returned last week from the World Trade Organization meeting in Qatar where Canada agreed to participate in the new round of negotiations. There has been a lot of talk about this being a development round. Will the minister tell the House what this means to Canadians?

Hon. Pierre Pettigrew (Minister for International Trade):

I am very proud to be back in the House having been in a position with all 142 countries of the planet to launch a new trade round at the WTO. I am very pleased because Canada has been able to meet all of its objectives.

I want to commend the work of my colleague, the Minister of Agriculture and Agri-Food, who has been able to put agriculture on the table. This is great news for Canadian farmers. We have also been able to adopt a TRIPS amendment that demonstrates all the flexibility we need for public health systems around the world.

(House of Commons Debates, November 19, 2001, p. 7263)
(Débats de la Chambre des Communes, le 19 novembre 2001, p. 7263)

Treaty Action Taken by Canada in 2001 / Mesures prises par le Canada en matière de traités en 2001

compiled by / préparé par
ANDRÉ BERGERON

André Bergeron is Treaty Registrar in the Legal Advisory Division at the Department of Foreign Affairs / Greffier des Traités, Direction des consultations juridiques, Ministère des Affaires étrangères.

I   BILATERAL

Agence Intergouvernementale de la Francophonie
Agreement between the Government of Canada and the Agence Intergouvernementale de la Francophonie. Paris, March 14, 2001. *Entered into force* March 14, 2001. CTS 2001/35.

Argentina
Treaty between the Government of Canada and the Government of the Argentine Republic on Mutual Assistance in Criminal Matters. Buenos Aires, January 12, 2000. *Entered into force* December 20, 2001. CTS 2001/31.

Australia
Agreement on Social Security between the Government of Canada and the Government of Australia. Ottawa, July 26, 2001. *Entered into force* January 1, 2003. CTS 2003/4.

Austria
Protocol between the Government of Canada and the Government of the Republic of Austria Amending the Convention for the Avoidance of Taxation and the Prevention of Fiscal Evasion with Respect to Taxes on Income and on Capital, signed at Vienna on the December 9, 1976. Vienna, June 15, 1999. *Entered into force* January 29, 2001. CTS 2001/8.

Barbados
Agreement between the Government of Canada and the Government of Barbados Regarding the Sharing of Forfeited or Confiscated Assets and Equivalent Funds. Barbados, February 26, 2001. *Entered into force* February 26, 2001. CTS 2001/36.

Belgium
Agreement between the Government of Canada and the Government of the Kingdom of Belgium on the Recognition of Driver's Licences. Brussels, December 14, 2001.

Bulgaria
Convention between the Government of Canada and the Government of the Republic of Bulgaria for the Avoidance of Double Taxation and the Prevention of Fiscal Evasion with Respect to Taxes on Income and on Capital; Protocol. Ottawa, March 3, 1999. Entered into force October 25, 2001.

Chile
Second Additional Protocol to the Free Trade Agreement between the Government of Canada and the Government of the Republic of Chile. Ottawa, October 25, 2001. *Entered into force* November 1, 2001. CTS 2001/33.

China (People's Republic of)
Agreement between the Government of Canada and the Government of the Hong Kong Special Administrative Region of the People's Republic of China on Mutual Legal Assistance in Criminal Matters. Hong Kong, February 16, 2001. Entered into force March 1, 2002.

Costa Rica
Free Trade Agreement between the Government of Canada and the Government of the Republic of Costa Rica. Ottawa, April 23, 2001. *Entered into force* November 1, 2002.

Agreement on Environmental Cooperation between the Government of Canada and the Government of the Republic of Costa Rica. Ottawa, April 23, 2001. *Entered into force* November 1, 2002.

Agreement on Labour Cooperation between the Government of Canada and the Government of the Republic of Costa Rica. Ottawa, April 23, 2001. *Entered into force* November 1, 2002.

Croatia
Agreement between the Government of Canada and the Government of the Republic of Croatia for the Promotion and Protection of Investments. Ottawa, February 3, 1997. Entered into force January 30, 2001. CTS 2001/4.

Czech Republic
Agreement on Social Security between Canada and the Czech Republic. Prague, May 24, 2001. *Entered into force* January 1, 2003. CTS 2003/3.

Convention between Canada and the Czech Republic for the Avoidance of Double Taxation and the Prevention of Fiscal Evasion with Respect to Taxes on Income. Prague, May 25, 2001. *Entered into force* May 28, 2002. CTS 2002/11.

Ecuador
Convention between the Government of Canada and the Government of the Republic of Ecuador for the Avoidance of Double Taxation and the Prevention of Fiscal Evasion with Respect to Taxes on Income. Quito, June 28, 2001. *Entered into force* December 20, 2001. CTS 2001/34.

European Community
Agreement between the Government of Canada and the European Community Renewing a Cooperation Programme in Higher Education and Training. Ottawa, December 19, 2000. *Entered into force* March 1, 2001. CTS 2001/16.

France
Amendment to the Agreement of October 4, 1956 between the Government of Canada and the Government of the French Republic on the Admission of Trainees to Canada and to France. Paris, February 6, 2001. Entered into force February 6, 2001. CTS 2001/6.

Agreement between the Government of Canada and the Government of the French Republic Concerning the Working Holiday Program. Paris, February 6, 2001. Entered into force June 1, 2001. CTS 2001/12.

Germany (Federal Republic of)
Agreement between Canada and the Federal Republic of Germany for the Avoidance of Double Taxation with Respect to Taxes on Income and Certain Other Taxes, the Prevention of Fiscal Evasion and the Assistance in Tax Matters; Protocol to the Agreement between Canada and the Federal Republic of Germany for the Avoidance of Double Taxation with Respect to Taxes on Income and Certain Other Taxes, the Prevention of Fiscal Evasion and the Assistance in Tax Matters.

Berlin, April 19, 2001. Entered into force March 28, 2002. CTS 2002/6.

Korea (Republic of)
Agreement between the Government of Canada and the Government of the Republic of Korea on the Production of the Bell Helicopter Textron Canada Model 427 Helicopter. Ottawa, June 4, 2001. Entered into force June 4, 2001. CTS 2001/18.

Exchange of Notes between the Government of Canada and the Government of the Republic of Korea Constituting an Agreement Relating to the Transfer of Tritium Items for the Wolsong Tritium Removal Facility. Seoul, January 19, 2001. *Entered into force* January 19, 2001. CTS 2001/5.

Agreement between the Government of Canada and the Government of the Republic of Korea on the Procurement of Telecommunications Equipment. Ottawa, July 5, 1999. Entered into force September 1, 2001. CTS 2001/24.

Luxembourg
Agreement between the Government of Canada and the Government of the Grand Duchy of Luxembourg Concerning the Sharing of Confiscated Property and Equivalent Amounts of Money. Brussels, Luxembourg, July 24, 2001. Entered into force July 24, 2001. CTS 2001/25.

Mexico
Exchange of Letters between the Government of Canada and the Government of the United Mexican States Constituting an Agreement Amending the Tariff Schedules to Annex 302.2 of the North American Free Trade Agreement (NAFTA). Ottawa, December 28, 2000. *Entered into force* January 1, 2001.

Exchange of Letters between the Government of Canada and the Government of the United Mexican States Constituting an Agreement Amending the Tariff Schedules to Annex 302.2 of the North American Free Trade Agreement. Mexico, Ottawa, December 12,

2001. Entered into force January 1, 2002. CTS 2002/15.

Agreement between the Government of Canada and the Government of the United Mexican States Regarding the Application of Their Competition Laws. Veracruz, November 15, 2001. Entered into force March 20, 2003.

Protocol between the Government of Canada and the Government of the United Mexican States Concerning the Transmission and Reception of Signals from Satellites for the Provision of Mobile-Satellite Services and Associated Feeder Links in Canada and in the United Mexican States. Mexico, January 16, 2001. Entered into force January 16, 2001. CTS 2001/13.

Protocol between the Government of Canada and the Government of the United Mexican States Concerning the Transmission and Reception from Satellites for the Provision of Fixed Satellite Services in Canada and in the United Mexican States. Mexico, January 16, 2001. *Entered into force* January 16, 2001. CTS 2001/14.

Netherlands
Agreement on Social Security between the Government of Canada and the Government of the Kingdom of the Netherlands; Protocol on Mutual Assistance pursuant to the Agreement on Social Security between the Government of Canada and the Government of the Kingdom of the Netherlands. Brantford, June 27, 2001.

Peru
Convention between the Government of Canada and the Government of the Republic of Peru for the Avoidance of Double Taxation and the Prevention of Fiscal Evasion with Respect to Taxes on Income and on Capital. Lima, July 20, 2001. *Entered into force* February 17, 2003.

Philippines
Supplementary Agreement to the Agreement on Social Security between

Canada and the Republic of the Philippines. Winnipeg, November 13, 1999. *Entered into force* July 1, 2001. CTS 2001/11.

Portugal

Convention between the Government of Canada and the Government of the Portuguese Republic for the Avoidance of Double Taxation and the Prevention of Fiscal Evasion with Respect to Taxes on Income; Protocol. Ottawa, June 14, 1999. *Entered into force* October 24, 2001. CTS 2001/27.

Russian Federation

Air Services Agreement between the Government of Canada and the Government of the Russian Federation. Ottawa, December 18, 2000. *Entered into force* March 9, 2001. CTS 2001/15.

Senegal

Convention between the Government of Canada and the Government of the Republic of Senegal for the Avoidance of Double Taxation and the Prevention of Fiscal Evasion with Respect to Taxes on Income. Dakar, August 2, 2001.

Slovak Republic

Agreement on Social Security between Canada and the Slovak Republic. Bratislava, May 21, 2001. *Entered into force* January 1, 2003. CTS 2003/2.

Agreement between the Government of Canada and the Government of the Slovak Republic for the Avoidance of Double Taxation and the Prevention of Fiscal Evasion with Respect to Taxes on Income and on Capital. Bratislava, May 22, 2001. *Entered into force* December 18, 2001. CTS 2001/37.

Slovenia

Agreement on Social Security between the Government of Canada and the Government of the Republic of Slovenia. Ljubljana, May 17, 1998. *Entered into force* January 1, 2001. CTS 2001/3.

South Africa

Treaty between the Government of Canada and the Government of the Republic of South Africa on Extradition. Durban, November 12, 1999. *Entered into force* May 4, 2001. CTS 2001/20.

Treaty between the Government of Canada and the Government of the Republic of South Africa on Mutual Legal Assistance in Criminal Matters. Durban, November 12, 1999. *Entered into force* May 4, 2001. CTS 2001/19.

Sweden

Treaty on Extradition between the Government of Canada and the Government of Sweden. Stockholm, February 15, 2000. *Entered into force* October 30, 2001. CTS 2001/28.

Treaty between the Government of Canada and the Government of Sweden on Mutual Assistance in Criminal Matters. Stockholm, February 15, 2000. Entered into force 1 December 2001. CTS 2001/29.

Switzerland

Agreement between the Government of Canada and the Swiss Confederation Concerning the Division of Confiscated Assets and Equivalent Sums of Money. Ottawa, May 22, 2001. *Entered into force* May 22, 2001. CTS 2001/17.

UNESCO

Agreement between the Government of Canada and the United Nations Educational, Scientific and Cultural Organization concerning the Establishment of the Seat of the Unesco Institute for Statistics. Paris, May 18, 2001. *Entered into force* May 18, 2001. CTS 2001/32.

United Arab Emirates

Agreement between the Government of Canada and the Government of the United Arab Emirates on Air Transport. Abu Dhabi, June 17, 2001. *Entered into force* June 17, 2001. CTS 2001/22.

United Kingdom of Great Britain and Northern Ireland

Agreement between the Government of Canada and the Government of the

United Kingdom of Great Britain and Northern Ireland Regarding the Sharing of Forfeited or Confiscated Assets or Their Equivalent Funds. London, February 21, 2001. *Entered into force* February 21, 2001. CTS 2001/9.

United States of America
Agreement on Air Transport Preclearance between the Government of Canada and the Government of the United States of America. Toronto, January 18, 2001. *Entered into force* May 2, 2003.

Second Protocol Amending the Treaty on Extradition between the Government of Canada and the Government of the United States of America. Ottawa, January 12, 2001. Entered into force April 30, 2003.

Venezuela
Convention between the Government of Canada and the Government of the Bolivarian Republic of Venezuela for the Avoidance of Double Taxation and the Prevention of Fiscal Avoidance and Evasion with Respect to Taxes on Income and on Capital. Caracas, July 10, 2001.

II   MULTILATERAL

Agriculture
Amendments to the International Plant Protection Convention of 1951, as amended in 1979. Rome, November 18, 1997. *Acceptance* by Canada October 22, 2001.

International Treaty on Plant Genetic Resources for Food and Agriculture. Rome, November 3, 2001. *Signed* by Canada June 10, 2002. *Ratified* by Canada June 10, 2002.

Aviation
Protocol Relating to an Amendment to the Convention on International Civil Aviation. Montréal, September 29, 1995. *Ratified* by Canada December 7, 2001.

Protocol on the Authentic Quinquelingual Text of the Convention on International Civil Aviation (Chicago, 1944). Montréal, September 29, 1995. *Acceptance* by Canada December 7, 2001.

Protocol Relating to an Amendment to the Convention on International Civil Aviation. Montréal, October 1, 1998. *Ratified* by Canada December 7, 2001.

Protocol on the Authentic Six-Language Text of the Convention on International Civil Aviation (Chicago, 1944). Montréal, October 1, 1998. *Acceptance* by Canada December 7, 2001.

Convention for the Unification of Certain Rules for International Carriage by Air. Montréal, May 28, 1999. *Signed* by Canada October 1, 2001. *Ratified* by Canada November 19, 2002.

Conservation
Convention on the Conservation and Management of Highly Migratory Fish Stocks in the Western and Central Pacific Ocean. Honolulu, September 5, 2000. *Signed* by Canada August 2, 2001.

Criminal International Law
Convention on Cybercrime. Budapest, November 23, 2001. *Signed* by Canada November 23, 2001.

Disarmament
Amendment to the Convention on Prohibitions or Restrictions on the Use of Certain Conventional Weapons Which May Be Deemed to be Excessively Injurious or to Have Indiscriminate Effects (with Protocols I, II and III). Geneva, December 21, 2001. *Acceptance* by Canada July 22, 2002.

Environment
Amendment to the Montreal Protocol on Substances That Deplete the Ozone Layer. Beijing, December 3, 1999. *Acceptance* by Canada February 9, 2001. *Entered into force* February 25, 2002.

Cartagena Protocol on Biosafety to the Convention on Biological Diversity.

Montréal, January 29, 2000. *Signed* by Canada April 19, 2001.

Stockholm Convention on Persistent Organic Pollutants. Stockholm, May 22, 2001. *Signed* by Canada May 23, 2001. *Ratified* by Canada May 23, 2001.

Human Rights
Optional Protocol to the Convention on the Rights of the Child on the Sale of Children, Child Prostitution and Child Pornography. New York, May 25, 2000. *Signed* by Canada November 10, 2001. *Entered into force* January 18, 2002.

Labour
Convention Concerning the Prohibition and Immediate Action for the Elimination of the Worst Forms of Child Labour. Geneva, June 17, 1999. *Ratified* by Canada June 6, 2000. *Entered into force* November 19, 2000. CTS 2001/2.

Law of the Sea
Agreement for the Implementation of the Provisions of the United Nations Convention on the Law of the Sea of 10 December 1982 Relating to the Conservation and Management of Straddling Fish Stocks and Highly Migratory Fish Stocks. New York, August 4, 1995. *Signed* by Canada December 4, 1995. *Ratified* by Canada August 3, 1999. *Entered into force* December 11, 2001.

Nuclear
Joint Convention on the Safety of Spent Fuel Management and on the Safety of Radioactive Waste Management. Vienna, September 5, 1997. *Signed* by Canada May 7, 1998. *Ratified* by Canada May 7, 1998. *Entered into force* June 18, 2001. CTS 2001/10.

Protocol Amending the Security Annex to the Agreement between the Parties to the North Atlantic Treaty for Co-operation Regarding Atomic Information. Brussels, June 2, 1998. *Signed* by Canada March 13, 2001. *Ratified* by Canada October 29, 2001.

Outer Space
Agreement among the Government of Canada, Governments of Member States of the European Space Agency, the Government of Japan, the Government of the Russian Federation and the Government of the United States of America Concerning Co-operation on the Civil International Space Station. Washington, January 29, 1998. *Signed* by Canada January 29, 1998. *Ratified* by Canada July 24, 2000. *Entered into force* March 27, 2001.

Patents
Patent Law Treaty. Geneva, June 2, 2000. *Signed* by Canada May 21, 2001.

Postal Matters
Sixth Additional Protocol to the Constitution of the Universal Postal Union; General Regulations of the Universal Postal Union; Universal Postal Convention; Postal Payment Services Agreement, Beijing, September 14, 1999. *Signed* by Canada September 14, 1999. *Ratified* by Canada February 23, 2001. *Entered into force* January 1, 2001.

Telecommunications
1998 Amendments to the International Mobile Satellite Organization (INMARSAT) Convention and Operating Agreement for the Restructuring of INMARSAT and Amendment to the Operating Agreement on the International Mobile Satellite Organization (with Annex for the Change of Name of the Organization), London, April 24, 1998. *Acceptance* by Canada July 20, 1999. *Entered into force* July 31, 2001.

Operating Agreement on the INMARSAT. London, April 24, 1998. *Signed* by Canada September 18, 1998. *Entered into force* July 31, 2001.

Tampere Convention on the Provision of Telecommunication Resources for Disaster Mitigation and Relief Operations. Tampere, June 18, 1998. *Signed* by Canada June 15, 1999. *Ratified* by Canada May 18, 2001.

Terrorism
International Convention for the Suppression of Terrorist Bombings. New York, December 15, 1997. *Signed* by Canada January 12, 1998. *Entered into force* May 23, 2001. *Ratified* by Canada April 3, 2002. CTS 2002/8.

Trade
Agreement Establishing the Advisory Centre on WTO Law. Seattle, November 30, 1999. *Signed* by Canada December 1, 1999. *Entered into force* July 15, 2001. CTS 2001/21.

Agreement on Mutual Recognition in Relation to Conformity Assessment between Canada and the Republic of Iceland, the Principality of Liechtenstein and the Kingdom of Norway. Brussels, July 4, 2000. *Signed* by Canada July 4, 2000. *Entered into force* January 1, 2001. CTS 2001/7.

Exchange of Letters (November 21 and December 12, 2002) Constituting an Agreement between Canada, the United Mexican States and the United States of America Rectifying Annex 300-B, Annex 401, Annex 403.1, the Uniform Regulations for Chapters Three and Five and the Uniform Regulations for Chapter Four of the North American Free Trade Agreement. Mexico, Ottawa, Washington, December 12, 2001. *Signed* by Canada December 12, 2001. *Entered into force* January 1, 2002. CTS 2002/17.

Agreement on Mutual Acceptance of Oenological Practices. Toronto, December 18, 2001. *Signed* by Canada December 18, 2001. *Ratified* by Canada November 27, 2002.

Transnational Crime
Protocol against the Illicit Manufacturing of and Trafficking in Firearms, Their Parts and Components and Ammunition, Supplementing the United Nations Convention against Transnational Organized Crime. New York,

May 31, 2001. *Signed* by Canada March 20, 2002.

I BILATÉRAUX

Afrique du Sud
Traité d'entraide judiciaire en matière pénale entre le gouvernement du Canada et le gouvernement de la République d'Afrique du Sud. Durban, 12 novembre 1999. *En vigueur* le 4 mai 2001. RTC 2001/19.

Traité d'extradition entre le gouvernement du Canada et le gouvernement de la République d'Afrique du Sud. Durban, 12 novembre 1999. *En vigueur* le 4 mai 2001. RTC 2001/20.

Agence intergouvernementale de la Francophonie
Accord entre le gouvernement du Canada et l'Agence intergouvernementale de la Francophonie. Paris, 14 mars 2001. *En vigueur* le 14 mars 2001. RTC 2001/35.

Allemagne (République fédérale d')
Accord entre le Canada et la République fédérale d'Allemagne en vue d'éviter les doubles impositions en matière d'impôts sur le revenu et de certains autres impôts, de prévenir l'évasion fiscale et de fournir assistance en matière d'impôts; Protocole à l'Accord entre le Canada et la République fédérale d'Allemagne en vue d'éviter les doubles impositions en matière d'impôts sur le revenu et de certains autres impôts, de prévenir l'évasion fiscale et de fournir assistance en matière d'impôts. Berlin, 19 avril 2001. *En vigueur* le 28 mars 2002. RTC 2002/6.

Argentine
Traité d'entraide judiciaire en matière pénale entre le gouvernement du Canada et le gouvernement de la République argentine. Buenos Aires, 12 janvier 2000. *En vigueur* le 20 décembre 2001. RTC 2003/4.

Autriche

Protocole entre le gouvernement du Canada et le gouvernement de la République d'Autriche modifiant la Convention tendant à éviter les doubles impositions et à prévenir l'évasion fiscale en matière d'impôts sur le revenu et sur la fortune, signée à Vienne le 9 décembre 1976. Vienne, 15 juin 1999. *En vigueur* le 29 janvier 2001. RTC 2001/8.

Barbade

Accord entre le gouvernement du Canada et le gouvernement de la Barbade au sujet du partage des biens confisqués ou des sommes d'argent équivalentes. Barbade, 26 février 2001. *En vigueur* le 26 février 2001. RTC 2001/36.

Belgique

Accord entre le gouvernement du Canada et le gouvernement du Royaume de Belgique sur la reconnaissance des permis de conduire. Bruxelles, 14 décembre 2001.

Bulgarie

Convention entre le gouvernement du Canada et le gouvernement de la République de Bulgarie en vue d'éviter les doubles impositions et de prévenir l'évasion fiscale en matière d'impôts sur le revenu et sur la fortune; Protocole. Ottawa, 3 mars 1999. *En vigueur* le 25 octobre 2001.

Chili

Deuxième Protocole supplémentaire au Traité de libre échange entre le gouvernement du Canada et le gouvernement de la République du Chili. Ottawa, 25 octobre 2001. *En vigueur* le 1er novembre 2001. RTC 2001/33.

Chine (République populaire de)

Accord d'entraide juridique en matière pénale entre le gouvernement du Canada et le gouvernement de la Région administrative spéciale de Hong Kong de la République populaire de Chine. Hong Kong, 16 février 2001. *En vigueur* le 1er mars 2002.

Communauté européenne

Accord entre le gouvernement du Canada et la Communauté européenne renouvelant un programme de coopération dans le domaine de l'enseignement supérieur et de la formation. Ottawa, 19 décembre 2000. *En vigueur* le 1er mars 2001. RTC 2001/16.

Corée (République de)

Accord entre le gouvernement du Canada et le gouvernement de la République de Corée relatif à la production de l'hélicoptère de Modèle 427 de Bell Helicopter Textron Canada. Ottawa, 4 juin 2001. *En vigueur* le 4 juin 2001. RTC 2001/18.

Échange de notes entre le gouvernement du Canada et le gouvernement de la République de Corée constituant un Accord relatif au transfert d'articles afférents au tritium destinés à l'usine d'extraction du tritium de Wolsong. Séoul, 19 janvier 2001. *En vigueur* le 19 janvier 2001. RTC 2001/5.

Accord entre le gouvernement du Canada et le gouvernement de la République de Corée sur les marchés d'équipements de télécommunications. Ottawa, 5 juillet 1999. En vigueur le 1er septembre 2001. RTC 2001/24.

Costa Rica

Accord de libre-échange entre le gouvernement du Canada et le gouvernement de la République du Costa Rica. Ottawa, 23 avril 2001. *En vigueur* le 1er novembre 2002

Accord de coopération environnementale entre le gouvernement du Canada et le gouvernement de la République du Costa Rica. Ottawa, 23 avril 2001. En vigueur le 1er novembre 2002.

Accord de coopération dans le domaine du travail entre le gouvernement du Canada et le gouvernement de la République du Costa Rica. Ottawa, 23 avril 2001. *En vigueur* le 1er novembre 2002.

Croatie
Accord entre le gouvernement du Canada et le gouvernement de la République de Croatie pour l'encouragement et la protection des investissements. Ottawa, 3 février 1997. *En vigueur* le 30 janvier 2001. RTC 2001/4.

Émirats arabes unis
Accord sur le transport aérien entre le gouvernement du Canada et le gouvernement des Émirats arabes unis. Abu Dhabi, 17 juin 2001. *En vigueur* le 17 juin 2001. RTC 2001/22.

Équateur
Convention entre le gouvernement du Canada et le gouvernement de la République de l'Équateur en vue d'éviter les doubles impositions et de prévenir l'évasion fiscale en matière d'impôts sur le revenu. Quito, 28 juin 2001. *En vigueur* le 20 décembre 2001. RTC 2001/34.

États-Unis d'Amérique
Accord entre le gouvernement du Canada et le gouvernement des États-Unis d'Amérique relatif au précontrôle dans le domaine du transport aérien. Toronto, 18 janvier 2001. *En vigueur* le 2 mai 2003.

Deuxième protocole modifiant le Traité d'extradition entre le gouvernement du Canada et le gouvernement des États-Unis d'Amérique. Ottawa, 12 janvier 2001. *En vigueur* le 30 avril 2003.

Fédération de Russie
Accord de transport aérien entre le gouvernement du Canada et le gouvernement de la Fédération de Russie. Ottawa, 18 décembre 2000. *En vigueur* le 9 mars 2001. RTC 2001/15.

France
Avenant à l'Accord du 4 octobre 1956 entre le gouvernement du Canada et le gouvernement de la République française relatif à l'admission de stagiaires au Canada et en France. Paris, 6 février 2001. *En vigueur* le 6 février 2001. RTC 2001/6.

Accord entre le gouvernement du Canada et le gouvernement de la République française relatif au programme vacances-travaux. Paris, 6 février 2001. *En vigueur* le 1er juin 2001. RTC 2001/12.

Luxembourg
Accord entre le gouvernement du Canada et le gouvernement du Grand-Duché de Luxembourg concernant le partage des biens confisqués et des sommes d'argent équivalentes. Bruxelles, Luxembourg, 24 juillet 2001. *En vigueur* le 24 juillet 2001. RTC 2001/25.

Mexique
Échange de lettres entre le gouvernement du Canada et le gouvernement des États-Unis du Mexique constituant un Accord modifiant les listes tarifaires de l'Annexe 302.2 de l'Accord de libre-échange nord-américain (ALÉNA). Ottawa, 28 décembre 2000. *En vigueur* le 1er janvier 2001.

Échange de lettres entre le gouvernement du Canada et le gouvernement des États-Unis du Mexique constituant un Accord modifiant les listes tarifaires de l'Annexe 302.2 de l'Accord de libre-échange nord-américain. Mexico, Ottawa, 12 décembre 2001. *En vigueur* le 1er janvier 2002. RTC 2002/15.

Accord entre le gouvernement du Canada et le gouvernement des États-Unis du Mexique concernant l'application de leurs lois sur la concurrence. Veracruz, 15 novembre 2001. *En vigueur* le 20 mars 2003.

Protocole entre le gouvernement du Canada et le gouvernement des États-Unis du Mexique relatif à l'émission et à la réception de signaux par satellite pour la fourniture de services mobiles par satellite de liaisons de connexion associées au Canada et aux États-Unis du Mexique. Mexico, 16 janvier 2001. *En vigueur* le 16 janvier 2001. RTC 2001/13.

Protocole entre le gouvernement du Canada et le gouvernement des États-Unis du Mexique relatif à l'émission et à la réception de signaux par satellite pour la fourniture de services fixes par satellite au Canada et aux États-Unis du Mexique. Mexico, 16 janvier 2001. *En vigueur* le 16 janvier 2001. RTC 2001/14.

Pays-Bas
Accord sur la sécurité sociale entre le gouvernement du Canada et le gouvernement du Royaume des Pays-Bas; Protocole sur l'assistance mutuelle en vertu de l'accord sur la sécurité sociale entre le gouvernement du Canada et le gouvernement du Royaume des Pays-Bas. Brantford, 27 juin 2001.

Pérou
Convention entre le gouvernement du Canada et le gouvernement de la République du Pérou en vue d'éviter les doubles impositions et de prévenir l'évasion fiscale en matière d'impôts sur le revenu et sur la fortune. Lima, 20 juillet 2001. *En vigueur* le 17 février 2003.

Philippines
Accord supplémentaire à l'Accord sur la sécurité sociale entre le Canada et la République des Philippines. Winnipeg, 13 novembre 1999. *En vigueur* le 1er juillet 2001. RTC 2001/11.

Portugal
Convention entre le gouvernement du Canada et le gouvernement de la République portugaise en vue d'éviter les doubles impositions et de prévenir l'évasion fiscale en matière d'impôts sur le revenu; Protocole. Ottawa, 14 juin 1999. *En vigueur* le 24 octobre 2001. RTC 2001/27.

République slovaque
Accord entre le gouvernement du Canada et le gouvernement de la République slovaque en vue d'éviter les doubles impositions et de prévenir l'évasion fiscale en matière d'impôts sur le revenu et sur la fortune. Bratislava, 22

mai 2001. *En vigueur* le 18 décembre 2001. RTC 2001/37.

Accord sur la sécurité sociale entre le Canada et la République slovaque. Bratislava, 21 mai 2001. En vigueur le 1er janvier 2003. RTC 2003/2.

République tchèque
Convention entre le Canada et la République tchèque en vue d'éviter les doubles impositions et de prévenir l'évasion fiscale en matière d'impôts sur le revenu. Prague, 25 mai 2001. *En vigueur* le 28 mai 2002. RTC 2002/11.

Accord sur la sécurité sociale entre le Canada et la République tchèque. Prague, 24 mai 2001. *En vigueur* le 1er janvier 2003. RTC 2003/3.

Royaume-Uni de Grande-Bretagne et d'Irlande du Nord
Accord entre le gouvernement du Canada et le gouvernement du Royaume-Uni de Grande-Bretagne et d'Irlande du Nord concernant le partage de biens confisqués ou des sommes d'argent équivalentes. Londres, 21 février 2001. *En vigueur* le 21 février 2001. RTC 2001/9.

Sénégal
Convention entre le gouvernement du Canada et le gouvernement de la République du Sénégal en vue d'éviter les doubles impositions et de prévenir l'évasion fiscale en matière d'impôts sur le revenu. Dakar, 2 août 2001.

Slovénie
Accord sur la sécurité sociale entre le gouvernement du Canada et le gouvernement de la République de Slovénie. Ljubljana, 17 mai 1998. *En vigueur* le 1er janvier 2001. RTC 2001/3.

Suède
Traité d'entraide judiciaire en matière pénale entre le gouvernement du Canada et le gouvernement de la Suède. Stockholm, 15 février 2000. *En vigueur* le 1er décembre 2001. RTC 2001/29.

Traité d'extradition entre le gouvernement du Canada et le gouvernement de la Suède. Stockholm, 15 février 2000. *En vigueur* le 30 octobre 2001. RTC 2001/28.

Suisse
Accord entre le gouvernement du Canada et la Confédération suisse concernant le partage des biens confisqués et des sommes d'argent équivalentes. Ottawa, 22 mai 2001. *En vigueur* le 22 mai 2001. RTC 2001/17.

UNESCO
Accord entre le gouvernement du Canada et l'Organisation des Nations Unies pour l'éducation, la science et la culture concernant l'établissement au Canada du siège de l'Institut de Statistique de l'UNESCO. Paris, 18 mai 2001. *En vigueur* le 18 mai 2001. RTC 2001/32.

Venezuela
Convention entre le gouvernement du Canada et le gouvernement de la République bolivarienne du Venezuela en vue d'éviter les doubles impositions et de prévenir l'évasion et la fraude fiscales en matière d'impôts sur le revenu et sur la fortune. Caracas, 10 juillet 2001.

II MULTILATÉRAUX

Agriculture
Amendements à la Convention internationale pour la protection des végétaux de 1951, tel qu'amendée en 1979. Rome, le 18 novembre 1997. *Acceptation* par le Canada le 22 octobre 2001.

Traité international sur les ressources phytogénétiques pour l'alimentation et l'agriculture. Rome, le 3 novembre 2001. Signé par le Canada le 10 juin 2002. Ratifié par le Canada le 10 juin 2002.

Aviation
Protocole concernant un amendement de la Convention relative à l'aviation civile internationale. Montréal, le 29 septembre 1995. *Ratifié* par le Canada le 7 décembre 2001.

Protocole concernant le texte authentique quinquélingue de la Convention relative à l'aviation civile internationale (Chicago, 1944). Montréal, le 29 septembre 1995. *Acceptation* par le Canada le 7 décembre 2001.

Protocole concernant un amendement de la Convention relative à l'aviation civile internationale. Montréal, le 1er octobre 1998. *Ratifié* par le Canada le 7 décembre 2001.

Protocole concernant le texte authentique en six langues de la Convention relative à l'aviation civile internationale (Chicago, 1944). Montréal, le 1er octobre 1998. *Acceptation* par le Canada le 7 décembre 2001.

Convention pour l'unification de certaines règles relatives au transport aérien international. Montréal, le 28 mai 1999. *Signée* par le Canada le 1er octobre 2001. *Ratifiée* par le Canada le 19 novembre 2002.

Brevets
Traité sur le droit des brevets. Genève, le 2 juin 2000. *Signé* par le Canada le 21 mai 2001.

Commerce
Accord instituant le Centre consultatif sur la législation de l'OMC. Seattle, le 30 novembre 1999. *Signé* par le Canada le 1er décembre 1999. *En vigueur* le 15 décembre 2001. RTC 2001/21.

Accord de reconnaissance mutuelle en matière d'évaluation de la conformité entre le Canada et la République d'Islande, la Principauté de Liechtenstein et le Royaume de Norvège. Bruxelles, le 4 juillet 2000. Signé par le Canada le 4 juillet 2000. *En vigueur* le 1er janvier 2001. RTC 2001/7.

Échange de lettres (21 novembre et 12 décembre 2002) constituant un accord entre le Canada, les États-Unis d'Amérique et les États-Unis du Mexique rectifiant l'annexe 300-B, l'annexe 401, l'annexe 403.1, le Règlement uniforme des chapitres trois et cinq et le Règlement uniforme du chapitre quatre de l'Accord de libre-échange nord-américain. Mexico, Ottawa, Washington, le 12 décembre 2001. *Signé* par le Canada le 12 décembre 2001. En vigueur le 1er décembre 2002. RTC 2002/17.

Accord d'acceptation mutuelle des pratiques œnologiques. Toronto, le 18 décembre 2001. *Signé* par le Canada le 18 décembre 2001. *Ratifié* par le Canada le 27 novembre 2002.

Conservation
Convention relative à la conservation et à la gestion de poissons grands migrateurs dans le Pacifique occidental et central. Honolulu, le 5 septembre 2000. *Signée* par le Canada le 2 août 2001.

Criminalité transnationale
Protocole contre la fabrication et le trafic illicites d'armes à feu, de leurs pièces, éléments et munitions, additionnel à la Convention des Nations Unies contre la criminalité transnationale organisée. New York, le 31 mai 2001. *Signé* par le Canada le 20 mars 2002.

Désarmement
Amendement à la Convention sur l'interdiction ou la limitation de l'emploi de certaines armes classiques qui peuvent être considérées comme produisant des effets traumatiques excessifs ou comme frappant sans discrimination (avec Protocoles I, II et III). Genève, le 21 décembre 2001. *Acceptation* par le Canada le 22 juillet 2002.

Droit de la mer
Accord aux fins de l'application des dispositions de la Convention des Nations Unies sur le droit de la mer du 10 décembre 1982 relatives à la conservation et à la gestion des stocks de poissons dont les déplacements s'effectuent tant à l'intérieur qu'au-delà des zones économiques exclusives (stocks chevauchants) et des stocks de poissons grands migrateurs. New York,

le 4 août 1995. *Signé* par le Canada le 4 décembre 1995. *Ratifié* par le Canada le 3 août 1999. *En vigueur* le 11 août 2001.

Droit pénal international
Convention sur la cybercriminalité. Budapest, le 23 novembre 2001. *Signée* par le Canada le 23 novembre 2001.

Droits de la personne
Protocole facultatif à la Convention relative aux droits de l'enfant, concernant la vente d'enfants, la prostitution des enfants et la pornographie mettant en scène des enfants. New York, le 25 mai 2000. *Signé* par le Canada le 10 novembre 2001. *En vigueur* le 18 novembre 2002.

Énergie nucléaire
Convention commune sur la sûreté de la gestion du combustible usé et sur la sûreté de la gestion des déchets radioactifs. Vienne, le 5 septembre 1997. *Signée* par le Canada le 7 mai 1998. *Ratifiée* par le Canada le 7 mai 1998. *En vigueur* le 18 mai 2001. RTC 2001/10.

Protocole modifiant l'Annexe de sécurité à l'Accord entre les États parties au Traité de l'Atlantique Nord sur la coopération dans le domaine des renseignements atomiques. Bruxelles, le 2 juin 1998. *Signé* par le Canada le 13 mars 2001. *Ratifié* par le Canada le 29 octobre 2001.

Environnement
Amendement au protocole de Montréal relatif aux substances qui appauvrissent la couche d'ozone. Beijing, le 3 décembre 1999. *Acceptation* par le Canada le 9 février 2001. *En vigueur* le 25 février 2002.

Protocole de Cartagena sur la prévention des risques biotechnologiques relatif à la Convention sur la diversité biologique. Montréal, le 29 janvier 2000. *Signé* par le Canada le 19 avril 2001.

Convention de Stockholm sur les polluants organiques persistants. Stockholm, le 22 mai 2001. *Signée* par le

Canada le 23 mai 2001. *Ratifiée* par le Canada le 23 mai 2001.

Espace extra-atmosphérique
Accord entre le gouvernement du Canada, les gouvernements d'États membres de l'Agence spatiale européenne, le gouvernement du Japon, le gouvernement de la Fédération de Russie et le gouvernement des États-Unis d'Amérique sur la coopération relative à la station spatiale internationale civile. Washington, le 29 janvier 1998. *Signé* par le Canada le 29 janvier 1998. *Ratifié* par le Canada le 24 juillet 2000. *En vigueur* le 27 juillet 2001.

Questions postales
Sixième Protocole additionnel à la Constitution de l'Union postale universelle, Règlement général de l'Union postale universelle, Convention postale universelle, Arrangement concernant les services de paiement de la poste. Beijing, le 14 septembre 1999. *Signé* par le Canada le 14 septembre 1999. *En vigueur* le 1ᵉʳ février 2001. *Ratifié* par le Canada le 23 février 2001.

Télécommunications
Amendements à la Convention portant création de l'organisation internationale de télécommunications mobiles par satellites et amendement à l'Accord d'exploitation relatif à l'Organisation internationale de télécommunications mobiles par satellites (avec Annexe modifiant le nom de l'Organisation. Londres, le 24 avril 1998. *Acceptation* par le Canada le 20 juillet 1999. *En vigueur* le 31 juillet 2001.

Accord d'exploitation relatif à l'Organisation internationale de télécommunications mobiles par satellites (INMARSAT). Londres, le 24 avril 1998. *Signé* par le Canada le 18 septembre 1998. *En vigueur* le 31 septembre 2001.

Convention de Tampere sur la mise à disposition de ressources de télécommunication pour l'atténuation des effets des catastrophes et pour les opérations de secours en cas de catastrophe. Tampere, le 18 juin 1998. *Signée* par le Canada le 15 juin 1999. *Ratifiée* par le Canada le 18 mai 2001

Terrorisme
Convention internationale pour la répression des attentats terroristes à l'explosif. New York, le 15 décembre 1997. *Signée* par le Canada le 12 janvier 1998. *En vigueur* le 23 avril 2001. *Ratifiée* par le Canada le 3 avril 2002. RTC 2002/8.

Travail
Convention concernant l'interdiction des pires formes de travail des enfants et l'action immédiate en vue de leur élimination. Genève, le 17 juin 1999. *Ratifiée* par le Canada le 6 juin 2000. *En vigueur* le 19 juin 2000. RTC 2001/2.

Cases / Jurisprudence

Canadian Cases in Public International Law in 2001-2 / Jurisprudence canadienne en matière de droit international public en 2001-2

compiled by / préparé par
KARIN MICKELSON

Diplomats — status in Canada

Copello v. *Canada (Minister of Foreign Affairs)*, [2002] 3 F.C. 24 (Federal Court Trial Division)

The applicant, a diplomat with the Italian Foreign Ministry posted to Ottawa, sought to quash a decision of the Minister of Foreign Affairs requesting that the applicant and his family depart Canada, as communicated to the Italian government through a diplomatic note.

The request for Mr. Copello's recall amounts to a declaration of *persona non grata*. The issue is whether that request was made pursuant to the exercise of the Crown prerogative or if it was made pursuant to a domestic statute. Article 9 of the Vienna Convention on Diplomatic Relations, which grants the receiving state the right to declare any member of the diplomatic staff of a country *persona non grata*, without having to explain its decision, is not given force of law in Canada through the Foreign Missions and International Organizations Act, S.C. 1991, c. 41. In the absence of implementation by Canada, Article 9 does not form part of domestic law. The exclusion of this article can only mean that Parliament intended that the expulsion of diplomats remain in the sphere of the Crown prerogative in the conduct of foreign affairs by Canada, and

Karin Mickelson is in the Faculty of Law at the University of British Columbia.

immune from judicial review. A declaration of *persona non grata* is not a legal issue and remains in the political arena.

Heneghan J. went on to deal briefly with the issues of standing and whether the applicant was owed a duty of fairness. With regard to the former, the decision was expressed in a diplomatic note, which is a communication between states. While the request for the recall of the applicant affected the applicant, it remained a matter of relations between states. The applicant was in Canada only in a representative capacity and, as such, he held no independent status. He lacks standing to challenge the actions of the minister. With regard to the latter, the declaration of *persona non grata* is not an administrative function carried out by the minister pursuant to the act. It is not analogous to a decision by the minister of citizenship and immigration to issue a deportation order. The applicant was in Canada solely as a representative of the Italian government and enjoyed the diplomatic immunity and privileges attached to that position. The degree of procedural fairness owed to him is dependent on whether it is a right or privilege that is at issue. It is apparent that this case involves the loss of a privilege, not a right. In the circumstances of this case the applicant was not owed a duty of fairness and, consequently, there was no breach of the duty of fairness.

Jurisdiction — application of Canadian law outside of Canada

R. v. Greco (2001), 159 C.C.C. (3d) 146 (Ontario Court of Appeal)

This was an appeal from a conviction on a charge of breach of probation. The appellant had assaulted his travelling companion while on holiday in Cuba. Upon his return to Canada, he was charged with breach of a 1997 probation order requiring that he keep the peace and be of good behaviour. The appeal raised the issues of whether the appellant was required to comply with the terms and conditions of the probation order while outside of Canada, and, if so, accepting that his assaultive conduct in Cuba would constitute a breach of probation, whether the Ontario Court of Justice had jurisdiction to try the offence and convict the appellant.

No rule or principle of international law deprives a judge of the Ontario or Superior Court of Justice of jurisdiction to make a probation order binding the conduct of a probationer both at home and abroad. The principle of "extraterritoriality" may impact on Canada's ability to enforce such orders. Yet these limitations on the ability of the court to enforce its orders should not be confused with the jurisdiction of the court in the first instance to prescribe orders that bind the conduct of probationers both at home and abroad. Subject to certain limitations, a state can extend the application of its laws and the jurisdiction of its courts to persons, property, and acts outside of its territory without offending against the principle of territoriality. Just as there is nothing in the principle of territoriality that prevents Canada from enacting laws enforceable in Canada that govern the conduct of persons outside of its territory, the principle of territoriality does not prevent courts from issuing orders, enforceable locally, that govern conduct outside of Canada.

Nor are there policy reasons for coming to a different conclusion. The notion that probationers are only bound by the terms and conditions of their probation orders while in Canada and that they can ignore or circumvent such orders with impunity by setting foot across the border, apart from being illogical, lacks justification once it is accepted that the requirements of comity remain sacrosanct and that Canadian courts will decline jurisdiction in cases where to do otherwise would result in a contravention of those requirements.

Policy considerations strongly favour an interpretation that makes the order binding on probationers regardless of where they happen to be. Conduct outside of Canada in breach of a probation order made in Canada can have a serious and immediate impact within Canada. The treatment, protection, and safety of the victim of this assault who lives in Canada are legitimate concerns of the Canadian criminal justice system. It is entirely consistent with those concerns that persons within the reach of Canadian courts be held to account for breaching an order made in Canada.

The only remaining question is whether to be effective abroad, the probation order must contain an express provision to that effect. Moldaver J.A. concluded that it need not. A common sense inference can and should be drawn that, subject to the requirements of comity, probation orders are meant to apply to probationers at all times wherever they might be, absent a specific term to the contrary.

The second issue, as to whether the Ontario Court of Justice had jurisdiction to convict the appellant because the conduct forming the breach occurred outside of Canada, turns on whether the offence of breach of probation was or was not committed in Canada. Moldaver J.A. applied the "real and substantial link" test set out by La Forest J. in *R. v. Libman*, [1985] 2 S.C.R. 178. Moldaver J.A.

observed that the requirements of comity, which LaForest J. believed might "well be coterminous" with "the outer limits of the test," are not engaged at all on the facts of this case. From the outset, the Cuban authorities made it clear that they had no interest in investigating or prosecuting the appellant for his conduct in Cuba. Moreover, there is no suggestion from anyone that the appellant's violent conduct was justified or condoned, let alone required, under Cuban law; nor is there any evidence that Cuba has ever registered a complaint with Canada over the prospect of the appellant's prosecution in Canada for the offence of breach of probation.

Once it is understood that Canada is the only country that has an interest in ensuring compliance with orders made by Canadian courts, little more need be said in terms of the "real and substantial link" test. The probation order in the instant case was imposed upon the appellant by an Ontario court. It required him to keep the peace and be of good behaviour both at home and abroad. Importantly, the offence in issue arises out of a breach of that order, a factor that is crucial in the application of the "real and substantial link" test. To the extent that he breached that order, Canada alone has an interest in bringing him to justice and it may do so. The requirements of international comity do not dictate otherwise.

Moldaver J.A. concluded that the offence of breach of probation was committed in Ontario; it follows that the Ontario Court of Justice had jurisdiction to try and to convict the appellant.

Note. See *R.* v. *Pilarinos*, [2001] B.C.S.C. 1690. The two accused sought to have an authorization permitting the Royal Canadian Mounted Police to intercept their private communications set aside on several bases, one of which was that the associate chief justice did not have the jurisdiction to issue the authorization. The authorization had been issued in California, and the defence argued that the associate chief justice had acted extraterritorially, in violation of the sovereignty of the United States and the state of California. Bennett J. notes that Canadian criminal law is not absolutely restricted to its territorial boundaries in terms of assuming jurisdiction over an offence. It is clear that the act of issuing the wiretap authorization from California did not interfere with the sovereignty of either the United States or the state of California. The actions of the Canadian authorities leading up to the issuance of the wiretap authorization also did not have any effect on the foreign jurisdiction. The powers exercised were all to take effect within

British Columbia, the jurisdiction of the superior court of criminal jurisdiction at issue. There is no reason in international law why superior court judges lose their status as judges if they cross a border. They have no authority or jurisdiction in the foreign state, but they may still exercise their jurisdiction for their territory, in this case, in British Columbia and, to a degree, in Canada.

Treaties and principles of international law — domestic application

Ahani v. *Canada (Attorney General)* (2002), 58 O.R. (3d) 107 (Ontario Court of Appeal)

The appellant, a convention refugee, was determined to be a terrorist and a danger to the security of Canada. The Minister of Citizenship and Immigration had ordered him deported to Iran. He challenged the deportation order, alleging that he would face torture in Iran. With the dismissal of his appeal by the Supreme Court of Canada on January 11, 2002, Ahani had exhausted all of his rights of review in Canada. He then filed a communication with the United Nations Human Rights Committee for relief under the Optional Protocol to the International Covenant on Civil and Political Rights, which Canada has ratified but not incorporated into its domestic law. The committee made an "interim measures" request, asking that Canada stay the deportation order until it considered Ahani's communication. The interim measures request is not binding, and Canada indicated it would not accede to it, and intended to deport Ahani immediately. This was an appeal from a decision of the Superior Court of Ontario dismissing Ahani's application for an injunction restraining his deportation pending the committee's consideration of his communication.

Writing for the majority, Laskin J.A. noted that while the Supreme Court had found that Ahani would be exposed to a minimal risk of "harm" if returned to Iran, Ahani is still a convention refugee. This court must therefore recognize that he still has a well-founded fear of persecution if returned to Iran. That is enough to trigger his section 7 rights. However, even if Ahani's section 7 rights are at stake, no principle of fundamental justice entitles him to remain in Canada until the committee considers his communication.

The content of the principles of fundamental justice can only be determined by balancing individual and state interests. Here, Ahani's interest is reflected in the opportunity to seek the committee's views on whether Canada's treatment of him breached the covenant. Canada's interest is reflected in two undisputed facts. The first fact is that Canada has never incorporated either the covenant or the protocol into Canadian law by implementing legislation. Absent implementing legislation, neither has any legal effect in Canada. The second fact is the nature of Canada's international commitment under the covenant and the protocol. In signing the protocol, Canada did not agree to be bound by the final views of the committee, nor did it even agree that it would stay its own domestic proceedings until the committee gave its views. In other words, neither the committee's views nor its interim measures requests are binding on Canada as a matter of international law, much less as a matter of domestic law. The party states that ratified the covenant and the optional protocol turned their minds to the question of whether they should agree to be bound by the committee's views, or whether they should at least agree to refrain from taking any action against an individual who had sought the committee's views until they were known. They decided as a matter of policy that they should not, leaving each party state, on a case-by-case basis, free to accept or reject the committee's final views, and equally free to accede to or not accede to an interim measures request. To give effect to Ahani's position would convert a non-binding request in a protocol, which has never been part of Canadian law, into a binding obligation enforceable in Canada by a Canadian court and, more, into a constitutional principle of fundamental justice. This is an untenable result.

By signing the protocol, Canada did provide an individual like Ahani an opportunity to seek the committee's views. Yet it qualified that right in two important ways. In any given case, Canada first reserved the right to reject the committee's views and, second, it reserved the right to enforce its own laws before the committee gave its views. In deporting Ahani, Canada was acting consistently with the terms under which it signed the protocol. It was not denying Ahani procedural fairness or depriving him of any remedy to which he is entitled. Even under the protocol, Ahani had no right to remain in Canada until the committee gives its views. He can therefore hardly claim that the principles of fundamental justice give him that right.

Laskin J.A. proceeded to deal with a number of the appellant's arguments, *inter alia,* that by agreeing to a procedure that it can choose to follow at its whim, Canada is not acting in good faith and, indeed, is acting contrary to its many pronouncements on the importance of international human rights. Laskin J.A. noted that on its face the argument that Canada will not be acting in good faith by deporting Ahani is now difficult to support. In deporting him, Canada would be enforcing its own laws and the decision of its highest court. It will be doing nothing more than it is entitled to do under the terms of the protocol. Moreover, Canada's domestic statutory regime for deporting convention refugees itself embodies a willingness to comply with international human rights standards. Ahani has had the full benefit of both statutory and Canadian Charter of Rights and Freedoms protections. Thus, the government of Canada would have every reason to hold a good faith belief that deporting Ahani now would not breach its obligations under the covenant. If, however, Canada has not acted in good faith, then it may justifiably be open to public criticism. If it falls short of the laudable goal of a full commitment to human rights conventions and treaties, other states may take it to task. However, the principles of fundamental justice lie in the basic tenets of our legal system. They are found in the domain of the judiciary, the guardian of the justice system. What Ahani complains about is a matter for the court of public or international opinion, not for a court of law.

Fundamentally, this case demonstrates the difference between the proper role of the executive and the proper role of the judiciary. Judges are not competent to assess whether Canada is acting in bad faith by rejecting the committee's interim measures request and instead deporting Ahani immediately. Canada has many international obligations to balance, not the least of which, in the wake of what occurred last September 11, is to ensure that it does not become a safe haven for terrorists. These are all considerations that lie within the executive's expertise in foreign relations. Courts have no expertise in these matters, and have no business intruding into them. Canada agreed to sign an international covenant and protocol that was not binding. It chose not to make these instruments part of its domestic law. It is not for the courts, under the guise of procedural fairness, to read in an enforceable constitutional obligation and commit Canada to a process that admittedly could take years, thus frustrating this country's wish to enforce its own laws by deporting a terrorist to a country where he will face at best a minimal risk of harm.

Laskin J.A. then dealt with the doctrine of legitimate expectations, emphasizing that it is a doctrine of procedural fairness only and creates no substantive rights. In this case, Ahani invoked the doctrine of legitimate expectations to support his contention that procedural fairness requires Canada not to deport him until the committee has considered his communication. His reliance on the doctrine is unusual in this sense: typically, individuals resort to legitimate expectations to obtain greater procedural fairness — greater participatory rights — from the administrative decision-maker. Yet Ahani did not seek more procedural fairness from the committee. He was content with the fairness of the committee's procedures. Instead, he tried to use the doctrine of legitimate expectations to impose procedural requirements on the other party to the dispute — Canada.

Even if he could overcome this obstacle, he would face two other hurdles, either of which show that he can have no legitimate expectation of remaining in Canada pending the committee's consideration of his communication. First, nothing in Canada's past practice with interim measures requests or in its dealings with Ahani could give rise to a legitimate expectation that it would permit Ahani to remain in the country until the committee considers his communication. Second, what Ahani seeks is not only procedural fairness but also a substantive right. He seeks the substantive right to remain in Canada until the committee delivers its views — a process that could take years. The law in Canada is clear: the doctrine of legitimate expectations does not create substantive rights.

Rosenberg, J.A., in dissent, asserted that where the legislature has established a statutory right to review a decision that could affect the security of the person, it is a principle of fundamental justice that the state cannot unreasonably frustrate that right. This principle of fundamental justice, although derived from a statutory right of review, can be applied by analogy to the process permitted by the covenant and the protocol. Individuals within Canada facing a deprivation of their right to life, liberty, or security of the person have a right under section 7 of the Charter, within reason, to have their petition reviewed by the Human Rights Committee free from any executive action that would render this review nugatory.

An aspect of the government's argument that the appellant has no right to await the decision of the committee is the principle that international conventions are not binding in Canada unless they have been specifically incorporated into Canadian law. This principle is to protect Parliament and the people of Canada from executive action. In this case, however, the government seeks to invoke the non-binding principle to shield the executive from the consequences of its voluntary decision to enter into and therefore be bound by the covenant and the protocol.

By signing the protocol, the federal government has conferred jurisdiction upon the committee. The non-binding principle goes only so far as to affirm that the covenant and the protocol do not create rights in the appellant that can be enforced in a domestic court. However, the appellant does not seek such an application of the covenant and the protocol. The appellant does not claim that the views of the committee about our process for removing him would create legal rights that could be enforced in a domestic court. He claims only the limited procedural right to reasonable access to the committee, upon which the federal government has conferred jurisdiction. He submits that the government having held out this right of review, however limited and non-binding, should not be entitled to render it practically illusory by returning him to Iran before he has had a reasonable opportunity to access it. Rosenberg J.A. expressed agreement with that submission and asserted that it is a principle of fundamental justice that individuals in Canada have fair access to the process in the protocol. By deporting the appellant to Iran, the government would deprive the appellant of this opportunity.

The application of this principle is more difficult in this context because of the difficulty for a Canadian court to assess the merits of a communication to the committee. However, there is a generally held consensus in Canada that in the human rights context an individual whose security is at stake should within reason be given the opportunity to access remedies at the international level and that the executive should not unreasonably frustrate the individual's attempt to do so. This is particularly the case where the individual seeks access to a body of the stature of the committee. While there may be no international consensus that governments that have ratified the optional protocol must await the views of the committee, this is not an obstacle to recognizing this principle of fundamental justice under the Charter. The principle is based upon a simple principle of justice that where there is a right there should be a remedy, a principle enshrined in the Charter and international conventions.

Rosenberg J.A. then commented on policy arguments made by counsel for the respondent that allowing the appellant to remain in Canada conflicts with its international obligation to fight terrorism. There is nothing inconsistent with according the appellant access to the committee and Canada complying with its international obligations. Canada is not harbouring terrorists or setting itself up as a haven for terrorists. The appellant has been in jail for over eight years. He seeks the views of a committee established in accordance with a United Nations covenant. If Canada is concerned that the optional protocol will be used as a vehicle to shield terrorists, it can denounce the protocol. It did not have to ratify the protocol; many nations have not done so. Furthermore, the committee is well positioned to balance the competing values in protecting convention refugees and the international obligation to eradicate terrorism.

Rosenberg J.A. also rejected the view that Canada ratified the covenant and the protocol because they created no enforceable obligations, noting that he found it difficult to accept that the federal government ratified the treaty because it knew it could not be made to comply with its binding obligations. This would undermine the good faith obligation inherent in ratifying treaties.

With regard to the content of the principle, Rosenberg J.A. noted that the right to access the Human Rights Committee is not absolute and the appellant may not have an unconditional right to stay in Canada indefinitely. While domestic courts have no jurisdiction to interpret international conventions, it is open to a court to make at least some preliminary assessment of the claim if for no other reason than to screen out the obviously frivolous claims. Further, this principle of fundamental justice may only be enforced in cases where the individual's life, liberty, or security of the person interests are implicated, as in the case of a convention refugee. The right to pursue the international remedy is not a means for delaying deportation in less serious cases. As well, it may be that the government can show in a particular case that the balance of convenience favours removal as where the applicant poses an unacceptable risk to public security even where, as in this case, he or she is being held in custody. Finally, there is a possibility that the government might be able to show that the committee process will result in such an intolerable delay that the balance of convenience favours deportation, although that would be an unusual case. In this case, the domestic procedures have occupied over eight years, and the appellant has remained in custody throughout. Canada can hardly complain about some delay at the committee level when it is a condition of invoking that jurisdiction that all domestic remedies have been exhausted.

Note. Both the majority and the dissent refered to a recent series of cases from the Judicial Committee of the Privy Council in death penalty cases out of the Caribbean, which have held that states subject to a constitutionally enshrined due process clause may be obliged to await the decision of international bodies. Laskin J.A. identified some significant differences in those cases from the present situation (most notably the fact that they involve capital punishment) but also noted that the reasoning in these cases conflicts directly with well-established Canadian law. In Canada, mere ratification of a treaty, without incorporating legislation, cannot make the international process part of our domestic criminal justice system. Rosenberg J.A. referred with approval to some of the Privy Council decisions but noted that he did so simply as an indication that countries with legal systems like ours have found that due process requires that individuals be given the opportunity to access international bodies and also indicated that he finds some of the reasoning strained.

Rahaman v. *Canada (Minister of Citizenship and Immigration)*, [2002] 3 F.C. 537 (Federal Court of Appeal)

The appellant was refused refugee status by the Convention Refugee Determination Division of the Immigration and Refugee Board. The board also concluded that there was "no credible basis" for the claim that Mr. Rahaman was a convention refugee, within the meaning of subsection 69.1(9.1) of the Immigration Act, R.S.C., 1985, c. I-2. The principal effects of a "no credible basis" finding are that the unsuccessful claimant for refugee status has no right to apply to remain as a member of the "post-determination refugee claimants in Canada" class and is liable to be removed from Canada seven days after the removal order is effective. This was an appeal by Mr. Rahaman from a decision dismissing an application for judicial review of the board's rejection of his refugee claim and of the "no credible basis" finding. The appeal focused on the "no credible basis" finding.

Counsel for Mr. Rahaman had argued, *inter alia,* that compliance with international norms requires that unsuccessful refugee claimants not be subject to *refoulement* pending the disposition of legal proceedings brought to review the rejection of their refugee claims, unless their claims are manifestly unfounded. For the court to interpret subsection 69.1(9.1) to include claims that cannot be said to be manifestly unfounded would put Canada out of line with international legal norms. Only when faced with completely unequivocal statutory language should the court conclude that an act of Parliament derogates from international norms respecting the protection of human rights.

Evans J.A. acknowledged that there is no doubt that, even when not incorporated by act of Parliament into Canadian law, international norms are part of the context within which domestic statutes are to be interpreted. The weight to be afforded to international norms that have not been incorporated by statute into Canadian law will depend on all the circumstances of the case, including the legal authoritativeness of their legal source, their specificity, and, in the case of customary international law, the uniformity of state practice. However, effect cannot be given to unincorporated international norms that are inconsistent with the clear provisions of an act of Parliament. Were it otherwise, the principle that treaties and other international norms only become part of the domestic law of Canada if enacted by Parliament would be undermined.

The question before the court is whether the prevailing interpretation of subsection 69.1 (9.1) authorizes the removal of unsuccessful refugee claimants contrary to international norms. This will occur if a claim supported by "no credible or trustworthy evidence" is not also "manifestly unfounded" as that phrase is understood in the international community.

The first step to answering that question is to ask if international norms require states to ensure that an unsuccessful refugee claimant is not returned to the country of alleged persecution pending the final disposition of a legal challenge to the dismissal of the refugee claim. This question is not expressly addressed in the United Nations Convention Relating to the Status of Refugees, or in the United Nations Protocol Relating to the Status of Refugees. However, considerable weight should be given to recommendations of the Executive Committee of the High Commissioner for Refugees on issues relating to refugee determination and protection that are designed to go some way to fill the procedural void in the convention itself. The Executive Committee has recommended that unsuccessful refugee claimants be given a reasonable opportunity to appeal from a refusal to recognize their claim and be permitted to remain in the country of refuge pending appeal, before they are returned to their home country where they may be subject to identifiable risk.

This and other material indicates the existence of an international norm that signatory states to the Geneva Convention should normally permit refugee claimants to remain in their territory until they have exhausted any right of appeal or review. This is what paragraph 49(1)(c) of the Immigration Act provides. However, it is also recognized in international instruments that states may derogate from the normal rule by providing more limited review and appeal rights to unsuccessful claimants whose claims have been held to be "manifestly unfounded." Thus, the Executive Committee has indicated a consensus on the problem created by the increase in applicants who "clearly have no valid claim" or whose claims are "manifestly unfounded" and that states must create separate national procedures to address this problem.

The restricted post-determination rights afforded by the Immigration Act to those whose claims are found to have no credible basis are not inconsistent with international norms as evidenced by the above instruments. "No credible basis" claimants may apply for judicial review and request the court to grant a stay pending the disposition of the application, and those found to be at serious risk in their country of origin will not be removed. A problem arises, however, if a claim can fall within this category, but is not "manifestly unfounded" as that term is commonly understood in the international community. A person whose claim is not "manifestly unfounded" should be permitted to remain pending the disposition of the appeal or review.

There is no doubt that some international instruments appear to give a very restricted meaning to the term "manifestly unfounded." More recent pronouncements, however, are less categorical, no doubt in response to a growing number of genuine and bogus refugee claims. There is evidence that there is as yet no international consensus on the scope of the term "manifestly unfounded"; as well as evidence of state practices that widen the categories of manifestly unfounded claims to include those that are supported by no credible evidence. It is not possible to conclude that a comprehensive international norm has emerged defining a manifestly unfounded or abusive application that would exclude a claim that has "no credible basis." It is also important to note in this regard that under Canadian law all eligible inland claimants have a right to a full adjudicative hearing before an independent administrative tribunal, and that a finding of "no credible basis" is only made on the basis of this process.

In view of the conclusion on the indeterminate state of international law on whether any claim that has no credible basis within the meaning of subsection 69.1 (9.1) is also manifestly unfounded, it is unnecessary to consider whether that provision should be interpreted to include only claims that are manifestly unfounded or clearly abusive. Evans J.A. noted, however, that although "manifestly unfounded or clearly abusive" is the phrase used in international instruments, Parliament has retained the term "no credible basis" in the act.

Evans J.A. concluded by asserting that the board should not routinely state that a claim has "no credible basis" whenever it concludes that the claimant is not a credible witness. Subsection 69.1(9.1) requires the board to examine all the evidence and to conclude that the claim has no credible basis only when there is no trustworthy or credible evidence that could support a recognition of the claim.

Suresh v. Canada (Minister of Citizenship and Immigration), [2002] 1 S.C.R. 3 (Supreme Court of Canada)

This was an appeal from a decision of the Federal Court of Appeal, noted in "Canadian Cases of Private International Law" (2000) 38 Can. Y.B. Int'l L. 433. Suresh came to Canada from Sri Lanka in 1990, was recognized as a convention refugee in 1991, and applied for landed immigrant status. In 1995, the government detained him and started proceedings to deport him to Sri Lanka on grounds that he was a member and fundraiser for the Liberation Tigers of Tamil Eelam (LTTE), an organization alleged to engage in terrorist activity in Sri Lanka. As the final step in the deportation process, the minister issued an opinion that Suresh constituted a danger to the security of Canada and should be deported pursuant to section 53(1)(b) of the Immigration Act, R.S.C. 1985, c. I-2, which permits the minister to deport a refugee even where the refugee's "life or freedom" would be threatened by the return. Suresh applied to the Federal Court for judicial review of the minister's decision; the application was dismissed both at the trial level and at the Court of Appeal.

The court began by discussing the appropriate standard of review and expressed agreement with Robertson J.A. of the Federal Court of Appeal that the reviewing court should adopt a deferential approach to this question and should set aside the minister's discretionary decision only if it is patently unreasonable in the sense that it was made arbitrarily or in bad faith, it cannot be supported on the evidence, or the minister failed to consider the appropriate factors. The court should not reweigh the factors or interfere merely because it would have come to a different conclusion. The court specifically addressed the question of the standard of review of the minister's decision on whether the refugee faced a substantial risk of torture upon deportation. Whether there was a substantial risk of torture if Suresh was deported is a threshold question. The threshold question is in large part a fact-driven inquiry. It requires consideration of the human rights record of the home state, the personal risk faced by the claimant, any assurances that the claimant will not be tortured and their worth, and, in this respect, the ability of the home state to control its own security forces, and more. It may also involve a reassessment of the refugee's initial claim and a determination of whether a third country is willing to accept the refugee. Such issues are largely outside the realm of expertise of reviewing courts and possesses a negligible legal dimension. The court is accordingly of the view that the threshold finding of whether Suresh faces a substantial risk of torture, as an aspect of the larger section 53(1)(b) opinion, attracts deference by the reviewing court to the minister's decision.

The court then turned to the question of whether the conditions for deportation in the act are constitutional. It began by considering whether the act permits deportation to torture contrary to section 7 of the Charter, which guarantees "the right to life, liberty and security of the person and the right not to be deprived thereof except in accordance with the principles of fundamental justice." The relevant principles of fundamental justice are determined by a contextual approach that takes into account the nature of the decision to be made. The approach is essentially one of balancing. Deportation to torture requires the court to consider a variety of factors, including the circumstances or conditions of the potential deportee, the danger that the deportee presents to Canadians or the country's security, and the threat of terrorism to Canada. In contexts in which the most significant considerations are general ones, it is likely that the balance will be struck the same way in most cases. It would be impossible to say in advance, however, that the balance will necessarily be struck the same way in every case. The notion of proportionality is fundamental to our constitutional system. Thus, the courts must ask whether the government's proposed response is reasonable in relation to the threat. In the past, the court has held that some responses are so extreme that they are *per se* disproportionate to any legitimate government interest. It must ask whether deporting a refugee to torture would be such a response.

The court considered the question of whether the government may, consistent with the principles of fundamental justice, expel a suspected terrorist to face torture elsewhere from two perspectives: first from the Canadian perspective and, second, from the perspective of the international norms that inform section 7. With respect to the former, the court noted that the inquiry is whether, viewed from a Canadian perspective, returning a refugee to the risk of torture because of security concerns violates the principles of fundamental justice where the deportation is effected for reasons of national security. A variety of phrases have been used to describe conduct that would violate fundamental justice. The most frequent is conduct that would "shock the Canadian conscience." The court has little difficulty in concluding that Canadians reject government-sanctioned torture in the domestic context. However, it noted that this appeal focuses on the prospect of Canada expelling a person to face torture in another country. This raises the question whether section 7 is implicated at all. On one theory, the inquiry need be concerned only with the minister's act of deporting and not with the possible consequences that the expelled refugee may face upon arriving in the destination country. If the court's section 7 analysis is confined to what occurs on Canadian soil as a necessary and immediate result of the minister's decision, torture does not enter the picture. If, on the other hand, that analysis must take into account what may happen to the refugee in the destination country, the court surely cannot ignore the possibility of grievous consequences such as torture and death, if a risk of those consequences is established.

The court found that the principle it articulated in *United States* v. *Burns*, [2001] 1 S.C.R. 283, noted at (2001) 39 Can. Y.B. Int'l L. 566, should apply in to this case despite the fact that it arises in the context of deportation and not extradition. The governing principle in *Burns* was a general one — namely, that the guarantee of fundamental justice applies even to deprivations of life, liberty, or security effected by actors other than our government, if there is a sufficient causal connection between our government's participation and the deprivation ultimately effected. The court reaffirmed that principle. At least where Canada's participation is a necessary precondition for the deprivation and where the deprivation is an entirely foreseeable consequence of Canada's participation, the government does not avoid the guarantee of fundamental justice merely because the deprivation in question would be effected by someone else's hand.

The courts therefore disagreed with the Federal Court of Appeal's suggestion that, in expelling a refugee to a risk of torture, Canada acts only as an "involuntary intermediary." Without Canada's action, there would be no risk of torture. Accordingly, the court could not pretend that Canada was merely a passive participant. That is not to say, of course, that *any* action by Canada that results in a person being tortured or put to death would violate section 7. There is always the question, as there is in this case, of whether there is a *sufficient* connection between Canada's action and the deprivation of life, liberty, or security.

The court noted that while it has never directly addressed the issue of whether deportation to torture would be inconsistent with fundamental justice, it has indicated on several occasions that extraditing a person to face torture would be inconsistent with fundamental justice. Canadian jurisprudence does not suggest that Canada may never deport a person to face treatment elsewhere that would be unconstitutional if imposed by Canada directly on Canadian soil. Again, the appropriate approach is essentially one of balancing. The outcome will depend not only on considerations inherent in the general context but also on considerations related to the circumstances and condition of the particular person whom the government seeks to expel. The state's genuine interest in combatting terrorism stands on the one hand, preventing Canada from becoming a safe haven for terrorists and protecting public security. On the other hand, Canada's constitutional commitment to liberty and fair process is found. This said, Canadian jurisprudence suggests that this balance will usually come down against expelling a person to face torture elsewhere.

The court then dealt with the international perspective. The provisions of the Immigration Act dealing with deportation must be considered in their international context. Similarly, the principles of fundamental justice expressed in section 7 of the Charter and the limits on rights that may be justified under section 1 of the Charter cannot be considered in isolation from the international norms that they reflect. International treaty norms are not, strictly speaking, binding in Canada unless they have been incorporated into Canadian law by enactment. However, in seeking the meaning of the Canadian constitution, the courts may be informed by international law.

The court began with the submission that the absolute prohibition on torture is a peremptory norm of customary international law or *jus cogens*. Peremptory norms develop over time and by general consensus of the international community. This is the difficulty in interpreting international law; it is often impossible to pinpoint when a norm is generally accepted and to identify who makes up the international community. In the case at bar, there are three compelling indicia that the prohibition of torture is a peremptory norm. First, there is the great number of multilateral instruments that explicitly prohibit torture. Second, Amnesty International submitted that no state has ever legalized torture or admitted to its deliberate practice and that governments accused of practising torture regularly deny their involvement, placing responsibility on individual state agents or groups outside the government's control. Therefore, it argues that the weight of these domestic practices is further evidence of a universal acceptance of the prohibition on torture. Counsel for the respondents, while not conceding this point, did not refer the court to any evidence of state practice to contradict this submission. However, it is noted in most academic writings that most, if not all states have officially prohibited the use of torture as part of their administrative practices. Last, a number of international authorities state that the prohibition on torture is an established peremptory norm. Others do not explicitly set it out as a peremptory norm; however, they do generally accept that the protection of human rights or humanitarian rights is a peremptory norm.

Although this court was not being asked to pronounce on the status of the prohibition on torture in international law, the fact that such a principle is included in numerous multilateral instruments, that it does not form part of any known domestic administrative practice, and that it is considered by many academics to be an emerging, if not established, peremptory norm, suggests that it cannot be easily derogated from. With this in mind, the court turned to the interpretation of the conflicting instruments at issue in this case. Deportation to torture is prohibited by both the International Covenant on Civil and Political Rights (ICCPR), which Canada ratified in 1976, and the Convention against Torture and other Cruel, Inhuman or Degrading Treatment or Punishment (CAT), which Canada ratified in 1987. While the provisions of the ICCPR do not themselves specifically address the permissibility of a state's expelling a person to face torture elsewhere, *General Comment 20* to the ICCPR makes clear that Article 7 is intended to cover this scenario. The court stated that it did not share Robertson J.A.'s view that *General Comment 20* should be disregarded because it "contradicts" the clear language of Article 7. There is no contradiction between the two provisions. *General Comment 20* does not run counter to Article 7; rather, it explains it. Nothing would prevent a state from adhering both to Article 7 and to *General Comment 20*, and *General Comment 20* does not detract from rights preserved or provided by Article 7. The clear import of the ICCPR, read together with the *General Comment 20*, is to foreclose a state from expelling a person to face torture elsewhere. The CAT takes the same stand — a state is not to expel a person to face torture, which includes both the physical and mental infliction of pain and suffering, elsewhere.

Robertson J.A. held that the CAT's clear proscription of deportation to torture must defer to Article 33(2) of the Refugee Convention, which permits a country to return (*refouler*) a refugee who is a danger to the country's security. The court acknowledged that Article 33 of the Refugee Convention appears on its face to stand in opposition to the categorical rejection of deportation to torture in the CAT. Robertson J.A., faced with this apparent contradiction, attempted to read the two conventions in a way that minimized the contradiction, holding that the anti-deportation provisions of the CAT were not binding, but derogable. The court stated that it was not convinced that the contradiction could be resolved in this way. It is not apparent to us that the clear prohibitions on torture in the CAT were intended to be derogable. First, the absence of an express prohibition against derogation in Article 3 of the CAT together with the "without prejudice" language of Article 16 do not seem to permit derogation. Nor does it follow from the assertion in Article 2(2) of CAT that "[n]o exceptional circumstances ... may be invoked as a justification of torture," that the absence of such a clause in the Article 3 *refoulement* provision permits acts leading to torture in exceptional circumstances. Moreover, the history of Article 16 of the CAT suggests that it was intended to leave the door open to other legal instruments providing greater protection, not to serve as the means for reducing protection. During the deliberations of the Working Group that drafted the CAT, Article 16 was characterized as a "saving clause affirming the continued validity of other instruments prohibiting punishments or cruel, inhuman, or degrading treatment." This undermines the suggestion that Article 16 can be used as a means of narrowing the scope of protection that the CAT was intended to provide.

In the court's view, the prohibition in the ICCPR and the CAT on returning a refugee to face a risk of torture reflects the prevailing international norm. Article 33 of the Refugee Convention protects, in a limited way, refugees from threats to life and freedom from all sources. By contrast, the CAT protects everyone, without derogation, from state-sponsored torture. Moreover, the Refugee Convention itself expresses a "profound concern for refugees" and its principal purpose is to "assure refugees the widest possible exercise of ... fundamental rights and freedoms." This negates the suggestion that the provisions of the Refugee Convention should be used to deny rights that other legal instruments make universally available to *everyone.*

The court concluded that the better view is that international law rejects deportation to torture, even where national security interests are at stake. This is the norm that best informs the content of the principles of fundamental justice under section 7 of the Charter. The court then proceeded to deal with section 53(1)(b) of the Immigration Act. The Canadian rejection of torture is reflected in the international conventions to which Canada is a party. The Canadian and international perspectives in turn inform our constitutional norms. The rejection of state action leading to torture generally, and deportation to torture specifically, is virtually categoric. Indeed, both domestic and international jurisprudence suggest that torture is so abhorrent that it will almost always be disproportionate to interests on the other side of the balance, even security interests. This suggests that, barring extraordinary circumstances, deportation to torture will generally violate the principles of fundamental justice protected by section 7 of the Charter. The question of whether the risk to national security is sufficient to justify the appellant's deportation cannot be answered by taking each allegation seriatim and deciding whether it has been established to some standard of proof. It is a question of evaluation and judgment, in which it is necessary to take into account not only the degree of probability of prejudice to national security but also the importance of the security interest at stake and the serious consequences of deportation for the deportee. In Canada, the balance struck by the minister must conform to the principles of fundamental justice under section 7 of the Charter. It follows that insofar as the Immigration Act leaves open the possibility of deportation to torture, the minister should generally decline to deport refugees where on the evidence there is a substantial risk of torture. The court did not exclude the possibility that in exceptional circumstances, deportation to face torture might be justified, either as a consequence of the balancing process mandated by section 7 of the Charter or under section 1. (A violation of section 7 will be saved by section 1 only in cases arising out of exceptional conditions.) Insofar as Canada is unable to deport a person where there are substantial grounds to believe he or she would be tortured on return, this is not because Article 3 of the CAT directly constrains the actions of the Canadian government, but because the fundamental justice balance under section 7 of the Charter generally precludes deportation to torture when applied on a case-by-case basis. The court may predict that it will rarely be struck in favour of expulsion where there is a serious risk of torture. However, as the matter is one of balance, precise prediction is elusive. The ambit of an exceptional discretion to deport to torture, if any, must await future cases. In these circumstances, section 53(1)(b) does not violate section 7 of the Charter. What is at issue is not the legislation, but the minister's obligation to exercise the discretion section 53 confers in a constitutional manner.

The court then turned to a consideration of whether the terms "danger to the security of Canada" and "terrorism" are unconstitutionally vague. In relation to the former, the court emphasized that it does not conflate section 19's reference to membership in a terrorist movement with "danger to the security of Canada." While the two may be related, "danger to the security of Canada" must mean something more than just "person described in section 19." Similarly, "danger to the security of Canada" must be distinguished from "danger to the public," although the two phrases may overlap. Subject to these qualifications, the court accepted that a fair, large, and liberal interpretation in accordance with international norms must be accorded to "danger to the security of Canada" in deportation legislation. It recognized that "danger to the security of Canada" is difficult to define and accepted that the determination of what constitutes a "danger to the security of Canada" is highly fact-based and political in a general sense. All of this suggests a broad and flexible approach to national security and a deferential standard of judicial review. Provided the minister is able to show evidence that reasonably supports a finding of danger to the security of Canada, courts should not interfere with the minister's decision.

The court addressed the question of whether the minister must present direct evidence of a specific danger to the security of Canada and considered the arguments that under international law the state must prove a connection between the terrorist activity and the security of the deporting country and that the *travaux préparatoires* to the Refugee Convention indicate that threats to the security of another state were not intended to qualify as a danger sufficient to permit *refoulement* to torture. Whatever the historic validity of insisting on direct proof of specific danger to the deporting country, as matters have evolved, courts may now conclude that the support

of terrorism abroad raises a possibility of adverse repercussions on
Canada's security. International conventions must be interpreted
in light of current conditions. It may once have made sense to suggest that terrorism in one country did not necessarily implicate
other countries. Yet after the year 2001, that approach is no longer
valid. First, the global transport and money networks that feed
terrorism abroad have the potential to touch all countries, including Canada, and to thus implicate them in the terrorist activity. Second, terrorism itself is a worldwide phenomenon. The terrorist
cause may focus on a distant locale, but the violent acts that support it may be close at hand. Third, preventive or precautionary
state action may be justified — not only an immediate threat but
also possible future risks must be considered. Fourth, Canada's
national security may be promoted by reciprocal cooperation
between Canada and other states in combating international terrorism. These considerations lead us to conclude that to insist on
direct proof of a specific threat to Canada as the test for "danger
to the security of Canada" is to set the bar too high. There must be
a real and serious possibility of adverse effect to Canada. Yet the
threat need not be direct; rather it may be grounded in distant
events that indirectly have a real possibility of harming Canadian
security.

While the phrase "danger to the security of Canada" must be
interpreted flexibly, and while courts need not insist on direct proof
that the danger targets Canada specifically, the fact remains that
to return (*refouler*) a refugee under section 53(1)(*b*) to torture
requires evidence of a serious threat to national security. To suggest
that something less than serious threats founded on evidence
would suffice to deport a refugee to torture would be to condone
unconstitutional application of the Immigration Act. Insofar as
possible, statutes must be interpreted to conform to the Constitution. This supports the conclusion that while "danger to the
security of Canada" must be given a fair, large and liberal interpretation, it nevertheless demands proof of a potentially serious
threat. A person constitutes a "danger to the security of Canada" if
he or she poses a serious threat to the security of Canada, whether
direct or indirect, and bearing in mind the fact that the security of
one country is often dependent on the security of other nations.
The threat must be "serious," in the sense that it must be grounded
on objectively reasonable suspicion based on evidence and in the
sense that the threatened harm must be substantial rather than
negligible.

In regard to "terrorism," the court noted the difficulties in ascertaining an authoritative definition of the term. However, the term "terrorism" is not so unsettled that it cannot set the proper boundaries of legal adjudication. The court discussed the difference between "functional" and "stipulative" approaches to the definition of terrorism, both of which are reflected in the recently negotiated International Convention for the Suppression of the Financing of Terrorism. While acknowledging some of the advantages of a functional approach, which defines terrorism by reference to specific acts of violence, the court adopted the stipulative definition found in the convention and concluded that "terrorism" in section 19 of the act includes any "act intended to cause death or serious bodily injury to a civilian, or to any other person not taking an active part in the hostilities in a situation of armed conflict, when the purpose of such act, by its nature or context, is to intimidate a population, or to compel a government or an international organization to do or to abstain from doing any act." This definition catches the essence of what the world understands by "terrorism." Particular cases on the fringes of terrorist activity will inevitably provoke disagreement. Parliament is not prevented from adopting more detailed or different definitions of terrorism. The issue is whether the term as used in the Immigration Act is sufficiently certain to be workable, fair, and constitutional. The court believed that it is.

Finally, the court considered the question of whether the procedures for deportation set out in the Immigration Act are constitutionally valid. In determining whether the procedural safeguards provided satisfy the demands of section 7, the court considered, *inter alia*, Canada's obligations under the Convention against Torture. Article 3 of the CAT, which explicitly prohibits the deportation of persons to states where there are "substantial grounds" for believing that the person would be "in danger of being subjected to torture," informs section 7 of the Charter. It is only reasonable that the same executive that bound itself to the CAT intends to act in accordance with the CAT's plain meaning. Given Canada's commitment to the CAT, the court found that the appellant had the right to procedural safeguards, at the section 53(1)(b) stage of the proceedings. More particularly, the phrase "substantial grounds" raises a duty to afford an opportunity to demonstrate and defend those grounds.

These procedural protections need not be invoked in every case, as not every case of deportation of a convention refugee under section 53(1)(b) will involve risk to an individual's fundamental right to be protected from torture or similar abuses. It is for the refugee to establish a threshold showing that a risk of torture or similar abuse exists before the minister is obliged to consider fully the possibility. This showing need not be *proof* of the risk of torture to that person, but the individual must make out a *prima facie* case that there *may* be a risk of torture upon deportation. If the refugee establishes that torture is a real possibility, the minister must provide the refugee with all the relevant information and advice she intends to rely on, provide the refugee with an opportunity to address that evidence in writing, and after considering all the relevant information, issue responsive written reasons. This is the minimum required to meet the duty of fairness and fulfill the requirements of fundamental justice under section 7 of the Charter.

Note. The court also dealt with the issue of whether deportation for membership in a terrorist organization unjustifiably violates Charter guarantees of freedom of expression and freedom of association. It pointed out that it has been established that section 2 of the Charter does not protect expressive or associational activities that constitute violence. The minister's discretion to deport under section 53 of the Immigration Act is confined, on any interpretation of the section, to persons who have been engaged in terrorism or are members of terrorist organizations, and who also pose a threat to the security of Canada. Persons associated with terrorism or terrorist organizations are, on the approach to terrorism suggested in these reasons, persons who are or have been associated with things directed at violence, if not violence itself. It follows that so long as the minister exercises her discretion in accordance with the act, there will be no sections 2(b) or (d) Charter violation.

Note. Veuillez voir *R. c. Peters*, [2002] J.Q. no. 701 (Court du Québec — Chambre criminelle et pénále). S'il est impossible de donner une définition exhaustive à la notion de "principes de justice fondamentale," la Cour suprême nous a enseigné que certains de ces principes étaient exprimés dans les conventions internationales sur les droits de la personne. Le droit international public reconnaît explicitement le droit qu'a un individu d'être jugé dans un délai raisonnable. Le paragraphe 14(3) du Pacte international relatif aux droits civils et politiques prévoit, en effet, que toute personne accusée d'une infraction pénale a droit d'être jugée sans retard excessif. Les statuts des tribunaux pénaux internationaux ainsi que celui de la Cour pénale internationale comportent aussi une disposition à cet égard. Les systèmes régionaux de protection des droits de la personne ont également prévu, dans leur convention respective, une disposition similaire.

Treaties — interpretation

Canada (Attorney General) v. *McNally Construction Inc.*, [2002] 4 F.C. 633 (Federal Court of Appeal)

This was an application for judicial review of a decision of the Canadian International Trade Tribunal that the North American Free Trade Agreement (NAFTA) and the Agreement on Government Procurement (AGP) applied to the procurement by the Department of Public Works and Government Services (DPWGS) on behalf of the Department of Fisheries and Oceans of a jet-propelled patrol boat for use in the coastal waters of the Maritime provinces. The DPWGS had contended before the tribunal that the procurement in issue was covered by specific exclusions for "ship-building and repair."

Having concluded that the proper standard of review is that of "patent unreasonableness" rather than "correctness," Stone J.A. noted that neither NAFTA nor the AGP defines the term "ship-building and repair." Having determined that the word "ship" has both a broad and narrower meaning, the tribunal decided to resolve the construction problem by selecting the meaning that it found to be most harmonious with the general purpose of the tendering provisions of NAFTA and the AGP and which it described as "to promote trade liberalization by insuring that tendering procedures are applied in a non-discriminatory and transparent manner." The language in which the exclusions are cast suggested to the tribunal that they were not intended to apply to any craft that might conceivably fall within a broad definition of that language but only to a large seagoing ship built or repaired on procurement of the federal government. Nothing in the record before the tribunal indicated that the "shipbuilding and repair" exclusions were intended by Canada to be applied to a "ship" in the broad sense in which that word has been defined. Stone J.A. accepted the tribunal's submission that the interpretation and application of the "shipbuilding and repair" exclusions requires an understanding of the procurement provisions of NAFTA and of the AGP, including the scheme of the exceptions and exemptions contained in them and called upon the tribunal's specialized expertise in interpreting these international treaties in the context of the act and the rules and regulations made thereunder.

Stone J.A. addressed a final argument put forward by the applicant in favour of according the word "ship" and the exclusions a broad meaning. The gist of the submission is that as the United States, a party to NAFTA, has adopted measures to protect its shipbuilding and repair industries and has excluded much of such activities from NAFTA, the exclusions under review mirror Canada's objective of obtaining a degree of reciprocity in this regard with the United States. However, the NAFTA agreement contains no similarly specific exclusions of procurement for ship construction or repair by Canada. Moreover, there is not in the record any evidence of the negotiating history that would throw light on the intended scope of the exclusions here in issue and certainly none that would support a confident conclusion that the Canadian exclusions were intended to bring about reciprocity with the United States. Thus, the tribunal's construction of the "shipbuilding and repair" exclusions in NAFTA and the AGP was not patently unreasonable.

Note. See *Zrig* v. *Canada (Minister of Citizenship and Immigration)*, [2002] 1 F.C. 559 (Federal Court Trial Division), regarding the interpretation of Article 1F(b) of the United Nations Convention Relating to the Status of Refugees, which provides that the convention shall not apply to any person with respect to whom there are serious reasons for considering that he has committed a serious non-political crime. The court held that although there is no Canadian precedent on the concept of complicity by association in connection with the application of Article 1F(b), the rules developed by the courts pursuant to Article 1F(a) and (c) of the convention can be applied with respect to Article 1F(b). Association with a person or organization responsible for crimes may constitute complicity if there is personal and knowing participation or toleration of the crimes. Mere membership in a group responsible for international crimes, unless it is an organization that has a "limited brutal purpose," is not enough. The closer one is to a position of leadership or command within an organization, the easier it will be to draw an inference of awareness of the crimes and participation in them.

Canadian Cases in
Private International Law in 2001-2 /
Jurisprudence canadienne en matière de
droit international privé en 2001-2

compiled by / préparé par
JOOST BLOM

A   *Jurisdiction / Compétence des tribunaux*

1   Common Law and Federal

(a)   Jurisdiction by consent — attornment

Note. See *Campagna* v. *Wong* (2002), 216 Sask. R. 142 (Q.B.). Although the plaintiff's action for assaults suffered over a seven-year period included torts committed in Hong Kong, the defendant was held to have submitted in respect of the whole of the action. See also *Stoymenoff* v. *Airtours Plc.* (2001), 17 C.P.C. (5th) 387 (Ont. S.C.J.), in which an English cruise line was held to have submitted to the court's jurisdiction in an action brought by the family of an Ontario-resident passenger who had died during a cruise. Parties were free to agree on the court for their dispute, according to art. 17(2) of the Athens Convention Relating to the Carriage of Passengers and Their Luggage by Sea (1974), which was implemented by Part 4 of the Marine Liability Act, S.C. 2001, c. 6.

Constitutionally based territorial limits on jurisdiction

Muscutt v. *Courcelles* (2002), 213 D.L.R. (4th) 577, 60 O.R. (3d) 20 (Ontario Court of Appeal)

In this and four other decisions, all given together, the Ontario Court of Appeal has endeavoured to lay down the law on jurisdiction *simpliciter* in a reasonably definitive way. Jurisdiction *simpliciter* is the question of whether the court of a province, when it exercises jurisdiction in a case that has strong connections with other legal

---

Joost Blom is in the Faculty of Law at the University of British Columbia.

jurisdictions, is acting within the territorial bounds that are impliedly set on provincial power by the Canadian constitution. Jurisdiction *simpliciter* is distinct from the issue of *forum non conveniens.* That is a matter, not of whether a court has power to act, but of whether a court that has power to act should nevertheless, in its discretion, refrain from exercising that power. The combined effect of *Morguard Investments Ltd.* v. *De Savoye,* [1990] 3 S.C.R. 1077, 76 D.L.R. (4th) 256, and *Hunt* v. *T & N Plc.,* [1993] 4 S.C.R. 289, 109 D.L.R. (4th) 16, was to lay down a constitutional requirement that, in order for a court to take jurisdiction over a case with extraprovincial connections, there must be a "real and substantial connection" between the facts of the case and the territory of the forum. An alternative formulation, also used in those cases, is that the exercise of jurisdiction must be compatible with "order and fairness."

In all five of the cases being discussed in this review, the primary connection of the litigation with Ontario was that the plaintiff lived there and, to some extent, suffered there from the consequences of the defendants' wrong. The Ontario Rules of Civil Procedure allow service *ex juris* without leave of the court in any case in which the claim is "in respect of damage sustained in Ontario arising from a tort, breach of contract, breach of fiduciary duty or breach of confidence, wherever committed" (Rules of Civil Procedure, R. 17.02(h)). The five actions stemmed from, respectively, the plaintiff's being injured as passenger in a motor vehicle accident in Alberta (*Muscutt* v. *Courcelles*); the plaintiff's being injured as a passenger in a motor vehicle accident in New York City (*Gajraj* v. *DeBernardo* (2002), 213 D.L.R. (4th) 651); the plaintiff's being injured when she fell on the premises of a restaurant near Buffalo, New York (*Sinclair* v. *Cracker Barrel Old Country Store Inc.* (2002), 213 D.L.R. (4th) 643); the plaintiff's suffering carbon monoxide poisoning in a taxi in Grenada, while on a shore excursion that was part of a Caribbean cruise (*Lemmex* v. *Sunflight Holidays Inc.* (2002), 213 D.L.R. (4th) 627); and the plaintiff's falling while rappelling off a high platform during a tour of a forest in Costa Rica as part of a package holiday (*Leufkens* v. *Alba Tours International Inc.* (2002), 213 D.L.R. (4th) 614). In each case, the Ontario court had jurisdiction as far as the rules for service *ex juris* were concerned, but the non-Ontario defendants (in the two holiday tour cases were Ontario defendants as well) argued that the court had no jurisdiction *simpliciter* because the action lacked a real and substantial connection with Ontario. The Court of Appeal held that jurisdiction *simpliciter* was established in the *Muscutt* case, but that the Ontario trial court lacked it in the other four.

Sharpe J.A., speaking for the court, agreed with earlier case law that took a broader approach to the question of jurisdiction than merely insisting on a certain accumulation of factual connections with the province. From the previous decisions, he drew eight factors that, he said, should go into the evaluation of whether jurisdiction *simpliciter* was present. The factors were as follows (at para. 75-110):

(1) the connection between the forum and the plaintiff's claim — this reflects the forum's "interest in protecting the legal rights of its residents and affording injured plaintiffs generous access for litigating claims against tortfeasors" (para. 77);

(2) the connection between the forum and the defendant — "If the defendant has done anything within the jurisdiction that bears upon the claim advanced by the plaintiff, the case for assuming jurisdiction is strengthened" (para. 82);

(3) unfairness to the defendant in assuming jurisdiction — "The principles of order and fairness require further consideration, because acts or conduct that are insufficient to render the defendant subject to the jurisdiction may still have a bearing on the fairness of assumed jurisdiction. Some activities, by their very nature, involve a sufficient risk of harm to extra-provincial parties that any unfairness in assuming jurisdiction is mitigated or eliminated" (para. 86);

(4) unfairness to the plaintiff in not assuming jurisdiction — "The principles of order and fairness should be considered in relation to the plaintiff as well as the defendant" (para. 88);

(5) the involvement of other parties to the suit — "The twin goals of avoiding a multiplicity of proceedings and avoiding the risk of inconsistent results are relevant considerations" (para. 91);

(6) the court's willingness to recognize and enforce an extra-provincial judgment rendered on the same jurisdictional basis — this stems from the proposition that *Morguard* made clear, namely, that "precisely the same real and substantial connection test [as applies to the recognition and enforcement of extra-provincial judgments] applies to the assumption of jurisdiction against an out-of-province defendant" (para. 38);

(7) whether the case is interprovincial or international in nature — "the decisions in *Morguard*, *Tolofson* (v. *Jensen*, [1994] 3 S.C.R. 1022, 120 D.L.R. (4th) 289) and *Hunt* suggest that the assumption of jurisdiction is more easily justified in interprovincial

cases than in international cases," because of the emphasis these cases placed on the constitutional imperatives that are implicit in the Canadian federal system (para. 95); and

(8) comity and the standards of jurisdiction, recognition, and enforcement prevailing elsewhere — in interprovincial cases, it is unnecessary to consider the standards that prevail in other jurisdictions, but "in international cases, it may be helpful to consider international standards, particularly the rules governing assumed jurisdiction and the recognition and enforcement of judgments in the location in which the defendant is situated" (para. 102).

On the basis of these factors, jurisdiction *simpliciter* was established only in the action with respect to the automobile accident in Alberta. In all five cases, factor (1) pointed towards jurisdiction, since the plaintiffs were from Ontario and their injuries affected them there, and factor (2) pointed away from it, because the defendants had done nothing in Ontario. In the Alberta case, factor (3) did not loom large because it was not unfair that defendants driving in Alberta should be liable to suit in another province by residents of that province whom they injured. In the other cases, the unfairness to the defendants was perceived to be greater. Even in the New York car accident case, the reasonable expectations of the New York defendants were said to be directed at litigation in their home state, not in Ontario, with which they had no connection (*Gajraj* at para. 17). Factor (4) played a role in the Alberta case because, given his injuries, it would be difficult for the plaintiff to litigate in Alberta, and he had no insurance that would cover the costs (*Muscutt* at para. 90). In the other cases, the court thought it was not unfair to require the plaintiffs to bring their claims in the defendants' home country. Factor (5) was not important in any of the cases, because in none of them were the claims against the non-Ontario defendants part of a group of interrelated claims for which Ontario was the more appropriate forum. Factor (6) featured in the four international cases, the Court of Appeal taking the view that an Ontario court would not recognize a judgment from the other country if the other country's court took jurisdiction over an Ontario defendant in the same circumstances as those that were put forward as being sufficient for an Ontario court to take jurisdiction. Factor (7) also militated against a finding of jurisdiction in the international cases and in favour of such a finding in the Alberta case. And factor (8) worked against finding jurisdiction in the international cases, because there was no evidence in any of the four that an Ontario judgment would be recognized in the defendants' home country.

Note. The multi-factored approach taken by the Ontario Court of Appeal in these five cases highlights the labile nature of the concept of jurisdiction *simpliciter.* This stems from the fact that the "order and fairness" side of *Morguard* predominates over the "real and substantial connection" side. Only the first two of the eight factors are strictly factual in nature. All the rest are designed, more or less explicitly, to assess the consequences of taking jurisdiction from the point of view of whether doing so would further the ends of justice.

The Court of Appeal's approach also highlights the extensive overlap, if its approach is correct, between jurisdiction *simpliciter* and *forum non conveniens.* Of the eight factors laid down by the court, only factor (6) (whether an Ontario court would recognize a foreign judgment given in parallel circumstances) would not usually be considered as part of a *forum conveniens* decision. All the factors have a clear bearing on the appropriateness of an Ontario forum as opposed to a foreign place of trial, the exact issue at stake in a *forum conveniens* dispute. Sharpe J.A. asserted that there is a distinction between the two concepts and that each has its role to play, but he did not venture into particulars:

The real and substantial connection test requires only *a* real and substantial connection, not *the most* real and substantial connection ... Further, the residual discretion to decline jurisdiction also suggests that the consideration of fairness and efficiency is not exhausted at the stage of assumed jurisdiction and that there is scope for considering these factors at the *forum non conveniens* stage. The residual discretion therefore provides both a significant control on assumed jurisdiction and a rationale for lowering the threshold required for the real and substantial connection test [emphasis in the original] (*Muscutt* at para. 44).

It is thus clear that a court can possess jurisdiction *simpliciter* but still be *forum non conveniens.* It is not clear whether the converse can occur, that is, whether there can ever be a case in which a court will lack jurisdiction *simpliciter* although, on the facts, it is the *forum conveniens.* Sharpe J.A.'s last sentence suggests that the answer is no. See also *O'Brien* v. *Canada (Attorney General),* which is cited immediately below.

The most important new element that these Ontario cases (leave to appeal to the Supreme Court of Canada has not been sought) add to the existing case law is the emphasis on jurisdiction *simpliciter* being the mirror-image of jurisdiction of a foreign court for the purpose of recognizing and enforcing a judgment. This is the converse of the idea, rejected in *Morguard* v. *De Savoye*, that we should recognize foreign courts as having jurisdiction if we would take jurisdiction in a parallel case. The principle is that we should not take jurisdiction ourselves unless we think we would be prepared to recognize a foreign judgment given in the same jurisdictional circumstances. This idea will operate, as it is designed to do, as a restraining influence on the usual wish to assist local plaintiffs by taking jurisdiction on the basis of a liberal rule for service *ex juris*. It is likely to operate more strongly in international cases than in interprovincial ones because, in international cases, there is no federal framework to provide assurance as to the standards of justice in, and ready access by defendants to, the extra-provincial court.

The Ontario Court of Appeal's decisions cast doubt on some earlier cases in which Ontario courts held that they had jurisdiction over claims against non-residents arising out of personal injuries suffered in another country. See *Furtado* v. *Gallant* (2001), 15 C.P.C. (5th) 98 (Ont. S.C.J.), the facts of which were similar to the *Gajraj* case (one of the *Muscutt* group of cases) but which reached the opposite result.

O'Brien v. *Canada (Attorney General)* (2002), 210 D.L.R. (4th) 668, 201 N.S.R. (2d) 338, application for leave to appeal dismissed, 24 Oct. 2002 (S.C.C.) (Nova Scotia Court of Appeal)

The plaintiff, an elderly man in poor health, brought an action in Nova Scotia against the defendants, doctors resident in New Brunswick, alleging that they were negligent in their treatment of him while he was a prisoner in an institution in New Brunswick. The defendants applied for an order setting aside the action on the ground that the Nova Scotia court lacked jurisdiction *simpliciter.* They argued that the mere facts that the plaintiff was now resident in Nova Scotia and was suffering health problems there were not sufficient to provide a real and substantial connection with Nova Scotia. The judge at first instance dismissed the application. The Court of Appeal affirmed. When applying the real and substantial connection test for jurisdiction *simpliciter,* the court must, as a matter of order and fairness, consider the personal circumstances of the parties. There was no patent injustice to the defendants if they had to defend an action in Nova Scotia. Their language of choice was French, but they could testify in French in a Nova Scotia court. On the other hand, considering the problems that the plaintiff would face if he were compelled to sue in New Brunswick, fairness favoured his side.

Note. This case was decided some months before the Ontario Court of Appeal decided *Muscutt* v. *Courcelles,* but the court's approach is similar, especially the weight — decisive in this case — given to "order and fairness," and thus to the individual circumstances of the parties, in the equation. It seems odd that the constitutionality of a court's assertion of jurisdiction should turn on such points as whether the plaintiff is a young ex-convict who can reasonably be expected to go to New Brunswick or an elderly one who is too sick to leave Nova Scotia, but that is the clear implication of the line that the courts have adopted.

See also *McNichol Estate* v. *Woldnik* (2001), 13 C.P.C. (5th) 61, 150 O.A.C. 68 (Ont. C.A.), application for leave to appeal dismissed June 20, 2002 (S.C.C.). In this case, the estate of an Ontario resident who had died in Florida brought malpractice actions in Ontario against four Ontario doctors and a Florida chiropractor who had treated the deceased the day before he died. The court held that the Ontario court had jurisdiction *simpliciter* in the action against the Florida defendant because it was desirable that the claim be decided in a single proceeding with the actions against the Ontario defendants. *Hyundai Auto Canada* v. *Bordeleau* (2002), 60 O.R. (3d) 641, 24 C.P.C. (5th) 81 (S.C.J. (Master)), was an action by an Ontario car distributor against various Québec parties for alleged warranty fraud. The conclusion that the court had jurisdiction *simpliciter* was based on virtually the same analysis as that used for *forum non conveniens,* including giving weight to the risk that the action was statute-barred in Québec.

Jurisdiction *simpliciter* was held not to exist in *Elawar* v. *Fédération des Clubs de Motoneigistes du Québec Inc.* (2001), 57 O.R. (3d) 232, 16 C.P.C. (5th) 307 (S.C.J.) (plaintiff suing with respect to personal injuries suffered in an accident in Quebec).

Teja v. *Rai* (2002), 209 D.L.R. (4th) 148, [2002] 2 W.W.R. 499 (British Columbia Court of Appeal)

The plaintiffs were the spouses of two people who were killed in a single-car accident in Washington State that was caused by the negligence of the defendant driver. The two deceased, the defendant, and three other passengers (who were also injured) were all residents of British Columbia at the time of the accident. By the time of trial, the defendant had become resident in Washington State, but she was willing to attorn to the jurisdiction of the British Columbia court. The plaintiffs, however, brought action against the defendant in Washington because the law of that state was in some respects more favourable to their claims. The defendant persuaded the Washington court to dismiss the action on the ground of *forum non conveniens.* The dismissal was subject to the condition that the British Columbia court take jurisdiction and accept the defendant's waiver of a limitation defence. The plaintiffs now sought a declaration from the British Columbia Supreme Court that it had no jurisdiction *simpliciter* because their actions had no real and substantial connection with the province.

The Court of Appeal, affirming the chambers judge, held that there was jurisdiction *simpliciter.* The real and substantial connection test for determining jurisdiction *simpliciter* had not displaced the old test that if the court has power over the defendant, by reason of presence in the jurisdiction or the defendant's voluntary submission to the authority of the court, the court has jurisdiction. The real and substantial connection test must be taken to incorporate the traditional elements — power over the defendant, situs of a tort, and place of performance of a contract — as relevant connecting factors. Taking into account the defendant's voluntary submission to the jurisdiction of the British Columbia court did not give unwarranted importance to her choice of forum and lesser weight to the plaintiffs' choice. Any unfairness to the plaintiffs arose, not out of the defendant's preference, but out of the action of the Washington court.

Note. Teja v. *Rai,* like the Ontario cases noted earlier, shows how little impact the advent of constitutional controls has so far had on the jurisdictional practice of Canadian courts. The Ontario cases show that jurisdiction over non-consenting defendants who are outside the province will be determined on a flexible standard that scarcely limits a court's ability to take jurisdiction where it sees itself as the *forum conveniens* compared with any alternative forum. The British Columbia case illustrates that jurisdiction *simpliciter* over consenting defendants, or defendants who are (apparently even temporarily) in the province at the time the action is commenced, will exist even if otherwise the action otherwise has very little connection with the province. In other words, the bases for jurisdiction that were accepted before *Morguard* have not been impaired by that case in any way. As Huddart J.A. pointed out in *Teja* (at para. 21-25), the Supreme Court of Canada's judgments in *Morguard* and *Hunt,* both given by La Forest J., include *dicta* supporting the view that the new constitutional parameter was meant only to underpin the courts' jurisdiction in new, non-traditional situations, not to erode their jurisdiction in traditional ones.

Service ex juris *— grounds*

Note. In *Integral Energy & Environmental Engineering Ltd.* v. *Schenker of Canada Ltd.* (2001), 206 D.L.R. (4th) 265, 293 A.R. 327 (C.A.), the court held that a first instance judge had been wrong to give leave to serve an Ontario shipping broker and a Belgian stevendoring firm *ex juris.* The action was brought in regard to damage to a boiler the plaintiff was having shipped from Ontario to Ghana and which was being transferred from one vessel to another in Belgium when it was damaged. It was true that the plaintiff had contracted with the Alberta office of another firm to arrange for the transportation, but any claim against the non-resident parties was necessarily in tort and the tort was not committed in Alberta, which would have been the only available ground for service *ex juris.* See also *Duracool Ltd.* v. *Wright* (2001), 267 A.R. 23 (Q.B.), upholding service *ex juris* on a number of American defendants and third parties, on the basis that the claims against them were for torts committed in Alberta because it was alleged that fraudulent misrepresentations by these parties had been received and acted on in Alberta.

Grounds for service *ex juris* were held not to exist in an action by a Saskatchewan-based insurer for a declaration that it was not bound to defend or indemnify an American insured to whom it had issued a liability insurance policy in connection with the insured's work on a construction project in Pennsylvania. On the facts, the insurance contract was neither made nor broken in Saskatchewan: *Kvaerner U.S. Inc.* v. *Liberty Mut. Ins. Co.* (2002), 217 Sask. R. 109 (C.A.).

Declining jurisdiction — exclusive choice of forum clause

Lamèque Quality Group Ltd. v. *A/S Nyborg Plast* (2001), 213 D.L.R. (4th) 301, 242 N.B.R. (2d) 98, application for leave to appeal dismissed, 23 May 2002 (S.C.C.) (New Brunswick Court of Appeal)

The plaintiff, a company based in New Brunswick, brought an action in that province against the Danish company from whom the plaintiff had purchased a quantity of plastic bags, which were said to be unfit for the purpose for which they had been bought. The confirmation form that the defendant had sent in reply to the plaintiff's order included among the delivery terms a clause: "Any dispute arising out of the agreement shall be settled according to Danish law and with the Maritime and Commercial Court of Copenhagen as venue." In the following clause, it provided that the seller could bring an action for non-payment of invoices "before any competent court or other authority." The defendant applied for a stay of proceedings or dismissal of the action on the ground that the court lacked jurisdiction or should decline it. The plaintiff said that it had not signed a contract with the defendant and so was not bound by the terms in question. The motions judge held that the action should proceed. The clauses were not a clear, exclusive choice of forum, and the defendant had failed to show that the balance of convenience favoured a trial in Denmark.

The Court of Appeal held that the proper course for the motions judge would have been to order a trial on the question of whether the clause formed part of the contract between the parties and defer a decision on interpreting the clause until then. However, it would be a waste of everyone's time and money if the Court of Appeal did not express a view on the interpretation of the clause. It was an exclusive jurisdiction clause. Among other factors, the exception in the following clause made sense only if the first clause was exclusive. If at trial the defendant established that the plaintiff was bound by the clause, the court would have to give effect to it unless the plaintiff met the heavy burden of showing why it should not be enforced. The mere fact that New Brunswick might be a more convenient forum from the plaintiff's perspective would not be a sufficient ground for the court to exercise its discretion against a stay or dismissal of the action. The action was remitted to the trial judge.

Note. In *Rosenthal* v. *Kingsway Gen. Ins. Co.* (2002), 20 C.P.C. (5th) 394 (Ont. S.C.J.), an exclusive choice of forum clause in favour of the English courts, contained in a bill of lading issued by the defendant English freight forwarder to the plaintiff Canadian customer, was not enforced. The court referred to the fact that much of the evidence in the dispute was located in Ontario, all parties to the dispute other than the defendant were closely connected to Ontario, and the defendant had attempted to impose the clause on the plaintiff unilaterally. The court also mentioned difficulties of an unspecified nature that the plaintiff would encounter in suing in England.

Exclusive choice of judicial forum clauses were enforced in *Doug's Recreation Centre Ltd.* v. *Polaris Industries Ltd./Industries Polaris Ltée* (2001), 244 N.B.R. (2d) 198 (C.A.) (clause in dealership contract that actions must be brought in courts of Manitoba), and *1349689 Ontario Inc.* v. *Hollyoake* (2002), 22 C.P.C. (5th) 329 (Ont. S.C.J.) (clause in franchise contract requiring disputes to be brought before courts of Ontario held not to be outweighed, on *forum conveniens* grounds, by other factors connecting the dispute to Manitoba). *Barber* v. *Height of Excellence Financial Planning Group Inc.* (2001), 213 Sask. R. 302 (C.A.), affirmed the decision noted in "Canadian Cases in Private International Law in 2000-1" (2001) 39 Can. Y.B. Int'l L. 592. The Court of Appeal disagreed with the first instance judge's view that the clause was not an exclusive choice of forum, but held that the clause, which was in a partnership contract, did not apply to the tort claims the plaintiff was making.

Declining jurisdiction — forum non conveniens — *defendant resident in the jurisdiction*

Somji v. *Somji* (2001), 292 A.R. 337, 21 R.F.L. (5th) 223 (Alberta Queen's Bench)

A daughter and her parents had immigrated to Canada from Tanzania in 1996 and 1993, respectively, and all were now resident in Alberta. The parents separated in 1994 and the daughter lived with her mother from the time she, the daughter, arrived in Canada. While divorce and matrimonial property proceedings between the parents were pending before the Alberta Queen's Bench, the daughter brought an action claiming a constructive trust over her parents' matrimonial property. The claim was based on the daughter's having helped her parents in the family clothing business in Tanzania from 1971 to 1984, when she was a dependent of her parents. The father applied for a declaration that the *forum conveniens* for the daughter's action was Tanzania and that her statement of claim should be struck out. The judge dismissed the father's application, referring to the fact that Canadian law had a well-developed jurisprudence on constructive trusts and unjust enrichment compared with Tanzania. Moreover, said the judge, Tanzania was a country with corruption, human rights violations, and an inefficient legal system. The daughter's action might not even be conceivable in a country where children were expected to work for their parents without compensation. The parties, the property, and much of the documentation in the case were all in Alberta. That outweighed the fact that the alleged unjust enrichment took place in Tanzania. Given the patriarchal nature of Tanzania and its legal system, to declare it the *forum conveniens* would effectively be to dismiss the daughter's action.

Note. As one of the factors in the *forum conveniens* equation, the judge referred to the fact that the daughter's claim would be governed by the law of Tanzania, as the law of the place where the unjust enrichment of the defendants took place, and said that proving the law of Tanzania would not be an insurmountable obstacle in an Alberta court. It is not easy to square the applicability of Tanzanian law with the judge's comments on the underdeveloped nature of Tanzania's law of restitution when compared with Canada's.

Lee v. *Li* (2002), 100 B.C.L.R. (3d) 291, 44 E.T.R. (2d) 126 (British Columbia Court of Appeal)

This was an estate dispute between three daughters, on the one hand, and the son and daughter-in-law, on the other, of a testator who had died resident in British Columbia but leaving a valuable immovable property in Taiwan. All the parties were resident in British Columbia. The son and his wife relied on a purported will of the testator. The daughters' action was brought for a declaration that the will was fraudulently made by the son and his wife, and for damages against them. Evidence was submitted that proceedings were taking place in Taiwan with respect to the estate, but there was no evidence as to the outcome. The defendants in the British Columbia action, the son and his wife, sought a stay of those proceedings. The first instance judge held that the trial should proceed because the defendants had delayed until almost the start of the trial before raising their jurisdictional objections. The judge went on to make a preliminary finding of fraud against the defendants, but deferred an assessment of damages until the outcome of the Taiwanese proceedings was known.

The Court of Appeal held that the judge should have stayed the action because there was no evidence that a decision of the British Columbia court would have any effect on the course of proceedings in Taiwan, where the immovable property was situated. Only the Taiwanese court had jurisdiction to deal with the property and therefore to deal with the issues about the genuineness of the will. Without evidence that the daughters had relied on the fraud or that the Taiwanese courts had accepted the fraudulent will, the daughters' claim for damages against their brother and sister-in-law had to fail as well. It was also appropriate, in deciding on the stay, to bear in mind the need for comity among the courts of different countries.

Note. Courts refused to stay proceedings on the ground of *forum non conveniens* in *Canadian National Ry. Co. v. Scott Steel Ltd.* (2001), 207 A.R. 302 (Q.B.) (construction contract was connected with Alberta although the actual project was in British Columbia, denial of stay made conditional on plaintiff's discontinuing a parallel action in British Columbia); *Vanderpol v. Aspen Trailer Co.* (2002), 100 B.C.L.R. (3d) 381 (C.A.) (wrongful dismissal action against a group of companies, the main one of which was based in British Columbia, by an employee who had worked for the defendants in Georgia); *Hodnett v. Taylor Manufacturing Industries Inc.* (2002), 22 C.P.C. (5th) 360 (Ont. S.C.J.) (very similar facts to *Vanderpol,* including the employee's having worked mainly in Georgia); and *ABB Inc. v. MSX International Inc.* (2001), 13 Const. L.R. (3d) 13 (Ont. S.C.J.) (action arising out of deficiencies in construction project in Ontario, both parties being international companies with offices in Ontario).

Declining jurisdiction — forum non conveniens — *defendant resident outside the jurisdiction*

SC International Enterprises Inc. v. Consolidated Freightways Corp. of Delaware (2002), 21 C.P.C. (5th) 238 (British Columbia Supreme Court)

The plaintiff, a British Columbia company, had arranged for a cargo of garments to be shipped from its plant in Mexico to New Jersey. Half the garments had gone missing. The plaintiff brought an action in British Columbia in negligence and breach of contract against CFM, the Mexican company that was responsible for shipment from Mexico to Texas, and CFD, the United States company that was responsible for the onward shipment. The defendants applied for a declaration that the British Columbia court lacked jurisdiction or should decline it. The chambers judge granted a stay, conditional on both defendants' consenting to the jurisdiction of the courts of both Texas and Mexico. The British Columbia court had jurisdiction *simpliciter.* The plaintiff had made a good arguable case that invoicing and payment for the shipments took place in the province and that the plaintiff suffered damage there. Most of the relevant witnesses were in Mexico or Texas and the alleged breach of contract or negligence took place in either or both of those jurisdictions. There was no evidence that the defendants would be subject to a juridical disadvantage in British Columbia. If both defendants consented to the jurisdiction of both Mexico and Texas so the plaintiff could proceed in either of those forums, then both of those jurisdictions would clearly be more appropriate for a trial of the dispute than British Columbia. Otherwise, however, British Columbia was more appropriate because a trial in that province would enable the entire matter to be resolved in one action.

Note. Courts refused to decline jurisdiction on the ground of *forum non conveniens* in the following cases brought against non-resident defendants: *Aimtronics Corp.* v. *Fattouche* (2002), 6 B.C.L.R. (4th) 336 (S.C.) (British Columbia firm suing an Alberta customer and, as guarantor, the customer's parent company; Alberta statutory restrictions on suing guarantors treated as one factor in favour of the plaintiff's chosen forum); and *Skylink Express Inc.* v. *All Canada Express Ltd.* (2001), 17 C.P.C. (5th) 380 (Ont. S.C.J.) (Ontario-based airline suing for damage to its airplane at an airport in Québec allegedly caused by the operator of another aircraft and by ground crew there).

Courts declined jurisdiction in *2916372 Manitoba Ltd.* v. *Kornberg* (2002), 164 Man. R. (2d) 1 (Q.B.) (ex-wife's action against Minnesota-resident former spouse, concerning his activities with respect to a Manitoba company that was set up as part of their matrimonial settlement, about which a great deal of litigation had already taken place in Minnesota); *1349689 Ontario Inc.* v. *Hollyoake* (2002), 22 C.P.C. (5th) 329 (Ont. S.C.J.) (breach of confidence action by Ontario franchisor against a franchisee's sons in respect of their conduct of an independent business in Manitoba); *Milligan* v. *Lines Overseas Management (Cayman) Ltd.* (2002), 18 C.C.E.L. (3d) 96 (Ont. S.C.J. (Master)) (Ontario resident suing international firm for wrongful dismissal from a position in its Cayman Islands office); *Aristocrat* v. *National Bank of the Republic of Kazakhstan* (2001), 21 C.P.C. (5th) 147 (Ont. S.C.J.) (action for loss on shares of a Kazakhstani private bank that was nationalized); and *Carlyle* v. *Lloydminster (City)* (2002), 220 Sask. R. 202 (Q.B.) (contract actions against Alberta-resident creators of a public monument installed in a Saskatchewan city that sits on the Alberta-Saskatchewan border).

BNP Paribas (Canada) v. *Mécs* (2002), 60 O.R. (3d) 205, 22 C.P.C. (5th) 341 (Ontario Superior Court of Justice)

The plaintiffs had obtained a judgment in the Quebec Superior Court against the defendants, who were residents of Hungary. The plaintiffs brought an action on the judgment in Ontario, serving the defendants *ex juris* under Civil Procedure Rule 17.02(m) ("the proceeding consists of a claim on a judgment of a court outside Ontario"). The defendants applied for a stay on the basis that Ontario was *forum non conveniens*. The judge dismissed the application. The concept of forum shopping, which underlies the *forum non conveniens* discretion, does not apply to enforcing foreign judgments. Rule 17.06, which deals with the discretion to decline jurisdiction, is worded permissively rather than mandatorily, and so accommodates the view that *forum non conveniens* is inapplicable to the enforcement of a Québec judgment. Principles of comity require that, absent issues of fraud or natural justice, the plaintiff should have the opportunity to enforce a Québec judgment in Ontario. Whether the defendants had assets in Ontario was irrelevant to the question whether the court should recognize the Québec judgment.

(b)   Class proceedings

Class including non-residents

Note. Wilson v. *Servier Canada Inc.* (2002), 213 D.L.R. (4th) 751, 59 O.R. (3d) 656 (Ont. S.C.J.), appeal quashed (2002), 220 D.L.R. (4th) 191 (Ont. C.A.), was a sequel to the Ontario Divisional Court's decision noted in "Canadian Cases in Private International Law in 2000-1" (2001) 39 Can. Y.B. Int'l L. 594. Four French corporations, which the representative plaintiff sought to add as defendants to the class action, repeated the argument made in the earlier case that an Ontario court could not constitutionally entertain an action by a national class, the result of which would be that non-Ontario plaintiffs, as part of the class, would be suing non-Ontario defendants for injuries suffered outside Ontario. The Superior Court rejected the argument on the same grounds as the Divisional Court had used. The constitutional imperative was that the assertion of jurisdiction over extra-provincial defendants be compatible with principles of order and fairness. There was a real and substantial connection with Ontario, based on the claim that the Ontario-resident members of the class had been injured in Ontario through the defendants' direct or indirect business activity in Ontario. If the interests of justice made it desirable that non-Ontario plaintiffs be included in the class, the Class Proceedings Act, S.O. 1992, c. 6, provided the machinery for doing so, which also allowed any non-resident to opt out of the class. The Ontario Court of Appeal quashed the appeal from the Superior Court's decision because the constitutional issue sought to be raised had already been decided in the earlier case, and the defendants had engaged in a proliferation of proceedings that had led to unacceptable delay. The matter should proceed to a decision on the merits.

See also *Hoy* v. *Medtronic Inc.* (2001), 94 B.C.L.R. (3d) 169, 12 C.P.C. 370 (B.C.S.C.), aff'd without reference to this point, 2003 B.C.C.A. 316, in which a national class was held appropriate in an action by patients who had had pacemakers implanted that were alleged to have had defective electric leads. Under section 16(2) of the Class Proceedings Act, R.S.B.C. 1996, c. 50, non-resident members of the class must opt into the litigation, whereas under the Ontario legislation they are automatically in unless they opt out.

As noted last year, the question remains whether courts in other provinces or countries would be bound to enforce a judgment in a class proceeding in so far as it purported to hold non-resident defendants liable to non-resident plaintiffs for injuries suffered outside the forum province. As far as the courts of other Canadian provinces are concerned, the issue is whether they will agree with the Ontario courts that the efficiency of having a national class supplies the necessary constitutional support for the taking of jurisdiction by the originating court. If they do, they are bound to recognize the judgment in the class proceeding under the *Morguard* principle. Even if they do not, there may still be a possible ground for enforcing the judgment on the basis of the defendant's attornment to the originating court's jurisdiction, assuming the defendant contested the case on the merits.

(c)   Actions relating to property

Bankruptcy and insolvency

Sam Lévy & Associates Inc. v. *Azco Mining Inc.*, [2001] 3 S.C.R. 978, 207 D.L.R. (4th) 385 (Supreme Court of Canada)

A corporation that carried on business in Québec was petitioned into bankruptcy. The Quebec Superior Court took jurisdiction under the Bankruptcy and Insolvency Act, R.S.C. 1985, c. B-3. The trustee applied to that court for an order to recover certain shares and warrants from an American venture capital company, whose main place of business was in British Columbia. The bankrupt's rights to the shares and warrants stemmed from a contract pursuant to which the bankrupt was developing a gold mining property in Africa in return for financing from the American company. The American corporation moved under section 187(7) of the act to transfer the proceeding to the British Columbia Supreme Court. It relied on what it argued was a choice of forum clause in the joint venture contract with the bankrupt, and on the fact that it wished to counterclaim against the bankrupt. Both the Superior Court and the Quebec Court of Appeal dismissed the motion.

The Supreme Court of Canada affirmed the dismissal. Under section 43 of the act, a bankruptcy petition must be presented to the court in the judicial district of the debtor's locality, which was the Quebec Superior Court. The act established a national scheme, thus giving the Québec court jurisdiction to deal with the debtor's assets throughout Canada. In order to make the system of a national bankruptcy jurisdiction effective, the powers of the court must be broadly interpreted. They extend to disputes related to the administration of the bankrupt's estate, but not to disputes with "strangers to the bankruptcy" or disputes that lack the "complexion of a matter in bankruptcy." The trustee's claim for the shares and warrants, or for money in lieu of them, was a remedy the Québec court could give under the act, because it was essentially a claim for specific property, not a claim for damages, which admittedly could only be brought in the ordinary civil courts.

There was no sufficient cause to transfer the proceedings to British Columbia. The contractual clause in question was not a choice of forum but only a choice of law clause. Even an exclusive choice of forum clause would not dictate a transfer. The policy of the act was to vest "single control" over the bankruptcy proceedings in one court for the sale of efficient administration, even if that inflicted additional cost on creditors and debtors in making their cases to the court. The connections that an individual dispute might have with another jurisdiction had to be balanced against the need to avoid fragmenting the bankruptcy proceedings among different courts. In any event, the connections of the contract in question with British Columbia were not particularly strong.

Note. See also *Holt Cargo Systems Inc.* v. *ABC Containerline N.V. (Trustees of)*, noted later under the heading (e) Admiralty, which also includes important observations on the exercise of bankruptcy jurisdiction by Canadian courts.

(d)   Infants and children

Custody — grounds for jurisdiction

Note. In *Turner* v. *Viau* (2002), 26 R.F.L. (5th) 440 (Ont. C.A.), jurisdiction in custody was held not to exist under section 22 of the Children's Law Reform Act, R.S.O. 1990, c. C.12, because the child was still habitually resident in Québec, despite the mother's having moved to Ontario with the child; there was no evidence the father had agreed to, or even acquiesced in, the move.

Custody — declining jurisdiction

Note. See *Brown* v. *Bezanson* (2002), 27 R.F.L. (5th) 1 (Sask. Q.B.), holding that proceedings to vary a custody order, which had been made as a corollary order in divorce proceedings, should be transferred to Nova Scotia on *forum conveniens* grounds pursuant to section 6(3) of the Divorce Act, R.S.C. 1985, c. 3 (2nd Supp.). In *DeRoussy* v. *Boekemeyer* (2001), 210 Sask. R. 319 (Q.B.), the court, although it had made the original custody order, declined jurisdiction to vary it because both parents and the child were now resident in Mexico, where proceedings had also been brought.

Custody — enforcement of extraprovincial custody order

Note. Ndegwa v. *Ndegwa* (2001), 20 R.F.L. (5th) 118 (Ont. S.C.J.), was an application to enforce a custody order made in Kenya in favour of the father. Enforcement was refused because the mother had neither had reasonable notice of the commencement of the Kenyan proceedings nor had an opportunity to be heard in them (sections 41(a) and (b), respectively, of the Children's Law Reform Act, R.S.O. 1990, c. C.12). Nor would the mother's custody application to the Ontario court be stayed, because the mother had presented credible evidence that returning the child to the father in Kenya would expose the child to a risk of serious harm (section 23 of the act).

Child abduction — Hague Convention on the Civil Aspects of International Child Abduction

Note. Orders for the return of a child under provincial statutes implementing the Hague Convention were made in *Zaman* v. *Khan* (2001), 20 R.F.L. (5th) 209 (Alta. Q.B.), *Aulwes* v. *Mai* (2002), 204 N.S.R. (2d) 349 (S.C.), and *Smushkevich* v. *Gartner* (2002), 29 R.F.L.

(5th) 412 (Ont. S.C.J.). Each was a case in which a parent had removed the child (in the *Aulwes* case, seven years ago) from the foreign jurisdiction without the knowledge of the other parent. In *Zimmerhansl* v. *Zimmerhansl* (2001), 20 R.F.L. (5th) 218 (Alta. Q.B.), the applicant parent was held to have consented and so there was no wrongful removal. In two other cases, the removal or retention was wrongful, but orders for the return of the child were refused on the ground that the child would be exposed to a grave risk of psychological harm or would be placed in an intolerable situation, if returned: *Kovacs* v. *Kovacs* (2002), 212 D.L.R. (4th) 711, 59 O.R. (3d) 671 (Ont. S.C.J.) (applicant parent was a fugitive from justice in Hungary, his country of residence); *Williams* v. *Elliott* (2001), 21 R.F.L. (5th) 247 (Ont. S.C.J.) (return refused because young children's separation from the mother would be intolerable for them, but jurisdiction in custody declined in favour of the court of the father's residence, North Carolina, and mother ordered not to leave Ontario until further order of that court).

(e)   Admiralty

Maritime lien claimant's action against ship — effect of foreign bankruptcy proceeding against shipowners

Holt Cargo Systems Inc. v. *ABC Containerline N.V. (Trustees of)*, [2001] 3 S.C.R. 907, 207 D.L.R. (4th) 577 (Supreme Court of Canada)

A United States company brought an action in the Federal Court of Canada against a ship for which it had supplied stevedoring and related services in a port in New Jersey. The ship was arrested just outside the Canadian port of Halifax. A week after the arrest, the ship's owners were adjudged bankrupt by a court in Belgium. The trustees applied to the Quebec Superior Court for an order recognizing the bankruptcy judgment and declaring it executory. The Québec court granted the order. Then the trustees obtained an order in Belgium requesting the Canadian courts' assistance in restraining actions against the bankrupt by creditors. The Québec court, exercising jurisdiction in bankruptcy, issued an order restraining all creditors and ordering the ship in Halifax, or the proceeds from its sale, to be delivered to the trustees. The Federal Court subsequently ordered the ship to be sold. The trustees claimed the proceeds. The Federal Court, Trial Division, refused to stay the proceedings for the sale of the ship and gave the United States company's maritime lien priority over the trustees' claim. The Federal Court of Appeal affirmed that decision.

On further appeal, the Supreme Court of Canada held that no order of the Québec court in bankruptcy could restrict the jurisdiction of the Federal Court to deal with the vessel. Comity was as much an obligation between domestic courts as between domestic and foreign courts. The Federal Court could have stayed the proceedings for sale of the ship if it was in the interests of justice to do so (section 50(1) of the Federal Court Act, R.S.C. 1985, c. F-7), but had not erred in principle in refusing a stay.

The creation and validity of the maritime lien were determined according to United States law, as the law of the place where the lien was said to have arisen. It was for Canadian law as the *lex fori* to grant the remedy and set the priorities. The United States company's lien right in a Canadian court was a legitimate advantage because the evidence was that a Belgian court would not give effect to its lien. Canadian law would recognize the order of a court of the bankrupt's domicile as effective to transfer of ownership of the vessel to the Belgian trustees. Under Canadian bankruptcy law, however, their title was subject to the prior claims of secured creditors, and a maritime lien holder was a secured creditor.

The trustees argued that Canadian law should embody a "universalist" approach to international bankruptcies and defer to the jurisdiction of a single bankruptcy court to determine all questions relating to the claims of creditors. That argument was rejected. While Canadian courts generally favour a process of universal distribution and recognize a foreign trustee's title to property, they also permit concurrent bankruptcies and protect the vested rights of what are regarded as secured creditors under Canadian law. With respect to the latter, the usual Canadian position has been that a foreign trustee in bankruptcy should have no higher claim on the *secured* assets of a bankrupt than if the bankruptcy had occurred in Canada. In order words, Canada has adhered to a "plurality approach" that recognizes that different jurisdictions may have a legitimate and concurrent interest in the conduct of an international bankruptcy, and that the interests asserted in Canadian courts may, but not necessarily must, be subordinated in a particular case to a foreign bankruptcy regime. The general approach reflects a desire for coordination rather than subordination, with deference being accorded only after due consideration of all the relevant circumstances rather than automatically accorded because of an abstract "universalist" principle.

According to the court, the pragmatism of the traditional approach commends itself still, and various features of Part XIII of the Bankruptcy and Insolvency Act, R.S.C. 1985, c. B-3, which was added in 1997 to deal with international insolvencies, are consistent with it. These include the ability of a court to restrict a Canadian trustee's authority to assets in Canada (section 268(2)), thus implying an acceptance of parallel bankruptcy proceedings; the specific provision that a court is not compelled to enforce an order made by a foreign court (section 268(6)); and the explicit denial of extraterritorial effect to foreign stay orders in so far as they relate to claims by creditors who reside or carry on business in Canada against property situated in Canada (section 269).

Therefore, a Canadian court sitting in admiralty, when asked to stay proceedings in order to further an international bankruptcy proceeding, must balance the need to promote the coordinated conduct of the bankruptcy against the need to do justice to the particular litigants who come before it. The judge of the Federal Court had done so appropriately in this case. A lien claimant had a legitimate advantage that it could reasonably expect the Federal Court to enforce under Canadian maritime law. The lack of connection between the dispute and Canada was a factor, but, given the lifestyle of ships, there would often be situations in which the claimant legitimately availed itself of the courts of a jurisdiction where the ship happened for the moment to be. The system of maritime commerce provided security to creditors, and that was to be weighed against the obligation of comity towards the Belgian bankruptcy court.

Note. The orders made by the Quebec Superior Court in regard to the vessel were set aside on appeal to the Quebec Court of Appeal, whose decision was affirmed by the Supreme Court of Canada in *Re Antwerp Bulkcarriers N.V.,* [2001] 3 S.C.R. 951, 207 D.L.R. (4th) 612. The bankruptcy jurisdiction of the Québec court did not extend to making orders that effectively countermanded valid orders made by the Federal Court. The proper remedy for the bankruptcy trustees, as the *Holt* case explains, was to seek a stay of the Federal Court proceedings against the ship.

2   Québec

(a)   Action personnelle

Compétence internationale — Article 3148 C.C.Q. — préjudice subi au Québec

Sorel-Tracy Terminal maritime c. F.S.L. Ltd., [2001] A.J.Q. N° 1515 (Cour supérieure du Québec)

La demanderesse, une société québécoise, a intenté une action en réclamation pour des services d'arrimage de marchandises dans le port de Sorel qu'elle a rendus à la codéfenderesse, une société constituée selon les lois de la République des îles Marshall. L'autre codéfenderesse, une société belge, est également poursuivie en sa qualité de caution. Le contrat de services contient une clause prévoyant que toute dispute devra être soumise aux tribunaux du Québec. La société caution invoque l'incompétence des tribunaux québécois pour entendre le litige à son égard puisque son obligation de garantie doit être exécutée en Belgique et qu'elle n'a pas convenu avec la codéfenderesse de soumettre le litige aux autorités québécoises. Elle demande également aux tribunaux québécois de décliner compétence en vertu du règle du *forum non conveniens*. Les deux sociétés étrangères sont dirigées par la même personne.

La Cour supérieure a rejeté l'exception déclinatoire. D'une part, l'action de la demanderesse vise distinctement deux défenderesses, l'une pour services rendus et l'autre à titre de caution, et, dans ce cas, l'article 3139 C.C.Q. ne permet pas l'assignation d'un défendeur étranger du simple fait que son codéfendeur a été légalement assigné au Québec. D'autre part, l'appauvrissement de la demanderesse ne saurait équivaloir au préjudice devant avoir été subi au Québec par un demandeur pour donner compétence aux tribunaux québécois selon l'article 3148 C.C.Q. S'il en était ainsi, il suffirait désormais qu'un demandeur ait un compte bancaire au Québec et qu'il allègue s'être appauvri pour donner compétence aux tribunaux québécois à l'égard d'un défendeur étranger. Par ailleurs, selon la lettre de garantie, la société caution doit exécuter à Québec son obligation de payer les factures adressées à la codéfenderesse. Cela rend les tribunaux québécois compétents à son endroit, peu importe qu'elle soit liée ou non par la clause d'élection de for. Quant au *forum non conveniens,* le présent litige ne présente pas de caractère exceptionnel fondant les tribunaux québécois à décliner compétence en faveur des tribunaux belges.

Élection de for — renvoi à l'arbitrage à l'étranger — faillite et insolvabilité

Peachtree Network (Proposition de), [2002] R.J.Q. 1938 (Cour supérieure du Québec)

Peachtree et l'intimée, Stime, ont signé une entente visant le développement d'un logiciel au benefice de cette dernière. Cette entente contenait une clause d'arbitrage avec élection de for. MyButler.com inc., qui avait conçu le logiciel, avait cédé tous ses droits à son égard à Peachtree. Ensuite, Peachtree a déposé un avis de son intention de faire une proposition à ses créanciers. Le syndic requérant a été nommé séquestre intérimaire. Stime a aussitôt mis le syndic en demeure de lui céder les codes sources du logiciel. Elle a obtenu une ordonnance de sauvegarde qui interdisait à Peachtree et au syndic de délaisser volontairement les codes sources en faveur de 3323455 Canada inc. Le tribunal a ratifié la proposition faite aux créanciers par Peachtree. Entre-temps, MyButler, qui est maintenant en faillite, a fait l'objet d'une ordonnance de sauvegarde semblable à celle rendue contre Peachtree. Le syndic a demandé le renvoi du litige à l'arbitrage devant le Tribunal de commerce, à Paris.

La Cour supérieure a décidé que le recours est prématuré. La clause d'arbitrage prévue à l'entente entre Peachtree et Stime prévoit une procédure préalable de conciliation. Or, cette étape n'a pas encore été franchie et il n'est pas possible de savoir si les parties utiliseront les procédures d'arbitrage. D'autre part, la demande de renvoi n'est pas fondée à l'égard de MyButler puisque celle-ci n'est pas partie aux conventions signées entre Peachtree et Stime. Les codes sources font partie du patrimoine de Peachtree ou de MyButler. Il s'agit de déterminer si Stime a des droits à faire valoir à cet égard. Pour décider de l'application d'une élection de for dans un contexte de faillite, il faut tenir compte des objectifs d'ordre public de la législation en matière de faillite. En sa qualité de syndic et de séquestre intérimaire, le requérant ne peut demander à un tribunal étranger de se prononcer sur la possession d'une partie de l'actif de l'une ou de l'autre débitrice. Dans la mesure où le litige porte sur des biens qui font partie du patrimoine dont le syndic a la saisine, seul un tribunal québécois siégeant en matière de faillite a compétence pour le trancher.

B   Procedure / *Procédure*

1   Common Law and Federal

(a)   Obtaining evidence abroad for local proceedings

Evidence given abroad subject to confidentiality order

Vitapharm Canada Ltd. v. *F. Hoffmann-LaRoche Ltd.* (2002), 212 D.L.R. (4th) 563, 18 C.P.R. (4th) 267, affirmed (2003), 223 D.L.R. (4th) 445, 23 C.P.R. (4th) 454 (Ont. C.A.) (Ontario Divisional Court)

The parties were engaged in class proceedings in Ontario about the alleged price-fixing by the defendant of its vitamin products. Similar proceedings involving some of the same parties were ongoing in the United States. Documents and information disclosed in the United States proceedings were the subject of a protective order by the United States court that was intended to preserve confidentiality of the information. The plaintiff in the Ontario proceedings applied to the United States court to be exempted from the protective order. The defendant brought a motion before the Ontario court for an injunction against the plaintiff's making this application. It was argued that the plaintiff was illegitimately seeking to use testimony obtained under compulsion in the United States for the purpose of Canadian proceedings.

Both the motions judge and the Divisional Court refused the injunction. The motion being made in the United States court was not to obtain rights of discovery but to secure access to the fruits of discovery conducted by parties in United States litigation. The evidence would have been disclosed if the Ontario proceedings had not existed. The United States motions should be governed by the applicable United States law in a United States court. Whether to entertain the motions or grant any relief was entirely for the United States court to determine. It would be unseemly for the Ontario court to purport to assume jurisdiction over proceedings pending in a foreign court. Even if the defendants had sought the intervention of the United States court in the Ontario litigation, it would not be necessary to grant injunctive relief before the hearing of the motions by the United States court.

Evidence sought in order to impugn foreign judgment

Note. In *Metalsac Ticdaret Ve Sanayi Ltd. STI* v. *Taylor Steel Inc.* (2001), 20 C.P.C. (5th) 277 (Ont. S.C.J.), the defendant in an action on a Turkish judgment moved to have the court issue a letter of request to the judicial authorities in Turkey, requesting that the Turkish court issue process against the court-appointed experts who had given evidence in the Turkish proceedings, ordering them to attend as witnesses in the Ontario enforcement proceedings. The motion was dismissed because the judgment debtor was seeking to impeach the foreign judgment on its merits by showing that the individuals had given biased testimony. With limited exceptions, an enforceable foreign judgment cannot be impeached on the merits.

(b) Obtaining evidence locally for foreign proceedings

Letter of request — scope of production and discovery of evidence

Note. OptiMight Communications Inc. v. *Innovance Inc.* (2002), 18 C.P.R. (4th) 362, 17 C.P.C. (5th) 238 (Ont. C.A.), held that a letter of request from a federal District Court in California was entitled to endorsement, but the motions judge should have limited the scope of the order because the full breadth of the request would subject the respondent corporation to overly broad, potentially irrelevant, and unduly burdensome production and discovery.

(c) Remedies

Damages — foreign currency — conversion

Note. In an action to enforce a United States arbitral award for US $35,000 under the International Commercial Arbitration Act, C.C.S.M., c. C151, the court held that the date for calculating the award in Canadian dollars must be the date of the Canadian judgment: *Proctor* v. *Schellenberg,* [2002] 7 W.W.R. 287, 22 B.L.R. (3d) 256 (Man. Q.B.), aff'd without reference to this point, [2003] 2 W.W.R. 621, 30 B.L.R. (3d) 1 (Man. C.A.). The court cited the Currency Act, R.S.C. 1985, c. C-52 as requiring this result, although the better view is that the statute does not dictate any particular conversion date, so the date of payment of the award would also be a possible date (and, in principle, is usually to be preferred).

C   Foreign Judgments / Jugements étrangers

1   Common Law and Federal

(a)   Defences applicable to enforcement by action or registration

Penal and revenue laws

Note. See *Re iTV Games Inc.,* noted later under D. Choice of Law; 1. Common Law and Federal; (c) Exclusion of foreign law — penal and revenue laws.

(b)   Enforcement of non-monetary orders

Note. Orders other than for the payment of money are not enforceable at common law, but some statutes make them enforceable among Canadian provinces. In *Jennings* v. *Alberta (Provincial Treasurer)* (2001), 92 Alta. L.R. (3d) 122 (Q.B.), a British Columbia

order, made in connection with divorce proceedings, giving the
wife a share of her husband's Alberta public sector pension, was
held operative in Alberta under the legislation that governed the
pension, which gives effect to matrimonial property orders made
in another Canadian jurisdiction. The Uniform Enforcement of
Canadian Judgments and Decrees Act, promulgated by the Uniform Law Conference of Canada in 1999, has been enacted in
British Columbia (S.B.C. 2003, c. 29, not yet in force) and Nova
Scotia (S.N.S. 2001, c. 30, not yet in force). This act puts non-
monetary orders on the same footing for enforcement purposes as
monetary orders, but gives the enforcing court power to vary the
order or limit its enforcement.

(c)   Registration under uniform reciprocal enforcement of
      judgments legislation or an international convention

Defences unique to registration statutes — registration ex parte

Note. The creditor under an Alberta judgment was held not entitled to have it registered *ex parte,* because the debtor neither was
personally served with process (notice was sent by registered mail)
nor submitted to the original court's jurisdiction (Reciprocal Enforcement of Judgments Act, R.S.N.W.T. 1988, c. R-1, s. 2(3)): *Hertz
Truck/Car Rentals* v. *Mendo* (2001), 14 C.P.C. (5th) 370 (N.W.T.S.C.).
The presence of a real and substantial connection between the litigation and Alberta was irrelevant to the operation of the statutory
rules.

(d)   Registration under uniform reciprocal enforcement of
      maintenance orders legislation

Final order — defences to registration

Note. See *Weller* v. *Davison* (2002), 26 R.F.L. (5th) 443, 203 N.S.R.
(2d) 353 (C.A.), which rejected an argument that a support order
should not have been registered because the respondent's participation in the original proceedings had been limited by the court.
The limitations had been appropriate in light of the respondent's
conduct.

Provisional order — making of order by original court — requirements

S.(M.B.) v. *L.(S.)* (2001), 93 Alta. L.R. (3d) 135, 22 R.F.L. (5th)
432 (Alberta Queen's Bench)

The Alberta court made an order for child support in an amount to be calculated on the basis of the father's income according to the federal Child Support Guidelines (made under the Divorce Act, R.S.C. 1985, c. 3 (2nd Supp.)). The court did not specify the guideline income of the father, because he was resident in Québec and the court did not have evidence as to his income. The Québec court refused to confirm this order because no specific quantum of support was ordered, as is required by the Loi sur l'Exécution réciproque d'ordonnances alimentaires, L.R.Q., c. E-19. The mother sought a ruling from the Alberta court on the validity of its provisional order. The court held that it must specify the quantum of support in a provisional order as if it were a final order and cannot accept such orders from other provinces without a specific quantum. Section 3(2) of the Reciprocal Enforcement of Maintenance Orders Act, R.S.A. 1980, c. 7.1, states that a provisional order may only include maintenance provisions that the court could have included in a final order. So in the provisional order, the court, using the applicant's evidence, should specify a quantum, which the confirming court can modify in light of the respondent's evidence.

Note. Compare *Baugh* v. *Samuels* (2001), 24 R.F.L. (5th) 270 (Ont. S.C.J.), in which a Georgia support order stating the judge's "opinion ... that the [respondent] owes a duty of support to the [applicant] and that such petition should be dealt with according to law," but giving no amount, was sufficient to constitute a provisional order under the Reciprocal Enforcement of Support Orders Act, R.S.O., c. R.7. Georgia law governed the applicant's entitlement to support, and Ontario law (the provincial statutory child support guidelines) would fill the gap as to quantum.

Provisional order — enforcement — distinction from final order

Note. Osborn v. *Towaij* (2002), 27 R.F.L. (5th) 410 (Ont. S.C.J.), deemed a purportedly final child support order of a court in Washington State to be provisional for the purposes of the Reciprocal Enforcement of Support Orders Act, R.S.O. 1990, c. R.7, because the Ontario-resident father had not received proper notice of the Washington proceedings (only fifteen days instead of the thirty that were customary in Ontario).

Confirmation of provisional order — evidence required

Note. See *Baugh* v. *Samuels,* noted earlier under the heading Provisional order — making of order by original court — requirements.

2   Québec

(a)   Motifs pour non-reconnaissance du jugement

Ordre public

DirecTV Inc. c. *Scullion,* [2002] R.J.Q. 2086 (Cour supérieure du Québec)

La demanderesse, une société américaine, exploite un système de télévision par satellite. Les défendeurs, des résidents québécois, ont manufacturé et distribué des cartes donnant accès au système de la demanderesse sans permission. Un jugement par défaut a été rendu par un tribunal américain condamnant les défendeurs à payer à la demanderesse plus de 19 millions de dollars. De leur côté, les défendeurs ont déposé devant les tribunaux québécois une action en dommages-intérêts contre la demanderesse et la Gendarmerie royale du Canada (GRC) pour abus de droit et perquisitions abusives. Aucune défense n'a encore été produite dans ce dossier. La demanderesse demande que le jugement américain soit homologué. Les défendeurs s'y opposent, alléguant, d'une part, que le jugement américain est incompatible avec l'ordre public parce que la condamnation en dommages est excessive et que la preuve a été obtenue illégalement de la GRC et, d'autre part, qu'une autre cause est pendante devant une autorité québécoise.

La Cour supérieure a accueilli la requête en reconnaissance et en exécution du jugement américain. D'une part, la condamnation d'ordre pécuniaire du tribunal américain n'est pas incompatible avec l'ordre public pusqu'il ne s'agit pas de dommages punitifs ou exemplaires, que l'évaluation des dommages n'est pas choquante, qu'elle est basée sur les revenus estimés provenant des activités pirates des défendeurs et qu'elle est calculée sur les pertes subies par la demanderesse selon la preuve. D'autre part, les allégations concernant la preuve obtenue illégalement de la GRC n'ont fait l'objet d'aucune plainte de la part des défendeurs et ne se trouvent pas dans leur déclaration produite dans leur recours contre la GRC. Par ailleurs, les défendeurs n'ont pas démontré une situation de litispendance. Les articles 3137 et 3155 C.C.Q. requièrent trois conditions pour qu'il y ait litispendance: identité de parties, identité d'objet et identité de faits. L'utilisation à ces articles des mots "fondé sur les mêmes faits" plutôt que "identité de cause" comme en droit interne s'explique par les difficultés propres à leur application en droit international privé. Il n'y a aucune décision rendue par les tribunaux québécois. De plus, il n'y avait aucune procédure judiciaire pendante devant les tribunaux québécois avant la signifi-cation des procédures américaines. Enfin, les faits allégués dans l'action des défendeurs ne sont pas les mêmes que ceux allégués dans l'action américaine et il ne s'agit pas de la même cause d'action.

(b)   Chose jugée

Désistement avec préjudice — chose jugée à l'égard des ayants droit

Jurak c. *Hooper,* [2001] A.J.Q. N° 1521 (Cour supérieure du Québec)

La défenderesse a obtenu des renseignements privilégiés alors qu'elle travaillait pour certaines compagnies liées à la famille du demandeur et qu'elle avait des liens avec l'autre défenderesse, qui était domestique dans cette famille. Elle a souscrit un affidavit détaillé qui a été utilisé dans le cadre de procédures opposant le demandeur à la veuve de son père devant les tribunaux américains. Dans la cause aux États-Unis, la défenderesse a été assignée à titre de défenderesse reconventionnelle par le demandeur. Un règlement hors cour est intervenu entre toutes les parties au litige américain et un désistement avec préjudice a été entériné par le tribunal américain. Le demandeur et sa compagnie poursuivent mainte-nant en dommage-intérêts, au Québec, la défenderesse ainsi que la domestique pour avoir violé leur vie privée. La défenderesse s'oppose à la recevabilité de ce recours, alléguant que le jugement américain a force de chose jugée. Le jugement américain a été reconnu au Québec en novembre 2000.

La Cour supérieure a accueilli la requête en irrecevabilité. Dans chacune des deux causes, c'est l'affidavit signé par la défenderesse et utilisé par la veuve dans ses procédures contre le demandeur qui constitue la base des réclamations du demandeur contre la dé-fenderesse. Selon un expert du droit américain, un désistement volontaire avec préjudice a le même effet qu'un jugement final dans une cause contestée et la doctrine de la *res judicata* s'applique. En l'espèce, il y a identité de cause et d'objet puisque les faits re-prochés dans les deux causes sont essentiellement les mêmes. Quant à l'identité des parties, la compagnie demanderesse n'était pas une partie au litige américain. Toutefois, la doctrine de la chose jugée vaut non seulement entre les parties en cause, mais aussi à l'égard de leurs "privies," c'est-à-dire de leurs ayants droit, ce qui inclut une compagnie qui, comme la codemanderesse, est détenue à 100 % par une partie à un litige réglé. Le fait de joindre cette dernière à titre de codemanderesse sans par ailleurs justifier quelque lien de droit que ce soit ou des dommages subis par cette compagnie par la faute de la défenderesse ne suffit pas à faire échec à la requête en irrecevabilité.

D   Choice of Law (including Status of Persons) / Conflits de lois
    (y compris statut personnel)

1   Common Law and Federal

(a)   Characterization

Substance or procedure

Somers v. *Fournier* (2002), 214 D.L.R. (4th) 611, 60 O.R. (3d) 225 (Ontario Court of Appeal)

The plaintiff, a resident of Ontario, was injured in a collision in New York State with a car driven by the defendant New York resident. The plaintiff brought an action in Ontario against the defendant and her own Ontario insurer, claiming damages for her personal injuries, prejudgment interest, and costs. The defendant moved for a declaration that the substantive law of New York applied to these issues. The motions judge held that New York law applied to the claim for damages but that Ontario law applied to the issues of prejudgment interest, costs, and the "cap" on non-pecuniary damages (a limit on non-pecuniary damages fixed in 1978 by the Supreme Court of Canada, which is currently an inflation-adjusted $280,000), because these were matters of procedure.

On appeal and cross-appeal, the Court of Appeal differed only on the issue of prejudgment interest. It affirmed that New York law applied to all issues of substantive law, because the plaintiff had not demonstrated sufficient injustice to warrant an exception to the *lex loci delicti* rule. (See *Wong* v. *Lee,* noted later under the heading (e) Torts). Costs were a procedural issue. The cap on non-pecuniary damages was a judicially imposed restriction on liability, a device developed to avoid excessive and unpredictable claims. The policy considerations that supported it militated in favour of characterizing this rule as one of procedural law as well. Prejudgment interest, by contrast, was akin to a head of damage available to respond to delay in the delivery of awarded compensation and should be characterized as substantive.

Note. Tolofson v. *Jensen,* [1994] 3 S.C.R. 1022, 120 D.L.R. (4th) 289, resolved a long-standing anomaly in the common law by deciding that statutes of limitation, no matter how they are worded, are to be characterized as substantive, not procedural. In *Castillo* v. *Castillo* (2002), 3 Alta. L.R. (4th) 84, 313 A.R. 189 (Q.B.), the court had to construe section 12 of the Limitations Act, R.S.A. 2000, c. L-12, which says: "The limitations law of the Province shall be applied whenever a remedial order is sought in this Province, notwithstanding that, in accordance with conflict of law rules, the claim will be adjudicated under the law of another jurisdiction." The court held that the section must not be read as substituting the limitations law of Alberta for the limitations law of the place of the tort, which *Tolofson* requires to be applied. Rather, the limitations law of the place of the tort must first be applied and, if by that law the claim is statute-barred, there is no valid claim on which the section can operate. The court was influenced by the fact that the 1989 Alberta Law Reform Institute report that prompted the enactment was intended to resolve the pre-*Tolofson* uncertainty about which law governs the issue of limitations. Its rationale had been superseded by *Tolofson* itself.

Contract or tort — subrogation right

Note. In *Kingsway Gen. Ins. Co.* v. *Canada Life Assurance Co.* (2001), 149 O.A.C. 303 (C.A.), the question was whether the insurer under a travel insurance policy, which had paid for the insured's medical expenses in Florida after she was injured in a motorcycle accident there, could make a subrogated claim for those expenses against the insurer under the motor vehicle policy for the motorcycle. Under Florida law, the claim was valid, but under Ontario law, the Insurance Act, R.S.O. 1990, c. I-8, s. 267.8(17), denies insurers a right of subrogation with respect to health care expenses. The issue was held to be, not one of tort, which would be governed by Florida law, but one of contract. It was thus governed by Ontario law as the proper law of the travel insurance policy. See also *Porto Seguro Companhia de Seguros, Gerais* v. *Belcan S.A.* (2001), 200 F.T.R. 44 (F.C.T.D.), recognizing a subrogated claim by the Brazilian insurer of a vessel damaged by another ship in the St. Lawrence Seaway.

(b)   Connecting factors

Domicile

Note. See *McCallum* v. *Ryan Estate,* noted later under the heading (f) Property — succession — testate succession.

(c)   Exclusion of foreign law

Penal and revenue laws

Note. In *Re iTV Games Inc.* (2002), 31 C.B.R. (4th) 279, 21 B.L.R. (3d) 258 (B.C.C.A.), the judgment debtor under a US $3.2 million judgment argued it could not be enforced because the judgment included an interest component that was so large as to involve a criminal interest rate (exceeding 60 per cent per annum) under Canadian law. The court rejected this argument on the facts and said that, even if the rate had exceeded the Canadian criminal level, the judgment would not have been penal for the purposes of private international law because the rate was not shown to be oppressive.

(d)   Contracts

Proper law — no agreed choice

Herman v. *Alberta (Public Trustee),* [2002] 7 W.W.R. 178, 2 Alta. L.R. (4th) 132 (Alberta Queen's Bench)

Three family members chartered a plane to fly themselves and two other family members from Ft. McMurray, Alberta, to La Loche, Saskatchewan. The plane crashed a few miles short of La Loche, well into Saskatchewan. Two of the passengers were killed and three others suffered serious injuries. The survivors brought actions in contract and in tort against, *inter alios,* the air carrier for their own injuries. They and other family members who were not on board brought actions in respect of the death of their two relatives under the Fatal Accidents Acts of either province, R.S.A. 2000, c. F-8, and R.S.S. 1978, c. F-11. The defendants conceded that Alberta was a *forum conveniens* and the plaintiffs conceded that Saskatchewan law governed the substantive issues relating to the tort claims because Saskatchewan was the place of the tort. One of the issues that had to be resolved was which law governed the contract.

The court held that the proper law of the contract was the law of Alberta, because that law had the closest and most real connection with the contract. The sales receipt was the only documentation of the contract. The subject matter of the contract was a neutral factor because it involved both provinces. The contract was made in Alberta for the transport of passengers from there to Saskatchewan. The majority of the performance occurred in Alberta, as the take-off and two-thirds of the flight were in Alberta. The passengers had a contractual obligation to pay the transportation cost in

Alberta. The location of the breach of contract was an irrelevant factor because it was not a circumstance existing when the contract was made. Even if it were relevant, the main breach took place in Alberta because it was there that the pilot took off without checking into the weather conditions at the destination, which omission was alleged to have been the cause of the crash. The fact that the head office of the carrier was in Alberta was a minor consideration, but it was relevant that the carrier and all but one of the parties to the contract were resident in Alberta.

Proper law — implied choice

Richardson International Ltd. v. *Mys Chikhacheva (The)*, [2002] 4 F.C. 80, 288 N.R. 96 (Federal Court of Appeal)

The plaintiff, a corporation incorporated in the state of Washington that conducted an international business of purchasing and marketing fish products, claimed a maritime lien over a fishing trawler that was arrested at the port of Nanaimo, British Columbia. Its claim was based on having supplied necessaries to the trawler, namely, financing for the vessel's refit. The trawler was registered out of Cyprus to its owner, Bering, and out of Russia to its bareboat charterer, Starodubskoe. The financing was supplied under a mortgage agreement and a marketing agreement with the charterer. The mortgage agreement covered the refit of two trawlers and a mother ship. The plaintiff took a mortgage over the mother ship. The terms provided: "To the extent not governed by the laws of Russia, the Mortgage shall in all respects be governed by and construed with the laws of the State of Washington." Under the marketing agreement, the plaintiff received title to all products produced on board the three vessels until its loan was repaid. After that time (as the court construed it), the cost of necessaries would be deducted from the value of product received. The marketing agreement included an arbitration clause, the place of arbitration being the state of Washington. The owner challenged the validity of the plaintiff's claim for a maritime lien.

The trial judge held that the maritime lien was governed by the law of Washington, as the proper law of the contract for the provision of necessaries, which was the marketing contract, to which the mortgage agreement was an accessory. By United States law, a supplier of necessaries under a contract with a bareboat charterer had a maritime lien against the vessel.

The Federal Court of Appeal dismissed the appeal. The marketing contract had no express choice of law clause, but the arbitration clause indicated the implied intention of the parties to have United States law apply. The legal terminology and the form of the documents also pointed towards that law, as the documents in their original form were drafted by United States lawyers. The currency of the agreement was United States dollars. The mortgage was incorporated by reference into the marketing contract by an addendum to it. Even though the contract was executed in Russia and partly performed there, it was clear that by implication the proper law was the law of the United States. Under that law, the failure to take a mortgage over the trawler in question did not defeat a maritime lien unless the lien was expressly waived in the contract, which was not the case. On the contrary, the contract included an express retention of lien rights against the mother ship, which suggested that, *a fortiori*, lien rights were retained against the unmortgaged trawlers.

Note. See also *Imperial Oil Ltd.* v. *Petromar Inc.*, noted later under the heading (f) Property — transfer *inter vivos* — maritime lien, in which the court also had to determine the law that governed a claim of a maritime lien but did not treat the proper law of the supply contract as decisive in the circumstances of that case.

Laws mandatorily applicable to the contract

Note. Day v. *Guarantee Co. of N. America* (2002), 200 N.S.R. (2d) 331 (S.C.), rev'd on other grounds, 2003 NCCA 13, was an action brought by an Ontario resident in Nova Scotia against her own Ontario insurer under the underinsured motorist coverage. The drivers of the other two vehicles involved in the accident could not be identified. The court held that section 127(1) of the Insurance Act, R.S.N.S. 1989, c. 231, must be construed to override the usual choice of law rules for both tort and contract claims. The section deprives an insurer of any defence that could not be set up if the insurance contract were evidenced by a policy issued in Nova Scotia. Thus, irrespective of the proper law of the contract, the Nova Scotia limitation statute applied to the contract claim.

(e) Torts

Applicable law

Wong v. *Lee* (2002), 211 D.L.R. (4th) 69, 58 O.R. (3d) 398 (Ontario Court of Appeal)

The plaintiff, an Ontario resident, was injured as a passenger in a single-vehicle accident in New York state. He brought actions against the driver, the owner, and the insurer of the automobile, all of whom were likewise resident in Ontario. The Insurance Act, R.S.O. 1990, c. I.8, section 267.1, bars an action for pecuniary losses and limits recovery in other ways in accordance with a no-fault insurance scheme. The parties stated a case for the court on the question of whether the law governing the tort issues was the law of New York or Ontario. The motions judge applied the *obiter dictum* in *Tolofson* v. *Jensen*, [1994] 3 S.C.R. 1022 at 1062, 120 D.L.R. (4th) 289 at 314, that in international cases, unlike interprovincial ones, an exception to the *lex loci delicti* rule may be justified in cases where the connections with the forum jurisdiction can be viewed as decisively preponderant. The judge held that, given all the connections with Ontario in this case, it would be unjust to apply New York law to the tort claims.

The Court of Appeal held by a majority of two to one that New York law applied. There was no ground for invoking the exception. The policy underlying the *lex loci delicti* rule is to create certainty in the choice of law rules so as to achieve fairness in the application of private international law. Further, the rule recognizes that international comity demands that recognition be given to the policy of the law of the place where the wrong occurred. A mere difference in policy between that jurisdiction and the forum did not qualify as an injustice and could not give rise to the exception. The Ontario statutory bar to pecuniary loss claims was substantive, not procedural, and therefore did not apply.

Note. The Ontario Court of Appeal seems to have all but closed off an avenue that was proving increasingly attractive to judges who were unhappy with the results of the strict *lex loci delicti* principle laid down in *Tolofson.* The court cites (at para. 11) with apparent disapproval a number of earlier cases that have applied the *lex fori* by way of exception. These cases included *Lebert* v. *Skinner Estate* (2001), 31 C.C.L.I. (3d) 61 (Ont. S.C.J.); *Wong* v. *Wei* (1999), 45 C.C.L.T. (2d) 105 (B.C.S.C.); and *Lau* v. *Li* (2001), 26 C.C.L.I. (3d) 94 (Ont. S.C.J.), leave to appeal denied, December 6, 2001 (Ont. Div. Ct.). (The last of these cases applied the exception to an interprovincial case, in flat disregard of what was said *Tolofson.*) The only earlier case departing from the *lex loci decliti* that the Court of Appeal seems to regard as acceptable is its own decision in *Hanlan* v. *Sernesky* (1998), 38 O.R. (3d) 479 (C.A.), aff'ng (1997),

35 O.R. (3d) 603 (Gen. Div.). At paragraph 16 of *Wong* v. *Lee,* this is explained on the basis that the issue in *Hanlan* was the non-recognition by the law of the place of the accident, Minnesota, of a complete category of claim, namely, the statutory cause of action that Ontario law gives the family members of the primary victim of the accident. From this comment, it would appear that, assuming all parties are from the forum province, an injustice sufficient to warrant departure from the *lex loci delicti* can be found where a whole class of claim is denied by the *lex loci delicti* but recognized by the *lex fori* (*Hanlan*), but not where a class of claim is barred by the *lex fori* but recognized by the *lex loci delicti* (*Wong*).

The pre-*Wong* v. *Lee* case of *Gracey* v. *Skinner Estate* (2001), 31 C.C.L.I. (3d) 61 (Ont. S.C.J.), applied the *lex fori* in the latter situation and must therefore be regarded as doubtful. The Court of Appeal applied *Wong* v. *Lee* in *Somers* v. *Fournier,* noted earlier under the heading (a) Characterization — substance or procedure.

Attempts to escape from the *lex loci delicti* were also rebuffed in the interprovincial cases of *Gill* v. *Canamex Trucking System Inc.* (2001), 16 C.P.C. (5th) 320 (Ont. S.C.J.) (*lex loci delicti* gave no-fault benefits on a lower scale than Ontario), and *Schultz* v. *Panorama Transportation Inc.* (2001), 31 C.C.L.I. (3d) 84 (Ont. S.C.J.) (*lex loci delicti* gave right of action in tort although the plaintiff was receiving no-fault benefits in Ontario).

Two other cases involved statutory responses that provinces have made to the disparity of laws with respect to liability for injuries in automobile accidents. *Hogan* v. *Doiron* (2001), 243 N.B.R. (2d) 263, 32 C.C.L.I. (3d) 12 (C.A.) (affirming the trial decision noted in "Canadian Cases in Private International Law in 2000-1" (2000) 38 Can. Y.B. Int'l L. 478), construed section 266(2) of the Motor Vehicle Act, R.S.N.B. 1973, c. M-17, which confines the "right of recovery" of non-residents, who are injured in an accident in New Brunswick, to the lesser of the right they would have in their home jurisdiction or the right that a New Brunswick resident would have if injured in the non-residents' home jurisdiction. The effect of this, the court held, was that Ontario residents injured on the roads of New Brunswick could not recover more in a New Brunswick tort action than the statutory accident benefits they would have received in Ontario if the accident had taken place there.

Chomos v. *Economical Mut. Ins. Co.* (2002), 216 D.L.R. (4th) 356, 61 O.R. (3d) 28 (C.A.), was a claim by Ontario residents under their Ontario underinsured motorist insurance policy, for damages owing to them by a resident of California who had injured them in that state. The statutorily prescribed terms of the policy said that issues of quantum were to be decided by Ontario law, and issues of liability by the law of the place of the accident. The statutory bar on tort claims arising out of automobile accidents (Insurance Act, R.S.O. 1990, c. I-8 (as amended by S.O. 1993, c. 10), ss. 267.1 and 267.2) was one of liability, not quantum, and so did not apply. *Wong* v. *Lee* had so held in relation to Ontario actions against the tort-feasor in an accident outside Ontario, and the same result had to follow in actions under an underinsured motorist policy where the accident took place outside Ontario. The intent of the legislature was to mirror the choice of law rule in *Tolofson.*

See also *Day* v. *Guarantee Co. of N. America,* noted earlier under the heading (d) Contracts — law mandatorily applicable to the contract, and *Kingsway Gen. Ins. Co.* v. *Canada Life Assurance Co.,* noted earlier under the heading (a) Characterization — contract or tort — subrogation right.

(f)   Property

Transfer inter vivos — *tangible movables — personal property security*

Northwest Equipment Inc. v. *Daewoo Heavy Industries America Corp.* (2002), 3 P.P.S.A.C. (3d) 101 (Alberta Court of Appeal)

An excavator was sold by Daewoo to Trainer Bros., an equipment seller and lessor located in British Columbia. Daewoo retained a security interest, which it registered in British Columbia. Trainer subsequently got into financial difficulties and, as part of a restruc-turing, transferred a quarter of its inventory to Northwest, a firm located in Washington state. Daewoo did not register its security interest in Washington until four months after the equipment was moved to that state, which is when Daewoo first learned of the move. Northwest later moved the excavator to Alberta and leased it there to Win Management, an Alberta firm. Eight months later, Daewoo learned of that series of transactions and registered its security interest in Alberta. It then seized the excavator from Win Northwest, which itself had registered a financing statement with respect to the excavator in Alberta when it leased it to Win, con-tested Daewoo's right to the property.

Both the trial judge and the Court of Appeal held that Daewoo was entitled to the property as against Northwest. The Personal Property Acts of both Alberta (R.S.A. 2000, c. P-7, s. 7(2)(a)) and British Columbia (R.S.B.C. 1996, c. 359, s. 7(2)) enact a choice of law rule that a security interest in property, such as the excavator, that can be used in more than one jurisdiction must be perfected according to the law of the place where the debtor was located at the time the security interest attached. That was British Columbia, and Daewoo had perfected its security interest there. The security interest had not been defeated by Trainer's sale of the excavator to Northwest because the sale was not in the ordinary course of Trainer's business (section 30(2) of the British Columbia Act). Nor had Daewoo consented to the transfer, of which Trainer had not advised it. Therefore, Daewoo's security interest continued to exist (section 28(1)(a)).

The interest had ceased to be perfected in British Columbia because it had not been perfected in Washington within sixty days of being transferred to a person located outside British Columbia (section 7(3)). (The rule refers to the earliest of that date or fifteen days of the secured party's having knowledge of the transfer, or the date when the interest ceases to be perfected in the original jurisdiction.) However, the fact that its interest ceased to be perfected in British Columbia did not mean that Daewoo lost its security interest as against the transferee of the property. A transferee for value without notice takes free of the security interest if the interest has not yet been perfected at the time of the transfer (section 20(c)), but that provision did not apply because the interest had been perfected at that time. A loss of perfection does not of itself extinguish or invalidate existing priorities.

Northwest could not set up its own interest, supposedly perfected in Alberta, as a perfected interest that took priority over Daewoo's unperfected interest (section 35(1)(b) of the British Columbia Act). Northwest was just a lessor and its interest was not a security interest. Even if its interest had been a security interest, Northwest could not use section 35(1)(b) to catapult its interest ahead of Daewoo's. Northwest was not a third party, and could have learned of Daewoo's interest by checking the British Columbia registry when it purchased the excavator. Moreover, by the time it registered its purported security interest in Alberta, Northwest had actual knowledge of Daewoo's interest.

Note. Re Steed (2001), 2 P.P.S.A.C. (3d) 92 (Alta. Q.B.), discussed when property is "brought into" Alberta for the purpose of the rule that a security interest must be registered in that province within sixty days of that date in order for the interest to continue perfected in Alberta. *Re Getz* (2002), 3 P.P.S.A.C. (3d) 151 (Sask. Q.B.), turned on the question of when a corporation had "knowledge" that an automobile over which it held a security interest had been taken out of Alberta into Saskatchewan. It was held to have "knowledge" as soon as it received notice from a trustee in Saskatchewan that the debtor had gone into bankruptcy. Notice of the debtor's location was constructive notice of the location of the debtor's vehicle. This notice set running a fifteen-day period for registration in Saskatchewan, which the corporation had missed.

Transfer inter vivos — *maritime lien*

Imperial Oil Ltd. v. *Petromar Inc.* (2001), [2002] 3 F.C. 190, 209 D.L.R. (4th) 158 (Federal Court of Appeal)

Petromar, a New York-based United States corporation, made a contract with Star Ship Management Limited, a United States corporation based in Florida, by which Petromar agreed to supply marine lubricants to ships managed by Star. The agreement was expressly governed by the law of New York. Petromar in turn arranged with Exxon International (ECI) for the supply of those lubricants. That contract, too, was expressly governed by New York law. It stipulated that ECI could perform its part of the agreement through designated suppliers, including Imperial Oil, a Canadian affiliated company. Imperial supplied lubricants on behalf of Petromar to two ships that were owned by Imperial itself but were chartered to Socanav, a Montreal-based firm, which had made a management contract with Star. The lubricants were supplied to the ships in Montreal, Québec, and Sarnia, Ontario. Socanav's charterparty was expressly governed by the maritime law of Canada and by Ontario law. The terms of Socanav's management agreement with Star were not in evidence. Petromar paid Imperial for the lubricants supplied to the vessels. It now claimed a maritime lien against Imperial's ships for these amounts because it, Petromar, had not been paid for the lubricants by Star or by Socanav. Imperial, as plaintiff, sought a declaration that Petromar and an associated company, as defendants, had no maritime lien against the vessels.

The trial judge held that the issue of the existence of the lien had its closest and most substantial connection with the United States, under whose law the supplier of necessaries obtains a maritime lien. Under Canadian law, the supplier gets an *in personam* right only, subject to narrow statutory exceptions. Imperial appealed.

The Court of Appeal held that Canadian law fell to be applied to the issue. The existence of a maritime lien did depend on the law of the jurisdiction that had the closest and most substantial connection with the transaction under which the lien was said to have arisen. However, the trial judge had attached too much weight to the contracts between Star and Petromar, and Petromar and ECI. Greater weight, rather, should have been given to the factors connecting the transaction to Canada. The latter included vessel registration, flag, ownership, possession in Canada by demise charterer, operation of the vessels from a base in Montreal, and the actual supply of lubricants in Canada. The factor deserving of significant weight was that the operations of Socanav were based in Canada at the time the lubricants were supplied and it was Canada, where the vessels traded and were based, that was economically most benefited by the lubricants. When the "base of operations" factor was weighed with other factors connecting the transaction to Canada, that which connected the transactions to the United States, the supply contracts, seemed less substantial.

Note. See also *Richardson International Ltd.* v. *Mys Chikhacheva (The),* noted earlier under (b) Contracts — proper law— implied choice, and *Finansbanken ASA* v. *GTS Katie* (2001), 214 F.T.R. 253 (F.C.T.D (prothonotary)) (rejecting on the facts a maritime lien claim that was put forward on the basis that Egyptian law had been agreed to govern a supply of bunkers in Gibraltar).

Administration of estates

Note. In *Monteiro* v. *Toronto Dominion Bank* (2001), 43 E.T.R. (2d) 74 (Ont. Div. Ct.), the executor appointed under the will of her mother, who died resident in Kuwait, claimed the balance of a bank account in Ontario in her mother's name. The bank claimed that it was owed money out of this account because of dealings with the testator's son. The daughter contended that these claims were being dealt with by the court in Kuwait, but the Ontario court held that evidence of those proceedings was insufficient to support a motion to stay or dismiss the bank's third party claim.

Succession — testate succession

McCallum v. *Ryan Estate* (2002), 45 E.T.R. (2d) 113 (Ontario Superior Court of Justice)

The testator was born and raised in Ontario and spent most of his working life there. He was divorced from his first wife in 1989. A daughter of the marriage remained with her mother. The court had made an order for the testator to pay child support. In 1997, the testator married his second wife, a United States citizen resident in Florida, and, not long after the marriage, they went to live in Florida. In July 1998, the testator moved to the state of Georgia, and his second wife joined him there in October 1998. The testator and his second wife separated in February 2000, and the wife commenced divorce proceedings in Georgia in April of that year. The testator continued to live in the matrimonial home in Georgia. In July 2000, he called his parents in Toronto and told them he was "coming home." He arrived in Toronto a few days later. He had applied for, but not yet obtained, permanent resident status in the United States. However, he opened a bank account in Ontario, deposited his US dollar savings there, and applied for welfare pending finding employment. He was killed in an automobile accident in September 2000, just before he was to undertake treatment for his alcoholism.

At the time of his death, the testator owed his first wife about $20,000 in arrears of child support. His second wife obtained an order from a court in Georgia awarding her one year's support from a Registered Retirement Savings Plan account that the testator had in Ontario. Although neither the daughter nor the first wife were parties to the proceeding, the Georgia court considered whether it should also make an order for support of the testator's daughter. It did not do so because the court held that the daughter, by now close to adulthood, was sufficiently provided for out of the proceeds of an insurance policy on the testator's life.

The first wife applied to the Ontario Superior Court for an order under the wills variation provisions of the Succession Law Reform Act, R.S.O. 1990, c. S.26 (as amended), that the daughter be awarded a share of the estate. The second wife filed an objection that the matter was *res judicata* because of the decision of the Georgia court and that the Ontario court lacked jurisdiction in any event because the testator died domiciled in Georgia.

The court held that the first wife had shown that the testator had abandoned his domicile of choice in Georgia when he returned to Ontario in July 2000. Thereupon his domicile of origin in Ontario revived. Succession to his movable property was therefore governed by Ontario law and the court had jurisdiction to make an order under the act to vary the disposition of property made in the testator's will. The matter of the testator's obligation to support his daughter was not *res judicata*. The Georgia court had not had jurisdiction because neither the first wife nor the daughter had submitted to the court's jurisdiction and there was no evidence that the merits of the support petition were pleaded before the Georgia court by them or on their behalf.

(g)   Husband and wife

Recognition of foreign divorce

Janes v. *Pardo* (2002), 208 Nfld. & P.E.I. R. 345, 24 R.F.L. (5th) 44 (Newfounland and Labrador Supreme Court)

The husband and wife were married in 1998 in New Mexico, and separated on July 4, 2000. The husband petitioned for divorce in Newfoundland on July 19, 2000. The wife was personally served with notice of the petition. She filed an answer on October 11, 2000, agreeing to a divorce but disputing any order as to costs. By this time, however, she had also petitioned for divorce in Montana, where she had been born and to where she had returned to live with her parents. That petition had been served on the husband on September 21, 2000. The husband filed documentation with the Montana court on October 13, 2000. The Montana court issued a decree of divorce on July 19, 2001. The husband applied to the court in Newfoundland and Labrador for a ruling on the validity of the Montana decree.

The Newfoundland court held that the decree should be recognized on the basis that the petitioner had a real and substantial connection with Montana, a common law test for recognition first used in *Indyka* v. *Indyka* (1967), [1969] 1 A.C. 33 (H.L.). Although she had not been ordinarily resident in Montana for a year before the presentation of her petition on September 21, 2000 (which would have brought the divorce within the recognition rule in section 22(1) of the Divorce Act, R.S.C. 1985, c. 3 (2nd Supp.)), she was living in Montana, she had registered as a voter there as of June 23, 2000, and she had obtained a driver's licence there in the same month. She therefore had a real and substantial connection with that state.

Note. It would appear that the wife's domicile of origin was Montana and that the domicile of origin revived when she resumed her residence there. If so, the divorce was also entitled to recognition under section 22(2) of the Divorce Act, because the Montana court had jurisdiction on the basis of her independent domicile in the state.

2   Québec

(a)   Enfants

Adoption — règles relatives à l'adoption internationale

A.B.M. (Dans la situation d'), [2002] R.J.Q. 1161 (Cour du Québec (Chambre de la jeunesse))

Les requérants sont musulmans et demeurent au Québec. Ils veulent adopter leur neveu de quatre ans, qui est né au Pakistan mais qui vit avec eux depuis presque deux ans. Les parents de l'enfant ont consenti à l'adoption. La directrice de la protection de la jeunesse et le procureur général du Québec s'opposent au placement en vue de l'adoption, invoquant que ce sont les lois du Pakistan qui s'appliquent en l'espèce puisque l'enfant y a son domicile. Ils allèguent qu'il n'existe pas de loi d'adoption dans ce pays et que l'adoption est interdite entre musulmans. Le jugement obtenu au Pakistan "appointing the Petitioners as guardians of the child" à la suite du consentement à l'adoption signé par les parents de l'enfant et assorti d'une "Declaration of willingness to act as guardians" ne serait qu'un acte de tutelle.

La Cour du Québec a rejeté les objections de la directrice de la protection de la jeunesse et le procureur général. Le domicile de l'enfant est chez les requérants, au Québec, à la suite du jugement ayant nommé la requérante sa tutrice. Toutefois, aux fins de l'adoption, on ne peut invoquer ce domicile actuel et faire fi des règles relatives à l'adoption internationale. L'article 3092 C.C.Q. s'applique et les règles relatives au consentement et à l'admissibilité à l'adoption sont celles du domicile d'origine, tandis que les effets de l'adoption sont soumis à la loi du domicile actuel. Or, le document que les parents ont signé au Pakistan devant un notaire est un véritable consentement à l'adoption. Le fait qu'on y mentionne que l'enfant pourra quand même hériter de ses parents n'altère en rien la validité du consetement et ne le limite pas. Cette clause ne vise que les effets de l'adoption. Un examen de toutes les procédures nécessaires à l'obtention du jugement de tutelle ainsi que du consentement à l'adoption et de l'acte d'adoption signés par les parents de l'enfant permet de conclure que celui-ci non seulement a été l'objet d'une tutelle mais est devenu admissible à l'adoption.

En ce qui concerne le droit étranger, les requérants ont allégué qu'il n'existait pas de loi d'adoption au Pakistan, mais l'article 2809 C.C.Q. ne permet pas de se contenter d'une telle allégation. Le procureur général a déposé une expertise d'un professeur d'université et un document du Haut Commissariat pour le Pakistan. Selon ces documents, l'adoption est interdite par la loi islamique au Pakistan, mais il existe une coutume voulant que ce pays reconnaisse le jugement d'adoption obtenu dans un autre pays si un jugement de tutelle a été prononcé et que les parents on permis que l'enfant sorte du pays. Pour être admis, un tel processus doit être conforme aux articles 3080 et 3081 C.C.Q. Les requérants on procédé selon la "coutume ou le processus habituel" reconnu par le Pakistan. Or, rien ne laisse croire qu'il est incompatible avec l'ordre public ou qu'il viole des conventions internationales.

Book Reviews / Recensions de livres

The Law of Subsidies under the GATT/WTO System. By Marc Benitah.
London: Kluwer Law International, 2001. 424 pages. US $92
(hardcover)

While many view the international economic disciplines imposed
on subsidies and countervailing duty measures to be a "patchwork of provisions" emanating from a number of agreements, Marc
Benitah attempts to tie this so-called patchwork together in his
book *The Law of Subsidies under the GATT/WTO System.*[1] Using the
analogy of the legal system's treatment of pollution, Benitah posits
that it is unrealistic to think that the system will provide absolute
protection to the party suffering the consequences of pollution;
rather, the dispute will be resolved through a weighing by judges
and policymakers of the damage suffered by the victim against the
social utility of the polluting activity. The same balancing of rights
occurs in the domain of subsidies and countervailing measures.
Subsidies, like the environment, can be understood in terms of a
theory of attenuated rights and obligations, rather than of absolute
rights and obligations.

The Law of Subsidies under the GATT/WTO System is divided into
three parts. Part 1 deals with the legal techniques for attenuating
entitlements granted to the party allegedly affected by a subsidy.
This portion of the book deals with explicit and implicit techniques
of attenuation as well as the relative weakness of attenuation in
the countervailing duty field. Part 2 deals with techniques of attenuation as a seed for the birth of legal disputes. In this second
part, Benitah examines disputes that have arisen as a result of the

---

[1] M. Benitah, *The Law of Subsidies under the GATT/WTO System* (London: Kluwer,
2001).

ambiguous interpretation of the General Agreement on Tariffs
and Trade (GATT)[2] / World Trade Organization (WTO) texts as
well as the disputes arising from poorly defined concepts within the
agreements. Part 3 scrutinizes the obstacles that remain in the way
of clarifying attenuated norms for subsidies and countervailing
measures through the case law process.

Benitah's book represents a significant contribution to the field
of international trade law, not only for those individuals in the legal
field but also for political scientists and trade economists interested
in the area of subsidies and a deeper understanding of the WTO
agreements (and their antecedents) dealing with subsidies and
countervailing measures. The book's strength lies in the breadth
of the illustrations used to demonstrate Benitah's common link of
attenuation. These illustrations amount to a compendium of WTO,
United States, and European Community (EC) case law dealing
with subsidies and countervailing measures and cover most, if not
all, of the major issues of current controversy.

Benitah offers a wealth of critical thought in his book. For example, in discussing upstream subsidies in agriculture, Benitah argues
that section 771B of the US Tariff Act of 1930,[3] which effectively
collapses upstream and downstream agricultural producers for
the purposes of countervailing duty analysis, is still at odds with the
GATT ruling in *Japan — Measures Affecting Imports of Pork* [4] and that
there is nothing in the Uruguay Round agreements that would
change the GATT Panel's analysis.[5] It is just a matter of time before
section 771B is put to the test.

One negative consequence of Benitah's critical focus and his
attempt to view all major issues through the prism of his theory of
attenuation is the tendency in places to characterize grey issues
in black and white terms. For example, in discussing Article 14
of the Subsidies and Countervailing Measures Agreement (SCM
Agreement),[6] Benitah characterizes Article 14's guidelines for

---

[2] General Agreement on Tariffs and Trade, April 15, 1994, WTO Agreement,
Annex 1A of the Marrakesh Agreement Establishing the World Trade Organization [hereinafter WTO Agreement], 33 ILM 1226 (1994).

[3] US Tariff Act, 19 U.S.C. 1202-1527, 46 Stat. 741.

[4] *Japan – Measures Affecting Imports of Pork,* January 31, 2001, WTO Doc. WT/
DS66/2.

[5] Benitah, *supra* note 1 at 211

[6] Subsidies and Countervailing Measures Agreement, Annex 1A of the WTO
Agreement, *supra* note 2 [hereinafter SCM Agreement].

determining whether a benefit has been conferred as inspired by the "simple" view of distortion.[7] The "simple" view of distortion is distinguished from the "sophisticated" view of distortion according to the scope of distortive effects created by a subsidy. Under the simple view of distortion, the misallocation of resources resulting from a subsidy is viewed as a *per se* unacceptable interference with the market and presumptively leads to disequilibrium in international economic relations. Under the "sophisticated" view of distortion, distortive subsidies are considered an acceptable exercise of the sovereign rights of a government, provided the distortive effects do not cross borders.

Whether or not Article 14 of the SCM Agreement embodies a "simple" or "sophisticated," or even an intermediate, view of distortion depends on how one interprets the term "market," which is used throughout the provision. Where a government is active in the economy, its participation can have a suppressive or even a stimulating effect on the "market" in question. To the extent that one interprets the references in Article 14 to the "market" benchmark as the prevailing market — that is, the market as it exists — without attempting to remove the suppressive or stimulative effects of government involvement, Article 14 may reflect a view of subsidies that is tolerant of distortions and, hence, may be more "sophisticated" than one may initially think.[8]

However, criticisms such as these are quibbles compared to the value added to various legal debates by Benitah's analysis. Chapter 44, which discusses a potential "legal dead end" contained in Article 15 of the SCM Agreement, is a modified version of an article by Benitah published in the *Journal of World Trade* in 1999. Benitah points out, correctly, that Article 15.2, 15.4, 15.5, and footnote 47 to the SCM Agreement can be interpreted as effectively collapsing the requirements of injury and causation in countervailing duty investigations.[9] A literal interpretation of footnote 47 would allow

---

[7] Benitah, *supra* note 1 at 90.

[8] This is exactly how Article 14(d) of the SCM Agreement, *supra* note 6, has been interpreted in the *United States — Preliminary Determinations with Respect to Certain Softwood Lumber from Canada*, September 27, 2002, WTO Doc. WT/DS 236/R at 7.49-7.58. A similar argument is being considered by the WTO in *United States — Final Countervailing Duty Determination with Respect to Softwood Lumber from Canada*, 2002, WTO Doc. WT 257 [hereinafter *Softwood Lumber* case].

[9] SCM Agreement, *supra* note 6, Article 15.5 provides that "[i]t must be demonstrated that the subsidized imports are, through the effects 47 of subsidies, causing injury within the meaning of this Agreement."

investigating authorities to find causation under Article 15.5 by simply finding that the volume of subsidized imports has increased and/or that there has been price undercutting by subsidized imports. The factors that are listed in Article 15.2 are clearly characterized in Article 15.1 as relevant to the legally distinct determination of *injury.*

Benitah offers a "second interpretive approach," pursuant to which paragraphs 2 and 4 of Article 15 are treated as related to the *effects of the subsidies.* Thus, injury and causation analysis in countervailing duty investigations requires an analysis of both the effects of *subsidized imports* and the *effects of the subsidy per se.* This interpretation gives meaning to footnote 47, not to mention the fact that it gives meaning to other paragraphs of Article 15, such as Article 15.7, which explicitly refer to the "nature of the subsidy" and "the trade effects likely to arise there from" (that is, from the subsidy) as factors to be examined. Put another way, if a subsidy is such that it does not produce a "trade effect" (that is, an increase in volume or price in the export market), it should not be countervailable.[10]

The final chapter of *The Law of Subsidies under the GATT/WTO System* contains a discussion of the lost opportunities for the development of the vibrant body of case law leading to the resolution of subsidy disputes. According to Benitah, these "lost opportunities" have been due to the politically charged nature of subsidy disputes

---

Footnote 47 states: "As set forth in paragraphs 2 and 4" Articles 15.2 and 15.4 discuss injury factors (that is, impact on price, quantity). Articles 15.1 and 15.2 provide in relevant part:

> A determination of injury ... shall be based on positive evidence and involve an objective examination of both (a) the volume of the subsidized imports and the effect of the subsidized imports on prices in the domestic market for like products and (b) the consequent impact of these imports on the domestic producers of such products.
>
> With regard to the volume of the subsidized imports, the investigating authorities shall consider whether there has been a significant increase in subsidized imports, either in absolute terms or relative to production or consumption in the importing Member.

[10] A similar argument is currently being made before a North American Free Trade Agreement panel in the ongoing *Softwood Lumber* litigation, *supra* note 8. In *Softwood Lumber,* it has been alleged that the International Trade Commission unlawfully disregarded a study submitted by the Canadian industry demonstrating that the domestic and export prices of softwood lumber are either unaffected by or in fact raised by the current system of stumpage in provincial forests and that the domestic production and exports of softwood lumber are either unaffected by or lowered by stumpage. This argument is in accordance with Benitah's "sophisticated" view of distortion.

and the fact that domestic lobbies have often been simply too powerful to allow unilateral modification of subsidy or countervailing duty practices. Benitah also notes that "the fact that subsidy issues systematically involved a technique of attenuation meant that the challenged party could have some hope that its case was legally viable."[11] Thus, there was no perceived need for immediate concessions. These "lost opportunities" have manifested themselves in the form of adopted (blocked) panel reports and what Benitah terms "abortive proceedings."

There have been considerable developments in WTO and other international case law dealing with subsidies and countervailing measures since the publication of Benitah's book. Despite attempts by Canada and the United States to resolve the recurring softwood lumber dispute, both sides are mired in litigation, and a body of WTO case law is beginning to emerge from the dispute.[12] In *Canada — Measures Affecting the Importation of Milk and the Exportation of Dairy Products*,[13] after years of WTO litigation, culminating in a December 2002 Appellate Body report confirming that Canada was providing illegal export subsidies to Canadian Dairy processors under its Commercial Export Milk program, Canada announced measures intended to bring its Dairy program into conformity with the WTO decision. The US trade representative has stated that "the WTO process has resulted in a positive solution."[14] Undoubtedly, domestic politics will continue to impede the resolution of these and other disputes relating to subsidies and countervailing measures. However, the upside to these bitter disputes is that the historical patchwork is slowly but surely coming together as a more coherent body of international economic law.

CHRISTOPHER KENT AND SAMER MUSALLAM
Wilmer, Cutler, Pickering and Ottawa

---

[11] Benitah, *supra* note 1 at 342

[12] *United States –Preliminary Determinations with Respect to Certain Softwood Lumber from Canada,* September 27, 2002, WTO Doc. WT-DS236/R. The interim report in *United States – Final Countervailing Duty Determination with Respect to Certain Softwood Lumber from Canada* is expected on May 20, 2003.

[13] *Canada – Measures Affecting the Importation of Milk and the Exportation of Dairy Products,* December 20, 2002, WTO Doc. WT/DS103/30.

[14] See office of the United States Trade Representative, "U.S. & Canada Reach Agreement Ending Legally Subsidized Canadian Dairy Exports to U.S.," May 9, 2003.

L'offense aux souverains et chefs de gouvernement étrangers par la voie de la presse. Par Jean-F. Marinus. Collection de droit international, Éditions Bruylant. Bruxelles: Éditions de l'Université de Bruxelles, 2002. 587 pp.

Proférer des injures, diffamer, calomnier, caricaturer les chefs d'État ou chefs de gouvernement à travers diverses formes de communication est presque devenu un sujet banal, un épiphénomène. Si les souverains d'hier étaient perçus comme des "dieux" sur terre et dont les sujets devaient se garder de profaner leur intégrité physique et morale, il en va tout autrement pour ceux de notre époque. Ces derniers, sous les forces conjuguées des libertés civiles et politiques et des exigences démocratiques garanties tant par les lois nationales que par le droit international ont perdu de leur caractère sacré même s'ils ont conservé certains privilèges et immunités dus à leur statut. En effet, les offenses faites aux chefs d'État ou de chefs de gouvernement étrangers, proférées alors qu'ils sont à l'étranger ou dans leur propre pays, n'émeuvent plus grand monde. La problématique posée par Jean-F. Marinus est celle-ci: existe-t-il des règles de droit international qui imposent aux États une obligation de sanctionner des offenses faites aux souverains ou chefs de gouvernement étrangers par la voie de la presse?

Pour répondre à cette question, Jean-F. Marinus a d'abord décrit et analysé dans la première partie de son ouvrage la législation, la pratique et la jurisprudence britannique en matière d'offenses envers les souverains et chefs d'État étrangers à travers les notions traditionnelles de *lèse-majesté* et de *libel*. L'auteur arrive à la conclusion qu'en Grande Bretagne, après la révolution de 1688 "ce qui était éventuellement réprimé ... n'était pas l'acte offensant en lui-même, dirigé contre la personne d'un souverain étranger, mais le risque d'un *breach of the peace* qui pouvait éventuellement en résulter." D'où la notion de *libel* séditieux qui, avec l'évolution de la pratique anglaise, n'existe pratiquement plus depuis la jurisprudence *Antonelli* et *Barberi* en 1905. L'évolution du droit britannique en la matière est étayée par des exemples historiques, confortée par des actes de législations et surtout par une jurisprudence abondante. On a pu retenir en définitive que la tendance actuelle, selon l'auteur, est à une protection faible des chefs d'État ou chefs de gouvernement étrangers. Il a ensuite analysé la pratique belge en matière d'offenses aux souverains et chefs de gouvernement étrangers en décrivant les délits de presse dans leur cadre constitutionnel, législatif et réglementaire. Il a ensuite défini ceux considérés par le code pénal belge comme étant des infractions de diffamation ou de calomnie et les actions en justice, civile et pénale, sanctionnant de telles offenses. La pratique belge de l'incrimination des délits de presse à l'endroit des personnalités publiques y est examinée depuis la loi "Faider" du 20 décembre 1852 jusqu'à nos jours. Toutefois, à l'instar de la Grande Bretagne, la Belgique a cessé d'intervenir sous sa propre initiative et au nom des principes démocratiques et des libertés publiques, pour réprimer les délits de presse contre les chefs d'État ou chefs de gouvernement étrangers dans la mesure où "l'exercice des libertés individuelles maintenant garanti par des textes internationaux est estimé supérieur à la protection de la dignité et de l'honneur d'une personnalité publique étrangère ou à un quelconque comportement requis de la part des États dans ce domaine." Outre la Grande-Bretagne et la Belgique, l'auteur a examiné les législations de plusieurs pays d'Europe et celles des pays anglo-saxons, notamment des États-Unis, du Canada, de la Nouvelle-Zélande, de l'Australie, etc. À ce niveau, la distinction est faite entre les États ayant adopté des lois spéciales, ceux ayant prévu simplement des dispositions dans leur code pénal et enfin ceux qui, expressément, n'ont fait aucune référence aux offenses faites aux chefs d'État ou chefs de gouvernement étrangers.

S'il existe des lois nationales qui érigent en crimes ou délits les offenses faites par de simples particuliers à l'endroit des souverains ou chefs de gouvernement étrangers par la voie de la presse, la question fondamentale se pose de savoir si ces législations répondent à des exigences de droit international ou à de simples règles de convenance ou de courtoisie entre souverains étatiques. À cette question, l'auteur a reconnu que le droit international n'impose pas aux États une obligation spéciale de vigilance pour les actes commis par des simples particuliers. En effet, la pratique des États est incertaine sur cette question et l'*opinio juris* nécessaire à sa consolidation fait défaut. Toutefois, il reste que d'une part la responsabilité de l'État pourrait être engagée pour les actes commis par ses propres organes et d'autre part qu'elle pourrait être établie pour manquement à une obligation générale de diligence à l'égard des actes des individus agissant sur son territoire.

Le sujet est brillamment traité. Il semble être toutefois dépassé par d'autres événements qui agitent la société internationale, à savoir le terrorisme international, les guerres, l'apparition de nouvelles maladies infectieuses qui ravagent des populations entières en maints endroits du monde. Même si pour l'heure, le sujet n'est pas l'objet d'une grande préoccupation, l'auteur a le mérite d'y consacrer une réflexion approfondie à travers une démarche bien structurée, laquelle rend sa lecture agréable. Enfin, l'ouvrage de Jean-F. Marinus se veut, nous semble-t-il, une interpellation non seulement des hommes de la presse, mais aussi des politiciens et des diplomates quant à l'équilibre à trouver entre libertés d'opinion, droit d'information du public et les principes du jeu démocratique dans toute société dite moderne.

CISSÉ YACOUBA

Faculté de droit, Université d'Ottawa

Evropeiskaia Konventsiia o pravakh cheloveka: teoreticheskie problemy i praktika realizatsii v sovremennoi Rossii. Edited by V.A. Achkasov. St. Petersburg: Izdatel'stvo S.-Peterburgskogo universiteta, 2002. 176 pages. ISBN 5-288-03053-7. US $16.95

On May 5, 1998, the Russian Federation ratified the European Convention for the Protection of Human Rights and Fundamental Freedoms (ECHR).[1] This historic step obliged Russian legislators, judges, and scholars of law, among others, to contemplate a series of interrelated issues.[2] It forced them earnestly to reassess the state's

---

The views advanced in the foregoing review are solely Eric Myles's views and should not be taken as expressing any view of the Department of Justice Canada.

[1] European Convention for the Protection of Human Rights and Fundamental Freedoms, November 4, 1950, 213 U.N.T.S. 221 (1950) [hereinafter ECHR]. B. Bowring, "Russia's Accession to the Council of Europe and Human Rights: Four Years On" (2000) 11(3) Helsinki Monitor 53 at 55. The Russian Federation made two reservations, both pertaining to its Criminal Procedure Code (at 55-60). The Criminal Procedure Code, which President Putin signed into law on December 17, 2001, apparently brings the Russian criminal justice system into compliance with the ECHR.

[2] The implications of the ECHR for the Russian Federation have been considered repeatedly in scholarly literature: V.A. Kartashkin, "Rossiia i Evropeiskaia konventsiia o zashchite prav cheloveka i osnovnykh svobod" (1996) 3 Moskovskii zhurnal mezhdunarodnogo prava 21; V.A. Kartashkin, "Powers and Activities of the Human Rights Commission of the President of the Russian Federation" (1998) 28 Israel Y.B. Human Rights 107; A. Kovler, "La Convenzione europea dei diritti dell'uomo e l'ordinamento giuridico russo" (2000) 13 Rivista internazionale dei diritti dell'uomo 441; G.E. Luk'iantsev, *Evropeiskie standarty v oblasti prav cheloveka: teoriia i praktika funktionirovaniia Evropeiskoi konventsii o zashchite prav cheloveka i osnovnykh svobod i protokoly k nei* (Moscow: Zven'ia, 2000); and S.A. Gorshakova, *Standarty Soveta Evropy po pravam cheloveka i rossiiskoe zakonodatel'stvo* (Moscow: NIMP, 2001).

role in guaranteeing the fundamental rights of Russian citizens.[3] Moreover, it required them practically to consider the ways by which the Russian Federation's political, economic, and legal environment might most effectively promote the rights that the ECHR prescribes. In September 2001, the Faculty of Philosophy at St. Petersburg State University held a seminar addressing the various issues surrounding the ECHR. The volume under review reproduces the eleven papers that were presented.[4]

When planning the seminar of September 2001, the Faculty of Philosophy at St. Petersburg State University eschewed a narrowly legal perspective in favour of a multidisciplinary approach. Among the participating staff of St. Petersburg State University were representatives of political science, international relations, and law. Other participants included the director of the Council of Europe's St. Petersburg Centre for Information and Documentation; the president of the St. Petersburg Institute "Strategiia"; and a judge of the St. Petersburg Constitutional Court. If a multidisciplinary approach to the issues surrounding the ECHR was to succeed, the papers presented needed to address the weightiest issues while remaining thematically coherent. Unfortunately, they fail to achieve this equilibrium.

Some weighty issues surrounding the ECHR receive inadequate treatment, if they are treated at all. One might wonder to what extent the Russian Federation has succeeded since May 5, 1998, in bringing into effect the rights that the ECHR prescribes. Three papers include remarks suggesting that the fundamental rights enjoined by the Russian Constitution or the ECHR all too often remain elusive in reality.[5] Important as these remarks are, they come

---

[3] In evoking this issue, it raised additionally the long-standing issue of the extent to which Russia should emulate the institutions in western European states. The Slavophiles and the Westernizers debated this issue passionately in the nineteenth century: A. Walicki, *The Slavophile Controversy: History of a Conservative Utopia in Nineteenth-Century Russian Thought* (Oxford: Clarendon Press, 1973), *passim*.

[4] V.A. Achkasov, ed., *Evropeiskaia Konventsiia o pravakh cheloveka»: teoreticheskie problemy i praktika realizatsii v sovremennoi Rossii* (St. Petersburg: Izdatel'stvo S.-Peterburgskogo universiteta, 2002).

[5] D.Z. Mutagirov, "Sostoianie prav i svobod cheloveka v Rossii," in Achkasov, *supra* note 4 at 35; A.V. Volkova, "Traditsii i prava cheloveka: problemy realizatsii Evropeiskoi Konventsii v rossiiskom zakonodatel'stve," in Achkasov, *supra* note 4 at 54; D.N. Baryshnikov, "Evropeiskaia Konventsiia o pravakh cheloveka o svobode SMI i praktika Evropeiskogo Suda," in Achkasov, *supra* note 4 at 144. Amnesty International has recently concurred in these remarks. "Amnesty Decries State of Russian Justice," *[Toronto] Globe and Mail* (October 30, 2002) A13.

en passant — they do not reflect a systematic attempt to appraise the practical effects of the ECHR. One might equally wonder how far the judgments of the European Court of Human Rights have forced earlier judgments of Russian courts to undergo revision. Nevertheless, the answer lies elsewhere.[6]

One can go a step further and observe that various papers give short shrift to the ECHR. S.A. Lantsov's paper on human rights in international relations mentions the ECHR only cursorily.[7] V.A. Achkasov's and S.G. Eremeev's paper on minorities' right to self-determination and the protection minority rights enjoy in practice includes scant mention of the ECHR.[8] V.A. Gutorov's and L.V. Davydov's paper on freedom of information contains an early acknowledgment that Article 10 of the ECHR protects freedom of opinion.[9] Then the ECHR sinks into oblivion, and the spotlight falls upon the governmental initiatives and the political machinations of media owners that have shaped the dissemination of news since 1991. M.A. Mogil'naia's paper on foreigners' right to participate in the activities of Russian local government organs includes no attempt to show that the ECHR is somehow engaged,[10] and A.A. Liverovskii's examination of judicial control over the procedures for adopting and propagating St. Petersburg's normative legal acts invites a similar observation.[11] If these papers had clear and convincing links with the ECHR, the volume's thematic coherence would have gained significantly.

---

[6] Compare with M. Ferschtman, "Reopening of Judicial Procedures in Russia: The Way to Implement the Future Decisions of ECHR Supervisory Organs?" in T. Barkhuysen, M.L. van Emmerik, and P.H.P.H.M.C. van Kempen, eds., *The Execution of Strasbourg and Geneva Human Rights Decisions in the National Legal Order* (The Hague: Martinus Nijhoff, 1999), 123.

[7] S.A. Lantsov, "Prava cheloveka v mezhdunarodnykh otnosheniiakh (teoreticheskie kontseptsii i sovremennaia praktika)" in Achkasov, *supra* note 4 at 121.

[8] V.A. Achkasov and S.G. Eremeev, "Printsip samoopredeleniia i zashchita prav natsional'nykh men'shinstv: teoreticheskie i prakticheskie problemy," in Achkasov, *supra* note 4 at 12.

[9] V.A. Gutorov and L.V. Davydov, "Svoboda informatsii v postkommunisticheskoi Rossii-mif ili real'nost'?," in Achkasov, *supra* note 4 at 58.

[10] M.A. Mogil'naia, "Osnovy politiko-pravovogo regulirovaniia uchastiia inostrantsev v deiatel'nosti organov mestnogo samoupravleniia v Rossiiskoi Federatsii," in Achkasov, *supra* note 4.

[11] A.A. Liverovskii, "Osushchestvlenie sudebnogo kontrolia za sobliudeniem protsedury priniatiia i opublikovaniia normativnykh pravovykh aktov (praktika Sankt-Peterburga)," in Achkasov, *supra* note 4.

Three papers deserve separate commentary because they include observations that illuminate most directly the circumstances in which the Russian Federation received the ECHR. In introducing the Russian Federation's experience of promoting human rights, V.E. Koptev-Dvornikov remarks that Moscow lawyers specializing in human rights have asked the Council of Europe to provide legal instruction.[12] Yet he refrains from developing this noteworthy statement.

A.S. Kartsov examines the approaches that European Court of Human Rights judges employ when interpreting the ECHR in concrete cases.[13] His examination is flawed because it presumes that the approaches of the judges mark them clearly as "liberals" and "conservatives." Surely a judge may be "liberal" on some issues and "conservative" on others. A more incisive examination could have resulted if Kartsov had probed the voting records of individual judges, blocs within the European Court of Human Rights, and so forth.[14] The approaches that Judge Anatolii Kovler, the Russian Federation's sitting judge in Strasbourg, has employed in interpreting the ECHR should have received mention, but they do not.

A.Iu. Sungorov's paper on the joint attempts of Russians and the Council of Europe to introduce ombudsmen in particular parts of the Russian Federation is unusually informative.[15] He furnishes absorbing glimpses into the realities of helping Russians assert human rights in the Republic of Northern Ossetia-Alania, the Krasnodar *krai*, and the Kaliningrad *oblast*. In his view, the experience of introducing ombudsmen in these parts of the Russian Federation offers instructive lessons for installing ombudsmen elsewhere.

Even if the remaining papers do not achieve the focus that Sungorov's paper attains,[16] the volume under review, reckoned as

---

[12] V.E. Koptev-Dvornikov, "Prava cheloveka i reformy: opty Rossii," in Achkasov, *supra* note 4 at 10.

[13] A.S. Kartsov, "Tolkovanie Konventsii: «konservatory» versus «liberaly»", Achkasov, *supra* note 4.

[14] Compare with P. McCormick, "Birds of a Feather: Alliances and Influences on the Lamer Court 1990-1997" (1998) 36 Osgoode Hall L.J. 339.

[15] A.Iu. Sungorov, "Instituty zashchity prav cheloveka: Evropeiskii opyt i ego sud'ba v rossiiskikh regionakh (na primere razvitiia instituta Upolnomochennogo po pravam cheloveka)," in Achkasov, *supra* note 4 at 102.

[16] Some papers contain fascinating tidbits relating less immediately to the assertion of human rights in the contemporary Russian Federation. A.V. Volkova relates (Volkova, in Achkasov, *supra* note 4 at 51) that on May 3, 2001, the

a whole, comprises a worthwhile contribution. The Faculty of Philosophy at the St. Petersburg State University deserves great praise for convening a seminar to examine ECHR-related issues. Twenty years ago, a seminar of this ilk would assuredly not have taken place. Hopefully, such a seminar will become an annual event in St. Petersburg. Furthermore, the papers submitted in September 2001 leave little doubt that international human rights issues are penetrating the discourse of the Russian Federation's political and legal scholars. Clearly, the seminar's participants reflected at length about international human rights norms. And the footnotes to various papers depict the authors as familiar with a broad spectrum of Western and Russian writings relating to international human rights. Canadians will be gratified to discover that the writings of Ronald St. John Macdonald, Will Kymlicka, Joan DeBardeleben, and other Canadian scholars receive mention.

In conclusion, the St. Petersburg State University seminar of September 2001 shows international human rights in today's Russian Federation as standing at a crossroads. On the one hand, the participants might have benefited from greater encouragement from Westerners in exploring how to promote the rights that the ECHR prescribes. On the other hand, the participants have demonstrated abundantly that they have already made great progress in comprehending international human rights issues. In this sense, the volume reviewed is to be welcomed. The participants' progress is sufficient to create hope that future Russian legislators, judges, and scholars of law will contemplate ways to bring the ECHR into effect in their homeland.

ERIC MYLES
Department of Justice Canada, Toronto

Supreme Court of Iakutia found unconstitutional almost half of the articles in Iakutia's Basic Law.

She does not explore further what the court's action implied. If it was enforced, however, it represented an important step in creating an independent Russian judiciary — a condition that is necessary if Russians are to have any realistic hope of challenging their government for breaching the rights prescribed by the ECHR and other human rights instruments.

Analytical Index / Index analytique

THE CANADIAN YEARBOOK OF INTERNATIONAL LAW

2 0 0 2

ANNUAIRE CANADIEN DE DROIT INTERNATIONAL

(A) Article; (NC) Notes and Comments; (Ch) Chronique;
(P) Practice; (C) Cases; (BR) Book Review
(A) Article; (NC) Notes et commentaires; (Ch) Chronique;
(P) Pratique; (C) Jurisprudence; (BR) Recension de livre

Index of Cases / Index de la jurisprudence

114957 Canada Ltée (Spraytech, Société d'arrosage) v. *Hudson (Town)*, 5 n. 9, 5 n. 11, 39 n. 159, 46-48, 50, 53, 57 n. 215, 260 n. 35
1349689 Ontario Inc. v. *Hollyoake*, 593, 596

ABB Inc. v. *MSX International Inc.*, 595
Abdulaziz, Cabales et Balkandi, 349 n. 17, 352 n. 34
A.B.M. (Dans la situation d'), 625-26
Affaire des produits en tôle d'acier non allié inoxydable en provenance du Canada, 426
Affaire des services transfrontières de camionnage, 423-24
Ahani v. *Canada (A.G.)*, 4-5 n. 7, 27 n. 106, 28-31, 561-67
Aimtronic Corp. v. *Fattouche*, 596
Alaska Boundary Tribunal (UK v. *USA), Award of*, 253 n. 9
Alberta (Workers' Compensation Board Appeals Commission) v. *Penny*, 337 n. 48
Anglo-Iranian Oil Co. Case (Interim Measures), 214 n. 69
Application of the Convention on the Prevention and Punishment of the Crime of Genocide (Bosnia and Herzegovina v. *Yugoslavia)*, 268 n. 11
Arbitration between the United Kingdom of Great Britain and Northern Ireland and the French Republic on the Delimitation of the Continental Shelf, 410 n. 203, 410 n. 205, 412-13
Argentina – Measures Affecting the Export of Bovine Hides and the Import of Finished Leather, 479-80
Aristocrat v. *National Bank of the Republic of Kazakhstan*, 596
Arrow River and Tributaries Slide & Boom Co. Ltd., 22 n. 83
Asylum Case (Columbia v. *Peru)*, 16 n. 57

Aulwes v. *Mai*, 600-1
Austro-German Customs Union Case, 214 n. 67, 222 n. 101

B. v. *France*, 312 n. 9
Baker v. *Canada (Minister of Citizenship and Immigration)*, 4 n. 7, 5-6, 7 n. 15, 8, 21 n. 77, 21 n. 78, 26 n. 103, 27, 33 n. 139, 35-42, 45-50, 53-54, 60, 254, 257 n. 26, 260 n. 34
Barber v. *Height of Excellence Financial Planning Group Inc.*, 593
Baugh v. *Samuels*, 609
Benjamin and Wilson v. *United Kingdom*, 315 n. 16
Bering Sea Fur-Seals (Gr. Brit. v. *U.S.)*, 120
Black v. *Chrétien*, 260 n. 38
Blaskic case, 470-71, 472-73
BNP Paribas (Canada) v. *Mécs*, 597
Botazzi v. *Italy*, 318
Bouzari v. *Iran*, 21 n. 75, 44 n. 175, 49 n. 197, 50 n. 202
Brésil – Programme de financement des exportations pour les aéronefs, 437
Brown v. *Bezanson*, 600

"Camouco" Case (Panama v. *France)*, 135, 140-41
Campagna v. *Wong*, 583
Canada – Crédits à l'exportation et garanties de prêtes accordés pour les aéronefs régionaux, 437 n. 67
Canada – Measures Affecting the Importation of Milk and the Exportation of Dairy Products, 433-34, 631
Canada – Mesures visant l'importation de lait et l'exportation de produits laitiers, 433-34, 631
Canada (A.G.) v. *McNally Construction Inc.*, 581-82
Canada (A.G.) v. *Ontario (A.G.)*, 22, 27

647